THE
ENDURING DEBATE

CLASSIC AND CONTEMPORARY READINGS
IN AMERICAN POLITICS

Sixth Edition

THE
ENDURING DEBATE

CLASSIC AND CONTEMPORARY READINGS
IN AMERICAN POLITICS

Sixth Edition

Edited by
David T. Canon
John J. Coleman
Kenneth R. Mayer

W. W. NORTON & COMPANY
NEW YORK   LONDON

W. W. Norton & Company has been independent since its founding in 1923, when William Warder Norton and Mary D. Herter Norton first published lectures delivered at the People's Institute, the adult education division of New York City's Cooper Union. The Nortons soon expanded their program beyond the Institute, publishing books by celebrated academics from America and abroad. By mid-century, the two major pillars of Norton's publishing program—trade books and college texts—were firmly established. In the 1950s, the Norton family transferred control of the company to its employees, and today—with a staff of 400 and a comparable number of trade, college, and professional titles published each year—W. W. Norton & Company stands as the largest and oldest publishing house owned wholly by its employees.

Composition: Bytheway Publishing Services
Production manager: Jane Searle
Manufacturing by Sheridan Printing Company

Library of Congress Cataloging-in-Publication Data
The enduring debate : classic and contemporary readings in American politics /
edited by David T. Canon, John J. Coleman, Kenneth R. Mayer. — 6th ed.
p. cm.
Includes bibliographical references.
ISBN 978-0-393-91205-0 (pbk.)
1. United States—Politics and government. I. Canon, David T. II. Coleman,
John J., 1959– III. Mayer, Kenneth R., 1960–
JK21.E53   2011
320.473—dc22   2011001522

W. W. Norton & Company Inc., 500 Fifth Avenue, New York, N.Y. 10110
www.wwnorton.com
W. W. Norton & Company Ltd., Castle House, 75/76 Wells Street, London W1T 3QT
1 2 3 4 5 6 7 8 9 0

Contents

PART II   Institutions

PART IV   Public Policy

CHAPTER 13   Politics and Policy   515

CHAPTER 14   Government and the Economy   550

xii Contents

Preface

We compiled this reader with two goals in mind. The first was to introduce students to some of the classic works in political science, so that they could see how these historic arguments connected to the broad themes generally covered in college-level introductory courses in American government. We also introduce students to classic primary-source documents. We think there is great value in reading Woodrow Wilson, David Truman, and V. O. Key, along with primary documents such as the *Federalist Papers*, the writings of Dr. Martin Luther King, Jr., and a major speech by Franklin Roosevelt, among others in this book. Combining these classic readings with more modern selections is a good way to show how the main themes in American politics endure. As the title suggests, many contemporary issues are similar to what earlier generations of Americans—and the Framers themselves—had to work out through existing political institutions and processes, or change those processes when they proved inadequate.

Our second goal was to expose students to debates on important contemporary political controversies. These debates give students examples of high-level political argumentation, showing how scholars and other expert commentators probe, analyze, attempt to persuade, and confront competing arguments. In some of the debates, authors directly challenge each other in a point/counterpoint format. In most of the debates the authors do not directly engage each other, but rather present a range of arguments on opposing sides of issues. Our hope is that students will see the value of real argument and become more discerning consumers of political information.

Finally, in addition to editing down selections to a manageable length while preserving the authors' central arguments, the book includes two pedagogical devices: the introductions to each article and debate, and discussion questions at the conclusion to each piece. The introductions provide students with the context of a given article or debate while briefly summarizing the argument. The questions provide the basis for students to engage some of the main ideas of an article.

THE
ENDURING DEBATE

CLASSIC AND CONTEMPORARY READINGS
IN AMERICAN POLITICS

Sixth Edition

PART I

The Constitutional System

CHAPTER 1

Political Culture

1

From *The Liberal Tradition in America: An Interpretation of American Political Thought Since the Revolution*

Louis Hartz

Political culture refers to the orientation of citizens toward the political system and toward themselves as actors in it. This includes the basic values, beliefs, attitudes, predispositions, and expectations that citizens bring to political life. Given the great diversity of the American population, one might expect a similarly diverse array of thought within political culture, with rival sets of political values challenging each other. In his classic and influential work, Louis Hartz argues that in fact there is broad agreement in the United States around a set of political beliefs. Hartz refers to this as the "liberal tradition"; the terms "liberal consensus" and "American Creed" have also been used by other authors. "Liberal" here means a focus on the individual and minimizing government intervention in daily life. Within the liberal tradition, the values of equality, private property, liberty, individualism, protection of religious freedom, and democracy are especially powerful. There is certainly debate over what these terms mean or how much to emphasize one versus another, and these clashes drive party politics, but we do not see successful political movements in the United States that directly challenge these values. On the contrary, most movements seek to show how their beliefs and principles are highly consistent with these basic American values. Hartz argues that it is the nature of American history that led to this unusual uniformity. Not having had a feudal stage, Americans also did not witness the revolutionary stages and ideologies that challenged feudalism in Europe. As Hartz puts it, "no feudalism, no socialism." This historical path does present some problems, in Hartz's view. Americans view liberalism as natural, as obvious. Indeed, to some extent, we are hardly aware of it as an ideology because it has been unchallenged. To Hartz, writing in the 1950s, this sometimes blinds Americans to policy alternatives, heightens our fears of social disharmony and "foreign" ideas, and makes it hard for Americans to understand other societies where a liberal tradition is not so dominant.

1. America and Europe

The analysis which this book contains is based on what might be called the storybook truth about American history: that America was settled by men who fled from the feudal and clerical oppressions of the Old World. If there is anything in this view, as old as the national folklore itself, then the outstanding thing about the American community in Western history ought to be the non-existence of those oppressions, or since the reaction against them was in the broadest sense liberal, that the American community is a liberal community. We are confronted * * * with * * * America skipping the feudal stage of history * * *. "Feudalism" refers technically to the institutions of the medieval era, and it is well known that aspects of the decadent feudalism of the later period, such as primogeniture, entail, and quitrents, were present in America even in the eighteenth century. "Liberalism" is an even vaguer term, clouded as it is by all sorts of modern social reform connotations, and even when one insists on using it in the classic Lockian sense, as I shall insist here, there are aspects of our original life in the Puritan colonies and the South which hardly fit its meaning.[1] But these are the liabilities of any large generalization, danger points but not insuperable barriers. What in the end is more interesting is the curious failure of American historians, after repeating endlessly that America was grounded in escape from the European past, to interpret our history in the light of that fact. * * *

*   *   *

2. "Natural Liberalism": The Frame of Mind

One of the central characteristics of a nonfeudal society is that it lacks a genuine revolutionary tradition, the tradition which in Europe has been linked with the Puritan and French revolutions: that it is "born free," as Tocqueville said. And this being the case, it lacks also a tradition of reaction * * *. Its liberalism is * * * a "natural" phenomenon. But the matter is curiously broader than this, for a society which begins with Locke, and thus transforms him, stays with Locke, by virtue of an absolute and irrational attachment it develops for him, and becomes as indifferent to the challenge of socialism in the later era as it was unfamiliar with the heritage of feudalism in the earlier one. It has within it, as it were, a kind of self-completing mechanism, which insures the universality of the liberal idea. * * * It is not accidental that America which has uniquely lacked a feudal tradition has uniquely lacked also a socialist tradition. The hidden origin of socialist thought everywhere in the West is to be found in the feudal ethos. * * *

America has presented the world with the peculiar phenomenon, not of a frustrated middle class, but of a *"frustrated aristocracy"*—of men, Aristotelian-like, trying to break out of the egalitarian confines of middle-class life but suffering guilt and failure in the process. The South before the Civil War is the case par excellence of this, though New England of course exemplifies it also. * * * The Southerners were thrown into fantastic contradictions by their iconoclastic conservatism, by what I have called the "Reactionary Enlightenment," and after the Civil War for good historical reasons they fell quickly into oblivion. The South, as John Crowe Ransom has said, has been the part of America closest to Old World Europe, but it has never really been Europe. It has been an alien child in a liberal family, tortured and confused, driven to a fantasy life which, instead of disproving the power of Locke in America, portrays more poignantly than anything else the tyranny he has had.

* * * Here we have one of the great and neglected relationships in American history: the common fecklessness of the Southern "feudalists" and the modern socialists. It is not accidental, but something rooted in the logic of all of Western history, that they should fail alike to leave a dent in the American liberal intelligence. * * * Socialism arises not only to fight capitalism but remnants of feudalism itself, so that the failure of the Southern [feudalists], in addition to setting the pattern for the failure of the later Marxists, robbed them in the process of a normal ground for growth. * * *

Surely, then, it is a remarkable force: this fixed, dogmatic liberalism of a liberal way of life. It is the secret root from which have sprung many of the most puzzling of American cultural phenomena. Take the unusual power of the Supreme Court and the cult of constitution worship on which it rests. Federal factors apart, judicial review as it has worked in America would be inconceivable without the national acceptance of the Lockian creed, ultimately enshrined in the Constitution, since the removal of high policy to the realm of adjudication implies a prior recognition of the principles to be legally interpreted. * * * If in England a marvelous organic cohesion has held together the feudal, liberal, and socialist ideas, it would still be unthinkable there that the largest issues of public policy should be put before nine Talmudic judges examining a single text. But this is merely another way of saying that law has flourished on the corpse of philosophy in America, for the settlement of the ultimate moral question is the end of speculation upon it. Pragmatism, interestingly enough America's great contribution to the philosophic tradition, does not alter this, since it feeds itself on the Lockian settlement. It is only when you take your ethics for granted that all problems emerge as problems of technique. Not that this is a bar in America to institutional innovations of highly non-Lockian kind. Indeed, as the New Deal shows, when you simply "solve problems" on the basis of a submerged and absolute liberal faith, you can depart from Locke with a kind of inventive freedom that European Liberal reformers and even European socialists, dominated by ideological systems, cannot duplicate. * * *

Here is a Lockian doctrine which in the West as a whole is the symbol of rationalism, yet in America the devotion to it has been so irrational that it has not even been recognized for what it is: liberalism. There has never been a "liberal movement" or a real "liberal party" in America: we have only had the American Way of Life, a nationalist articulation of Locke which usually does not know that Locke himself is involved; and we did not even get that until after the Civil War when the Whigs of the nation, deserting the Hamiltonian tradition, saw the capital that could be made out of it. This is why even critics who have noticed America's moral unity have usually missed its substance. Ironically, "liberalism" is a stranger in the land of its greatest realization and fulfillment. But this is not all. Here is a doctrine which everywhere in the West has been a glorious symbol of individual liberty, yet in America its compulsive power has been so great that it has posed a threat to liberty itself. * * *

I believe that this is the basic ethical problem of a liberal society: not the danger of the majority which has been its conscious fear, but the danger of unanimity, which has slumbered unconsciously behind it: the "tyranny of opinion" that Tocqueville saw unfolding as even the pathetic social distinctions of the Federalist era collapsed before his eyes. But in recent times this manifestation of irrational Lockianism, or of "Americanism," to use a favorite term of the American Legion, * * * has neither slumbered nor been unconscious. It has been very much awake in a red scare hysteria which no other nation in the West has really been able to understand. And this suggests a very significant principle: that when a liberal community faces military and ideological pressure from without it transforms eccentricity into sin, and the irritating figure of the bourgeois gossip flowers into the frightening figure of an A. Mitchell Palmer or a Senator McCarthy. * * *

The decisive domestic issue of our time may well lie in the counter resources a liberal society can muster against this deep and unwritten tyrannical compulsion it contains. They exist. Given the individualist nature of the Lockian doctrine, there is always a logical impulse within it to transcend the very conformitarian spirit it breeds in a Lockian society * * *.

But the most powerful force working to shatter the American absolutism is, paradoxically enough, the very international involvement which tensifies it. This involvement is complex in its implications. If in the context of the Russian Revolution it elicits a domestic redscare, in the context of diplomacy it elicits an impulse to impose Locke everywhere. * * * Thus to say that world politics shatters "Americanism" at the moment it intensifies it is to say a lot: it is to say that the basic horizons of the nation both at home and abroad are drastically widened by it. * * * [W]hen has the nation appreciated more keenly the limits of its own cultural pattern as applied to the rest of the world? * * * [W]hen has the meaning of civil liberties been more ardently understood than now? * * * The outcome of the battle between intensified "Americanism" and new enlightenment is still an open question.

*   *   *

3.' The Dynamics of a Liberal Society

So far I have spoken of natural liberalism as a psychological whole, embracing the nation and inspiring unanimous decisions. We must not assume, however, that this is to obscure or to minimize the nature of the internal conflicts which have characterized American political life. * * * What we learn from the concept of a liberal society, lacking feudalism and therefore socialism and governed by an irrational Lockianism, is that the domestic struggles of such a society have all been projected with the setting of Western liberal alignments. * * *

*   *   *

That society has been a triumph for the liberal idea, but we must not assume that this ideological victory was not helped forward by the magnificent material setting it found in the New World. The agrarian and proletarian strands of the American democratic personality, which in some sense typify the whole of American uniqueness, reveal a remarkable collusion between Locke and the New World. Had it been merely the liberal spirit alone which inspired the American farmer to become capitalistically oriented, to repudiate save for a few early remnants the village organization of Europe, to produce for a market and even to enter capitalist occupations on the side such as logging and railroad building, then the difficulties he encountered would have been greater than they were. But where land was abundant and the voyage to the New World itself a claim to independence, the spirit which repudiated peasantry and tenantry flourished with remarkable ease. Similarly, had it merely been an aspect of irrational Lockianism which inspired the American worker to think in terms of the capitalist setup, the task would have been harder than it was.

But social fluidity was peculiarly fortified by the riches of a rich land, so that there was no small amount of meaning to Lincoln's claim in 1861 that the American laborer, instead of "being fixed to that condition for life," works for "a while," then "saves," then "hires another beginner" as he himself becomes an entrepreneur. And even when factory industrialism gained sway after the Civil War, and the old artisan and cottage-and-mill mentality was definitely gone, it was still a Lockian* idea fortified by material resources which inspired the triumph of the job mentality of Gompers rather than the class mentality of the European worker. The "petit-bourgeois" giant of America, though ultimately a triumph for the liberal idea, could hardly have chosen a better material setting in which to flourish.

* * *

One cannot say of the liberal society analysis that by concentrating on national unities it rules out the meaning of domestic conflict. Actually it discovers that meaning * * *. The argument over whether we should "stress" solidarity or conflict in American politics misleads us by advancing a false set of alternatives.

* * *

DISCUSSION QUESTIONS

1. Do you agree with Hartz that Americans have a hard time understanding other societies because of ideological uniformity in the United States?

2. Do you think Hartz is correct in saying that Americans are in agreement on the values of the liberal tradition? Are there parts of American history or society today that make you doubt his thesis?

3. Without limiting yourself to Hartz's observations, what do you think might be some of the advantages and disadvantages of a high degree of agreement on basic values for American society and politics?

---

*"Lockian" refers to John Locke, a British political theorist. Locke's ideas of individualism, liberty, property rights, and limited government influenced political leaders at the time of the American Revolution [Editors].

2

From *The Creation of the American Republic 1776–1787*

Gordon S. Wood

*In the 1960s, a group of historians took issue with the depiction of American so-
ciety as fundamentally and uniformly liberal. Perhaps American society in the
twentieth century was dominated by the liberal tradition, historians such as
Gordon Wood argued, but in the colonial and revolutionary period, it was classical republicanism that most shaped public thought about politics. The liberal
tradition emphasizes the primacy of the individual in society; classical republicanism draws individuals' attention to society and the community. A contemporary term for this approach is "communitarianism." To classical republicans,
individuals are not self-made—society makes individuals what they are and individuals owe something to society in return. The classical republican approach
doesn't disagree that individuals have personal responsibility and need to work
hard and diligently. It would, however, suggest that the point of self-improvement
is to better serve the community and society. Wood notes that in this view, politics is not primarily about achieving one's self-interest. Rather, the focus is on
civic duty. Participation was expected, for the social good. Individuals are to be
motivated not by self-interest but by morality and virtue. Although Wood argues
elsewhere that classical republicanism failed in the 1780s and made way for liberal politics to become dominant and embraced by the Constitution, other historians suggest that the classical republican ideals continued to influence American
politics through various reform movements over the course of U.S. history.*

* * *

The Public Good

The sacrifice of individual interests to the greater good of the whole
formed the essence of republicanism and comprehended for Americans the idealistic goal of their Revolution. From this goal flowed all of
the Americans' exhortatory literature and all that made their ideology
truly revolutionary. This republican ideology both presumed and helped
shape the Americans' conception of the way their society and politics
should be structured and operated—a vision so divorced from the realities of American society, so contrary to the previous century of American
experience, that it alone was enough to make the Revolution one of the

great utopian movements of American history. By 1776 the Revolution came to represent a final attempt, perhaps—given the nature of American society—even a desperate attempt, by many Americans to realize the traditional Commonwealth ideal of a corporate society, in which the common good would be the only objective of government.

*   *   *

To make the people's welfare—the public good—the exclusive end of government became for the Americans, as one general put it, their "Polar Star," the central tenet of the Whig faith, shared not only by Hamilton and Paine at opposite ends of the Whig spectrum, but by any American bitterly opposed to a system which held "that a Part is greater than its Whole; or, in other Words, that some Individuals ought to be considered, even to the Destruction of the Community, which they compose." No phrase except "liberty" was invoked more often by the Revolutionaries than "the public good." It expressed the colonists' deepest hatreds of the old order and their most visionary hopes for the new. * * *

From the logic of belief that "all government . . . is or ought to be, calculated for the general good and safety of the community," for which end "the most effectual means that human wisdom hath ever been able to devise, is frequently appealing to the body of the people," followed the Americans' unhesitating adoption of republicanism in 1776. The peculiar excellence of republican government was that it was "wholly characteristical of the purport, matter, or object for which government ought to be instituted." By definition it had no other end than the welfare of the people: *res publica*, the public affairs, or the public good. "The word *republic*," said Thomas Paine, "means the *public good*, or the good of the whole, in contradistinction to the despotic-form, which makes the good of the sovereign, or of one man, the only object of the government." * * *

Since in a free government the public good was identical with the people's welfare, a "matter of COMMON FEELING" and founded on the "COMMON CONSENT" of the people, the best way of realizing it in the Whig mind was to allow the people a maximum voice in the government. "That the great body of the people," as even the Tory William Smith of Philadelphia admitted, "can have any interest separate from their country, or (when fairly understood) pursue any other, is not to be imagined," "unless," as John Sullivan said, "we suppose them idiots or self-murderers." Therefore any government which lacked "a proper representation of the people" or was in any way even "independent of the people" was liable to violate the common good and become tyrannical. Most Whigs had little doubt of the people's honesty or even of their ability to discern what was good for themselves. It was a maxim, declared a New York patriot, "that whatever may be the particular opinions of Individuals, the bulk of the people, both mean, and think right." Was there ever any fear, James Burgh had gone so far as to ask, that the people might be "*too free to* consult the general good?" Of course even the most radical English Whigs admitted that the people might sometimes mistake their own interest and might often be unable to affect it even when they did correctly perceive it. Most Americans therefore assumed that the people, in their representational expression of their collective liberty in the houses of representatives, could not run the whole government. "Liberty, though the most essential requisite in government," Richard Price had written, "is not the only one; wisdom, union, dispatch, secrecy, and vigour are likewise requisite"—qualities best supplied by a magistracy and a senate.

Yet such governors and upper houses, however necessary, must be electively dependent on the people. Republicanism with its elective magistracy would not eliminate the problems of politics and the threat of power, but it did promise a new era of stability and cooperation between rulers and ruled. * * * For decades, and especially in recent years, the Crown's presence in America had played havoc with the colonists' political life and was the real source of that factious behavior of which royal officials had so repeatedly and unjustly accused them. "Every man that has lived any time in America, under regal government, knows what frequent, and almost continual opposition there is between the country interest and those in power." "By keeping clear of British government," the Americans could at last be rid of those "jars and contentions between Governors and Assemblies." By allowing the people to elect their magistracy, republicanism would work to "blend the interests of the people and their rulers" and thus "put down every animosity among the people." In the kind of states where *their governors shall proceed from the midst of them* the people could be surer that their interests exclusively would be promoted, and therefore in turn would "pay obedience to officers properly appointed" and maintain "no discontents on account of their advancement."

What made the Whig conception of politics and the republican emphasis on the collective welfare of the people comprehensible was the assumption that the people, especially when set against their rulers, were a homogeneous body whose "interests when candidly considered are one." Since everyone in the community was linked organically to everyone else, what was good for the whole community was ultimately good for all the parts. The people were in fact a single organic piece (*"for God hath so tempered the body that there should be no Schism in the body, but that the Members should have the same care for one another"*) with a unitary concern that was the only legitimate objective of governmental policy. This common interest was not, as we might today think of it, simply the sum or consensus of the particular interests that made up the community. It was rather an entity in itself, prior to and distinct from the various private interests of groups and individuals. As Samuel Adams said in 1776, paraphrasing Vattel, the state was "a moral person, having an interest and will of its own." Because politics was conceived to be not the reconciling but the transcending of the different interests of the society in the search for the single common good, the republican state necessarily had to be small in territory and generally similar in interests. Despite sporadic suggestions in the press for "a simple government" of a strong continental congress chosen "by the people, (not by their representatives)," and uniting all the people "in one great republick," few Americans thought that such an extensive continental republic, as distinct from a league of states, was feasible in 1776—however much they may have differed over the desirable strength of the expected confederation.

No one, of course, denied that the community was filled with different, often clashing combinations of interests. But apart from the basic conflict between governors and people these were not to be dignified by their incorporation into formal political theory or into any serious discussion of what ought to be. In light of the assumption that the state was "to be considered as one moral whole" these interests and parties were regarded as aberrations or perversions, indeed signs of sickness in the body politic. Although some eighteenth-century thinkers were in fact beginning to perceive the inevitability, even the desirability, of faction in a free state, most continued to regard division among the people as "both dangerous and destructive," arising "from false ambition, avarice, or revenge." Men lost control of their basest passions and were unwilling to sacrifice their immediate desires for the corporate good. Hence, "party differences," however much they may infect the society, could never ideally be admitted into the institutions of government, but "would be dropped at the threshold of the state house." The representatives of the people would not act as spokesmen for private and partial interests, but all would be "disinterested men, who could have no interest of their own to seek," and "would employ their whole time for the public good; then there would be but one interest, the good of the people at large."

*   *   *

Yet ironically it was precisely internal discord and conflict for which republics were most widely known. Throughout history "free republican governments have been objected to, as if exposed to factions from an excess of liberty." But this was because liberty had been misunderstood and falsely equated with licentiousness or the liberty of man in a state of nature which was "a state of war, rapine and murder." True liberty was "natural liberty restrained in such manner, as to render society one great family; where everyone must consult his neighbour's happiness, as well as his own." In a republic "each individual gives up all private interest that is not consistent with the general good, the interest of the whole body." For the republican patriots of 1776 the commonweal was all-encompassing—a transcendent object with a unique moral worth that made partial considerations fade into insignificance. "Let regard be had only to the good of the whole" was the constant exhortation by publicists and clergy. Ideally, republicanism obliterated the individual. "A Citizen," said Samuel Adams, "owes everything to the Commonwealth." "Every man in a republic," declared Benjamin Rush, "is public property. His time and talents—his youth—his manhood—his old age—nay more, life, all belong to his country." "No man is a true republican," wrote a Pennsylvanian in 1776, "that will not give up his single voice to that of the public."

Individual liberty and the public good were easily reconcilable because the important liberty in the Whig ideology was public or political liberty. In 1776 the solution to the problems of American politics seemed to rest not so much in emphasizing the private rights of individuals against the general will as it did in stressing the public rights of the collective people against the supposed privileged interests of their rulers. "Civil Liberty," as one colonist put it, was not primarily individual; it was "the freedom of bodies politic, or States." Because, as Josiah Quincy said, the people "as a body" were "never interested to injure themselves," and were "uniformly desirous of the general welfare," there could be no real sense of conflict between public and personal liberty. Indeed, the private liberties of individuals depended upon their collective public liberty. * * *

Thus in the minds of most Whigs in 1776 individual rights, even the basic civil liberties that we consider so crucial, possessed little of their modern theoretical relevance when set against the will of the people. This is why, for example, throughout the eighteenth century the Americans could contend for the broadest freedom of speech against the magistracy, while at the same time punishing with a severe strictness any seditious libels against the representatives of the people in the colonial assemblies. Anyone who tried to speak against the interests of the people "should be held in execration. . . . Every word, that tends to weaken the hands of the people is a crime of devilish dye"; indeed, "it is the *unpardonable Sin* in politics." Thus it was "no *Loss of Liberty*, that court-minions can complain of, when they are silenced. No man has right to say a word, which may lame the liberties of his country." * * *

* * *

Even at the beginning, however, there were some good Whigs who perceived the inherent conflict between individual liberty and traditional republican theory. Ancient Sparta, William Moore Smith told the members of the Continental Congress in the spring of 1775, had demonstrated the problem. Knowing that luxury was the great enemy of republicanism and liberty, Lycurgus had sought to avoid the evil by eliminating wealth itself. But in doing so he undermined the very basis of freedom. "He seems not to have reflected that there can be no true liberty without security of property; and where property is secure, industry begets wealth; and wealth is often productive of a train of evils naturally destructive to virtue and freedom!" "Here, then," said Smith, "is a sad dilemma in politics." If the people "exclude *wealth*, it must be by regulations intrenching too far upon civil *liberty.*" But if wealth is allowed to flourish, "the siren *luxury*" soon follows at its heels and gradually contaminates the whole society. "What is to be done in this case?" Must the society, "to secure the first of blessings, *liberty*," strangle wealth, the first offspring of liberty, in its birth and thus in effect destroy liberty as well? "Or, is there no proper use of *wealth* and *civil happiness*, the genuine descendants of *civil liberty*, without abusing them to the nourishment of *luxury* and *corruption?*" Smith, like other Whigs in 1776, thought there was an answer to the dilemma in the more enlightened policy and "purer system of *religion*" of this modern age—"to regulate the use of wealth, but not to exclude it."

* * *

The Need for Virtue

Perhaps everyone in the eighteenth century could have agreed that in theory no state was more beautiful than a republic, whose whole object by definition was the good of the people. * * * The very greatness of republicanism, its utter dependence on the people, was at the same time its source of weakness. In a republic there was no place for fear; there could be no sustained coercion from above. The state, like no other, rested on the consent of the governed freely given and not compelled. In a free government the laws, as the American clergy never tired of repeating, had to be obeyed by the people for conscience's sake, not for wrath's.

* * *

In a monarchy each man's desire to do what was right in his own eyes could be restrained by fear or force. In a republic, however, each man must somehow be persuaded to submerge his personal wants into the greater good of the whole. This willingness of the individual to sacrifice his private interests for the good of the community—such patriotism or love of country—the eighteenth century termed "public virtue." A republic was such a delicate polity precisely because it demanded an extraordinary moral character in the people. Every state in which the people participated needed a degree of virtue; but a republic which rested solely on the people absolutely required it. * * * The eighteenth-century mind was thoroughly convinced that a popularly based government "cannot be supported without *Virtue.*" Only with a public-spirited, self-sacrificing people could the authority of a popularly elected ruler be obeyed, but "more by the virtue of the people, than by the terror of his power." Because virtue was truly the lifeblood of the republic, the thoughts and hopes surrounding this concept of public spirit gave the Revolution its socially radical character—an expected alteration in the very behavior of the people, "laying the foundation in a constitution, not without or over, but within the subjects."

This public virtue, "this endearing and benevolent passion," was "the noblest which can be displayed" and represented all that men of the eighteenth century sought in social behavior. "Its grand source" lay in the attitudes and actions of the individuals who made up the society, "in that charity which forms every social connection." In other words, public virtue, the willingness of the people to surrender all, even their lives, for the good of the state, was primarily the consequence of men's individual private virtues. * * * For most Americans in 1776 vicious behavior by an individual could have only disastrous results for the community. A man racked by the selfish passions of greed, envy, and hate lost his conception of order; "his sense of a connection with the *general* system—his benevolence—his desire and freedom of *doing good*, ceased." It seemed obvious that a republican society could not "be maintained without justice, benevolence and the social virtues." * * * Somehow, as a Boston writer argued * * * the individual's widening and traditionally weakening circles of love—from himself to his family to the community—must be broken into; men must be convinced that their fullest satisfaction would come from the subordination of their individual loves to the greater good of the whole. It was man's duty and interest to be benevolent. "The happiness of every individual" depended "on the happiness of society." * * * Once men correctly perceived their relation to the commonwealth they would never injure what was really their personal interest to protect and sustain.

Equality

* * *

Even the most radical republicans in 1776 admitted the inevitability of all natural distinctions: weak and strong, wise and foolish—and even of incidental distinctions: rich and poor, learned and unlearned. Yet, of course, in a truly republican society the artificial subsidiary distinctions would never be extreme, not as long as they were based solely on natural distinctions. It was widely believed that equality of opportunity would necessarily result in a rough equality of station, that as long as the social channels of ascent and descent were kept open it would be impossible for any artificial aristocrats or overgrown rich men to maintain themselves for long. With social movement founded only on merit, no distinctions could have time to harden. * * * And projected public educational systems would open up the advantages of learning and advancement to all.

Great consequences were expected to flow from such an egalitarian society. If every man realized that his associations with other men and the state depended solely on his merit, then, as former Massachusetts Governor Thomas Pownall told the Americans, there would be an end to the jealousy and the contentions for "unequal Dominion" that had beset communities from time immemorial. Indeed, equality represented the social source from which the anticipated harmony and public virtue of the New World would flow. "It is this principle of equality . . . ," wrote one Virginian in 1776, "which alone can inspire and preserve the virtue of its members, by placing them in a relation to the publick and to their fellow-citizens, which has a tendency to engage the heart and affections to both."

It was a beautiful but ambiguous ideal. The Revolutionaries who hoped for so much from equality assumed that republican America would be a community where none would be too rich or too poor, and yet at the same time believed that men would readily accede to such distinctions as emerged as long as they were fairly earned. But ironically their ideal contained the sources of the very bitterness and envy it was designed to eliminate. For if the promised equality was the kind in which "one should consider himself as good a man as another, and not be brow beaten or intimidated by riches or supposed superiority," then their new republican society would be no different from that in which they had lived, and the Revolution would have failed to end precisely what it was supposed to end. Indeed, although few Americans could admit it in 1776, it was the very prevalence of this ambivalent attitude toward equality that had been at the root of much of their squabbling during the eighteenth century.

* * *

DISCUSSION QUESTIONS

1. Do classical republican values sound impractical for contemporary American politics? Or do you think these values have more influence in politics than someone like Louis Hartz would acknowledge?

2. What are the key components of the classical republican outlook, as presented by Wood? How do they differ from the liberal tradition?

3. Wood notes at several points that some of the strengths of republican thought would also prove to make it difficult for republicanism to thrive. Identify and describe these strengths.

3

"Beyond Tocqueville, Myrdal, and Hartz: The Multiple Traditions in America"

Rogers M. Smith

Where liberalism points to notions of equality, Rogers Smith argues that there is another tradition in American political thought that has been influential. He does not deny the significance in American political history of liberalism or of republicanism, which argues for a more society-centered perspective on government than does liberalism. Smith, however, contends that an equally significant strand of thought, "ascriptive hierarchy," has been important across U.S. history. In this way of thinking, society is a hierarchy, where some groups are on top and others are below. Those on top are deserving of all the rights and benefits the liberal tradition can offer; those below are not. The most glaring examples of this throughout American history were the treatment of racial minorities, especially blacks, and the treatment of women. Smith notes that those holding these illiberal views were not on the fringes of society but, rather, were probably the majority view. We cannot, Smith argues, marginalize the impact of "ascriptive American" hierarchy or those who held these views. American public policy at the highest levels was influenced by its premises. Moreover, the same individuals often held these illiberal views in tandem with their liberal or republican views and expended great intellectual energy to make these views seem acceptable in the light of fundamental American beliefs.

Since the nation's inception, analysts have described American political culture as the preeminent example of modern liberal democracy, of government by popular consent with respect for the equal rights of all. They have portrayed American political development as the working out of liberal democratic or republican principles, via both "liberalizing" and "democratizing" socioeconomic changes and political efforts to cope with tensions inherent in these principles. Illiberal, undemocratic beliefs and practices have usually been seen only as expressions of ignorance and prejudice, destined to marginality by their lack of rational defenses. * * *

[Alexis de] Tocqueville's thesis—that America has been most shaped by the unusually free and egalitarian ideas and material conditions that prevailed at its founding—captures important truths. Nonetheless, the purpose of this essay is to challenge that thesis by showing that its adherents fail to give due weight to inegalitarian ideologies and conditions that have shaped the participants and the substance of American politics just as deeply. For over 80% of U.S. history, its laws declared most of the world's population to be ineligible for full American citizenship solely because of their race, original nationality, or gender. For at least two-thirds of American history, the majority of the domestic adult population was also ineligible for full citizenship for the same reasons. * * *

The Tocquevillian story is thus deceptive because it is too narrow. It is centered on relationships among a minority of Americans (white men, largely of northern European ancestry) analyzed via reference to categories derived from the hierarchy of political and economic statuses men have held in Europe: monarchs and aristocrats, commercial burghers, farmers, industrial and rural laborers, and indigents. Because most European observers and British American men have regarded these categories as politically fundamental, it is understandable that they have always found the most striking fact about the new nation to be its lack of one type of ascriptive hierarchy. There was no hereditary monarchy or nobility native to British America, and the revolutionaries rejected both the authority of the British king and aristocracy and the creation of any new American substitutes. Those features of American political life made the United States appear remarkably egalitarian by comparison with Europe.

But the comparative moral, material, and political egalitarianism that prevailed at the founding among moderately propertied white men was surrounded by an array of other fixed, ascriptive systems of unequal status, all largely unchallenged by the American revolutionaries. Men were thought naturally suited to rule over women, within both the family and the polity. White northern Europeans were thought superior culturally—and probably biologically—to black Africans, bronze Native Americans, and indeed all other races and civilizations. Many British Americans also treated religion as an inherited condition and regarded Protestants as created by God to be morally and politically, as well as theologically, superior to Catholics, Jews, Muslims, and others.

These beliefs were not merely emotional prejudices or "attitudes." Over time, American intellectual and political elites elaborated distinctive justifications for these ascriptive systems, including inegalitarian scriptural readings, the scientific racism of the "American school" of ethnology, racial and sexual Darwinism, and the romantic cult of Anglo-Saxonism in American historiography. All these discourses identified the true meaning of *Americanism* with particular forms of cultural, religious, ethnic, and especially racial and gender hierarchies. Many adherents of ascriptive Americanist outlooks insisted that the nation's political and economic structures should formally reflect natural and cultural inequalities, even at the cost of violating doctrines of universal rights. Although these views never entirely prevailed, their impact has been wide and deep.

Thus to approach a truer picture of America's political culture and its characteristic conflicts, we must consider more than the familiar categories of (absent) feudalism and socialism and (pervasive) bourgeois liberalism and republicanism. The nation has also been deeply constituted by the ideologies and practices that defined the relationships of the white male minority with subordinate groups, and the relationships of these groups with each other. When these elements are kept in view, the flat plain of American egalitarianism mapped by Tocqueville and others suddenly looks quite different. We instead perceive America's initial conditions as exhibiting only a rather small, recently leveled valley of relative equality nestled amid steep mountains of hierarchy. And though we can see forces working to erode those mountains over time, broadening the valley, many of the peaks also prove to be volcanic, frequently responding to seismic pressures with outbursts that harden into substantial peaks once again.

To be sure, America's ascriptive, unequal statuses, and the ideologies by which they have been defended have always been heavily conditioned and constrained by the presence of liberal democratic values and institutions. The reverse, however, is also true. Although liberal democratic ideas and practices have been more potent in America than elsewhere, American politics is best seen as expressing the interaction of multiple political traditions, including *liberalism, republicanism*, and *ascriptive forms of Americanism*, which have collectively comprised American political culture, without any constituting it as a whole. Though Americans have often struggled over contradictions among these traditions, almost all have tried to embrace what they saw as the best features of each.

Ascriptive outlooks have had such a hold in America because they have provided something that neither liberalism nor republicanism has done so well. They have offered creditable intellectual and psychological reasons for many Americans to believe that their social roles and personal characteristics express an identity that has inherent and transcendant worth, thanks to nature, history, and God. Those rationales have obviously aided those who sat atop the nation's political, economic, and social hierarchies. But many Americans besides elites have felt that they have gained meaning, as well as material and political benefits, from their nation's traditional structures of ascribed places and destinies.

Conventional narratives, preoccupied with the absence of aristocracy and socialism, usually stress the liberal and democratic elements in the rhetoric of even America's dissenters. These accounts fail to explain how and why liberalizing efforts have frequently lost to forces favoring new forms of racial and gender hierarchy. Those forces have sometimes negated major liberal victories, especially in the half-century following Reconstruction; and the fate of that era may be finding echoes today.

My chief aim here is to persuade readers that many leading accounts of American political culture are inadequate. * * * This argument is relevant to contemporary politics in two ways. First, it raises the possibility that novel intellectual, political, and legal systems reinforcing racial, ethnic, and gender inequalities might be rebuilt in America in the years ahead. That prospect does not seem plausible if the United States has always been essentially liberal democratic, with all exceptions marginal and steadily eliminated. It seems quite real, however, if liberal democratic traditions have been but contested parts of American culture, with inegalitarian ideologies and practices often resurging even after major enhancements of liberal democracy. Second, the political implications of the view that America has never been completely liberal, and that changes have come only through difficult struggles and then have often not been sustained, are very different from the complacency—sometimes despair—engendered by beliefs that liberal democracy has always been hegemonic.

* * *

The Multiple-Traditions Thesis of American Civic Identity

It seems prudent to stress what is not proposed here. This is not a call for analysts to minimize the significance of white male political actors or their conflicts with each other. Neither is it a call for accounts that assail "Eurocentric" white male oppressors on behalf of diverse but always heroic subjugated groups. The multiple-traditions thesis holds that Americans share a *common* culture but one more complexly and multiply constituted than is usually acknowledged. Most members of all groups have shared and often helped to shape all the ideologies and institutions that have structured American life, including ascriptive ones. A few have done so while resisting all subjugating practices. But members of every group have sometimes embraced "essentialist" ideologies valorizing their own ascriptive traits and denigrating those of others, to bleak effect. Cherokees enslaved blacks, champions of women's rights disparaged blacks and immigrants, and blacks have often been hostile toward Hispanics and other new immigrants. White men, in turn, have been prominent among those combating invidious exclusions, as well as those imposing them.

Above all, recognition of the strong attractions of restrictive Americanist ideas does not imply any denial that America's liberal and democratic traditions have had great normative and political potency, even if they have not been so hegemonic as some claim. Instead, it sheds a new—and, in some respects, more flattering—light on the constitutive role of liberal democratic values in American life. Although some Americans have been willing to repudiate notions of democracy and universal rights, most have not; and though many have tried to blend those commitments with exclusionary ascriptive views, the illogic of these mixes has repeatedly proven a major resource for successful reformers. But we obscure the difficulty of those reforms (and thereby diminish their significance) if we slight the ideological and political appeal of contrary ascriptive traditions by portraying them as merely the shadowy side of a hegemonic liberal republicanism.

At its heart, the multiple-traditions thesis holds that the definitive feature of American political culture has been not its liberal, republican, or "ascriptive Americanist" elements but, rather, this more complex pattern of apparently inconsistent combinations of the traditions, accompanied by recurring conflicts. Because standard accounts neglect this pattern, they do not explore how and why Americans have tried to uphold aspects of all three of these heterogeneous traditions in combinations that are longer on political and psychological appeal than on intellectual coherency.

A focus on these questions generates an understanding of American politics that differs from Tocquevillian ones in four major respects. First, on this view, purely liberal and republican conceptions of civic identity are seen as frequently unsatisfying to many Americans, because they contain elements that threaten, rather than affirm, sincere, reputable beliefs in the propriety of the privileged positions that whites, Christianity, Anglo-Saxon traditions, and patriarchy have had in the United States. At the same time, even Americans deeply attached to those inegalitarian arrangements have also had liberal democratic values. Second, it has therefore been typical, not aberrational, for Americans to embody strikingly opposed beliefs in their institutions, such as doctrines that blacks should and should not be full and equal citizens. But though American efforts to blend aspects of opposing views have often been remarkably stable, the resulting tensions have still been important sources of change. Third, when older types of ascriptive inequality, such as slavery, have been rejected as unduly illiberal, it has been normal, not anomalous, for many Americans to embrace new doctrines and institutions that reinvigorate the hierarchies they esteem in modified form. Changes toward greater inequality and exclusion, as well as toward greater equality and inclusiveness, thus can and do occur. Finally, the dynamics of American development cannot simply be seen as a rising tide of liberalizing forces progressively submerging contrary beliefs and practices. The national course has been more serpentine. The economic, political, and moral forces propelling the United States toward liberal democracy have often been heeded by American leaders, especially since World War II. But the currents pulling toward fuller expression of alleged natural and cultural inequalities have also always won victories. In some eras they have predominated, appearing to define not only the path of safety but that of progress. In all eras, including our own, many Americans have combined their allegiance to liberal democracy with beliefs that the presence of certain groups favored by history, nature, and God has made Americans an intrinsically "special" people. Their adherents have usually regarded such beliefs as benign and intellectually well founded; yet they also have always had more or less harsh discriminatory corollaries.

To test these multiple-traditions claims, consider the United States in 1870. By then the Civil War and Reconstruction had produced dramatic advances in the liberal and democratic character of America's laws. Slavery was abolished. All persons born in the United States and subject to its jurisdiction were deemed citizens of the United States and the states in which they resided, regardless of their race, creed or gender. None could be denied voting rights on racial grounds. The civil rights of all were newly protected through an array of national statutes. The 1790 ban on naturalizing Africans had been repealed, and expatriation declared a natural right. Over the past two decades women had become more politically engaged and had begun to gain respect as political actors.

* * *

[Neither liberal or republican analyses] would have had the intellectual resources to explain what in fact occurred. Over the next fifty years, Americans did not make blacks, women, and members of other races full and equal citizens, nor did racial and gender prejudices undergo major erosion. Neither, however, were minorities and women declared to be subhuman and outside the body politic. And although white Americans engaged in extensive violence against blacks and Native Americans, those groups grew in population, and no cataclysm loomed. Instead, intellectual and political elites worked out the most elaborate theories of racial and gender hierarchy in U.S. history and partially embodied them in a staggering array of new laws governing naturalization, immigration, deportation, voting rights, electoral institutions, judicial procedures, and economic rights—but only partially. The laws retained important liberal and democratic features, and some were strengthened. They had enough purchase on the moral and material interests of most Americans to compel advocates of inequality to adopt contrived, often clumsy means to achieve their ends.

The considerable success of the proponents of inegalitarian ideas reflects the power these traditions have long had in America. But after the Civil War, * * * evolutionary theories enormously strengthened the intellectual prestige of doctrines presenting the races and sexes as naturally arrayed into what historians have termed a "raciocultural hierarchy," as well as a "hierarchy of sex." Until the end of the nineteenth century, most evolutionists * * * thought acquired characteristics could be inherited. Thus beliefs in biological differences were easily merged with the * * * historians' views that peoples were the products of historical and cultural forces. Both outlooks usually presented the current traits of the races as fixed for the foreseeable future. Few intellectuals were shy about noting the implications of these views for public policy. Anthropologist Daniel

G. Brinton made typical arguments in his 1895 presidential address to the American Association for the Advancement of Science. He contended that the "black, brown and red races" each had "a peculiar mental temperament which has become hereditary," leaving them constitutionally "recreant to the codes of civilization." Brinton believed that this fact had not been adequately appreciated by American lawmakers. Henceforth, conceptions of "race, nations, tribes" had to "supply the only sure foundations for legislation; not *a priori* notions of the rights of man."

As Brinton knew, many politicians and judges had already begun to seize on such suggestions. In 1882, for example, California senator John Miller drew on the Darwinian "law of the 'survival of the fittest'" to explain that "forty centuries of Chinese life" had "ground into" the Chinese race characteristics that made them unbeatable competitors against the free white man. They were "automatic engines of flesh and blood," of "obtuse nerve," marked by degradation and demoralization, and thus far below the Anglo-Saxon, but were still a threat to the latter's livelihood in a market economy. Hence, Miller argued, the immigration of Chinese laborers must be banned. His bill prevailed, many expressing concern that these Chinese would otherwise become American citizens. The Chinese Exclusion Act was not a vestige of the past but something new, the first repudiation of America's long history of open immigration; and it was justified in terms of the postwar era's revivified racial theories.

Yet although men like Miller not only sustained but expanded Chinese exclusions until they were made virtually total in 1917 (and tight restrictions survived until 1965), they never managed to deny American citizenship to all of the "Chinese race." Until 1917 there were no restrictions on the immigration of upper-class Chinese, and in 1898 the Supreme Court declared that children born on U.S. soil to Chinese parents were American citizens (*United States* v. *Wong Kim Ark* 1898). Birthplace citizenship was a doctrine enshrined in common law, reinforced by the Fourteenth Amendment, and vital to citizenship for the children of *all* immigrant aliens. Hence it had enough legal and political support to override the Court's recognition of Congress's exclusionary desires. Even so, in other cases the Court sustained bans on Chinese immigration while admitting the racial animosities behind them, as in the "Chinese Exclusion Case" (*Chae Chan Ping* v. *United States* 1889); upheld requirements for Chinese-Americans to have certificates of citizenship not required of whites (*Fong Yue Ting* v. *United States* 1893); and permitted officials to deport even Chinese persons who had later been judged by courts to be native-born U.S. citizens (*United States* v. *Ju Toy* 1905).

The upshot, then, was the sort of none-too-coherent mix that the multiple-traditions thesis holds likely. Chinese were excluded on racial grounds, but race did not bar citizenship to those born in the United States; yet Chinese ancestry could subject some American citizens to burdens, including deportation, that others did not face. The mix was not perfect from any ideological viewpoint, but it was politically popular. It maintained a valued inclusive feature of American law (birthplace citizenship) while sharply reducing the resident Chinese population. And it most fully satisfied the increasingly powerful champions of Anglo-Saxon supremacy.

From 1887 on, academic reformers and politicians sought to restrict immigration more generally by a means that paid lip service to liberal norms even as it aimed at racist results—the literacy test. On its face, this measure expressed concern only for the intellectual merits of immigrants. But the test's true aims were spelled out in 1896 by its sponsor, Senator Henry Cabot Lodge, a Harvard Ph.D. in history and politics. Committee research, he reported, showed that the test would exclude "the Italians, Russians, Poles, Hungarians, Greeks, and Asiatics," thereby preserving "the quality of our race and citizenship." Citing "modern history" and "modern science," Thomas Carlyle and Gustave le Bon, Lodge contended that the need for racial exclusion arose from "something deeper and more fundamental than anything which concerns the intellect." Race was above all constituted by moral characteristics, the "stock of ideas, traditions, sentiments, modes of thought" that a people possessed as an "accumulation of centuries of toil and conflict." These mental and moral qualities constituted the "soul of a race," an inheritance in which its members "blindly believe," and upon which learning had no effect. But these qualities could be degraded if "a lower race mixes with a higher"; thus, exclusion by race, not reading ability, was the nation's proper goal.

When the literacy test finally passed in 1917 but proved ineffective in keeping out "lower races," Congress moved to versions of an explicitly racist national-origins quota system. It banned virtually all Asians and permitted European immigration only in ratios preserving the northern European cast of the American citizenry. Congressman Albert Johnson, chief author of the most important quota act in 1924, proclaimed that through it, "the day of indiscriminate acceptance of all races, has definitely ended." The quota system, repealed only in 1965, was a novel, elaborate monument to ideologies holding that access to American citizenship should be subject to racial and ethnic limits. It also served as the prime model for similar systems in Europe and Latin America.

*   *   *

But despite the new prevalence of such attitudes on the part of northern and western elites in the late nineteenth century, the Reconstruction amendments and statutes were still on the books, and surviving liberal sentiments made repealing them politically difficult. Believers in racial inequality were, moreover, undecided on just what to do about blacks. * * * "Radical" racists * * * argued that blacks, like other lower races, should be excluded from American society and looked hopefully for evidence that they were dying out. Their position was consistent with Hartz's claim that Americans could not tolerate permanent unequal statuses; persons must either be equal citizens or outsiders. But * * * "Conservatives" believed * * * that blacks and other people of color might instead have a permanent "place" in America, so long as "placeness included hierarchy." Some still thought that blacks, like the other "lower races," might one day be led by whites to fully civilized status, but no one expected progress in the near future. Thus blacks should instead be segregated, largely disfranchised, and confined to menial occupations via inferior education and discriminatory hiring practices—but not expelled, tortured, or killed. A few talented blacks might even be allowed somewhat higher stations.

* * * The result was a system closest to Conservative desires, one that kept blacks in their place, although that place was structured more repressively than most Conservatives favored. And unlike the ineffective literacy test, here racial inegalitarians achieved much of what they wanted without explicitly violating liberal legal requirements. Complex registration systems, poll taxes, and civics tests appeared race-neutral but were designed and administered to disfranchise blacks. This intent was little masked. * * * These efforts succeeded. Most dramatically, in Louisiana 95.6% of blacks were registered in 1896, and over half (130,000) voted. After disfranchising measures, black registration dropped by 90% and by 1904 totaled only 1,342. The Supreme Court found convoluted ways to close its eyes to these tactics.

By similar devices, blacks were virtually eliminated from juries in the south, where 90% of American blacks lived, sharply limiting their ability to have their personal and economic rights protected by the courts. "Separate but equal" educational and business laws and practices also stifled the capacities of blacks to participate in the nation's economy as equals, severely curtailed the occupations they could train for, and marked them—unofficially but clearly—as an inferior caste. Thus here, as elsewhere, it was evident that the nation's laws and institutions were not meant to confer the equal civic status they proclaimed for all Americans; but neither did they conform fully to doctrines favoring overt racial hierarchy. They represented another asymmetrical compromise among the multiple ideologies vying to define American political culture.

So, too, did the policies governing two groups whose civic status formally improved during these years: Native Americans and women. * * *

*   *   *

This period also highlights how the influence of inegalitarian doctrines has not been confined to white male intellectuals, legislators, and judges. The leading writer of the early twentieth-century women's movement, Charlotte Perkins Gilman, was a thoroughgoing Darwinian who accepted that evolution had made women inferior to men in certain respects, although she insisted that these differences were usually exaggerated and that altered social conditions could transform them. And even as he

attacked Booker T. Washington for appearing to accept the "alleged inferiority of the Negro race," W. E. B. DuBois embraced the widespread La-
marckian view that racial characteristics were socially conditioned but
then inherited as the "soul" of a race. He could thus accept that most
blacks were "primitive folk" in need of tutelage. * * *

The acceptance of ascriptive inegalitarian beliefs by brilliant and politically dissident female and black male intellectuals strongly suggests that
these ideas had broad appeal. Writers whose interests they did not easily
serve still saw them as persuasive in light of contemporary scientific theories and empirical evidence of massive inequalities. It is likely, too, that for
many the vision of a meaningful natural order that these doctrines provided
had the psychological and philosophical appeal that such positions have
always had for human beings, grounding their status and significance in
something greater and more enduring than their own lives. * * *

In sum, if we accept that ideologies and institutions of ascriptive hierarchy have shaped America in interaction with its liberal and democratic
features, we can make more sense of a wide range of inegalitarian policies newly contrived after 1870 and perpetuated through much of the
twentieth century. Those policies were dismantled only through great
struggles, aided by international pressures during World War II and the
Cold War; and it is not clear that these struggles have ended. The novel-
ties in the policies and scientific doctrines of the Gilded Age and Progressive Era should alert us to the possibility that new intellectual systems
and political forces defending racial and gender inequalities may yet gain
increased power in our own time.

*   *   *

The achievements of Americans in building a more inclusive democracy certainly provide reasons to believe that illiberal forces will not prevail. But just as we can better explain the nation's past by recognizing
how and why liberal democratic principles have been contested with frequent success, we will better understand the present and future of American politics if we do not presume they are rooted in essentially liberal or
democratic values and conditions. Instead, we must analyze America as
the ongoing product of often conflicting multiple traditions.

Discussion Questions

1. According to Smith, what are some examples of how Americans in
   the late nineteenth century simultaneously held liberal and ascriptive hierarchical views?

2. What are the key components of the classical republican outlook, as
   presented by Smith? How do they differ from the liberal tradition?

3. Do you believe that ascriptive hierarchy is still a powerful strain of thought in American political culture? If so, what are some examples?

4. How would you know if ascriptive hierarchy was as widespread as Smith contends? What kind of evidence would you look for?

5. How might an advocate of liberalism, republicanism, and ascriptive hierarchy define "the public good"?

Debating the Issues: What Does It Mean to Be an American?

What does it mean to be an American? This deceptively simple question is challenging to answer. Because the United States encompasses a vast array of ethnicities, religions, and cultures, it can be difficult to define "American" by reference to those criteria. The country's geography differs dramatically from area to area, and the economic way of life accordingly differs greatly as well. And in many ways, diverse groups of Americans have experienced American history differently, so a common historical identity is not obviously the answer either. One popular argument is that the United States is united by a set of political ideals. As far back as the early nineteenth century, scholars have tried to identify the nature of American political culture: Is it a commitment to individualism? A belief in equality? A shared set of values about the appropriate role of government? Openness?

Sarah Song reviews three ways in which ideals might provide what she refers to as civic solidarity. Constitutional patriotism says that the key to the American identity is fidelity to and support of ideals set forth in the major texts of American political culture such as the Declaration of Independence and the Constitution. Liberal nationalism argues that adherence to a set of ideals is not sufficient for a national identity. It also must include these four features: "a shared belief among a group of individuals that they belong together, historical continuity stretching across generations, connection to a particular territory, and a shared set of characteristics constituting a national culture." Last, Song argues most strongly for "deep diversity," a multicultural understanding of the United States in which an acceptance of difference is the key idea that glues society together—the search for a common culture shared by all is set aside. In this view, acceptance and encouragement of different languages, beliefs, and values are themselves the unifying value that unites a society's understanding of itself. Song presents Canada as an example of deep diversity.

Steven Warshawsky argues that American identity centers around a commonly held set of ideas that can be considered the American way of life. This way of life includes beliefs in liberty, equality, property rights, religious freedom, limited government, and a common language for conducting political and economic life. Although we have always been a nation of immigrants, from the original settlers to the mass immigration of the late nineteenth and early twentieth centuries, Warshawsky sees assimilation into American political culture as critical to American national identity. He also notes that America, including the scope and reach of government, has changed dramatically over time. Warshawsky asks whether these changes also changed what it means to be "an American." He argues this is a difficult question but concludes that straying too far from the principles of the Founders means "we will cease to be 'Americans' in any meaningful sense of the word."

Daniel Elazar provides a different way of approaching the question of what it means to be an American. He argues that political beliefs in the United States are distributed unevenly across the country. In large part, this has to do with migration patterns. Once certain ethnic groups and nationalities predominated in a particular area, the institutions they built and the practice of politics tended to become ingrained with their political and cultural beliefs. Elazar sees three types of value systems across the country: moralism, individualism, and traditionalism. Moralism is focused on the community and engaging in politics to do good. Individualism focuses on individual rights and tends to view governing as a set of transactions among various individuals and groups. Traditionalism attempts to use the power of government to preserve existing social arrangements. These three approaches vary in their prevalence across the country, and even within states there may be variation as to which of the three predominates. Some areas have a mixture of two of these value systems, whereas other areas are more purely of one type.

4

"What Does It Mean to Be an American?"

Sarah Song

It is often said that being an American means sharing a commitment to a set of values and ideals. Writing about the relationship of ethnicity and American identity, the historian Philip Gleason put it this way:

> To be or to become an American, a person did not have to be any particular national, linguistic, religious, or ethnic background. All he had to do was to commit himself to the political ideology centered on the abstract ideals of liberty, equality, and republicanism. Thus the universalist ideological character of American nationality meant that it was open to anyone who willed to become an American.

To take the motto of the Great Seal of the United States, *E pluribus unum*—"From many, one"—in this context suggests not that manyness should be melted down into one, as in [the] image of the melting pot, but that, as the Great Seal's sheaf of arrows suggests, there should be a coexistence of many-in-one under a unified citizenship based on shared ideals.

Of course, the story is not so simple, as Gleason himself went on to note. America's history of racial and ethnic exclusions has undercut the universalist stance; for being an American has also meant sharing a national culture, one largely defined in racial, ethnic, and religious terms. * * * In this essay, I explore different ideals of civic solidarity with an eye toward what they imply for newcomers who wish to become American citizens.

Why does civic solidarity matter? First, it is integral to the pursuit of distributive justice. * * * The underlying idea is that people are more likely to support redistributive schemes when they trust one another, and they are more likely to trust one another when they regard others as like themselves in some meaningful sense.

Second, genuine democracy demands solidarity. If democratic activity involves not just voting, but also deliberation, then people must make an effort to listen to and understand one another. Moreover, they must be willing to moderate their claims in the hope of finding common ground on which to base political decisions. Such democratic activity cannot be realized by individuals pursuing their own interests; it requires some concern for the common good. A sense of solidarity can help foster mutual sympathy and respect, which in turn support citizens' orientation toward the common good.

Third, civic solidarity offers more inclusive * * * models of political community as an alternative to the racial, ethnic, or religious narratives that have permeated political life. The challenge, then, is to develop a model of civic solidarity that is "thick" enough to motivate support for justice and democracy while also "thin" enough to accommodate racial, ethnic, and religious diversity.

We might look first to [the] idea of constitutional patriotism * * *. On this view, what binds citizens together is their common allegiance to the ideals embodied in a shared political culture.

* * *

The basis of American solidarity is not any particular racial or ethnic identity or religious beliefs, but universal moral ideals embodied in American political culture and set forth in such seminal texts as the Declaration of Independence, the U.S. Constitution and Bill of Rights, Abraham Lincoln's Gettysburg Address, and Martin Luther King, Jr.'s "I Have a Dream" speech. * * *

What does constitutional patriotism suggest for the sort of reception immigrants should receive? There has been a general shift in Western Europe and North America in the standards governing access to citizenship from cultural markers to values, and this is a development that constitutional patriots would applaud. In the United States those seeking to become citizens must demonstrate basic knowledge of U.S. government and history. A newly revised U.S. citizenship test was instituted in October 2008 with the hope that it will serve, in the words of the chief of the Office of Citizenship, Alfonso Aguilar, as "an instrument to promote civic learning and patriotism." The revised test attempts to move away from civics trivia to emphasize political ideas and concepts. * * * The new test asks more open-ended questions about government powers and political concepts: "What does the judicial branch do?" "What stops one branch of government from becoming too powerful?" "What is freedom of religion?" "What is the 'rule of law'?"

Constitutional patriots would endorse this focus on values and principles. * * * All that should be expected of immigrants is that they embrace the constitutional principles as interpreted by the political culture, not that they necessarily embrace the majority's ethical-cultural forms [such as language].

Yet * * * government decisions about the language of public institutions, public holidays, and state symbols unavoidably involve recognizing and supporting particular ethnic and religious groups over others. In the United States, English language ability has been a statutory qualification for naturalization since 1906, originally as a requirement of oral ability and later as a requirement of English literacy. Indeed, support for the principles of the Constitution has been interpreted as requiring English literacy. The language requirement might be justified as a practical matter (we need some language to be the common language of schools, government, and the workplace, so why not the language of the majority?), but for a great many citizens, the language requirement is also viewed as a key marker of national identity. The continuing centrality of language in naturalization policy prevents us from saying that what it means to be an American is purely a matter of shared values.

Another misconception about constitutional patriotism is that it is necessarily more inclusive of newcomers than [other] models of solidarity. Its inclusiveness depends on which principles are held up as the polity's shared principles. * * * Consider ideological requirements for naturalization in U.S. history. The first naturalization law of 1790 required nothing more than an oath to support the U.S. Constitution. The second naturalization act added two ideological elements: the renunciation of titles or orders of nobility and the requirement that one be found to have "behaved as a man . . . attached to the principles of the constitution of the United States." This attachment requirement was revised in 1940 from a behavioral qualification to a personal attribute, but this did not help clarify what attachment to constitutional principles requires. Not surprisingly, the "attachment to constitutional principles" requirement has been interpreted as requiring a belief in representative government, federalism, separation of powers, and constitutionally guaranteed individual rights. It has also been interpreted as disqualifying anarchists, polygamists, and conscientious objectors for citizenship. In 1950, support for communism was added to the list of grounds for disqualification from naturalization—as well as grounds for exclusion and deportation. The 1990 Immigration Act retained the McCarthy-era ideological qualifications for naturalization; current law disqualifies those who advocate or affiliate with an organization that advocates communism or opposition to all organized government. Patriotism * * * is capable of excess and pathology, as evidenced by loyalty oaths and campaigns against "un-American" activities.

In contrast to constitutional patriots, liberal nationalists acknowledge that states cannot be culturally neutral even if they tried. States cannot avoid coercing citizens into preserving a national culture of some kind because state institutions and laws define a political culture, which in turn shapes the range of customs and practices of daily life that constitute a national culture. David Miller, a leading theorist of liberal nationalism, defines national identity according to the following elements: a shared belief among a group of individuals that they belong together, historical continuity stretching across generations, connection to a particular territory, and a shared set of characteristics constituting a national culture. It is not enough to share a common identity rooted in a shared history or a shared territory; a shared national culture is a necessary feature of national identity. I share a national culture with someone, even if we never meet, if each of us has been initiated into the traditions and customs of a national culture.

What sort of content makes up a national culture? Miller says more about what a national culture does not entail. It need not be based on biological descent. Even if nationalist doctrines have historically been based on notions of biological descent and race, Miller emphasizes that sharing a national culture is, in principle, compatible with people belonging to a diversity of racial and ethnic groups. In addition, every member need not have been born in the homeland. Thus, "immigration need not pose problems, provided only that the immigrants come to share a common national identity, to which they may contribute their own distinctive ingredients."

Liberal nationalists focus on the idea of culture, as opposed to ethnicity. * * * Both nationality and ethnicity have cultural components, but what is said to distinguish "civic" nations from "ethnic" nations is that the latter are exclusionary and closed on grounds of biological descent; the former are, in principle, open to anyone willing to adopt the national culture.

Yet the civic-ethnic distinction is not so clear-cut in practice. Every nation has an "ethnic core."

* * *

Why, then, if all national cultures have ethnic cores, should those outside this core embrace the national culture? * * *

The major difficulty here is that national cultures are not typically the product of collective deliberation in which all have the opportunity to participate. The challenge is to ensure that historically marginalized groups, as well as new groups of immigrants, have genuine opportunities to contribute "on an equal footing" to shaping the national culture. * * *

Cultural nationalist visions of solidarity would lend support to immigration and immigrant policies that give weight to linguistic and ethnic preferences and impose special requirements on individuals from groups deemed to be outside the nation's "core culture." One example is the practice in postwar Germany of giving priority in immigration and naturalization policy to ethnic Germans; they were the only foreign nationals who were accepted as permanent residents set on the path toward citizenship. They were treated not as immigrants but "resettlers" (Aussiedler) who acted on their constitutional right to return to their country of origin. In contrast, non-ethnically German guestworkers (Gastarbeiter) were designated as "aliens" (Ausländer) under the 1965 German Alien Law and excluded from German citizenship. Another example is the Japanese naturalization policy that, until the late 1980s, required naturalized citizens to adopt a Japanese family name. The language requirement in contemporary naturalization policies in the West is the leading remaining example of a cultural nationalist integration policy; it reflects not only a concern with the economic and political integration of immigrants but also a nationalist concern with preserving a distinctive national culture.

Constitutional patriotism and liberal nationalism are accounts of civic solidarity that deal with what one might call first-level diversity. Individuals have different group identities and hold divergent moral and religious outlooks, yet they are expected to share the same idea of what it means to be American: either patriots committed to the same set of ideals or co-nationals sharing the relevant cultural attributes. [A]n alternative approach [is] the idea of "deep diversity."

* * *

What leads people to support [deep] diversity is both the desire to be a member of the political community and the recognition of disagreement about what it means to be a member.

* * * The United States has a need for acknowledgment of diverse modes of belonging based on the distinctive histories of different groups. Native Americans, African Americans, Irish Americans, Vietnamese Americans, and Mexican Americans: across these communities of people, we can find not only distinctive group identities, but also distinctive ways of belonging to the political community.

*   *   *

While attractive for its inclusiveness, the deep diversity model may be too thin a basis for civic solidarity in a democratic society. Can there be civic solidarity without citizens already sharing a set of values or a culture in the first place? * * * In contrast to liberal nationalism, deep diversity does not aim at specifying a common national culture that must be shared by all. What matters is not so much the content of solidarity, but the ethos generated by making the effort at mutual understanding and respect.

Canada's approach to the integration of immigrants may be the closest thing there is to "deep diversity." Canadian naturalization policy is not so different from that of the United States: a short required residency period, relatively low application fees, a test of history and civics knowledge, and a language exam. Where the United States and Canada diverge is in their public commitment to diversity. Through its official multiculturalism policies, Canada expresses a commitment to the value of diversity among immigrant communities through funding for ethnic associations and supporting heritage language schools. Constitutional patriots and liberal nationalists say that immigrant integration should be a two-way process, that immigrants should shape the host society's dominant culture just as they are shaped by it. Multicultural accommodations actually provide the conditions under which immigrant integration might genuinely become a two-way process. Such policies send a strong message that immigrants are a welcome part of the political community and should play an active role in shaping its future evolution.

*   *   *

What is now formally required of immigrants seeking to become American citizens most clearly reflects the first two models of solidarity: professed allegiance to the principles of the Constitution (constitutional patriotism) and adoption of a shared culture by demonstrating the ability to read, write, and speak English (liberal nationalism). The revised citizenship test makes gestures toward respect for first-level diversity and inclusion of historically marginalized groups with questions such as, "Who lived in America before the Europeans arrived?" "What group of people was taken to America and sold as slaves?" "What did Susan B. Anthony do?" "What did Martin Luther King, Jr. do?" The election of the first African American president of the United States is a significant step forward. A more inclusive American solidarity requires the recognition not only of the fact that Americans are a diverse people, but also that they have distinctive ways of belonging to America.

"What Does It Mean to Be an American?"

STEVEN M. WARSHAWSKY

"Undocumented Americans." This is how Senate Majority Leader Harry Reid recently described the estimated 12–20 million illegal aliens living in America. What was once a Mark Steyn joke has now become the ideological orthodoxy of the Democratic Party.

Reid's comment triggered an avalanche of outrage among commentators, bloggers, and the general public. Why? Because it strikes at the heart of the American people's understanding of themselves as a nation and a civilization. Indeed, opposition to the ongoing push for "comprehensive immigration reform"—i.e., amnesty and a guest worker program—is being driven by a growing concern among millions of Americans that massive waves of legal and illegal immigration—mainly from Mexico, Latin America, and Asia—coupled with the unwillingness of our political and economic elites to mold these newcomers into red-white-and-blue Americans, is threatening to change the very character of our country. For the worse.

I share this concern. I agree with the political, economic, and cultural arguments in favor of sharply curtailing immigration into the United States, as well as refocusing our immigration efforts on admitting those foreigners who bring the greatest value to—and are most easily assimilated into—American society. * * * But this essay is not intended to rehash these arguments. Rather, I wish to explore the question that underlies this entire debate: What does it mean to be an American? This may seem like an easy question to answer, but it's not. The harder one thinks about this question, the more complex it becomes.

Clearly, Harry Reid has not given this question much thought. His implicit definition of "an American" is simply: Anyone living within the geopolitical boundaries of the United States. In other words, mere physical location on Earth determines whether or not someone is "an American." Presumably, Reid's definition is not intended to apply to tourists and other temporary visitors. Some degree of permanency—what the law in other contexts calls "residency," i.e., a subjective intention to establish one's home or domicile—is required. In Reid's view, therefore, a Mexican from Guadalajara, a Chinese from Shanghei [sic], an Indian from Delhi, or a [fill in the blank] become "Americans" as soon as they cross into U.S.

territory and decide to live here permanently, legally or not. Nothing more is needed.

This is poppycock, of course. A Mexican or a Chinese or an Indian, for example, cannot transform themselves into Americans simply by moving to this country, any more than I can become a Mexican, a Chinese, or an Indian simply by moving to their countries. Yet contemporary liberals have a vested interest in believing that they can. This is not just a function of immigrant politics, which strongly favors the Democratic Party (hence the Democrats' growing support for voting rights for non-citizens). It also reflects the liberals' (and some libertarians') multicultural faith, which insists that it is morally wrong to make distinctions among different groups of people, let alone to impose a particular way of life—what heretofore has been known as the American way of life—on those who believe, speak, and act differently. Even in our own country.

In short, diversity, not Americanism, is the multicultural touchstone.

What's more, the principle of diversity, taken to its logical extreme, inevitably leads to a *rejection* of Americanism. Indeed, the ideology of multiculturalism has its roots in the radical—and anti-American—New Left and Black Power movements of the 1960s and 1970s. Thus the sorry state of U.S. history and civics education in today's schools and universities, which are dominated by adherents of this intellectual poison. Moreover, when it comes to immigration, multiculturalists actually *prefer* those immigrants who are as unlike ordinary Americans as possible. This stems from their deep-rooted opposition to traditional American society, which they hope to undermine through an influx of non-western peoples and cultures.

This, in fact, describes present U.S. immigration policy, which largely is a product of the 1965 Immigration Act (perhaps Ted Kennedy's most notorious legislative achievement). The 1965 Immigration Act eliminated the legal preferences traditionally given to European immigrants, and opened the floodgates to immigration from less-developed and non-western countries. For example, in 2006 more immigrants came to the United States from Columbia, Peru, Vietnam, and Haiti (not to mention Mexico, China, and India), than from the United Kingdom, Germany, Italy, and Greece. And once these immigrants arrive here, multiculturalists believe we should accommodate *our* society to the needs and desires of the newcomers, not the other way around. Thus, our government prints election ballots, school books, and welfare applications in foreign languages, while corporate America asks customers to "press one for English."

Patriotic Americans—those who love our country for its people, its history, its culture, and its ideals—reject the multiculturalists' denuded, and ultimately subversive, vision of what it means to be "an American." While the American identity is arguably the most "universal" of all major nationalities—as evidenced by the millions of immigrants the world over who have successfully assimilated into our country over the years—it is not an empty, meaningless concept. It has substance. Being "an American" is *not* the same thing as simply living in the United States. Nor, I would add, is it the same thing as holding U.S. citizenship. After all, a baby born on U.S. soil to an illegal alien is a citizen. This hardly guarantees that this baby will grow up to be *an American*.

So what, then, does it mean to be an American? I suspect that most of us believe, like Supreme Court Justice Potter Stewart in describing pornography, that we "know it when we see it." For example, John Wayne, Amelia Earhart, and Bill Cosby definitely are Americans. The day laborers standing on the street corner probably are not. But how do we put this inner understanding into words? It's not easy. Unlike most other nations on Earth, the American nation is not strictly defined in terms of race or ethnicity or ancestry or religion. George Washington may be the Father of Our Country (in my opinion, the greatest American who ever lived), but there have been in the past, and are today, many millions of patriotic, hardworking, upstanding Americans who are not Caucasian, or Christian, or of Western European ancestry. Yet they are undeniably as American as you or I (by the way, I am Jewish of predominantly Eastern European ancestry). Any definition of "American" that excludes such folks—let alone one that excludes me!—cannot be right.

Consequently, it is just not good enough to say, as some immigration restrictionists do, that this is a "white-majority, Western country." Yes, it is. But so are, for example, Ireland and Sweden and Portugal. Clearly, this level of abstraction does not take us very far towards understanding what it means to be "an American." Nor is it all that helpful to say that this is an English-speaking, predominately Christian country. While I think these features get us closer to the answer, there are millions of English-speaking (and non-English-speaking) Christians in the world who are not Americans, and millions of non-Christians who are. Certainly, these fundamental historical characteristics are important elements in determining who we are as a nation. Like other restrictionists, I am opposed to public policies that seek, by design or by default, to significantly alter the nation's "demographic profile." Still, it must be recognized that demography alone does not, and cannot, explain what it means to be an American.

So where does that leave us? I think the answer to our question, ultimately, must be found in the realms of ideology and culture. What distinguishes the United States from other nations, and what unites the disparate peoples who make up our country, are our unique political, economic, and social values, beliefs, and institutions. Not race, or religion, or ancestry.

Whether described as a "proposition nation" or a "creedal nation" or simply just "an idea," the United States of America is defined by *our way of life*. This way of life is rooted in the ideals proclaimed in the

Declaration of Independence; in the system of personal liberty and limited government established by the Constitution; in our traditions of self-reliance, personal responsibility, and entrepreneurism; in our emphasis on private property, freedom of contract, and merit-based achievement; in our respect for the rule of law; and in our commitment to affording equal justice to all. Perhaps above all, it is marked by our abiding belief that, as Americans, we have been called to a higher duty in human history. We are the "city upon a hill." We are "the last, best hope of earth."

Many immigration restrictionists and so-called traditionalists chafe at the notion that the American people are not defined by "blood and soil." Yet the truth of the matter is, we aren't. One of the greatest patriots who ever graced this nation's history, Teddy Roosevelt, said it best: "Americanism is a matter of the spirit and of the soul." Roosevelt deplored what he called "hyphenated Americanism," which refers to citizens whose primary loyalties lie with their particular ethnic groups or ancestral lands. Such a man, Roosevelt counseled, is to be "unsparingly condemn[ed]."

But Roosevelt also recognized that "if he is heartily and singly loyal to this Republic, then no matter where he was born, he is just as good an American as any one else." Roosevelt's words are not offered here to suggest that all foreigners are equally capable of assimilating into our country. Clearly, they aren't. Nevertheless, the appellation "American" is open to anyone who adopts our way of life and loves this country above all others.

Which brings me to the final, and most difficult, aspect of this question: How do we define the "American way of life"? This is the issue over which our nation's "culture wars" are being fought. Today the country is divided between those who maintain their allegiance to certain historically American values, beliefs, and institutions (but not all—see racial segregation), and those who want to replace them with a very different set of ideas about the role of government, the nature of political and economic liberty, and the meaning of right and wrong. Are both sides in this struggle equally "American"?

Moreover, the "American way of life" has changed over time. We no longer have the Republic that existed in TR's days. The New Deal and Great Society revolutions—enthusiastically supported, I note, by millions of white, Christian, English-speaking citizens—significantly altered the political, economic, and social foundations of this country. Did they also change what it means to be "an American"? Is being an American equally compatible, for example, with support for big government versus small government? the welfare state versus rugged individualism? socialism versus capitalism? And so on. Plainly, this is a much harder historical and intellectual problem than at first meets the eye.

Personally, I do not think the meaning of America is nearly so malleable as today's multiculturalists assume. But neither is it quite as narrow as many restrictionists contend. Nevertheless, I am convinced that being *an American* requires something more than merely living in this country, speaking English, obeying the law, and holding a job (although this would be a very good start!). What this "something more" is, however, is not self-evident, and, indeed, is the subject of increasingly bitter debate in this country.

Yet one thing is certain: If we stray too far from the lines laid down by the Founding Fathers and the generations of great American men and women who built on their legacy, we will cease to be "Americans" in any meaningful sense of the word. As Abraham Lincoln warned during the secession era, "America will never be destroyed from the outside. If we falter and lose our freedoms, it will be because we destroyed ourselves." Today the danger is not armed rebellion, but the slow erasing of the American national character through a process of political and cultural redefinition. If this ever happens, it will be a terrible day for this country, and for the world.

6

"The Three Political Cultures"

Daniel J. Elazar

The United States is a single land of great diversity inhabited by what is now a single people of great diversity. The singleness of the country as a whole is expressed through political, cultural, and geographic unity. Conversely, the country's diversity is expressed through its states, subcultures, and sections. In this section, we will focus on the political dimensions of that diversity-in-unity—on the country's overall political culture and its subculture.

Political culture is the summation of persistent patterns of underlying political attitudes and characteristic responses to political concerns that is manifest in a particular political order. Its existence is generally unperceived by those who are part of that order, and its origins date back to the very beginnings of the particular people who share it. Political culture is an intrinsically political phenomenon. As such, it makes its own demands on the political system. For example, the definition of what is "fair" in the political arena—a direct manifestation of political culture—is likely to be different from the definition of what is fair in family or business relationships. Moreover, different political cultures will define fairness in politics differently. Political culture also affects all other questions confronting the political system. For example, many factors go into shaping public expectations regarding government services, and political culture will be significant among them. Political systems, in turn, are in some measure the products of the political cultures they serve and must remain in harmony with their political cultures if they are to maintain themselves.

* * *

Political-culture factors stand out as particularly influential in shaping the operations of the national, state, and local political systems in three ways: (1) by molding the perceptions of the political community (the citizens, the politicians, and the public officials) as to the nature and purposes of politics and its expectations of government and the political process; (2) by influencing the recruitment of specific kinds of people to become active in government and politics—as holders of elective offices, members of the bureaucracy, and active political workers; and (3) by subtly directing the actual way in which the art of government is practiced by citizens, politicians, and public officials in the light of their perceptions. In turn, the cultural components of individual and group behavior are manifested in civic behavior as dictated by conscience and internalized ethical standards, in the forms of law-abidingness (or laxity in such matters) adhered to by citizens and officials, and in the character of the positive actions of government.

* * *

The national political culture of the United States is itself a synthesis of three major political subcultures. These subcultures jointly inhabit the country, existing side by side or sometimes overlapping one another. All three are of nationwide proportions, having spread, in the course of time, from coast to coast. Yet each subculture is strongly tied to specific sections of the country, reflecting the streams and currents of migration that have carried people of different origins and backgrounds across the continent in more or less orderly patterns.

Given the central characteristics that define each of the subcultures and their centers of emphasis, the three political subcultures may be called individualistic, moralistic, and traditionalistic. Each reflects its own particular synthesis of the marketplace and the commonwealth.

It is important, however, not only to examine this description and the following ones very carefully but also to abandon the preconceptions associated with such idea-words as individualistic, moralistic, marketplace, and so on. Thus, for example, nineteenth-century individualistic conceptions of minimum intervention were oriented toward *laissez-faire*, with the role of government conceived to be that of a policeman with powers to act in certain limited fields. And in the twentieth century, the notion of what constitutes minimum intervention has been drastically expanded to include such things as government regulation of utilities, unemployment

compensation, and massive subventions to maintain a stable and growing economy—all within the framework of the same political culture. The
demands of manufacturers for high tariffs in 1865 and the demands of
labor unions for worker's compensation in 1965 may well be based on the
same theoretical justification that they are aids to the maintenance of a
working marketplace. Culture is not static. It must be viewed dynami-
cally and defined so as to include cultural change in its very nature.

The Individualistic Political Culture

The *individualistic political culture* emphasizes the conception of the democratic order as a marketplace. It is rooted in the view that government is
instituted for strictly utilitarian reasons, to handle those functions demanded by the people it serves. According to this view, government need
not have any direct concern with questions of the "good society" (except
insofar as the government may be used to advance some common conception of the good society formulated outside the political arena, just
as it serves other functions). Emphasizing the centrality of private concerns, the individualistic political culture places a premium on limiting
community intervention—whether governmental or nongovernmental—
into private activities, to the minimum degree necessary to keep the marketplace in proper working order. In general, government action is to be
restricted to those areas, primarily in the economic realm, that encourage
private initiative and widespread access to the marketplace.

The character of political participation in systems dominated by the
individualistic political culture reflects the view that politics is just another means by which individuals may improve themselves socially and
economically. In this sense politics is a "business," like any other that
competes for talent and offers rewards to those who take it up as a career.
Those individuals who choose political careers may rise by providing the
governmental services demanded of them and, in return, may expect to
be adequately compensated for their efforts.

Interpretation of officeholders' obligations under the individualistic
political culture vary among political systems and even among individuals within a single political system. Where the standards are high, such
people are expected to provide high-quality government services for the
general public in the best possible manner in return for the status and
economic rewards considered their due. Some who choose political careers clearly commit themselves to such norms; others believe that an
office-holder's primary responsibility is to serve him- or herself and those
who have supported him or her directly, favoring them at the expense of
others. In some political systems, this view is accepted by the public as
well as by politicians.

Political life within an individualistic political culture is based on a
system of mutual obligations rooted in personal relationships. Whereas

in a simple civil society those relationships can be direct ones, those with individualistic political cultures in the United States are usually too complex to maintain face-to-face ties. So the system of mutual obligation is harnessed through political parties, which serve as "business corporations" dedicated to providing the organization necessary to maintain that system. Party regularity is indispensable in the individualistic political culture because it is the means for coordinating individual enterprise in the political arena; it is also the one way of preventing individualism in politics from running wild.

In such a system, an individual can succeed politically, not by dealing with issues in some exceptional way or by accepting some concept of good government and then by striving to implement it, but by maintaining his or her place in the system of mutual obligations. A person can do this by operating according to the norms of his or her particular party, to the exclusion of other political considerations. Such a political culture encourages the maintenance of a party system that is competitive, but not overtly so, in the pursuit of office. Its politicians are interested in office as a means of controlling the distribution of the favors or rewards of government rather than as a means of exercising governmental power for programmatic ends; hence competition may prove less rewarding than accommodation in certain situations.

Since the individualistic political culture eschews ideological concerns in its "business-like" conception of politics, both politicians and citizens tend to look upon political activity as a specialized one—as essentially the province of professionals, of minimum and passing concern to laypersons, and with no place for amateurs to play an active role. Furthermore, there is a strong tendency among the public to believe that politics is a dirty—albeit necessary—business, better left to those who are willing to soil themselves by engaging in it. In practice, then, where the individualistic political culture is dominant, there is likely to be an easy attitude toward the limits of the professional's perquisites. Since a fair amount of corruption is expected in the normal course of things, there is relatively little popular excitement when any is found, unless it is of an extraordinary character. It is as if the public were willing to pay a surcharge for services rendered, rebelling only when the surcharge becomes too heavy. Of course, the judgments as to what is "normal" and what is "extraordinary" are themselves subjective and culturally conditioned.

Public officials, committed to "giving the public what it wants," are normally not willing to initiate new programs or open up new areas of government activity on their own initiative. They will do so when they perceive an overwhelming public demand for them to act, but only then. In a sense, their willingness to expand the functions of government is based on an extension of the *quid pro quo* "favors" system, which serves as the central core of their political relationships. New and better services are the reward they give the public for placing them in office. The value mix and legitimacy of change in the individualistic political culture are directly related to commercial concerns.

The individualistic political culture is ambivalent about the place of bureaucracy in the political order. In one sense, the bureaucratic method of operation flies in the face of the favor system that is central to the individualistic political process. At the same time, the virtues of organizational efficiency appear substantial to those seeking to master the market. In the end, bureaucratic organization is introduced within the framework of the favor system; large segments of the bureaucracy may be insulated from it through the merit system, but the entire organization is pulled into the political environment at crucial points through political appointment at the upper echelons and, very frequently, also through the bending of the merit system to meet political demands.

*   *   *

The Moralistic Political Culture

To the extent that American society is built on the principles of "commerce" (in the broadest sense) and that the marketplace provides the model for public relationships, all Americans share some of the attitudes that are of great importance in the individualistic political culture. At the same time, substantial segments of the American people operate politically within the framework of two political cultures—the moralistic and traditionalistic political cultures—whose theoretical structures and operational consequences depart significantly from the individualistic pattern at crucial points.

The *moralistic political culture* emphasizes the commonwealth conception as the basis for democratic government. Politics, to this political culture, is considered one of the great human activities: the search for the good society. True, it is a struggle for power, but it is also an effort to exercise power for the betterment of the commonwealth. Accordingly, in the moralistic political culture, both the general public and the politicians conceive of politics as a public activity centered on some notion of the public good and properly devoted to the advancement of the public interest. Good government, then, is measured by the degree to which it promotes the public good and in terms of the honesty, selflessness, and commitment to the public welfare of those who govern.

In the moralistic political culture, individualism is tempered by a general commitment to utilizing communal (preferably nongovernmental, but governmental if necessary) power to intervene in the sphere of "private" activities when it is considered necessary to do so for the public good or the well-being of the community. Accordingly, issues have an important place in the moralistic style of politics, functioning to set the tone for political concern. Government is considered a positive instrument with a responsibility to promote the general welfare, although definitions of what its positive role should be may vary considerably from era to era.

As in the case of the individualistic political culture, the change from nineteenth- to twentieth-century conceptions of what government's positive role should be has been great; for example, support for Prohibition has given way to support for wage and hour regulation. At the same time, care must be taken to distinguish between a predisposition toward communal activism and a desire for federal government activity. For example, many representatives of the moralistic political culture oppose federal aid for urban renewal without in any way opposing community responsibility for urban development. The distinction they make (implicitly, at least) is between what they consider legitimate community responsibility and what they believe to be central government encroachment; or between communitarianism, which they value, and "collectivism," which they abhor. Thus, on some public issues we find certain such representatives taking highly conservative positions despite their positive attitudes toward public activity generally. Such representatives may also prefer government intervention in the social realm—that is, censorship or screening of books and movies—over government intervention in the economy, holding that the former is necessary for the public good and the latter, harmful.

Since the moralistic political culture rests on the fundamental conception that politics exists primarily as a means for coming to grips with the issues and public concerns of civil society, it embraces the notion that politics is ideally a matter of concern for all citizens, not just those who are professionally committed to political careers. Indeed, this political culture considers it the duty of every citizen to participate in the political affairs of his or her commonwealth.

Accordingly, there is a general insistence within this political culture that government service is public service, which places moral obligations upon those who participate in government that are more demanding than the moral obligations of the marketplace. There is an equally general rejection of the notion that the field of politics is a legitimate realm for private economic enrichment. Of course, politicians may benefit economically because of their political careers, but they are not expected to *profit* from political activity; indeed, they are held suspect if they do.

Since the concept of serving the community is the core of the political relationship, politicians are expected to adhere to it even at the expense of individual loyalties and political friendships. Consequently, party regularity is not of prime importance. The political party is considered a useful political device, but it is not valued for its own sake. Regular party ties can be abandoned with relative impunity for third parties, special local parties, or nonpartisan systems if such changes are believed to be helpful in gaining larger political goals. People can even shift from party to party without sanctions if such change is justified by political belief.

In the moralistic political culture, rejection of firm party ties is not to be viewed as a rejection of politics as such. On the contrary, because politics is considered potentially good and healthy within the context of that culture, it is possible to have highly political nonpartisan systems. Certainly nonpartisanship is instituted not to eliminate politics but to improve it, by widening access to public office for those unwilling or unable to gain office through the regular party structure.

In practice, where the moralistic political culture is dominant today, there is considerably more amateur participation in politics. There is also much less of what Americans consider to be corruption in government and less tolerance of those actions considered to be corrupt. Hence politics does not have the taint it so often bears in the individualistic environment.

By virtue of its fundamental outlook, the moralistic political culture creates a greater commitment to active government intervention in the economic and social life of the community. At the same time, the strong commitment to *communitarianism* characteristic of that political culture tends to channel the interest in government intervention into highly localistic paths, such that a willingness to encourage local government intervention to set public standards does not necessarily reflect a concomitant willingness to allow outside governments equal opportunity to intervene. Not infrequently, public officials themselves will seek to initiate new government activities in an effort to come to grips with problems as yet unperceived by a majority of the citizenry. The moralistic political culture is not committed to either change or the status quo *per se* but, rather, will accept either depending upon the morally defined ends to be gained.

The major difficulty of this political culture in adjusting bureaucracy to the political order is tied to the potential conflict between communitarian principles and the necessity for large-scale organization to increase bureaucratic efficiency, a problem that could affect the attitudes of moralistic culture states toward federal activity of certain kinds. Otherwise, the notion of a politically neutral administrative system creates no problem within the moralistic value system and even offers many advantages. Where merit systems are instituted, they are rigidly maintained.

*   *   *

The Traditionalistic Political Culture

The *traditionalistic political culture* is rooted in an ambivalent attitude toward the marketplace coupled with a paternalistic and elitist conception of the commonwealth. It reflects an older, precommercial attitude that accepts a substantially hierarchical society as part of the ordered nature of things, authorizing and expecting those at the top of the social structure to take a special and dominant role in government. Like its moralistic

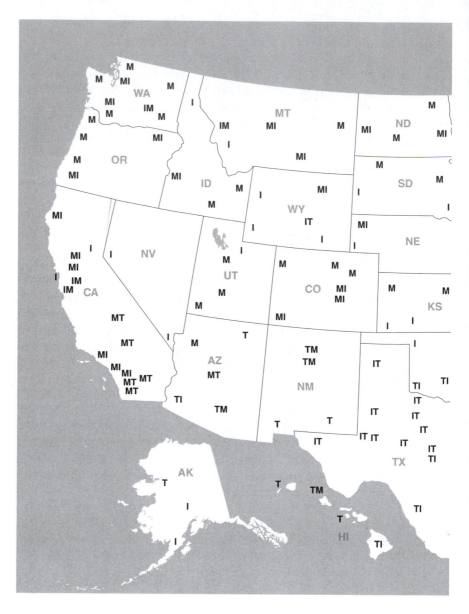

Map 1   The Regional Distribution of Political Cultures Within the States. *Source:* Daniel J. Elazar, *American Federalism: A View from the States*, 3d ed. (New York: Harper and Row Publishers, 1984), pp. 124–25. Reprinted by permission of HarperCollins Publishers.

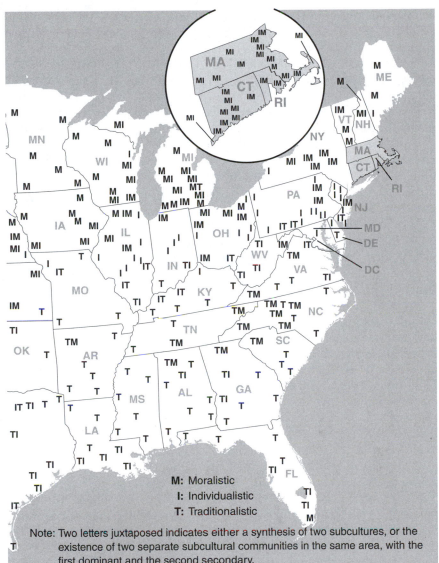

M: Moralistic
I: Individualistic
T: Traditionalistic

Note: Two letters juxtaposed indicates either a synthesis of two subcultures, or the existence of two separate subcultural communities in the same area, with the first dominant and the second secondary.

counterpart, the traditionalistic political culture accepts government as an actor with a positive role in the community, but in a very limited sphere—mainly that of securing the continued maintenance of the existing social order. To do so, it functions to confine real political power to a relatively small and self-perpetuating group drawn from an established elite who often inherit their "right" to govern through family ties or social position. Accordingly, social and family ties are paramount in a traditionalistic political culture; in fact, their importance is greater than that of personal ties in the individualistic political culture, where, after all is said and done, a person's first responsibility is to him- or herself. At the same time, those who do not have a definite role to play in politics are not expected to be even minimally active as citizens. In many cases, they are not even expected to vote. In return, they are guaranteed that, outside of the limited sphere of politics, family rights (usually labeled "individual rights") are paramount, not to be taken lightly or ignored. As in the individualistic political culture, those active in politics are expected to benefit personally from their activity, though not necessarily through direct pecuniary gain.

Political parties are of minimal importance in a traditionalistic political culture, inasmuch as they encourage a degree of openness and competition that goes against the fundamental grain of an elite-oriented political order. Their major utility is to recruit people to fill the formal offices of government not desired by the established power-holders. Political competition in a traditionalistic political culture is usually conducted through factional alignments, as an extension of the personalistic politics that is characteristic of the system; hence political systems within the culture tend to have a loose one-party orientation if they have political parties at all.

Practically speaking, a traditionalistic political culture is found only in a society that retains some of the organic characteristics of the pre-industrial social order. "Good government" in the political culture involves the maintenance and encouragement of traditional patterns and, if necessary, their adjustment to changing conditions with the least possible upset. Where the traditionalistic political culture is dominant in the United States today, political leaders play conservative and custodial rather than initiatory roles unless pressed strongly from the outside.

Whereas the individualistic and moralistic political cultures may encourage the development of bureaucratic systems of organization on the grounds of "rationality" and "efficiency" in government (depending on their particular situations), traditionalistic political cultures tend to be instinctively anti-bureaucratic. The reason is that bureaucracy by its very nature interferes with the fine web of informal interpersonal relationships that lie at the root of the political system and have been developed by following traditional patterns over the years. Where bureaucracy is introduced, it is generally confined to ministerial functions under the aegis of the established power-holders.

*   *   *

The Distribution and Impact of Political Subcultures

Map 1 on pages 46–47 shows how migrational patterns have led to the concentration of specific political subcultures in particular states and localities. The basic patterns of political culture were set during the period of the rural-land frontier by three great streams of American migration that began on the East Coast and moved westward after the colonial period. Each stream moved from east to west along more or less fixed paths, following lines of least resistance that generally led them due west from the immediately previous area of settlement.

*   *   *

Political Culture: Some Caveats

By now the reader has no doubt formed his or her own value judgments as to the relative worth of the three political subcultures. For this reason a particular warning against *hasty* judgments must be added here. Each of the three political subcultures contributes something important to the configuration of the American political system, and each possesses certain characteristics that are inherently dangerous to the survival of that system.

The moralistic political culture, for example, is the primary source of the continuing American quest for the good society, yet there is a noticeable tendency toward inflexibility and narrow-mindedness among some of its representatives. The individualistic political culture is the most tolerant of out-and-out political corruption, yet it has also provided the framework for the integration of diverse groups into the mainstream of American life. When representatives of the moralistic political culture, in their striving for a better social order, try to limit individual freedom, they usually come up against representatives of the individualistic political culture, to whom individual freedom is the cornerstone of their pluralistic order, though not for any noble reasons. Conversely, of course, the moralistic political culture acts as a restraint against the tendencies of the individualistic political culture to tolerate anything as long as it is in the marketplace.

The traditionalistic political culture contributes to the search for continuity in a society whose major characteristic is change; yet in the name of continuity, its representatives have denied African-Americans (as well as Native Americans and Latinos) their civil rights. When it is in proper working order, the traditionalistic culture has produced a unique group of first-rate national leaders from among its elites; but without a first-rate elite to draw upon, traditionalistic political-culture systems degenerate into oligarchies of the lowest level. Comparisons like these should induce caution in any evaluation of a subject that, by its very nature, evokes value judgments.

It is equally important to use caution in identifying individuals and groups as belonging to one cultural type or another on the basis of their public political behavior at a given moment in time. Immediate political responses to the issues of the day may reveal the political culture of the respondents, but not necessarily. Often, in fact, people will make what appear to be the same choices for different reasons—especially in public affairs, where the choices available at any given time are usually quite limited. Deeper analysis of what is behind those responses is usually needed. In other words, the names of the political cultures are not substitutes for the terms *conservative* and *liberal*, and should not be taken as such.

*   *   *

Discussion Questions

1. Making English a government's official language means that all official documents, ballots, and school instruction would be in English, with no translations provided by the government (although private organizations would be free to provide translations). Should English be the "official" language of the United States? What are the advantages and disadvantages in using only a single language for all government activity? Does having a common language foster assimilation and national unity?

2. Should the United States, as a deliberate strategy, seek to reinforce what it perceives as "shared American values"? If so, how? If not, why not? Should it take the ideology and political values of potential immigrants explicitly into account?

3. Political scientists and historians often refer to "American exceptionalism," or the idea that the United States is unique. For example, compared to other democratic countries, Americans place more emphasis on individual rights and much greater decentralization of political power across the branches and levels of government. Do these outcomes require the kind of shared beliefs discussed by Warshawsky? Or could they arise under the alternative scenarios presented by Song and Elazar?

4. Consider the definitions Elazar presents in his analysis. What would you say are the fundamental differences and similarities among the three approaches?

5. A visitor from another country asks you, "What does it mean to be an American?" What do you say?

CHAPTER 2

Constructing the Government: The Founding and the Constitution

7

"The Nature of American Constitutionalism," from *The Origins of the American Constitution*

MICHAEL KAMMEN

The Constitution is a remarkably simple document that has provided a frame-work of governance for the United States for more than 220 years. It establishes a shared sovereignty between the states and the federal government, a separation and checking of powers between three branches of government, qualifications for citizenship and holding office, and a delineation of the rights considered so fundamental their restriction by the government requires extensive due process and a compelling national or state concern. Yet the Constitution's simple text produces constant controversy over its interpretation and efforts to bend, twist, and nudge its application to changing economic markets, technology, social trends, and family structures. The document's durability and flexibility amidst conflict and social change is a tribute not only to the men who drafted the Constitution in 1787, but to the American people and their willingness to embrace the challenges of self-governance at the time of the Revolution and today.

In the following article Michael Kammen argues that in order to begin to understand the Constitution and the continuous debate surrounding its interpretation, we must look to the history of American constitutionalism. Informed by John Locke's Second Treatise of Government, the British constitution, and a colonial experience deemed an affront to basic liberties and rights, Americans plunged into the writing of the Constitution as a means to delegate power from the sovereign people to their elected and appointed agents. It is, as Kammen notes, quite remarkable that the American states chose to draft state constitutions in the midst of a revolutionary battle for independence, rather than establish provisional governments. It is similarly remarkable that these state constitutions have grown significantly in length over the years and are so readily amended and even rewritten, in contrast to the relatively short and difficult-to-amend Constitution of the United States.

Kammen suggests that the Constitution's simplicity and durability lies in both the historic need for compromise between conflicting interests, as well as the surprising common ground that nevertheless existed over basic principles: the need to protect personal liberty, the commitment to a republican form of government, and the importance of civic virtue for preserving citizen sovereignty. This embrace of basic governing principles could explain the deeper devotion to the U.S. Constitution, in contrast to the state documents, as well as the fear that an amended or completely altered Constitution might prove less malleable and accommodating for the governance of a diverse nation.

The Nature of American Constitutionalism

"Like the Bible, it ought to be read again and again." Franklin Delano Roosevelt made that remark about the U.S. Constitution in March 1937, during one of those cozy "fireside chats" that reached millions of Americans by radio. "It is an easy document to understand," he added. And six months later, speaking to his fellow citizens from the grounds of the Washington Monument on Constitution Day—a widely noted speech because 1937 marked the sesquicentennial of the Constitution, and because the President had provoked the nation with his controversial plan to add as many as six new justices to the Supreme Court—Roosevelt observed that the Constitution was "a layman's document, not a lawyer's contract," a theme that he reiterated several times in the course of this address.

It seems fair to say that Roosevelt's assertions were approximately half true. No one could disagree that the Constitution ought to be read and reread. Few would deny that it was meant to be comprehended by laymen, by ordinary American citizens and aspirants for citizenship. Nevertheless, we must ponder whether it is truly "an easy document to understand." Although the very language of the Constitution is neither technical nor difficult, and although it is notably succinct—one nineteenth-century expert called it "a great code in a small compass"—abundant evidence exists that vast numbers of Americans, ever since 1787, have not understood it as well as they might. Even the so-called experts (judges, lawyers, political leaders, and teachers of constitutional law) have been unable to agree in critical instances about the proper application of key provisions of the Constitution, or about the intentions of those who wrote and approved it. Moreover, we do acknowledge that the Constitution developed from a significant number of compromises, and that the document's ambiguities are, for the most part, not accidental.

Understanding the U.S. Constitution is essential for many reasons. One of the most urgent is that difficult issues are now being and will continue to be settled in accordance with past interpretations and with our jurists' sense of what the founders meant. In order to make such difficult determinations, we begin with the document itself. Quite often, however, we also seek guidance from closely related or contextual documents, such as the notes kept by participants in the Constitutional Convention held at Philadelphia in 1787, from the correspondence of delegates and other prominent leaders during the later 1780s, from *The Federalist* papers, and even from some of the Anti-Federalist tracts written in opposition to the Constitution. In doing so, we essentially scrutinize the origins of American constitutionalism.

If observers want to know what is meant by constitutionalism, they must uncover several layers of historical thought and experience in public affairs. Most obviously we look to the ideas that developed in the United States during the final quarter of the eighteenth century—unquestionably the most brilliant and creative era in the entire history of American political thought. We have in mind particularly, however, a new set of assumptions that developed after 1775 about the very nature of a constitution. Why, for example, when the colonists found themselves nearly in a political state of nature after 1775, did they promptly feel compelled to write state constitutions, many of which contained a bill of rights? The patriots were, after all, preoccupied with fighting a revolution. Why not simply set up provisional governments based upon those they already had and wait until Independence was achieved? If and when the revolution succeeded, there would be time enough to write permanent constitutions.

The revolutionaries did not regard the situation in such casual and pragmatic terms. They shared a strong interest in what they called the science of politics. They knew a reasonable amount about the history of political theory. They believed in the value of ideas applied to problematic developments, and they felt that their circumstances were possibly unique in all of human history. They knew with assurance that their circumstances were changing, and changing rapidly. They wanted self-government, obviously, but they also wanted legitimacy for their newborn governments. Hence a major reason for writing constitutions. They believed in the doctrine of the social contract (about which Jean-Jacques Rousseau had written in 1762) and they believed in government by the consent of the governed: two more reasons for devising written constitutions approved by the people or by their representatives.

The men responsible for composing and revising state constitutions in the decade following 1775 regarded constitutions as social compacts that delineated the fundamental principles upon which the newly formed polities were agreed and to which they pledged themselves. They frequently used the word "experiment" because they believed that they were making institutional innovations that were risky, for they seemed virtually unprecedented. They intended to create republican governments and assumed that to do so successfully required a fair amount of social homogeneity, a high degree of consensus regarding moral values, and a pervasive capacity for virtue, by which they meant unselfish, public-spirited behavior.

Even though they often spoke of liberty, they meant civil liberty rather than natural liberty. The latter implied unrestrained freedom—absolute liberty for the individual to do as he or she pleased. The former, by contrast, meant freedom of action so long as it was not detrimental to others and was beneficial to the common weal. When they spoke of *political* liberty they meant the freedom to be a participant, to vote and hold public office, responsible commitments that ought to be widely shared if republican institutions were to function successfully.

The colonists' experiences throughout the seventeenth and eighteenth centuries had helped to prepare them for this participatory and contractual view of the nature of government. Over and over again, as the circles of settlement expanded, colonists learned to improvise the rules by which they would be governed. They had received charters and had entered into covenants or compacts that may be described as protoconstitutional, i.e., cruder and less complete versions of the constitutional documents that would be formulated in 1776 and subsequently. These colonial charters not only described the structure of government, but frequently explained what officials (often called magistrates) could or could not do.

As a result, by the 1770s American attitudes toward constitutionalism were simultaneously derivative as well as original. On the one hand, they extravagantly admired the British constitution ("unwritten" in the sense that it was not contained in a single document) and declared it to be the ultimate achievement in the entire history of governmental development. On the other hand, as Oscar and Mary Handlin have explained, Americans no longer conceived of constitutions in general as the British had for centuries.

> In the New World the term, constitution, no longer referred to the actual organization of power developed through custom, prescription, and precedent. Instead it had come to mean a written frame of government setting fixed limits on the use of power. The American view was, of course, closely related to the rejection of the old conception that authority descended from the Crown to its officials. In the newer view—that authority was derived from the consent of the governed—the written constitution became the instrument by which the people entrusted power to their agents.

*   *   *

Issues, Aspirations, and Apprehensions in 1787–1788

The major problems that confronted the Constitution-makers, and the issues that separated them from their opponents, can be specified by the key words that recur so frequently in the documents that follow in this collection. The Federalists often refer to the need for much more energy, stability, and efficiency in the national government. They fear anarchy and seek a political system better suited to America's geographical expanse: "an extensive sphere" was Madison's phrase in a letter to Jefferson.

The Anti-Federalists were apprehensive about "unrestrained power" (George Mason's words), about the great risk of national "consolidation" rather than a true confederation, about the failure to include a bill of rights in the new Constitution, about the prospect of too much power in the federal judiciary, about the "tendency to aristocracy" (see the "Federal Farmer"*), about insufficient separation of powers, and a government unresponsive to the needs of diverse and widely scattered people.

Because the two sides disagreed so strongly about the nature of the proposed government—was it genuinely federal or really national?—it is all too easy to lose sight of the common ground that they shared, a common ground that made it possible for many Anti-Federalists to support the Constitution fully even before George Washington's first administration came to a close in 1793. Both sides felt an absolute commitment to republicanism and the protection of personal liberty, as we have already seen. Both sides acknowledged that a science of politics was possible and ought to be pursued, but that "our own experience" (Madison's view, though held by "Brutus"† also) ought to be heeded above all. A majority on both sides accepted the inevitable role that interests would play in public affairs and recognized that public opinion would be a powerful force. The phrase "public opinion" appears eleven times explicitly in *The Federalist* papers, and many other times implicitly or indirectly.

The desire for happiness was invoked constantly. Although admittedly a vague and elusive concept, it clearly meant much more than the safeguarding of property (though the protection of property belonged under the rubric of happiness in the minds of many). For some it simply meant personal contentment; but increasingly there were leaders, such as George Washington, who spoke of "social happiness," which referred to harmony among diverse groups. David Humphreys's "Poem on the Happiness of America" (1786) provides an indication that this notion had national as well as individual and societal connotations.

Although both sides believed that the preservation of liberty was one of the most essential ends of government, the continued existence of chattel slavery in a freedom-loving society created considerable awkwardness for the founders. In 1775–1776, when the revolutionaries had explained the reasons for their rebellion, they frequently referred to a British plot to "enslave" Americans. The constant invocation of that notion has puzzled many students because whatever the wisdom or unwisdom of imperial

* The pen name of Richard Henry Lee of Virginia, a noted Anti-Federalist [*Editors*].
† The pen name of Robert Yates, an Anti-Federalist [*Editors*].

policy in general, there most certainly was no conspiracy in London to enslave America.

There really should be no mystery about the colonists' usage, however, because as good Lockeans they knew full well the argument in chapter four of John Locke's *Second Treatise of Government*, entitled "Of Slavery" (an argument reiterated in Rousseau's *Social Contract*). "The liberty of man in society," Locke wrote, "is to be under no other legislative power but that established by consent in the commonwealth, nor under the dominion of any will or restraint of any law but what that legislative shall enact according to the trust put in it." The denial of *full* freedom quite simply meant "slavery."

Slavery and the international slave trade were discussed extensively in 1787 at the Constitutional Convention. By then, however, "slavery" was not often used as a theoretical and general synonym for unfreedom. It meant the permanent possession of one person (black) by another (white), usually for life, the slaveowner being entitled to own the children of his or her chattel as well. We must remember that the Convention met in secret session, and that the delegates agreed not to divulge information about their proceedings for fifty years. Consequently not very much was said publicly about slavery in 1787–1788 in connection with the Constitution. Not until 1840, when the U.S. government published James Madison's detailed notes on the Convention debates, did Americans learn just how much had been compromised at Philadelphia in order to placate South Carolina and Georgia. The Constitution essentially protected slavery where it existed, and remained mute about the legality of slavery in territories that might one day become additional states. Accommodation had prevailed in 1787, which meant, as it turned out, postponing for seventy-four years the moral and political crisis of the Union.

Legacies of American Constitutionalism

Although it is difficult for us fully to imagine the complexities of interest group politics, regional rivalries, and ideological differences in 1787, the instrumental achievement of that extraordinary Convention has generally been appreciated over the years. Even such a sardonic mind as H. L. Mencken's conceded as much. "The amazing thing about the Constitution," he wrote, "is that it is as good as it is—that so subtle and complete a document emerged from that long debate. Most of the Framers, obviously, were second-rate men; before and after their session they accomplished nothing in the world. Yet during that session they made an almost perfect job of the work in hand."

Their accomplishment was, indeed, remarkable. The distribution and separation of powers among three branches at the national level, and the development of federalism as a means of apportioning sovereignty between the nation and the states, have received broad recognition and the compliment of imitation by many other nations.

Equally appreciated is the fact that the U.S. Constitution is the oldest written national constitution in the world. (The Massachusetts Constitution of 1780, although amended and revised many times, is even older.) Its endurance is genuinely remarkable. We should therefore note that the framers deserve much of the credit for that endurance, not simply because they transcended their own limitations, * * * but because they contrived to restrict the ease with which the Constitution might be revised or reconsidered. There was considerable talk in 1787–1788 about holding a second convention in order to refine the product of the first. Anti-Federalists and many who were undecided wanted such a course of action. George Washington, however, regarded that idea as impractical. Hamilton, despite his dissatisfaction with many aspects of the Constitution, doubted whether a second convention could possibly be as successful as the first; and Madison feared a serious erosion of what had been accomplished in 1787.

It is easy to forget that the Philadelphia Convention vastly exceeded its authority, and that the men who met there undertook what amounted to a usurpation of legitimate authority. As [President] Franklin Delano Roosevelt pointed out on Constitution Day in 1937, contemporaries who opposed the newly drafted document "insisted that the Constitution itself was unconstitutional under the Articles of Confederation. But the ratifying conventions overruled them." The right of revolution had been explicitly invoked in 1776 and implicitly practiced in 1787. Having done their work, however, most of the delegates did not believe that it ought to be repealed or casually revised.

The complexity of changing or adding to the original document had profound implications for the subsequent history of American constitutionalism. First, it meant that in order to gain acceptance of their handiwork, the Federalists had to commit themselves, unofficially, to the formulation of a bill of rights when the first Congress met in 1789, even though many Federalists felt that such a list of protections was superfluous. They protested that a finite list of specified safeguards would imply that numerous other liberties might not be protected against encroachment by the government. The point, ultimately, is that promulgation of the U.S. Constitution required two sets of compromises rather than one: those that took place among the delegates to the Convention, and the subsequent sense that support for ratification would be rewarded by the explicit enumeration of broad civil liberties.

Next, the existence of various ambiguities in the Constitution meant that explication would subsequently be required by various authorities, such as the Supreme Court. The justices' interpretations would become part of the total "package" that we call American constitutionalism; but the justices did not always agree with one another, and the rest of the nation did not always agree with the justices. Those realities gave rise to an ongoing pattern that might be called conflict-within-consensus.

Some of those disputes and ambiguities involved very basic questions: What are the implications and limits of consent? Once we have participated in the creation of a polity and agreed to abide by its rules, then what? How are we to resolve the conflict that arises when the wishes or needs of a majority diminish the liberties or interests of a minority? This last question was the tough issue faced by the New England states in 1814, when they contemplated secession, and by South Carolina in 1828–1833 when a high tariff designed to protect northern manufacturing threatened economic distress to southern agricultural interests. And that, of course, was the thorny issue that precipitated southern secession and the greatest constitutional crisis of all in 1860–1861.

There is yet another ambiguity, or contradiction, in American constitutional thought—though it is less commonly noticed than the one described in the previous paragraph. As we have observed, the founders were not eager for a second convention, or for easy revisions or additions to their handiwork. They did provide for change; but they made the process complicated and slow. They did not believe that the fundamental law of a nation should be casually altered; and most Americans have accepted that constraint.

Nevertheless, on the *state* level Americans have amended, expanded, revised, and totally rewritten their constitutions with some frequency. A great deal of so-called positive law (i.e., legislative enactments) finds its way into state constitutions, with the result that many modern ones exceed one hundred pages in length. There is no clear explanation for this striking pattern of divergence between constitutionalism on the national and state levels. The curious pattern does suggest, however, that Americans have regarded the U.S. Constitution of 1787 as more nearly permanent than their state constitutions. Perhaps the pattern only tells us that achieving a national consensus for change in a large and diverse society is much more difficult than achieving a statewide consensus for change.

Whatever the explanation for this dualism in American constitutionalism, the paradox does not diminish the historical reality that writers of the federal as well as the first state constitutions all tried to establish charters clearly suited to the cultural assumptions and political realities of the American scene. Even though the founders explored the history of political thought in general and the history of republics in particular, they reached the commonsense conclusion that a constitution must be adapted to the character and customs of a people. Hence the debate in 1787–1788 over the relative merits of "consolidation" versus "confederation." Hence the concern about what sort of governmental system would work most effectively over a large geographical expanse. James Madison conveyed this sense of American exceptionalism several times in a letter to Thomas

Jefferson (then U.S. minister to France) in 1788, when a bill of rights was under consideration.

On August 28, 1788, a month after New York became the eleventh state to ratify the Constitution, George Washington sent Alexander Hamilton a letter from his temporary retirement at Mount Vernon. The future president acknowledged that public affairs were proceeding more smoothly than he had expected. Consequently, he wrote, "I hope the political Machine may be put in motion, without much effort or hazard of miscarrying." As he soon discovered, to put the new constitutional machine in motion would require considerable effort. It did not miscarry because the "machine" had been so soundly designed. A concerted effort would be required, however, to keep the machine successfully in operation. That should not occasion surprise. The founders had assumed an involved citizenry; and the governmental system they created functions best when their assumption is validated. That is the very essence of democratic constitutionalism.

DISCUSSION QUESTIONS

1. In your view, what would Kammen think about recent efforts to amend the Constitution to ban abortion, ban gay marriage, mandate a balanced budget, protect the flag against desecration, and protect victims' rights?

2. Although the flexibility of the Constitution helps explain its longevity, that flexibility comes at a price: ambiguity and gaps in constitutional language. What are some examples of constitutional language that is ambiguous?

3. One reason that Kammen argues it is important to understand the origins of American constitutionalism is that many judges today use their understanding of the Founders' intentions to inform their decisions. To what extent should the Founders' intentions influence modern court decisions? What are the advantages and disadvantages of this "original intent" perspective on jurisprudence?

8

The Federalist, No. 15

ALEXANDER HAMILTON

Despite the deference given the Constitution today, it did not command instant respect in 1787. The fight for ratification was bitter between the Federalists (those who supported the Constitution) and the Anti-Federalists (who feared that the new national government would become too powerful).

The Federalist Papers, originally written as a series of newspaper editorials intended to persuade New York to ratify the Constitution, remains the most valuable exposition of the political theory underlying the Constitution. In The Federalist, No. 15, *reprinted below, Alexander Hamilton is at his best arguing for the necessity of a stronger central government than that established under the Articles of Confederation. He points out the practical impossibility of engaging in concerted action when each of the thirteen states retains virtual sovereignty, and the need for a strong central government to hold the new country together politically and economically.*

In the course of the preceding papers I have endeavored, my fellow-citizens, to place before you in a clear and convincing light the importance of Union to your political safety and happiness. * * * [T]he point next in order to be examined is the "insufficiency of the present Confederation to the preservation of the Union." * * * There are material imperfections in our national system and * * * something is necessary to be done to rescue us from impending anarchy. The facts that support this opinion are no longer objects of speculation. They have forced themselves upon the sensibility of the people at large, and have at length extorted . . . a reluctant confession of the reality of those defects in the scheme of our federal government which have been long pointed out and regretted by the intelligent friends of the Union.

We may indeed with propriety be said to have reached almost the last stage of national humiliation. There is scarcely anything that can wound the pride or degrade the character of an independent nation which we do not experience. Are there engagements to the performance of which we are held by every tie respectable among men? These are the subjects of constant and unblushing violation. Do we owe debts to foreigners and to our own citizens contracted in a time of imminent peril for the preservation of our political existence? These remain without any proper or satisfactory provision for their discharge. * * * Are we in a condition to resent or to repel the aggression? We have neither troops, nor treasury, nor government. * * * Is public credit an indispensable resource in time of public danger? We seem to have abandoned its cause as desperate and irretrievable. Is commerce of importance to national wealth? Ours is at the lowest point of declension. Is respectability in the eyes of foreign powers a safeguard against foreign encroachments? The imbecility of our government even forbids them to treat with us. . . . Is private credit the friend and patron of industry? That most useful kind which relates to borrowing and lending is reduced within the narrowest limits, and this still more from an opinion of insecurity than from a scarcity of money. * * *

This is the melancholy situation to which we have been brought by those very maxims and counsels which would now deter us from adopting the proposed Constitution; and which, not content with having conducted us to the brink of a precipice, seem resolved to plunge us into the abyss that awaits us below. Here, my countrymen, impelled by every motive that ought to influence an enlightened people, let us make a firm stand for our safety, our tranquility, our dignity, our reputation. Let us at last break the fatal charm which has too long seduced us from the paths of felicity and prosperity.

* * * While [opponents of the Constitution] admit that the government of the United States is destitute of energy, they contend against conferring upon it those powers which are requisite to supply that energy. * * * This renders a full display of the principal defects of the Confederation necessary in order to show that the evils we experience do not proceed from minute or partial imperfections, but from fundamental errors in the structure of the building, which cannot be amended otherwise than by an alteration in the first principles and main pillars of the fabric.

The great and radical vice in the construction of the existing Confederation is in the principle of LEGISLATION FOR STATES OR GOVERNMENTS, in their CORPORATE OR COLLECTIVE CAPACITIES, and as contradistinguished from the INDIVIDUALS of whom they consist. Though this principle does not run through all the powers delegated to the Union, yet it pervades and governs those on which the efficacy of the rest depends. Except as to the rule of apportionment, the United States have an indefinite discretion to make requisitions for men and money; but they have no authority to raise either by regulations extending to the individual citizens of America. The consequence of this is that though in theory their resolutions concerning those objects are laws constitutionally binding on the members of the Union, yet in practice they are mere recommendations which the States observe or disregard at their option. * * *

There is nothing absurd or impracticable in the idea of a league or alliance between independent nations for certain defined purposes precisely stated in a treaty regulating all the details of time, place, circumstance, and quantity, leaving nothing to future discretion, and depending for its execution on the good faith of the parties. * * *

If the particular States in this country are disposed to stand in a similar relation to each other, and to drop the project of a general DISCRETIONARY SUPERINTENDENCE, the scheme would indeed be pernicious and would entail upon us all the mischiefs which have been enumerated under the first head; but it would have the merit of being, at least, consistent and practicable. Abandoning all views towards a confederate government, this would bring us to a simple alliance offensive and defensive; and would place us in a situation to be alternate friends and enemies of each other, as our mutual jealousies and rivalships, nourished by the intrigues of foreign nations, should prescribe to us.

But if we are unwilling to be placed in this perilous situation; if we still will adhere to the design of a national government, or, which is the same thing, of a superintending power under the direction of a common council, we must resolve to incorporate into our plan those ingredients which may be considered as forming the characteristic difference between a league and a government; we must extend the authority of the Union to the persons of the citizens—the only proper objects of government.

Government implies the power of making laws. It is essential to the idea of a law that it be attended with a sanction; or, in other words, a penalty or punishment for disobedience. If there be no penalty annexed to disobedience, the resolutions or commands which pretend to be laws will, in fact, amount to nothing more than advice or recommendation. This penalty, whatever it may be, can only be inflicted in two ways: by the agency of the courts and ministers of justice, or by military force; by the COERCION of the magistracy, or by the COERCION of arms. The first kind can evidently apply only to men; the last kind must of necessity be employed against bodies politic, or communities, or States. * * * In an association where the general authority is confined to the collective bodies of the communities that compose it, every breach of the laws must involve a state of war; and military execution must become the only instrument of civil obedience. Such a state of things can certainly not deserve the name of government, nor would any prudent man choose to commit his happiness to it.

There was a time when we were told that breaches by the States of the regulations of the federal authority were not to be expected; that a sense of common interest would preside over the conduct of the respective members, and would beget a full compliance with all the constitutional requisitions of the Union. This language, at the present day, would appear as wild as a great part of what we now hear from the same quarter will be thought, when we shall have received further lessons from that best oracle of wisdom, experience. It at all times betrayed an ignorance of the true springs by which human conduct is actuated, and belied the original inducements to the establishment of civil power. Why has government been instituted at all? Because the passions of men will not conform to the dictates of reason and justice without constraint. * * *

In addition to all this * * * it happens that in every political association which is formed upon the principle of uniting in a common interest a number of lesser sovereignties, there will be found a kind of eccentric tendency in the subordinate or inferior orbs by the operation of which there will be a perpetual effort in each to fly off from the common center. This tendency is not difficult to be accounted for. It has its origin in the love of power. Power controlled or abridged is almost always the rival and enemy of that power by which it is controlled or abridged. This simple proposition will teach us how little reason there is to expect that the persons intrusted with the administration of the affairs of the particular members of a confederacy will at all times be ready with perfect good humor and an unbiased regard to the public weal to execute the resolutions or decrees of the general authority. * * *

If, therefore, the measures of the Confederacy cannot be executed without the intervention of the particular administrations, there will be little prospect of their being executed at all. * * * [Each state will evaluate every federal measure in light of its own interests] and in a spirit of interested and suspicious scrutiny, without that knowledge of national circumstances and reasons of state, which is essential to a right judgment, and with that strong predilection in favor of local objects, which can hardly fail to mislead the decision. The same process must be repeated in every member of which the body is constituted; and the execution of the plans, framed by the councils of the whole, will always fluctuate on the discretion of the ill-informed and prejudiced opinion of every part. * * *

In our case the concurrence of thirteen distinct sovereign wills is requisite under the Confederation to the complete execution of every important measure that proceeds from the Union. It has happened as was to have been foreseen. The measures of the Union have not been executed; and the delinquencies of the States have step by step matured themselves to an extreme, which has, at length, arrested all the wheels of the national government and brought them to an awful stand. Congress at this time scarcely possess the means of keeping up the forms of administration, till the States can have time to agree upon a more substantial substitute for the present shadow of a federal government. * * * Each State yielding to the persuasive voice of immediate interest or convenience has successively withdrawn its support, till the frail and tottering edifice seems ready to fall upon our heads and to crush us beneath its ruins.

Publius

DISCUSSION QUESTIONS

1. Do you think the national government is sufficiently held in check as Hamilton argues? Or is the exercise of its authority so vast as to give credence to the Anti-Federalist fears? To put it another way, would the Framers be surprised or pleased with the scope of government powers today?

2. According to Hamilton, what are the weaknesses of a "league" compared to a government?

3. What is the significance of Hamilton's statement that "we must extend the authority of the Union to the persons of the citizens?"

The Federalist, No. 51

JAMES MADISON

Such well-known patriots as Patrick Henry—"give me liberty or give me death!"—opposed the new Constitution. The proposed national government was stronger than its predecessor, but this was precisely the problem for the Anti-Federalists. A stronger national government could act in a more concerted manner in matters of foreign affairs and interstate commerce, but it also held the power to oppress the very people who gave it sovereignty. Arguments over this delicate balance of power animated debates over constitutional ratification.

James Madison concurred with Hamilton on the need for a stronger national government, but also recognized the importance of a limited government. In one of the most famous passages of The Federalist *Papers, Madison notes in* The Federalist, *No. 51, "If men were angels, no government would be necessary. If angels were to govern men, neither external nor internal controls on government would be necessary." But because angels do not govern us, Madison argued for the importance of controls on government. Here is where Madison attempts to address the concerns of the Anti-Federalists by arguing for a "double security" against majority tyranny. To achieve this security, the power of government must be divided across (between state and national governments) and within levels of government (among the courts, the president, and Congress). Such a division insured that if any one institution tried to become too powerful, the others would step in to counteract it. This essay remains one of the most eloquent defenses of our system of checks and balances and separation of powers.*

To the People of the State of New York:

To what expedient, then, shall we finally resort for maintaining in practice the necessary partition of power among the several departments as laid down in the Constitution? The only answer that can be given is, that as all these exterior provisions are found to be inadequate, the defect must be supplied by so contriving the interior structure of the government as that its several constituent parts may, by their mutual relations, be the means of keeping each other in their proper places. Without presuming to undertake a full development of this important idea, I will hazard a few general observations, which may perhaps place it in a clearer light, and enable us to form a more correct judgment of the principles and structure of the government planned by the convention.

In order to lay a due foundation for that separate and distinct exercise of the different powers of government, which to a certain extent is admitted on all hands to be essential to the preservation of liberty, it is evident that each department should have a will of its own; and consequently should be so constituted that the members of each should have as little agency as possible in the appointment of the members of the others. Were this principle rigorously adhered to, it would require that all the appointments for the supreme executive, legislative, and judiciary magistracies should be drawn from the same fountain of authority, the people, through channels having no communication whatever with one another. Perhaps such a plan of constructing the several departments would be less difficult in practice than it may in contemplation appear. Some difficulties, however, and some additional expense would attend the execution of it. Some deviations, therefore, from the principle must be admitted. In the constitution of the judiciary department in particular, it might be inexpedient to insist rigorously on the principle: first, because peculiar qualifications being essential in the members, the primary consideration ought to be to select that mode of choice which best secures these qualifications; secondly, because the permanent tenure by which the appointments are held in that department must soon destroy all sense of dependence on the authority conferring them.

It is equally evident, that the members of each department should be as little dependent as possible on those of the others for the emoluments annexed to their offices. Were the executive magistrate or the judges not independent of the legislature in this particular, their independence in every other would be merely nominal.

But the great security against a gradual concentration of the several powers in the same department, consists in giving to those who administer each department the necessary constitutional means and personal motives to resist encroachments of the others. The provision for defence must in this, as in all other cases, be made commensurate to the danger of attack. Ambition must be made to counteract ambition. The interest of the man must be connected with the constitutional rights of the place. It may be a reflection on human nature, that such devices should be necessary to control the abuses of government. But what is government itself, but the greatest of all reflections on human nature? If men were angels, no government would be necessary. If angels were to govern men, neither external nor internal controls on government would be necessary. In framing a government which is to be administered by men over men, the great difficulty lies in this: you must first enable the government to control the governed; and in the next place oblige it to control itself. A dependence on the people is, no doubt, the primary control on the government; but experience has taught mankind the necessity of auxiliary precautions.

This policy of supplying, by opposite and rival interests, the defect of better motives might be traced through the whole system of human affairs, private as well as public. We see it particularly displayed in all the subordinate distributions of power, where the constant aim is to divide and arrange the several offices in such a manner as that each may be a check on the other—that the private interest of every individual may be a sentinel over the public rights. These inventions of prudence cannot be less requisite in the distribution of the supreme powers of the State.

But it is not possible to give to each department an equal power of self-defence. In republican government the legislative authority necessarily predominates. The remedy for this inconveniency is to divide the legislature into different branches; and to render them, by different modes of election and different principles of action, as little connected with each other as the nature of their common functions and their common dependence on the society will admit. It may even be necessary to guard against dangerous encroachments by still further precautions. As the weight of the legislative authority requires that it should be thus divided, the weakness of the executive may require, on the other hand, that it should be fortified. An absolute negative on the legislature appears, at first view, to be the natural defence with which the executive magistrate should be armed. But perhaps it would be neither altogether safe nor alone sufficient. On ordinary occasions it might not be exerted with the requisite firmness, and on extraordinary occasions it might be perfidiously abused. May not this defect of an absolute negative be supplied by some qualified connection between this weaker department and the weaker branch of the stronger department, by which the latter may be led to support the constitutional rights of the former, without being too much detached from the rights of its own department?

If the principles on which these observations are founded be just . . . and they be applied as a criterion to the several State constitutions and to the federal Constitution, it will be found that if the latter does not perfectly correspond with them, the former are infinitely less able to bear such a test.

There are, moreover, two considerations particularly applicable to the federal system of America, which place that system in a very interesting point of view.

First. In a single republic, all the power surrendered by the people is submitted to the administration of a single government; and the usurpations are guarded against by a division of the government into distinct and separate departments. In the compound republic of America, the power surrendered by the people is first divided between two distinct governments, and then the portion allotted to each subdivided among distinct and separate departments. Hence a double security arises to the rights of the people. The different governments will control each other, at the same time that each will be controlled by itself.

Second. It is of great importance in a republic not only to guard the society against the oppression of its rulers, but to guard one part of the society against the injustice of the other part. Different interests necessarily exist in different classes of citizens. If a majority be united by a common interest, the rights of the minority will be insecure. There are but two methods of providing against this evil: the one by creating a will in the community independent of the majority—that is, of the society itself; the other by comprehending in the society so many separate descriptions of citizens as will render an unjust combination of a majority of the whole very improbable, if not impracticable. The first method prevails in all governments possessing an hereditary or self-appointed authority. This, at best, is but a precarious security; because a power independent of the society may as well espouse the unjust views of the major, as the rightful interests of the minor party, and may possibly be turned against both parties. The second method will be exemplified in the federal republic of the United States. Whilst all authority in it will be derived from and dependent on the society, the society itself will be broken into so many parts, interests and classes of citizens, that the rights of individuals or of the minority will be in little danger from interested combinations of the majority. In a free government the security for civil rights must be the same as that for religious rights. It consists in the one case in the multiplicity of interests and in the other in the multiplicity of sects. The degree of security in both cases will depend on the number of interests and sects; and this may be presumed to depend on the extent of country and number of people comprehended under the same government. This view of the subject must particularly recommend a proper federal system to all the sincere and considerate friends of republican government, since it shows that in exact proportion as the territory of the Union may be formed into more circumscribed Confederacies or States, oppressive combinations of a majority will be facilitated; the best security under the republican forms for the rights of every class of citizens will be diminished; and consequently the stability and independence of some member of the government, the only other security, must be proportionally increased. Justice is the end [that is, the goal] of government. It is the end of civil society. It ever has been and ever will be pursued until it be obtained, or until liberty be lost in the pursuit. In a society under the forms of which the stronger faction can readily unite and oppress the weaker, anarchy may as truly be said to reign as in a state of nature, where the weaker individual is not secured against the violence of the stronger; and, as in the latter state even the stronger individuals are prompted, by the uncertainty of their condition, to submit to a government which may protect the weak as well as themselves; so, in the former state will the more powerful factions or parties be gradually induced by a like motive to wish for a government which will protect all parties, the weaker as well as the more powerful. It can be little doubted that if the State of Rhode Island was separated from the Confederacy and left to itself, the insecurity of rights under the popular form of government within such narrow limits would be displayed by such reiterated oppressions of factious majorities that some power altogether independent of the people would soon be called for by the voice of the very factions whose misrule had proved the necessity of it. In the extended republic of the United States and among the great variety of interests, parties, and sects which it embraces, a coalition of a majority of the whole society could seldom take place on any other principles than those of justice and the general good; whilst there being thus less danger to a minor from the will of a major party, there must be less pretext, also, to provide for the security of the former, by introducing into the government a will not dependent on the latter, or, in other words, a will independent of the society itself. It is no less certain than it is important, notwithstanding the contrary opinions which have been entertained, that the larger the society, provided it lie within a practical sphere, the more duly capable it will be of self-government. And happily for the *republican cause*, the practicable sphere may be carried to a very great extent by a judicious modification and mixture of the *federal principle*.

PUBLIUS

DISCUSSION QUESTIONS

1. According to Madison, the principles of "separation of powers" and "checks and balances" operate to limit the authority of the national government. How? Discuss at least one current issue involving these two principles and the constitutional issues at stake.

2. Is the system of "separation of powers" and "checks and balances" too inefficient to handle the challenges posed by the modern and dangerous world? Would the United States be better off with a more efficient form of government that would allow quicker action and more accountability?

Debating the Issues: Should the Constitution Be Fundamentally Changed?

Veneration for the Constitution is a classic American value; indeed, it is often said that the essence of being an American is a set of shared values and commitments expressed within the four corners of that document, most notably equality and liberty. The Constitution is the embodiment of those values, celebrated as the first, and most enduring, written constitution in human history. We celebrate the first words of the preamble, "We the people," salute the Framers as men of historic wisdom and judgment, and honor the structures and processes of government.

We also note the practical wisdom of the Framers, in their ability to reconcile competing tensions in creating a government powerful enough to function, but not at the risk of giving majorities the right to trample minority rights. Political theory at the time held that efforts to create democracies inevitably devolved into one of two end results: either mob rule, as majorities took control and used their power to oppress political minorities; or autocracy, as elites assumed control and did not give it up. The many carefully considered elements of constitutional structure—bicameralism, the balance between federal and state power, the equilibrium of checks and balances—have lasted for more than two centuries. And apart from one exceptional period of civil war, the structures have channeled political conflict peacefully.

Is that veneration truly warranted? Sanford Levinson, a professor at the University of Texas Law School, thinks not. He considers the Constitution to be a seriously flawed document in need of fundamental change. As originally written, the Constitution came nowhere near the aspirations of the Preamble, explicitly allowing slavery, and even after amendments retains several antidemocratic elements, including the electoral college; the vastly unequal representation in the Senate, in which Wyoming (population 544,000) has the same voting power as California (population 37 million, over sixty times as large); and lifetime tenure for judges. These features fail to live up to the Preamble, which Levinson considers to be the foundation of the rest of the Constitution—the whole point of the constitutional enterprise. Levinson points out that several key figures of the American founding—Thomas Jefferson especially—believed that the Constitution would require frequent updating. This was the purpose of Article V, which sets out the process for amending the document. And, Levinson notes, many of the features of the Constitution that we venerate were not thought through but were instead the product of pure compromise, in which the Framers took vastly inconsistent positions when necessary in order to secure sufficient support for ratification. So, far from being a philosophically perfect document or system, the Constitution created a cumbersome and inequitable system, one that no other democratic system has chosen to copy since.

The problem with amending the Constitution is that the features Levinson considers most offensive—especially the unequal representation in the Senate—are virtually impossible to change. Article V specifies that no state can be deprived of its equal representation in the Senate without its consent (something that no state could ever be expected to do). The only recourse is a constitutional convention, in which delegates would consider fundamental reform. Levinson regards this as essential in order to allow the national government to respond to the challenge of modern economic and political times.

Eric Lane and Michael Oreskes take the more traditional stance that the Constitution is fine as it is; they argue that it is the people who must change. The key problem is that people do not understand the purpose of checks and balances or other features of the Constitution that frustrate their policy demands. But the Constitution is not just a mechanism for giving each of us what we want: the Constitution, they argue, is a vehicle for protecting liberty and providing the opportunity for individuals to pursue what they want through political and economic freedom. Instead of evaluating our legislators by how well they fulfill their constitutional duties, we base our evaluation on how much pork they can deliver to the folks at home. We are looking for an institutional fix through constitutional change when the problem is that our own fidelity to constitutional principles is waning. Evidence that the Constitution got it right comes from the fact that it produced the richest, freest, and most powerful country that has ever existed.

If there is one area of agreement between Levinson and Lane and Oreskes, it is that democracy is fragile, though they arrive at that conclusion for different reasons: Levinson because government fails to give the public what it wants, Lane and Oreskes because we are using our power to demand the wrong things.

"The Ratification Referendum: Sending the Constitution to a New Convention for Repair"

SANFORD LEVINSON

The U.S. Constitution is radically defective in a number of important ways. Unfortunately, changing the Constitution is extremely difficult, for both political and constitutional reasons. But the difficulty of the task does not make it any less important that we first become aware of the magnitude of the deficiencies in the current Constitution and then turn our minds, as a community of concerned citizens, to figuring out potential solutions. This [reading] is organized around the conceit that Americans in 2008 will have the opportunity to vote on the following proposal: "Shall Congress call a constitutional convention empowered to consider the adequacy of the Constitution, and, if thought necessary, to draft a new constitution that, upon completion, will be submitted to the electorate for its approval or disapproval by majority vote? Unless and until a new constitution gains popular approval, the current Constitution will continue in place."

Although such a referendum would be unprecedented with regard to the U.S. Constitution, there is certainly nothing "un-American" about such a procedure. As Professor John J. Dinan has noted in his recent comprehensive study of what he terms "the American state constitutional tradition," fourteen American states in their own constitutions explicitly give the people an opportunity "to periodically vote on whether a convention should be called." Article XIX of the New York Constitution, for example, provides that the state electorate be given the opportunity every twenty years to vote on the following question: "Shall there be a convention to revise the constitution and amend the same?" Should the majority answer in the affirmative, then the voters in each senate district will elect three delegates "at the next ensuring general election," while the state-wide electorate "shall elect fifteen delegates-at-large." It should occasion no surprise that one author has described such a "mandatory referendum" as a means of "enforcing the people's right to reform their government."

It is no small matter to give people a choice with regard to the mechanisms—as well as the abstract principles—by which they are to be governed. The imagined referendum would allow "We the People of the United States of America," in whose name the document is ostensibly "ordain[ed]," to examine the fit between our national aspirations, set out in the Preamble to the Constitution, and the particular means chosen to realize those goals.

I am assuming that those reading this * * * are fellow Americans united by a deep and common concern about the future of our country. * * * I hope to convince you that, as patriotic Americans truly committed to the deepest principles of the Constitution, we should vote yes and thus trigger a new convention. My task is to persuade you that the Constitution we currently live under is grievously flawed, even in some ways a "clear and present danger" to achieving the laudable and inspiring goals to which this country professes to be committed, including republican self-government.

I believe that the best way to grasp the goals of our common enterprise is to ponder the inspiring words of the Preamble to the Constitution:

> We the People of the United States, in Order to form a more perfect Union, establish Justice, insure domestic tranquility, provide for the common defence, promote the general Welfare, and secure the Blessings of Liberty to ourselves and our Posterity, do ordain and establish this Constitution for the United States of America.

It is regrettable that law professors rarely teach and that courts rarely cite the Preamble, for it is *the single most important part* of the Constitution. The reason is simple: It announces the *point* of the entire enterprise. The 4,500 or so words that followed the Preamble in the original, unamended Constitution were all in effect merely means that were thought to be useful to achieving the great aims set out above. It is indeed the ends articulated in the Preamble that justify the means of our political institutions. And to the extent that the means turn out to be counterproductive, then we should revise them.

It takes no great effort to find elements in the original Constitution that run counter to the Preamble. It is impossible for us today to imagine how its authors squared a commitment to the "Blessings of Liberty" with the toleration and support of chattel slavery that is present in various articles of the Constitution. The most obvious example is the bar placed on Congress's ability to forbid the participation by Americans in the international slave trade until 1808. The most charitable interpretation of the framers, articulated by Frederick Douglass, is that they viewed these compromises with the acknowledged evil of slavery as temporary; the future would see its eradication through peaceful constitutional processes.

One might believe that the Preamble is incomplete because, for example, it lacks a commitment to the notion of equality. Political scientist Mark Graber has suggested that the reference to *"our* Posterity" suggests a potentially unattractive limitation of our concerns *only* to members of the American political community, with no notice taken of the posterity of other societies, whatever their plight. Even if one would prefer a more explicitly cosmopolitan Preamble, I find it hard to imagine rejecting any of the overarching values enunciated there. In any event, I am happy to endorse the Preamble as the equivalent of our creedal summary of America's civil religion.

There are two basic responses to the discovery that ongoing institutional practices are counterproductive with regard to achieving one's announced goals. One is to adjust the practices in ways that would make achievement of the aims more likely. This is, often, when we mean by the very notion of rationality: One does not persist in behaviors that are acknowledged to make more difficult the realization of one's professed hopes. Still, a second response, which has its own rationality, is to adjust the goals to the practices. Sometimes, this makes very good sense if one comes to the justified conclusion that the goals may be utopian. In such cases, it is a sign of maturity to recognize that we will inevitably fall short in our aims and that "the best may be enemy of the good" if we are tempted to throw over quite adequate, albeit imperfect, institutions in an attempt to attain the ideal.

Perhaps one might even wish to defend the framer's compromises with slavery on the ground that they were absolutely necessary to the achievement of the political union of the thirteen states. One must believe that such a union, in turn, was preferable to the likely alternative, which would have been the creation of two or three separate countries along the Atlantic coast. Political scientist David Hendrickson has demonstrated that many of the framers—and many other theorists as well—viewed history as suggesting a high probability that such separate countries would have gone to war with one another and made impossible any significant measure of "domestic tranquility." Hendrickson well describes the Constitution as a "peace pact" designed to prevent the possibility of war. If there is one thing we know, it is that unhappy compromises must often be made when negotiating such pacts. Of course, American slaves—and their descendants—could scarcely be expected to be so complacently accepting of these compromises, nor, of course, should *any* American who takes seriously the proclamation of the Pledge of Allegiance that ours is a system that takes seriously the duty to provide "liberty and justice for all."

Not only must we restrain ourselves from expecting too much of any government; we must also recognize that the Preamble sets out potentially conflicting goals. It is impossible to maximize the achievement of all of the great ends of the Constitution. To take an obvious example, providing for the "common defence" may require on occasion certain incursions into the "Blessings of Liberty." One need only refer to the military draft, which was upheld in 1918 by the Supreme Court against an attack claiming that it constituted the "involuntary servitude"—that is, slavery—prohibited by the Thirteenth Amendment. We also properly accept certain limitations on the freedom of the press with regard, say, to publishing certain information—the standard example is troop movements within a battle zone—deemed to be vital to American defense interests. The year 2005 ended with the beginning of a great national debate about the propriety of warrantless interceptions of telephone calls and other incursions on traditional civil liberties in order, ostensibly, to protect ourselves against potential terrorists.

Even if one concedes the necessity of adjusting aims in light of practical realities, it should also be readily obvious that one can easily go overboard. At the very least, one should always be vigilant in assessing such adjustments lest one find, at the end of the day, that the aims have been reduced to hollow shells. It is also necessary to ask if a rationale supporting a given adjustment that might well have been convincing at time A necessarily continues to be present at time B. Practical exigencies that required certain political compromises in 1787 no longer obtain today. We have long since realized this about slavery. It is time that we apply the same critical eye to the compromise of 1787 that granted all states an equal vote in the Senate.

To criticize that particular compromise—or any of the other features of the Constitution that I shall examine below—is not necessarily to criticize the founders themselves. My project—and, therefore, your own vote for a new convention, should you be persuaded by what follows—requires no denigration of the founders. They were, with some inevitable exceptions, an extraordinary group of men who performed extraordinary deeds, including drafting a Constitution that started a brand-new governmental system. By and large, they deserve the monuments that have been erected in their honor. But they themselves emphasized the importance—indeed, necessity—of learning from experience.

They were, after all, a generation that charted new paths by overturning a centuries-long notion of the British constitutional order because it no longer conformed to their own sense of possibility (and fairness). They also, as it happened, proved ruthlessly willing to ignore the limitations of America's "first constitution," the Articles of Confederation. Although Article XIII of that founding document required unanimous approval by the thirteen state legislatures before any amendment could take affect, Article VII of the Constitution drafted in Philadelphia required the approval of only nine of the thirteen states, and the approval was to be given by state conventions rather than by the legislatures.

The most important legacies handed down by the founding generation were, first, a remarkable willingness to act in bold and daring ways when they believed that the situation demanded it, coupled with the noble visions first of the Declaration of Independence and then of the Preamble. Both are as inspiring—and potentially disruptive—today as when they were written more than two centuries ago. But we should also be inspired by the copious study that Madison and others made of every available history and analysis of political systems ranging from ancient Greece to the Dutch republic and the British constitutional order. We best honor the framers by taking the task of creating a republican political order as seriously as they did and being equally willing to learn from what the history of the past 225 years, both at home and abroad, can teach us about how best to achieve and maintain such an order. At the time of its creation, we could legitimately believe that we were the only country committed to democratic self-governance. That is surely no longer the case, and we might well have lessons to learn from our co-ventures in that enterprise. To the extent that experience teaches us that the Constitution in significant aspects demeans "the consent of the governed" and has become an impediment to achieving the goals of the Preamble, we honor rather than betray the founders by correcting their handiwork.

Overcoming Veneration

* * * I suspect * * * that at least some readers might find it difficult to accept even the possibility that our Constitution is seriously deficient because they venerate the Constitution and find the notion of seriously criticizing it almost sacrilegious.

In an earlier book, *Constitutional Faith*, I noted the tension between the desire of James Madison that Americans "venerate" their Constitution and the distinctly contrasting views of his good friend Thomas Jefferson that, instead, the citizenry regularly subject it to relentless examination. Thus, whatever may have been Jefferson's insistence on respecting what he called the "chains" of the Constitution, he also emphasized that the "Creator has made the earth for the living, not the dead." It should not be surprising, then, that he wrote to Madison in 1789, "No society can make a perpetual constitution, or even a perpetual law."

Jefferson and Madison might have been good friends and political associates, but they disagreed fundamentally with regard to the wisdom of subjecting the Constitution to critical analysis. Jefferson was fully capable of writing that "[w]e may consider each generation as a distinct nation, with a right, by the will of its majority, to bind themselves, but none to bind the succeeding generation, more than the inhabitants of another country." His ultimate optimism about the Constitution lay precisely in its potential for change: "Happily for us, that when we find our constitutions defective and insufficient to secure the happiness of our people, we can assemble with all the coolness of philosophers, and set it to rights, while every other nation on earth must have recourse to arms to amend or restore their constitutions." * * *

Madison, however, would have none of this. He treated 1787 almost as a miraculous and singular event. Had he been a devotee of astrology, he might have said that the stars were peculiarly and uniquely aligned to allow the drafting of the Constitution and then its ratification. Though Madison was surely too tactful to mention this, part of the alignment was the absence of the famously contentious Jefferson and John Adams. Both were 3,000 miles across the sea, where they were serving as the first ambassadors from the new United States to Paris and London, respectively. Moreover, it certainly did not hurt that Rhode Island had refused to send any delegates at all and therefore had no opportunity to make almost inevitable mischief, not to mention being unable to vote in an institutional structure where the vote of one state could make a big difference. And, if pressed, Madison would presumably have agreed that the Constitutional Convention—and the ratifying conventions thereafter—would never have succeeded had the delegates included American slaves, Native Americans, or women in the spirit of Abigail Adams. She had famously—and altogether unsuccessfully—told her husband that leaders of the new nation should "remember the ladies." One need not see the framers in Philadelphia as an entirely homogeneous group—they were not—in order to realize that the room was devoid of those groups in America that were viewed as merely the *objects*, and not the active *subjects*, of governance.

Madison sets out his views most clearly in the *Federalist*, No. 49, where he explicitly takes issue with Jefferson's proposal for rather frequent constitutional conventions that would consider whether "alter[ation]" of the constitution might be desirable. Madison acknowledges the apparent appeal, in a system where "the people are the only legitimate fountain of power," of "appeal[ing] to the people themselves." However, "there appear to be insuperable objections against the proposed recurrence to the people." Perhaps the key objection is that *"frequent appeal to the people would carry an implication of some defect in the government [and] deprive the government of that veneration which time bestows on every thing, and without which perhaps the wisest and freest governments would not possess the requisite stability."* Only "a nation of philosophers" can forgo this emotion of veneration—and, therefore, feel free of guilt-ridden anxiety about the idea of constitutional change. However, "a nation of philosophers is as little to be expected as the philosophical race of kings wished for by Plato."

Madison is thus fearful of "disturbing the public tranquillity by interesting too strongly the public passions." The success of Americans in replacing a defective Articles of Confederation with a better Constitution does not constitute a precedent for future action. We should "recollect," he says, "that all the existing constitutions were formed in the midst of a danger which repressed the passions most unfriendly to order and concord." Moreover, the people at large possessed "an enthusiastic confidence . . . in their patriotic leaders," which, he says, fortunately "stifled the ordinary diversity of opinions on great national questions." He is extremely skeptical that the "future situations in which we must expect to be usually placed" will "present any equivalent security against the danger" of an excess of public passion, disrespect for leaders, and the full play of diverse opinions. In case there is any doubt, he writes of his fear that the *"passions*, therefore, not the *reasons*, of the public would sit in judgment."

Madison's view of his fellow Americans was far closer to that of

Alexander Hamilton, with whom he had coauthored the *Federalist*. One can doubt that Madison expressed any reservations when hearing Hamilton, addressing his fellow delegates to the Philadelphia convention on June 18, 1787, denounce the conceit that "the voice of the people" is "the voice of God." On the contrary, said Hamilton: "The people are turbulent and changing; they seldom judge or determine right." Although Madison was not opposed to constitutional amendment as such, he clearly saw almost no role for a public that would engage in probing questions suggesting that there might be serious "defects" in the Constitution. Only philosophers (like himself?) or, perhaps, "patriotic leaders" could be trusted to engage in dispassionate political dialogue and reasoning. In contrast, the general public should be educated to feel only "veneration" for their Constitution rather than be encouraged to use their critical faculties and actually assess the relationship between the great ends set out in the Preamble and the instruments devised for their realization.

* * *

This is a mistake. To the extent that we continue thoughtlessly to venerate, and therefore not subject to truly critical examination, our Constitution, we are in the position of the battered wife who continues to profess the "essential goodness" of her abusive husband. To stick with the analogy for a moment, it may well be the case that the husband, when sober or not gambling, is a decent, even loving, partner. The problem is that such moments are more than counterbalanced by abusive ones, even if they are relatively rare. And he becomes especially abusive when she suggests the possibility of marital counseling and attendant change. Similarly, that there are good features of our Constitution should not be denied. But there are also significantly abusive ones, and it is time for us to face them rather than remain in a state of denial.

Trapped Inside the Article V Cage

The framers of the Constitution were under no illusion that they had created a perfect document. The best possible proof for this proposition comes from George Washington himself. As he wrote to his nephew Bushrod two months after the conclusion of the Philadelphia convention over which he had presided, *"The warmest friends and the best supporters the Constitution has do not contend that it is free from imperfections;* but they found them unavoidable and are sensible if evil is likely to arise there from, the remedy must come hereafter." Sounding a remarkably Jeffersonian note, Washington noted that the "People (for it is with them to Judge) can, as they will have the advantage of experience on their Side, decide with as much propriety on the alteration[s] and amendment[s] which are necessary." Indeed, wrote the man described as the Father of Our Country, "I do not think we are more inspired, have more wisdom, or possess more virtue, than those who will come after us."

Article V itself is evidence of the recognition of the possibility—and inevitable reality—of imperfection, else they would have adopted John Locke's suggestion in a constitution that he drafted for the Carolina colonies that would have made the document unamendable. It is an unfortunate reality, though, that Article V, practically speaking, brings us all too close to the Lockean dream (or nightmare) of changeless stasis.

As University of Houston political scientist Donald Lutz has conclusively demonstrated, the U.S. Constitution is the most difficult to amend of any constitution currently existing in the world today. Formal amendment of the U.S. Constitution generally requires the approval of two-thirds of each of the two houses of our national Congress, followed by the approval of three-quarters of the states (which today means thirty-eight of the fifty states). Article V does allow the abstract possibility that amendments could be proposed through the aegis of a constitutional convention called by Congress upon the petition of two-thirds of the states; such proposals, though, would still presumably have to be ratified by the state legislatures or, in the alternative, as was done with regard to the Twenty-first Amendment repealing the prohibition of alcohol required by the Eighteenth Amendment, by conventions in each of the states. As a practical matter, though, Article V makes it next to impossible to amend the Constitution with regard to genuinely controversial issues, even if substantial—and intense—majorities advocate amendment.

As I have written elsewhere, some significant change functionally similar to "amendment" has occurred informally, outside of the procedures set out by Article V. One scholar has aptly described this as a process of "constitutional change off-the-books." Yale law professor Bruce Ackerman has written several brilliant books detailing the process of "non-Article V" amendment, and I warmly commend them to the reader. Yet it is difficult to argue that such informal amendment has occurred, or is likely to occur, with regard to the basic *structural* aspects of the American political system with which this book is primarily concerned.

It is one thing to argue, as Ackerman has done, that the New Deal worked as a functional amendment of the Constitution by giving Congress significant new powers to regulate the national economy. Similarly, one could easily argue that the president, for good or for ill, now possesses powers over the use of armed forces that would have been inconceivable to the generation of the framers. Whatever the text of the Constitution may say about the power of Congress to "declare war" or whatever the original understanding of this clause, it is hard to deny that many presidents throughout our history have successfully chosen to take the country to war without seeking a declaration of war (or, in some cases, even prior congressional approval of any kind). Ackerman and David Golove have also persuasively argued that the Treaty Clause, which requires that two-thirds of the Senate assent to any treaty, has been transformed through the use of "executive agreements." Although such agreements are unmentioned in the text of the Constitution, presidents have frequently avoided the strictures of the Treaty Clause by labeling an "agreement" what earlier would have been viewed as a "treaty." Thus, the North American Free Trade Agreement did not have to leap the hurdles erected by the Treaty Clause; instead, it was validated by majority votes of both the House of Representatives and the Senate.

These developments are undoubtedly important, and any complete analysis of our constitutional system should take account of such flexibility. But we should not overemphasize our system's capacity to change, and it is *constitutional stasis* rather than the potential for adaptation that is my focus.

* * *

* * * One cannot, as a practical matter, litigate the obvious inequality attached to Wyoming's having the same voting power in the Senate as California. Nor can we imagine even President George W. Bush, who has certainly not been a shrinking violet with regard to claims of presidential power, announcing that Justice John Paul Stevens—appointed in 1976 and embarking on this fourth decade of service on the Supreme Court at the age of eighty-six—is simply "too old" or has served "long enough," and that he is therefore nominating, and asking the Senate to confirm, a successor to Justice Stevens in spite of the awkward fact that the justice has not submitted his resignation.

In any event, * * * the Constitution makes it unacceptably difficult to achieve the inspiring goals of the Preamble and, therefore, warrants our disapproval. * * *

Although I am asking you to take part in a hypothetical referendum and to vote no with regard to the present Constitution, I am *not* asking you to imagine simply tearing it up and leaping into the unknown of a fanciful "state of nature." All you must commit yourself to is the proposition that the Constitution is sufficiently flawed to justify calling a new convention authorized to scrutinize all aspects of the Constitution and to suggest such changes as are felt to be desirable. The new convention would be no more able to bring its handiwork into being by fiat than were the framers in Philadelphia. All proposals would require popular approval in a further national referendum. This leaves open the possibility that, even after voting to trigger the convention, you could ultimately decide that the "devil you know" (the present Constitution) is preferable to the "devil you don't" (the proposed replacement). But the important thing, from my perspective, is to recognize that there are indeed "devilish" aspects of our present Constitution that should be confronted and, if at all possible, exorcised. To complete this metaphor, one might also remember that "the devil is in the details." * * *

11

"We"

ERIC LANE AND MICHAEL ORESKES

We live in a remarkable political age. More people than ever before in history, possibly a majority of all the people on earth, live under governments that could reasonably be described as democracies. The enormity of this can only be grasped by going back * * * to that moment in the late 1700s when democracy as we now know it barely existed in the world. Indeed, the word *democracy* was essentially an insult, a synonym for *mob rule*. Yes, there were places where the king had ceded some measure of power to aristocracies or even to semirepresentative parliaments. There were also commercial cities in Europe that had allowed considerable popular participation in decision making.

But nowhere was there anything like what a group of men, desperately trying to save their fledgling country, invented in Philadelphia in the summer of 1787. They wrote "a Constitution which . . . has brought such a happy order out of so gloomy a chaos," James Madison said of his handiwork many years later. They wrote a Constitution that invented a new kind of representative government. It ushered in what we can now see as the Age of Democracy in which "representative government bottomed on the principle of popular sovereignty . . . has become the political norm." In a recent book on the rise of democracy, the British scholar John Dunn finds Madison's pride understandable given the far-reaching effects of his invention: "It secured the new Republic extremely effectively, and, as we now know, for a very long time. In doing so, it turned the United States into the most politically definite, the best consolidated and the most politically self-confident society on earth. It also, over time . . . opened the way for it to become overwhelmingly the most powerful state in human history."

Quite an impressive summer's work.

But where are we in the life span of this invention? The American experiment has now lasted longer than any democracy in history. (Athens, for example, lasted only around 170 years as a democracy.) It has also spawned and inspired many others to pursue democracy. After much spillage of words and blood across the twentieth century, there is no longer even a serious intellectual challenger to representative democracy as the best and most legitimate way to organize government. What a long way we have come from 1787! "The United States is now the oldest enduring republic in world history, with a set of political institutions and traditions that have stood the test of time," wrote the historian Joseph J. Ellis.

The framers would have been stunned by this success. They knew the lessons of history were against them. They had learned from experience that individuals set free pursued their own interests. Large numbers of individuals pursuing their own interests led to chaos. Chaos invited dictators, homegrown or external, to intervene to restore order, snuffing out the very liberty people had fought to establish. They understood this cycle from their reading and, more, from the first eleven years of their own nation, which by 1787 seemed to them to be descending into the gloomy chaos Madison wrote of later.

That is why they saw democracy as "fragile."

Fragile because the framers had come to understand that in pursuit of their self-interests, Americans, like everyone else, would be willing to trample the "democracy" of others thus endangering their own.

Fragile because it was dependent on the broad participation of Americans in the nation's political processes.

Fragile because it was dependent on the willingness of Americans to acquiesce to the results of such a process.

Fragile because of the Constitution's delicate arrangement of checks and balances.

Fragile because it was a system for institutionalizing compromise. There would always be citizens searching for a more perfect system, some system that promised more wealth, or more security, or more equality, or a more glorious future, or just more of whatever it is they particularly wanted.

That was the challenge the framers confronted in 1787. People wanted what they wanted for themselves. The framers' solution, wonderfully modern and, in 1787, totally original, was to adopt a more realistic view of people and adapt their design for government to that view. They enlisted vice "on the side of virtue." They set out to prove how a representative democracy could operate without special public virtue, how "an avaricious society can form a government able to defend itself against the avarice of its members." In other words, this was not a government as good as its people. It was a government designed to produce results better than the desires of each individual person! And that is how the people ensured their own liberty. Out of many one, *E Pluribus Unum*.

To accept democracy as it emerged from Philadelphia meant to accept, as Franklin said, that this was no perfect system, just the closest to perfection a human design could come.

The framers worried that their new democracy would last only a few years. But amazingly it succeeded. Two hundred and twenty years later, the many offshoots of modern representative democracy have triumphed around the world. How ironic, then, that its original American version, with its complicated checks and balances, faces meaningful challenge in the place where it was born.

This is not the first such challenge in American history, of course, and we hope not the last. It won't be if we face it, as previous generations faced their constitutional challenges. The challenge takes new forms each time. But at heart the issue is always the same: We want what we want, and we are convinced that the system that is stopping us is wrong, flawed, broken or outmoded.

This is the essence of our present challenge. The bond between government and governed has become strained. Americans are deeply frustrated with the workings of their government. They see it as unresponsive, unrepresentative, ineffective, crippling. Can you image even a handful of Americans acknowledging today that the purpose of their government is to produce results better than the desires of the people as individuals? Not likely.

We Americans love the framers. We consume books about them and revere their words. But we have lost our connection to what they actually invented and how that invention over time created in us what we have come to call a Constitutional Conscience. We have lost the narrative thread that connects us to the story of our constitutional democracy. That story tells us two things. First, how the framers learned a series of lessons between 1776 and 1787 and used these lessons to craft our government, the blueprint for which became the Constitution. And second, how we, the people, created a Constitutional Conscience from the essential meaning of that Constitution—its freedoms and its processes and tradeoffs— and guided by these principles were then able to adapt time and again through our history to an evolving America.

This narrative thread is vital to us. It is the story that makes us Americans, ties us to our government and ties our government to us. Without it we have begun, without being totally conscious of what we are doing, to drift away from our constitutional system. We are drifting away because our knowledge of our system has grown thin. From the 1960s onward, according to Derek Bok, civic education has been declining and by the 1980s had nearly vanished. "It is striking how little energy is devoted to trying to engage citizens more actively in the affairs of government. Civic education in the public schools has been almost totally eclipsed by a preoccupation with preparing the workforce of a global economy. Most universities no longer treat the preparation of citizens as an explicit goal of their curriculum."

Reports have documented this steady decline in civic understanding. In 1998, the Department of Education found that 75 percent of high school seniors were "not proficient in civics; one third lacked even a basic comprehension of how the government operates, while only 9 percent could give two reasons why citizens should participate in the democratic process." A report in 2002 concluded "that the nation's citizenry is woefully under-educated about the fundamentals of our American Democracy."

This lack of connection is producing a dangerous spiral of frustration and disenchantment. On the one hand, Americans take the existence of our democracy for granted, while, on the other hand, being frustrated with its workings. This produces a dangerous spiral of frustration and disenchantment. Observed Bok: "Americans have expectations for politics and the political process that are often unrealistic. Convinced that presidents can often accomplish more than is humanly possible, that legislators should be able to arrive at sensible decisions without prolonged disagreement or controversy, and that politicians should refrain from pandering to the voters yet still reflect the views of their constituents, the public seems fated to endure repeated disappointment over the government and those who run it."

Some Americans respond to this disappointment by demanding changes in the system, others by distancing themselves from the system, which leaves those who stay engaged more powerful to push for the agenda they want.

Those demands for change come in two basic forms, although proponents of each argue that their proposals would make the system more democratic by shifting power. There are the Lloyd Cutlers, Oliver Norths and Dick Cheneys who want to shift more power to the president so he can either force the rest of the government to respond or just act without being fettered by the process. And there are others who want to shift more power directly to citizens so they can force government to respond, or simply go around the process. That they want such changes is within their rights. But any meaningful argument for them must occur in the context of the lessons the framers learned long ago. Without this context, we risk making changes that dismantle what has been proven right about our system and even endanger the freedoms it was built to guarantee.

It might be helpful to restate those lessons, in a simple form that everyone can paste on their refrigerator.

The framers boiled their experience down to a Constitution. We have boiled their experience down to these five lessons.

1. Everyone is selfish. This is not to say that people cannot act well or perform acts of great nobility. But essentially people act to achieve their own self-interest, particularly at the level at which government operates: regulating conduct and redistributing wealth. People are, however, willing to trade one benefit for another and sometimes even sacrifice a narrow interest for a broader one that they feel will ultimately do them more good. The government's job is to find those areas of common ground. That is where we can build a common good.

2. Government is the steam valve of society. It funnels and relieves the pressures that build from competing interests.

3. Political process is more important than product. Consensus around a flawed plan can still produce great progress. (The Constitution itself is the best example.) But a "perfect plan" without consensus will only produce conflict and deadlock. (The Clinton health care debacle is one example.) Respect for the system is thus a vital prerequisite for progress. When respect is in such short supply, it is no surprise that progress is, as well.
4. The strength of consensus is directly related to the breadth of representation and the depth of deliberation. A sound-bite society where civic education has vanished has little basis for forging strong consensus.
5. Every interest is a special one. The founders would no doubt be amazed by the scale and power of modern corporations and trade unions. But they would have no difficulty at all with the idea that everyone has wants and desires and that these drive their views and their allegiances to groups and factions. To them, the only meaningful definition of the *common good* would be the agreement that emerged from an inclusive political and legislative process to resolve competing (special) interests.

Our world is very different from that of the framers. People have powers now they could not have dreamed of then. Information, the lifeblood of democracy, moved then at the speed of sail. It moves now at the speed of light.

But there is no evidence that people have changed. Therefore, we see no reason to abandon the lessons the framers formed about people or the system they built from those lessons. Indeed, some of the changes, most particularly the speed with which society can now move, only reinforce the need for care in our political deliberations and for the speed bumps in the process that prevent us from rushing to judgment. That is what the framers built for us.

Recent experience reminds us that we make mistakes as a country when we move away from how our system was built to work. When people say now they wish the Congress and the media had done more to question the march to war in Iraq, they are saying, too, that they wish the leaders of Congress and of the press had done more to assert their authority, and fulfill their responsibilities, under, respectively, Article I and the First Amendment to the Constitution. Even many proponents of the war concede now that the checks and balances did not work well. We believe this failure was due to the weakening of our sense of constitutional roles, of our Constitutional Conscience.

We as Americans need to continue to remind ourselves of the framers' concern that democracy was fragile.

So far, unlike in the past, no one is openly arguing for an abandonment of democracy. Indeed, what many Americans think we need is what they see as more democracy. Both the proponents of strengthened presidential power and the proponents of direct democracy argue that their proposals would make the system more representative of the general public: the president as the only nationally elected official, and direct democracy as the only means to involve Americans more directly in the decision-making processes. Either way, the argument is for a more direct engagement and less entanglement in Washington process. We understand those feelings. They rise historically from a treasured strain of American belief running back to, at least, Tom Paine, the Declaration of Independence and the Articles of Confederation.

But we must not forget the warning of the framers that the most likely undoing of democracy would be in the name of more democracy.

That thought is why we wrote this book. We wanted to pick up the dropped narrative thread of the American democratic story, to remind ourselves that the democratic thinking of 1776 is only the first half of our legacy. The second half was born of Madison and his colleagues in 1787. The framers in 1787 saw liberty and direct democracy is inadequate on their own to ensure the very democracy they purported to further. For in the real world in which government works, this directly democratic perspective translates into one group getting its way over the interest of other groups or one branch, whether a powerful legislature or monarchical president, getting too much power over everyone else.

The framers' ideas transformed the thirst for liberty into a real nation. Madison and his colleagues invented a form of government whose purpose, as the historian Gordon Wood summed it up, was not to transcend our differences but to reconcile them.

Americans' current frustration and anger with their government is sapping their commitment to the principles that have made the country work. Rather than drift away from the Constitution, we should renew our connection to it. We should remember that consultation and process and debate are good things, even when they slow and complicate decisions. Most of all, we should remind each other that compromise is a show of strength, not weakness. Reaffirming these constitutional principles will actually address our frustration better than inventing something different, or more accurately, returning to what did not work between 1776 and 1787.

People say that what they want is compromise and consensus. The framers believed in that. It is why the most important and radical word in the Constitution was the first word, *We*. The government was the people and is the people. The power of each branch of government is a grant from the people, and each branch to one degree or another is accountable to them. Nothing like this had ever been created before. One British political leader, comparing the evolution of Britain's unwritten constitution to the seemingly overnight drafting of the U.S. Constitution, called the latter "the most wonderful work ever struck off at a given time by the brain and purpose of man."

But Americans in practice, in the grind of life, are no longer seeing it this way. For one thing, they do not connect their desire for consensus with the Constitution's governmental design. For another, they routinely, and predictably, define the consensus they want as the achievement of their own goals, not something larger. Americans' demands on government are today broad and deeply diverse. And when they are in an uncompromising mood, when they are divided fifty-fifty, red from blue, their representative government reflects this division, and it stalls.

The problem is not that government is unrepresentative. The problem, if you want to call it that, is that the government is very representative. The message we are hearing is that our government does not work. The message we should be hearing is that our government is a reflection of our own divisions. What we need is not a new system of government. We need a renewed willingness to work out our differences and find compromises, consensus and that other now-popular phrase, common ground.

The purpose of American-style democracy is not to guarantee each of us what we want individually. It is to give each of us as large an opportunity as possible to pursue what we want within the limits the Constitution and our Constitutional Conscience impose on us. This tension between individual liberty and community restraint has over time produced a great deal of good for a great many people and worked better than any alternative yet tried. It is still the best system for our sprawling, complicated nation.

To say that ours is the best system is not to say that it is a perfect system. It is not and never will be perfect. It can't be. It is composed of we, the people, with all our flaws. That is the point. We make it work. Our drive. Our demands. Our participation! In 1888, the poet and editor James Russell Lowell remarked on the "splendid complacency" he found among his fellow Americans who were "neglectful" of their "political duties." He traced this neglect back to a widespread but mistaken belief that the framers of the Constitution had "invented a machine that would go of itself." Lowell said he admired the ability of Americans to let "confidence in our luck" and "absorption with material interests" subsume attention to the state of our democracy.

*   *   *

These problems have been building for years. By the end of the 1980s, politicians in Washington were in open despair that the political system was unable to deal with the problems facing the country.

The political deterioration has grown steadily worse. Not surprisingly, since it is our most representative branch of government, the dysfunction is most visible in the Congress. In a nation of citizens so lacking in an understanding of our system, it is hardly surprising that, increasingly, the men and women they send to Washington don't make an adherence to constitutional principles an important part of their daily work. "People revere the Constitution yet know so little about it—and that goes for some of my fellow senators," said the Senate's top institutionalist, Robert Byrd of West Virginia.

The framers counted on a balance of power between Congress and the president. They were, critically, intended to watch each other. But * * * Congress has wavered in the exercise of its constitutional duty.

The weakness of the legislature throws off the whole design of the system. The strong reassertions of presidential prerogatives would not have surprised the framers. They would have expected this, although some may have been surprised at the degree. "You must . . . oblige [the government] to control itself," Madison wrote. The American system counts on each branch asserting its authority, just as it counts on each individual to press his or her wishes. Balance is essential to the framers' design, but to find the right balance each participant has to push and pull. The danger comes when one branch pushes and the other folds.

*   *   *

The imbalance we refer to here is far more than the common instinct of members of Congress trying to protect a president of the same party. To some extent, this will always happen. But American history is marked with examples of members of Congress of each party asserting their institutional, constitutional role and challenging a president of their own party. Senator Harry S. Truman investigated President Roosevelt's administration, and Senator Lyndon B. Johnson investigated president Truman's administration. It was a Republican senator, Howard Baker, whose incessant questions crystallized the belief that a Republican president knew more about Watergate than he had told. And it was a Democratic senator, Daniel Patrick Moynihan, who blocked the Democratic president and his wife from their plan to overhaul American health care. Moynihan's critique was a classic defense of constitutional process. The Clintons drafted their plan, Moynihan complained, behind closed doors and failed to consult the Congress or build a consensus. And a few Republican legislators had begun challenging President George W. Bush's Iraq policy by the end of 2006.

But over the last few years on Capitol Hill, the Republican leadership seemed to disown the institutional role in the constitutional design. * * * Without amending the Constitution, both Senator Bill Frist and Speaker Dennis Hastert effectively gave President Bush the parliamentary type of system that Lloyd Cutler had so desperately wanted for President Carter. They operated as the president's floor leaders in the Congress, rather than as his separate and coequal partners in government.

Congress of course is not a piece of machinery. It is 535 individual members. They are the ones who decide how assertive to be. The single most important factor in that decision is the question of how assertive

American voters expect them to be. Senator Frist and Speaker Hastert followed their path because it was easy, because they did not feel political pressure to assert their institutional roles under the Constitution. We can blame the voters for not pressuring the leaders. Or we can blame the leaders for not leading the citizens. Both are true. If two of the top elected figures in the country have such little regard for the institutional obligations handed down to them, how can we expect ordinary Americans to pay attention to the Constitution? Yet it is also hard to ask politicians to exercise institutional responsibilities that we give them no credit for exercising.

Both sides of the problem are an outgrowth of how far we have fallen away from an intimate knowledge of or connection to our Constitutional Conscience. We judge our politicians heavily by what we want and how well they deliver. We measure them in the present tense alone. We don't praise honest men and women for taking clear stands on constitutional principle or exercising those institutional responsibilities. We want to know what they have done for us lately; not what they have done to faithfully exercise the responsibilities given them by the Constitution. And how could it be otherwise, for we have little idea what those responsibilities are. * * *

The 2006 election sent a message to the incumbents in Congress. In very much the way the Federalists were tossed out in 1800, after President Adams failed to stop a Federalist Congress from plunging forward with the reviled Sedition Act, the Republicans were tossed out of Congress in 2006 for failing to check a Republican president's plunge into an unpopular war. Elections, as vital as they are, are in effect a last resort— the voters passing judgment after the fact. The system was designed to produce better results before the fact, when it is allowed to work. Whether you in the end supported or opposed American entry into Iraq, that decision, and more particularly the decision of the president and Congress, would have been stronger and more effective if it had been subject to more oversight in Congress and more debate in public. Perhaps you think the more effective policy would have been to stay out of war. Or perhaps you wish the war and its aftermath had been more effectively executed. As it turned out, Congress did not watch over the president, and the country got neither peace nor effective war. In both 1800 and 2006, the election produced dramatic shifts because classic checks and balances failed and thus produced policies that angered the voters. The election results were a punishment. But punishment by itself did not correct the more basic reasons the system of checks and balances failed.

The downward spiral will continue unless we get to the root of the problem. And what is the root of the problem? All of us, Americans, and each of us. A public opinion survey once asked Americans to "suppose the President and Congress have to violate a Constitutional principle to pass an important law the public wanted. Would you support them in this action?" Only 49 percent of the public said no. The other half were a mix of yes (22 percent) and undecided or neither (29 percent). Even on a simple statement of a bedrock principle of our system, we are divided. That is a shaky foundation on which to rest the most important government on earth.

Why does our constitutional commitment seem so thin? At one level, we have come to mistake longevity for permanence. We take for granted the existence of what not so long ago was remarkable and revolutionary. We assume that because we have been a free and successful democracy for our lifetimes and our parents' and grandparents' lifetimes that we will remain such for our children's and our children's children's lifetimes, too. That alone would be worrisome. When citizens take their democracy for granted, they undermine its most basic tenet. Democracy dissolves without the commitment to it of its citizens. That loss of commitment is what the framers most feared.

In our own time, the historian Sean Wilentz put it this way: "Democracy is never a gift bestowed by benevolent, far seeing rulers who seek to reinforce their own legitimacy. It must always be fought for, by political coalitions that cut across distinctions of wealth, power, and interest. It succeeds and survives only when it is rooted in the lives and expectations of its citizens and continually reinvigorated in each generation. Democratic successes are never irreversible."

But instead of reinvigorating our representative government, current generations are disparaging it. We are not fighting for it. Instead, we as a people are frustrated with the day-to-day workings of government and restlessly search for some "fix" for the system.

Perhaps our confidence in the permanence of our democracy has left us feeling free to attack its workings. To a point, that is healthy. The system was built for robust debate, and it has survived a great deal of it. But robust debate requires engagement and information. It requires the debaters to have some context, some sense of shared ground.

Where do we find that common ground? By looking behind the trouble signs. We said that taking our democracy for granted while also being frustrated with our government seems almost contradictory. We said "almost" because in fact we believe they rise from the same source.

Americans don't know their own government anymore. They don't know their own history. We take our democracy for granted because we don't understand how hard it was to build it, how much courage (not just on the battlefield) it took to preserve it, and how close it came to failure on several occasions from the Alien and Sedition Acts, through the Civil War to the Great Depression. And we are frustrated with how it works today because no one is explaining that how it works (most of time) is how the framers, benefiting from the real-life experience of the early nation, designed it to work. Defending the system is not a politically popular thing to do. And in our hurry-up society, no one wants to sit still long enough to hear explanations of the system, let alone defenses. This is frightening. The framers expected flaws to emerge in their design. They expected fixes to be needed.

What is dangerous now is that the debate over the system has lost the context of how the system got to be what it is. In an environment where citizens do not particularly understand the system's basic design, many of the fixes are actually challenges to the overall design. Madison and his colleagues envisioned the Senate, with its members chosen for longer terms from entire states, as a balance and a check to the House, with its larger membership with shorter terms from narrower constituencies. Together they would check the president, with a term halfway between that in the House and that in the Senate. Yet today former senator Gravel is running for president on the express platform of creating a national system of referendum to circumvent the Congress. His campaign is welcome to the extent that it encourages a debate that teaches Americans about the design of the Constitution. Americans are free to change that design. But they should understand what they are doing and what they are abandoning if they do.

We hope the result will be an embrace of improvements, rather than a dismantling of constitutional principles. But if only 49 percent of the country is willing to speak up for a fundamental constitutional principle, we are perilously close to undoing the system itself. The wrong crisis at the wrong moment could push us over the edge before we realize what we have done. Indeed, all that protects us in this situation is the framers' prescience in creating a system where a majority of one is not enough to make radical changes. But then of course we become frustrated that we can't get the change we want, and the spiral starts all over again.

Thomas Jefferson said that the tree of liberty needs to be refreshed from time to time with the blood of patriots and tyrants. What a wonderful bit of Jeffersonian poetry. But we think something less dramatic, but perhaps harder in its own way, is needed right now. We as Americans need to tend our own garden. We need to renew not just our faith in but our understanding of the system the framers gave us. That understanding requires more than some sound bites about liberty and freedom. We need to embrace that our liberty and freedom flow directly from less glamorous but still vital ideas, such as compromise, and checks and balances, and representation and process. A dash of humility would not hurt either.

Two of our most important modern presidents, Franklin Roosevelt and Ronald Reagan, each saw the importance of renewing our understanding of American constitutional government.

Roosevelt became president in the middle of the worst crisis of American democracy since the Civil War. The link between the American political system and its economic success had snapped. Around the world, dictatorships of the left and the right were on the rise. There were people who came to FDR—serious, important people—to advise him that he might have to take authoritarian powers himself. Looking back, we came much closer than many people realize to the loss of our democracy. But we did not lose it, thanks to the resolve of FDR and the strength in the American people of what we have come to describe as our Constitutional Conscience. Four years later, Roosevelt, in his first fireside chat of his second term as president, said he hoped the American people had reread their Constitution in the last few weeks. "Like the Bible," he said "it ought to be read again and again." Ironically, Roosevelt made this remark in a speech in which he argued for a plan to weaken the Supreme Court and strengthen the power of the presidency and the Congress by putting more of his appointees on the Court. It is a testament to the strength of our Constitutional Conscience that Roosevelt's way of arguing for this plan was to present it as a defense of the Constitution, not an infringement of it. The system stopped him anyway, and even without those expanded powers he guided the country out of the Depression. The Court-packing plan he outlined in that fireside chat has vanished into history. It turns out that the more important notion of that speech was Roosevelt's insistence that we reconnect with the Constitution regularly.

Half a century later, Ronald Reagan was saying farewell after eight years as president. He had come to office in the midst of a crisis of confidence. Watergate, stagflation, the Iran hostage crisis, the residue of the 1960s had combined to shake Americans' faith in their country. Reagan had worked with considerable success to rebuild that faith. As he said farewell, he took pride in that accomplishment. But he recognized that the job was only partly done: "This national feeling is good, but it won't count for much and it won't last unless it is grounded in thoughtfulness and knowledge. An informed patriotism is what we want. And are we doing a good enough job teaching our children what America is and what she represents in the long history of the world? Those of us who are over thirty five or so years of age grew up in a different America. We were taught, very directly, what it means to be an American. And we absorbed, almost in the air, a love of country and an appreciation of its institutions."

But as America prepared to enter the 1990s, Reagan warned, the fashion had changed. "Younger parents aren't sure that an unambivalent appreciation of America is the right thing to teach modern children. And as for those who create the popular culture, well-grounded patriotism is no longer the style. Our spirit is back, but we haven't reinstitutionalized it."

Roosevelt and Reagan are the touchstone presidents of the American Century. In some ways they could not represent more different political moments. The first brought a powerful centralized federal government into our domestic lives. The other drew the line to limit it. Yet across the half century that separated them, they each affirmed the centrality of connecting Americans to their democratic heritage.

"So we've got to teach history based not on what's in fashion but what's important," said Reagan. He concluded: "If we forget what we did, we won't know who we are. Let's start with some basics: more attention to American history and a greater emphasis on civic ritual."

We agree. Indeed, we think we owe it to the framers and all succeeding Americans who have struggled for the Constitution to renew our connection to our own history. But even more, we owe it to the future, which will be shaped by our actions.

There is a strong sense that we have become selfish and self-involved as a people. It is hard to say whether we are more self-interested than Americans at the time the Constitution was written. It was written because the framers thought we were very selfish, and they decided they could not fight human nature, only harness it. That was the genius of their system. It accepted us for who we are and yet still offered the optimistic vision that we could, as a nation, compromise our differences to agree to do great things.

We are all for ideas to make us less selfish or self-interested. But we are with the framers in doubting that human nature can be fundamentally changed.

They were right that our more selfish impulses can be channeled. Americans throughout their history have understood that it was in their own interest, ultimately, to preserve this system that balanced everyone's demands. That understanding is what we mean by our Constitutional Conscience. It is what Sean Wilentz is talking about when he describes coalitions that cut across lines of wealth, power and interest. It is noble to try to make people different. We admire those who try. But politics is the art of the possible. The framers made it possible for us to live together in liberty and community. The 220-year history of our Constitution is a history of Americans repeatedly rekindling their belief that their own interests are served by this system that grants extensive liberty in exchange for a willingness to compromise and tolerate differences. We Americans need to rekindle that belief once more.

If this [reading] has one message, it is that there is nothing about our past success that guarantees our future success. Each generation must do that for itself. Nevertheless, this is a hopeful message, because we are not alone in our struggle. We have been given a great gift and with it a great responsibility. We are the inheritors of the longest democratic tradition in the world. We still hold in great respect the men who began that tradition and the men and women who carried it forth and bequeathed it to us. That respect is a resource for us now. The struggles we are having, the frustrations we are feeling, are exactly the struggles and frustrations the framers anticipated when they designed our democracy. We can lean on them and their experience. By reaching backward to them and their ideas, we can move forward.

Discussion Questions

1. Most of the time, people become critical of the Constitution when they don't get the policy results they want. When Congress fails to pass legislation because of the power of small-state senators, when the Supreme Court issues a ruling they oppose, when the president makes a decision regarding the use of force that they oppose, the immediate impulse is to blame the system and call for change that would make the preferred policies more likely. Is this a valid reason for wanting the system to change?

2. The Constitution was written over two hundred years ago by a group of white men who had very "unmodern" views about democracy and equality. On what basis should we be bound by the decisions that they made? What is the foundation of constitutional fidelity? What would be the result if each generation were permitted to remake the rules?

3. Often, opinions about the Constitution divide along philosophical lines. On one side are people who believe that the most important purpose of a constitution is to limit government size and power. On the other are people who believe that the Constitution must protect rights and promote equality (which almost always involves expanding the size and power of government). Who has the better case? Why?

CHAPTER 3

Federalism

12

The Federalist, No. 46

JAMES MADISON

Some of the most divisive and bitter political battles in our nation's history have occurred over interpretations of the constitutional principle of federalism—the division of powers and functions between the state governments and the national government. The struggle for desegregation and the civil rights of minorities, the legalization of abortion, the selective incorporation of the Bill of Rights into the Fourteenth Amendment, slavery and the Civil War all ultimately turned on the question, Who has the authority to govern: the states, or the national government? Our federal system is a delicate balance of power and shared responsibility between nation and states, each with constitutional authority to pass laws, levy taxes, and protect the interests and rights of citizens. It is a dynamic balance of power, easily destabilized by economic crises, political initiatives, and Supreme Court rulings, but often resolved in more recent years by the question, Who will pay the price for implementing and enforcing government policy?

The "double security" that James Madison discussed in The Federalist, *No. 51, in the previous chapter, did not satisfy those who feared that the national powers would encroach on state sovereignty. In* The Federalist, *No. 46, Madison went to great lengths to reassure the states that they would continue to wield a high degree of power, arguing that "the first and most natural attachment of the people will be to the governments of their respective states." While recognizing the potential for conflicts between state and federal governments, Madison concluded that the power retained by the states would be sufficient to resist arrogation by the newly established national government.*

I proceed to inquire whether the federal government or the State governments will have the advantage with regard to the predilection and support of the people. Notwithstanding the different modes in which they are appointed, we must consider both of them as substantially dependent on the great body of the citizens of the United States. * * * The federal and State governments are in fact but different agents and trustees of the people, constituted with different powers and designed for different purposes. The adversaries of the Constitution seem to have lost sight of the people altogether in their reasonings on this subject; and to have viewed these different establishments not only as mutual rivals and enemies, but as uncontrolled by any common superior in their efforts to usurp the authorities of each other. These gentlemen must here be reminded of their error. They must be told that the ultimate authority, wherever the derivative may be found, resides in the people alone, and that it will not depend merely on the comparative ambition or address of the different governments whether either, or which of them, will be able to enlarge its sphere of jurisdiction at the expense of the other. Truth, no less than decency, requires that the event in every case should be supposed to depend on the sentiments and sanction of their common constituents.

Many considerations * * * seem to place it beyond doubt that the first and most natural attachment of the people will be to the governments of their respective States. Into the administration of these a greater number of individuals will expect to rise. From the gift of these a greater number of offices and emoluments will flow. By the superintending care of these, all the more domestic and personal interests of the people will be regulated and provided for. With the affairs of these, the people will be more familiarly and minutely conversant. And with the members of these will a greater proportion of the people have the ties of personal acquaintance and friendship, and of family and party attachments; on the side of these, therefore, the popular bias may well be expected most strongly to incline.

The remaining points on which I propose to compare the federal and State governments are the disposition and the faculty they may respectively possess to resist and frustrate the measures of each other.

It has been already proved that the members of the federal will be more dependent on the members of the State governments than the latter will be on the former. It has appeared also that the prepossessions of the people, on whom both will depend, will be more on the side of the State governments than of the federal government. So far as the disposition of each towards the other may be influenced by these causes, the State governments must clearly have the advantage. But in a distinct and very important point of view, the advantage will lie on the same side. The prepossessions, which the members themselves will carry into the federal government, will generally be favorable to the States; whilst it will rarely happen that the members of the State governments will carry into the public councils a bias in favor of the general government. A local spirit will infallibly prevail much more in the members of Congress than a national spirit will prevail in the legislatures of the particular States.

* * * What is the spirit that has in general characterized the proceedings of Congress? A perusal of their journals, as well as the candid acknowledgments of such as have had a seat in that assembly, will inform us that the members have but too frequently displayed the character rather of partisans of their respective States than of impartial guardians of a common interest; that where on one occasion improper sacrifices have been made of local considerations to the aggrandizement of the federal government, the great interests of the nation have suffered on a hundred from an undue attention to the local prejudices, interests, and views of the particular States. I mean not by these reflections to insinuate that the new federal government will not embrace a more enlarged plan of policy than the existing government may have pursued; much less that its views will be as confined as those of the State legislatures; but only that it will partake sufficiently of the spirit of both to be disinclined to invade the rights of the individual States, or the prerogatives of their governments.

Were it admitted, however, that the federal government may feel an equal disposition with the State governments to extend its power beyond the due limits, the latter would still have the advantage in the means of defeating such encroachments. If an act of a particular State, though unfriendly to the national government, be generally popular in that State, and should not too grossly violate the oaths of the State officers, it is executed immediately and, of course, by means on the spot and depending on the State alone. The opposition of the federal government, or the interposition of federal officers, would but inflame the zeal of all parties on the side of the State, and the evil could not be prevented or repaired, if at all, without the employment of means which must always be resorted to with reluctance and difficulty. On the other hand, should an unwarrantable measure of the federal government be unpopular in particular States, which would seldom fail to be the case, or even a warrantable measure be so, which may sometimes be the case, the means of opposition to it are powerful and at hand. The disquietude of the people; their repugnance and, perhaps, refusal to co-operate with the officers of the Union; the frowns of the executive magistracy of the State; the embarrassments created by legislative devices, which would often be added on such occasions, would oppose, in any State, difficulties not to be despised; would form, in a large State, very serious impediments; and where the sentiments of several adjoining States happened to be in unison, would present obstructions which the federal government would hardly be willing to encounter.

But ambitious encroachments of the federal government on the authority of the State governments would not excite the opposition of a single State, or of a few States only. They would be signals of general alarm. Every government would espouse the common cause. A correspondence would be opened. Plans of resistance would be concerted.

One spirit would animate and conduct the whole. The same combinations, in short, would result from an apprehension of the federal, as was produced by the dread of a foreign yoke; and unless the projected innovations should be voluntarily renounced, the same appeal to a trial of force would be made in the one case as was made in the other.

The only refuge left for those who prophesy the downfall of the State governments is the visionary supposition that the federal government may previously accumulate a military force for the projects of ambition. The reasonings contained in these papers must have been employed to little purpose indeed, if it could be necessary now to disprove the reality of this danger. That the people and the States should, for a sufficient period of time, elect an uninterrupted succession of men ready to betray both; that the traitors should, throughout this period, uniformly and systematically pursue some fixed plan for the extension of the military establishment; that the governments and the people of the States should silently and patiently behold the gathering storm and continue to supply the materials until it should be prepared to burst on their own heads must appear to everyone more like the incoherent dreams of a delirious jealousy, or the misjudged exaggerations of a counterfeit zeal, than like the sober apprehensions of genuine patriotism. Extravagant as the supposition is, let it, however, be made. Let a regular army, fully equal to the resources of the country, be formed; and let it be entirely at the devotion of the federal government: still it would not be going too far to say that the State governments with the people on their side would be able to repel the danger.

Besides the advantage of being armed, which the Americans possess over the people of almost every other nation, the existence of subordinate governments, to which the people are attached and by which the militia officers are appointed, forms a barrier against the enterprises of ambition, more insurmountable than any which a simple government of any form can admit of.

Let us not insult the free and gallant citizens of America with the suspicion that they would be less able to defend the rights of which they would be in actual possession than the debased subjects of arbitrary power would be to rescue theirs from the hands of their oppressors. Let us rather no longer insult them with the supposition that they can ever reduce themselves to the necessity of making the experiment by a blind and tame submission to the long train of insidious measures which must precede and produce it.

The argument under the present head may be put into a very concise form, which appears altogether conclusive. Either the mode in which the federal government is to be constructed will render it sufficiently dependent on the people, or it will not. On the first supposition, it will be restrained by that dependence from forming schemes obnoxious to their constituents. On the other supposition, it will not possess the confidence of the people, and its schemes of usurpation will be easily defeated by the State governments, who will be supported by the people.

On summing up the considerations stated in this and the last paper, they seem to amount to the most convincing evidence that the powers proposed to be lodged in the federal government are as little formidable to those reserved to the individual States as they are indispensably necessary to accomplish the purposes of the Union; and that all those alarms which have been sounded of a meditated and consequential annihilation of the State governments must, on the most favorable interpretation, be ascribed to the chimerical fears of the authors of them.

PUBLIUS

DISCUSSION QUESTIONS

1. Is Madison right when he states that people are more attached to their state governments than to the national government? Why or why not? If not, would it better facilitate the democratic process if they were more attached to state governments?

2. Would your answer change at all during different political times? For example, were people more attached to the national government in the wake of the terrorist attacks on our country than they were before September 11, 2001? Do people lose their faith in the national government during tough economic times?

From *The Price of Federalism*

PAUL PETERSON

In this concise overview of American federalism, Paul Peterson argues that both the early and more modern system of shared sovereignty between the national government and the states have had their disadvantages. From the early period of "dual federalism" to the more modern system of a dominant national government, the battle over national and state government jurisdiction and power has led to bloodshed and war; the denial of political, social, and economic rights; and regional inequalities among the states.

Nevertheless, Peterson argues, there are advantages to federalism. Federalism has also facilitated capital growth and development, the creation of infrastructures, and social programs that greatly improved the quality of life for millions of Americans. Once the national government took responsibility for guaranteeing civil rights and civil liberties, the states "became the engines of economic development." Not all states are equally wealthy, but the national government has gradually diminished some of these differences by financing many social and economic programs. One battle over the proper form of federal relations involved welfare policy in the 1990s. Republicans in Congress wanted to give back to states the power to devise their own programs, whereas most Democrats and President Clinton initially wanted to retain a larger degree of federal government control. However, President Clinton eventually agreed to end welfare as an entitlement and return substantial control over the program to the states. The long-term verdict on this landmark legislation is still an open question. There is considerable debate over the proper balance between federal and state funding for the state-level welfare programs.

These same debates have cropped up in more recent years in homeland security policy. Ideally, this policy would be run at the national level, and resources would be allocated to parts of the country that pose the greatest security risks. However, every state wants its share of the federal pie, so resources are not always allocated in the most efficient manner. Federalism also poses challenges for coordinating policy for "first responders" in a time of crisis: Who is responsible for coming to the aid of people in distress: local, state, or national agencies?

The Price of Early Federalism

As a principle of government, federalism has had a dubious history. It remains on the margins of political respectability even today. I was recently invited to give a presentation on metropolitan government before a United Nations conference. When I offered to discuss how the federal principle could be used to help metropolitan areas govern themselves more effectively, my sponsors politely advised me that this topic would be poorly received. The vast majority of UN members had a unified form of government, I was told, and they saw little of value in federalism. We reached a satisfactory compromise. I replaced "federal" with "two-tier form of government."

Thomas Hobbes, the founder of modern political thought, would have blessed the compromise, for he, too, had little room for federalism in his understanding of the best form of government. Hobbes said that people agreed to have a government over them only because they realized that in a state of nature, that is, when there is no government, life becomes a war of all against all. If no government exists to put malefactors in jail, everyone must become a criminal simply to avoid being a victim. Life becomes "nasty, brutish and short." To avoid the violent state of nature, people need and want rule by a single sovereign. Division of power among multiple sovereigns encourages bickering among them. Conflicts become inevitable, as each sovereign tries to expand its power (if for no other reason than to avoid becoming the prey of competing sovereigns). Government degenerates into anarchy and the world returns to the bitter state of nature from which government originally emerged.

The authors of *The Federalist* papers defended dual sovereignty by turning Hobbes's argument in favor of single sovereignty on its head. While Hobbes said that anything less than a single sovereign would lead to war of all against all, *The Federalist* argued that the best way of preserving liberty was to divide power. If power is concentrated in any one place, it can be used to crush individual liberty. Even in a democracy there can be the tyranny of the majority, the worst kind of tyranny because it is so stifling and complete. A division of power between the national and state governments reduces the possibility that any single majority will be able to control all centers of governmental power. The national government, by defending the country against foreign aggression, prevents external threats to liberty. The state governments, by denying power to any single dictator, reduce threats to liberty from within. As James Madison said in his defense of the Constitution, written on the eve of its ratification,

> The power surrendered by the people is first divided between two distinct governments, and then the portion allotted to each subdivided among distinct and separate departments. Hence a double security arises to the rights of the people. The different governments will control each other, at the same time that each will be controlled by itself. [*The Federalist*, No. 51]

Early federalism was built on the principle of dual sovereignty. The Constitution divided sovereignty between state and nation, each in control of its own sphere. Some even interpreted the Constitution to mean that state legislatures could nullify federal laws. Early federalism also gave both levels of government their own military capacity. Congress was given the power to raise an army and wage war, but states were allowed to maintain their own militia.

The major contribution of early federalism to American liberties took place within a dozen years after the signing of the Constitution. Liberty is never established in a new nation until those in authority have peacefully ceded power to a rival political faction. Those who wrote the Constitution and secured its ratification, known as the Federalists, initially captured control of the main institutions of the national government: Congress, the presidency, and the Supreme Court. Those opposed to the new constitutional order, the antifederalists, had to content themselves with an opposition role in Congress and control over a number of state governments, most notably Virginia's.

The political issues dividing the two parties were serious. The Federalist party favored a strong central government, a powerful central bank that could facilitate economic and industrial development, and a strong, independent executive branch. Federalists had also become increasingly disturbed by the direction the French Revolution had taken. They were alarmed by the execution of thousands, the confiscation of private property, and the movement of French troops across Europe. They called for the creation of a national army and reestablished close ties with Britain.

The antifederalists, who became known as Democratic-Republicans, favored keeping most governmental power in the hands of state governments. They were opposed to a national bank, a strong presidency, and industrial government. They thought the United States would remain a free country only if it remained a land of independent farmers. They bitterly opposed the creation of a national army for fear it would be used to repress political opposition. Impressed by the French Revolution's commitment to the rights of man, they excused its excesses. The greater danger, they thought, was the reassertion of British power, and they denounced the Federalists for seeming to acquiesce in the seizure of U.S. seamen by the British navy.

The conflict between the two sides intensified after George Washington retired to his home in Mount Vernon. In 1800 Thomas Jefferson, founder of the Democratic-Republican party, waged an all-out campaign to defeat Washington's Federalist successor, John Adams. In retrospect, the central issue of the election was democracy itself. Could an opposition party drive a government out of power? Would political leaders accept their defeat?

So bitter was the feud between the two parties that Representative Matthew Lyon, a Democratic-Republican, spit in the face of a Federalist on the floor of Congress. Outside the Congress, pro-French propagandists relentlessly criticized Adams. To silence the opposition, Congress, controlled by the Federalists, passed the Alien and Sedition Acts. One of the

Alien Acts gave President Adams the power to deport any foreigners "concerned in any treasonable or secret machinations against the government." The Sedition Act made it illegal to "write, print, utter, or publish . . . any false, scandalous and malicious writing . . . against . . . the Congress of the United States, or the President."

The targets of the Sedition Acts soon became clear. Newspaper editors supporting the Democratic-Republicans were quickly indicted, and ten were brought to trial and convicted by juries under the influence of Federalist judges. Matthew Lyon was sentenced to a four-month jail term for claiming, presumably falsely, that President Adams had an "unbounded thirst for ridiculous pomp, foolish adulation, and selfish avarice." Even George Washington lent his support to this political repression.

Federalism undoubtedly helped the fledgling American democracy survive this first constitutional test. When the Federalists passed the Alien and Sedition Acts, Democratic-Republicans in the Virginia and Kentucky state legislatures passed resolutions nullifying the laws. When it looked as if Jefferson's victory in the election of 1800 might be stripped away by a Federalist-controlled House of Representatives, both sides realized that the Virginia state militia was at least as strong as the remnants of the Continental Army. Lacking the national army they had tried to establish, the Federalists chose not to fight. They acquiesced in their political defeat in part because their opponents had military as well as political power, and because they themselves could retreat to their own regional base of power, the state and local governments of New England and the mid-Atlantic states.

Jefferson claimed his victory was a revolution every bit as comprehensive as the one fought in 1776. The Alien and Sedition Acts were discarded, nullified not by a state legislature but by the results of a national election. President Adams returned to private life without suffering imprisonment or exile. Many years later, he and Jefferson reconciled their differences and developed through correspondence a close friendship. They died on the same day, the fiftieth anniversary of the Declaration of Independence. To both, federalism and liberty seemed closely intertwined.

The price to be paid for early federalism became more evident with the passage of time. To achieve the blessings of liberty, early federalism divided sovereign power. When Virginia and Kentucky nullified the Alien and Sedition Acts, they preserved liberties only by threatening national unity. With the election of Jefferson, the issue was temporarily rendered moot, but the doctrine remained available for use when southerners once again felt threatened by encroaching national power.

The doctrine of nullification was revived in 1830 by John C. Calhoun, sometime senator from South Carolina, who objected to high tariffs that protected northern industry at the expense of southern cotton producers. When Congress raised the tariff, South Carolina's legislature threatened to declare the law null and void. Calhoun, then serving as Andrew

Jackson's vice president, argued that liberties could be trampled by national majorities unless states could nullify tyrannical acts. Andrew Jackson, though elected on a state's rights ticket, remained committed to national supremacy. At the annual Democratic banquet honoring the memory of Thomas Jefferson, Calhoun supporters sought to trap Jackson into endorsing the doctrine. But Jackson, aware of the scheme, raised his glass in a dramatic toast to "Our federal union: it must be preserved!" Not to be outdone, Calhoun replied in kind: "The union, next to our liberty, most dear!"

A compromise was found to the overt issue, the tariff, but it was not so easy to resolve the underlying issue of slavery. In the infamous Dred Scott decision, the Supreme Court interpreted federalism to mean that boundaries could not be placed on the movements of masters and slaves. Northern territories could not free slaves that came within their boundaries; to do so deprived masters of their Fifth Amendment right not to be deprived of their property without due process of law. The decision spurred northern states to elect Abraham Lincoln president, which convinced southern whites that their liberties, most dear, were more important than federal union.

To Lincoln, as to Jackson, the union was to be preserved at all costs. Secession meant war. War meant the loss of 1 million lives, the destruction of the southern economy, the emancipation of African Americans from slavery, the demise of the doctrine of nullification, and the end to early federalism. Early federalism, with its doctrine of dual sovereignty, may have initially helped to preserve liberty, but it did so at a terrible price. As Hobbes feared, the price of dual sovereignty was war.

Since the termination of the Civil War, Americans have concluded that they can no longer trust their liberties to federalism. Sovereignty must be concentrated in the hands of the national government. Quite apart from the dangers of civil war, the powers of state and local governments have been used too often by a tyrannical majority to trample the rights of religious, racial, and political minorities. The courts now seem a more reliable institutional shelter for the nation's liberties.

But if federalism is no longer necessary or even conducive to the preservation of liberty, then what is its purpose? Is it merely a relic of an outdated past? Are the majority of the members of the United Nations correct in objecting to the very use of the word?

The Rise of Modern Federalism

The answers to these questions have been gradually articulated in the 130 years following the end of the Civil War. Although the states lost their sovereignty, they remained integral to the workings of American government. Modern federalism no longer meant dual sovereignty and shared military capacity. Modern federalism instead meant only that each level of government had its own independently elected political leaders and its own separate taxing and spending capacity. Equipped with these tools of quasi-sovereignty, each level of government could take all but the most violent of steps to defend its turf.

Although sovereignty and military capacity now rested firmly in the hands of the national government, modern federalism became more complex rather than less so. Power was no longer simply divided between the nation and its states. Cities, counties, towns, school districts, special districts, and a host of additional governmental entities, each with its own elected leaders and taxing authority, assumed new burdens and responsibilities.

Just as the blessings bestowed by early federalism were evident from its inception, so the advantages of modern federalism were clear from the onset. If states and localities were no longer the guarantors of liberty, they became the engines of economic development. By giving state and local governments the autonomy to act independently, the federal system facilitated the rapid growth of an industrial economy that eventually surpassed its European competitors. Canals and railroads were constructed, highways and sewage systems built, schools opened, parks designed, and public safety protected by cities and villages eager to make their locality a boomtown.

The price to be paid for modern federalism did not become evident until government attempted to grapple with the adverse side effects of a burgeoning capitalist economy. Out of a respect for federalism's constitutional status and political durability, social reformers first worked with and through existing components of the federal system, concentrating much of their reform effort on state and local governments. Only gradually did it become clear that state and local governments, for all their ability to work with business leaders to enhance community prosperity, had difficulty meeting the needs of the poor and the needy.

It was ultimately up to the courts to find ways of keeping the price of modern federalism within bounds. Although dual sovereignty no longer meant nullification and secession, much remained to be determined about the respective areas of responsibility of the national and state governments. At first the courts retained remnants of the doctrine of dual sovereignty in order to protect processes of industrialization from governmental intrusion. But with the advent of the New Deal, the constitutional power of the national government expanded so dramatically that the doctrine of dual sovereignty virtually lost all meaning. Court interpretations of the constitutional clauses on commerce and spending have proved to be the most significant.

According to dual sovereignty theory, article 1 of the Constitution gives Congress the power to regulate commerce "among the states," but the regulation of intrastate commerce was to be left to the states. So, for example, in 1895 the Supreme Court said that Congress could not break up a sugar monopoly that had a nationwide impact on the price of sugar, because the monopoly refined its sugar within the state of Pennsylvania. The mere fact that the sugar was to be sold nationwide was only "incidental" to its production. As late as 1935, the Supreme Court, in a 6 to 3 decision, said that Congress could not regulate the sale of poultry because the regulation took effect after the chickens arrived within the state of Illinois, not while they were in transit.

Known as the "sick chicken" case, this decision was one of a series in which the Supreme Court declared unconstitutional legislation passed in the early days of President Franklin Roosevelt's efforts to establish his New Deal programs. Seven of the "nine old men" on the Court had been appointed by Roosevelt's conservative Republican predecessors. By declaring many New Deal programs in violation of the commerce clause, the Supreme Court seemed to be substituting its political views for those of elected officials. In a case denying the federal government the right to protect workers trying to organize a union in the coal industry, the Republican views of the Court seemed to lie just barely below the surface of a technical discussion of the commerce clause. Justice George Sutherland declared, "The relation of employer and employee is a local relation . . . over which the federal government has no legislative control."

The Roosevelt Democrats were furious at decisions that seemed to deny the country's elected officials the right to govern. Not since Dred Scott* had judicial review been in such disrepute. Roosevelt decided to "pack the court" by adding six new judges over and above the nine already on the Court. Although Roosevelt's court-packing scheme did not survive the political uproar on Capitol Hill, its effect on the Supreme Court was noticeable. In the midst of the court-packing debate, Justices Charles Hughes and Owen Roberts, who had agreed with Sutherland's opinion in the coal case, changed their mind and voted to uphold the Wagner Act, a new law designed to facilitate the formation of unions. In his opinion, Hughes did not explicitly overturn the coal miner decision (for which he had voted), but he did say: "When industries organize themselves on a national scale, . . . how can it be maintained that their industrial labor relations constitute a forbidden field into which Congress may not enter?" Relations between employers and their workers, once said to be local, suddenly became part of interstate commerce.

The change of heart by Hughes and Roberts has been called "the switch in time that saved nine." The New Deal majority that emerged on the court was soon augmented by judges appointed by Roosevelt. Since the New Deal, the definition of interstate commerce has continued to expand. In 1942 a farmer raising twenty-three acres of wheat, all of which might be fed to his own livestock, was said to be in violation of the crop

---

*In *Dred Scott v. Sanford* (1857), the Court declared the antislavery provision of the Missouri Compromise of 1820 to be unconstitutional [*Editors*].

quotas imposed by the Agricultural Adjustment Act of 1938. Since he was feeding his cows himself, he was not buying grain on the open market, thereby depressing the worldwide price of grain. With such a definition of interstate commerce, nothing was local.

The expansion of the meaning of the commerce clause is a well-known part of American political history. The importance to federalism of court interpretations of the "spending clause" is less well known. The constitutional clause in question says that Congress has the power to collect taxes to "provide for the . . . general welfare." But how about Congress's power to collect taxes for the welfare of specific individuals or groups?

The question first arose in a 1923 case, when a childless woman said she could not be asked to pay taxes in order to finance federal grants to states for programs that helped pregnant women. Since she received no benefit from the program, she sued for return of the taxes she had paid to cover its costs. In a decision that has never been reversed, the Supreme Court said that she had suffered no measurable injury and therefore had no right to sue the government. Her taxes were being used for a wide variety of purposes. The amount being spent for this program was too small to be significant. The court's decision to leave spending issues to Congress was restated a decade later when the social security program was also challenged on the grounds that monies were being directed to the elderly, not for the general welfare. Said Justice Benjamin N. Cardozo for a court majority: "The conception of the spending power . . . [must find a point somewhere] between particular and general . . . . There is a middle ground . . . in which discretion is large. The discretion, however, is not confided to the Court. The discretion belongs to Congress, unless the choice is clearly wrong."

The courts have ever since refused to review Congress's power to spend money. They have also conceded to Congress the right to attach any regulations to any aid Congress provides. In 1987 Congress provided a grant to state governments for the maintenance of their highways, but conditioned 5 percent of the funds on state willingness to raise the drinking age from eighteen to twenty-one. The connection between the appropriation and the regulation was based on the assumption that youths under the age of twenty-one are more likely to drive after drinking than those over twenty-one. Presumably, building more roads would only encourage more inebriated young people to drive on them. Despite the fact that the connection between the appropriation and the regulation was problematic, the Supreme Court ruled that Congress could attach any reasonable conditions to its grants to the states. State sovereignty was not violated, because any state could choose not to accept the money.

In short, the courts have virtually given up the doctrine of judicial review when it comes to matters on which Congress can spend money. As a consequence, most national efforts to influence state governments come in the form of federal grants. Federal aid can also be used to influence local governments, such as counties, cities, towns, villages, and school districts. These local governments, from a constitutional point of view, are mere creatures of the state of which they are part. They have no independent sovereignty.

The Contemporary Price of Federalism

If constitutional doctrine has evolved to the point that dual sovereign theory has been put to rest, this does not mean that federalism has come to an end. Although ultimate sovereignty resides with the national government, state and local governments still have certain characteristics and capabilities that make them constituent components of a federal system. * * * Two characteristics of federalism are fundamental. First, citizens elect officials of their choice for each level of government. Unless the authority of each level of government rests in the people, it will become the agent of the other. Second, each level of government raises money through taxation from the citizens residing in the area for which it is responsible. It is hard to see how a system could be regarded as federal unless each level of government can levy taxes on its residents. Unless each level of government can raise its own fiscal resources, it cannot act independently.

Although the constitutional authority of the national government has steadily expanded, state and local governments remain of great practical significance. Almost half of all government spending for domestic (as distinct from foreign and military) purposes is paid for out of taxes raised by state and local governments.

The sharing of control over domestic policy among levels of government has many benefits, but federalism still exacts its price. It can lead to great regional inequalities. Also, the need for establishing cooperative relationships among governments can contribute to great inefficiency in the administration of government programs.

DISCUSSION QUESTIONS

1. What is the constitutional basis for federalism?

2. How has the relationship between state governments and the national government changed since the early years of the Republic?

3. Does a federal system serve our needs today? Does the federal government have too much power relative to the states? What would be the advantages and disadvantages of a reduced federal presence in state matters?

14

"Jumping Frogs, Endangered Toads, and California's Medical-Marijuana Law"

George J. Annas

From welfare reform to health care, educational funding to inner-city develop-ment, state governments have sought more control over public policy within their borders. In the 1970s and 1980s, when this devolution of power to the states was called "New Federalism," the debate was pretty simple. Republicans favored devolution because state governments were "closer to the people" and could bet-ter determine their needs. Democrats resisted the transfer of power from Wash-ington, fearing that many states would not adequately care for and protect minorities and poor people, or protect the environment without prodding from Washington. To the extent that the courts got involved in the debate, they tended to favor the transfer of power to the states.

The debate over developing power from the national government to the states has grown increasingly complicated in the past several years: the partisan nature of the debate shifted, the Courts have played a larger, but inconsistent role, and issues of "states' rights" increasingly tend to cut across normal ideological and partisan divisions. While Republicans continued to favor greater state control, a Democratic President, Bill Clinton, supported devolution to the states in several areas in the 1990s, especially welfare policy. Since the mid-1990s, the Supreme Court has played a central role in the shift of power to the states, but two recent cases involving medical marijuana (Gonzales v. Raich) and assisted suicide (Gonzales v. Oregon) show how the typical debate between national and state power can shift when a moral dimension is introduced.

In both cases, state voters supported liberal policies (approving medical mari-juana in California and assisted suicide in Oregon). Therefore, the "states' rights" position on federalism in these cases represented the liberal perspective, which in partisan terms means mostly Democratic, rather than the conservative positions on race, labor, market regulation, and welfare that state-centered feder-alism is typically associated with. What's a good liberal or conservative to do? Social liberals supported the medical marijuana law (and thus the minority in Raich) and the assisted suicide law in Oregon (the majority in Gonzales). Moral conservatives were the opposite (pro-Raich, anti-Gonzales). However, on the central question of federal versus state power, which has been a central ideo-logical divide in this nation since the Federalists and Anti-Federalists battled it out at the Constitutional Convention, liberals and conservatives would have to flip their views. So a national-power liberal would have supported the Raich *decision and opposed the* Gonzales *decision (the opposite of the social liberal), whereas a state-power conservative would have opposed* Raich *and supported* Gonzales *(which is the reverse of a moral conservative's positions). That means that a national power liberal and the moral conservative would have the same views (national power would be used to regulate medical marijuana and assisted suicide), while states' rights advocates share the views of the social liberals (because voters in California approved medical marijuana and Oregon voters supported assisted suicide).*

Somewhat surprisingly, there was almost no consistency among the eight justices who voted on both cases (William Rehnquist was replaced by John Roberts between the two cases): only Justice O'Connor supported the states' rights position in both cases, and Scalia voted as a moral conservative (which runs strongly counter to his previously articulated views on national power and federalism). All of the other six justices mixed their views. The Court as a whole was inconsistent on the question of federalism as well: in the medical marijuana case, the Court upheld Congress's power to prohibit the medical use of marijuana under the Controlled Substances Act. But in the assisted suicide case, the Court said that Congress did not give the U.S. attorney general the power under that same law to limit the drugs that doctors in Oregon could prescribe for use in an assisted suicide.

George Annas looks at the medical marijuana case (and touches on the assisted suicide case) from the perspective of doctors. Writing in the New England Journal of Medicine, *one of the leading medical journals in the nation, Annas points out the "most interesting, and disturbing aspect of the case to physicians" is the Court's reference to "unscrupulous physicians who overprescribe when it is sufficiently profitable to do so." Annas says that such cases are rare and that the California law was narrowly written to make sure that such abuses would not occur. This article is also very useful for its excellent overview of Congress's commerce clause powers and its importance in federalism cases.*

Mark Twain wasn't thinking about federalism or the structure of American government when he wrote "The Celebrated Jumping Frog of Calaveras County." Nonetheless, he would be amused to know that today, almost 150 years later, the Calaveras County Fair and Jumping Frog Jubilee not only has a jumping frog contest but also has its own Frog Welfare Policy. The policy includes a provision for the "Care of Sick or Injured Frogs" and a limitation entitled "Frogs Not Permitted to Participate," which stipulates that "under no circumstances will a frog listed on the endangered species list be permitted to participate in the Frog Jump." This fair, like medical practice, is subject to both state and federal laws. Care of the sick and injured (both frogs and people) is primarily viewed as a matter of state law, whereas protection of endangered species is primarily regulated by Congress under its authority to regulate interstate commerce.

Not to carry the analogy too far, but it is worth recalling that Twain's famous frog, Dan'l Webster, lost his one and only jumping contest because his stomach had been filled with quail shot by a competitor. The loaded-down frog just couldn't jump. Until the California medical-marijuana case, it seemed to many observers that the conservative Rehnquist Court had succeeded in filling the commerce clause with quail shot—and had effectively prevented the federal government from regulating state activities. In the medical-marijuana case, however, a new majority of justices took the lead out of the commerce clause so that the federal government could legitimately claim jurisdiction over just about any activity, including the practice of medicine. The role of the commerce clause in federalism and the implications of the Court's decision in the California medical-marijuana case for physicians are the subjects I explore in this article.

The Commerce Clause

The U.S. Constitution determines the areas over which the federal government has authority. All other areas remain, as they were before the adoption of the Constitution, under the authority of the individual states. Another way to say this is that the states retain all governmental authority they did not delegate to the federal government, including areas such as criminal law and family-law matters. These are part of the state's "police powers," usually defined as the state's sovereign authority to protect the health, safety, and welfare of its residents. Section 8 of Article I of the Constitution contains 18 clauses specifying delegated areas (including the military, currency, postal service, and patenting) over which "Congress shall have power," and these include the commerce clause—"to regulate commerce with foreign nations, and among the several states, and with the Indian tribes."

Until the Great Depression (and the disillusionment with unregulated markets), the Supreme Court took a narrow view of federal authority that could be derived from the commerce clause by ruling consistently that it gave Congress the authority only to regulate activities that directly involved the movement of commercial products (such as pharmaceuticals) from one state to another. Since then, and at least until 1995, the Court's interpretation seemed to be going in the opposite direction: Congress was consistently held to have authority in areas that had almost any relationship at all to commerce.

Guns in Schools and Violence Against Women

Under modern commerce clause doctrine, Congress has authority to regulate in three broad categories of activities: the use of the channels of interstate commerce (e.g., roads, air corridors, and waterways); the instrumentalities of interstate commerce (e.g., trains, trucks, and planes) and persons and things in interstate commerce; and "activities having a substantial relation to interstate commerce." The first two categories are easy ones in that they involve activities that cross state lines. The third category, which does not involve crossing a state line, is the controversial one. The interpretation question involves the meaning and application of the concept of "substantially affecting" interstate commerce.

In a 1937 case that the Court characterized as a "watershed case" it concluded that the real question was one of the degree of effect. Intrastate activities that "have such a close and substantial relation to interstate commerce that their control is essential or appropriate to protect that commerce from burdens and obstructions" are within the power of Congress to regulate. Later, in what has become perhaps its best-known commerce-clause case, the Court held that Congress could enforce a statute that prohibited a farmer from growing wheat on his own farm even if the wheat was never sold but was used only for the farmer's personal consumption. The Court concluded that although one farmer's personal use of home-grown wheat may be trivial (and have no effect on commerce), "taken together with that of many others similarly situated," its effect on interstate commerce (and the market price of wheat) "is far from trivial."

The 1995 case that seemed to presage a states' rights revolution (often referred to as "devolution") involved the federal Gun-Free School Zones Act of 1990, which made it a federal crime "for any individual knowingly to possess a firearm at a place that the individual knows, or has reasonable cause to believe, is a school zone." In a 5-to-4 opinion, written by the late Chief Justice William Rehnquist, the Court held that the statute exceeded Congress's authority under the commerce clause and only the individual states had authority to criminalize the possession of guns in school.

The federal government had argued (and the four justices in the minority agreed) that the costs of violent crime are spread out over the entire population and that the presence of guns in schools threatens "national productivity" by undermining the learning environment, which in turn decreases learning and leads to a less productive citizenry and thus a less productive national economy. The majority of the Court rejected these arguments primarily because they thought that accepting this line of reasoning would make it impossible to define "any limitations on federal power, even in areas such as criminal law enforcement or education, where states historically have been sovereign."

In 2000, in another 5-to-4 opinion written by Rehnquist, using the same rationale, the Court struck down a federal statute, part of the Violence against Women Act of 1994, that provided a federal civil remedy for victims of "gender-motivated violence." In the Court's words:

> Gender-motivated crimes of violence are not, in any sense of the phrase, economic activity. . . . Indeed, if Congress may regulate gender-motivated violence, it would be able to regulate murder or any other type of violence since

gender-motivated violence, as a subset of all violent crime, is certain to have lesser economic impacts than the larger class of which it is a part.

The Court, specifically addressing the question of federalism, concluded that "the Constitution requires a distinction between what is truly national and what is truly local. . . . Indeed, we can think of no better example of the police power, which the Founders denied to the National Government and reposed in the States, than the suppression of violent crime and vindication of its victims."

Medical Marijuana in California

The next commerce-clause case involved physicians, albeit indirectly, and the role assigned to them in California in relation to the protection of patients who used physician-recommended marijuana from criminal prosecution. The question before the Supreme Court in the recent medical-marijuana case (*Gonzales v. Raich*) was this: Does the commerce clause give Congress the authority to outlaw the local cultivation and use of marijuana for medicine if such cultivation and use complies with the provisions of California law?

The California law, which is similar to laws in at least nine other states, creates an exemption from criminal prosecution for physicians, patients, and primary caregivers who possess or cultivate marijuana for medicinal purposes on the recommendation of a physician. Two patients for whom marijuana had been recommended brought suit to challenge enforcement of the federal Controlled Substances Act after federal Drug Enforcement Administration agents seized and destroyed all six marijuana plants that one of them had been growing for her own medical use in compliance with the California law. The Ninth Circuit Court of Appeals ruled in the plaintiffs' favor, finding that the California law applied to a separate and distinct category of activity, "the intrastate, noncommercial cultivation and possession of *cannabis* for personal medical purposes as recommended by a patient's physician pursuant to valid California state law," as opposed to what it saw as the federal law's purpose, which was to prevent "drug trafficking." In a 6-to-3 opinion, written by Justice John Paul Stevens, with Justice Rehnquist dissenting, the Court reversed the appeals court's opinion and decided that Congress, under the commerce clause, did have authority to enforce its prohibition against marijuana—even state-approved, homegrown, noncommercial marijuana, used only for medicinal purposes on a physician's recommendation.

The majority of the Court decided that the commerce clause gave Congress the same power to regulate homegrown marijuana for personal use that it had to regulate homegrown wheat. The question was whether homegrown marijuana for personal medical consumption substantially affected interstate commerce (albeit illegal commerce) when all affected patients were taken together. The Court concluded that Congress "had a rational basis for concluding that leaving home-consumed marijuana outside federal control" would affect "price and market conditions." The Court also distinguished the guns-in-school and gender-violence cases on the basis that regulation of drugs is "quintessentially economic" when economics is defined as the "production, distribution, and consumption of commodities."

This left only one real question open: Is the fact that marijuana is to be used only for medicinal purposes on the advice of a physician, as the Ninth Circuit Court had decided, sufficient for an exception to be carved out of otherwise legitimate federal authority to control drugs? The Court decided it was not, for several reasons. The first was that Congress itself had determined that marijuana is a Schedule I drug, which it defined as having "no acceptable medical use." The Court acknowledged that Congress might be wrong in this determination, but the issue in this case was not whether marijuana had possible legitimate medical uses but whether Congress had the authority to make the judgment that it had none and to ban all uses of the drug. The dissenting justices argued that personal cultivation and use of marijuana should be beyond the authority of the commerce clause. The Court majority disagreed, stating that if it accepted the dissenting justices' argument, personal cultivation for recreational use would also be beyond congressional authority. This conclusion, the majority argued, could not be sustained:

> One need not have a degree in economics to understand why a nationwide exemption for the vast quantity of marijuana (or other drugs) locally cultivated for personal use (which presumably would include use by friends, neighbors, and family members) may have a substantial impact on the interstate market for this extraordinarily popular substance. The congressional judgment that an exemption for such a significant segment of the total market would undermine the orderly enforcement of the entire [drug] regulatory scheme is entitled to a strong presumption of validity.

The other primary limit to the effect of the California law on interstate commerce is the requirement of a physician's recommendation on the basis of a medical determination that a patient has an "illness for which marijuana provides relief." And the Court's discussion of this limit may be the most interesting, and disturbing, aspect of the case to physicians. Instead of concluding that physicians should be free to use their best medical judgment and that it was up to state medical boards to decide whether specific physicians were failing to live up to reasonable medical standards—as the Court did, for example, in its cases related to restrictive abortion laws—the Court took a totally different approach. In the Court's words, the broad language of the California medical-marijuana law allows "even the most scrupulous doctor to conclude that some recreational uses would be therapeutic. And our cases have taught us that there are some unscrupulous physicians who overprescribe when it is sufficiently profitable to do so."

The California law defines the category of patients who are exempt from criminal prosecution as those suffering from cancer, anorexia, AIDS, chronic pain, spasticity, glaucoma, arthritis, migraine, and "any other chronic or persistent medical symptom that substantially limits the ability of a person to conduct one or more major life activities . . . or if not alleviated may cause serious harm to the patient's safety or physical or mental health." These limits are hardly an invitation for recreational-use recommendations. Regarding "unscrupulous physicians," the Court cited two cases that involve criminal prosecutions of physicians for acting like drug dealers, one from 1919 and the other from 1975, implying that because a few physicians might have been criminally inclined in the past, it was reasonable for Congress (and the Court), on the basis of no actual evidence, to assume that many physicians may be so inclined today. It was not only physicians that the Court found untrustworthy but sick patients and their caregivers as well:

> The exemption for cultivation by patients and caregivers [patients can possess up to 8 oz. of dried marijuana and cultivate up to 6 mature or 12 immature plants] can only increase the supply of marijuana in the California market. The likelihood that all such production will promptly terminate when patients recover or will precisely match the patients' medical needs during their convalescence seems remote; whereas the danger that excesses will satisfy some of the admittedly enormous demand for recreational use seems obvious.

Justice Sandra Day O'Connor's dissent merits comment, because it is especially relevant to the practice of medicine. She argues that the Constitution requires the Court to protect "historic spheres of state sovereignty from excessive federal encroachment" and that one of the virtues of federalism is that it permits the individual states to serve as "laboratories," should they wish, to try "novel social and economic experiments without risk to the rest of the country." Specifically, she argues that the Court's new definition of economic activity is "breathtaking" in its scope, creating exactly what the gun case rejected—a federal police power. She also rejects reliance on the wheat case, noting that under the Agricultural Adjustment Act in question in that case, Congress had exempted the planting of less than 200 bushels (about six tons), and that when Roscoe Filburn, the farmer who challenged the federal statute, himself harvested his wheat, the statute exempted plantings of less than six acres.

In O'Connor's words, the wheat case "did not extend Commerce Clause authority to something as modest as the home cook's herb garden." O'Connor is not saying that Congress cannot regulate small quantities of a product produced for personal use, only that the wheat case "did not hold or imply that small-scale production of commodities is always economic, and automatically within Congress' reach." As to potential "exploitation [of the act] by unscrupulous physicians" and patients, O'Connor finds no factual support for this assertion and rejects the conclusion that simply by "piling assertion upon assertion" one can make a case for meeting the "substantiality test" of the guns-in-school and gender-violence cases.

It is important to note that the Court was not taking a position on whether Congress was correct to place marijuana in Schedule I or a position against California's law, any more than it was taking a position in favor of guns in schools or violence against women in the earlier cases. Instead, the Court was ruling only on the question of federal authority under the commerce clause. The Court noted, for example, that California and its supporters may one day prevail by pursuing the democratic process "in the halls of Congress." This seems extremely unlikely. More important is the question not addressed in this case—whether suffering patients have a substantive due-process claim to access to drugs needed to prevent suffering or a valid medical-necessity defense should they be prosecuted for using medical marijuana on a physician's recommendation. Also not addressed was the question that will be decided during the coming year: whether Congress has delegated to the U.S. attorney general its authority to decide what a "legitimate medical use" of an approved drug is in the context of Oregon's law governing physician-assisted suicide. What is obvious from this case, however, is that Congress has the authority, under the commerce clause, to regulate both legal and illegal drugs whether or not the drugs in question actually cross state lines. It would also seem reasonable to conclude that Congress has the authority to limit the uses of approved drugs.

Federalism and Endangered Species

Because *Gonzales v. Raich* is a drug case, and because it specifically involves marijuana, the Court's final word on federalism may not yet be in. Whether the "states' rights" movement has any life left after medical marijuana may be determined in the context of the Endangered Species Act. Two U.S. Circuit Courts of Appeals, for example, have recently upheld application of the federal law to protect endangered species that, unlike the descendants of Mark Twain's jumping frog, have no commercial value. Even though the Supreme Court refused to hear appeals from both of the lower courts, the cases help us understand the contemporary reach of congressional power under the commerce clause. One case involves the protection of six tiny creatures that live in caves (the "Cave Species")—three arthropods, a spider, and two beetles—from a commercial developer. The Fifth Circuit Court of Appeals noted that the Cave Species are not themselves an object of economics or commerce, saying: "There is no market for them; any future market is conjecture. If the speculative future medicinal benefits from the Cave Species makes their regulation commercial, then almost anything would be. . . . There is no historic trade in the Cave Species, nor do tourists come to Texas to view them." Nonetheless, the court concluded that Congress had the authority, under the commerce clause, to view life as an "interdependent web" of all species; that destruction of endangered species can be aggregated, like home-grown wheat; and that the destruction of multiple species has a substantial effect on interstate commerce.

The other case, from the District of Columbia Court of Appeals, involves the arroyo south-western toad, whose habitat was threatened by a real-estate developer. In upholding the application of the Endangered Species Act to the case, the appeals court held that the commercial activity being regulated was the housing development itself, as well as the "taking" of the road by the planned commercial development. The court noted that the "company would like us to consider its challenge to the ESA [Endangered Species Act] only as applied to the arroyo toad, which it says has no 'known commercial value'—unlike, for example, Mark Twain's celebrated jumping frogs [sic] of Calaveras County." Instead, the court concluded that application of the Endangered Species Act, far from eroding states' rights, is consistent with "the historic power of the federal government to preserve scarce resources in one locality for the future benefit of all Americans.

On a request for a hearing by the entire appeals court, which was rejected, recently named Chief Justice John Roberts—who at the time was a member of the appeals court—wrote a dissent that was not unlike Justice O'Connor's dissent in the marijuana case. In it he argued that the court's conclusion seemed inconsistent with the guns-in-school and gender-violence cases and that there were real problems with using an analysis of the commerce clause to regulate "the taking of a hapless toad that, for reasons of its own, lives its entire life in California." The case has since been settled. The development is going ahead in a way that protects the toad's habitat.

The Future of the Commerce Clause

Twain's short story has been termed "a living American fairy tale, acted out annually in Calaveras County." In what might be termed a living American government tale, nominees to the Supreme Court are routinely asked to explain their judicial philosophy of constitutional and statutory interpretation to the Senate Judiciary Committee. Asked about his "hapless toad" opinion during the Senate confirmation hearings on his nomination to replace Rehnquist as chief justice, Roberts said: "The whole point of my argument in the dissent was that there was another way to look at this [i.e., the approach taken by the Fifth Circuit Court in the Cave Species case]. . . . I did not say that even in this case that the decision was wrong. . . . I simply said, let's look at those other grounds for decision because that doesn't present this problem." These hearings provide an opportunity for all Americans to review their understanding of our constitutional government and the manner in which it allocates power between the federal government and the 50 states. To the extent that this division of power is determined by the Court's view of the commerce clause, a return to an expansive reading of this clause seems both likely and, given the interdependence of the national and global economies, proper.

Of course, the fact that Congress has authority over a particular subject—such as whether to adopt a system of national licensure for physicians—does not mean that its authority is unlimited or even that Congress will use it. Rather, as Justice Stevens noted, cases such as the California medical-marijuana case lead to other central constitutional questions, as yet unresolved. These questions include whether patients, terminally ill or not, have a constitutional right not to suffer—at least, when their physicians know how to control their pain.

DISCUSSION QUESTIONS

1. *What would you do?* If you were a state legislator or a judge, how would you decide these issues? Specifically, as a matter of policy, do you think that doctors should be able to prescribe marijuana to alleviate pain? Should they be able to prescribe lethal drugs to be used by terminally ill patients? What about as a matter of law? Do you agree with the Supreme Court's decisions on these issues?

2. Do you support a state-centered or nation-centered perspective on federalism? Now go back and look at your answers to the last questions. Did you take positions that were consistent with your views on federalism or as a policy concern?

3. What does Mark Twain's jumping frog represent in Annas's article? Which Supreme Court case breathed life back into the frog? Why?

DEBATING THE ISSUES: NULLIFYING HEALTH CARE REFORM

For many years, federalism was viewed as a relatively sleepy, unexciting part of American politics. Certainly, it was important to understand federalism's role in the American political system, Madison's "double security," and how intergovernmental relations have evolved. But relations between the national government and the states had settled into a stable system of cooperative federalism in most policy areas, so there were not many new and exciting developments. That all has changed in the past couple of decades. The Supreme Court has generally been shifting power from the national government to the states (with some exceptions). New struggles with "coercive federalism" have emerged as the national government tries to shape policy in the states. From education policy to the environment, immigration, welfare, gun rights, and now health care, the states are often at odds with Washington, D.C.

The states have raised the stakes of this intergovernmental struggle in recent years by reviving the early nineteenth century idea of "nullification." As the historian Sean Wilentz explains, the idea was developed by Thomas Jefferson in response to the Alien and Sedition Acts' limits on the First Amendment and asserts that the states can ignore national laws that they believe are unconstitutional. Jefferson used the term "interposition" to describe states interposing themselves between the unconstitutional acts of the national government and the people. John C. Calhoun developed this idea as a justification for southern opposition to a protective tariff, as a broad statement of states' rights, and ultimately the rationale for southern secession over the issue of slavery. This view also played a prominent role in the "massive resistance" to the integration of southern public schools after the *Brown v. Board of Education* decision in 1954.

States have recently applied nullification to federal policies concerning medical marijuana, gun control, immigration, and most prominently, health care. In each instance, states have passed laws or statewide referenda that contradict federal law. Attorneys general from twenty states have filed lawsuits challenging the constitutionality of Obama's health care reform, arguing that the federal government does not have the power to compel individuals to purchase health insurance; many of these suits also claim that the federal government cannot force states to fund expanded Medicaid coverage or administer health insurance exchanges (markets where individuals can purchase insurance). One of the lead attorneys in the lawsuit, David Rivkin, calls it "the most important constitutional challenge in our generation, and one of the two or three most important in our history." At least thirty-nine states have initiated legislation to overturn parts of the law. Three states have passed legislation voiding the individual mandate, and four more have put the issue to voters in a referendum on a constitutional amendment.

One example of the latter is a proposed amendment to the Arizona constitution that says, "A law or rule shall not compel, directly or indirectly, any person, employer, or health care provider to participate in any health care system."

Will these challenges to the national health care law succeed? Most constitutional experts give the state challenges little chance of success because of broad congressional powers recognized by the U.S. Supreme Court under the commerce clause, the necessary and proper clause, and Congress's taxing and spending powers. However, several federal district court judges have ruled in favor of the challenges, meaning that the question may well be left to the Supreme Court to resolve.

Timothy Jost agrees that these are not frivolous arguments but asserts that the "argument that the mandate [that individuals buy health insurance] is constitutional is overwhelming." Instead, he sees the push for nullification being driven by politics. Its real significance is that it is "an invitation to civil disobedience" to ignore the federal mandate, much like the current battle over medical marijuana and the historical "massive resistance" to the integration of southern schools discussed by Wilentz.

Clint Bolick defends the Health Care Freedom Act on several grounds. He sidesteps the question of nullification (by arguing that the Arizona amendment would not nullify part of the federal statute because people would still have the right to participate—they simply would not be forced to do so). He points out that national supremacy does not automatically mean that the national government can do whatever it wants: the national government would have to justify its right to require people to buy health insurance. He outlines a series of Supreme Court cases in which the states' position was upheld over the national government's regulatory and commerce powers. Whether the Court agrees with the states on the Health Care Freedom Act remains to be seen, but these are serious constitutional arguments.

15

"States of Anarchy: America's Long, Sordid Affair with Nullification"

SEAN WILENTZ

Historical amnesia is as dangerously disorienting for a nation as for an individual. So it is with the current wave of enthusiasm for "states' rights," "interposition," and "nullification"—the claim that state legislatures or special state conventions or referendums have the legitimate power to declare federal laws null and void within their own state borders. The idea was broached most vociferously in defense of the slave South by John C. Calhoun in the 1820s and '30s, extended by the Confederate secessionists in the 1850s and '60s, then forcefully reclaimed by militant segregationists in the 1950s and '60s. Each time it reared its head, it was crushed as an assault on democratic government and the nation itself—in Abraham Lincoln's words, "the essence of anarchy." The issue has been decided time and again, not least by the deaths of more than 618,000 Americans on Civil War battlefields. Yet there are those who now seek to reopen this wound in the name of resisting federal legislation on issues ranging from gun control to health care reform. Proclaiming themselves heralds of liberty and freedom, the new nullifiers would have us repudiate the sacrifices of American history—and subvert the constitutional pillars of American nationhood.

The origins of nullification date back to the stormy early decades of the republic. In 1798, a conservative Federalist Congress, fearing the rise of a political opposition headed by Thomas Jefferson, passed the Alien and Sedition Acts, which outlawed criticism of the federal government. Coming before the Supreme Court had assumed powers of judicial review, the laws, signed by President John Adams, were steps toward eradicating political dissent. In a panic, Jefferson and his ally, James Madison, wrote sets of resolutions duly passed by the legislatures of Virginia and Kentucky, which called upon the state governments to resist and, as Madison put it, "interpose" themselves between the federal government and the citizenry. But the other state legislatures either ignored or repudiated the resolutions as affronts to the Constitution, and the crisis was ended by the democratic means of an election when Jefferson won the presidency two years later—the wholly peaceable and constitutional "revolution of 1800."

The concept was revived by John C. Calhoun, who expanded it into a theory of nullification and Southern states' rights in 1828. The specific issue at stake was a protective tariff that Southerners believed unfair to their section, but behind it lay a growing fear that the federal government might interfere with the institution of slavery. Calhoun declared that, as "irresponsible power is inconsistent with liberty," individual states had the right to nullify laws they deemed unconstitutional. He asserted further that, should the federal government try to suppress nullification, individual states had the right to secede from the Union. In 1832, the South Carolina legislature passed a formal ordinance nullifying the tariff. But President Andrew Jackson proclaimed nullification pernicious nonsense. The nation, Jackson proclaimed, was not created by sovereign state governments—then, as now, a basic misunderstanding propagated by pro-nullifiers. Ratified in order "to form a more perfect union," the Constitution was a new framework for a nation that already existed under the Articles of Confederation. "The Constitution of the United States," Jackson declared, created "a government, not a league."

Although state governments had certain powers reserved to them, these did not include voiding laws duly enacted by the people's representatives in Congress and by the president. Calhoun and South Carolina were isolated by Jackson's firm stand. The aging James Madison sided with the president, deploring "the strange doctrines and misconceptions" of the South Carolinians, charging that they were a perversion of the Virginia Resolutions and insisting that the "Constitution & laws of the U.S. should be the supreme law of the Land." (Madison also wrote of nullification that "[n]o man's creed was more opposed to such an inversion of the Repubn. order of things" than Thomas Jefferson's.) Other Southern states refused to join in the nullification movement, and Congress approved a compromise tariff bill.

Calhoun's radical ideas about states' rights resurfaced during the sectional crisis over slavery in the 1850s. The Civil War began as a struggle over democracy and U.S. government, focused on a key question: Could the slave interests in individual states, dissatisfied with the outcome of a presidential election, declare that election null and void and secede from the Union? Lincoln, like Jackson before him, declared such extreme views of state sovereignty a direct attack on democratic republican government.

After four years of the Civil War, in a "new birth of freedom" that resurrected the Union, Calhoun's states' rights doctrines were utterly disgraced—but they did not disappear forever. Nearly a century later, they were exhumed to justify the so-called "massive resistance" of the segregationist South against civil rights and, in particular, the Supreme Court's ruling on *Brown v. Board of Education* in 1954. The current rage for nullification is nothing less than another restatement, in a different context, of musty neo-Confederate dogma.

Following the *Brown* decision, James J. Kilpatrick, the prosegregationist editor of *The Richmond News Leader*, dressed up nullification under the milder sounding "interposition," borrowed from Madison's Virginia Resolutions. Kilpatrick hoped that adopting lofty Madisonian language would lift resistance to *Brown* "above the sometimes sordid level of race and segregation." Despite his rhetorical sleight of hand, his intent was radical—supporting resistance not only to acts of Congress or the outcome of a presidential election, but also to the decisions of the ultimate court. Not surprisingly, not a single Supreme Court justice then or since, including the fiercest advocates of states' rights, has ever ruled the concept a valid response to federal law or judicial rulings. All have recognized that nullification under any name would leave controversial laws or court decisions open to state-by-state popular referendums—a recipe for chaos that would undercut judicial review, the cornerstone of

American constitutional jurisprudence. And the justices have recognized the explicit language of Article VI of the Constitution, that federal laws made in pursuance of the Constitution "shall be the supreme Law of the Land; and the Judges of every State shall be bound thereby." Yet, in their last-ditch efforts to save Jim Crow, segregationists like Kilpatrick grasped and distorted the words of James Madison from 1798. In the spirit of John C. Calhoun and the Confederacy, they then vaunted their idea of "interposition" above the words of the Constitution, of which Madison is considered the father.

Kilpatrick's gambit caught on among his fellow white supremacists in Southern state governments—most notably Virginia's—and they passed resolutions of interdiction in defiance of the *Brown* decision. (The Alabama legislature went further, bluntly declaring *Brown*, "as a matter of right, null, void, and of no effect.") Those resolutions came to lie at the heart of what Senator Harry F. Byrd of Virginia announced in February 1956 as a policy of "massive resistance" to *Brown*. For several years, the strategy succeeded in fending off federal authority, resulting in mob violence against blacks and federal officials, as well as the closure of entire public school systems in the South—including the shutdown of public education in Virginia's Prince Edward County for five years, beginning in 1959. But determined efforts by the administrations of Dwight D. Eisenhower, John F. Kennedy, and Lyndon B. Johnson eventually broke the back of the segregationist campaign. And, as early as January 1960, state and federal courts negated the Virginia nullification laws meant to implement massive resistance. Segregationists found other temporary means to preserve racial separation in the schools, including, for a time, the creation of private "segregation academies." But, in time, Virginia, as well as the rest of the South, finally acceded to the legitimacy of the *Brown* decision. The repudiated doctrines of interposition and nullification were repudiated once more.

Less than a year ago, on July 16, 2009, the *Richmond Times-Dispatch* ran an editorial apologizing for its role and that of its sister newspaper, the *News Leader*, in instigating and supporting massive resistance, which it called "a dreadful doctrine." It is all the more ironic that the legal fictions used to justify that doctrine should now be reappearing in new circumstances. "Who is the sovereign, the state or the federal government?" demanded state Representative Chris N. Herrod, a Republican, amid a recent session of the Utah legislature that affirmed it had the power to nullify heath care reform. Last month, Governor Mike Rounds of South Dakota, a Republican, signed into law a bill that invalidated all federal regulation of firearms regarding weapons manufactured and used in South Dakota. The day before, Wyoming's governor, Dave Freudenthal, a Democrat, signed similar legislation for his state. Meanwhile, the Oklahoma House of Representatives resolved that Oklahomans should be permitted to vote on a state constitutional amendment that would allow them to ignore the impending reform of the health care system. And, in Virginia, the home of massive resistance, Attorney General Ken Cuccinelli, a Republican, has argued that a recently enacted state law prohibiting the government from requiring the people to buy health insurance counters federal health care reform, which, he insists, is unconstitutional.

Now, as in the 1860s and 1960s, nullification and interposition are pseudoconstitutional notions taken up in the face of national defeat in democratic politics. Unable to prevail as a minority and frustrated to the point of despair, its militant advocates abandon the usual tools of democratic politics and redress, take refuge in a psychodrama of "liberty" versus "tyranny," and declare that, on whatever issue they choose, they are not part of the United States or subject to its laws—that, whenever they say so, the Constitution in fact forms a league, and not a government. Although not currently concerned with racial supremacy, the consequence of their doctrine would uphold an interpretation of the constitutional division of powers that would permit the majority of any state to reinstate racial segregation and inequality up to but not including enslavement, if it so chose.

That these ideas resurfaced 50 years ago, amid the turmoil of civil rights, was as harebrained as it was hateful. But it was comprehensible if only because interposition and nullification lay at the roots of the Civil War. Today, by contrast, the dismal history of these discredited ideas resides within the memories of all Americans who came of age in the 1950s and '60s—and ought to, on that account, be part of the living legacy of the rest of the country. Only an astonishing historical amnesia can lend credence to such mendacity.

Arizona House Concurrent Resolution 2014: A Concurrent Resolution Proposing an Amendment to the Constitution of Arizona; Amending Article XXVII, by Adding Section 2, Constitution of Arizona; Relating to Health Care Services

Section 2.

A. To preserve the freedom of Arizonans to provide for their health care:
 1. A law or rule shall not compel, directly or indirectly, any person, employer or health care provider to participate in any health care system.
 2. A person or employer may pay directly for lawful health care services and shall not be required to pay penalties or fines for paying directly for lawful health care services. A health care provider may accept direct payment for lawful health care services and shall not be required to pay penalties or fines for accepting direct payment from a person or employer for lawful health care services.
B. Subject to reasonable and necessary rules that do not substantially limit a person's options, the purchase or sale of health insurance in private health care systems shall not be prohibited by law or rule.
C. This section does not:
 1. Affect which health care services a health care provider or hospital is required to perform or provide.
 2. Affect which health care services are permitted by law.
 3. Prohibit care provided pursuant to Article XVII, Section 8 of this constitution or any statutes enacted by the legislature relating to worker's compensation.
 4. Affect laws or rules in effect as of January 1, 2009.
 5. Affect the terms or conditions of any health care system to the extent that those terms and conditions do not have the effect of punishing a person or employer for paying directly for lawful health care services or a health care provider or hospital for accepting

direct payment from a person or employer for lawful health care services.
D. For the purposes of this section:
   1. "Compel" includes penalties or fines.
   2. "Direct payment or pay directly" means payment for lawful health care services without a public or private third party, not including an employer, paying for any portion of the service.
   3. "Health care system" means any public or private entity whose function or purpose is the management of, processing of, enrollment of individuals for or payment for, in full or in part, health care services or health care data or health care information for its participants.
   4. "Lawful health care services" means any health-related service or treatment to the extent that the service or treatment is permitted or not prohibited by law or regulation that may be provided by persons or business otherwise permitted to offer such services.
   5. "Penalties or fines" means any civil or criminal penalty or fine, tax, salary or wage withholding or surcharge or any named fee with similar effect established by law or rule by a government established, created or controlled agency that is used to punish or discourage the exercise of rights protected under this section.

17

"Can the States Nullify Health Care Reform?"

TIMOTHY S. JOST

On February 1, the Virginia Senate passed a bill stating that "No resident of this Commonwealth . . . shall be required to obtain or maintain a policy of individual insurance coverage." In considering this legislation, Virginia joins numerous other states with pending legislation aimed at limiting, changing, or opposing national health care reforms. What is going on here?

Whereas states generally adopt laws to achieve a legal effect, nullification laws are pure political theater. On its face, the Virginia bill exempts residents of the Commonwealth from having to comply with a law requiring the purchase of heath insurance. Although the bill is phrased in the passive voice, its intent is clearly to block the implementation of a federal mandate requiring all individuals to carry health insurance. But achieving this aim is constitutionally impossible.

The Supremacy Clause of the United States Constitution (article VI, clause 2) states, "This Constitution, and the Laws of the United States . . . shall be the supreme Law of the Land; . . . any Thing in the Constitution or Laws of any State to the Contrary notwithstanding." Indeed, one of the primary reasons for adopting our Constitution in place of the Articles of Confederation was to establish the supremacy of national over state law. Our only civil war was fought over the question of whether national or state law was ultimately supreme.

Within the past 60 years, the most important confrontation between federal law and states' rights concerned school desegregation. Faced with federal law commanding the desegregation of its schools, Arkansas amended its constitution to prohibit integration. In *Cooper v. Aaron* (1958), the only Supreme Court opinion I know of that was signed individually by each of the Court's nine justices, the Court decisively reaffirmed the supremacy of federal law and rejected the state's claimed right to nullification. More recently, a number of federal courts have rejected claims that a state could refuse Medicaid coverage of abortions in cases of rapes and incest after the Hyde amendment (which originally prohibited the use of federal funds for coverage of abortion except when the mother's life was at risk) was changed to permit federal funding for abortions under these circumstances. These decisions held that state constitutional provisions must yield even to federal regulations. State law cannot nullify federal law. This principle is simply beyond debate, and state legislators, many of them lawyers, know that.

The purpose of these laws, therefore, is not legal but rather political. The Virginia bill is a second-generation nullification statute. Earlier proposals in other states, including a constitutional amendment proposed by the Arizona legislature, are worded differently. These bills protect a right to pay health care providers directly for services and to purchase private health insurance. In other words, they were proposed to oppose a single-payer system or mandatory public option, neither of which has ever been part of the current federal reform legislation. These antireform bills were based on model legislation put forward by the American Legislative Exchange Council, an organization funded by wealthy right-wing foundations to support conservative state legislative causes, which was reportedly aided in this endeavor by the insurance industry. Because these bills were not aimed at any actual federal legislation, they seem to have simply been part of a larger campaign to mischaracterize federal legislative efforts and stir up opposition to any federal health care reform.

The Virginia bill, in contrast, is aimed at an actual provision of the federal health care reform bill—the individual mandate. As the legislative findings that accompany the individual mandate in the Senate bill emphasize, the mandate is fundamental to the legislation. The government cannot require insurers to take all comers, regardless of health status and preexisting conditions, unless the healthy as well as the unhealthy are required to purchase health insurance. We will not be able to reduce providers' burden of uncompensated care or the alarming rate of medical bankruptcies unless all Americans who can afford health insurance buy it.

The individual mandate, however, is uniquely vulnerable. First, it is strongly opposed by conservatives and libertarians. The fact that five of the Virginia Senate's Democrats voted for the state senate bill sends a clear message to Virginia's congressional delegation that a federal bill containing such a mandate is going to be very unpopular with many of their constituents.

Second, the individual mandate is somewhat vulnerable constitutionally. Although the argument that the mandate is constitutional is overwhelming, as Balkin noted in a recent issue of the *Journal*, it is hard to think of a direct precedent for it. And the argument against it is not frivolous, unlike most of the other constitutional arguments that have been raised against the pending legislation. The state bills can be read as briefs to the Supreme Court on this issue.

Third, the mandate is particularly vulnerable from an enforcement perspective. It essentially imposes a tax penalty (to begin in 2014 and to be fully phased in by 2016) on uninsured individuals who do not purchase health insurance, subject to a number of exceptions for those who cannot afford health insurance or who oppose it for religious reasons. Individuals are supposed to pay this penalty with their annual income taxes, but the Senate bill waives criminal penalties and prohibits the Internal Revenue Service (IRS) from imposing liens or levies on a taxpayer's property for failure to pay. Compliance will, therefore, be largely voluntary (although the IRS can still make a tax resister's life miserable, whether or not it can ultimately collect). The state bills can thus be seen as invitations to civil disobedience that counsel state citizens to "violate the federal law, wave this statute in their face, and dare them to come after you."

I know of two other significant state campaigns—one ongoing, one historical—to rally or support state citizens in resisting federal law. In the ongoing effort, more than a quarter of the states have now legalized medical marijuana in the face of a federal prohibition. Although the Supreme Court has emphatically upheld the authority of the federal government to outlaw medical marijuana, the Justice Department announced last fall that the prosecution of users of the medical marijuana was not "an efficient use of limited federal resources." It is possible that the federal government will eventually conclude that it is not possible to enforce the individual mandate for health insurance. But if individuals successfully resist accepting responsibility for being insured, there will be no way of expanding affordable coverage in a system that depends on private insurers. If government funding of health care must therefore be increased, it may not be the result resisters want.

In the historical effort, demagogues such as the late Senator Harry Byrd (D-VA) mounted the Campaign for Massive Resistance to school desegregation in Virginia and other states during the 1950s and 1960s. Virginia passed a series of statutes intended to maintain the strict segregation of its schools, even going so far as to close the public schools in one county for 6 years. The legislation was held unconstitutional by the federal courts, and the campaign eventually collapsed. Today, most Virginians regard the whole episode as an embarrassment. The state legislature has even adopted reparations legislation to help people who were denied an education during the campaign. Perhaps if health care reform is successfully implemented and Americans come to fully appreciate its benefits, they will look back at the current efforts with similar embarrassment.

These resistance efforts are not about law—they are about politics. But of course at this point, health care reform is only about politics, except insofar as it is still about the morality of equal treatment for all.

18

"The Health Care Freedom Act: Questions & Answers"

CLINT BOLICK

The Health Care Freedom Act will appear as a proposed constitutional amendment on Arizona's 2010 election ballot, and similar measures are under consideration in more than 30 other states. With the possibility that Congress will enact some sort of national health insurance legislation, questions are being raised about the scope of the Health Care Freedom Act and its effect should a federal bill become law. In the following pages, Clint Bolick, who helped to author the Health Care Freedom Act, answers frequently asked questions.

Q: What is the Health Care Freedom Act?

A: The Health Care Freedom Act is a proposed amendment to the Arizona Constitution that would preserve certain existing rights that individuals have regarding health care. It was initially proposed by two Arizona physicians, Dr. Eric Novack and Dr. Jeffrey Singer, with drafting assistance from the Goldwater Institute. The measure qualified as a voter initiative on the 2008 ballot, and despite a well-financed opposition campaign, it was defeated by less than one-half of 1 percent of the vote.

Changes were made to address concerns raised by the opponents, and the Arizona Legislature voted to refer the revised version to the 2010 ballot.

The American Legislative Exchange Council adopted model legislation based on the Arizona measure, and activists and legislators in at least 35 additional states are pursuing constitutional amendments or statutes based on the Arizona model.

Q: What are the key provisions?

A: Although the precise language varies from state to state, the Health Care Freedom Act seeks to protect two essential rights. First, it protects a person's right to participate or not in any health care system, and prohibits the government from imposing fines or penalties on that person's decision. Second, it protects the right of individuals to purchase—and the right of doctors to provide—lawful medical services without government fine or penalty. The Health Care Freedom Act would place these essential rights in the state constitution (or, in some states, it would protect them by statute).

Q: What motivated the Health Care Freedom Act?

A: No one questions the need for serious health care reform. However, the proponents of the Health Care Freedom Act believe that regardless of how such reform is fashioned, either at the state or federal level, the essential rights protected by the Health Care Freedom Act should be preserved. Many advocates of a larger government role in regulating or providing health insurance support a mandate that would compel individuals to join a government-approved health insurance plan, whether or not they can afford it and whether or not the system best fits their needs. In some countries in which government plays a large role in providing health insurance, medical services are rationed and individuals are prevented or discouraged from obtaining otherwise lawful medical services. Supporters of the Health Care Freedom Act have a variety of perspectives on the form that health care reform should take. But they agree that no matter what legislation is passed, it should not take from Americans their precious right to control their own medical affairs.

Q: By what authority can states pass the Health Care Freedom Act?

A: It is well-established that the U.S. Constitution provides a baseline for the protection of individual rights, and that state constitutions may provide additional protections—and all of them do. For instance, some states provide greater protections of freedom of speech or due process rights. Because the Health Care Freedom Act offers greater protection than the federal constitution, states are allowed to enact it.

Q: Does it matter whether the Health Care Freedom Act is passed as a statute or as a constitutional amendment?

A: A state constitution is the organic law of the state, reflecting the most fundamental values shared by the citizens of the state. Moreover, a state constitutional amendment will ensure that state legislature can never infringe upon the protected rights. So a constitutional amendment is preferable, especially to protect against legislative tinkering. However, for purposes of a federalism defense against excessive federal legislation, it should not matter whether the people of the state have acted through their constitution or by statute.

Q: Does the Health Care Freedom Act attempt to "nullify" federal health insurance legislation?

A: Absolutely not. If federal legislation is enacted, individuals would still have the option to participate in federal health insurance programs. This act simply protects a person's right not to participate.

Q: To the extent that the Health Care Freedom Act conflicts with provisions of federal legislation, isn't the state law automatically preempted by the Supremacy Clause of the U.S. Constitution?

A: No. In any clash between state and federal provisions, at least four federal constitutional provisions are relevant. The Supremacy Clause establishes the Constitution as the supreme law of the land and provides that federal laws prevail over conflicting state laws where Congress has the legitimate authority to enact the legislation and where it does not impermissibly tread upon state sovereignty. The federal government will have to demonstrate that its legislation legitimately is derived from congressional authority to regulate interstate commerce. It will also have to show the legislation does not violate the 10th Amendment, which reserves to the states all government power not expressly delegated to the national government; and the 11th Amendment, which protects states from being used as mere instrumentalities of the national government. This constitutional construct is known as federalism.

Q: Are certain provisions of proposed federal health care legislation vulnerable to constitutional challenge without the Health Care Freedom Act?

A: Yes, in at least three ways. First, to the extent that the legislation purports to regulate transactions that do not directly affect interstate commerce, such as mandating insurance for individuals. Congress may lack authority to do so under the Commerce Clause. Several relatively recent decisions by the U.S. Supreme Court have invalidated federal legislation on this basis. In *U.S. v. Lopez* (1995), the Court struck down federal laws that restricted guns in school zones; and in *U.S. v. Morrison*, it struck down a federal statute involving violence against women. In both cases, the Court found the subject matter of the federal laws did not "substantially affect" interstate commerce, so Congress had no power to regulate it under the circumstances presented.

Second, to the extent the legislation interferes with the individual's right to choose health insurance providers, doctors, or lawful medical services, it may violate the right to medical self-determination recognized under the U.S. Constitution. As the Court declared in *Griswold v. Connecticut* (1965), "We have recognized that the special relationship between patient and physician will often be encompassed within the domain of private life protected by the Due Process Clause." Several of the early abortion cases involved what Justice William O. Douglas, concurring in *Doe v. Bolton* (1973), described as the "right to seek advice on one's health and the right to place reliance on the physician of one's choice." Whether or not one agrees with those abortion rulings, they establish a strong basis for challenging certain federal and state intrusions.

Third, several recent decisions have invalidated federal laws that "commandeer" state governments to do their bidding. In *New York v. United States* (1992), for instance, the Court struck down federal rules requiring states to take ownership of certain radioactive waste and to expose themselves to liability. Speaking for the Court, Justice Sandra Day O'Connor ruled that "no matter how powerful the federal interest involved, the Constitution simply does not give Congress the authority to require the States to regulate." Tellingly, she added "the Constitution protects us from our own best intentions: It divides power among sovereigns ... precisely so that we may resist the temptation to concentrate power in one location as an expedient solution to the crisis of the day." To the extent that federal health insurance legislation forces states to implement its provisions, it could be subject to robust constitutional challenge.

Q: Could the Health Care Freedom Act provide additional protection against federal health insurance legislation that violates protected rights?

A: Yes. Although the federal government usually prevails in federalism clashes, the current U.S. Supreme Court is the most pro-federalism Court in decades. There are no cases precisely on point, but the Court under Chief Justice John Roberts has sided with the states in at least three major recent federalism clashes. In the case most closely on point, *Gonzales v. Oregon* (2006), the Court upheld the state's "right-to-die" law, which was enacted by Oregon voters, over the objections of the U.S. Attorney General, who argued that federal law pre-empted the state law. Applying "the structure and limitations of federalism," the Court observed that states have great latitude in regulating health and safety, including medical standards, which are primarily and historically a matter of local concern. Holding that the attorney general's reading of the federal statute would mark "a radical shift of authority from the States to the Federal Government to define general standards of medical practice in every locality," the Court interpreted the statute to allow Oregon to protect the rights of its citizens.

Horne v. Flores (2009) considered a measure adopted by Arizona voters to require English immersion as the state's educational policy for students for whom English is a second language. Lower federal courts had imposed an injunction based on a finding that Arizona was failing to comply with federal bilingual education requirements. The Supreme Court held that injunctions affecting "areas of core state responsibility, such as public education," should be lifted as quickly as circumstances warrant. It observed that "federalism concerns are heightened when . . . a federal court decree has the effect of dictating state or local budget priorities." The Court remanded the case to lower courts to reconsider the injunction.

In *Northwest Austin Municipal Utility District No. 1 v. Holder* (2009), the Court examined a challenge to section 5 of the Voting Rights Act, which places certain states and localities in a penalty box, requiring them to obtain "pre-clearance" by the U.S. Department of Justice for any changes that impact voting. The Court was sharply critical of the "federalism costs" imposed upon the covered jurisdictions. It avoided the constitutional question by applying the federal law in a way that allowed the utility district to "bail out" from pre-clearance requirements under section 5.

In each of these cases, the Court sided with states in federalism disputes with the federal government.

Q: Will the Health Care Freedom Act affect future state legislation regarding health insurance?

A: Yes. If it is passed as a constitutional amendment, it would prevent any future legislation that infringes upon the rights protected by the amendment.

Q: Won't this be really expensive for the states to defend in court?

A: The Goldwater Institute has offered to defend the constitutionality of the Health Care Freedom Act at no cost to any state. Because legal challenges would involve purely constitutional issues and would not require expensive trials, to the extent that states become involved in litigation, they should be able to do so within existing Attorney General litigation budgets. Moreover, depending on the details of national health insurance legislation, the cost of federal mandates is likely to far exceed the cost of litigation.

Q: Even if the states and individuals did not prevail in a challenge to intrusive federal health insurance legislation, would there be reasons to support the Health Care Freedom Act?

A: Yes. First, if these rights are given additional protection under state constitutions, they will create an absolute barrier to future state legislation that violates those rights. Moreover, efforts to enact the Health Care Freedom Act send a powerful message to our nation's capitol that people at the grassroots take these rights very seriously and intend to protect them.

*   *   *

DISCUSSION QUESTIONS

1. When should the national government direct policy? When should it step back and let the states have their way? Should the national government have the power to compel people to buy health insurance (while providing subsidies to those who cannot afford it)?

2. Sean Wilentz argues that if states can simply ignore national laws they disagree with, this would be a recipe for anarchy. Do you agree? Are there any instances in which the states should be able to ignore national laws? What about assisted suicide, medical marijuana, or gun rights?

3. Do you agree with Timothy Jost that the most important implications of the legal challenges by the states are political, rather than legal? If so, will "massive resistance" to the law be a problem?

4. Are you convinced by Clint Bolick's case for the legal arguments in favor of the Arizona state constitutional amendment on health care? On which points, if any, do you think the health care law is vulnerable to constitutional challenge?

CHAPTER 4

The Constitutional Framework and the Individual: Civil Liberties and Civil Rights

In the next two selections, Abraham Lincoln and Martin Luther King, Jr., take opposing points of view about how to achieve peaceful change in a civil society. What happens when the fight for justice and equality comes into conflict with the rule of law? Are people ever justified in breaking laws for what they perceive to be the greater good? Is civil disobedience justified in some contexts?

In a speech that he delivered twenty-three years before becoming president, Lincoln argues that the laws must be followed, as without adherence to laws we have no civil society. Change, Lincoln stresses, must come from working within the system. King disagrees, arguing that while people have a moral obligation to follow just laws, they have an equally compelling duty to break unjust laws through nonviolent means. In his "Letter from Birmingham Jail," which he addressed to more conservative religious leaders in the civil rights movement who were concerned about his tactics, King outlined procedures for distinguishing between just and unjust laws, and for resisting those laws that are unjust. It is ironic that despite Lincoln's admonitions about working within the system, it was under his leadership that the nation fought its bloodiest war precisely because the central issues of states' rights and slavery could not be solved within the system. King, on the other hand, who argued in favor of breaking unjust laws, was actually instrumental in putting pressure on Congress (the "system") to change those laws that he and others in the civil rights movement considered unjust.

Current battles over abortion and the environment show the debate between Lincoln and King to be timeless. Activists in both policy areas have been decried as "radical" or "extremist" because of occasional civil disobedience against legal activities. Some environmentalists have prevented lumber harvesting by putting spikes in trees; some pro-life activists have blocked women's access to abortion clinics. And in the abortion case, as in the Lincoln-King debate, issues of civil rights and civil liberties intersect.

19

"The Perpetuation of Our Political Institutions"

Abraham Lincoln

In the great journal of things happening under the sun, we, the American People, find our account running, under date of the nineteenth century of the Christian era. We find ourselves in the peaceful possession, of the fairest portion of the earth, as regards extent of territory, fertility of soil, and salubrity of climate. We find ourselves under the government of a system of political institutions, conducing more essentially to the ends of civil and religious liberty, than any of which the history of former times tells us. We, when mounting the stage of existence, found ourselves the legal inheritors of these fundamental blessings. We toiled not in the acquirement or establishment of them—they are a legacy bequeathed us, by a *once* hardy, brave, and patriotic, but *now* lamented and departed race of ancestors. Theirs was the task (and nobly they performed it) to possess themselves, and through themselves, us, of this goodly land; and to up-rear upon its hills and its valleys, a political edifice of liberty and equal rights; 'tis ours only, to transmit these, the former, unprofaned by the foot of an invader; the latter, undecayed by the lapse of time and untorn by usurpation, to the latest generation that fate shall permit the world to know. This task of gratitude to our fathers, justice to ourselves, duty to posterity, and love for our species in general, all imperatively required us faithfully to perform.

How then shall we perform it? At what point shall we expect the approach of danger? By what means shall we fortify against it? Shall we expect some transatlantic military giant, to step the ocean, and crush us at a blow? Never! All the armies of Europe, Asia and Africa combined, with all the treasure of the earth (our own excepted) in their military chest; with a Buonaparte for a commander, could not by force take a drink from the Ohio, or make a track on the Blue Ridge, in a trial of a thousand years.

At what point then is the approach of danger to be expected? I answer, if it ever reach us, it must spring up amongst us. It cannot come from abroad. If destruction be our lot, we must ourselves be its author and finisher. As a nation of freemen, we must live through all time, or die by suicide.

I hope I am over wary; but if I am not, there is, even now, something of ill-omen amongst us. I mean the increasing disregard for law which pervades the country; the growing disposition to substitute the wild and furious passions, in lieu of the sober judgment of Courts; and the worse than savage mobs, for the executive ministers of justice. This disposition is awfully fearful in any community; and that it now exists in ours, though grating to our feelings to admit, it would be a violation of truth, and an insult to our intelligence, to deny. Accounts of outrages committed by mobs, form the everyday news of the times. They have pervaded the country, from New England to Louisiana; they are neither peculiar to the eternal snows of the former, nor the burning suns of the latter; they are not the creature of climate—neither are they confined to the slaveholding, or the non-slaveholding States. Alike, they spring up among the pleasure hunting masters of Southern slaves, and the order loving citizens of the land of steady habits. Whatever, then, their cause may be, it is common to the whole country.

It would be tedious, as well as useless, to recount the horrors of all of them. Those happening in the State of Mississippi, and at St. Louis, are, perhaps, the most dangerous in example and revolting to humanity. In the Mississippi case, they first commenced by hanging the regular gamblers; a set of men, certainly not following for a livelihood, a very useful, or very honest occupation; but one which, so far from being forbidden by the laws, was actually licensed by an act of the Legislature, passed but a single year before. Next, negroes, suspected of conspiring to raise an insurrection, were caught up and hanged in all parts of the State: then, white men, supposed to be leagued with the negroes; and finally, strangers, from neighboring States, going thither on business, were, in many instances, subjected to the same fate. Thus went on this process of hanging, from gamblers to negroes, from negroes to white citizens, and from these to strangers; till, dead men were seen literally dangling from the boughs of trees upon every road side; and in numbers almost sufficient, to rival the native Spanish moss of the country, as a drapery of the forest.

Turn, then, to that horror-striking scene at St. Louis. A single victim was only sacrificed there. His story is very short; and is, perhaps, the most highly tragic, of anything of its length, that has ever been witnessed in real life. A mulatto man, by the name of McIntosh, was seized in the street, dragged to the suburbs of the city, chained to a tree, and actually burned to death; and all within a single hour from the time he had been a freeman, attending to his own business, and at peace with the world.

Such are the effects of mob law; and such are the scenes, becoming more and more frequent in this land so lately famed for love of law and order; and the stories of which have even now grown too familiar, to attract any thing more than an idle remark.

But you are, perhaps, ready to ask, "What has this to do with the perpetuation of our political institutions?" I answer, it has much to do with it. Its direct consequences are, comparatively speaking, but a small evil; and much of its danger consists, in the proneness of our minds, to regard its direct as its only consequences. Abstractly considered, the hanging of the gamblers at Vicksburg was of but little consequence. They constitute a portion of population that is worse than useless in any community; and their death, if no pernicious example be set by it, is never matter of reasonable regret with anyone. If they were annually swept from the stage of existence by the plague or small pox, honest men would, perhaps, be much profited by the operation. Similar too, is the correct reasoning, in regard to the burning of the negro at St. Louis. He had forfeited his life, by the perpetration of an outrageous murder, upon one of the most worthy and respectable citizens of the city; and had he not died as he did, he must have died by the sentence of the law, in a very short time afterwards. As to him alone, it was as well the way it was, as it could otherwise have been. But the example in either case was fearful. When men take it in their heads today, to hang gamblers, or burn murderers, they should recollect, that, in the confusion usually attending such transactions, they will be as likely to hang or burn someone who is neither a gambler nor a murderer as one who is; and that, acting upon the example they set, the mob of tomorrow, may, and probably will, hang or burn some of them by the very same mistake. And not only so; the innocent, those who have ever set their faces against violations of law in every shape, alike with the guilty, fall victims to the ravages of mob law; and thus it goes on, step by step, till all the walls erected for the defence of the persons and property of individuals, are trodden down, and disregarded. But all this even, is not the full extent of the evil. By such examples, by instances of the perpetrators of such acts going unpunished, the lawless in spirit are encouraged to become lawless in practice; and having been used to no restraint, but dread of punishment, they thus become absolutely unrestrained. Having ever regarded Government as their deadliest bane, they make a jubilee of the suspension of its operations; and pray for nothing so much as its total annihilation. While, on the other hand, good men, men who love tranquility, who desire to abide by the laws, and enjoy their benefits, who would gladly spill their blood in the defence of their country; seeing their property destroyed; their families insulted, and their lives endangered; their persons injured; and seeing nothing in prospect that forebodes a change for the better; become tired of, and disgusted with, a Government that offers them no protection; and are not much averse to a change in which they imagine they have nothing to lose. Thus, then, by the operation of this mobocratic spirit, which all must admit is now abroad in the land, the strongest bulwark of any Government, and particularly of those constituted like ours, may effectually be broken down and destroyed—I mean the *attachment* of the People. Whenever this effect shall be produced among us, whenever the vicious portion of population shall be permitted to gather in bands of hundreds and thousands, and burn churches, ravage and rob provision-stores, throw printing presses into rivers, shoot editors, and hang and burn obnoxious persons at pleasure, and with impunity, depend on it, this Government cannot last. By such things, the feelings of the best citizens will become more or less alienated from it; and thus it will be left without friends, or with too few, and those few too weak, to make their friendship effectual. At such a time and under such circumstances, men of sufficient talent and ambition will not be wanting to seize the opportunity, strike the blow, and overturn that fair fabric which for the last half century has been the fondest hope of the lovers of freedom, throughout the world.

I know the American People are *much* attached to their Government; I know they would suffer *much* for its sake; I know they would endure evils long and patiently, before they would ever think of exchanging it for another. Yet, notwithstanding all this, if the laws be continually despised and disregarded, if their rights to be secure in their persons and property are held by no better tenure than the caprice of a mob, the alienation of their affections from the Government is the natural consequence; and to that, sooner or later, it must come.

Here then, is one point at which danger may be expected.

The question recurs, "how shall we fortify against it?" The answer is simple. Let every American, every lover of liberty, every well-wisher to his posterity, swear by the blood of the Revolution never to violate in the least particular the laws of the country; and never to tolerate their violation by others. As the patriots of seventy-six did to the support of the Declaration of Independence, so to the support of the Constitution and Laws, let every American pledge his life, his property, and his sacred honor; let every man remember that to violate the law is to trample on the blood of his father, and to tear the character of his own, and his children's liberty. Let reverence for the laws be breathed by every American mother to the lisping babe that prattles on her lap—let it be taught in schools, in seminaries, and in colleges; let it be written in Primers, spelling books, and in Almanacs; let it be preached from the pulpit, proclaimed in legislative halls, and enforced in courts of justice. And, in short, let it become the *political religion* of the nation; and let the old and the young, the rich and the poor, the grave and the gay, of all sexes and tongues, and colors and conditions, sacrifice unceasingly upon its altars.

While ever a state of feeling, such as this, shall universally, or even, very generally prevail throughout the nation, vain will be every effort, and fruitless every attempt, to subvert our national freedom.

When I so pressingly urge a strict observance of all the laws, let me not be understood as saying there are no bad laws, nor that grievances may not arise, for the redress of which, no legal provisions have been made. I mean to say no such thing. But I do mean to say that, although bad laws, if they exist, should be repealed as soon as possible, still while they continue in force, for the sake of example they should be religiously observed. So also in unprovided cases. If such arise, let proper legal provisions be made for them with the least possible delay; but, till then, let them, if not too intolerable, be borne with.

There is no grievance that is a fit object of redress by mob law. In any case that arises, as for instance, the promulgation of abolitionism, one of two positions is necessarily true; that is, the thing is right within itself, and therefore deserves the protection of all law and all good citizens; or, it is wrong, and therefore proper to be prohibited by legal enactments; and in neither case, is the interposition of mob law, either necessary, justifiable, or excusable.

* * *

But this state of feeling *must fade, is fading, has faded,* with the circumstances that produced it.

I do not mean to say, that the scenes of the revolution *are now* or *ever will* be entirely forgotten; but that like everything else, they must fade upon the memory of the world, and grow more and more dim by the lapse of time. In history, we hope, they will be read of, and recounted, so long as the bible shall be read; but even granting that they will, their influence *cannot be* what it heretofore has been. Even then, they *cannot be* so universally known, nor so vividly felt, as they were by the generation just gone to rest. At the close of that struggle, nearly every adult male had been a participator in some of its scenes. The consequence was, that of those scenes, in the form of a husband, a father, a son or a brother, *a living history* was to be found in every family—a history bearing the indubitable testimonies of its own authenticity, in the limbs mangled, in the scars of wounds received, in the midst of the very scenes related—a history, too, that could be read and understood alike by all, the wise and the ignorant, the learned and the unlearned. But *those* histories are gone. They *can* be read no more forever. They *were* a fortress of strength; but, what invading foeman could *never do*, the silent artillery of time *has done*; the leveling of its walls. They are gone. They *were* a forest of giant oaks; but the all-resistless hurricane has swept over them, and left only, here and there, a lonely trunk, despoiled of its verdure, shorn of its foliage; unshading and unshaded, to murmur in a few more gentle breezes, and to combat with its mutilated limbs, a few more ruder storms, then to sink, and be no more.

They *were* the pillars of the temple of liberty; and now that they have crumbled away, that temple must fall, unless we, their descendants, supply their places with other pillars, hewn from the solid quarry of sober reason. Passion has helped us; but can do so no more. It will in future be our enemy. Reason, cold, calculating, unimpassioned reason, must furnish all the materials for our future support and defence. Let those materials be molded into *general intelligence, sound morality,* and, in particular, *a reverence for the constitution and laws:* and, that we improved to the last; that we remained free to the last; that we revered his name to the last; that, during his long sleep, we permitted no hostile foot to pass over or desecrate his resting place; shall be that which to learn the last trump shall awaken our WASHINGTON.

Upon these let the proud fabric of freedom rest, as the rock of its basis; and as truly as has been said of the only greater institution, *"the gates of hell shall not prevail against it."*

20

"Letter from Birmingham Jail"

Martin Luther King, Jr.

My Dear Fellow Clergymen:
    While confined here in the Birmingham City Jail, I came across your recent statement calling my present activities "unwise and untimely." Seldom do I pause to answer criticism of my work and ideas. If I sought to answer all the criticism that cross my desk, my secretaries would have little time for anything other than such correspondence in the course of the day, and I would have no time for constructive work. But since I feel that you are men of genuine goodwill and that your criticisms are sincerely set forth, I want to try to answer your statement in what I hope will be patient and reasonable terms.

I think I should indicate why I am here in Birmingham, since you have been influenced by the view which argues against "outsiders coming in." I have the honor of serving as president of the Southern Christian Leadership Conference, an organization operating in every Southern state, with headquarters in Atlanta, Georgia. We have some eighty-five affiliate organizations across the South, and one of them is the Alabama Christian Movement for Human Rights. Frequently, we share staff, educational, and financial resources with our affiliates. Several months ago the affiliate here in Birmingham asked us to be on call to engage in a nonviolent direct-action program if such were deemed necessary. We readily consented, and when the hour came we lived up to our promise. So I, along with several members of my staff, am here because I was invited here. I am here because I have organizational ties here.

But more basically, I am in Birmingham because injustice exists here. Just as the prophets of the 8th century B.C. left their villages and carried their "thus saith the Lord" far afield, and just as the apostle Paul left his village of Tarsus and carried the gospel of Jesus Christ to the far corners of the Greco-Roman world, so am I compelled to carry the gospel of freedom beyond my own hometown. Like Paul, I must constantly respond to the Macedonian call for aid.*

Moreover, I am cognizant of the interrelatedness of all communities and states. I cannot sit idly by in Atlanta and not be concerned about what happens in Birmingham. Injustice anywhere is a threat to justice

* See Acts 16:9 [*Editors*].

everywhere. We are caught in an inescapable network of mutuality, tied in a single garment of destiny. Whatever affects one directly affects all indirectly. Never again can we afford to live with the narrow, provincial "outside agitator" idea. Anyone who lives inside the United States can never be considered an outsider anywhere within its bounds.

You deplore the demonstrations taking place in Birmingham. But your statement, I am sorry to say, fails to express a similar concern for the conditions that brought about the demonstrations. I am sure that none of you would want to rest content with the superficial kind of social analysis that deals merely with effects and does not grapple with underlying causes. It is unfortunate that demonstrations are taking place in Birmingham, but it is even more unfortunate that the city's white power structure left the Negro community with no alternative.

* * *

You may well ask, "Why direct action? Why sit-ins, marches, etc.? Isn't negotiation a better path?" You are quite right in calling for negotiation. Indeed, this is the very purpose of direct action. Nonviolent direct action seeks to foster such a tension that a community which has constantly refused to negotiate is forced to confront the issue. It seeks so to dramatize the issue that it can no longer be ignored. My citing the creation of tension as part of the work of the nonviolent resister may sound rather shocking. But I readily acknowledge that I am not afraid of the word "tension." I have earnestly opposed violent tension, but there is a type of constructive, nonviolent tension which is necessary for growth. Just as Socrates felt that it was necessary to create a tension in the mind so that individuals could shake off the bondage of myths and half-truths and rise to the realm of creative analysis and objective appraisal, so must we see the need for nonviolent gadflies to create the kind of tension in society that will help men rise from the dark depths of prejudice and racism to the majestic heights of understanding and brotherhood.

The purpose of our direct-action program is to create a situation so crisis-packed that it will inevitably open the door to negotiation. I therefore concur with you in your call for negotiation. Too long has our beloved Southland been bogged down in a tragic effort to live in monologue rather than dialogue.

* * *

We have waited for more than 340 years for our constitutional and God-given rights. The nations of Asia and Africa are moving with jetlike speed toward gaining political independence, but we still creep at horse-and-buggy pace toward gaining a cup of coffee at a lunch counter. Perhaps it is easy for those who have never felt the stinging darts of segregation to say "Wait." But when you have seen vicious mobs lynch your mothers and fathers at will and drown your sisters and brothers at whim; when you have seen hate-filled policemen curse, kick, and even kill your black brothers and sisters with impunity; when you see the vast majority of your 20 million Negro brothers smothering in an air-tight cage of poverty in the midst of an affluent society; when you suddenly find your tongue twisted as you seek to explain to your six-year-old daughter why she can't go to the public amusement park that has just been advertised on television, and see tears welling up when she is told that Funtown is closed to colored children, and see ominous clouds of inferiority beginning to form in her little mental sky, and see her beginning to distort her personality by unconsciously developing a bitterness toward white people; when you have to concoct an answer for a five-year-old son asking, "Daddy, why do white people treat colored people so mean?"; when you take a cross-country drive and find it necessary to sleep night after night in the uncomfortable corners of your automobile because no motel will accept you; when you are humiliated day in and day out by nagging signs reading "white" and "colored"; when your first name becomes "nigger," your middle name becomes "boy" (however old you are), and your last name becomes "John," and your wife and mother are never given the respected title "Mrs."; when you are harried by day and haunted by night by the fact that you are a Negro, never quite knowing what to expect next, and are plagued with inner fears and outer resentments; when you are forever fighting a degenerating sense of "nobodiness"—then you will understand why we find it difficult to wait. There comes a time when the cup of endurance runs over, and men are no longer willing to be plunged into an abyss of injustice where they experience the bleakness of corroding despair. I hope, sirs, you can understand our legitimate and unavoidable impatience.

You express a great deal of anxiety over our willingness to break laws. This is certainly a legitimate concern. Since we so diligently urge people to obey the Supreme Court's decision of 1954 outlawing segregation in the public schools, at first glance it may seem rather paradoxical for us consciously to break laws. One may well ask, "How can you advocate breaking some laws and obeying others?" The answer lies in the fact that there are two types of laws: just and unjust. I agree with St. Augustine that "an unjust law is no law at all."

* * *

Let us consider some of the ways in which a law can be unjust. A law is unjust, for example, if the majority group compels a minority group to obey the statute but does not make it binding on itself. By the same token, a law in all probability is just if the majority is itself willing to obey it. Also, a law is unjust if it is inflicted on a minority that, as a result of being denied the right to vote, had no part in enacting or devising the law. Who can say that the legislature of Alabama which set up that state's segregation laws was democratically elected? Throughout Alabama all sorts of devious methods are used to prevent Negroes from becoming registered voters, and there are some counties in which, even though Negroes constitute a majority of the population, not a single Negro is registered. Can any law enacted under such circumstances be considered democratically structured?

Sometimes a law is just on its face and unjust in its application. For instance, I have been arrested on a charge of parading without a permit. Now there is nothing wrong in having an ordinance which requires a permit for a parade. But such an ordinance becomes unjust when it is used to maintain segregation and to deny citizens the First Amendment privilege of peaceful assembly and protest.

I hope you are able to see the distinction I am trying to point out. In no sense do I advocate evading the law, as would the rabid segregationist. That would lead to anarchy. One who breaks an unjust law must do so *openly*, *lovingly*, and with a willingness to accept the penalty. I submit that an individual who breaks a law that conscience tells him is unjust and who willingly accepts the penalty of imprisonment in order to arouse the conscience of the community over its injustice is in reality expressing the highest respect for law.

*   *   *

I must make two honest confessions to you, my Christian and Jewish brothers. First, I must confess that over the past few years I have been gravely disappointed with the white moderate. I have almost reached the regrettable conclusion that the Negro's great stumbling block in his stride toward freedom is not the White Citizen's Counciler or the Ku Klux Klanner but the white moderate who is more devoted to "order" than to justice; who prefers a negative peace which is the absence of tension to a positive peace which is the presence of justice; who constantly says "I agree with you in the goal you seek, but I cannot agree with your methods"; who paternalistically believes he can set the timetable for another man's freedom; who lives by a mythical concept of time and who constantly advises the Negro to wait for a "more convenient season." Shallow understanding from people of goodwill is more frustrating than absolute misunderstanding from people of ill will. Lukewarm acceptance is much more bewildering than outright rejection.

I had hoped that the white moderate would understand that law and order exist for the purpose of establishing justice and that when they fail in this purpose they block social progress. I had hoped that the white moderate would understand that the present tension in the South is a necessary phase of the transition from an obnoxious negative peace, in which the Negro passively accepted his unjust plight, to a substantive and positive peace, in which all men will respect the dignity and worth of human personality. Actually, we who engage in nonviolent direct action are not the creators of tension. We merely bring to the surface the hidden tension that is already alive. We bring it out in the open where it can be seen and dealt with. Like a boil that can never be cured so long as it is covered up but must be opened with all its pus-flowing ugliness to the natural medicines of air and light, injustice must be exposed, with all the tension its exposure creates, to the light of human conscience and the air of national opinion before it can be cured.

* * *

You speak of our activity in Birmingham as extreme. At first I was rather disappointed that fellow clergymen would see my nonviolent efforts as those of an extremist. I began thinking about the fact that I stand in the middle of two opposing forces in the Negro community. One is a force of complacency made up of Negroes who, as a result of long years of oppression, are so completely drained of self-respect and a sense of "somebodiness" that they have adjusted to segregation, and of a few middle-class Negroes who, because of a degree of academic and economic security and because in some ways they profit by segregation, have unconsciously become insensitive to the problems of the masses. The other force is one of bitterness and hatred, and it comes perilously close to advocating violence. It is expressed in the various black nationalist groups that are springing up across the nation, the largest and best-known being Elijah Muhammad's Muslim movement. Nourished by the Negro's frustration over the continued existence of racial discrimination, this movement is made up of people who have lost faith in America, who have absolutely repudiated Christianity, and who have concluded that the white man is an incorrigible "devil."

I have tried to stand between these two forces, saying that we need emulate neither the "do-nothingism" of the complacent nor the hatred of the black nationalist. For there is the more excellent way of love and non-violent protest. I am grateful to God that, through the influence of the Negro church, the way of nonviolence became an integral part of our struggle.

If this philosophy had not emerged, by now many streets of the South would, I am convinced, be flowing with blood. And I am further convinced that if our white brothers dismiss as "rabble-rousers" and "outside agitators" those of us who employ nonviolent direct action and if they refuse to support our nonviolent efforts, millions of Negroes will, out of frustration and despair, seek solace and security in black nationalist ideologies—a development that would inevitably lead to a frightening racial nightmare.

* * *

Let me take note of my other major disappointment. Though there are some notable exceptions, I have also been disappointed with the white church and its leadership. I do not say this as one of those negative critics who can always find something wrong with the church. I say this as a minister of the gospel, who loves the church; who was nurtured in its bosom; who has been sustained by its spiritual blessings and who will remain true to it as long as the cord of life shall lengthen.

When I was suddenly catapulted into the leadership of the bus protest in Montgomery, Alabama, a few years ago, I felt we would be supported by the white church. I felt that the white ministers, priests, and rabbis of the South would be among our strongest allies. Instead, some have been outright opponents, refusing to understand the freedom movement and misrepresenting its leaders; all too many others have been more cautious than courageous and have remained silent and secure behind stained-glass windows.

In spite of my shattered dreams I came to Birmingham with the hope that the white religious leadership of this community would see the justice of our cause and with deep moral concern would serve as the channel through which our just grievances could reach the power structure. But again I have been disappointed.

I have heard numerous Southern religious leaders admonish their worshipers to comply with a desegregation decision because it is the *law*, but I have longed to hear white ministers declare, "Follow this decree because integration is morally *right* and because the Negro is your brother." In the midst of blatant injustices inflicted upon the Negro I have watched white churchmen stand on the sideline and mouth pious irrelevancies and sanctimonious trivialities. In the midst of a mighty struggle to rid our nation of racial and economic injustice I have heard many ministers say, "Those are social issues with which the gospel has no real concern," and I have watched many churches commit themselves to a completely otherworldly religion which makes a strange, unbiblical distinction between body and soul, between the sacred and the secular.

We are moving toward the close of the twentieth century with a religious community largely adjusted to the status quo—a taillight behind other community agencies rather than a headlight leading men to higher levels of justice.

*   *   *

But the judgment of God is upon the church as never before. If today's church does not recapture the sacrificial spirit of the early church, it will lose its authenticity, forfeit the loyalty of millions, and be dismissed as an irrelevant social club with no meaning for the twentieth century. Every day I meet young people whose disappointment with the church has turned into outright disgust.

Perhaps I have once again been too optimistic. Is organized religion too inextricably bound to the status quo to save our nation and the world? Perhaps I must turn my faith to the inner spiritual church, the church within the church, as the true *ecclesia* and the hope of the world. But again

I am thankful to God that some noble souls from the ranks of organized religion have broken loose from the paralyzing chains of conformity and joined us as active partners in the struggle for freedom. They have left their secure congregations and walked the streets of Albany, Georgia, with us. They have gone down the highways of the South on torturous rides for freedom. Yes, they have gone to jail with us. Some have been kicked out of their churches, have lost the support of their bishops and fellow ministers. But they have acted in the faith that right defeated is stronger than evil triumphant. Their witness has been the spiritual salt that has preserved the true meaning of the gospel in these troubled times. They have carved a tunnel of hope through the dark mountain of disappointment.

I hope the church as a whole will meet the challenge of this decisive hour. But even if the church does not come to the aid of justice, I have no despair about the future. I have no fear about the outcome of our struggle in Birmingham, even if our motives are at present misunderstood. We will reach the goal of freedom in Birmingham and all over the nation, because the goal of America is freedom.

*   *   *

Before closing I feel impelled to mention one other point in your statement that has troubled me profoundly. You warmly commended the Birmingham police force for keeping "order" and "preventing violence." I doubt that you would have so warmly commended the police force if you had seen its angry dogs sinking their teeth into six unarmed, nonviolent Negroes. I doubt that you would so quickly commend the policemen if you were to observe their ugly and inhuman treatment of Negroes here in the City Jail; if you were to watch them push and curse old Negro women and young Negro girls; if you were to see them slap and kick old Negro men and young boys; if you were to observe them, as they did on two occasions, refuse to give us food because we wanted to sing our grace together. I cannot join you in your praise of the Birmingham Police Department.

It is true that the police have exercised discipline in handling the demonstrators. In this sense they have conducted themselves rather "nonviolently" in public. But for what purpose? To preserve the evil system of segregation. Over the past few years I have consistently preached that nonviolence demands that the means we use must be as pure as the ends we seek. I have tried to make clear that it is wrong to use immoral means to attain moral ends. But now I must affirm that it is just as wrong, or perhaps even more so, to use moral means to preserve immoral ends. Perhaps Mr. Connor and his policemen have been rather nonviolent in public, as was Chief Pritchett in Albany, Georgia, but they have used the moral means of nonviolence to maintain the immoral end of racial injustice. As T. S. Eliot has said, there is no greater treason than to do the right deed for the wrong reason.

I wish you had commended the Negro sit-inners and demonstrators of Birmingham for their sublime courage, their willingness to suffer and their amazing discipline in the midst of great provocation. One day the South will recognize its real heroes. . . . One day the South will know that when these disinherited children of God sat down at lunch counters they were in reality standing up for what is best in the American dream and for the most sacred values in our Judeo-Christian heritage, thereby bringing our nation back to those great wells of democracy which were dug deep by the founding fathers in their formulation of the Constitution and the Declaration of Independence.

DISCUSSION QUESTIONS

1. What are the main points of disagreement between the King and Lincoln views?

2. Many of those involved in social protest movements (from anti-abortion protestors to environmental activists) draw parallels between their efforts and King's legacy of civil disobedience, in an effort to establish their right to disobey laws they find unjust. Are such applications of King's argument legitimate? Why or why not?

21

"In Defense of Prejudice"

Jonathan Rauch

Some political theorists argue that democracies must not only prevent the intrusion of government on basic liberties, but also must play a positive role in bolstering and protecting the rights of all their citizens. The challenge is admirable but difficult, as governments in practice are often faced with trade-offs between the two values. Consider free speech, a right enshrined in the First Amendment. The right to speak freely is fundamental to democratic governance. Yet it is not absolute. Is there a line where my right to speak freely impinges upon your wish not to hear what I have to say, particularly when my words are perceived as offensive, harmful, and prejudicial? What role should the government play in drawing the line, if any? Should it limit speech in order to protect others from the insult words can bring? If there is such a line, who decides where it is drawn?

In the following article Jonathan Rauch stands "in defense of prejudice" and in opposition to those who call for government regulation of speech that is insulting to or stigmatizes individuals based on their sex, race, color, handicap, religion, sexual orientation; or national and ethnic origin. In the workplace, universities, public school curricula, the media, and criminal law, speech is increasingly regulated by codes aimed at eradicating prejudice. Rauch argues that regulating speech this way is foolish. In his view, the only way to challenge and correct prejudice is through the free flow of speech, some of which we might not want to hear. Government best protects liberty when it works to preserve rather than prevent the free flow of speech, no matter how distasteful or hurtful that speech may be.

The war on prejudice is now, in all likelihood, the most uncontroversial social movement in America. Opposition to "hate speech," formerly identified with the liberal left, has become a bipartisan piety. In the past year, groups and factions that agree on nothing else have agreed that the public expression of any and all prejudices must be forbidden. On the left, protesters and editorialists have insisted that Francis L. Lawrence resign as president of Rutgers University for describing blacks as "a disadvantaged population that doesn't have that genetic, hereditary background to have a higher average." On the other side of the ideological divide, Ralph Reed, the executive director of the Christian Coalition, responded to criticism of the religious right by calling a press conference to denounce a supposed outbreak of "name-calling, scapegoating, and religious bigotry." Craig Rogers, an evangelical Christian student at California State University, recently filed a $2.5 million sexual-harassment suit against a lesbian professor of psychology, claiming that anti-male bias in one of her lectures violated campus rules and left him feeling "raped and trapped."

In universities and on Capitol Hill, in workplaces and newsrooms, authorities are declaring that there is no place for racism, sexism, homophobia, Christian-bashing, and other forms of prejudice in public debate or even in private thought. "Only when racism and other forms of prejudice are expunged," say the crusaders for sweetness and light, "can minorities be safe and society be fair." So sweet, this dream of a world without prejudice. But the very last thing society should do is seek to utterly eradicate racism and other forms of prejudice.

I suppose I should say, in the customary I-hope-I-don't-sound-too-defensive tone, that I am not a racist and that this is not an article favoring racism or any other particular prejudice. It is an article favoring intellectual pluralism, which permits the expression of various forms of bigotry and always will. Although we like to hope that a time will come when no one will believe that people come in types and that each type belongs with its own kind, I doubt such a day will ever arrive. By all indications, *Homo sapiens* is a tribal species for whom "us versus them" comes naturally and must be continually pushed back. Where there is genuine freedom of expression, there will be racist expression. There will also be people who believe that homosexuals are sick or threaten children or—especially among teenagers—are rightful targets of manly savagery. Homosexuality will always be incomprehensible to most people, and what is incomprehensible is feared. As for anti-Semitism, it appears to be a hardier virus than influenza. If you want pluralism, then you get racism and sexism and homophobia, and communism and fascism and xenophobia and tribalism, and that is just for a start. If you want to believe in intellectual freedom and the progress of knowledge and the advancement of science and all those other good things, then you must swallow hard and accept this: for as thickheaded and wayward an animal as us, the realistic question is how to make the best of prejudice, not how to eradicate it.

Indeed, "eradicating prejudice" is so vague a proposition as to be meaningless. Distinguishing prejudice reliably and nonpolitically from non-prejudice, or even defining it crisply, is quite hopeless. We all feel we know prejudice when we see it. But do we? At the University of Michigan, a student said in a classroom discussion that he considered homosexuality a disease treatable with therapy. He was summoned to a formal disciplinary hearing for violating the school's policy against speech that "victimizes" people based on "sexual orientation." Now, the evidence is abundant that this particular hypothesis is wrong, and any American homosexual can attest to the harm that the student's hypothesis has inflicted on many real people. But was it a statement of prejudice or of misguided belief? Hate speech or hypothesis? Many Americans who do not regard themselves as bigots or haters believe that homosexuality is a treatable disease. They may be wrong, but are they all bigots? I am unwilling to say so, and if you are willing, beware. The line between a prejudiced belief and a merely controversial one is elusive, and the harder you look the more elusive it becomes. "God hates homosexuals" is a statement of fact, not of bias, to those who believe it; "American criminals are disproportionately black" is a statement of bias, not of fact, to those who disbelieve it.

Who is right? You may decide, and so may others, and there is no need to agree. That is the great innovation of intellectual pluralism . . . We cannot know in advance or for sure which belief is prejudice and which is truth, but to advance knowledge we don't need to know. The genius of intellectual pluralism lies not in doing away with prejudices and dogmas but in channeling them—making them socially productive by pitting prejudice against prejudice and dogma against dogma, exposing all to withering public criticism. What survives at the end of the day is our base of knowledge.

*   *   *

Pluralism is the principle that protects and makes a place in human company for that loneliest and most vulnerable of all minorities, the minority who is hounded and despised among blacks and whites, gays and straights, who is suspect or criminal among every tribe and in every nation of the world, and yet on whom progress depends: the dissident. I am not saying that dissent is always or even usually enlightened. Most of the time it is foolish and self-serving. No dissident has the right to be taken seriously, and the fact that Aryan Nation racists or Nation of Islam anti-Semites are unorthodox does not entitle them to respect. But what goes around comes around. As a supporter of gay marriage, for example, I reject the majority's view of family, and as a Jew I reject its view of God. I try to be civil, but the fact is that most Americans regard my views on marriage as a reckless assault on the most fundamental of all institutions, and many people are more than a little discomfited by the statement "Jesus Christ was no more divine than anybody else" (which is why so few people ever say it). Trap the racists and anti-Semites, and you lay a trap for me too. Hunt for them with eradication in your mind, and you have brought dissent itself within your sights.

The new crusade against prejudice waves aside such warnings. Like earlier crusades against antisocial ideas, the mission is fueled by good (if cocksure) intentions and a genuine sense of urgency. Some kinds of error are held to be intolerable, like pollutants that even in small traces poison the water for a whole town. Some errors are so pernicious as to damage real people's lives, so wrongheaded that no person of right mind or good-will could support them. Like their forebears of other stripe—the Church in its campaigns against heretics, the McCarthyites in their campaigns against Communists—the modern anti-racist and anti-sexist and anti-homophobic campaigners are totalists, demanding not that misguided ideas and ugly expressions be corrected or criticized but that they be eradicated. They make war not on errors but on error, and like other totalists they act in the name of public safety—the safety, especially, of minorities.

The sweeping implications of this challenge to pluralism are not, I think, well enough understood by the public at large. Indeed, the new brand of totalism has yet even to be properly named. "Multiculturalism," for instance, is much too broad. "Political correctness" comes closer but is too trendy and snide. For lack of anything else, I will call the new anti-pluralism "purism," since its major tenet is that society cannot be just until the last traces of invidious prejudice have been scrubbed away. Whatever you call it, the purists' way of seeing things has spread through American intellectual life with remarkable speed, so much so that many people will blink at you uncomprehendingly or even call you a racist (or sexist or homophobe, etc.) if you suggest that expressions of racism should be tolerated or that prejudice has its part to play.

The new purism sets out, to begin with, on a campaign against words, for words are the currency of prejudice, and if prejudice is hurtful then so must be prejudiced words. "We are not safe when these violent words are among us," wrote Mari Matsuda, then a UCLA law professor. Here one imagines gangs of racist words swinging chains and smashing heads in back alleys. To suppress bigoted language seems, at first blush, reasonable, but it quickly leads to a curious result. A peculiar kind of verbal shamanism takes root, as though certain expressions, like curses or magical incantations, carry in themselves the power to hurt or heal—as though words were bigoted rather than people. "Context is everything," people have always said. The use of the word "nigger" in *Huckleberry Finn* does not make the book an "act" of hate speech—or does it? In the new view, this is no longer so clear. The very utterance of the word "nigger" (at least by a non-black) is a racist act. When a *Sacramento Bee* cartoonist put the word "nigger" mockingly in the mouth of a white supremacist, there were howls of protest and 1,400 canceled subscriptions and an editorial apology, even though the word was plainly being invoked against racists, not against blacks.

Faced with escalating demands of verbal absolutism, newspapers issue lists of forbidden words. The expressions "gyp" (derived from "Gypsy") and "Dutch treat" were among the dozens of terms stricken as "offensive" in a much-ridiculed (and later withdrawn) *Los Angeles Times* speech code. The University of Missouri journalism school issued a *Dictionary of Cautionary Words and Phrases*, which included *"Buxom*: Offensive reference to a woman's chest. Do not use. See 'Woman.' *Codger*: Offensive reference to a senior citizen."

As was bound to happen, purists soon discovered that chasing around after words like "gyp" or "buxom" hardly goes to the roots of the problem. As long as they remain bigoted, bigots will simply find other words. If they can't call you a kike then they will say Jewboy, Judas, or Hebe, and when all those are banned they will press words like "oven" and "lampshade" into their service. The vocabulary of hate is potentially as rich as your dictionary, and all you do by banning language used by cretins is to let them decide what the rest of us may say. The problem, some purists have concluded, must therefore go much deeper than laws: it must go to the deeper level of ideas. Racism, sexism, homophobia, and the rest must be built into the very structure of American society and American patterns of thought, so pervasive yet so insidious that, like water to a fish, they are both omnipresent and unseen. The mere existence of prejudice constructs a society whose very nature is prejudiced.

This line of thinking was pioneered by feminists, who argued that pornography, more than just being expressive, is an act by which men construct an oppressive society. Racial activists quickly picked up the argument. Racist expressions are themselves acts of oppression, they said. "All racist speech constructs the social reality that constrains the liberty of nonwhites because of their race," wrote Charles R. Lawrence III, then a law professor at Stanford. From the purist point of view, a society with even one racist is a racist society, because the idea itself threatens and demeans its targets. They cannot feel wholly safe or wholly welcome as long as racism is present. Pluralism says: There will always be some racists. Marginalize them, ignore them, exploit them, ridicule them, take pains to make their policies illegal, but otherwise leave them alone. Purists say: That's not enough. Society cannot be just until these pervasive and oppressive ideas are searched out and eradicated.

And so what is now under way is a growing drive to eliminate prejudice from every corner of society. I doubt that many people have noticed how far-reaching this anti-pluralist movement is becoming.

In universities: Dozens of universities have adopted codes proscribing speech or other expression that (this is from Stanford's policy, which is more or less representative) "is intended to insult or stigmatize an individual or a small number of individuals on the basis of their sex, race, color, handicap, religion, sexual orientation or national and ethnic origin." Some codes punish only persistent harassment of a targeted individual, but many, following the purist doctrine that even one racist is too many, go much further. At Penn, an administrator declared: "We at the University of Pennsylvania have guaranteed students and the community that they can live in a community free of sexism, racism, and homophobia." Here is the purism that gives "political correctness" its distinctive combination of puffy high-mindedness and authoritarian zeal.

In school curricula: "More fundamental than eliminating racial segregation has to be the removal of racist thinking, assumptions, symbols, and materials in the curriculum," writes theorist Molefi Kete Asante. In practice, the effort to "remove racist thinking" goes well beyond striking egregious references from textbooks. In many cases it becomes a kind of mental engineering in which students are encouraged to see prejudice everywhere; it includes teaching identity politics as an antidote to internalized racism; it rejects mainstream science as "white male" thinking; and it tampers with history, installing such dubious notions as that the ancient Greeks stole their culture from Africa or that an ancient carving of a bird is an example of "African experimental aeronautics."

In criminal law: Consider two crimes. In each, I am beaten brutally; in each, my jaw is smashed and my skull is split in just the same way. However, in the first crime my assailant calls me an "asshole"; in the second he calls me a "queer." In most states, in many localities, and, as of September 1994, in federal cases, these two crimes are treated differently: the crime motivated by bias—or deemed to be so motivated by prosecutors and juries—gets a stiffer punishment. "Longer prison terms for bigots," shrilled Brooklyn Democratic Congressman Charles Schumer, who introduced the federal hate-crimes legislation, and those are what the law now provides. Evidence that the assailant holds prejudiced beliefs, even if he doesn't actually express them while committing an offense, can serve to elevate the crime. Defendants in hate-crimes cases may be grilled on how many black friends they have and whether they have told racist jokes. To increase a prison sentence only because of the defendant's "prejudice" (as gauged by prosecutor and jury) is, of course, to try minds and punish beliefs. Purists say, Well, they are dangerous minds and poisonous beliefs.

In the workplace: Though government cannot constitutionally suppress bigotry directly, it is now busy doing so indirectly by requiring employers to eliminate prejudice. Since the early 1980s, courts and the Equal Employment Opportunity Commission have moved to bar workplace speech deemed to create a hostile or abusive working environment for minorities. The law, held a federal court in 1988, "does require that an employer take prompt action to prevent . . . bigots from expressing their opinions in a way that abuses or offends their co-workers," so as to achieve "the goal of eliminating prejudices and biases from our society." So it was, as UCLA law professor Eugene Volokh notes, that the EEOC charged that a manufacturer's ads using admittedly accurate depictions of samurai, kabuki, and sumo were "racist" and "offensive to people of Japanese origin"; that a Pennsylvania court found that an employer's printing Bible verses on paychecks was religious harassment of Jewish employees; that an employer had to desist using gender-based job titles like "foreman" and "draftsman" after a female employee sued.

On and on the campaign goes, darting from one outbreak of prejudice to another like a cat chasing flies. In the American Bar Association, activists demand that lawyers who express "bias or prejudice" be penalized. In the Education Department, the civil-rights office presses for a ban on computer bulletin board comments that "show hostility toward a person or group based on sex, race or color, including slurs, negative stereotypes, jokes or pranks." In its security checks for government jobs, the FBI takes to asking whether applicants are "free of biases against any class of citizens," whether, for instance, they have told racist jokes or indicated other "prejudices." Joke police! George Orwell, grasping the close relationship of jokes to dissent, said that every joke is a tiny revolution. The purists will have no such rebellions.

The purist campaign reaches, in the end, into the mind itself. In a lecture at the University of New Hampshire, a professor compared writing to sex ("You and the subject become one"); he was suspended and required to apologize, but what was most insidious was the order to undergo university-approved counseling to have his mind straightened out. At the University of Pennsylvania, a law lecturer said, "We have ex-slaves here who should know about the Thirteenth Amendment"; he was banished from campus for a year and required to make a public apology, and he, too, was compelled to attend a "sensitivity and racial awareness" session. Mandatory re-education of alleged bigots is the natural consequence of intellectual purism. Prejudice must be eliminated!

* * * "Nobody escapes," said a Rutgers University report on campus prejudice. Bias and prejudice, it found, cross every conceivable line, from sex to race to politics: "No matter who you are, no matter what the color of your skin, no matter what your gender or sexual orientation, no matter what you believe, no matter how you behave, there is somebody out there who doesn't like people of your kind." Charles Lawrence writes: "Racism is ubiquitous. We are all racists." If he means that most of us think racist thoughts of some sort at one time or another, he is right. If we are going to "eliminate prejudices and biases from our society," then the work of the prejudice police is unending. They are doomed to hunt and hunt and hunt, scour and scour and scour.

What is especially dismaying is that the purists pursue prejudice in the name of protecting minorities. In order to protect people like me (homosexual), they must pursue people like me (dissident). In order to bolster minority self-esteem, they suppress minority opinion. There are, of course, all kinds of practical and legal problems with the purists' campaign: the incursions against the First Amendment; the inevitable abuses by prosecutors and activists who define as "hateful" or "violent" whatever speech they dislike or can score points off of; the lack of any evidence that repressing prejudice eliminates rather than inflames it. But minorities, of all people, ought to remember that by definition we cannot prevail by numbers, and we generally cannot prevail by force. Against the power of ignorant mass opinion and group prejudice and superstition, we have only our voices. If you doubt that minorities' voices are powerful weapons, think of the lengths to which Southern officials went to silence the Reverend Martin Luther King, Jr. (recall that the city commissioner of Montgomery, Alabama, won a $500,000 libel suit, later overturned in *New York Times v. Sullivan* [1964], regarding an advertisement in the *Times* placed by civil-rights leaders who denounced the Montgomery police). Think of how much gay people have improved their lot over twenty-five years simply by refusing to remain silent. Recall the Michigan student who was prosecuted for saying that homosexuality is a treatable disease, and notice that he was black. Under that Michigan speech code, more than twenty blacks were charged with racist speech, while no instance of racist speech by whites was punished. In Florida, the hate-speech law was invoked against a black man who called a policeman a "white cracker"; not so surprisingly, in the first hate-crimes case to reach the Supreme Court, the victim was white and the defendant black.

In the escalating war against "prejudice," the right is already learning to play by the rules that were pioneered by the purist activists of the left. Last year leading Democrats, including the President, criticized the Republican Party for being increasingly in the thrall of the Christian right. Some of the rhetoric was harsh ("fire-breathing Christian radical right"), but it wasn't vicious or even clearly wrong. Never mind: when Democratic Representative Vic Fazio said Republicans were "being forced to the fringes by the aggressive political tactics of the religious right," the chairman of the Republican National Committee, Haley Barbour, said, "Christian-bashing" was "the left's preferred form of religious bigotry." Bigotry! Prejudice! "Christians active in politics are now on the receiving end of an extraordinary campaign of bias and prejudice," said the conservative leader William J. Bennett. One discerns, here, where the new purism leads. Eventually, any criticism of any group will be "prejudice."

DISCUSSION QUESTIONS

1. Do you agree or disagree that some groups need to be protected against offensive or hurtful ideas or speech? How do you define "hurtful" or "offensive"? What is the basis for your position? Where is the First Amendment in this debate?

2. Would a campus newspaper be justified in rejecting a paid advertisement from (a) a group or individual that denied the Holocaust had occurred; (b) a group or individual that argued against any sort of affirmative action; or (c) an environmental group that advocated violence against the property of corporations that polluted the environment? Would you support a "speech code" that prohibited someone from making these arguments on campus? Defend your answer.

Debating the Issues: Corporate and Labor Spending in Campaigns and the First Amendment

The First Amendment says that "Congress shall make no law . . . abridging the freedom of speech." The Supreme Court must define the boundaries of what that broad prohibition means: Does it apply to pornography, commercial speech, or speech that advocates the overthrow of the government or incites violence? Political advertising and campaign spending generate a difficult set of questions. The Court has recognized a government interest in promoting fair elections that are free from corruption, so some regulation of campaign speech is warranted. But the question is where to draw the line between permissible speech and corrupting speech.

Most of you are probably familiar with the saying "Money talks." With the recent Supreme Court decision in *Citizens United v. Federal Election Commission* (FEC), the speaking power of money just got much stronger. In this decision, the Court decided that the First Amendment protects the right of corporations, nonprofit groups, and labor unions to spend directly in political campaigns, rather than having to set up political action committees to run so-called electioneering ads (that specifically call for the election or defeat of a candidate). One controversial aspect of this decision was that corporations, not just individuals, have free-speech rights.

Ronald Dworkin, a law professor at New York University, says the decision "threatens democracy" because it will create "an avalanche of negative political commercials financed by huge corporate wealth." He also is concerned that the decision has "generated open hostilities among the three branches of our government," pointing to comments from President Obama in his 2010 State of the Union message and the subsequent negative reaction from Supreme Court Justices Alito and Roberts. Dworkin argues that this radical a decision cannot be grounded in any theory of the First Amendment, ignored relevant precedent (despite the conservative majority's avowed belief in judicial restraint), and opened American electoral campaigns to influence from foreign corporations. Dworkin concludes with a plea for stronger disclosure laws and public financing for congressional elections.

Bradley Smith, a former chair of the Federal Election Commission, strongly disagrees. He calls the decision a "wonderful affirmation of the primacy of political speech in First Amendment jurisprudence." Furthermore, he says, the impact of the decision is almost certainly overstated: Twenty-eight states already allow corporations to advertise in state elections, and most large corporations are unlikely to start spending huge amounts of money because they prefer lobbying to spending money in elections. Also, the decision empowers not only corporations but also labor unions, which are more likely to want to spend in elections. Though downplaying the radical nature of the decision, Smith clearly indicates (and hopes) that it may be a foot in the door for more significant changes down the road such as allowing unlimited corporate donations to candidates and more corporate spending against "tax and spend, pro-regulatory politicians."

22

"The Decision That Threatens Democracy"

RONALD DWORKIN

No Supreme Court decision in decades has generated such open hostilities among the three branches of our government as has the Court's 5–4 decision in *Citizens United v. FEC* in January 2010. The five conservative justices, on their own initiative, at the request of no party to the suit, declared that corporations and unions have a constitutional right to spend as much as they wish on television election commercials specifically supporting or targeting particular candidates. President Obama immediately denounced the decision as a catastrophe for American democracy and then, in a highly unusual act, repeated his denunciation in his State of the Union address with six of the justices sitting before him.

"With all due deference to separation of powers," he said, "last week the Supreme Court reversed a century of law that I believe will open the floodgates for special interests—including foreign corporations—to spend without limit in our elections." As he spoke one of the conservative justices, Samuel Alito, in an obvious breach of decorum, mouthed a denial, and a short time later Chief Justice John Roberts publicly chastised the President for expressing that opinion on that occasion. The White House press secretary, Robert Gibbs, then explained Obama's remarks: "The President has long been committed to reducing the undue influence of special interests and their lobbyists over government. That is why he spoke out to condemn the decision and is working with Congress on a legislative response." Democrats in Congress have indeed called for a constitutional amendment to repeal the decision and several of them, more realistically, have proposed statutes to mitigate its damage.

The history of the Court's decision is as extraordinary as its reception. At least since 1907, when Congress passed the Tillman Act at the request of President Theodore Roosevelt, it had been accepted by the nation and the Court that corporations, which are only fictitious persons created by law, do not have the same First Amendment rights to political activity as real people do. In 1990, in *Austin v. Michigan Chamber of Commerce*, the Court firmly upheld that principle. In 2002, Congress passed the Bipartisan Campaign Reform Act (BCRA) sponsored by Senators John McCain and Russell Feingold, which forbade corporations to engage in television electioneering for a period of thirty days before a primary for federal office and sixty days before an election. In 2003, in *McConnell v. Federal Election Commission (FEC)*, the Court upheld the constitutionality of that prohibition.

In the 2008 presidential primary season a small corporation, Citizens United, financed to a minor extent by corporate contributions, tried to broadcast a derogatory movie about Hillary Clinton. The FEC declared the broadcast illegal under the BCRA. Citizens United then asked the Supreme Court to declare it exempt from that statute on the ground, among others, that it proposed to broadcast its movie only on a pay-per-view channel. It did not challenge the constitutionality of the act. But the five conservative justices—Chief Justice Roberts and Justices Samuel Alito, Anthony Kennedy, Antonin Scalia, and Clarence Thomas—decided on their own initiative, after a rehearing they themselves called for, that they wanted to declare the act unconstitutional anyway.

They said that the BCRA violated the First Amendment, which declares that Congress shall make no law infringing the freedom of speech. They agreed that their decision was contrary to the *Austin* and *McConnell* precedents; they therefore overruled those decisions as well as repealing a century of American history and tradition. Their decision threatens an avalanche of negative political commercials financed by huge corporate wealth, beginning in this year's midterm elections. Overall these commercials can be expected to benefit Republican candidates and to injure candidates whose records dissatisfy powerful industries. The decision gives corporate lobbyists, already much too influential in our political system, an immensely powerful weapon. It is important to study in some detail a ruling so damaging to democracy.

The First Amendment, like many of the Constitution's most important provisions, is drafted in the abstract language of political morality: it guarantees a "right" of free speech but does not specify the dimensions of that right—whether it includes a right of cigarette manufacturers to advertise their product on television, for instance, or a right of a Ku Klux Klan chapter publicly to insult and defame blacks or Jews, or a right of foreign governments to broadcast political advice in American elections. Decisions on these and a hundred other issues require interpretation and if any justice's interpretation is not to be arbitrary or purely partisan, it must be guided by principle—by some theory of why speech deserves exemption from government regulation in principle. Otherwise the Constitution's language becomes only a meaningless mantra to be incanted whenever a judge wants for any reason to protect some form of communication. Precedent—how the First Amendment has been interpreted and applied by the Supreme Court in the past—must also be respected. But since the meaning of past decisions is also a matter of interpretation, that, too, must be guided by a principled account of the First Amendment's point.

A First Amendment theory is therefore indispensible to responsible adjudication of free speech issues. Many such theories have been offered by justices, lawyers, constitutional scholars, and philosophers, and most of them assign particular importance to the protection of political speech—speech about candidates for public office and about issues that are or might be topics of partisan political debate. But none of these theories—absolutely none of them—justifies the damage the five conservative justices have just inflicted on our politics.

The most popular of these theories appeals to the need for an informed electorate. Freedom of political speech is an essential condition of an effective democracy because it ensures that voters have access to as wide and diverse a range of information and political opinion as possible. Oliver Wendell Holmes Jr., Learned Hand, and other great judges and scholars argued that citizens are more likely to reach good decisions if no ideas, however radical, are censored. But even if that is not so, the basic justification of majoritarian democracy—that it gives power to the informed and settled opinions of the largest number of people—nevertheless requires what Holmes called a "free marketplace of ideas."

Kennedy, who wrote the Court's opinion in *Citizens United* on behalf of the five conservatives, appealed to the "informed electorate" theory. But he offered no reason for supposing that allowing rich corporations to swamp elections with money will in fact produce a better-informed public—and there are many reasons to think it will produce a worse-informed one. Corporations have no ideas of their own. Their ads will promote the opinions of their managers, who could publish or broadcast those opinions on their own or with others of like mind through political action committees (PACs) or other organizations financed through voluntary individual contributions. So though allowing them to use their stockholders' money rather than their own will increase the volume of advertising, it will not add to the diversity of ideas offered to voters.

Corporate advertising will mislead the public, moreover, because its volume will suggest more public support than there actually is for the opinions the ads express. Many of the shareholders who will actually pay for the ads, who in many cases are members of pension and union funds, will hate the opinions they pay to advertise. Obama raised a great deal of money on the Internet, mostly from small contributors, to finance his presidential campaign, and we can expect political parties, candidates, and PACs to tap that source much more effectively in the future. But these contributions are made voluntarily by supporters, not by managers using the money of people who may well be opposed to their opinions. Corporate advertising is misleading in another way as well. It purports to offer opinions about the public interest, but in fact managers are legally required to spend corporate funds only to promote their corporation's own financial interests, which may very well be different.

There is, however, a much more important flaw in the conservative justices' argument. If corporations exercise the power that the Court has now given them, and buy an extremely large share of the television time available for political ads, their electioneering will undermine rather than improve the public's political education. Kennedy declared that speech may not be restricted just to make candidates more equal in their financial resources. But he misunderstood why other nations limit campaign expenditures. This is not just to be fair to all candidates, like requiring a single starting line for runners in a race, but to create the best conditions for the public to make an informed decision when it votes—the main purpose of the First Amendment, according to the marketplace theory. The Supreme Court of Canada understands the difference between these different goals. Creating "a level playing field for those who wish to engage in the electoral discourse," it said, " . . . enables voters to be better informed; no one voice is overwhelmed by another."

Monopolies and near monopolies are just as destructive to the marketplace of ideas as they are to any other market. A public debate about climate change, for instance, would not do much to improve the understanding of its audience if speaking time were auctioned so that energy companies were able to buy vastly more time than academic scientists. The great mass of voters is already very much more aware of electoral advertising spots constantly repeated, like beer ads, in popular dramatic series or major sports telecasts than of opinions reported mainly on public broadcasting news programs. Unlimited corporate advertising will make that distortion much greater.

The difference between the two goals I distinguished—aiming at electoral equality for its own sake and reducing inequality in order to protect the integrity of political debate—is real and important. If a nation capped permissible electoral expenditure at a very low level, it would achieve the greatest possible financial equality. But it would damage the quality of political debate by not permitting enough discussion and by preventing advocates of novel or unfamiliar opinion from spending enough funds to attract any public attention. Delicate judgment is needed to determine how much inequality must be permitted in order to ensure robust debate and an informed population. But allowing corporations to spend their corporate treasure on television ads conspicuously fails that test. Judged from the perspective of this theory of the First Amendment's purpose— that it aims at a better-educated populace—the conservatives' decision is all loss and no gain.

A second popular theory focuses on the importance of free speech not to educate the public at large but to protect the status, dignity, and moral development of individual citizens as equal partners in the political process. Justice John Paul Stevens summarized this theory in the course of his very long but irresistibly powerful dissenting opinion in *Citizens United*. Speaking for himself and Justices Stephen Breyer, Ruth Ginsburg, and Sonia Sotomayor, he said that "one fundamental concern of the First Amendment is to 'protec[t] the individual's interest in self-expression.'" Kennedy tried to appeal to this understanding of the First Amendment to justify free speech for corporations. "By taking the right to speak from some and giving it to others," he stated, "the Government deprives the disadvantaged person or class of the right to use speech to strive to establish worth, standing, and respect for the speaker's voice." But this is bizarre. The interests the First Amendment protects, on this second theory, are only the moral interests of individuals who would suffer frustration and indignity if they were censored. Only real human beings can have those emotions or suffer those insults. Corporations, which are only artificial legal inventions, cannot. The right to vote is surely at least as important a badge of equal citizenship as the right to speak, but not even the conservative justices have suggested that every corporation should have a ballot.

A third widely accepted purpose of the First Amendment lies in its contribution to honesty and transparency in government. If government were free to censor its critics, or to curtail the right to a free press guaranteed in a separate phrase of the First Amendment, then it would be harder for the public to discover official corruption. The Court's *Citizens United* decision does nothing to serve that further purpose. Corporations do not need to run television ads in the run-up to an election urging votes against particular candidates in order to report discoveries they may make about official dishonesty, or in order to defend themselves against any accusation of dishonesty made against them. And of course they have everyone else's access to print and television reporters.

Though the Court's decision will do nothing to deter corruption in that way, it will do a great deal to encourage one particularly dangerous form of it. It will sharply increase the opportunity of corporations to tempt or intimidate congressmen facing reelection campaigns. Obama and Speaker Nancy Pelosi had great difficulty persuading some members of the House of Representatives to vote for the health care reform bill, which finally passed with a dangerously thin majority, because those members feared they were risking their seats in the coming midterm elections. They knew, after the Court's decision, that they might face not just another party and candidate but a tidal wave of negative ads financed by health insurance companies with enormous sums of their shareholders' money to spend.

Kennedy wrote that there is no substantial risk of such corrupting influence so long as corporations do not "coordinate" their electioneering with any candidate's formal campaign. That seems particularly naive. Few congressmen would be unaware of or indifferent to the likelihood of a heavily financed advertising campaign urging voters to vote for him, if he worked in a corporation's interests, or against him if he did not. No coordination—no role of any candidate or his agents in the design of the ads—would be necessary.

Kennedy's naiveté seems even stranger when we notice the very substantial record of undue corporate influence laid before Congress when it adopted the BCRA. Before that act, corporations and other organizations were free to broadcast "issue" ads that did not explicitly endorse or oppose any candidates. The district court judge who first heard the *Citizens United* case found that, according to testimony of lobbyists and political consultants, at least some "Members of Congress are particularly grateful when negative issue advertisements are run by these organizations . . . [that] . . . use issue advocacy as a means to influence various Members of Congress." That influence can be expected to be even greater now that the Court has permitted explicit political endorsements or opposition as well. Kennedy's optimism went further: he denied that heavy corporate spending would lead the public to suspect that form of corruption. But the district court judge had reported that

> 80 percent of Americans polled are of the view that corporations and other organizations that engage in electioneering communications, which benefit specific elected officials, receive special consideration from those officials when matters arise that affect these corporations and organizations.

So the radical decision of the five conservative justices is not only not supported by any plausible First Amendment theory but is condemned by them all. Was their decision nevertheless required by the best reading of past Supreme Court decisions? That seems initially unlikely because, as I said, the decision overruled the two most plainly pertinent such decisions: *Austin* and *McConnell*. Nothing had happened to the country, or through further legislation, that cast any doubt on those decisions. The change that made the difference was simply Justice Sandra Day O'Connor's resignation in 2006 and President George W. Bush's appointment of Alito to replace her.

Overruling these decisions is itself remarkable, particularly for Roberts and Alito, who promised to respect precedent in their Senate confirmation hearings. One of the reasons that Kennedy offered to justify his decision is alarming. He said that since the conservative justices who dissented in those past cases and who remain on the Court had continued to complain about them, the decisions were only weak precedents. "The simple fact that one of our decisions remains controversial," he announced, "is, of course, insufficient to justify overruling it. But it does undermine the precedent's ability to contribute to the stable and orderly development of the law." In other words, if the four more liberal justices who dissented in this case continue to express their dissatisfaction with it, they would be free to overrule it if the balance of the Court shifts again. That novel view would mean the effective end of the doctrine of precedent on the Supreme Court.

* * *

* * * [T]he central issue in *Citizens United* * * * is whether corporations are entitled to the First Amendment protection that individuals and groups of individuals have. We have already noticed a variety of arguments that they do not. Very few individuals have anything like the capital accumulation of any of the Fortune 500 corporations, the smallest of which had revenues of $5 billion (the top of the list—Exxon Mobil—had $443 billion) in 2008. Individuals speak and spend for themselves, together or in association with other individuals, while corporations speak for their commercial interests and spend other people's money, not their own. Individuals have rights, on which their dignity and standing depend, to play a part in the nation's government; corporations do not. No one thinks corporations should vote, and their rights to speak as institutions have been limited for over a century. * * *

* * *

Two Democrats—Senator Charles Schumer of New York and Representative Chris Van Hollen of Maryland—have announced proposals for legislation to protect the country from the Court's ruling. The Court might reject some of their proposals—forbidding corporate advertising by TARP recipients who have not paid back the government's loan, for example—as unconstitutional attempts to ban speech according to the speaker's identity. Kennedy left open the possibility, however, that Congress might constitutionally accept another of their proposals: banning electioneering by corporations controlled by foreigners.

He also explicitly recognized the constitutionality of another of the Democrats' proposals: he said that Congress might require public disclosure of a corporation's expenses for electioneering. (Thomas dissented from that part of Kennedy's ruling.) Congress should require prompt disclosures on the Internet so that the information could be made quickly available to voters. It would be even more important for Congress to provide for ample disclosure within a television advertisement itself. The disclosure should name not only fronting organizations, like Citizens United, but also at least the major corporate contributors to that organization. Congress should also require that any corporation that wished to engage in electioneering obtain at least the annual consent of its stockholders to that activity and to a proposed budget for it, and that the required disclosure in an ad report the percentage of stockholders who have refused that blanket consent. Finally, Congress should require that the CEO of the major corporate contributor to any ad appear in that ad to state that he or she believes that broadcasting it is in the corporation's own financial interests.

The conservative justices might object that such disclosure requirements would unduly burden corporate speech and impermissibly target one type of speaker for special restriction. They might say, to use one of Kennedy's favorite terms, that these requirements would "chill" corporate speech. But we must distinguish measures designed to deter speech from those designed to guard against deception. The in-ad disclosures I describe need not take significantly more broadcast time than the "Stand By My Ad" rule that now requires a candidate to declare in his campaign's ad that he approves it. If several corporations finance an ad together, much of the required information—the amount of shareholder dissent, for instance—could be disclosed as an aggregate figure. If these requirements discourage a corporation's speech not because of the expense but for the different reason that managers are unwilling to report shareholder opposition or to acknowledge their fiduciary duty to act only in the financial interests of their own company, then their fear only shows the pertinence of Kennedy's own claim that "shareholder democracy" is the right remedy to protect shareholders who oppose a corporation's politics.

*   *   *

The Supreme Court's conservative phalanx has demonstrated once again its power and will to reverse America's drive to greater equality and more genuine democracy. It threatens a step-by-step return to a constitutional stone age of right-wing ideology. Once again it offers justifications that are untenable in both constitutional theory and legal precedent. Stevens's remarkable dissent in this case shows how much we will lose when he soon retires. We must hope that Obama nominates a progressive replacement who not only is young enough to endure the bad days ahead but has enough intellectual firepower to help construct a rival and more attractive vision of what our Constitution really means.

23

"*Citizens United* We Stand"

BRADLEY A. SMITH

March 24, 2009, was a turning point in the long-running battle to restrict political speech, aka "campaign finance reform." On that day, the Supreme Court heard oral argument in *Citizens United v. Federal Election Commission*, in which the conservative activist group Citizens United challenged the provisions of the McCain-Feingold law that had prohibited it from airing a documentary film, *Hillary: The Movie*, through video on demand within 30 days of any 2008 Democratic presidential primary.

In the course of the argument, Deputy Solicitor General Malcolm Stewart, an experienced Supreme Court litigator, argued that a 1990 precedent, *Austin v. Michigan Chamber of Commerce*, gave the government the power to limit any political communication funded by a corporation, even a nonprofit such as Citizens United. Justice Samuel Alito asked Stewart if that power would extend to censoring political books published by corporations. Stewart responded—consistent with the government's position at all stages of the case—that yes, it would. There was an audible hush—if such a thing is possible—in the court. Then Justice Alito, appearing to speak for the room, merely said, "I find that pretty incredible."

Incredible or not, that was, and had been for many years, the position of the U.S. government. But until that moment, it seemed to have never quite sunken in with the justices. Americans are willing to accept far more abridgements of free speech than we sometimes like to believe, but the idea of banning books strikes an emotional chord that something described simply as "prohibitions and limits on campaign spending" does not. Americans may not always live up to the Bill of Rights, but Americans do not ban books. A stunned Court eventually asked the parties to reargue the case, to consider whether *Austin* should be overruled.

On reargument last September, Solicitor General Elena Kagan tried to control the damage, arguing that the government never actually had tried to censor books, even as she reaffirmed its claimed authority to do just that. She also stated that "pamphlets," unlike books, were clearly fair game for government censorship. (Former Federal Election Commissioner Hans von Spakovsky has noted that in fact the FEC has conducted lengthy investigations into whether certain books violated campaign finance laws, though it has not yet held that a book publisher violated the law through publication. And the FEC has attempted to penalize publishers of magazines and financial newsletters, only to be frustrated by the courts.) With the endgame of "campaign finance reform" finally laid out plainly, the Supreme Court's decision seemed a foregone conclusion. Sure enough, in January, the Court ruled that corporations, as associations of natural persons, have a right to spend funds from their general treasuries to support or oppose political candidates and causes—including through the publication or distribution of books and movies.

Though this ruling is obviously a correct interpretation of the First Amendment, reaction to the Court's decision in *Citizens United* has been loud, often disingenuous, and in some cases nearly hysterical. President Obama used his State of the Union address to publicly scold the Court, in the process so mischaracterizing the Court's decision that he prompted Judge Alito's now famous, spontaneous rejoinder, "Not true."

Meanwhile, Democrats in Congress and the states have been working overtime to come up with "fixes," ranging from the absurd (a Vermont legislator proposed forcing corporate sponsors to be identified every five seconds during any broadcast ad), to the merely pernicious (such as proposals that seek to immobilize corporate speech by forcing corporations to hold a majority vote of shareholders before each and every expenditure). The fact that virtually all of these proposed "fixes" have been sponsored by Democrats, with the aim of silencing what they perceive to be the pro-Republic voices of the business community, merely illustrates once again the basic problem with campaign finance reform that *Citizens United* sought to alleviate: the desire to manipulate the law for partisan purposes.

Citizens United is at once both a potential game-changer and a decision whose "radicalism" has been widely overstated. Why overstated? Well, to start, one would never guess from the left's hysteria that even prior to *Citizens United*, 28 states, representing roughly 60 percent of the U.S. population, already allowed corporations and unions to make expenditures promoting or opposing candidates for office in state elections; in 26 states, such corporate and union expenditures were unlimited. Moreover, while the first bans on corporate spending were enacted more than a century ago, prior to the 1990 *Austin* decision, the Supreme Court had never upheld a ban, or even a limitation, on independent expenditures supporting or opposing a political candidate. It was the misleading contention that the decision overturned "100 years of law and precedent," that appears to have evoked Justice Alito's "not true" response to the president's State of the Union comments.

The president also stated, again misleadingly, that the decision would open the door for foreign corporations to spend unlimited sums in American elections. In fact, another provision of federal law, not at issue in the case, already prohibits any foreign national, including foreign corporations, from spending money in any federal campaign. FEC regulations, which have the force of the law, further prohibit any foreign national from playing any role in the political spending decisions of any U.S. corporation, political action committee, or association. And the Court specifically stated that *Citizens United* was not addressing these laws at all. So while some states may tweak their state rules in the wake of *Citizens United* to limit the ability of U.S. incorporated and headquartered subsidiaries of foreign corporations to spend money in campaigns, the "foreign corporation" bogeyman is little more than leftist demagoguery.

What is much more alarming than the prospect of U.S. corporations with some foreign ownership participating in campaigns is the fact that the four most liberal justices on the Supreme Court would have upheld the *Austin* precedent, and with it the authority of the federal government to censor books and movies published, produced, or distributed by U.S. corporations. But by affirming the rights of citizens to speak out on political issues, even when organized through the corporate form, the Supreme Court quite rightly put political speech back at the core of the First Amendment.

After four decades in which the Court had given greater First Amendment protection to such activities as topless dancing, simulated child pornography, Internet porn, flag burning, and the transfer of stolen information than to political speech, *Citizens United* is a wonderful reaffirmation of the primacy of political speech in the First Amendment jurisprudence. In that respect, the case has already been a constitutional game-changer. Future litigation is sure to follow, building on the success of *Citizens United* to free up the political system and strike down the still extensive web of regulation that envelops political speech.

Some of these challenges are already well under way. For example, under current federal law, an individual such as George Soros is free to spend $20 million to promote his favored candidates, but if two or more individuals get together to do the same thing, neither can contribute more than $5,000 to the effort. It is hard to see what anti-corruption purpose such a dichotomy serves, and in *SpeechNow.org v. FEC*, argued before the U.S. Court of Appeals for the District of Columbia Circuit in January, plaintiffs argue if it is not corrupting for one person to spend unlimited sums on independent expenditures, it is not corrupting if two or more people combine their resources to promote the candidates of their choice. A decision is expected soon. Expect, too, legal challenges to the federal prohibition on contributions by corporations directly to candidates—if a $2,300 contribution from a corporate CEO or PAC is not corrupting, it is hard to see how a $2,300 contribution directly from a corporate treasury is corrupting.

Much less clear is whether *Citizens United* will be a game-changer in electoral politics. The general consensus is that *Citizens United* favors

Republicans, based on the widely held perception that corporations are more likely to support Republicans than Democrats. But this perception may not be true. Even before *Citizens United*, the federal government and most states also allowed corporations to operate political action committees (PACs), which could then solicit the corporation's managers and shareholders for voluntary contributions to the PAC, which in turn could contribute limited amounts to candidates or make independent expenditures to support candidates. But whereas corporate PACs typically gave about two-thirds of their contributions to Republicans during the 1990s and the first part of the last decade, peaking in the 2004 cycle at nearly 10 to 1 for the GOP, over the past three years corporate PACs have devoted a slim majority of the contributions to Democrats.

More importantly, there is good reason to doubt that *Fortune* 500 companies are going to start making large expenditures in political campaigns. As noted, even before *Citizens United*, 28 states allowed corporate and union spending on state and local political races, yet large-scale corporate spending was very rare in those states. Another sign that corporations are not eager to jump headfirst into political spending comes from the relatively low level of activity by corporate PACs. Among the *Fortune* 500—huge corporations that are all heavily regulated by the government—only about 60 percent actually maintained PACs.

These PACs are subject to extensive regulation, which runs up operating costs to the point that the operating costs of PACs often total more than half of their total revenue. Corporations can, however, pay these operating costs directly from their corporate treasuries. Yet roughly half of these PACs' operating expenses were paid not by the corporations that established them, but out of funds donated to the PACs. In other words, even before *Citizens United*, corporate America could have roughly doubled the amount of money available in their PACs to use for political expenditures simply by paying the administrative and legal costs of operating the PAC from their general treasuries. Yet they did not. And only about 10 percent of PACs contributed the maximum legal amount in any election. All this suggests a lack of interest in political participation.

The truth is, the *Fortune* 500 prefer lobbying to campaigning. Even prior to McCain-Feingold, when corporations could support parties with "soft money," the *Fortune* 500 spent roughly 10 times as much money on lobbying as on political expenditures. As Edward Kangas, former chairman of Deloitte Touche Tohmatsu and of the Committee for Economic Development said in the *New York Times*, explaining his support for McCain-Feingold, "We have lobbyists."

But if large corporations may be reluctant to spend on political races, Big Labor is not. Labor unions also benefit from the *Citizens United* decision, and have historically been much more partisan in their political activity than has big business. The relatively small number of unions makes it easier for them to coordinate their activity. Add in the lack of any need to avoid offending a portion of their customer base, and unions are well positioned to take advantage of *Citizens United*. Indeed, within weeks of the *Citizens United* decision, three unions pledged to spend $1 million each to try to defeat U.S. senator Blanche Lincoln in the Democratic primary in Arkansas, finding her insufficiently dedicated to Big Labor's agenda.

Thus, if *Citizens United* ultimately works to favor conservatives, it may be less due to the *Fortune* 500 than to the small business community. These small and midsized companies usually cannot afford the high administrative costs of maintaining a PAC, and often don't have enough employees eligible for solicitation to make forming a PAC worthwhile in any case. Moreover, unlike *Fortune* 500 companies, small businesses typically do not maintain permanent large lobbying operations in Washington, and because they are less likely to be heavily regulated or engaged in government contracting, their contact with Washington is likely to be more sporadic. For these companies, the ability to speak directly to the public is potentially a great benefit.

This small business community is generally much more conservative in its politics than is the *Fortune* 500, and in particular much more hostile to government regulation. But these small companies are unlikely to undertake major campaigns on their own. Thus it may be up to trade associations and business groups, such as chambers of commerce, to organize business efforts.

Meanwhile, managers and executives, particularly of large, publicly traded companies, will need to do some serious rethinking about their obligations to shareholders. Do they have an obligation to their shareholders to try to maximize long-term value by opposing tax and spend, pro-regulatory politicians, and working to elect officials who appreciate pro-growth policies? Or do they play it safe, avoid political activity, and hope that the regulators will eat them last? The decisions they make may ultimately determine the real importance of *Citizens United*.

Discussion Questions

1. How should the Supreme Court balance the need for elections that are free from corruption and the First Amendment's protection for political speech?

2. Do you agree with Dworkin's argument that none of the five theories of the First Amendment apply to corporate speech? Which of the five would have the strongest basis for justifying a First Amendment protection for corporate speech?

3. Should corporations be treated as people for purposes of political speech? If yes, why isn't it sufficient that the individuals who work

for the corporations can spend their own money independently in elections? If not, why should individuals give up their free speech rights just because they incorporate?

4. Setting aside for now the First Amendment questions, whose arguments about the implications of the decision do you find more compelling? Do you agree with Dworkin, who sees it as a threat to democracy? Or Bradley, who thinks the consequences are exaggerated?

PART II

Institutions

CHAPTER 5

Congress: The First Branch

24

Speech to the Electors of Bristol

EDMUND BURKE

We often hear a politician say that "I vote my conscience" or "I do the right thing" rather than giving in to political expedience or the temporary whims of the voters. We also suspect that such behavior is relatively uncommon, given the desire of most politicians to stay on the good side of the voters and not be booted from office.

The following speech by Edmund Burke is the classic statement of a representative following his or her conscience, even if it means going against constituents' wishes. Indeed, the politician who behaves this way is often called a "Burkean trustee." Burke gave this speech after being elected in 1774 to represent Bristol in the House of Commons. Burke argues for independent judgment, saying, "Your Representative owes you, not his industry only, but his judgement [sic]; and he betrays, instead of serving you, if he sacrifices it to your opinion." He also argues for a general, common good rather than local interests as the proper focus of a representative's efforts. He says, "Parliament is a deliberative Assembly of one Nation, with one Interest, that of the whole; where, not local Purposes, not local Prejudices ought to guide, but the general Good, resulting from the general Reason of the whole. You chuse a Member indeed; but when you have chosen him, he is not Member of Bristol, but he is a Member of Parliament."

Burke practiced what he preached and went against his constituents on several issues involving trade (which were quite important in this port city). However, this approach had its political costs—by 1780 it was clear he would not be reelected. So he decided not to run for reelection in Bristol, but instead accepted a safe seat from his parliamentary patron, Lord Rockingham, which he held until his retirement in 1794.

*Mr. Edmund Burke's Speech to the Electors of Bristol [On his being declared by
the Sheriffs, duly elected one of the Representatives in Parliament for that City,
on Thursday the 3d of November, 1774]*

GENTLEMEN,
    I cannot avoid sympathizing strongly with the feelings of the
Gentleman who has received the same honour that you have conferred
on me. * * *

* * *

But how should I appear to the Voters themselves? If I had gone round
to the citizens intitled to Freedom, and squeezed them by the hand—"Sir,
I humbly beg your Vote—I shall be eternally thankful—may I hope for
the honour of your support?—Well!—come—we shall see you at the
Council-house."—If I were then to deliver them to my managers, pack
them into tallies, vote them off in court, and when I heard from the Bar—
"Such a one only! and such a one for ever!—he's my man!"—"Thank you,
good Sir—Hah! my worthy friend! thank you kindly—that's an honest
fellow—how is your good family?"—Whilst these words were hardly out
of my mouth, if I should have wheeled round at once, and told them—
"Get you gone, you pack of worthless fellows! you have no votes—you
are Usurpers! you are intruders on the rights of real freemen! I will have
nothing to do with you! you ought never to have been produced at this
Election, and the sheriffs ought not to have admitted you to poll."
    Gentlemen, I should make a strange figure, if my conduct had been of
this sort. I am not so old an acquaintance of yours as the worthy Gentleman. Indeed I could not have ventured on such kind of freedoms with
you. But I am bound, and I will endeavour, to have justice done to the
rights of Freemen; even though I should, at the same time, be obliged to
vindicate the former part of my antagonist's conduct against his own
present inclinations.
    I owe myself, in all things, to all the freemen of this city. My particular
friends have a demand on me, that I should not deceive their expectations. Never was cause or man supported with more constancy, more activity, more spirit. I have been supported with a zeal indeed and heartiness
in my friends, which (if their object had been at all proportioned to their
endeavours) could never be sufficiently commended. They supported me
upon the most liberal principles. They wished that the members for Bristol should be chosen for the City, and for their Country at large, and not
for themselves.
    So far they are not disappointed. If I possess nothing else, I am sure I
possess the temper that is fit for your service. I know nothing of Bristol,
but by the favours I have received, and the virtues I have seen exerted
in it.

I shall ever retain, what I now feel, the most perfect and grateful attachment to my friends—and I have no enmities; nor resentment. I never can consider fidelity to engagements, and constancy in friendships, but with the highest approbation; even when those noble qualities are employed against my own pretensions. The Gentleman, who is not fortunate as I have been in this contest, enjoys, in this respect, a consolation full of honour both to himself and to his friends. They have certainly left nothing undone for his service.

As for the trifling petulance, which the rage of party stirs up in little minds, though it should shew itself even in this court, it has not made the slightest impression on me. The highest flight of such clamorous birds is winged in an inferior region of the air. We hear them, and we look upon them, just as you, Gentlemen, when you enjoy the serene air on your lofty rocks, look down upon the Gulls, that skim the mud of your river, when it is exhausted of its tide.

I am sorry I cannot conclude, without saying a word on a topick touched upon by my worthy Colleague. I wish that topick had been passed by; at a time when I have so little leisure to discuss it. But since he has thought proper to throw it out, I owe you a clear explanation of my poor sentiments on that subject.

He tells you, that "the topick of Instructions has occasioned much altercation and uneasiness in this City"; and he expresses himself (if I understand him rightly) in favour of the coercive authority of such instructions.

Certainly, Gentlemen, it ought to be the happiness and glory of a Representative, to live in the strictest union, the closest correspondence, and the most unreserved communication with his constituents. Their wishes ought to have great weight with him; their opinion high respect; their business unremitted attention. It is his duty to sacrifice his repose, his pleasures, his satisfactions, to theirs; and, above all, ever, and in all cases, to prefer their interest to his own. But, his unbiassed opinion, his mature judgement, his enlightened conscience, he ought not to sacrifice to you; to any man, or to any sett of men living. These he does not derive from your pleasure; no, nor from the Law and the Constitution. They are a trust from Providence, for the abuse of which he is deeply answerable. Your Representative owes you, not his industry only, but his judgement; and he betrays, instead of serving you, if he sacrifices it to your opinion.

My worthy Colleague says, his Will ought to be subservient to yours. If that be all, the thing is innocent. If Government were a matter of Will upon any side, yours, without question, ought to be superior. But Government and Legislation are matters of reason and judgement, and not of inclination; and, what sort of reason is that, in which the determination precedes the discussion; in which one sett of men deliberate, and another decide; and where those who form the conclusion are perhaps three hundred miles distant from those who hear the arguments?

To deliver an opinion, is the right of all men; that of Constituents is a weighty and respectable opinion, which a Representative ought always to rejoice to hear; and which he ought always most seriously to consider. But authoritative instructions; Mandates issued, which the Member is bound blindly and implicitly to obey, to vote, and to argue for, though contrary to the clearest conviction of his judgement and conscience; these are things utterly unknown to the laws of this land, and which arise from a fundamental Mistake of the whole order and tenour of our Constitution.

Parliament is not a Congress of Ambassadors from different and hostile interests; which interests each must maintain, as an Agent and Advocate, against other Agents and Advocates; but Parliament is a deliberative Assembly of one Nation, with one Interest, that of the whole; where, not local Purposes, not local Prejudices ought to guide, but the general Good, resulting from the general Reason of the whole. You chuse a Member indeed; but when you have chosen him, he is not Member of Bristol, but he is a Member of Parliament. If the local Constituent should have an Interest, or should form an hasty Opinion, evidently opposite to the real good of the rest of the Community, the Member for that place ought to be as far, as any other, from any endeavour to give it Effect. I beg pardon for saying so much on this subject. I have been unwillingly drawn into it; but I shall ever use a respectful frankness of communication with you. Your faithful friend, your devoted servant, I shall be to the end of my life: A flatterer you do not wish for. On this point of instructions, however, I think it scarcely possible, we ever can have any sort of difference. Perhaps I may give you too much, rather than too little trouble.

From the first hour I was encouraged to court your favour to this happy day of obtaining it, I have never promised you any thing, but humble and persevering endeavours to do my duty. The weight of that duty, I confess, makes me tremble; and whoever well considers what it is, of all things in the world will fly from what has the least likeness to a positive and precipitate engagement. To be a good Member of Parliament, is, let me tell you, no easy task; especially at this time, when there is so strong a disposition to run into the perilous extremes of servile compliance, or wild popularity. To unite circumspection with vigour, is absolutely necessary; but it is extremely difficult. We are now Members for a rich commercial City; this City, however, is but a part of a rich commercial Nation, the Interests of which are various, multiform, and intricate. We are Members for that great Nation, which however is itself but part of a great Empire, extended by our Virtue and our Fortune to the farthest limits of the East and of the West. All these wide-spread Interests must be considered; must be compared; must be reconciled if possible. We are Members for a free Country; and surely we all know, that the machine of a free Constitution is no simple thing; but as intricate and as delicate, as it is valuable. We are Members in a great and ancient Monarchy; and we must preserve religiously, the true legal rights of the Sovereign, which form the Key-stone that binds together the noble and well-constructed Arch of our Empire and our Constitution. A Constitution made up of balanced Powers must ever be a critical thing. As such I mean to touch that part of it which comes within my reach. I know my Inability, and I wish for support from every Quarter. In particular I shall aim at the friendship, and shall cultivate the best Correspondence, of the worthy Colleague you have given me.

I trouble you no farther than once more to thank you all; you, Gentlemen, for your Favours; the Candidates for their temperate and polite behaviour; and the Sheriffs, for a Conduct which may give a Model for all who are in public Stations.

DISCUSSION QUESTIONS

1. Is it possible for members of Congress to act as "Burkean trustees" today? Or would they not survive politically?

2. Can you think of any examples of Burkean "profiles in courage" in which the politician does the right thing, rather than what is politically popular?

3. What do you think of Burke's claim that "he is not Member of Bristol, but he is a Member of Parliament." How would you feel about your member of Congress if he or she took this view?

4. For some issues, would it be better to have a representative who behaved like Burke? For others, would it be better for the representative to listen to the constituents? What would be some examples of each?

25

From *Congress: The Electoral Connection*

David R. Mayhew

Is Edmund Burke right? Are members of Congress motivated by the desire to make good public policy that will best serve the public and national interest? Are they willing to go against their constituents' opinions when they think it is the right thing to do? The political scientist David Mayhew argues the motivation is not so idealistic or complex. Members of Congress simply want to be reelected, and most of their behavior—advertising, credit claiming, and position taking—is designed to make reelection easier. Further, Mayhew argues that the structure of Congress is ideally suited to facilitate the reelection pursuit. Congressional offices and staff advertise member accomplishments, committees allow for the specialization necessary to claim credit for particularistic benefits provided to the district, and the political parties in Congress do not demand loyalty when constituent interests run counter to the party line.

Mayhew's argument is not universally accepted. Many political scientists accept his underlying premise as a given: elected officials are self-interested, and this is manifest in their constant pursuit of reelection. But others disagree with the premise. Motivations, they argue, are far more complex than allowed for by such a simple statement or theory. People often act unselfishly, and members of Congress have been known to vote their consciences even if it means losing an election. Others have pointed out that parties now put stronger constraints on congressional behavior than they did when Mayhew was writing in the early 1970s.

[1.] The organization of Congress meets remarkably well the electoral needs of its members. To put it another way, if a group of planners sat down and tried to design a pair of American national assemblies with the goal of serving members' electoral needs year in and year out, they would be hard pressed to improve on what exists. * * * [2.] Satisfaction of electoral needs requires remarkably little zero-sum conflict among members. That is, one member's gain is not another member's loss; to a remarkable degree members can successfully engage in electorally useful activities without denying other members the opportunity successfully to engage in them. In regard to credit claiming, this second point requires elaboration further on. Its application to advertising is perhaps obvious. The members all have different markets, so that what any one member does is not an inconvenience to any other. There are exceptions here—

House members are sometimes thrown into districts together, senators have to watch the advertising of ambitious House members within their states, and senators from the same state have to keep up with each other—but the case generally holds. With position taking the point is also reasonably clear. As long as congressmen do not attack each other—and they rarely do—any member can champion the most extraordinary causes without inconveniencing any of his colleagues.

* * *

A scrutiny of the basic structural units of Congress will yield evidence to support both these * * * points. First, there are the 535 Capitol Hill *offices*, the small personal empires of the members. * * * The Hill office is a vitally important political unit, part campaign management firm and part political machine. The availability of its staff members for election work in and out of season gives it some of the properties of the former; its case-work capabilities, some of the properties of the latter. And there is the franking privilege for use on office emanations. * * * A final comment on congressional offices is perhaps the most important one: office resources are given to all members regardless of party, seniority, or any other qualification. They come with the job.

Second among the structural units are the *committees*. * * * Committee membership can be electorally useful in a number of different ways. Some committees supply good platforms for position taking. The best example over the years is probably the House Un-American Activities Committee (now the Internal Security Committee), whose members have displayed hardly a trace of an interest in legislation. [Theodore] Lowi has a chart showing numbers of days devoted to HUAC public hearings in Congresses from the Eightieth through the Eighty-ninth. It can be read as a supply chart, showing biennial volume of position taking on subversion and related matters; by inference it can also be read as a measure of popular demand (the peak years were 1949–56). Senator Joseph McCarthy used the Senate Government Operations Committee as his investigative base in the Eighty-third Congress; later on in the 1960s Senators Abraham Ribicoff (D., Conn.) and William Proxmire (D., Wis.) used subcommittees of this same unit in catching public attention respectively on auto safety and defense waste. With membership on the Senate Foreign Relations Committee goes a license to make speeches on foreign policy. Some committees perhaps deserve to be designated "cause committees"; membership on them can confer an ostentatious identification with salient public causes. An example is the House Education and Labor Committee, whose members, in Fenno's analysis, have two "strategic premises": "to prosecute policy partisanship" and "to pursue one's individual policy preferences regardless of party." Committee members do a good deal of churning about on education, poverty, and similar matters. In recent years Education and Labor has attracted media-conscious members such as Shirley Chisholm (D., N.Y.), Herman Badillo (D., N.Y.), and Louise Day Hicks (D., Mass.).

Some committees traffic in particularized benefits.

* * *

Specifically, in giving out particularized benefits where the costs are diffuse (falling on taxpayer or consumer) and where in the long run to reward one congressman is not obviously to deprive others, the members follow a policy of universalism. That is, every member, regardless of party or seniority, has a right to his share of benefits. There is evidence of universalism in the distribution of projects on House Public Works, projects on House Interior, projects on Senate Interior, project money on House Appropriations, project money on Senate Appropriations, tax benefits on House Ways and Means, tax benefits on Senate Finance, and (by inference from the reported data) urban renewal projects on House Banking and Currency. The House Interior Committee, in Fenno's account, "takes as its major decision rule a determination to process and pass *all* requests and to do so in such a way as to maximize the chances of passage in the House. Succinctly, then, Interior's major strategic premise is: *to secure House passage of all constituency-supported, Member-sponsored bills.*"

* * *

Particularism also has its position-taking side. On occasion members capture public attention by denouncing the allocation process itself; thus in 1972 a number of liberals held up some Ways and Means "members' bills" on the House floor. But such efforts have little or no effect. Senator Douglas used to offer floor amendments to excise projects from public works appropriations bills, but he had a hard time even getting the Senate to vote on them.

Finally, and very importantly, the committee system aids congressmen simply by allowing a division of labor among members. The parceling out of legislation among small groups of congressmen by subject area has two effects. First, it creates small voting bodies in which membership may be valuable. An attentive interest group will prize more highly the favorable issue positions of members of committees pondering its fortunes than the favorable positions of the general run of congressmen. Second, it creates specialized small-group settings in which individual congressmen can make things happen and be perceived to make things happen. "I put that bill through committee." "That was my amendment." "I talked them around on that." This is the language of credit claiming. It comes easily in the committee setting and also when "expert" committee members handle bills on the floor. To attentive audiences it can be believable. Some political actors follow committee activities closely and mobilize electoral resources to support deserving members.

* * *

The other basic structural units in Congress are the *parties*. The case here will be that the parties, like the offices and committees, are tailored to suit members' electoral needs. They are more useful for what they are not than for what they are.

* * *

What is important to each congressman, and vitally so, is that he be free to take positions that serve his advantage. There is no member of either house who would not be politically injured—or at least who would not think he would be injured—by being made to toe a party line on all policies (unless of course he could determine the line). There is no congressional bloc whose members have identical position needs across all issues. Thus on the school busing issue in the Ninety-second Congress, it was vital to Detroit white liberal Democratic House members that they be free to vote one way and to Detroit black liberal Democrats that they be free to vote the other. In regard to these member needs the best service a party can supply to its congressmen is a negative one; it can leave them alone. And this in general is what the congressional parties do. Party leaders are chosen not to be program salesmen or vote mobilizers, but to be brokers, favor-doers, agenda-setters, and protectors of established institutional routines. Party "pressure" to vote one way or another is minimal. Party "whipping" hardly deserves the name. Leaders in both houses have a habit of counseling members to "vote their constituencies."

DISCUSSION QUESTIONS

1. If members are motivated by the desire to be reelected, is this such a bad thing? After all, shouldn't members of Congress do things that will keep the voters happy? Does the constant quest for reelection have a positive or negative impact on "representation"?

2. How could the institutions of Congress (members' offices, committees, and parties) be changed so that the collective needs of the institution would take precedence over the needs of individual members? Would there be any negative consequences for making these changes?

3. Some have argued that term limits are needed to break the never-ending quest for reelection. Do you think that term limits for members of Congress are a good idea?

26

"Too Much of a Good Thing: More Representative Is Not Necessarily Better"

John R. Hibbing and Elizabeth Theiss-Morse

David Mayhew describes an institution that should be highly responsive to voters. If members of Congress want to get reelected, they need to do what their constituents want them to do. However, John Hibbing and Elizabeth Theiss-Morse argue that having institutions that are too representative may be "too much of a good thing." That is, it may not be in the nation's interest to always do what the public wants, especially when it comes to issues of institutional reform. On questions of reform, the public is usually convinced that the only thing preventing ideal policies is that the "people in power" are serving their own interests rather than the public's interests. According to this view, the obvious—but wrong according to Hibbing and Theiss-Morse—solution is to weaken political institutions through "reforms" such as term limits, reducing the salaries of members of Congress, and requiring Congress to balance the federal budget every year. Hibbing and Theiss-Morse argue that these reforms might make people even more disillusioned when they discover that weakening Congress will not solve our nation's problems.

The authors also argue that the public generally does not have a very realistic understanding of the inherent nature of conflict in the political process. The public believes that there is substantial consensus on most issues and that only small "fringe" groups disagree on a broad range of issues. If this were true, why people are frustrated with Congress would certainly be understandable. But in reality, as the authors point out, the nation is deeply divided about the proper course of action. This makes conflict and compromise an inherent part of the legislative process and, at the same time, dims the prospects for simple reforms.

Reform sentiments are much in evidence on the American political scene as we approach the end of the [twentieth] century, and improving the way public opinion is represented in political institutions is often the major motivation of reformers. This is clear * * * from the activities of contemporary political elites, and from the mood of ordinary people. Gross dissatisfaction exists with the nature of representation perceived to be offered by the modern political system. People believe the political

process has been commandeered by narrow special interests and by political parties whose sole aim is to contradict the other political party.
Given the centrality of representation in the U.S. polity, the organizers
and contributors to this symposium are to be commended. It is laudable
to want to consider ways of improving the system and, thereby, making
people happier with their government. Many of the ideas described in
the accompanying essays have considerable merit.

We do, however, wish to raise two important cautions: one briefly and
the second in greater detail. Perhaps these cautions are not needed; the
authors of the accompanying pieces are almost certainly aware of them.
Still, general debate often neglects these two points. Therefore, quite apart
from whether it is a good idea or a bad idea, say, to reform campaign finance, enact term limits, or move toward proportional representation and
away from single-member districts, it is important * * * to keep in mind
that 1) "because the people want them" is not a good justification for
adopting procedural reforms and 2) actual enactment of the reforms
craved by the people will not necessarily leave us with a system that is
more liked even by the people who asked for the reforms in the first
place. We take each point in turn.

Ignoring the People's Voice on Process Matters Is Not Evil

It would be easy at this point to slip into a discussion of the political acumen possessed by the American public and, relatedly, of the extent to
which elected officials and political institutions should listen to the people. But such a discussion has been going on at least since the time of
Plato and it is unlikely we would add much to it here. Instead, we merely
wish to point out that, whatever the overall talents of the rank and file,
political change in the realm of process should *not* be as sensitive to the
public's wishes as political change in the realm of policy.

It is one thing to maintain that in a democracy the people should get
welfare reform if they want it. It is quite another to maintain that those
same people should get term limits if they want them. Process needs to
have some relative permanence, some "stickiness." This is the *definiens* of
institutional processes. Without this trait, policy legitimacy would be
compromised. The U.S. Constitution (like all constitutions) drives home
this contention by including much on process (vetoes, impeachments,
representational arrangements, terms of officials, minimum qualifications
for holding particular offices, etc.) and precious little about policy. What
policy proclamations *are* to be found in the Constitution have faced a
strong likelihood of being reversed in subsequent actions (slavery and
the 13th Amendment; tax policy and the 16th Amendment; prohibition
and the 21st Amendment). Constitutions are written not to enshrine policy but to enshrine a system that will then make policy. These systemic
structures should not be subjected lightly to popular whimsy.

The Framers took great efforts to insulate processes from the momentary fancies of the people; specifically, they made amending the Constitution difficult. It is not unusual for reformers, therefore, to run up against the Constitution and its main interpreters—the courts. Witness recent decisions undermining the ability of citizens to impose legislative term limits on members of Congress save by constitutional amendment. This uphill battle to enact procedural reform is precisely what the founders intended—and they were wise to do so.

It may be that the people's will should be reflected directly in public policy, perhaps through initiatives or, less drastically, through the actions of citizen-legislators who act as delegates rather than Burkean trustees. But this does not mean that the rules of the system themselves should change with public preferences in the same way health care policy should change with public preferences.

There may be many good reasons to change the processes of government—possibly by making government more representative—but a persuasive defense of process reforms is *not* embedded in the claim that the people are desirous of such reform. Just as the Bill of Rights does not permit a simple majority of the people to make decisions that will restrict basic rights, so the rest of the Constitution does not permit a simple majority of the people to alter willy-nilly the processes of government. There are good reasons for such arrangements.

Be Careful What You Wish For

One important reason we should be glad ordinary people are not in a position to leave their every mark on questions of political process and institutional design is the very good possibility that people will not be happy with the reforms they themselves advocate. The people generally clamor for reforms that would weaken institutions and strengthen the role of the people themselves in policy decisions. They advocate people's courts, an increased number of popular initiatives and referenda, devolution of authority to institutions "closer" to the people, term limits, staff cuts, emaciating the bureaucracy, elimination of committees, cessation of contact between interest groups and elected officials, and a weakening of political parties. These changes would clear the way for people to have greater influence on decisions, and this is what the people want, right?

Actually, our research suggests this is *not* what the people really want. The public does not desire direct democracy; it is not even clear that people desire democracy at all, although they are quite convinced they do. People want no part of a national direct democracy in which they would be asked to register their preferences, probably electronically, on important issues of the day. Proposals for such procedures are received warmly by a very small minority of citizens. Observers who notice the public's enthusiasm for virtually every populist notion sometimes go the next step of assuming the public wants direct democracy. This is simply an inaccurate assumption.

However, the public *does* want institutions to be transformed into something much closer to the people. The public sees a big disconnect between how they want representation to work and how they believe it is working. Strong support of populist government (not direct democracy) has been detected in innumerable polls conducted during the last couple of decades. That the public looks favorably upon this process agenda is beyond dispute. A national survey we conducted in 1992 found strong support for reforms that would limit the impact of the Washington scene on members of Congress. For example, seven out of 10 respondents supported a reduction in congressional salaries, eight out of 10 supported term limitations, and nine out of 10 supported a balanced-budget amendment. What ties these reforms together is the public's desire to make elected officials more like ordinary people. In focus groups we conducted at the same time as the survey, participants stated many times that elected officials in Washington had lost touch with the people. They supported reforms believed to encourage officials to start keeping in touch. Elected officials should balance the budget just like the people back home. Elected officials should live off modest salaries just like the people back home. And elected officials should face the prospect of getting a real job back home rather than staying in Washington for years and years. These reforms would force elected officials to understand the needs of their constituents rather than get swept up in the money and power that run Washington.

If these reforms were put into place, would the public suddenly love Congress? We do not think so. Certain reforms, such as campaign finance reform, may help, since they would diminish the perception that money rules politics in Washington. But the main reason the public is disgruntled with Congress and with politics in Washington is because they are dissatisfied with the processes intrinsic to the operation of a democratic political system—debates, compromises, conflicting information, inefficiency, and slowness. This argument may seem odd on its face, so in the next few paragraphs we provide our interpretation of why the public questions the need for democratic processes.

The public operates under the erroneous assumption that the majority of the American people agrees on policy matters. In focus groups we conducted in 1997, participants adamantly stated that "80 percent of the American people agree on what needs to be done [about serious societal problems], but it's the other 20 percent who have the power." This pervasive and persistent belief in the existence of popular consensus on tough policy issues is, of course, grossly mistaken. Virtually every well-worded survey question dealing with salient policy issues of the day reveals deep divisions in the American public. From welfare reform to health care; from remaining in Bosnia to the taxes-services trade-off; from a constitutional amendment on flag desecration to the situations in which abortion is believed to be properly permitted, the people are at odds with each other.

This level of popular disagreement would be quite unremarkable except for the fact that the people will not admit that the disagreement actually exists. Instead, people project their own particular views, however ill-formed, onto a clear majority of other "real" people. Those (allegedly) few people who allow it to be known that they do not hold these views are dismissed as radical and noisy fringe elements that are accorded far too much influence by polemical parties, self-serving special interests, and spineless, out-of-touch elected officials. Thus, the desire to move the locus of decision making closer to the people is based on a faulty assumption right off the bat. Many believe that if decisions emanated from the people themselves, we would get a welcome break from the fractious politics created by politicians and institutions. Pastoral, common-sensical solutions will instead quietly begin to find their way into the statute books. The artificial conflict to which we have unfortunately become accustomed will be no more and we can then begin to solve problems.

Given people's widespread belief in popular consensus, it is no wonder they despise the existing structure of governmental institutions. All that these institutions—and the people filling them—do is obscure the will of the people by making it look as though there is a great deal of divisiveness afoot. Who then can condone debate and compromise among elected officials if these processes only give disproportionate weight to nefarious fringe elements that are intent upon subverting the desires of healthy, red-blooded Americans? Who then can condone inefficiency and slowness when we all agree on what needs to be done and politicians ought just to do it? Democratic processes merely get in the way. People react positively to the idea that we ought to run government like a business—it would be efficient, frugal, and quick to respond to problems. Of course, what people tend not to realize is that it would also be undemocratic.

Too many people do not understand political conflict: they have not been taught to deal with it; they have not come to realize it is a natural part of a culture such as ours. When they are confronted with it, they conclude it is an indication something is woefully amiss and in need of correction. They jump at any solution perceived to have the potential of reducing conflict; solutions such as giving authority over to potentially autocratic and hierarchical business-like arrangements or to mythically consensual ordinary people.

Our fear is that, if the people were actually given what they want, they might soon be even more disillusioned with the political system than ever. Suppose people *were* made to feel more represented than they are now; suppose authority *were* really pushed toward the common person. The first thing people would learn is that these changes will have done nothing to eliminate political conflict. The deep policy divisions that polls now reveal among the citizenry would be of more consequence since these very views would now be more determinative of public policy. Conflict would still be pervasive. Popular discontent would not have been ameliorated. Quite likely, people would quickly grow ever more cynical about the potential for reform to accomplish what they want it to accomplish.

Instead of allowing the people to strive for the impossible—an open and inclusive democracy that is devoid of conflict—we need to educate the people about the unrealistic nature of their desires. Instead of giving the people every reform for which they agitate, we need to get them to see where their wishes, if granted, are likely to lead them. The people pay lip service to democracy but that is the extent of it. They claim to love democracy more than life itself, but they only love the concept. They do not love the actual practice of democracy because it suggests differences, because it is ponderous, because it revolves around debate (bickering) and compromise (selling out) and divisions (gridlock).

Conclusion

We hasten to point out that we are not opposed to reforms. For what it is worth, we believe the United States polity could certainly benefit from selective modifications to current institutional arrangements. But we *are* opposed to the tendency of many ordinary people to try to enact reforms intended to weaken political institutions even though these same people evince no real plan describing where that power should be transferred. It is often assumed that the people are populists and that they therefore want power in their own hands. As we have indicated, they do not in actuality want power. They only want to know that they could have this power if they wanted it. They only want to know that this power is not being exercised by those who are in a position to use it to their own advantage. They only want decisions to be made nonconflictually. And they are willing to entertain a variety of possible structures (some far from democratic) if those reforms appear to offer hope of bringing about all these somewhat contradictory desires.

Altering representational arrangements should be considered. The current system can and must be improved. The campaign finance system is an embarrassment and the dispute over drawing oddly-shaped districts for the purpose of obtaining majority-minority districts lays bare the very real problems of single member districts. But we should not jump to enact all reforms simply because people think they want them. No one said that in a democracy the people would get to shape processes however they wanted. It is not inconsistent to have democratic governmental structures that are themselves rather impervious to popular sentiments for change in those procedures. What makes the system democratic is the ability of people to influence policy, not the ability of people to influence process.

This is fortunate because the people's ideas about process are fundamentally flawed. People (understandably) think well of the American public writ large, and people (understandably) dislike conflict, so people (nonsensically) assume the two cannot go together in spite of the impressive array of factual evidence indicating that conflict and the American people—indeed any free people, as Madison so eloquently related in *Federalist* 10—go hand in hand. As a result of their misconception, the people will undoubtedly be quite dissatisfied with the actual consequences of most attempts to expand representation via campaign finance reform, term limits, or proportional representation. There may be good reasons to enact such reforms, but, we submit, neither a public likely to be suddenly pleased with the post-reform political system nor a public that is somehow deserving of a direct voice in process reform is one of them.

DISCUSSION QUESTIONS

1. In one of the more provocative claims in their article, Hibbing and Theiss-Morse say, "The public does not desire direct democracy; it is not even clear that people desire democracy at all, although they are quite convinced they do." Do you agree? What evidence do they provide to support this claim?

2. If the public had a more complex understanding of the political process, what types of reforms would it favor?

3. Is it possible to have a political system that is too responsive?

Debating the Issues: Pork-Barrel Politics

In an era of enormous budget deficits, federal spending is under intense scrutiny. One type of spending—"pork-barrel" policies that are targeted to a specific district or project—is especially controversial because it raises questions about the capacity of Congress to deal effectively with national problems and priorities. However, the debate over pork-barrel politics illustrates the difficulties of defining national interests as opposed to parochial, or local, interests and the role of Congress in policy making.

Pork may take many forms. The most common legislative vehicle for distributing pork is the "earmark," which identifies specific, targeted spending, usually as part of a larger bill. Transportation bills and water projects are two of the traditional outlets for pork-barrel spending, but in recent years even bills funding the war against terrorism, homeland security, and the wars in Iraq and Afghanistan have been full of pork. For example, charges of wasteful spending have been made concerning the rebuilding of Iraq as contractors received "no-bid" contracts for securing and restoring oil fields, among other lucrative projects.

The Cato Institute is a libertarian think tank that is highly critical of wasteful government spending. The selection from the Cato Handbook provides a general example of how special interests win over the general interests, specific instances of pork in recent years (including grants for the Shedd Aquarium in Chicago and the Rock and Roll Hall of Fame in Cleveland), and the broader implications of pork for the policy-making process. Cato's overall critique of pork is that the American taxpayer should not be funding these programs. Rather, the private sector should provide funding (if any). Pork contributes to the ballooning federal deficit and debt and is the "currency of corruption." The selection ends with a call for more transparency in pork spending and its eventual elimination.

Where Cato sees waste and abuse of the nation's resources, however, James Inhofe, a Republican senator from Oklahoma, and Jonathan Rauch see many positive virtues. In an interview with Brian Friel, Inhofe characterizes earmark reform as a phony issue. Inhofe sees earmarks as maintaining Congress's control over spending. Otherwise, the power to decide which projects get funded would shift to unelected bureaucrats. Also, Inhofe argues that national interests can be served by allowing local interests to dip into the pork barrel. Although Inhofe has vowed to fight any ban on earmarks, one possible area of common ground between him and earmark reformers would be limiting earmarks to spending that has been authorized by a congressional committee (rather than just tacked on to a spending bill).

Rauch agrees that the power of the purse should remain with

Congress rather than the executive branch, but also points out that a recent bill that was criticized as being "full of pork" had less than 2 percent of the offending spending. (Overall, pork accounts for less than 1 percent of federal spending.) Furthermore, much of the accountability and transparency Cato calls for is already in place: it isn't that easy to get an earmark, and earmark sponsors are made public. Other supporters of pork have called it the "glue" of legislating. If it takes a little pork for the home district or state to get important legislation through Congress, so be it. Also, one person's pork could be another person's essential spending. Members of Congress are best able to determine that need.

27

"Corporate Welfare and Earmarks," from *Cato Handbook for Policymakers*

When considering budget issues, federal policymakers are supposed to have the broad public interest in mind. Unfortunately, that is not how the federal budget process usually works in practice. Many federal programs are sustained by special-interest groups working with policymakers seeking narrow benefits at the expense of taxpayers and the general public.

* * *

How can special interests regularly triumph over the broad public interest in our democracy? For one thing, recipients of federal handouts have a strong incentive to create organizations to lobby Congress to keep the federal gravy train flowing. By contrast, average citizens have no strong incentive to lobby against any particular subsidy program because each program costs just a small portion of their total tax bill.

When average citizens do speak out against particular programs, they are usually outgunned by the professionals who are paid to support programs. Those professionals have an informational advantage over citizens because the workings of most federal programs are complex. The lobby groups that defend subsidy programs are staffed by top program experts, and they are skilled at generating media support. One typical gambit is to cloak the narrow private interests of subsidy recipients in public interest clothing, and proclaim that the nation's future depends on increased funding.

TABLE 1
Majority Voting Does Not Ensure That a Project's
Benefits Outweigh Costs

Legislator	Vote	Benefits Received by Constituents	Taxes Paid by Constituents
Clinton	Yea	$12	$10
Cochran	Yea	$12	$10
Collins	Yea	$12	$10
Carper	Nay	$2	$10
Coburn	Nay	$2	$10
Total	Pass	$40	$50

Another reason it is hard to challenge spending programs is that lobby groups, congressional supporters, and federal agencies rarely admit that any program is a failure. Washington insiders become vested in the continued funding of programs because their careers, pride, and reputations are on the line, and they will battle against any cuts or reforms.

How do dubious spending programs get enacted in the first place? Table 1 shows how Congress can pass special-interest legislation in which the costs outweigh the benefits. The table assumes that legislators vote in the narrow interest of their districts. The hypothetical project shown creates benefits of $40 and costs taxpayers $50, and is thus a loser for the nation. Nonetheless, the project gains a majority vote. The program's benefits are more concentrated than its costs, and that is the key to gaining political support.

The pro-spending bias of Congress is strengthened by the complex web of vote trading, or logrolling, that often occurs. Table 2 shows that

TABLE 2
Logrolling Allows Passage of Subsidies That Benefit Minorities
of Constituents

Legislator	Project A		Project B		Vote on a Bill Including Projects A and B
	Benefits Received by Constituents	Taxes Paid by Constituents	Benefits Received by Constituents	Taxes Paid by Constituents	
Clinton	$15	$10	$8	$10	Yea
Cochran	$15	$10	$8	$10	Yea
Collins	$4	$10	$20	$10	Yea
Carper	$3	$10	$2	$10	Nay
Coburn	$3	$10	$2	$10	Nay
Total	$40	$50	$40	$50	Pass

because of logrolling, projects that are net losers to society can pass even if they do not have majority support. Because Projects A and B would fail with stand alone votes, Clinton, Cochran, and Collins enter an agreement to mutually support the two projects. That is, they logroll. The result is that the two projects get approved, even though each imposes net costs on society and benefits only a minority of voters.

The popularity of logrolling means that programs that make no economic sense and have only minimal public support are enacted all the time.

* * *

Earmarks

The federal budget practice of "earmarking" has exploded during the last 15 years. Earmarks are line items in spending bills inserted by legislators for specific projects in their home states. Some infamous earmarks funded a $50 million indoor rain forest in Iowa and a $223 million "bridge to nowhere" in Alaska. Earmarks can provide recipients with federal grant money, contracts, loans, or other types of benefits. Earmarks are often referred to as "pork" spending.

* * * [T]he number of pork projects increased from fewer than 2,000 annually in the mid-1990s to almost 14,000 in 2005. Various scandals and the switch to Democratic control of Congress then slowed the pace of earmarking for a couple of years. But earmarking is on the rise again. The fiscal year 2008 omnibus appropriations bill was bloated with 11,610 spending projects inserted by members of Congress for their states and districts.

Earmarked projects are generally those that have not been requested by the president and have not been subject to expert review or competitive bidding. Thus, if the government had $1 billion to spend on bioterrorism research, it might be earmarked to go to laboratories in the districts of important politicians, rather than to labs chosen by a panel of scientists. Earmarking has soared in most areas of the budget, including defense, education, housing, scientific research, and transportation.

The main problem with earmarking is that most spending projects chosen by earmark are properly the responsibility of state and local governments or the private sector, not the federal government. The rise in earmarks is one manifestation of Congress's growing intrusion into state affairs, . . . Consider these earmarks from the FY08 omnibus appropriations bill:

1. $1,648,850 for the private Shedd Aquarium in Chicago, which is also awash with corporate funding;
2. $787,200 for "green design" changes at the Museum of Natural History in Minneapolis;

3. $492,000 for the Rocky Flats Cold War Museum in Arvada, Colorado;
4. $1,950,000 for a library and archives at the Charles B. Rangel Center for Public Service at the City College of New York;
5. $2,400,000 for renovations to Haddad Riverfront Park in Charleston;
6. $500,000 for upgrades to Barracks Row, a swank Capitol Hill neighborhood;
7. $742,764 for fruit fly research, partly conducted in France;
8. $188,000 for the Lobster Institute in Maine; and
9. $492,000 for fuel cell research for Rolls-Royce Group of Canton, Ohio.

Projects 1 to 3 give taxpayer money to groups that should be funding their own activities from admissions fees and charitable contributions. Interestingly, the nonprofit Shedd Aquarium has spent hundreds of thousands of dollars on lobbyists to secure federal earmarks, and its chief executive earned a huge $600,000 salary in 2006. Or consider that the Rock and Roll Hall of Fame in Cleveland has received federal grants, even though there are thousands of music industry millionaires who should be footing the bill.

Projects 4 to 6 are examples of items that state and local governments should fund locally. Unfortunately, state and local officials are increasingly asking Washington for handouts, and lobby groups such as Cassidy and Associates are helping them "mine" the federal budget for grants.

Projects 7 to 9 fund activities that should be left to the private sector. Industries should fund their own research, which is likely to be more cost-effective than government efforts. Besides, successful research leads to higher profits for private businesses, and it makes no sense for taxpayers to foot the bill for such private gains.

Earmarks' Erosion of Fiscal Responsibility

Defenders of earmarks argue that they are no big deal since they represent just a small share of overall federal spending. The problem is that earmarking has contributed to the general erosion in fiscal responsibility in Washington. Earmarks have exacerbated the parochial mindset of most members, who spend their time appeasing state and local interest groups rather than tackling issues of broad national concern. Many politicians complain about the soaring federal deficit, yet their own staff members spend most of their time trying to secure earmarks in spending bills.

The rise in earmarking has encouraged a general spendthrift attitude in Congress. Why should rank-and-file members restrain themselves when their own leaders are usually big recipients of pork? Sen. Tom Coburn (R-OK) is right that the problem with earmarks is "the hidden cost of perpetuating a culture of fiscal irresponsibility. When politicians fund pork projects they sacrifice the authority to seek cuts in any other program." Similarly, Rep. Jeff Flake (R-AZ) concludes that "earmarking . . . has become the currency of corruption in Congress. . . . Earmarks are used as inducements to get members to sign on to large spending measures."

Reforms to Increase Transparency and Downsize the Government

A first step toward eliminating earmarks, corporate welfare, and other special-interest spending is to further increase transparency in the congressional and agency spending processes. Under pressure from reformers, the government has set up a searchable database of federal grants and contracts at www.usaspending.gov. A second step is for citizens to use this website and other tools to research federal spending, and then to call their members of Congress and tell them what programs should be cut.

Citizens should also ask their members to support reforms to the budget process. One idea for cutting corporate welfare is to set up a commission akin to the successful military base–closing commissions of the 1990s. It would draw up a list of current subsidies and present it to Congress, which would vote on the cuts as a package without amendment. To make the package a political winner, all budget savings would go toward immediate tax cuts for families.

Ultimately, earmarking and corporate welfare should be abolished, and spending on activities that are legitimate federal functions should be determined by a system of competitive bidding and expert review. Of course, it will not be easy to reform the spending practices of Congress. Members often feel committed to expanding spending in their districts and on their favored programs. But taxpayers fund all those programs, and they need to do a better job of convincing their members to cut unneeded programs and pass much leaner federal budgets.

—Prepared by Chris Edwards and Jeff Patch

28

"Inhofe: Earmarks Are Good for Us"

Brian Friel

Sen. James Inhofe, R-Okla., the ranking member on the Senate Environment and Public Works Committee, spent the past eight years battling liberals over climate change and arguing that predictions of catastrophic global warming are a "hoax." Now Inhofe is taking on what he describes as another "phony" issue—earmark reform. But this crusade puts him at odds with fellow conservatives in his own party.

In recent years, taxpayer watchdog groups and anti-pork-barrel lawmakers—including Sens. John McCain, R-Ariz.; Jim DeMint, R-S.C.; and Inhofe's home-state colleague and fellow Republican, Tom Coburn—have turned earmarks into a dirty word. They contend that lawmakers' longstanding practice of earmarking funding for pet projects promotes waste, big spending, and corruption. The Senate foes regularly offer floor amendments attempting to strip earmarks from legislation.

Inhofe, who ranked as the most conservative senator in *National Journal*'s 2009 vote ratings, launched a campaign this week to recast earmarks as a tool that conservatives should embrace, not deride. He noted that most people took global warming as a fact eight years ago, and he contended that he has effectively shown that it is not. His earmark battle is aimed at showing that what everyone believes about earmarks is also untrue, he said.

"They're winning on the phrase," Inhofe said of anti-earmarkers, in an interview. "It's fraudulent."

Elected to the House in 1986 and to the Senate in 1994, Inhofe says that his efforts on global warming ultimately led to the recent demise of cap-and-trade climate-change legislation. To environmentalists and many congressional Democrats, he is a villain. Dan Lashof, the climate center director of the Natural Resources Defense Council, calls Inhofe "the Senate's chief spokesman for climate deniers." But the Oklahoman has become a star in conservative circles for his outspoken and often lonely fight on the issue.

Armed with those bona fides, Inhofe is planning to take his pro-earmark campaign to rank-and-file conservatives. He said he was inspired, in part, by a column that Jonathan Rauch wrote in this magazine. . . . Inhofe is slated to speak to a "tea party" group in Jacksonville, Fla., later this month, where he expects to test-drive his message. He has drafted an op-ed outlining his views on the "phony issue of earmarks." He also hopes to convince conservative talk-radio hosts that their frequent earmark-bashing misses the more important goal: reducing overall spending to ensure greater fiscal responsibility in Washington.

"You don't save anything by cutting earmarks," Inhofe said. He maintained that eliminating lawmakers' earmarks doesn't shrink the overall budget; it just leaves it to federal agencies—currently controlled by the Democratic Obama administration—to decide how to distribute the money. "These nonelected bureaucrats are the ones who are making the decisions."

As an example, Inhofe pointed to a transportation program that pays for low-budget initiatives such as bike trails, streetscapes, and congestion mitigation. In 2008, Congress distributed the millions of dollars in program funding through earmarks that boosted 102 projects in 35 states. The year before, when no earmarks were permitted, the Transportation Department funded projects through a grant competition in just five big cities—Miami, Minneapolis-St. Paul, New York City, San Francisco, and Seattle.

Inhofe argues that earmarks have funded many programs that conservatives support, particularly in national defense. As the second-ranking Republican on the Armed Services Committee, behind McCain, Inhofe notes that Congress has used earmarks to keep several military programs chugging along despite executive branch objections, including additional C-17 cargo planes that President Obama fought against last year. McCain offered an amendment to the Defense appropriations bill that would have nixed the funds for the extra planes, but Inhofe and 63 other senators defeated it.

Instead of imposing an earmark moratorium, Inhofe proposes a freeze in nonsecurity appropriations at fiscal 2008 levels, a move that he says would save $600 billion more than Obama's proposal in February to freeze such spending at fiscal 2010 levels. He also maintains that individual projects should be assessed on their merits, not on whether they are deemed to be earmarks.

Opponents counter, though, that earmarked congressional projects have become a symbol of what is wrong with Washington.

"I think there is a justifiable argument for earmarks, that we as legislators probably know better in some instances than bureaucrats in Washington about how money should be spent," Sen. George LeMieux, R-Fla., conceded. "But earmarks are, unfortunately, the engine that drives the train that gets us into these huge spending problems. If I put an earmark in a particular appropriations bill, and then that appropriations bill is 15 percent more than it was last year, and I say I can't support that, they'll say, well, your earmark is in there. So the earmark is what buys you into bigger spending."

"Railing against earmarks helps those who vote for the billion-dollar spending bills seem more conservative than they really are."
—James Inhofe

While not naming names, Inhofe argues that some Republican senators use their anti-earmark credentials as a fig leaf to cover their votes to authorize massive spending programs. As examples, he cited the $700 billion bank bailout in October 2008; the Fannie Mae and Freddie Mac takeover in July 2008; and a bill the same month to increase funding for HIV/AIDS programs in Africa from $15 billion to $50 billion.

"If you look at those three things, you're well over a trillion dollars," he said. "And you look at the Republicans who voted for them. They've been able to use earmarks to distract people."

DeMint voted with Inhofe against all three measures. McCain voted for the bank bailout; and Coburn voted for both the bank bill and the AIDS legislation. DeMint, McCain, and Coburn are among the sponsors of earmark-moratorium legislation introduced last month.

Inhofe said that if Congress bans earmarks, his fallback position is that they should be defined only as projects that receive appropriations without having been previously authorized by Congress. Inhofe is a chief authorizer—for transportation programs at the Environment and Public Works Committee and for military programs at the Armed Services Committee. He and other authorizers regularly struggle for power with appropriators, who often have their own ideas about which projects to fund in their annual spending bills.

In a brief interview, McCain defended his anti-earmark stance. "My record is very clear," he said. "For 20 years I've fought against earmarks and their corruption. They breed corruption, and they've bred corruption."

McCain said he believes that the root of the problem is unauthorized appropriations. "You've got to get the definition of an earmark: that is, an unauthorized appropriation. If you authorize it, even if I disagree with it, that's the right process," he said. "What [earmarks] have done is totally circumvent what we should be doing: that is, authorizing and *then* appropriating."

Sen. Saxby Chambliss, R-Ga.—the ranking member on the Senate Agriculture, Nutrition, and Forestry Committee, another key authorizing panel—said that giving authorizers more power to say where money should be spent could be one part of earmark reform. He is a co-sponsor of the earmark moratorium. "I hope we get some sort of meaningful earmark reform as a result of continuing to stir that issue up," Chambliss said.

Inhofe's pro-earmark campaign will certainly cause a stir among his colleagues. Some House and Senate Republicans have urged the party to unilaterally adopt an earmark moratorium to paint a strong contrast to the Democrats. Inhofe counters that doing so would simply give more money to Obama to spend on liberal-supported projects and that it would distract attention from the core issues that the GOP can ride to victory in November.

"The Republican Party has the greatest issues ever in the history of politics in America—health care, cap-and-trade, closing Gitmo—that's terrorists coming into the United States, and the deficit, and the debt," Inhofe said. "Making an issue out of earmarks serves to only mislead voters by providing cover for big spenders. Railing against earmarks helps those who vote for the billion-dollar spending bills seem more conservative than they really are."

29

"Earmarks Are a Model, Not a Menace"

JONATHAN RAUCH

Naturally, when a gigantic omnibus appropriations bill came to the Senate floor last week, 98 percent of it got almost no attention. "Member projects—aka earmarks or 'pork'—account for less than 2 percent of spending in the $410 billion omnibus bill on the floor of the Senate this week, but they're drawing most of the opposition fire," *The Christian Science Monitor* reported. Less than 2 percent! Of course, this orgy of waste offended me for the same reason it offended everyone else: I was not getting an earmark.

I decided to get an earmark. Seemed easy enough. Just call someone in a congressional office, make a silly request—propose converting pig vomit into drywall, that sort of thing—and voila, I would have my very own "pet project."

So I called my congressman, Rep. Jim Moran, D-Va., who, handily enough, is a member of the Appropriations Committee. Imagine my shock when I got a staffer who insisted that I would have to *apply*.

Apply? For a *pet project*? Right. There was a form. As in, paperwork. The exact form would depend on which Appropriations subcommittee has jurisdiction. And I would need to meet with legislative aides to explain why my project deserved funding. And they would probably vet my request with the relevant federal agency.

Oh. But then I'm in, right?

Not quite. Moran told me he will get a thousand earmark applications this year. "It actually goes up every year." He will accept only the best hundred or so.

But *then* I'm in?

No, then the relevant Appropriations subcommittee further whittles the list. About three dozen of Moran's earmarks will get funded, he figures.

So my chances of scoring boodle were on the order of only 3 percent. I didn't fill out the form, even though it was only a page long. Down in Norfolk, Rep. Bobby Scott, D-Va., requires earmark applicants to fill out a seven-page form that looks like my tax return—and I itemize. "Please check *all* that apply: . . . This project is largely for EPA consent decree. . . . Preliminary planning and engineering design is completed." Really, it takes all the thrill out of pet projects.

Beating up on earmarks is fun. But if you interrupt the joy long enough to take a closer look, you may discover that the case against earmarks has pretty much evaporated over the past few years. In fact, reformers seem to want to hound out of existence a system that actually works better than much of what Washington does.

When former Rep. Jim Kolbe, R-Ariz., entered Congress in 1985, "there were no earmarks," he told me recently. Perhaps, you say, this was because appropriators were indifferent to how much federal money flowed to their districts? Sorry, bad guess.

In those days, according to Kolbe (an Appropriations Committee member who retired in 2007), appropriators felt little need to write earmarks into law. Instead, subcommittee chairmen and ranking members just dropped money into program accounts. Then they called up executive branch bureaucrats with advice on how to spend it.

"Most agencies didn't need to be threatened if the chairman of their subcommittee called," says Scott Lilly, a former House Appropriations Committee staff director and now a senior fellow with the Center for American Progress. Sometimes, Lilly says, "you'd increase the entire national program in order that it would have a better chance that it would spill into your state."

In the 1980s and 1990s, the once-sequestered system cracked open. The number of earmarks increased by a factor of 25 between 1991 and 2005. Earmarks were often invisible, at least until after they were enacted. "The bill would be passed before people even started digging into what was in there," Lilly says. Public outrage swelled.

On its heels, however, came reform, notably in the last couple of years. Every earmark request now must be made public before Congress votes on it. The sponsoring member, the amount and nature of the request, and the name and address of the beneficiary must all be disclosed. You can find all this stuff online. As I was miffed to discover, many congressional offices have formalized the application procedure. Getting an earmark now is a lot like applying for a grant.

As transparency has taken over, the case against earmarks has melted away. Their budgetary impact is trivial in comparison with entitlements and other large programs. Obsessing about earmarks, indeed, has the perverse, if convenient, effect of distracting the country from its real spending problems, thus substituting indignation for discipline.

Earmarks are often criticized for rewarding political clout rather than merit. If earmarks were merit-based, says Steve Ellis of the watchdog group Taxpayers for Common Sense, you wouldn't see them flowing disproportionately to Appropriations Committee members. And earmarks, he adds, reflect parochial rather than national priorities. "There's no way the Appropriations Committee is able to vet the thousands of earmarks worth billions of dollars."

Fair enough. But if you think that executive branch decisions are strictly apolitical and merit-based, I have two words for you: Karl Rove. "The idea that the only politicians in the government are in the Congress is just false," Lilly says. If you think that executive branch decision-making is transparent, I have two more words for you: Dick Cheney.

And if you think Congress is parochial, take it up with Mr. Madison. He wrote the Constitution, which says, in terms that leave no room for quibbling, that the power of the purse belongs to Congress. The Founders' notion was that accountability to local voters was the best safeguard for the people's money. "The idea that unless something is in the president's budget Congress shouldn't consider it turns the Constitution on its head," Kolbe says.

"The problem with a lot of federal programs is that they have to take a cookie-cutter approach," Moran says. Big, conventionally authorized programs, with their funding formulas and contracting rules and national purview, may be too slow to meet urgent local needs, too rigid to support innovation, too formulaic to finance a one-shot project.

Kolbe recalls an earmark that sped up an approved but languishing highway project in Arizona. "It was desperately needed; there were huge backups on the interstate," he says. "Seeing the growing need, not anticipated at the time of its initial approval, we simply jumped it up on the priority list."

Political discretion can be abused, and one would certainly not want most federal spending to be subject to it. But, provided that transparency is assured, shouldn't there be a place in government for elected officials to exercise judgment in the use of taxpayer money? In fact, if you wanted to create a nonbureaucratic, transparent system of rapid-response grants for pressing local concerns, you would come up with something very much like today's earmarking system (and you'd call it "reinventing government").

Some earmark spending is silly, but then so is some non-earmark spending, and there is a lot more of the latter. Competition for funding, combined with flexibility and local knowledge, makes earmarks "often some of the best expenditures the federal government makes in a particular area," Lilly says. "I would say, on the whole, earmarks proba-bly provide as much value-added as non-earmarked federal spending."

And earmark spending today is, if anything, more transparent, more accountable, and more promptly disclosed than is non-earmark spend-ing. Indeed, executive agencies could stand to emulate some of the online disclosure rules that apply to earmarks.

These days, the problem is not so much with earmarking as with Con-gress's and the public's obsession with it. "It just takes too damn much time," Lilly says. "Congress is spending an inordinate amount of time on 1 percent of the budget and giving the executive branch much too free a rein on the other 99 percent."

Reformers who want to ban earmarking might think again. "You're never going to abolish earmarks," Moran says. "What you'll wind up abolishing is the transparency, the accountability." If unable to earmark, legislators will inveigle executive agencies behind the scenes, fry bureau-crats at hearings, and expand or rewrite entire programs to serve paro-chial needs. This, of course, is the way things worked in the bad old days. "I think you'll wind up going back to that system," Kolbe cautions.

A better approach is to improve transparency and further routinize the earmarking process, as President Obama proposed on Wednesday when he signed the omnibus spending bill. But here is a reform that would help much more: Declare earmarking an ex-problem and move on. Next time you come across someone who looks at a giant federal spending bill and sees only the 2 percent that happens to be earmarked, tell that person to get over it.

DISCUSSION QUESTIONS

1. How would you define pork-barrel projects? Are all pork projects contrary to the national interest? How do we distinguish between local projects that are in the national interest and those that are not?

2. Consider Cato's list of examples of pork. If you were a member of Congress, which of these would you clearly support? Which would you clearly oppose? Which would you want to find out more about before deciding?

3. Members of Congress face strong incentives to serve constituent needs and claim credit for delivering federal dollars. Pork-barrel projects provide the means to do just that. What changes in Con-gress or the political process might be made to alter legislative be-havior, or to change the incentives legislators face when securing re-election? Do we want members of Congress to be focused pri-marily on broad national issues rather than local priorities?

CHAPTER 6

The President: From Chief Clerk to Chief Executive

30

"The Power to Persuade," from *Presidential Power*

Richard Neustadt

An enduring theme in analyses of the presidency is the gap between what the public expects of the office and the president's actual powers. Neustadt, who wrote the first edition of Presidential Power *in 1960, offered a new way of looking at the office. His main point is that formal powers (the constitutional powers set out in Article II and the statutory powers that Congress grants) are not the president's most important resource. The president cannot, Neustadt concluded, expect to get his way by command—issuing orders to subordinates and other government officials with the expectation of immediate and unquestioning compliance. In a system of "separate institutions sharing power," other political actors have their own independent sources of power and therefore can refuse to comply with presidential orders. Nobody, Neustadt argues, sees things from the president's perspective (or "vantage point"). Legislators, judges, cabinet secretaries, all have their own responsibilities, constituencies, demands of office, and resources, and their interests and the president's will often differ. The key to presidential power is the power to persuade—to convince others that they should comply with the president's wishes because doing so is in their interest. Presidents persuade by bargaining: making deals, reaching compromise positions; in other words, the give and take that is part of politics.*

The limits on command suggest the structure of our government. The constitutional convention of 1787 is supposed to have created a government of "separated powers." It did nothing of the sort. Rather, it created a government of separated institutions *sharing* powers. "I am part of the legislative process," Eisenhower often said in 1959 as a reminder of his veto. Congress, the dispenser of authority and funds, is no less part of the administrative process. Federalism adds another set of separated institutions. The Bill of Rights adds others. Many public purposes can only be achieved by voluntary acts of private institutions; the press, for one, in Douglass Cater's phrase, is a "fourth branch of government." And with the coming of alliances abroad, the separate institutions of a London, or a Bonn, share in the making of American public policy.

What the Constitution separates our political parties do not combine. The parties are themselves composed of separated organizations sharing public authority. The authority consists of nominating powers. Our national parties are confederations of state and local party institutions, with a headquarters that represents the White House, more or less, if the party has a President in office. These confederacies manage presidential nominations. All other public offices depend upon electorates confined within the states. All other nominations are controlled within the states. The President and congressmen who bear one party's label are divided by dependence upon different sets of voters. The differences are sharpest at the stage of nomination. The White House has too small a share in nominating congressmen, and Congress has too little weight in nominating Presidents for party to erase their constitutional separation. Party links are stronger than is frequently supposed, but nominating processes assure the separation.

The separateness of institutions and the sharing of authority prescribe the terms on which a President persuades. When one man shares authority with another, but does not gain or lose his job upon the other's whim, his willingness to act upon the urging of the other turns on whether he conceives the action right for him. The essence of a President's persuasive task is to convince such men that what the White House wants of them is what they ought to do for their sake and on their authority.

Persuasive power, thus defined, amounts to more than charm or reasoned argument. These have their uses for a President, but these are not the whole of his resources. For the men he would induce to do what he wants done on their own responsibility will need or fear some acts by him on his responsibility. If they share his authority, he has some share in theirs. Presidential "powers" may be inconclusive when a President commands, but always remain relevant as he persuades. The status and authority inherent in his office reinforce his logic and his charm.

* * *

A President's authority and status give him great advantages in dealing with the men he would persuade. Each "power" is a vantage point for him in the degree that other men have use for his authority. From the veto to appointments, from publicity to budgeting, and so down a long list, the White House now controls the most encompassing array of vantage points in the American political system. With hardly an exception, the men who share in governing this country are aware that at some time, in some degree, the doing of *their* jobs, the furthering of *their* ambitions, may depend upon the President of the United States. Their need for presidential action, or their fear of it, is bound to be recurrent if not actually continuous. Their need or fear is his advantage.

A President's advantages are greater than mere listing of his "powers" might suggest. The men with whom he deals must deal with him until the last day of his term. Because they have continuing relationships with him, his future, while it lasts, supports his present influence. Even though there is no need or fear of him today, what he could do tomorrow may supply today's advantage. Continuing relationships may convert any "power," any aspect of his status, into vantage points in almost any case. When he induces other men to do what he wants done, a President can trade on their dependence now *and* later.

The President's advantages are checked by the advantages of others. Continuing relationships will pull in both directions. These are relationships of mutual dependence. A President depends upon the men he would persuade; he has to reckon with his need or fear of them. They too will possess status, or authority, or both, else they would be of little use to him. Their vantage points confront his own; their power tempers his.

* * *

The power to persuade is the power to bargain. Status and authority yield bargaining advantages. But in a government of "separated institutions sharing powers," they yield them to all sides. With the array of vantage points at his disposal, a President may be far more persuasive than his logic or his charm could make him. But outcomes are not guaranteed by his advantages. There remain the counter pressures those whom he would influence can bring to bear on him from vantage points at their disposal. Command has limited utility; persuasion becomes give-and-take. It is well that the White House holds the vantage points it does. In such a business any President may need them all—and more.

* * *

This view of power as akin to bargaining is one we commonly accept in the sphere of congressional relations. Every textbook states and every legislative session demonstrates that save in times like the extraordinary Hundred Days of 1933—times virtually ruled out by definition at midcentury—a President will often be unable to obtain congressional action on his terms or even to halt action he opposes. The reverse is equally accepted: Congress often is frustrated by the President. Their formal powers are so intertwined that neither will accomplish very much, for very long, without the acquiescence of the other. By the same token, though, what one demands the other can resist. The stage is set for that great game, much like collective bargaining, in which each seeks to profit from the other's needs and fears. It is a game played catch-as-catch-can, case by case. And everybody knows the game, observers and participants alike.

* * *

Like our governmental structure as a whole, the executive establishment consists of separated institutions sharing powers. The President heads one of these; Cabinet officers, agency administrators, and military commanders head others. Below the departmental level, virtually independent bureau chiefs head many more. Under mid-century conditions, Federal operations spill across dividing lines on organization charts; almost every policy entangles many agencies; almost every program calls for interagency collaboration. Everything somehow involves the President. But operating agencies owe their existence least of all to one another—and only in some part to him. Each has a separate statutory base; each has its statutes to administer; each deals with a different set of subcommittees at the Capitol. Each has its own peculiar set of clients, friends, and enemies outside the formal government. Each has a different set of specialized careerists inside its own bailiwick. Our Constitution gives the President the "take-care" clause and the appointive power. Our statutes give him central budgeting and a degree of personnel control. All agency administrators are responsible to him. But they *also* are responsible to Congress, to their clients, to their staffs, and to themselves. In short, they have five masters. Only after all of those do they owe any loyalty to each other.

"The members of the Cabinet," Charles G. Dawes used to remark, "are a President's natural enemies." Dawes had been Harding's Budget Director, Coolidge's Vice-President, and Hoover's Ambassador to London; he also had been General Pershing's chief assistant for supply in the First World War. The words are highly colored, but Dawes knew whereof he spoke. The men who have to serve so many masters cannot help but be somewhat the "enemy" of any one of them. By the same token, any master wanting service is in some degree the "enemy" of such a servant. A President is likely to want loyal support but not to relish trouble on his doorstep. Yet the more his Cabinet members cleave to him, the more they may need help from him in fending off the wrath of rival masters. Help, though, is synonymous with trouble. Many a Cabinet officer, with loyalty ill-rewarded by his lights and help withheld, has come to view the White House as innately hostile to department heads. Dawes's dictum can be turned around.

* * *

The more an officeholder's status and his "powers" stem from sources independent of the President, the stronger will be his potential pressure *on* the President. Department heads in general have more bargaining power than do most members of the White House staff; but bureau chiefs may have still more, and specialists at upper levels of established career services may have almost unlimited reserves of the enormous power which consists of sitting still. As Franklin Roosevelt once remarked:

> The Treasury is so large and far-flung and ingrained in its practices that I find it almost impossible to get the action and results I want—even with Henry [Morgenthau] there. But the Treasury is not to be compared with the State Department. You should go through the experience of trying to get any changes in the thinking, policy, and action of the career diplomats and then you'd know what a real problem was. But the Treasury and the State Department put together are nothing compared with the Na-a-vy. The admirals are really something to cope with—and I should know. To change anything in the Na-a-vy is like punching a feather bed. You punch it with your right and you punch it with your left until you are finally exhausted, and then you find the damn bed just as it was before you started punching.

*   *   *

There is a widely held belief in the United States that were it not for folly or for knavery, a reasonable President would need no power other than the logic of his argument. No less a personage than Eisenhower has subscribed to that belief in many a campaign speech and press conference remark. But faulty reasoning and bad intentions do not cause all quarrels with Presidents. The best of reasoning and of intent cannot compose them all. For in the first place, what the President wants will rarely seem a trifle to the men he wants it from. And in the second place, they will be bound to judge it by the standard of their own responsibilities, not his. However logical his argument according to his lights, their judgment may not bring them to his view.

The men who share in governing this country frequently appear to act as though they were in business for themselves. So, in a real though not entire sense, they are and have to be. When Truman and MacArthur fell to quarreling, for example, the stakes were no less than the substance of American foreign policy, the risks of greater war or military stalemate, the prerogatives of Presidents and field commanders, the pride of a proconsul and his place in history. Intertwined, inevitably, were other stakes, as well: political stakes for men and factions of both parties; power stakes for interest groups with which they were or wished to be affiliated. And every stake was raised by the apparent discontent in the American public mood. There is no reason to suppose that in such circumstances men of large but differing responsibilities will see all things through the same glasses. On the contrary, it is to be expected that their views of what ought to be done and what they then should do will vary with the differing perspectives their particular responsibilities evoke. Since their duties are not vested in a "team" or a "collegium" but in themselves, as individuals, one must expect that they will see things *for* themselves. Moreover, when they are responsible to many masters and when an event or policy turns loyalty against loyalty—a day by day occurrence in the nature of the case—one must assume that those who have the duties to perform will choose the terms of reconciliation. This is the essence of their personal responsibility. When their own duties pull in opposite directions, who else but they can choose what they will do?

* * *

Outside the Executive Branch the situation is the same, except that loyalty to the President may often matter *less.* . . . And when one comes to congressmen who can do nothing for themselves (or their constituents) save as they are elected, term by term, in districts and through party structures *differing* from those on which a President depends, the case is very clear. An able Eisenhower aide with long congressional experience remarked to me in 1958: "The people on the Hill don't do what they might *like* to do, they do what they think they *have* to do in their own interest as *they* see it. . . ." This states the case precisely.

The essence of a President's persuasive task with congressmen and everybody else, *is to induce them to believe that what he wants of them is what their own appraisal of their own responsibilities requires them to do in their interest, not his.* Because men may differ in their views on public policy, because differences in outlook stem from differences in duty—duty to one's office, one's constituents, oneself—that task is bound to be more like collective bargaining than like a reasoned argument among philosopher kings. Overtly or implicitly, hard bargaining has characterized all illustrations offered up to now. This is the reason why: persuasion deals in the coin of self-interest with men who have some freedom to reject what they find counterfeit.

Let me introduce a case . . . : the European Recovery Program of 1948, the so-called Marshall Plan. This is perhaps the greatest exercise in policy *agreement* since the cold war began. When the then Secretary of State, George Catlett Marshall, spoke at the Harvard commencement in June of 1947, he launched one of the most creative, most imaginative ventures in the history of American foreign relations. What makes this policy most notable for present purposes, however, is that it became effective upon action by the 80th Congress, at the behest of Harry Truman, in the election year of 1948.

Eight months before Marshall spoke at Harvard, the Democrats had lost control of both Houses of Congress for the first time in fourteen years. Truman, whom the Secretary represented, had just finished his second troubled year as President-by-succession. Truman was regarded with so little warmth in his own party that in 1946 he had been urged *not* to participate in the congressional campaign. At the opening of Congress in January 1947, Senator Robert A. Taft, "Mr. Republican," had somewhat the attitude of a President-elect. This was a vision widely shared in

Washington, with Truman relegated, thereby, to the role of caretaker-on-term. Moreover, within just two weeks of Marshall's commencement address, Truman was to veto two prized accomplishments of Taft's congressional majority: the Taft-Hartley Act and tax reduction. Yet scarcely ten months later the Marshall Plan was under way on terms to satisfy its sponsors, its authorization completed, its first-year funds in sight, its administering agency in being: all managed by as thorough a display of executive-congressional cooperation as any we have seen since the Second World War. For any President at any time this would have been a great accomplishment. In years before mid-century it would have been enough to make the future reputation of his term. And for a Truman, at this time, enactment of the Marshall Plan appears almost miraculous.

How was the miracle accomplished? How did a President so situated bring it off? In answer, the first thing to note is that he did not do it by himself. Truman had help of a sort no less extraordinary than the outcome. Although each stands for something more complex, the names of Marshall, Vandenberg, . . . Bevin, Stalin, tell the story of that help.

In 1947, two years after V-J Day, General Marshall was something more than Secretary of State. He was a man venerated by the President as "the greatest living American," literally an embodiment of Truman's ideals. He was honored at the Pentagon as an architect of victory. He was thoroughly respected by the Secretary of the Navy, James V. Forrestal, who that year became the first Secretary of Defense. On Capitol Hill Marshall had an enormous fund of respect stemming from his war record as Army Chief of Staff, and in the country generally no officer had come out of the war with a higher reputation for judgment, intellect, and probity. Besides, as Secretary of State, he had behind him the first generation of matured foreign service officers produced by the reforms of the 1920's, and mingled with them, in the departmental service, were some of the ablest of the men drawn by the war from private life to Washington.

*   *   *

Taken together, these are exceptional resources for a Secretary of State. In the circumstances, they were quite as necessary as they obviously are relevant. The Marshall Plan was launched by a "lame duck" Administration "scheduled" to leave office in eighteen months. Marshall's program faced a congressional leadership traditionally isolationist and currently intent upon economy. European aid was viewed with envy by a Pentagon distressed and virtually disarmed through budget cuts, and by domestic agencies intent on enlarged welfare programs. It was not viewed with liking by a Treasury intent on budget surpluses. The plan had need of every asset that could be extracted from the personal position of its nominal author and from the skills of his assistants.

Without the equally remarkable position of the senior Senator from Michigan, Arthur H. Vandenberg, it is hard to see how Marshall's assets could have been enough. Vandenberg was chairman of the Senate Foreign Relations Committee. Actually, he was much more than that. Twenty years a senator, he was the senior member of his party in the Chamber. Assiduously cultivated by F.D.R. and Truman, he was a chief Republican proponent of "bipartisanship" in foreign policy, and consciously conceived himself its living symbol to his party, to the country, and abroad. Moreover, by informal but entirely operative agreement with his colleague Taft, Vandenberg held the acknowledged lead among Senate Republicans in the whole field of international affairs. This acknowledgement meant more in 1947 than it might have meant at any other time. With confidence in the advent of a Republican administration two years hence, most of the gentlemen were in a mood to be responsive and responsible. The war was over, Roosevelt dead, Truman a caretaker, theirs the trust. That the Senator from Michigan saw matters in this light, his diaries make clear. And this was not the outlook from the Senate side alone; the attitudes of House Republicans associated with the Herter Committee and its tours abroad suggest the same mood of responsibility. Vandenberg was not the only source of help on Capitol Hill. But relatively speaking, his position there was as exceptional as Marshall's was downtown.

*   *   *

At Harvard, Marshall had voiced an idea in general terms. That this was turned into a hard program susceptible of presentation and support is due, in major part, to Ernest Bevin, the British Foreign Secretary. He well deserves the credit he has sometimes been assigned as, in effect, co-author of the Marshall Plan. For Bevin seized on Marshall's Harvard speech and organized a European response with promptness and concreteness beyond the State Department's expectations. What had been virtually a trial balloon to test reactions on both sides of the Atlantic was hailed in London as an invitation to the Europeans to send Washington a bill of particulars. This they promptly organized to do, and the American Administration then organized in turn for its reception without further argument internally about the pros and cons of issuing the "invitation" in the first place. But for Bevin there might have been trouble from the Secretary of the Treasury and others besides.

If Bevin's help was useful at that early stage, Stalin's was vital from first to last. In a mood of self-deprecation Truman once remarked that without Moscow's "crazy" moves "we would never have had our foreign policy . . . we never could have got a thing from Congress." George Kennan, among others, had deplored the anti-Soviet overtone of the case made for the Marshall Plan in Congress and the country, but there is no doubt that this clinched the argument for many segments of American opinion. There also is no doubt that Moscow made the crucial contributions to the case.

* * *

The crucial thing to note about this case is that despite compatibility of views on public policy, Truman got no help he did not pay for (except Stalin's). Bevin scarcely could have seized on Marshall's words had Marshall not been plainly backed by Truman. Marshall's interest would not have comported with the exploitation of his prestige by a President who undercut him openly, or subtly, or even inadvertently, at any point. Vandenberg, presumably, could not have backed proposals by a White House which begrudged him deference and access gratifying to his fellow-partisans (and satisfying to himself). Prominent Republicans in private life would not have found it easy to promote a cause identified with Truman's claims on 1948—and neither would the prominent New Dealers then engaged in searching for a substitute.

Truman paid the price required for their services. So far as the record shows, the White House did not falter once in firm support for Marshall and the Marshall Plan. Truman backed his Secretary's gamble on an invitation to all Europe. He made the plan his own in a well-timed address to the Canadians. He lost no opportunity to widen the involvements of his own official family in the cause. Averell Harriman the Secretary of Commerce, Julius Krug the Secretary of the Interior, Edwin Nourse the Economic Council Chairman, James Webb the Director of the Budget—all were made responsible for studies and reports contributing directly to the legislative presentation. Thus these men were committed in advance. Besides, the President continually emphasized to everyone in reach that he did not have doubts, did not desire complications and would foreclose all he could. Reportedly, his emphasis was felt at the Treasury, with good effect. And Truman was at special pains to smooth the way for Vandenberg. The Senator insisted on "no politics" from the Administration side; there was none. He thought a survey of American resources and capacity essential; he got it in the Krug and Harriman reports. Vandenberg expected advance consultation; he received it, step by step, in frequent meetings with the President and weekly conferences with Marshall. He asked for an effective liaison between Congress and agencies concerned; Lovett and others gave him what he wanted. When the Senator decided on the need to change financing and administrative features of the legislation, Truman disregarded Budget Bureau grumbling and acquiesced with grace. When, finally, Vandenberg desired a Republican to head the new administering agency, his candidate, Paul Hoffman, was appointed despite the President's own preference for another. In all of these ways Truman employed the sparse advantages his "powers" and his status then accorded him to gain the sort of help he had to have.

*   *   *

Had Truman lacked the personal advantages his "powers" and his status gave him, or if he had been maladroit in using them, there probably would not have been a massive European aid program in 1948. . . . The President's own share in this accomplishment was vital. He made his contribution by exploiting his advantages. Truman, in effect, lent Marshall and the rest the perquisites and status of his office. In return they lent him their prestige and their own influence. The transfer multiplied *his* influence despite his limited authority in form and lack of strength politically. Without the wherewithal to make this bargain, Truman could not have contributed to European aid.

*   *   *

DISCUSSION QUESTIONS

1. Considering recent presidents (Barack Obama and George W. Bush), identify and discuss some examples of Neustadt's argument that presidents cannot get their way by "command" but must bargain to get what they want.

2. Can you think of any recent examples when a president has been able to get what he wants by giving a command (that is, to someone not in the military)?

3. How should a president convince a member of Congress to pass a piece of legislation that the president favors?

31

"Perspectives on the Presidency," from *The Presidency in a Separated System*

CHARLES O. JONES

Just how powerful is the president? Have the fears of some of the Framers—that the president would degrade into an imperial despot—been realized, or does the separation of powers effectively check the president's ability to misuse the powers of office? Charles Jones argues that we should view the president as only one of the players in American government; the presidency exists only as one part of a set of institutions where responsibility is diffused, where the bulk of political activity takes place independent of the presidency, and where the different players and institutions learn to adjust to the others. Consider, for example, that President George W. Bush faced a Senate controlled by the Democrats for most of his first two years in office and had to work with them to achieve some of his major goals such as education reform. Or that President Barack Obama left it to Congress to work out many details of health care reform, in contrast to President Bill Clinton, who unsuccessfully attempted to get Congress to enact a major health care reform plan produced by an administration task force. Ultimately, Jones argues, the president is only a part of a larger "separated system," in which Congress, the courts, and the bureaucracy can shape policy.

The president is not the presidency. The presidency is not the government. Ours is not a presidential system.

I begin with these starkly negative themes as partial correctives to the more popular interpretations of the United States government as presidency-centered. Presidents themselves learn these refrains on the job, if they do not know them before. President Lyndon B. Johnson, who had impressive political advantages during the early years of his administration, reflected later on what was required to realize the potentialities of the office:

> Every President has to establish with the various sectors of the country what I call "the right to govern." Just being elected to the office does not guarantee him that right. Every President has to inspire the confidence of the people. Every President has to become a leader, and to be a leader he must attract people who are willing to follow him. Every President has to develop a moral underpinning to his power, or he soon discovers that he has no power at all.

To exercise influence, presidents must learn the setting within which it has bearing. [Then] President-elect Bill Clinton recognized the complexities of translating campaign promises into a legislative program during a news conference shortly after his election in 1992:

> It's all very well to say you want an investment tax credit, and quite another thing to make the 15 decisions that have to be made to shape the exact bill you want.
> It's all very well to say . . . that the working poor in this country . . . should be lifted out of poverty by increasing the refundable income tax credit for the working poor, and another thing to answer the five or six questions that define how you get that done.

For presidents, new or experienced, to recognize the limitations of office is commendable. Convincing others to do so is a challenge. Presidents become convenient labels for marking historical time: the Johnson years, the Nixon years, the Reagan years. Media coverage naturally focuses more on the president: there is just one at a time, executive organization is oriented in pyramidal fashion toward the Oval Office, Congress is too diffuse an institution to report on as such, and the Supreme Court leads primarily by indirection. Public interest, too, is directed toward the White House as a symbol of the government. As a result, expectations of a president often far exceed the individual's personal, political, institutional, or constitutional capacities for achievement. Performance seldom matches promise. Presidents who understand how it all works resist the inflated image of power born of high-stakes elections and seek to lower expectations. Politically savvy presidents know instinctively that it is precisely at the moment of great achievement that they must prepare themselves for the setback that will surely follow.

Focusing exclusively on the presidency can lead to a seriously distorted picture of how the national government does its work. The plain fact is that the United States does not have a presidential system. It has a *separated* system. It is odd that it is so commonly thought of as otherwise since schoolchildren learn about the separation of powers and checks and balances. As the author of *Federalist* 51 wrote, "Ambition must be made to counteract ambition." No one, least of all presidents, the Founders reasoned, can be entrusted with excessive authority. Human nature, being what it is, requires "auxiliary precautions" in the form of competing legitimacies.

The acceptance that this is a separated, not a presidential, system, prepares one to appraise how politics works, not to be simply reproachful and reformist. Thus, for example, divided (or split-party) government is accepted as a potential or even likely outcome of a separated system, rooted as it is in the separation of elections. Failure to acknowledge the authenticity of the split-party condition leaves one with little to study and much to reform in the post–World War II period, when the government has been divided more than 60 percent of the time.

Simply put, the role of the president in this separated system of governing varies substantially, depending on his resources, advantages, and strategic position. My strong interest is in how presidents place

themselves in an ongoing government and are fitted in by other participants, notably those on Capitol Hill. The central purpose of this book
is to explore these "fittings." In pursuing this interest, I have found little
value in the presidency-centered, party government perspective, as I
will explain below. As a substitute, I propose a separationist, diffused-
responsibility perspective that I find more suited to the constitutional,
institutional, political, and policy conditions associated with the American system of governing.

*   *   *

The Dominant Perspective

The presidency-centered perspective is consistent with a dominant and
well-developed perspective that has been highly influential in evaluating
the American political system. The perspective is that of party government, typically one led by a strong or aggressive president. Those advocating this perspective prefer a system in which political parties are
stronger than they normally can be in a system of separated elections.

*   *   *

The party government perspective is best summarized in the recommendations made in 1946 by the Committee on Political Parties of the
American Political Science Association.

> The party system that is needed must be democratic, responsible and effec-
> tive. . . .
> An effective party system requires, first, that the parties are able to bring
> forth programs to which they commit themselves and, second, that the parties
> possess sufficient internal cohesion to carry out these programs. . . .
> The fundamental requirement of such accountability is a two-party system
> in which the opposition party acts as the critic of the party in power, develop-
> ing, defining, and presenting the policy alternatives which are necessary for a
> true choice in reaching public decisions.

Note the language in this summary: party in power, opposition party,
policy alternatives for choice, accountability, internal cohesion, programs
to which parties commit themselves. As a whole, it forms a test that a
separated system is bound to fail.

I know of very few contemporary advocates of the two-party responsibility model. But I know many analysts who rely on its criteria when judging the political system. One sees this reliance at work when reviewing
how elections are interpreted and presidents are evaluated. By this standard, the good campaign and election have the following characteristics:

- Publicly visible issues that are debated by the candidates during the
  campaign.
- Clear differences between the candidates on the issues, preferably deriving from ideology.

- A substantial victory for the winning candidate, thus demonstrating public support for one set of issue positions.
- A party win accompanying the victory for the president, notably an increase in the presidential party's share of congressional seats and statehouses so that the president's win can be said to have had an impact on other races (the coattail effect).
- A greater than expected win for the victorious party, preferably at both ends of Pennsylvania Avenue.
- A postelection declaration of support and unity from the congressional leaders of the president's party.

The good president, by this perspective, is one who makes government work, one who has a program and uses his resources to get it enacted. The good president is an activist: he sets the agenda, is attentive to the progress being made, and willingly accepts responsibility for what happens. He can behave in this way because he has demonstrable support.

It is not in the least surprising that the real outcomes of separated elections frustrate those who prefer responsible party government. Even a cursory reading of the Constitution suggests that these demanding tests will be met only by coincidence. Even an election that gives one party control of the White House and both houses of Congress in no way guarantees a unified or responsible party outcome. And even when a president and his congressional party leaders appear to agree on policy priorities, the situation may change dramatically following midterm elections. Understandably, advocates of party government are led to propose constitutional reform.

* * *

An Alternative Perspective

The alternative perspective for understanding American national politics is bound to be anathema to party responsibility advocates. By the rendition promoted here, responsibility is not focused, it is diffused. Representation is not pure and unidirectional; it is mixed, diluted, and multidirectional. Further, the tracking of policy from inception to implementation discourages the most devoted advocate of responsibility theories. In a system of diffused responsibility, credit will be taken and blame will be avoided by both institutions and both parties. For the mature government (one that has achieved substantial involvement in social and economic life), much of the agenda will be self-generating, that is, resulting from programs already on the books. Thus the desire to propose new programs is often frustrated by demands to sustain existing programs, and substantial debt will constrain both.

Additionally there is the matter of who *should* be held accountable for what and when. This is not a novel issue by any means. It is a part of the common rhetoric of split-party government. Are the Democrats responsible for how Medicare has worked because it was a part of Lyndon Johnson's Great Society? Or are the Republicans responsible because their presidents accepted, administered, and revised the program? Is President Carter responsible for creating a Department of Energy or President Reagan responsible for failing to abolish it, or both? The partisan rhetoric on deficits continues to blame the Democrats for supporting spending programs and the Republicans for cutting taxes. It is noteworthy that this level of debate fails to treat more fundamental issues, such as the constitutional roadblocks to defining responsibility. In preventing the tyranny of the majority, the founders also made it difficult to specify accountability.

Diffusion of responsibility, then, is not only a likely result of a separated system but may also be a fair outcome. From what was said above, one has to doubt how reasonable it is to hold one institution or one party accountable for a program that has grown incrementally through decades of single- and split-party control. Yet reforming a government program is bound to be an occasion for holding one or the other of the branches accountable for wrongs being righted. If, however, politics allows crossing the partisan threshold to place both parties on the same side, then agreements may be reached that will permit blame avoidance, credit taking, and, potentially, significant policy change. This is not to say that both sides agree from the start about what to do, in a cabal devoted to irresponsibility (though that process is not unknown). Rather it is to suggest that diffusion of responsibility may permit policy reform that would have been much less likely if one party had to absorb all of the criticism for past performance or blame should the reforms fail when implemented.

Institutional competition is an expected outcome of the constitutional arrangements that facilitate mixed representation and variable electoral horizons. In recent decades this competition has been reinforced by Republicans settling into the White House, the Democrats comfortably occupying the House of Representatives, and, in very recent times, both parties hotly contending for majority status in the Senate. Bargains struck under these conditions have the effect of perpetuating split control by denying opposition candidates (Democratic presidential challengers, Republican congressional challengers) both the issues upon which to campaign and the means for defining accountability.

The participants in this system of mixed representation and diffused responsibility naturally accommodate their political surroundings. Put otherwise, congressional Democrats and presidential Republicans learn how to do their work. Not only does each side adjust to its political circumstances, but both may also be expected to provide themselves with the resources to participate meaningfully in policy politics.

Much of the above suggests that the political and policy strategies of presidents in dealing with Congress will depend on the advantages they have available at any one time. One cannot employ a constant model of the activist president leading a party government. Conditions may encourage the president to work at the margins of president-congressional interaction (for example, where he judges that he has an advantage, as with foreign and defense issues). He may allow members of Congress to take policy initiatives, hanging back to see how the issue develops. He may certify an issue as important, propose a program to satisfy certain group demands, but fail to expend the political capital necessary to get the program enacted. The lame-duck president requires clearer explication. The last months and years of a two-term administration may be one of congressional initiative with presidential response. The point is that having been relieved of testing the system for party responsibility, one can proceed to analyze how presidents perform under variable political and policy conditions.

* * *

In a separated system of diffused responsibility, these are the expectations:

- Presidents will enter the White House with variable personal, political, and policy advantages or resources. Presidents are not equally good at comprehending their advantages or identifying how these advantages may work best for purposes of influencing the rest of the government.
- White House and cabinet organization will be quite personal in nature, reflecting the president's assessment of strengths and weaknesses, the challenges the president faces in fitting into the ongoing government, and the political and policy changes that occur during the term of office. There is no formula for organizing the presidency, though certain models can be identified.
- Public support will be an elusive variable in analyzing presidential power. At the very least, its importance for any one president must be considered alongside other advantages. "Going public" does not necessarily carry a special bonus, though presidents with limited advantages otherwise may be forced to rely on this tactic.
- The agenda will be continuous, with many issues derived from programs already being administered. The president surely plays an important role in certifying issues and setting priorities, but Congress and the bureaucracy will also be natural participants. At the very least, therefore, the president will be required to persuade other policy actors that his choices are the right ones. They will do the same with him.
- Lawmaking will vary substantially in terms of initiative, sequence, partisan and institutional interaction, and productivity. The challenge is to comprehend the variable role of the president in a government that is designed for continuity and change.
- Reform will be an especially intricate undertaking since, by constitutional design, the governmental structure is antithetical to efficient goal achievement. Yet many, if not most, reforms seek to achieve efficiency

within the basic separated structure. There are not many reforms designed to facilitate the more effective working of split-party government.

DISCUSSION QUESTIONS

1. The conventional wisdom is that presidential power increases, often dramatically, during war and other national crises. How was President Barack Obama's ability to exercise power affected by the economic and financial crises occurring as he took office?

2. How do President Obama's first two years—declining popularity, Democratic majorities in Congress, and much partisan conflict between Republicans and the president—affect your view of Jones's argument?

3. How can Jones's view of the presidency be squared with the popular view that the president is the most powerful person in the world?

Debating the Issues: Is Obama a Transformational President?

When Barack Obama announced his presidential campaign in January 2007, the odds seemed long. Yet he defeated New York State Senator Hillary Clinton in one of the most closely contested presidential nomination contests in decades, and then went on to defeat the far more experienced Republican senator John McCain to win the presidency.

Throughout the campaign, Obama dazzled audiences with soaring rhetoric about "changing Washington," announcing that his campaign was about "hope and change." "It's time for us to change America," Obama said as he accepted his party's nomination for president, time to "cast off the worn-out ideas and politics of the past." Obama presented himself as a transformational president, someone who would introduce a new kind of politics. All presidents promise change—that's the main reason for running against incumbents or the incumbent political party. But Obama held out the prospect of a fundamental alteration of political arrangements and incentives, a shift in who held political power. As the first African American president, Obama certainly represented symbolic change in the kind of person who could get elected. Would he be able to deliver? Would he truly change the way politics operated and change the distribution of political power? Progressives and liberals were euphoric, certain that their time had come after eight years of George W. Bush's conservatism and wartime policy. Conservatives were alarmed that Obama would usher in a major expansion of government's role in the economy and weaken national security policy.

What can we now say about President Obama? Will he be compared to Andrew Jackson, Franklin Roosevelt, Thomas Jefferson, or Abraham Lincoln, presidents who fundamentally altered political arrangements and power? Will he be just another president who promised big and failed to deliver? Or is there a middle ground?

David Greenberg occupies the middle ground in this debate. The soaring hopes of January 2009 have dissipated in the face of the realities of governing, which has always been much, much harder than campaigning. But, Greenberg argues, that is inevitable, because "in the modern age, presidents are never able to meet" the expectations of transformative change. Presidents always confront limits and, given the expectations generated during the campaign, they must always disappoint. But that is hardly synonymous with failure, and Greenberg notes that other historic presidents—including Lincoln, Roosevelt, Kennedy—and Reagan, although Greenberg doesn't mention him—had rough early days.

Writing from the left, Katrina Vanden Heuvel and Robert L. Borosage express disappointment, especially over Obama's policies toward the financial sector, which they see as enriching Wall Street bankers while leaving families behind, and his surge in troop commitments in Afghanistan. "Many wonder," they write, "what happened to the transformational presidency." They argue that the president, despite his promises, has not been bold enough in confronting entrenched interests and has proven reluctant to mobilize his liberal base in the face of conservative obstructionism. The result has been timid compromises on health care reform and a reluctance to confront conservative arguments head on. These authors urge the president to move sharply to the left. They also call on progressives to organize large-scale protests that take advantage of the same enthusiasm that motivated many supporters during the 2008 campaign.

Richard Lowry and Ramesh Ponnuru see Obama as transformative, but not in a positive way. In their view, Obama is the first president explicitly to reject the notion of American exceptionalism—the idea that the United States is historically unique and has always differed from other democracies. They claim that liberals have always been uncomfortable with this notion, and that the Left is more likely to see the United States as the source of many of the world's problems, not its best hope. And Obama, in their eyes, embodies this rejection of American exceptionalism. They note his efforts to expand greatly the size and scope of government regulatory power, his "hesitance to advocate American ideals," and his defensiveness in the international arena. They claim that Obama's problems stem from the public's repudiation of his principal policies.

32

"The Honeymooners"

DAVID GREENBERG

The promise and selling point of Barack Obama's 2008 campaign—breaking with the past, delivering something new—was the oldest promise in American politics. Since European settlers crossed the Atlantic imagining (mistakenly) a "new world" without history, Americans have rewarded talk of new beginnings. The early colonists sought to create a society de novo in ways that Europe—with its religious wars, social stratification, and finitude of land—made impossible. To the Revolutionary generation, the acts of declaring independence and drafting a constitution seemed to ratify this mythology. And in every era since, Americans have fallen, starry-eyed, for leaders who speak of a future unencumbered by history's weight. Theodore Roosevelt's New Nationalism, Woodrow Wilson's New Freedom, FDR's New Deal, JFK's New Frontier, even George H. W. Bush's New World Order—all began with the promise of the new.

Of course, after the flush of a campaign, both voters and presidents have invariably discovered that history imposes constraints. After the Civil War, a cohort of young intellectuals invested hope in Ulysses S. Grant, only to see rampant corruption persist and the dream of reconstructing the South dissolve. After World War I, the crash-and-burn of Wilson's noble quest for "peace without victory" soured Americans on an energetic executive for a decade. Bill Clinton's New Covenant, a dead-on-arrival slogan, presaged the letdown that came as his followers realized that liberalism's revival would require more than a few token compromises.

Obama in 2008 was just the latest aspirant to talk of beginning anew. He bested Hillary Clinton for the Democratic nomination in part by saddling her with the record of not one but two past presidents: the residual regret over her husband's supposedly small-bore and blandly centrist Third Way agenda, and the collective buyers' remorse over the Iraq War. In contrast to the dreaded "incrementalism" of the Clintons, Obama's candidacy tantalized voters with a chance for what he called "transformational" or "fundamental" change.

One year later, transformation looks like a fleeting dream. No one knows whether Obama can deliver massive change on the scale of Lincoln, Wilson, FDR, or LBJ. But right now, the opportunity that loomed last fall seems to have passed. Conservatives—uncharacteristically mute last winter—have regained their voice, nearly derailing Obama's health-care plan and keeping the administration on defense in the daily media wars. Meanwhile, liberals and leftists, who largely muffled their doubts when Obama had a presidency to win, are suddenly seething over his moderation and compromises—keeping suspected terrorists jailed indefinitely, countenancing his treasury secretary's coziness with financial CEOs, letting center-right senators weaken his health-care plan. Washington pundits, for their part, intoned throughout 2009 that in taking on health care, energy, and financial reform in his first year, the president was attempting "too much."

Yet the now-prevalent pessimism about Obama's presidency is surely unwarranted. True, we can no longer expect Obama to be the agent of a post-partisan politics, or an uncorrupted anti-politician incapable of spin or triangulation, or America's most civil-libertarian president, or a socialist. But in the modern age, presidents are never able to meet such expectations. Our hunger for presidential intervention, leadership, and salvation now exceeds any individual's capacities. So the eclipse of these campaign-trail fantasies about Obama's presidency hardly signals its death. On the contrary, it marks the true beginning.

"If there is anything that history has taught us," John F. Kennedy said on the campaign trail in 1960, "it is that the great accomplishments of Woodrow Wilson and of Franklin Roosevelt were made in the early days, months, and years of their administrations. That was the time for maximum action." But Kennedy was wrong—unless you choose to focus exclusively on the word *years* instead of *days* and *months*. As rich in opportunity as presidential honeymoons can be—and the best executives have used them to get important things done—a president's real work doesn't occur when he has what Obama calls the righteous wind at his back. It occurs when he has to soldier on into a fight, despite blustery headwinds.

Like the unit of 100 days, the benchmark of a president's first year matters a lot to journalists but relatively little to historians. The 100-days concept itself, which originated with Roosevelt's flurry of activity in early 1933, soon devolved into a transparent public-relations gimmick, as media-age presidents sweated over how to boost their grades on what soon came to be recognized as the president's initial report card. Similarly, the now-ritualized year-one evaluation, though harmless as an exercise in journalistic stock-taking, offers a weak basis for predicting future performance. Indeed, none of the three presidents Obama has taken as his role models—Lincoln, FDR, and Kennedy—enjoyed a first year that foretold the direction of his presidency. Transformation doesn't happen overnight.

Abraham Lincoln is Obama's favorite president and his aspirational model. In 2007, the senator from Illinois launched his bid for the Oval Office in Lincoln's shadow, on the steps of the Springfield Old State Capitol. With his message of national conciliation, Obama often echoed Lincoln's second inaugural address. Even when he attacked his rivals, he suggested that he was merely combating their retrogressive politics while he was summoning the better angels of our nature. At times, the Lincoln comparisons taxed credulity: Obama's devotees even pointed to Lincoln's one-term service in Congress—and his subsequent rise to become America's greatest president—to answer the charge that Obama hadn't accomplished enough in his career to earn him the White House. It was no surprise when, in January 2009, the incoming president took his inaugural oath on the Bible Lincoln had used, and presided over festivities branded as "A New Birth of Freedom."

Yet as Obama surely knows, Lincoln—a transformative president if there ever was one—started his administration on a shaky note. His inaugural address fumblingly extended on olive branch to the seceding states of the South, promising (to no avail) that he would enforce the fugitive-slave law and uphold slavery in the states where it was legal. The Confederate attack on Fort Sumter forced Lincoln to change course. But on the crucial matter of slavery, the president—who had never considered himself an abolitionist—remained fairly conservative. "If I could save the Union without freeing *any* slave I would do it, and if I could save it by freeing *all* the slaves I would do it," he wrote to Horace Greeley in 1862, "and if I could save it by freeing some and leaving others alone I would also do that." Few foresaw that his presidency would end with the abolition of slavery and a redefinition of freedom, union, and equality.

Lincoln also needed time to gain his footing as commander in chief. Unsure of himself in military affairs, he was at the mercy of his generals, including the aging and detached Winfield Scott. Dispiriting defeats—notably at the First Battle of Bull Run, in July 1861—emboldened the South. Even after Lincoln mustered the wisdom to replace Scott, George B. McClellan, his new top commander, frustrated the president by declining to advance against Confederate forces. As for his domestic agenda, Lincoln, like most 19th-century presidents, followed Congress's lead. But even there, despite a Republican leadership eager to exploit the sudden absence of Southerners, major laws—the Homestead Act, the Pacific Railway Act, and the Morrill Land Grant Act—didn't get the president's signature until 1862.

No one could say that Franklin Roosevelt began his first year in office hesitantly. His first 100 days were indeed a whirlwind of legislative and executive feats. But FDR geared his first-year efforts almost entirely toward recovery—a necessary but hardly transformative goal.

Certain measures—like solving the banking crisis, which had reached catastrophic proportions on the eve of his inauguration—made a palpable difference. But the core elements of FDR's "First New Deal" turned out to be, on the whole, ineffectual or unconstitutional—or both. The National Recovery Administration, the centerpiece of it all, which relied on industry leaders to agree to production codes, was flawed in both conception and execution, and it failed miserably. When the Supreme Court unanimously ruled it unconstitutional, Roosevelt's aide Robert Jackson called the decision a blessing in disguise, since it spared the president from having to watch Congress decline to renew the act. The Agricultural Adjustment Act, which regulated farm production through central planning, was also struck down. And then there was Roosevelt's Economy Act, a misguided effort in budget balancing taken up before Washington discovered the wisdom of deficit spending.

Most of the New Deal's lasting elements didn't come until 1935. Only after taking a beating on the airwaves from demagogic populists like Senator Huey Long of Louisiana and the radio priest Charles Coughlin did FDR sign on to the Social Security Act, which created unemployment insurance, old-age pensions, and a safety net for the disabled. And not until his second term did his administration embrace a Keynesian strategy of aggressive spending to lift the economy out of crisis. If Roosevelt's first year was historic for its activist spirit and purposeful intervention, its economic philosophy left little mark.

While Obama styled himself Lincolnian in his rhetoric of reconciliation, and Rooseveltian in his steadfastness in the face of economic distress, he just as often summoned the Kennedy mystique, presenting himself as the telegenic, inspirational torchbearer of an ascendant generation. Obama suggested that he wanted to "move the country in a fundamentally different direction," as he believed Kennedy had. Just as Kennedy's election shattered the anti-Catholic taboo in presidential politics, Obama's promised to topple an age-old wall of racial prejudice. The Baby Boomers who flocked to Obama's candidacy said he brought back memories of JFK. The claim was echoed most tellingly by the fallen president's own brother, who anointed Obama as JFK's successor after perceiving a slight to the family name in Hillary Clinton's assertion that the skill of Lyndon Johnson—she didn't mention Jack—had been instrumental in passing the 1964 Civil Rights Act.

In fact, on civil rights, as in other areas, Kennedy's first-year performance dismayed his enthusiasts. As a candidate, he had vowed to desegregate federal housing with "a stroke of the presidential pen." But once in office, he demurred; fearful of alienating powerful southern Democrats whose support he needed on other issues, he focused instead on foreign-policy problems. Not until he'd cleared the 1962 midterm elections did Kennedy issue the housing proclamation. Caution likewise informed his response to the Freedom Riders—the activists who rode buses across the South starting in May 1961 to force the government to uphold the Supreme Court's desegregation of interstate travel. When white southerners brutally beat the activists, Kennedy and his aides, unprepared, at first tried to stop the rides, sending in federal marshals only when it seemed that the violence might turn deadly.

In foreign policy, too, the biggest developments of JFK's debut year yielded little positive transformation. The Bay of Pigs invasion, all ill-conceived CIA scheme hatched under Dwight Eisenhower, redounded to Kennedy's benefit only because he had the sense not to duck responsibility. At his June summit in Vienna with Nikita Khrushchev, the new president felt he was verbally pummeled by the Soviet premier, in what Kennedy called the "roughest thing in my life." Kennedy's tepid response may have encouraged Khrushchev to erect the Berlin Wall that fall. When that happened, too, JFK was slow to act (KENNEDY: YOU CAN'T STOP TANKS WITH WORDS, read one West Berliner's protest sign), and even his decision to send retired General Lucius Clay and Vice President Johnson to West Berlin to boost morale did nothing to deter the Soviets. At the end of 1961, Kennedy's aide Ted Sorensen mentioned that two reporters were

considering writing books about the year gone by. Kennedy was mystified: "Who would want to read a book on disasters?"

The presidency that Obama's resembles most so far isn't any of these but,
ironically, that of Bill Clinton—ironic because Obama, speaking in January 2008 about what makes a good president, implicitly denigrated Clinton even as he praised Ronald Reagan for having "changed the trajectory
of America" and "put us on a fundamentally different path." Obama,
many speculated at the time, may have been playing head games with
his peevish predecessor, goading him into another outburst that would
thrill the press pack. Even so, it was a strange reading of history. Reagan's election, after all, did not initiate but culminated a long conservative effort to gain control of the levers of power; his decisions as president
moved his party to the right, but they also introduced fissures and frustrations into the conservative alliance. Clinton's tenure, in contrast, began
a new era for the Democrats, and after his eight years, virtually all of the
party's leading lights embraced what had been controversial stands in
1992: an internationalist foreign policy, growth-centered economics, and
a willingness to link social policies to family values.

The point would be trivial had Obama not reached for Clinton's 1992
playbook during the fall 2008 campaign. Obama's battle with John Mc-
Cain, which centered on the hard-pressed middle class, showed that
Obama represented less a repudiation of Clinton (as the primaries had
suggested) than a continuation. His rhetoric wafted to earth to focus on
everyday economic concerns. His convention speech opened, after the
preliminaries, not with soaring visions of post-partisan unity, but with
issue-based, it's-the-economy-stupid plain language:

> Tonight, more Americans are out of work and more are working harder for
> less. More of you have lost your homes and even more are watching your
> home values plummet. More of you have cars you can't afford to drive, credit-
> card bills you can't afford to pay, and tuition that's beyond your reach.

Obama discovered this idiom just in time for the financial chaos and the
debates with McCain.

Obama's successes and struggles in his first year bear striking resem-
blances to Clinton's. Both men were elected with similar mandates—
Clinton won 370 electoral voles, Obama 365—and majorities in both
houses of Congress. Both opened their first years well by signing a few
queued-up executive orders and bills—including the Family and Medical
Leave Act, for Clinton, and the Lilly Ledbetter Fair Pay Act and the expansion of the Children's Health Insurance Program, for Obama. And
both made economic revival their first priority. Both men also entered office facing tooth-and-nail resistance from a right wing that had just lost
the presidency. The right imagined Clinton, as it does Obama, to be far

more radical than he really was, and it thus tried to delegitimize him. A short line connects the "Who shot Vince Foster?" conspiracy theories to those surrounding Obama's citizenship.

Republicans also forced Clinton to pass his first economic plan without their support, much as they tried to scuttle Obama's stimulus package. And despite losing the legislative battle, they succeeded in shaping public perception of these economic bills after their passage. Clinton's 1993 budget—which not only set the government on course for a record surplus, but also cut taxes for millions while raising them on very few—was nonetheless portrayed, and viewed by most Americans, as a tax hike. In parallel fashion, economic evidence suggests that Obama's spring stimulus bill has already done some appreciable good. But according to an August Gallup poll, Americans consider it too big and are uncertain about its benefits. And while Obama seems likely, as of this writing, to emerge from his first health-care fight with more to show for it than Clinton did from his, the final bill probably won't be more than an incremental step or two forward—less like Medicare than like the 1996 Kennedy-Kassebaum Act, a now-forgotten consolation prize that Clinton garnered later in his presidency.

The reassertion of political limits and the deflation of campaign-season euphoria make it unlikely that Obama's presidency will be "transformational" in the sense that he spoke of on the campaign trail—Lincolnian in its boldness, Rooseveltian in its activism, or Kennedyesque in its uplift. More likely, it will resemble Clinton's presidency, with eight years of muddling through, frequent bouts of sharp partisan opposition, fluctuating poll ratings, and dashed hopes.

This should be no cause for distress. Obama could do worse than to emulate Clinton, who, at the end of day, left the country better off than when he took office. Clinton's record remains undervalued, partly because a misleading narrative took hold (that his impeachment cost him the chance to do more), and partly because many of his gains were achieved not through the big-ticket stand-alone legislation that journalists recite in their year-end summaries but through less visible allocations within the interstices of the federal budget. No single law or presidential order gave us the longest economic expansion in history, the lowest unemployment rates in three decades, or the declines in poverty, crime, and teen pregnancy. Nor does Clinton deserve sole credit for these feats. But all were accomplished during his eight years.

Twenty-five years ago, the political scientist Theodore Lowi published a book called *The Personal President*. It argued that the increasingly large responsibilities placed on the president since Franklin Roosevelt's time—of regulation, social provision, and economic management, to say nothing of the leadership of the free world—have exploded into impossible expectations. Every postwar chief executive, Lowi noted—and the observation still holds—has begun his presidency with high approval ratings and left office with the public chastened of its early optimism, if not disillusioned altogether. (The president who has exited the White House with the highest approval ratings, post-FDR, is Clinton.)

It is easy to propose that we lower our expectations for our new presidents—even, or perhaps especially, for presidents who come bearing lofty promises of transformation. But we can't correct the problem, Lowi's diagnosis suggested, simply by resolving to demand less from our chief executives or by vowing to learn from the past. The problem is rooted in nothing less than the presidency's assumption of immense powers, and of a central role in our imagination. Candidates have no better path to victory than by inspiring us with dreams of a new political era, and presidents have no choice but to attempt "too much." In doing so, however, they can only disappoint us.

33

"Change Won't Come Easy"

Katrina Vanden Heuvel and Robert L. Borosage

President Obama hailed the healthcare reform bill coming out of the Senate as the "most important piece of social legislation since the Social Security Act passed in the 1930s." Former Democratic Party chair Howard Dean denounced it as a "giveaway to insurance companies."

Larry Summers, Obama's lead economic adviser, described the $780 billion recovery plan as the largest stimulus plan in the country's history. Economists like Nobel laureate Joseph Stiglitz warned from the beginning that it was too small to lift us out of the Great Recession.

The president described the administration's financial reform package as a "sweeping overhaul," a "transformation on a scale not seen since . . . the Great Depression." Former Federal Reserve chair Paul Volcker warned that the proposed "safety net" for big banks would encourage much greater "risk taking."

Congressman Ed Markey, chair of the House Select Committee on Energy Independence, hailed the energy bill that was passed by the House as "the most important energy and environmental bill in our nation's history." Environmental leaders were underwhelmed; some considered it worse than the current law.

The discordant reality of these times is that these conflicting statements are all essentially true. "I want you to be ready," Bill Clinton warned bloggers about healthcare reform at the Netroots Conference in August, to "accept less than a full loaf." He could easily have been talking about the Obama presidency itself. Progressives must determine how to respond now that the fierce resistance to change has revealed itself.

The euphoria of a year ago is dissipating. Then, in the wake of a calamitous and discredited conservative government, Americans voted for change, electing a stunningly gifted leader and large Democratic majorities in both houses of Congress. A mobilized activist base appeared ready to throw itself into the fray, and an emerging majority coalition suggested the potential for a long-term realignment.

Now the struggles of the first year of the Obama administration are generating increasing demoralization and anger. Disappointment about reforms in motion—healthcare, jobs, climate change—marks those who care the most. The recovery plan, which has revived Wall Street but not working families, is fueling dangerous right-wing populism. Substituting an unwinnable "good war" in Afghanistan for the unwinnable "bad war" in Iraq, along with a military budget exceeding that of George W. Bush, is a recipe for failure. The administration's foreign policy—despite the promise in Cairo of engaging the Muslim world and in Prague of embracing disarmament—is increasingly described by neocons as providing more continuity than change from the Bush years. Democrats cringe at prospects for the fall elections. Despite all the obvious eloquence and intelligence of the new president, many wonder what happened to the transformational presidency.

It Ain't Easy; Everything's Broken

Turns out, Obama is not the Messiah, and those who thought so were always fooling themselves. The disappointments of Obama's first year are less the product of his failures than of the balance of forces he faces in Washington and in the country. Many progressives thought we had taken back America with the election of 2008, but in reality the work had only just begun.

In fact, the president has been bolder than many expected, summoning the country to address fundamental challenges it can no longer afford to ignore. Yet the ambition of Obama's vision has been accompanied by a marked caution in conception and execution. Obama clearly aspires to a historic presidency, one that defines a new era as FDR's or Reagan's did. But he has never been a movement progressive the way Reagan was a movement conservative. He has surrounded himself with the brightest and best of the Democratic establishment, drawn inevitably from those marinated in the Clinton years. Many of his leading advisers—from Larry Summers and Timothy Geithner to Robert Gates—were directly implicated in the decisions that helped to drive us off the cliff. These voices are not advocates of transformation.

So the reform proposals that emerge from the administration often fall short not only of the hopes of progressives but of the objectives the president himself defines and the change the country needs. Obama outlined a new foundation for the economy in his "Sermon on the Mount," but the big banks were rescued, not reorganized, and no industrial policy accompanied the commitment to a new economy. Bankers were chastised for their bonuses, but there was no drive to hold executives accountable and empower workers, both central to an economy that sustains a broad middle class. The president shelved Bush's failed cowboy bellicosity, but the decision to escalate in Afghanistan accedes to the Bush folly of waging war against terrorism rather than intensifying global law enforcement.

Most surprising has been the reluctance to engage the right boldly in the war of ideas. Reagan consolidated the conservative era in part by bludgeoning reigning liberalism with a relentless conservative critique. He attacked and retreated on policy when necessary, but his ideological assault never faltered. Obama has a rare ability to frame the contrast with the right, to counter its market fundamentalism and virulent nihilism with a compelling statement of our shared values, with government as the necessary instrument of our common purpose.

But for much of the year, Democrats have been having policy debates—on the public opinion, on cap and trade, on systemic risk regulation—while Republicans and the resurgent right have been waging an argument about values and ideas, on liberty and free markets, freedom and small government. Although the administration has reminded Americans of the catastrophic legacy left by the Bush years, it has seldom indicted the conservative ideas that were the source of the calamity. Instead the president prefers to blame the process—"partisanship . . . politics . . . ever quickening news cycles . . . endless campaigns focused on scoring points instead of meeting our common challenges."

That default complements an insider Congressional strategy that prefers backroom compromise to public mobilization. This president enunciates the elements of his reform proposals and then lets Congress and his aides to do their work off-stage. But that cedes the terrain to the legions of the old order that are mobilized to fend off real reform.

The past months have exposed the elements of that resistance—the cynical Republican strategy of lockstep obstruction, the Senate rules that empower a handful of small-state conservatives and the embittered Joe Lieberman. (It is worth remembering that there were majorities in both houses of Congress for a bolder stimulus and far better healthcare reform.)

And of course, at the heart of the opposition are the entrenched corporate complexes that feed off public subsidies and a corrupt Congress. These have been boom times for Democratic lobbyists and former officeholders. The commercial banks deployed nearly 417 registered lobbyists in 2009. The insurance and drug lobbies spent about $1.4 million a day, with 350 former legislators and staffers lined up to weaken healthcare reform. Legislators in both parties succumbed to the pervasive corruptions of our money politics.

The result is that even when historic reforms like healthcare emerge, they are so battered that supporters end up dispirited. Democrats face going into the 2010 midterm elections with double-digit unemployment, rescued bankers awarding themselves million-dollar bonuses, rising casualties in Afghanistan, the right mobilized and progressive activists dismayed. If Republicans score major victories in the election, that will make everything harder; the administration will become more cautious, not less. Clearly, if we are not to squander the best opportunity for progressive reform in thirty years, something will have to change.

Going Grassroots

The president warned that change wouldn't come easy. From the start, the administration devoted energy and resources to organizing a unified base of activists. Organizing for Obama promised use of an unmatched list of activists and supporters built during the campaign. Donors were tapped to set up new entities—Common Purpose Project, Unity '09, etc.— to coordinate messages and field operations. Significant resources went to coalitions to help drive healthcare, climate change and immigration reform. The administration's argument was and is compelling. This is a reform moment with the most liberal president in memory. It is time to unite, provide support for his leadership and help drive reform.

Progressives and grassroots networks across the country rallied to that call. Remarkable work has been done. Broad coalitions were built, arming activists with more capacity and better coordination in the process of lobbying legislators. New constituencies—the faith community, young people and small business owners—have been enlisted. Resources were devoted to conservative districts and states where key swing votes had to be won.

These efforts have propelled the president's key reforms. When tea-baggers threatened to torpedo heathcare reform, progressives—led by Health Care for America Now, unions and MoveOn—mobilized and soon overwhelmed them in town hall meetings.

But there were costs associated with channeling progressive energy through the administration. Obama aides, led by Chief of Staff Rahm Emanuel, argued fiercely against going after the Democrats—Blue Dogs and New Dems—who were impeding reform, and the White House chose not to mobilize its base to pressure them. Groups were often blindsided by backroom deals like the one with the drug companies that sustained the ban on negotiating lower drug prices.

One unintended consequence was that populist anger has been channeled by the right, not the left. Tea-baggers, well funded by established interests, turned rage against those trying to dig out of the hole rather than those who got us into it. Their voice was inchoate, but at the core was a fury at Big Government, Big Banks and Big Business, which were taking their jobs, pocketing public subsidies and helping "those people" while raising their taxes. On the left, there has been no movement comparable to the labor and socialist demonstrations in the '30s or the civil rights movement in the '60s that forced the pace of change.

Moving Forward: Ideas Matter

Cynicism is the cheap coin of politics. The left blogosphere is rife with the complaints of the disillusioned (denouncing politicians as crooks, the government as corrupt and Obama as compromised) and threats to give up and stay home. That would be a profound mistake. This country is enmeshed in a fierce debate about its future. Can we summon up the will and the majorities needed to meet the critical challenges we face? Or will we continue our decline, ceding ground to the entrenched corporate cronyism that profits from conservative misrule?

Winning this debate requires new thinking as well as independent organizing. Progressives should be moving outside the Beltway, working to organize protest movements for social justice and giving voice to the displaced and the unemployed. We should be helping to chart a new course while exposing the false idols and powerful interests that stand in the way.

And we should be directly joining the argument with the resurgent right. One basic lesson must be repeated and elaborated upon: the mess that we are in results not from inaction or partisan stalemate but from the failure of conservative policies and ideas in action. Only by coming together to demand an accountable democratic government on our side, free from the special interests that feed off it, can we build a stronger, more just and more vibrant America.

Reform Matters

A renewed focus on building protest movements can bolster, not weaken, reform efforts. National debates over fundamental reforms will provide the grist for such organizing. In 2010, assuming healthcare finally passes, the legislative agenda will turn to jobs and financial accountability, two issues that are vital to building the new economy. Politically, the fall elections will likely depend on which candidates and which party can convince skeptical voters that they are on the side of working people and for curbing Wall Street's excesses.

Here progressive organizing and protests that challenge the limits of the current debate are essential. On jobs, the fundamental questions are whether a commitment will be made of sufficient scale to meet the deepening jobs crisis and whether that initiative will be sufficiently targeted to impact those areas most devastated. Republicans and Blue Dog Demo-crats are already declaiming against any new program. The administra-tion, badgered about deficits and believing the economy is on the road to recovery, it likely to support a face-lift when reconstructive surgery is needed.

The stakes here couldn't be higher. If Democrats don't deliver on jobs, the economy won't recover, and the 2010 election may well snuff out any chance for reforms. At the very least, they have to show Americans that they're fighting for jobs. Independent organizing that gives voice to the unemployed, already begun by labor unions and civil rights groups, is essential. The House Progressive Caucus can play a major role in raising the bar and forcing the issue.

Similarly, the debate on financial reform should provide the context for progressive protest organizing. The White House plans to pick a fight with the banking lobby over the proposed Consumer Financial Protec-tion Agency, which would create an independent cop to police banks and protect consumers from financial frauds and abuses. In the House, Re-publicans voted with the banks against reform. In contrast, progressives are pushing sweeping reforms that go to the heart of the financial ex-cesses of the past years—auditing the Federal Reserve; breaking up the big banks; taxing windfall profits, excess bonuses and speculation; out-lawing exotic instruments; and limiting usurious interest rates.

Independent organizing can tap into a wellspring of public fury. Muck-raking is needed to detail and broadcast the systemic frauds and corrup-tions. Creative demonstrations can embarrass the bank lobby and the legislators on the take. It is only if the big banks' money becomes toxic that there is any hope of gaining the reforms needed to curb their power. Here is where the creativity and energy of the Obama activists, many frus-trated by the timidity of Organizing for America, can find expression.

Pundits predict that the other issues on the president's agenda—cli-mate change, immigration reform, employee free choice—will have a dif-ficult time getting a hearing before the 2010 elections. Progressives will have to push hard to ensure that these reforms—vital to both the new economy and to consolidating the emerging progressive majority—are not shunted to the side.

Because of the botched terrorist attempt to bomb a plane on Christmas Day, the administration enters the year on the defensive on terrorism. The furor will add to bipartisan support for an enlarged military budget and for military escalation in Afghanistan, Yemen and elsewhere. The president will sound more bellicose notes on terrorism. The opposition to escalation in Afghanistan, which probably still enjoys majority support among Democrats in the House, will have to redouble its work, educat-ing Americans about the costs and the stakes and offering common-sense alternative strategies to meet the threat of terrorism.

Challenge Those Who Stand in the Way

Democratic prospects look grim for the fall elections. In low-turnout midterm elections, the passion of base supporters plays a large role. Clearly, the right will be mobilized. Progressives will have to confound the widespread expectation that they will not match the right's fervor.

The elections will turn into a national referendum on the country's direction. Will Americans punish those pushing for reform, or those standing in the way? The clear focus must be to make certain that Republicans pay for their irresponsible strategy of obstruction. Here the GOP's opposition to creating jobs and curbing banks should provide a clear picture of what side they are on.

But this cannot be a purely partisan effort. Democrats who have consistently opposed or weakened vital reforms should not get a free pass. Progressives should be organizing primary challenges against the most egregious Blue Dogs—exemplified by Representative Melissa Bean, who gilded her campaign war chest by leading the banks' lobby efforts to weaken financial reform. It would be best to do this in districts or states where Democrats are strong, so the seats are not lost; but that may not be possible. Organizing formidable challenges in a couple of districts will send an important message.

The Audacity of Hope

As Frederick Douglass taught, "power concedes nothing without a demand. It never did and never will." Digging out of the hole that conservatives left Americans in can't be done overnight. The president has called on the country to face daunting challenges. Every step of reform is contested by powerful interests. Ruinous policies—such as our commitment to policing the world—have broad bipartisan support. Yet we haven't had this kind of moment since the 1960s. With persistence, work, rededication and struggle, we can issue the demands that change requires. This is a time for neither the innocent nor the cynical. It is a time for passion, for tenacity and, yes, for hope.

34

"An Exceptional Debate"

Richard Lowry and Ramesh Ponnuru

It's almost commonplace on the left that conservatives are "nihilists" for their opposition to President Obama. It's opposition for opposition's sake, an unprincipled exercise in partisan obstruction—mindless, toxic, destructive. When directed at Obama, "no" is an indefensible word, devoid of philosophical content.

Another, different charge has traditionally been leveled at conservatives—that they are "radicals." This criticism was made of *National Review* right at the beginning. Conservatives want to tear down the state, overturn precedent, reverse the direction of history. They are imprudent and incautious in their pursuit of a blinkered ideological agenda, in other words, fundamentally unconservative.

So conservatives get it coming and going. Our opposition to the Left is deemed nihilistic and our affirmative agenda radical. These dueling critiques point to a paradox at the heart of American conservatism. We aren't Tories, concerned with preserving the prerogatives of an aristocratic elite or defending tradition at all costs. Instead, we're advocates of the dynamism of an open society. Through most of human history and still in many places in the world, that would make us the opposite of conservatives. Not in America.

What do we, as American conservatives, want to *conserve*? The answer is simple: the pillars of American exceptionalism. Our country has always been exceptional. It is freer, more individualistic, more democratic, and more open and dynamic than any other nation on earth. These qualities are the bequest of our Founding and of our cultural heritage. They have always marked America as special, with a unique role and mission in the world: as a model of ordered liberty and self-government and as an exemplar of freedom and a vindicator of it, through persuasion when possible and force of arms when absolutely necessary.

The survival of American exceptionalism as we have known it is at the heart of the debate over Obama's program. It is why that debate is so charged. In his first year, Obama tried to avoid the cultural hot buttons that tripped up Bill Clinton and created the "gays, guns, and God" backlash of 1994. But he has stoked a different type of cultural reaction. The level of spending, the bailouts, and the extent of the intervention in the economy contemplated in health-care and cap-and-trade legislation have created the fear that something elemental is changing in the country. At stake isn't just a grab bag of fiscal issues, but the meaning of America and the character of its people: the ultimate cultural issue.

*   *   *

Liberty is the most important element of the creed. To secure it, the Founders set about strictly limiting government within carefully specified bounds. Immediately upon the collapse of British government in America, the states drew up written constitutions and neutered their executives. They went as far as they could possibly go to tame the government—indeed, they went farther, and had to start over to get a functioning state. But even this second try produced a Constitution that concentrated as much on what government could not do as on what it could.

The Founders knew what men were capable of, in the positive sense if their creative energies were unleashed and in the negative sense if they were given untrammeled power over others. "It may be a reflection on human nature," Madison wrote in a famous passage in *Federalist* No. 51 describing the checks in the Constitution, "that such devices should be necessary to control the abuses of government. But what is government itself, but the greatest of all reflections on human nature? If men were angels, no government would be necessary. If angels were to govern men, neither external nor internal controls on government would be necessary."

The Constitution's negative character reflected its basic goal: to protect people in their liberty. In stark contrast, European constitutions, even prior to World War II, established positive rights to government benefits. As Mary Ann Glendon notes, these differences "are legal manifestations of divergent, and deeply rooted, cultural attitudes toward the state and its functions."

This framework of freedom made possible the flourishing of the greatest commercial republic in history. * * *

*   *   *

In a telling coincidence, the publication of Adam Smith's world-changing free-market classic, *The Wealth of Nations*, coincided with the Declaration of Independence in 1776. Many of the Founders read the book. Without the medieval encumbrances and the powerful, entrenched special interests that plagued other countries, the United States could make Smith's ideas the basis of its economic dispensation. Gordon writes, "The United States has consistently come closer to the Smithian ideal over a longer period of time than any other major nation."

In the latitude provided by this relatively light-handed government, a commerce-loving, striving, and endlessly inventive people hustled its way to become the greatest economic power the world has ever known.

In America, there really hasn't been a disaffected proletariat—because the proletariat has gotten rich. Friedrich Engels had it right when he carped that "America is so purely bourgeois, so entirely without a feudal past and therefore proud of its purely bourgeois organization."

The traditional Marxist claim about the U.S. was that it was governed by the executive committee of the bourgeoisie. This was not intended as a compliment, but it was largely true. Look at the archetypal American, Benjamin Franklin, whose name comes from the Middle English meaning freeman, someone who owns some property. Napoleon dismissed the British as "a nation of shopkeepers"; we are a nation of Franklins.

Abraham Lincoln, a de facto Founding Father, is an exemplar of this aspect of America. "I hold the value of life," Lincoln said, "is to improve one's condition." There are few things he hated more than economic stasis. He couldn't abide Thomas Jefferson's vision of a nation of yeoman farmers living on their land forevermore, blissfully untouched by the forces of modern economic life. (Appropriately enough, Jefferson died broke.) Lincoln captured the genius of American life when he said, "The man who labored for another last year, this year labors for himself and next year he will hire others to labor for him."

That sentiment is at the heart of the American economic gospel. American attitudes toward wealth and its creation stand out within the developed world. Our income gap is greater than that in European countries, but not because our poor are worse off. In fact, they are better off than, say, the bottom 10 percent of Britons. It's just that our rich are phenomenally wealthy.

This is a source of political tension, but not as much as foreign observers might expect, thanks partly to a typically American attitude. A 2003 Gallup survey found that 31 percent of Americans expect to get rich, including 51 percent of young people and more than 20 percent of Americans making less than $30,000 a year. This isn't just cockeyed optimism. America remains a fluid society, with more than half of people in the bottom quintile pulling themselves out of it within a decade.

And so we arrived in the 21st century still a country apart. Prior to its recent run-up, total government spending was still only about 36 percent of GDP in the U.S. In Europe, the figure was much higher—44 percent in Britain, 53 percent in France, and 56 percent in Sweden. (The difference is starker when only nondefense spending is compared.)

Politically, we have always been more democratic, more populist than other countries. Edmund Burke said of the low-church Protestants who flocked here, "They represent the dissidents of dissent and the protest wing of the Protestant religion." The Scotch-Irish who settled the hinterlands were even more cussed. It wasn't very easy to tell any of these people what to do, as colonial governors learned to their regret.

*   *   *

Today, we still have more elections for more offices more often than other countries. Even many judges and law-enforcement officials are elected. In the federal government, political appointees have greater sway over the civil service than is the case in other developed countries. As Edward C. Banfield and James Q. Wilson have written, "There is virtually no sphere of 'administration' apart from politics."

* * *

We have managed to preserve a remarkable national spirit. At over 70 percent, more Americans express pride in their country than Western Europeans do in theirs. In terms of demography, we are the youngest advanced country in the world, and our population continues to grow as that of Western Europe is projected to decline.

Americans are more religious than Europeans. In the 18th century, American religious dissenters supported overthrowing state-supported churches because it would allow them to compete on an even playing field with other denominations. In that competition, America saw an explosion of religious feeling and became the most evangelical country in the world.

Religion gained authority and vitality from its separation from the state, and religion-inspired reform movements, from abolitionism to the civil-rights movement, have been a source of self-criticism and renewal. Today, 73 percent of Americans believe in God, compared with 27 percent of Frenchmen and 35 percent of Britons, according to a 2006 *Financial Times* survey.

All of this means that America has the spirit of a youthful, hopeful, developing country, matched with the economic muscle of the world's most advanced society and the stability of its oldest democratic institutions.

* * *

None of this is to say, of course, that America is perfect. No nation can be. But one can only regard with wonderment what America stands for and all that it has accomplished in its amazing, utterly distinct adventure in liberty.

There have always been those who take exception to American exceptionalism. Europeans developed a cottage industry in travel writing about America, most of it—although not all, with Tocqueville the most important exception—scandalized by the riotous freedoms of these restless, stubborn, commerce-crazy, God-soaked barbarians. The America of these portraits was simultaneously primitive and decadent: "grotesque, obscene, monstrous, stultifying, stunted, leveling, deadening, deracinating, roofless, uncultured," as James Ceaser summarizes the critique in *Reconstructing America*. Many of America's European critics hoped that, over time, America would lose its distinctiveness. It would become just another developed Western country: more centralized, more elitist, more secular, less warlike, and less free. In short, a *quieter*, more *civilized* place.

The American Left has shared this maddened perplexity at its country's character and this hope for its effacement. Marxists at home and abroad were always mystified by the failure of socialism in the U.S. They thought that, as the most advanced capitalist society, we would have had the most restive proletariat. Instead we have had a broad and largely satisfied middle class. Even our unions, in their early history, were antistatist, their radicalism anarchistic rather than socialist. * * *

* * *

New Deal intellectuals gushed over Bolshevism in the 1930s. FDR Brain Truster Stuart Chase enthused, "Why should Russians have all the fun of remaking a world?" His statement captured the utopian underpinnings of the progressive project and the yearning for the kind of radical remaking of society that was readily attainable only in countries that gave themselves over entirely to the state. The other model was Italian fascism, which New Dealers studied closely and in important respects aped.

The New Deal was a watershed, but America didn't lurch all the way to socialism. The power of the central government increased, a welfare state was born, and unionization advanced. But even in the midst of the Great Depression, typically American attitudes still prevailed. In a 1935 Gallup survey, Americans by a wide margin thought the government was spending too much.

After World War II, a Left that had been gaining strength in Europe for decades finally realized its social-democratic ambitions. The U.S. followed a different course. In the academy, a perverse version of American exceptionalism took root: an exceptionalism of criminality, conquest, and oppression. America was special only in its misdeeds and failings; all cultures were to be celebrated except our own. The exceptionalism of Howard Zinn and Noam Chomsky, in milder form, occupied the commanding heights of our education system. It has worked to trash our Founding, to wipe out our historical memory, and to create a guilty conscience among our ruling elite.

In politics, however, the country's progress away from its character continued to be "unaccountably slow." American government continued to grow, particularly during the Johnson and Nixon years; the states became ever more one of the federal government's key client groups rather than checks on its power. But the individualistic American character began to reassert itself after its mid-century dormancy. Americans saw the stagflation of the 1970s as an indictment of Big Government rather than a crisis of capitalism. Ronald Reagan won the presidency of a nation that, by European standards, was still a freewheeling cowboy economy and democracy—and made it even freer.

Deregulation exposed unions to competitive pressures that they could not survive. The U.S. quickly came out of its post-Vietnam defensive crouch. And religion, rather than fading away, became more publicly assertive in response to perceived threats. Bill Clinton's Democratic presidency did more to confirm than to alter these trends.

The Left's search for a foreign template to graft onto America grew more desperate. Why couldn't we be more like *them*—like the French, like the Swedes, like the Danes? Like any people with a larger and busier government overawing the private sector and civil society? You can see it in *Sicko*, wherein Michael Moore extols the British national health-care system, the French way of life, and even the munificence of Cuba; you can hear it in all the admonitions from left-wing commentators that every other advanced society has government child care, or gun control, or mass transit, or whatever socialistic program or other infringement on our liberty we have had the wisdom to reject for decades.

President Obama's first year in office should be seen in the context of contemporary liberalism's discomfort with American exceptionalism.

The president has signaled again and again his unease with traditional American patriotism. As a senator he notoriously made a virtue of not wearing a flag pin. As president he has been unusually detached from American history: When a foreign critic brought up the Bay of Pigs, rather than defend the country's honor he noted that he was a toddler at the time. And while acknowledging that America has been a force for good, he has all but denied the idea that America is an exceptional nation. Asked whether he believed in American exceptionalism during a European trip last spring, Obama said, "I believe in American exceptionalism, just as I suspect that the Brits believe in British exceptionalism and the Greeks believe in Greek exceptionalism." (Is it just a coincidence that he reached for examples of former hegemons?)

In this respect the president reflects the mainstream sentiment of American liberals. We do not question the sincerity of his, or their, desire to better the lot of his countrymen. But modern liberal intellectuals have had a notoriously difficult time coming up with a decent account of patriotism even when they have felt it. * * *

Given the liberal gestalt, it is perhaps unsurprising that every important aspect of American exceptionalism has been under threat from President Obama and his allies in Washington. Obama has frankly and correctly described their project as to change the country fundamentally.

* * *

Already we are catching up to the European norm for government power. In 2010, government spending in the U.S. will reach an estimated 44 percent of GDP. With entitlements for the elderly on a path to explode with the retirement of the Baby Boomers, the trend is toward more convergence. In a strange reversal, last year it was an American president urging *continental Europeans* to spend more to combat the recession. Two if his highest priorities would drastically, and probably irreversibly, expand the government's footprints.

American liberals have long been embarrassed about our country's supposedly retrograde policies on health care and energy, especially compared with Europe's nationalized health insurance and carbon rationing. So they tried to use their unprecedented power after the 2008 elections to bring the U.S. into line. They sought to limit carbon emissions. That legislation would simultaneously represent a massive indirect tax increase, an extension of the tentacles of government regulation into every sector of the economy, and an empowerment of new bureaucratic instruments to control and direct economic development.

Obama's health-care policy would change the relationship of people to government, probably forever, by further nationalizing our system. It would have the federal government, for the first time, order all Americans to purchase a specified product. And socialized health-care systems in other lands have become endless warrants for more taxing and spending, as both are justified as necessary to delivering adequate health care. Once the public is hooked on government health care, its political attitudes shift leftward. (The system's flaws, such as rationing, tend to be attributed to underfunding, so that even discontent with it ends up entrenching it.)

Free labor markets have been an expression of American individualism and a contributor to American dynamism. But President Obama has attempted to upend seven decades of American labor law in order to make it easier for unions to collect new members. Democrats hope to reverse the unions' decline. Tellingly, after the United Auto Workers helped wreck GM and Chrysler, the Obama administration handed it a large share of control over the two companies.

Corporations, meanwhile, are also becoming more dependent on government handouts. Rivalry between business and political elites has helped to safeguard American liberty. What we are seeing now is the possible emergence of a new political economy in which Big Business, Big Labor, and Big Government all have cozy relations of mutual dependence. The effect would be to suppress both political choice and economic dynamism.

The retreat from American exceptionalism has a legal dimension as well. Obama's judicial nominees are likely to attempt to bring our Constitution into line with European norms. Here, again, he is building on the work of prior liberals who used the federal courts as a weapon against aspects of American exceptionalism such as self-government and decentralization. Increasingly, judicial liberals look to putatively enlightened foreign, and particularly European, opinion as a source of law capable of displacing the law made under our Constitution.

Liberal regulators threaten both our dynamism and our self-government. They are increasingly empowered to make far-reaching policy decisions on their own—for instance, the EPA has the power to decide, even in the absence of cap-and-trade legislation passed by Congress, how to regulate carbon emissions. The agency thus has extraordinary sway over the economy, without any meaningful accountability to the electorate. The Troubled Asset Relief Program has turned into a honeypot for the executive branch, which can dip into it for any purpose that suits it. Government is increasingly escaping the control of the people from whom it is supposed to derive its powers.

Inevitably, the transformation of America at home is being accompanied by a shift in its policies toward the rest of the world. Since the 1940s America has been the crucial undergirding of the international order. Its power and sway are a stabilizing influence in every region of the world, and it provides international public goods, from the policing of sea lanes to humanitarian interventions. It is also, in keeping with its missionary history, the chief exponent of liberty in the world.

Obama is turning his back both on the overarching vision of freedom and on the prudence, and mislabeling his approach "realism." He has been positively allergic to the word "democracy." His administration has shown very little interest in defending human rights around the world, whether in China or in Cuba. During the Iranian election crisis, he was even cooler to the protesters in the streets than the Europeans were.

His hesitance to advocate American ideals is not a return to the realpolitik of Nixon or the first Bush. A deep naïveté informs his policy. He believes that our enemies can be persuaded, merely through sweet talk and blandishments, to abandon their cold-blooded interests and their most deeply held ambitions. This is impossible without developing the kind of leverage over them in which Obama seems to have little interest. Yes, Reagan negotiated with the Soviets, but only when they had a leader who was a reformer and the arms build-up and the prospect of SDI had tilted the correlation of forces—to use the Marxist argot—in our direction. Under the sway of Obama's anti-idealism, the U.S. is less interested in serving as a champion of liberty; his policies will also reduce our power, and thus our effectiveness should we choose to wield it again.

In many of Obama's performances overseas (the Nobel acceptance speech is an exception), there has been a dismaying defensiveness. It's almost as though he doesn't think we deserve to stand up for our ideals or for our interests, and believes that our record of sins, hypocrisies, and affronts makes a posture of apologetic passivity the only appropriate one. This posture raises a disturbing possibility: that the waning of America's civilizational self-confidence is part and parcel of the change Obama is effecting.

In Europe, we see a civilization that is not willing to defend itself: nations that will surrender their sovereignty, cultures that will step aside to be supplanted by an alien creed, peoples that will no longer make the most meaningful investment in the future by reproducing. There is a sense that history is over and Europeans are just waiting for someone to turn out the last light in the last gallery of the Louvre.

The popular revolt against Obama's policies is a sign that Americans are not prepared to go gentle into that good night. Other factors are of course in play—most important, the weak economy—but the public is saying "No" to a rush to social democracy.

Although the conservatives, libertarians, and independents who oppose Obama's health-care initiative may not put it in quite these terms, they sense that his project will not just increase insurance premiums but undermine what they cherish about America. Those Americans who want to keep our detention facility at Guantanamo Bay think it necessary to protect our security—but they also worry, more profoundly, that our leaders are too apologetic to serve our interests. Americans may want change, even fundamental change, but most of them would rather change our institutions than our national character.

It is madness to consider President Obama a foreigner. But it is blindness to ignore that American exceptionalism has homegrown enemies—people who misunderstand the sources of American greatness or think them outdated. If they succeed, we will be less free, less innovative, less rich, less self-governing, and less secure. We will be less.

As will the world. The Europeans can afford a foreign policy devoted nearly exclusively to "soft power" because we are here to defend them and mount the forward defense of freedom. Who is going to do that for us, when we are no longer doing it for ourselves? Who will answer the call when America is no longer home?

If our politics seems heated right now, that is because the central question before us is whether to abandon our traditional sense of ourselves as an exceptional nation. To be exceptional is of course not to be perfect. The old anti-imperialist saying—"My country right or wrong; if right, to be kept right; if wrong, to be set right"—has considerable wisdom. But Americans are right not to want to become exceptional only in the 230-year path we took to reach the same lackluster destination as everyone else.

Discussion Questions

1. If you were David Axelrod, President Obama's main political advisor, what political strategy would you urge? Would you recommend that Obama tack left and push hard on the progressive agenda? Or move to the center with a more moderate agenda? What would influence your recommendations: the 2010 midterm election results, reelection, maintaining popularity, getting policies through Congress, or some other consideration?

2. Greenberg argues that the problem is our expectations. The public *says* it wants a president who will shake things up, but when faced

with the prospect of major change, we retreat to a more centrist posture, content with "muddling through" and nervous about dramatic
change. Is he right?

3. When a president announces a desire to "change politics," what
does that mean? Does it mean that political power will shift to
groups currently outside the walls of power? That Democrats will
call the shots instead of Republicans (or vice versa)? Something
more fundamental? Or is it simply rhetoric, designed to impress but
without much substance? What evidence would you use to decide?

CHAPTER 7

Bureaucracy in a Democratic System

35

"The Study of Administration"

Woodrow Wilson

Until the late nineteenth century, almost no one paid attention to how the government actually worked. Administrative positions were generally filled by political appointees who were supporters of elected officials, and there was little that resembled "management" in the contemporary sense. However, a great deal of money was distributed at the national level, and as scandals mounted over the manner in which the money was distributed, the demand for government accountability grew.

Reformers argued that government employees should be hired on the basis of their merit, rather than because of their political allegiance to one candidate or another. Others called for reforms in the administration of public programs. Nearly thirty years before he was president, Woodrow Wilson, then a professor at Bryn Mawr College, wrote an article for Political Science Quarterly *arguing that political scientists had neglected the study of public administration—the problems involved in managing public programs. He argued that public administration should be carried out in accordance with scientific principles of management and efficiency, an argument that would recur every few decades in demands to reform and "reinvent" government.*

It is the object of administrative study to discover, first, what government can properly and successfully do, and, secondly, how it can do these proper things with the utmost possible efficiency and at the least possible cost either of money or of energy. On both these points there is obviously much need of light among us; and only careful study can supply that light.

* * *

The science of administration is the latest fruit of that study of the science of politics which was begun some twenty-two hundred years ago. It is a birth of our own century, almost of our own generation.

Why was it so late in coming? Why did it wait till this too busy century of ours to demand attention for itself? Administration is the most obvious part of government; it is government in action; it is the executive, the operative, the most visible side of government, and is of course as old as government itself. It is government in action, and one might very naturally expect to find that government in action had arrested the attention and provoked the scrutiny of writers of politics very early in the history of systematic thought.

But such was not the case. No one wrote systematically of administration as a branch of the science of government until the present century had passed its first youth and had begun to put forth its characteristic flower of systematic knowledge. Up to our own day all the political writers whom we now read had thought, argued, dogmatized only about the *constitution* of government; about the nature of the state, the essence and seat of sovereignty, popular power and kingly prerogative; about the greatest meanings lying at the heart of government, and the high ends set before the purpose of government by man's nature and man's aims. * * * The question was always: Who shall make law, and what shall that law be? The other question, how law should be administered with enlightenment, with equity, with speed, and without fiction, was put aside as "practical detail" which clerks could arrange after doctors had agreed upon principles.

*   *   *

[However,] if difficulties of government action are to be seen gathering in other centuries, they are to be seen culminating in our own.

This is the reason why administrative tasks have nowadays to be so studiously and systematically adjusted to carefully tested standards of policy, the reason why we are having now what we never had before, a science of administration. The weightier debates of constitutional principle are even yet by no means concluded; but they are no longer of more immediate practical moment than questions of administration. It is getting to be harder to *run* a constitution than to frame one.

*   *   *

There is scarcely a single duty of government which was once simple which is not now complex; government once had but a few masters; it now has scores of masters. Majorities formerly only underwent government; they now conduct government. Where government once might follow the whims of a court, it must now follow the views of a nation.

And those views are steadily widening to new conceptions of state duty; so that at the same time that the functions of government are every day becoming more complex and difficult, they are also vastly multiplying in number. Administration is everywhere putting its hands to new undertakings. * * * Seeing every day new things which the state ought to do, the next thing is to see clearly how it ought to do them.

This is why there should be a science of administration which shall seek to straighten the paths of government, to make its business less businesslike, to strengthen and purify its organization, and to crown its dutifulness. This is one reason why there is such a science.

But where has this science grown up? Surely not on this side [of] the sea. Not much impartial scientific method is to be discerned in our administrative practices. The poisonous atmosphere of city government, the crooked secrets of state administration, the confusion, sinecurism, and corruption ever and again discovered in the bureaus at Washington forbid us to believe that any clear conceptions of what constitutes good administration are as yet very widely current in the United States.

* * *

American political history has been a history, not of administrative development, but of legislative oversight—not of progress in governmental organization, but of advance in law-making and political criticism. Consequently, we have reached a time when administrative study and creation are imperatively necessary to the well-being of our governments saddled with the habits of a long period of constitution-making. * * * We have reached * * * the period * * * when the people have to develop administration in accordance with the constitutions they won for themselves in a previous period of struggle with absolute power.

* * *

It is harder for democracy to organize administration than for monarchy. The very completeness of our most cherished political successes in the past embarrasses us. We have enthroned public opinion; and it is forbidden us to hope during its reign for any quick schooling of the sovereign in executive expertness or in the conditions of perfect functional balance in government. The very fact that we have realized popular rule in its fullness has made the task of *organizing* that rule just so much the more difficult. * * * An individual sovereign will adopt a simple plan and carry it out directly: he will have but one opinion, and he will embody that one opinion in one command. But this other sovereign, the people, will have a score of differing opinions. They can agree upon nothing simple: advance must be made through compromise, by a compounding of differences, by a trimming of plans and a suppression of too straightforward principles. There will be a succession of resolves running through a course of years, a dropping fire of commands running through a whole gamut of modifications.

* * *

Wherever regard for public opinion is a first principle of government, practical reform must be slow and all reform must be full of compromises. For wherever public opinion exists it must rule.

* * *

The field of administration is a field of business. It is removed from the hurry and strife of politics; it at most points stands apart even from the debatable ground of constitutional study. It is a part of political life only as the methods of the counting-house are a part of the life of society; only as machinery is part of the manufactured product. But it is, at the same time, raised very far above the dull level of mere technical detail by the fact that through its greater principles it is directly connected with the lasting maxims of political wisdom, the permanent truths of political progress.

The object of administrative study is to rescue executive methods from the confusion and costliness of empirical experiment and set them upon foundations laid deep in stable principle.

* * *

[A]dministration lies outside the proper sphere of *politics*. Administrative questions are not political questions. Although politics sets the tasks for administration, it should not be suffered to manipulate its offices.

* * *

There is another distinction which must be worked into all our conclusions, which, though but another side of that between administration and politics, is not quite so easy to keep sight of: I mean the distinction between *constitutional* and administrative questions, between those governmental adjustments which are essential to constitutional principle and those which are merely instrumental to the possibly changing purposes of a wisely adapting convenience.

* * *

A clear view of the difference between the province of constitutional law and the province of administrative function ought to leave no room for misconception; and it is possible to name some roughly definite criteria upon which such a view can be built. Public administration is detailed and systematic execution of public law. Every particular application of general law is an act of administration. The assessment and raising of taxes, for instance, the hanging of a criminal, the transportation and delivery of the mails, the equipment and recruiting of the army, and navy, etc., are all obviously acts of administration; but the general laws which direct these things to be done are as obviously outside of and above administration. The broad plans of governmental action are not administrative; the detailed execution of such plans is administrative. Constitutions, therefore, properly concern themselves only with those instrumentalities of government which are to control general law. Our federal constitution observes this principle in saying nothing of even the greatest of the purely executive offices, and speaking only of that President of the Union who was to share the legislative and policy-making functions of government, only of those judges of highest jurisdiction who were to interpret and guard its principles, and not of those who were merely to give utterance to them.

* * *

There is, [however,] one point at which administrative studies trench on constitutional ground—or at least upon what seems constitutional ground. The study of administration, philosophically viewed, is closely connected with the study of the proper distribution of constitutional authority. To be efficient it must discover the simplest arrangements by which responsibility can be unmistakably fixed upon officials; the best way of dividing authority without hampering it, and responsibility without obscuring it. And this question of the distribution of authority, when taken into the sphere of the higher, the originating functions of government, is obviously a central constitutional question.

* * *

To discover the best principle for the distribution of authority is of greater importance, possibly, under a democratic system, where officials serve many masters, than under others where they serve but a few. All sovereigns are suspicious of their servants, and the sovereign people is no exception to the rule; but how is its suspicion to be allayed by *knowledge*? If that suspicion could be clarified into wise vigilance, it would be altogether salutary; if that vigilance could be aided by the unmistakable placing of responsibility, it would be altogether beneficient. Suspicion in itself is never healthful either in the private or in the public mind. *Trust is strength* in all relations of life; and, as it is the office of the constitutional reformer to create conditions of trustfulness, so it is the office of the administrative organizer to fit administration with conditions of clearcut responsibility which shall insure trustworthiness.

And let me say that large powers and unhampered discretion seem to me the indispensable conditions of responsibility. Public attention must be easily directed, in each case of good or bad administration, to just the man deserving of praise or blame. There is no danger in power, if only it be not irresponsible. If it be divided, dealt out in shares to many, it is obscured; and if it be obscured, it is made irresponsible. But if it be centered in heads of the service and in heads of branches of the service, it is easily watched and brought to book. If to keep his office a man must achieve open and honest success, and if at the same time he feels himself intrusted with large freedom of discretion, the greater his power the less likely is he to abuse it, the more is he nerved and sobered and elevated by it. The less his power, the more safely obscure and unnoticed does he feel his position to be, and the more readily does he relapse into remissness.

Just here we manifestly emerge upon the field of that still larger question—the proper relations between public opinion and administration.

To whom is official trustworthiness to be disclosed, and by whom is it to be rewarded? Is the official to look to the public for his meed of praise and his push of promotion, or only to his superior in office? Are the people to be called in to settle administrative discipline as they are called in to settle constitutional principles? These questions evidently find their root in what is undoubtedly the fundamental problem of this whole study. That problem is: What part shall public opinion take in the conduct of administration?

The right answer seems to be, that public opinion shall play the part of authoritative critic.

But the *method* by which its authority shall be made to tell? Our peculiar American difficulty in organizing administration is not the danger of losing liberty, but the danger of not being able or willing to separate its essentials from its accidents. Our success is made doubtful by that besetting error of ours, the error of trying to do too much by vote. Self-government does not consist in having a hand in everything, any more than housekeeping consists necessarily in cooking dinner with one's own hands. The cook must be trusted with a large discretion as to the management of the fires and the ovens.

*   *   *

The problem is to make public opinion efficient without suffering it to be meddlesome. Directly exercised, in the oversight of the daily details and in the choice of the daily means of government, public criticism is of course a clumsy nuisance, a rustic handling delicate machinery. But as superintending the greater forces of formative policy alike in politics and administration, public criticism is altogether safe and beneficent, altogether indispensable. Let administrative study find the best means for giving public criticism this control and for shutting it out from all other interference.

But is the whole duty of administrative study done when it has taught the people what sort of administration to desire and demand, and how to get what they demand? Ought it not to go on to drill candidates for the public service?

*   *   *

If we are to improve public opinion, which is the motive power of government, we must prepare better officials as the *apparatus* of government.

* * * It will be necessary to organize democracy by sending up to the competitive examinations for the civil service men definitely prepared for
standing liberal tests as to technical knowledge. A technically schooled
civil service will presently have become indispensable.

I know that a corps of civil servants prepared by a special schooling
and drilled, after appointment, into a perfected organization, with appropriate hierarchy and characteristic discipline, seems to a great many very
thoughtful persons to contain elements which might combine to make an
offensive official class—a distinct, semi-corporate body with sympathies
divorced from those of a progressive, free-spirited people, and with hearts
narrowed to the meanness of a bigoted officialism.

*   *   *

But to fear the creation of a domineering, illiberal officialism as a result
of the studies I am here proposing is to miss altogether the principle upon
which I wish most to insist. That principle is, that administration in the
United States must be at all points sensitive to public opinion. A body of
thoroughly trained officials serving during good behavior we must have
in any case: that is a plain business necessity. But the apprehension that
such a body will be anything un-American clears away the moment it is
asked, What is to constitute good behavior? For that question obviously
carries its own answer on its face. Steady, hearty allegiance to the policy
of the government they serve will constitute good behavior. That *policy*
will have no taint of officialism about it. It will not be the creation of permanent officials, but of statesmen whose responsibility to public opinion
will be direct and inevitable. Bureaucracy can exist only where the whole
service of the state is removed from the common political life of the people, its chiefs as well as its rank and file. Its motives, its objects, its policy,
its standards, must be bureaucratic.

*   *   *

The ideal for us is a civil service cultured and self-sufficient enough to
act with sense and vigor, and yet so intimately connected with the popular thought, by means of elections and constant public counsel, as to find
arbitrariness or class spirit quite out of the question.

Having thus viewed in some sort the subject-matter and the objects of
this study of administration, what are we to conclude as to the methods
best suited to it—the points of view most advantageous for it?

Government is so near us, so much a thing of our daily familiar handling, that we can with difficulty see the need of any philosophical study
of it, or the exact point of such study, should it be undertaken. We have
been on our feet too long to study now the art of walking. We are a practical people, made so apt, so adept in self-government by centuries of
experimental drill that we are scarcely any longer capable of perceiving
the awkwardness of the particular system we may be using, just because

it is so easy for us to use any system. We do not study the art of governing: we govern. But mere unschooled genius for affairs will not save us from sad blunders in administration. Though democrats by long inheritance and repeated choice, we are still rather crude democrats. Old as democracy is, its organization on a basis of modern ideas and conditions is still an unaccomplished work. The democratic state has yet to be equipped for carrying those enormous burdens of administration which the needs of this industrial and trading age are so fast accumulating.

*   *   *

We can borrow the science of administration [developed elsewhere] with safety and profit if only we read all fundamental differences of condition into its essential tenets. We have only to filter it through our constitutions, only to put it over a slow fire of criticism and distil away its foreign gases.

*   *   *

Our own politics must be the touchstone for all theories. The principles on which to base a science of administration for America must be principles which have democratic policy very much at heart. And, to suit American habit, all general theories must, as theories, keep modestly in the background, not in open argument only, but even in our own minds— lest opinions satisfactory only to the standards of the library should be dogmatically used, as if they must be quite as satisfactory to the standards of practical politics as well. Doctrinaire devices must be postponed to tested practices. Arrangements not only sanctioned by conclusive experience elsewhere but also congenial to American habit must be preferred without hesitation to theoretical perfection. In a word, steady, practical statesmanship must come first, closet doctrine second. The cosmopolitan what-to-do must always be commanded by the American how-to-do-it.

Our duty is to supply the best possible life to a *federal* organization, to systems within systems; to make town, city, county, state, and federal governments live with a like strength and an equally assured healthfulness, keeping each unquestionably its own master and yet making all interdependent and co-operative, combining independence with mutual helpfulness. The task is great and important enough to attract the best minds.

This interlacing of local self-government with federal self-government is quite a modern conception. * * * The question for us is, how shall our series of governments within governments be so administered that it shall always be to the interest of the public officer to serve, not his superior alone but the community also, with the best efforts of his talents and the soberest service of his conscience? How shall such service be made to his commonest interest by contributing abundantly to his sustenance, to his dearest interest by furthering his ambition, and to his highest interest by advancing his honor and establishing his character? And how shall this be done alike for the local part and for the national whole?

If we solve this problem we shall again pilot the world.

Discussion Questions

1. Do you agree with Wilson's central proposition that politics and administration are separate things? Can you think of any examples where the two overlap? Is it possible, or even desirable, to separate politics and administration?

2. Should there be an expectation of neutral efficiency that separates politicians' policy views from the work of government agencies?

3. Should government officials be able to take into account whether someone supports an agency's goals when deciding whom to hire? Does your answer differ depending on whether the agency is involved in foreign policy, domestic policy, or national security?

36

From *Bureaucracy: What Government Agencies Do and Why They Do It*

JAMES Q. WILSON

Woodrow Wilson was merely the first in a long line of reformers to suggest that government might be more efficient if it ran more like a business. The sentiment remains today. Perhaps a more "businesslike" government would issue our income tax refunds more promptly, protect the environment at lower cost, and impose fewer burdens on citizens. The catch is, we want all this at low cost and minimal intrusiveness in our lives, yet we want government bureaucracies to be held strictly accountable for the authority they exercise.

James Q. Wilson argues that government will never operate like a business, nor should we expect it to. His comparison of the Watertown, Massachusetts, Registry of Motor Vehicles (representing any government bureaucracy) with a nearby McDonald's (representing any private profit-seeking organization) shows that the former will most likely never service its clientele as well as the latter. The problem is not bureaucratic laziness, or any of the conventional criticisms of government agencies, but is instead due to the very different characteristics of public versus private enterprises. In order to understand "what government agencies do and why they do it," Wilson argues we must first understand that government bureaucracies operate in a political marketplace, rather than an economic one. The annual revenues and personnel resources of a government agency are determined by elected officials, not by the agency's ability to meet the demands of its customers in a cost-efficient manner. The government agency's internal structure and decision-making procedures are defined by legislation, regulation, and executive orders, whereas similar decisions in a private business are made by executive officers and management within the organization. And, perhaps most critical, a government agency's goals are often vague, difficult if not impossible to measure, and even contradictory. In business, by contrast, the task is clearer. The basic goal of a private business has always been to maximize the bottom line: profit. Although suggesting we should not approach the reform of government agencies the way we might a private bureaucracy, James Q. Wilson notes in this 1980s analysis that we should nevertheless try to make government bureaucracies operate more effectively and efficiently.

By the time the office opens at 8:45 A.M., the line of people waiting to do business at the Registry of Motor Vehicles in Watertown,

Massachusetts, often will be twenty-five deep. By midday, especially if it is near the end of the month, the line may extend clear around the building. Inside, motorists wait in slow-moving rows before poorly marked windows to get a driver's license or to register an automobile. When someone gets to the head of the line, he or she is often told by the clerk that it is the wrong line: "Get an application over there and then come back," or "This is only for people getting a new license; if you want to replace one you lost, you have to go to the next window." The customers grumble impatiently. The clerks act harried and sometimes speak brusquely, even rudely. What seems to be a simple transaction may take 45 minutes or even longer. By the time people are photographed for their driver's licenses, they are often scowling. The photographer valiantly tries to get people to smile, but only occasionally succeeds.

Not far away, people also wait in line at a McDonald's fast-food restaurant. There are several lines; each is short, each moves quickly. The menu is clearly displayed on attractive signs. The workers behind the counter are invariably polite. If someone's order cannot be filled immediately, he or she is asked to step aside for a moment while the food is prepared and then is brought back to the head of the line to receive the order. The atmosphere is friendly and good-natured. The room is immaculately clean.

Many people have noticed the difference between getting a driver's license and ordering a Big Mac. Most will explain it by saying that bureaucracies are different from businesses. "Bureaucracies" behave as they do because they are run by unqualified "bureaucrats" and are enmeshed in "rules" and "red tape."

But business firms are also bureaucracies, and McDonald's is a bureaucracy that regulates virtually every detail of its employees' behavior by a complex and all-encompassing set of rules. Its operations manual is six hundred pages long and weighs four pounds. In it one learns that french fries are to be nine-thirty-seconds of an inch thick and that grill workers are to place hamburger patties on the grill from left to right, six to a row for six rows. They are then to flip the third row first, followed by the fourth, fifth, and sixth rows, and finally the first and second. The amount of sauce placed on each bun is precisely specified. Every window must be washed every day. Workers must get down on their hands and knees and pick up litter as soon as it appears. These and countless other rules designed to reduce the workers to interchangeable automata were inculcated in franchise managers at Hamburger University located in a $40 million facility. There are plenty of rules governing the Registry, but they are only a small fraction of the rules that govern every detail of every operation at McDonald's. Indeed, if the DMV manager tried to impose on his employees as demanding a set of rules as those that govern the McDonald's staff, they would probably rebel and he would lose his job.

It is just as hard to explain the differences between the two organizations by reference to the quality or compensation of their employees. The Registry workers are all adults, most with at least a high-school education; the McDonald's employees are mostly teenagers, many still in school. The Registry staff is well-paid compared to the McDonald's workers, most of whom receive only the minimum wage. When labor shortages developed in Massachusetts during the mid-1980s, many McDonald's stores began hiring older people (typically housewives) of the same sort who had long worked for the Registry. They behaved just like the teenagers they replaced.

Not only are the differences between the two organizations not to be explained by reference to "rules" or "red tape" or "incompetent workers," the differences call into question many of the most frequently mentioned complaints about how government agencies are supposed to behave. For example: "Government agencies are big spenders." The Watertown office of the Registry is in a modest building that can barely handle its clientele. The teletype machine used to check information submitted by people requesting a replacement license was antiquated and prone to errors. Three or four clerks often had to wait in line to use equipment described by the office manager as "personally signed by Thomas Edison." No computers or word processors were available to handle the preparation of licenses and registrations; any error made by a clerk while manually typing a form meant starting over again on another form.

Or: "Government agencies hire people regardless of whether they are really needed." Despite the fact that the citizens of Massachusetts probably have more contact with the Registry than with any other state agency, and despite the fact that these citizens complain more about Registry service than about that of any other bureau, the Watertown branch, like all Registry offices, was seriously understaffed. In 1981, the agency lost 400 workers—about 25 percent of its work force—despite the fact that its workload was rising.

Or: "Government agencies are imperialistic, always grasping for new functions." But there is no record of the Registry doing much grasping, even though one could imagine a case being made that the state government could usefully create at Registry offices "one-stop" multi-service centers where people could not only get drivers' licenses but also pay taxes and parking fines, obtain information, and transact other official business. The Registry seemed content to provide one service.

In short, many of the popular stereotypes about government agencies and their members are either questionable or incomplete. To explain why government agencies behave as they do, it is not enough to know that they are "bureaucracies"—that is, it is not enough to know that they are big, or complex, or have rules. What is crucial is that they are *government* bureaucracies. * * * [N]ot all government bureaucracies behave the same way or suffer from the same problems. There may even be registries of motor vehicles in other states that do a better job than the one in

Massachusetts. But all government agencies have in common certain characteristics that tend to make their management far more difficult than managing a McDonald's. These common characteristics are the constraints of public agencies.

The key constraints are three in number. To a much greater extent than is true of private bureaucracies, government agencies (1) cannot lawfully retain and devote to the private benefit of their members the earnings of the organization, (2) cannot allocate the factors of production in accordance with the preferences of the organization's administrators, and (3) must serve goals not of the organization's own choosing. Control over revenues, productive factors, and agency goals is all vested to an important degree in entities external to the organization—legislatures, courts, politicians, and interest groups. Given this, agency managers must attend to the demands of these external entities. As a result, government management tends to be driven by the *constraints* on the organization, not the *tasks* of the organization. To say the same thing in other words, whereas business management focuses on the "bottom line" (that is, profits), government management focuses on the "top line" (that is, constraints). Because government managers are not as strongly motivated as private ones to define the tasks of their subordinates, these tasks are often shaped by [other] factors.

* * *

Revenues and Incentives

In the days leading up to September 30, the federal government is Cinderella, courted by legions of individuals and organizations eager to get grants and contracts from the unexpended funds still at the disposal of each agency. At midnight on September 30, the government's coach turns into a pumpkin. That is the moment—the end of the fiscal year— at which every agency, with a few exceptions, must return all unexpended funds to the Treasury Department.

Except for certain quasi-independent government corporations, such as the Tennessee Valley Authority, no agency may keep any surplus revenues (that is, the difference between the funds it received from a congressional appropriation and those it needed to operate during the year). By the same token, any agency that runs out of money before the end of the fiscal year may ask Congress for more (a "supplemental appropriation") instead of being forced to deduct the deficit from any accumulated cash reserves. Because of these fiscal rules agencies do not have a material incentive to economize: Why scrimp and save if you cannot keep the results of your frugality?

Nor can individual bureaucrats lawfully capture for their personal use any revenue surpluses. When a private firm has a good year, many of its officers and workers may receive bonuses. Even if no bonus is paid, these employees may buy stock in the firm so that they can profit from any growth in earnings (and, if they sell the stock in a timely manner, profit from a drop in earnings). Should a public bureaucrat be discovered trying to do what private bureaucrats routinely do, he or she would be charged with corruption.

We take it for granted that bureaucrats should not profit from their offices and nod approvingly when a bureaucrat who has so benefited is indicted and put on trial. But why should we take this view? Once a very different view prevailed. In the seventeenth century, a French colonel would buy his commission from the king, take the king's money to run his regiment, and pocket the profit. At one time a European tax collector was paid by keeping a percentage of the taxes he collected. In this country, some prisons were once managed by giving the warden a sum of money based on how many prisoners were under his control and letting him keep the difference between what he received and what it cost him to feed the prisoners. Such behavior today would be grounds for criminal prosecution. Why? What has changed?

Mostly we the citizenry have changed. We are creatures of the Enlightenment: We believe that the nation ought not to be the property of the sovereign; that laws are intended to rationalize society and (if possible) perfect mankind; and that public service ought to be neutral and disinterested. We worry that a prison warden paid in the old way would have a strong incentive to starve his prisoners in order to maximize his income; that a regiment supported by a greedy colonel would not be properly equipped; and that a tax collector paid on a commission basis would extort excessive taxes from us. These changes reflect our desire to eliminate moral hazards—namely, creating incentives for people to act wrongly. But why should this desire rule out more carefully designed compensation plans that would pay government managers for achieving officially approved goals and would allow efficient agencies to keep any unspent part of their budget for use next year?

Part of the answer is obvious. Often we do not know whether a manager or an agency has achieved the goals we want because either the goals are vague or inconsistent, or their attainment cannot be observed, or both. Bureau chiefs in the Department of State would have to go on welfare if their pay depended on their ability to demonstrate convincingly that they had attained their bureaus' objectives.

But many government agencies have reasonably clear goals toward which progress can be measured. The Social Security Administration, the Postal Service, and the General Services Administration all come to mind. Why not let earnings depend importantly on performance? Why not let agencies keep excess revenues?

* * *

But in part it is because we know that even government agencies with clear goals and readily observable behavior only can be evaluated by making political (and thus conflict-ridden) judgments. If the Welfare Department delivers every benefit check within 24 hours after the application is received, Senator Smith may be pleased but Senator Jones will be irritated because this speedy delivery almost surely would require that the standards of eligibility be relaxed so that many ineligible clients would get money. There is no objective standard by which the trade-off between speed and accuracy in the Welfare Department can be evaluated. Thus we have been unwilling to allow welfare employees to earn large bonuses for achieving either speed or accuracy.

The inability of public managers to capture surplus revenues for their own use alters the pattern of incentives at work in government agencies. Beyond a certain point additional effort does not produce additional earnings. (In this country, Congress from time to time has authorized higher salaries for senior bureaucrats but then put a cap on actual payments to them so that the pay increases were never received. This was done to insure that no bureaucrat would earn more than members of Congress at a time when those members were unwilling to accept the political costs of raising their own salaries. As a result, the pay differential between the top bureaucratic rank and those just below it nearly vanished.) If political constraints reduce the marginal effect of money incentives, then the relative importance of other, nonmonetary incentives will increase. . . .

That bureaucratic performance in most government agencies cannot be linked to monetary benefits is not the whole explanation for the difference between public and private management. There are many examples of private organizations whose members cannot appropriate money surpluses for their own benefit. Private schools ordinarily are run on a nonprofit basis. Neither the headmaster nor the teachers share in the profit of these schools; indeed, most such schools earn no profit at all and instead struggle to keep afloat by soliciting contributions from friends and alumni. Nevertheless, the evidence is quite clear that on the average, private schools, both secular and denominational, do a better job than public ones in educating children. Moreover, as political scientists John Chubb and Terry Moe have pointed out, they do a better job while employing fewer managers. Some other factors are at work. One is the freedom an organization has to acquire and use labor and capital.

Acquiring and Using the Factors of Production

A business firm acquires capital by retaining earnings, borrowing money, or selling shares of ownership; a government agency (with some exceptions) acquires capital by persuading a legislature to appropriate it. A business firm hires, promotes, demotes, and fires personnel with considerable though not perfect freedom; a federal government agency is told by Congress how many persons it can hire and at what rate of pay, by the Office of Personnel Management (OPM) what rules it must follow in selecting and assigning personnel, by the Office of Management and Budget (OMB) how many persons of each rank it may employ, by the Merit Systems Protection Board (MSPB) what procedures it must follow in demoting or discharging personnel, and by the courts whether it has faithfully followed the rules of Congress, OPM, OMB, and MSPB. A business firm purchases goods and services by internally defined procedures (including those that allow it to buy from someone other than the lowest bidder if a more expensive vendor seems more reliable), or to skip the bidding procedure altogether in favor of direct negotiations; a government agency must purchase much of what it uses by formally advertising for bids, accepting the lowest, and keeping the vendor at arm's length. When a business firm develops a good working relationship with a contractor, it often uses that vendor repeatedly without looking for a new one; when a government agency has a satisfactory relationship with a contractor, ordinarily it cannot use the vendor again without putting a new project out for a fresh set of bids. When a business firm finds that certain offices or factories are no longer economical it will close or combine them; when a government agency wishes to shut down a local office or military base often it must get the permission of the legislature (even when formal permission is not necessary, informal consultation is). When a business firm draws up its annual budget each expenditure item can be reviewed as a discretionary amount (except for legally mandated payments of taxes to government and interest to banks and bondholders); when a government agency makes up its budget many of the detailed expenditure items are mandated by the legislature.

All these complexities of doing business in or with the government are well-known to citizens and firms. These complexities in hiring, purchasing, contracting, and budgeting often are said to be the result of the "bureaucracy's love of red tape." But few, if any, of the rules producing this complexity would have been generated by the bureaucracy if left to its own devices, and many are as cordially disliked by the bureaucrats as by their clients. These rules have been imposed on the agencies by external actors, chiefly the legislature. They are not bureaucratic rules but *political* ones. In principle the legislature could allow the Social Security Administration, the Defense Department, or the New York City public school system to follow the same rules as IBM, General Electric, or Harvard University. In practice they could not. The reason is politics, or more precisely, democratic politics.

* * *

Public versus Private Management

What distinguishes public from private organizations is neither their size nor their desire to "plan" (that is, control) their environments but rather the rules under which they acquire and use capital and labor. General Motors acquires capital by selling shares, issuing bonds, or retaining earnings; the Department of Defense acquires it from an annual appropriation by Congress. GM opens and closes plants, subject to certain government regulations, at its own discretion; DOD opens and closes military bases under the watchful guidance of Congress. GM pays its managers with salaries it sets and bonuses tied to its earnings; DOD pays its managers with salaries set by Congress and bonuses (if any) that have no connection with organizational performance. The number of workers in GM is determined by its level of production; the number in DOD by legislation and civil-service rules.

What all this means can be seen by returning to the Registry of Motor Vehicles and McDonald's. Suppose you were just appointed head of the Watertown office of the Registry and you wanted to improve service there so that it more nearly approximated the service at McDonald's. Better service might well require spending more money (on clerks, equipment, and buildings). Why should your political superiors give you that money? It is a cost to them if it requires either higher taxes or taking funds from another agency; offsetting these real and immediate costs are dubious and postponed benefits. If lines become shorter and clients become happier, no legislator will benefit. There may be fewer complaints, but complaints are episodic and have little effect on the career of any given legislator. By contrast, shorter lines and faster service at McDonald's means more customers can be served per hour and thus more money can be earned per hour. A McDonald's manager can estimate the marginal product of the last dollar he or she spends on improving service; the Registry manager can generate no tangible return on any expenditure he or she makes and thus cannot easily justify the expenditure.

Improving service at the Registry may require replacing slow or surly workers with quick and pleasant ones. But you, the manager, can neither hire nor fire them at will. You look enviously at the McDonald's manager who regularly and with little notice replaces poor workers with better ones. Alternatively, you may wish to mount an extensive training program (perhaps creating a Registration University to match McDonald's Hamburger University) that would imbue a culture of service in your employees. But unless the Registry were so large an agency that the legislature would neither notice nor care about funds spent for this purpose— and it is not that large—you would have a tough time convincing anybody that this was not a wasteful expenditure on a frill project.

If somehow your efforts succeed in making Registry clients happier, you can take vicarious pleasure in it; in the unlikely event a client seeks you out to thank you for those efforts, you can bask in a moment's worth of glory. Your colleague at McDonald's who manages to make customers happier may also derive some vicarious satisfaction from the improvement but in addition he or she will earn more money owing to an increase in sales.

In time it will dawn on you that if you improve service too much, clients will start coming to the Watertown office instead of going to the Boston office. As a result, the lines you succeeded in shortening will become longer again. If you wish to keep complaints down, you will have to spend even more on the Watertown office. But if it was hard to persuade the legislature to do that in the past, it is impossible now. Why should the taxpayer be asked to spend more on Watertown when the Boston office, fully staffed (naturally, no one was laid off when the clients disappeared), has no lines at all? From the legislature's point of view the correct level of expenditure is not that which makes one office better than another but that which produces an equal amount of discontent in all offices.

Finally, you remember that your clients have no choice: The Registry offers a monopoly service. It and only it supplies drivers' licenses. In the long run all that matters is that there are not "too many" complaints to the legislature about service. Unlike McDonald's, the Registry need not fear that its clients will take their business to Burger King or to Wendy's. Perhaps you should just relax.

If this were all there is to public management it would be an activity that quickly and inevitably produces cynicism among its practitioners. But this is not the whole story. For one thing, public agencies differ in the kinds of problems they face. For another, many public managers try hard to do a good job even though they face these difficult constraints.

DISCUSSION QUESTIONS

1. Wilson argues that McDonald's and the Registry of Motor Vehicles operate differently because of the inherent differences between public and private organizations. Apply his reasoning to other cases, for instance the U.S. Postal Service and Fed Ex, or any other area where the government and the private sector compete for business. Think about the goals of the organizations, who controls them, how you distinguish success from failure, and the consequences of failure.

2. What are the advantages and disadvantages of trying to run the government more like a business? How would you define the basic parameters of a "businesslike" government—such as, Who are the "customers"?

3. Some critics of government inefficiency argue that nearly every domestic government function—from schools to road building—could be run more efficiently if it were "privatized"—turned over to private contractors. Do you agree? Are there any government functions that do not lend themselves to privatization?

Debating the Issues: Policy "Czars" and Presidential Control of the Bureaucracy

All presidents want the federal bureaucracy—meaning executive branch agencies—to be responsive to presidential policies and preferences. Bringing agencies into line, however, is a difficult challenge. Not only do agencies or, more properly, the people in the agencies, seek to please multiple entities, including Congress, the courts, interest groups, and clientele groups who interact with various agencies on regulatory or benefit issues, but bureaucracies are also inherently resistant to change. The scale of the executive branch makes this task even harder, because it is difficult to monitor and assess the thousands of programs in the many different departments, regulatory agencies, government corporations, boards, and commissions.

The president appoints the people at the top of federal agencies. Most of them serve at the pleasure of the president, meaning that the president can fire them without giving a reason. Other agency leaders, particularly in the independent regulatory agencies such as the Federal Reserve Board or the Securities and Exchange Commission, are insulated from political pressure, and the president can only remove them under certain conditions. Even those whom the president has the option to fire can, in Washington lingo, "go native," meaning that they advocate the agency's views more than the president's.

Eventually, every president becomes frustrated with a lack of responsiveness among the agencies. Different presidents have come up with a variety of ways of combating this phenomenon, but the one common feature is that presidents increasingly centralize policy-making control within the White House. Rather than relying on agencies to create policy, presidents come to rely on White House personnel and processes to devise, implement, and monitor policy.

One of President Obama's tools in policy centralization is the use of so-called czars, presidential advisors who work in the White House on a particular policy area, and answer only to the president. Some of these czars occupy positions created by statute. The most noteworthy is the head of the White House Office of National Drug Control Policy, usually referred to as the drug czar. President Obama has made extensive use of these positions, relying on these advisors across a wide range of policy—environment, green energy, financial industry oversight, the automobile industry, and Afghanistan.

The readings provide three perspectives on the czar position. James Pfiffner, a presidential scholar, notes that the controversy over Obama's use of these advisors is nothing new and reflects the long-standing tension between administrative neutrality and responsiveness to presidential policy preferences. Presidents want to control policy, and that means having people who answer only to the president responsible for crafting and monitoring policy proposals.

Matthew Spalding offers a less sanguine take, noting that the existence of czars reflects a much broader debate over how policy should be made: by technical experts who do not have to answer to the public, or by elected representatives. Like Pfiffner, Spalding connects the use of czars to the long-standing presidential desire for bureaucratic control. But unlike many critics of Obama's extensive use of czars, Spalding sees their proliferation as a sign of deeper trouble: the increasing difficulty of controlling a bureaucracy that is, apart from the judiciary, the least accountable institution in the national government. The real problem, as Spalding sees it, is the fact that government has grown so large, intrusive, and potentially uncontrollable.

Finally, Will Englund provides three examples of policy czar types, noting the conditions under which they will succeed or fail. He argues that there have been some quiet successes, especially the coordinating effort carried out by the Clinton Y2K (year 2000) czar John Koskinen. For those of you too young to remember, there was a good deal of nervousness about how computers would respond when 1999 turned into 2000. Many older computers could store only two-digit dates, meaning that on January 1, 2000, they might read a date as 00 and interpret that to mean 1900, which could have caused problems with software involved with everything from electrical utilities to finance to aircraft flight management. Ultimately, January 1, 2000, came and went without incident.

37

"Presidential Use of White House 'Czars'"

James P. Pfiffner

The term "czar" has no generally accepted definition within the context of American government. It is a term loosely used by journalists to refer to members of a president's administration who seem to be in charge of a particular policy area. For my purposes, the term "czar" refers to members of the White House staff who have been designated by the president to coordinate a specific policy that involves more than one department or agency in the executive branch; they do not hold Senate-confirmed positions, nor are they officers of the United States.

Article II Section 2 of the Constitution says that the president "shall nominate, and by and with the Advice and Consent of the Senate, shall appoint . . . Officers of the United States." The positions held by these officers are created in law and most of them exercise legal authority to commit the United States government to certain policies (within the law) and expend resources in doing so.

In contrast, members of the White House staff are appointed by the president without Senate confirmation. They are legally authorized only to advise the president; they cannot make authoritative decisions for the government of the United States. There is a parallel between the concepts of "line" and "staff" in the U.S. military. Staff personnel can advise line officers, but only line officers can make authoritative decisions, such as hiring and firing personnel or committing budgetary resources.

For practical purposes, however, staff personnel may have considerable "power" or influence, as opposed to authority. But this power is derivative from the line officer for whom they work. Thus White House staffers may communicate orders from the president, but they cannot legally give those orders themselves. In the real world, of course, White House staffers often make important decisions, but the weight of their decisions depends entirely on the willingness of the president to back them up.

Growth of the White House Staff

Both the advantages and disadvantages of White House czars are illustrated by the significant growth of the White House staff in the Modern Presidency [sic] . Although presidents have always had advisers and confidants in the White House, the formal White House staff was established in 1939 when Congress gave Franklin Roosevelt authority to create the Executive Office of the President and hire six formal White House staffers. The expected role of the White House staff was articulated by the classic statement of Franklin Roosevelt's Brownlow Committee in 1937:

> These aides would have no power to make decisions or issue instructions in their own right. They would not be interposed between the president and the heads of his departments. They would not be assistant presidents in any sense. . . . They would remain in the background, issue no orders, make no decisions, emit no public statements. . . . [T]hey would not attempt to exercise power on their own account. They should be possessed of high competence, great physical vigor, and a passion for anonymity.

Despite the fact that these precepts have gone by the wayside and the White House staff now includes hundreds of people, some of whom enjoy high public visibility and wield significant power, the norms established in the Brownlow Committee Report still define the ideal for White House aides.

Over the following decades, presidents initiated major changes in the size and scope of their staffs. Dwight Eisenhower created the position of chief of staff to the president and began to institutionalize the White House. John Kennedy, after the Bay of Pigs debacle, told McGeorge Bundy to put together "a little State Department" in the White House that would consider national security policy from his own perspective rather than through the narrower lenses of the Departments of State and Defense. The Assistant to the President for National Security Affairs, (national security advisor) has played major roles in every presidential administration since then. It reached its zenith of power when Henry Kissinger held that position at the same time he was Secretary of State in the Nixon Administration.

When Richard Nixon came to office, his distrust of the executive branch bureaucracies led him to expand considerably the White House staff. In addition to increasing the number of White House staffers in the White House Office, he created the position of domestic policy adviser and designated John Ehrlichmann to be its director. Subsequent presidents have continued to use these White House positions and to create new ones to meet their needs.

A certain amount of the centralization of policy control through expanding staff in the White House was inevitable and useful. Executive branch departments and cabinet secretaries necessarily and reasonably view national policy from their own perspective, and they often clash with other departments over the formulation and implementation of presidential policies. These conflicts and differing perspectives must be resolved and integrated by presidents, but someone short of the president must be able to narrow the range of alternatives for the president to consider. This coordination role is the most important role of the White House staff; and talented people are necessary to do the job. That being said, too much centralization and too many White House staffers can impair effective presidential leadership. White House staffers are ambitious people, and may try to use the president's power as their own. Thus the White House staff must be carefully policed and kept on a short leash.

The Appropriate Role of Czars

This brings the focus back to White House czars. Presidents designate czars in order to coordinate policy making across different departments and agencies. They thus play essential roles and lift the burden of coordination from the president. They help reduce the range of options to the essentials necessary for presidential decision. But if the number of czars proliferates, they can clog and confuse the policy making process. In addition to coordinating policy among departments and agencies, someone then must coordinate the czars and their access to the president. Czars may also create layers of aides between the president and departmental secretaries. Too many czars can result in managerial overload.

From the president's perspective, a proliferation of czars replicates the divisions already present in the departments and agencies of the executive branch. A large White House staff with many czars must be disciplined and coordinated by the president's chief of staff, a position used by every president since the Nixon administration. Perhaps the greatest challenge that the use of czars presents to coherent policy making is the question: who is in charge of this policy area short of the president? Conflict will abound, and members of Congress as well as other national leaders may be confused as to the locus of authoritative decisions. When this happens in foreign policy, as it has at times in recent decades, foreign leaders do not know who speaks for the president. In addition, a too active czar can pull problems into the White House that could be settled at the cabinet level. Only those issues that are central to a president's policy agenda should be brought into the White House; others should be delegated to the cabinet secretaries who have responsibility for their implementation.

From the czar's perspective, the title can be a mixed blessing. The czar enjoys the prestige and perks of being on the White House staff. He or she gets national news coverage and has the opportunity to exercise leadership and sometimes power. On the other hand, czars are often frustrated because they are supposed to be in charge of policy, yet they do not have authority commensurate with their responsibilities. While a czar may have the spotlight and the president's ear in the short term, he or she cannot enforce decisions on departments and agencies. Unlike cabinet secretaries, czars control neither personnel appointments nor budgets. For these they must depend on cabinet secretaries, and if they disagree with the cabinet secretary, they are at a disadvantage. They might appeal to the president to back up their decisions, but presidents have limited time, and czars can go back to that well only so many times. Persons who have been designated the "drug czar," the director of the Office of National Drug Control Policy, have thus had mixed success in their efforts to coordinate harmful substances policy across the executive branch. The Secretary of Homeland Security has more resources at her command than does the Assistant to the President for Homeland Security.

From the perspective of the department secretary, the presence of White House czars is most often frustrating. Throughout the modern presidency White house staffers have been the natural enemy of cabinet secretaries. Each vies for the president's ear, and each resents the other's "interference." White House staffers enjoy proximity to the president and can drop everything else in order to focus on whatever policy the president is considering. Cabinet secretaries, in contrast, must worry about managing their departments and the many policies for which they are responsible. Absent a close relationship with the president, cabinet secretaries are often at a disadvantage in securing presidential attention, and they often resent a czar who is interposed between them and the president.

Managing the Presidency

In the real world, presidents must balance their desire for centralized control with the managerial imperatives for delegation. No president can do an effective job without talented people on the White House staff. Yet if the president allows White House staffers to shut out cabinet secretaries, he or she will not be exposed to the crucial perspectives that cabinet secretaries provide: institutional memory, an operational point of view, and a broader political sensitivity than a single czar can provide. Thus the question of the best balance comes down to presidential judgment and managerial insight. Some czars, such as the National Security Advisor, are clearly necessary. And major presidential policy priorities must be coordinated out of the White House. Secondary issues should be pushed down to the departmental level.

A czar, seen as a symbol of presidential priorities, can be useful for that purpose and not pose an impediment to clear lines of policy making. But a czar who is charged with policy coordination and who uses his or her influence to undercut cabinet secretaries can create confusion and undermine effective policy making. So the real question of the impact of czars must be judged by the roles they play and their approach to their responsibilities rather than merely counting their numbers.

Thus insofar as President Obama's czars take active roles in policy making (as opposed to advising), attempt to shut out cabinet secretaries, and exercise power in their own right, they dilute authority and confuse the chain of command. But if they work closely with cabinet secretaries and help coordinate policy advice to the president, they can be very useful. So the effect of czars and their usefulness depends on their behavior. That said, the larger the White House staff and the more czars that the president designates, the more likely the White House will be difficult to manage, and relations between cabinet secretaries and White House staff will be strained.

Congressional Oversight of Executive Branch Policy

Members of Congress are sometimes frustrated in their attempts to oversee executive branch policies and chafe at presidential attempts to circumvent Congress in its legitimate policy making role and responsibilities for oversight of the executive branch. And it is possible that presidents may use their White House staffs to frustrate legitimate congressional participation. Presidents often resist requests for White House staff to testify before Congress and they use claims of executive privilege, sometimes legitimately, sometimes not. Thus Congress can be frustrated when it seems that the president is refusing to let it exercise legitimate oversight of executive branch policy and actions. But Congress is not without constitutional authority to oversee the executive branch.

* * *

Congress has alternatives other than calling White House staffers to testify. Policy making in the executive branch is the responsibility of the president, who is accountable to Congress and the public. If Congress is concerned with policies or their implementation, it can call cabinet secretaries (or subordinate officers of the government) to testify about policy making and implementation. Congress can exercise its power of the purse and authorization power to curb or direct policy implementation. Executive branch departments and agencies exist and are authorized only in law, and Congress can change those laws. As a matter of comity, the president is entitled to the confidentiality of his or her staff, just as members of Congress are entitled to confidentiality of their staff and Supreme Court Justices are entitled to confidentiality of their clerks.

If Congress suspects that White House staffers are illegitimately interfering with policy making or implementation, it can call in cabinet secretaries to explain the policies or programs for which they are responsible. If White House staffers seem to be actually implementing policies, there is certainly cause for concern and Congress has a right to demand explanations. But the keys to congressional control are its authorization and appropriation powers.

In my judgment, there are much more significant threats to congressional constitutional authority than the existence of czars in the White House. The explosion of the use of signing statements to imply that the president may not faithfully execute the law presents a fundamental threat to the constitutional role of Congress, which possesses "All legislative powers" granted in the Constitution.

If presidents create secret programs that effectively nullify or circumvent the laws, they are placing themselves above the law and claiming the authority to suspend the laws, which the Framers of the Constitution explicitly rejected.

If presidents use the state secrets privilege to avoid the disclosure of or accountability for their actions, the role of the courts can be undercut.

If presidents claim the right to suspend *habeas corpus*, they are treading on Article I of the Constitution.

Although some presidents have abused their power by making extraordinary claims to constitutional authority, it is also the duty of Congress as a co-equal branch of government to assert its own constitutional prerogatives. Congress has all the authority it needs to ensure effective oversight of executive branch implementation of policy. The use of czars by presidents presents serious questions of policy making and management, but the constitutional prerogatives of Congress are more seriously undermined by the claims of presidents to have the right to set aside the laws in favor of their own policy priorities.

38

"Examining the History and Legality of Executive Branch Czars"

Matthew Spalding

L et me begin by commending the Senate Judiciary Committee, and especially Senator Feingold, for calling this hearing and giving serious consideration to this issue. Who would have thought that over 200 years after the Declaration of Independence indicted George III for having "erected a multitude of New Offices, and sent hither swarms of Officers to harass our people and eat out their substance" we would be debating the number and proliferation of "czars" in the administration of American government?

The very word, of course, is itself a significant part of the problem. An endless source of humor, it is both confusing and revealing. It is a confusing term because no one officially holds the title; it is a shorthand popularization used by the media and commentators, as well as individuals in government, to describe certain individuals in the administration who seem to be coordinating national policy and particular policy issues across agencies and programs. We don't know how many there are, as there is no official list. Complicating the matter further is that, of those who have been dubbed "czars," some are in positions created by Congress and have been confirmed by the Senate while others are not in such positions and have not been confirmed.

Yet the term is also revealing. While it is a clever label meant to simplify the proliferation of long, formal job titles, it clearly was meant as well to imply in certain positions a breadth of authority and level of status beyond the particulars of the formal title, and seemingly beyond the confines of the normal administrative process. Americans have always bristled at such claims of undefined authority, and calling it by a title historically associated with lawlessness and despotism only serves to underscore the problem.

The use of the term is not new, of course. [President] Nixon seems to have had the first in the modern era, and there were a couple under both Ronald Reagan and George Herbert Walker Bush and President Clinton had a few more. But there seems to have been a proliferation of the title in the previous and the current administration. I say "seems" because there is significant information we do not know about these positions, their duties and responsibilities, and their line of authority. This is why

Congress—and here I note the letters from Senator Feingold, as well as a letter from Representatives Issa and Smith—is absolutely correct in asking for more information about the activities and authority of several of the individual czars.

My guess is that there are actually many more individuals that could fairly be called "czars" in the administration. I say that because the problem is not in the title *per se*, or who made or didn't make the czar list, but with the activities associated with the particular position, and whether there is a general trend toward a centralization of czar power in the White House. Congress, both in terms of preserving its own powers and checking those of the executive as well as encouraging open deliberation and responsibility in government, ought to be keenly interested in this question.

The issue is not whether the proliferation of "czars" amounts to a usurpation of power by the executive branch. Rather, the fundamental issue is how the rise of modern administrative government has put us in an unsolvable dilemma: whether policy should be made by technical experts, insulated from public accountability and control, or whether policy should be made by our elected representatives in Congress and the executive branch. The rise of government by bureaucrats—due to the delegation of power from Congress to administrative agencies, combined with the removal of those agencies from the President's control—has given rise to efforts by Presidents from both parties to get the bureaucratic state under control through various mechanisms. The rise of "czars" in the current administration is just another manifestation—albeit, an unfortunate one—of this phenomenon.

To understand this argument, a quick synopsis of some background history is necessary. During the late nineteenth and early twentieth centuries (also known as the "Progressive Era"), leading intellectuals and politicians sought to transform American government, which they believed was set up to circumvent the public interest for the sake of narrow and parochial interests.

The problem, in their view, was that policy was being made politically—that is, by inexpert officials chosen by the people, who were unfamiliar with the practicalities of modern society. The solution they devised was to transfer policymaking authority to administrative experts, removed from day-to-day politics and political control, who would be social scientists, educated at top universities and trained to apply cutting-edge scientific research to modern problems. As one leading Progressive, John Dewey, argued, "the question of method in formation and execution of policies is the central thing in liberalism. The method indicated is that of maximum reliance upon intelligence."

Technical intelligence, rather than the will of the people expressed through elected representatives, would be the basis for policymaking in the Progressives' new state. Authority to make policy would have to be transferred *out* of the elected branches of government and *into* newly created administrative boards and commissions, which would be staffed with these experts and tasked with making policy appropriate for a modern society.

The result of this movement was to transfer the authority to make law from Congress, filled with inexpert politicians, to administrative experts housed in administrative agencies. But politics would still exert a pernicious influence on these agencies unless they were also insulated from the control of the President, who was also an elected official and tied to the political impulses of his constituency. Therefore, two things had to be achieved: the delegation of legislative power to agencies, and the removal of presidential control over these new institutions. Both were achieved before and during the New Deal, with the creation of "independent regulatory commissions" which were not located within the executive branch. Rather, they would be outside of the traditional branches of government and not directly accountable to any of those traditional branches.

In practice, this meant that the expansion of administrative agencies *appeared* to involve an expansion of executive power, but it actually resulted in a decline of executive control and responsibility for administrative policy. This led to the paradox of the expansion of administrative agencies, but the decline of presidential control over those agencies. Harry Truman famously predicted the difficulty that Dwight Eisenhower would have in setting policy priorities for the administration: "He will sit here and he will say, 'Do this!, Do that!' And nothing will happen. Poor Ike—it won't be a bit like the Army." It was President Truman who breathlessly complained, "I thought I was the President, but when it comes to these bureaucrats, I can't do a damn thing." The Progressive impulse to put technical experts in charge of national policy led to the unfortunate consequence of popularly elected Presidents being unable to change national policy. The ideal of scientific policy had been elevated over the principle of the consent of the governed.

This created a fundamental dilemma: how can the bureaucratic state the Progressives created be organized and controlled? Is it destined to result in a collection of disconnected, uncoordinated independent agencies that each pursue a focused goal such as workplace safety or the regulation of communications? How will these bureaucrats be held accountable to the people, if they do not answer to the President?

From the perspective of the domestic policy agenda of the President, the story of the twentieth century is the history of attempts by individual Presidents to regain control of agencies which are ostensibly executive and which are primarily staffed with officials that the President cannot remove.

Nearly every President, from both parties, has devised a plan for bringing the bureaucracy under the control of the chief executive. Congress has always had several tools for controlling administrative officials—

most notably the powers to authorize and fund agencies. But without the power to remove administrative officials, how can the vast administrative state be controlled?

Presidents have tried many devices for bringing agencies under their supervision. Administrative re-organization was a prominent agenda, employed both by the FDR and Nixon Administrations. The President's control over the administration was expanded by Presidents Carter and Reagan, most notably in the latter's creation of a regulatory review process in the Office of Information and Regulatory Analysis (OIRA), which is now headed by the legal scholar Cass Sunstein, otherwise known as President Obama's "regulatory czar." (Incidentally, Sunstein's nomination was approved by the Senate, despite the "czar" moniker.) Elena Kagan, the [former] Solicitor General, wrote a famous law review article outlining the ways in which President Clinton had established a firmer grip on administrative agencies.

President Obama's attempt to centralize control over administrative agencies is therefore nothing new, nor is it peculiar to one of the two major parties in America. It is a symptom of a much more serious sickness— the fact that Congress has transferred a great deal of its authority to administrative agencies, and neglected to put anyone in charge of the whole structure. This entire framework is in tension with the original Constitution, but the Constitution nevertheless can give us some basic principles for thinking about the question of "czars" in the White House.

The United States Constitution does not create or *require* a cabinet under the executive branch, though it clearly anticipates the managerial structure and recognizes the significance of department heads to assist the President in overseeing the executive branch. From the very beginning, every President has used such a structure to manage the executive branch. The most recent example of strong cabinet government, revived after the failed executive models of the Nixon administration's heavy-handed centralization of White House authority as well as the Carter administration's small-minded micromanaging style, was the presidency of Ronald Reagan, who regularly turned to cabinet secretaries directly for advice and to carry out policy and who created "cabinet councils" to coordinate the activities of the cabinet and respective departments. Presidents since, however, seem to be moving away from the cabinet structure and more in the direction of centralizing more authority directly in the Executive Office of the President.

The President has the authority to appoint his own staff and advisors to assist in the work of his office. It is perfectly legitimate for presidential staff to advance the president's policy objectives within the administration as a matter of course, and Presidents often appoint particular advisors to advance particular, high-level policies. The executive has this authority as a separate and independent matter from officers created by the legislature to carry out the law, and Congress cannot infringe on that authority.

Nevertheless, through its legislative and oversight functions, and more specifically through the Senate's participation in the appointment of officers under Article II, Congress also has significant responsibilities over the general activities of the administration in carrying out the operations of the federal government. With this legislative power in mind, a number of Senators have focused their attention on eighteen czar positions in the administration that may overstep Congress's express statutory assignment of responsibility and its oversight responsibilities.

Where can the line be drawn between executive privilege and legislative responsibility? If executive authority is being used as a subterfuge to thwart confirmation requirements and accountability, and so evade constitutional requirements for individuals performing operational and managerial functions normally the responsibility of cabinet secretaries and department and agency executives that require Senate confirmation, that would certainly violate the spirit and probably the letter of the Constitution. A possible example of this problem may be Climate Czar Carol Browner who, according to reports, was the lead negotiator in establishing new automobile emissions standards, stemming from the Supreme Court's interpretation of the Clean Air Act. In addition to seeming to be beyond congressional legislative intent, it also seems to circumvent the authority of the EPA [Environmental Protection Agency] administrator.

As the number of czars expands, and the President's policy staff grows, and there are more and more individuals acting more and more as administrative heads rather than advisors, Congress should raise questions as to whether those individuals should be subject to executive privilege or can be compelled to testify before Congress. The President cannot have it both ways.

In addition to the constitutional questions, I would also like to note concerns about the administrative problems inherent in this new executive management paradigm. Having policy operations run out of the White House causes confusion of responsibility for one thing. Who is in charge of health care reform: Kathleen Sebelius, the Secretary of Health and Human Services, or Nancy DeParle, the health care czar? In general, running operations out of the White House can become very problematic: recall again the Nixon Administration, and the activities of Mr. Haldeman and Mr. Erlichman. More recently, the Tower Commission warned against White House staff acting outside of the regular structure of policy decision-making. There will always be a temptation to use White House authority—real or implied—to exercise political influence over normal departmental activities. As long as that influence is not accountable, and thus responsible—which seems to have been the case in recent stories concerning a conference call with the National Endowment for the Arts encouraging policy-oriented art or the issuance of curricula to accompany the President's recent speech to students—it is more likely than not to be inappropriate.

In all of these cases, congressional oversight would serve as an important and legitimate check on executive authority. But additional oversight, with the requirement for approval of and testimony from as many presidential staff as possible, will not solve the fundamental problem behind the current czar wars, which I think has more to do with the general nature of modern administrative government and a growing popular concern about the limits (or lack thereof) on its activities.

For some time now, Congress has developed the habit of delegating vast amounts of authority to the executive branch to address a problem and after the fact looks to manage the exercise of that authority, as opposed to writing clear and detailed laws to be executed by the President. The Troubled Asset Relief Program (TARP), meant to purchase assets and equity from financial institutions as a way to address the subprime mortgage crisis, is a perfect example. Unbounded delegations allowed the Secretary of the Treasury to spend up to $700 billion at will to purchase "troubled" assets of any financial institution. Lo and behold, the United States is now majority owner of General Motors and there is a Car Czar. Setting aside the wisdom of the policy, can it fairly be said that this was the intention of Congress?

And in some cases the delegation of czar-like authority is even clearer. The health care legislation in the House of Representatives creates a "Health Choices Commissioner" at the head of a new Health Choices Administration. This duly created, and presumably Senate confirmed, Health Insurance Czar would exercise enormous control over the nation's insurance industry, an enormous concentration of power in one person.

The modern executive, on the other hand, increasingly attempts to get control of the vast bureaucracy under their authority and, in the most recent iteration of the battle, appoints *uber*-bureaucrats to shift that bureaucracy in the President's policy directions. This is partly a misconception of executive authority that seems to see cabinet officers as independent of that authority, or at least an unwillingness to exert authority over executive branch policy through the cabinet. But it also seems to be a general attempt to circumvent congressional oversight (or interference, depending on how you look at it) in shaping policies within the discretion of the executive branch. An executive desire to do more and more things outside of legislative authority, and with vast sums of money appropriated by Congress to do more and more things, makes matters all the worse.

The combination of these two trends creates a situation where more and more laws—in the form of rulemaking, regulations, and policy pronouncements—are made by administrative agents not only outside of the open and transparent requirements of responsible government, and without congressional approval and oversight, but generally beyond the principle that legitimate government arises out of the consent of the governed. And the more government regularly operates as a matter of course outside of popular consent, the more we become clients rather than rulers of a vast and distant government, the less we are self-governing, and the less we control our own fate. And that, as Alexis de Tocqueville warned in *Democracy in America,* is the recipe for a benign form of despotism that truly imperils our democratic experiment.

39

"Czar Wars"

Will Englund

The way the people around Obama describe it, his system of multiple czars is intended to ensure that agencies are on the same page, that consequences that an individual department wouldn't normally consider are taken into account, that policies are drawn up with contributions from all involved, that follow-up isn't neglected. They argue that the administration has useful precedents to replicate—if [Bush's Homeland Security Advisor Frances] Townsend, for instance, didn't think of herself as a "czar," that's fine, because what matters is the way she went about doing her job. Some White House veterans think that the Obama people have a case.

"If you look back, just to give you a couple of reference points, the idea that the White House is the place to coordinate interagency policy and drive decisions of the president is a long-standing tradition, most strongly embedded in the creation of the National Security Council in 1947," says John Podesta, who was chief of staff for President Clinton and headed Obama's transition team. He mentions Clinton's use of the National Economic Council as a mechanism inside the White House where ideas were generated and policy was coordinated.

"It doesn't displace the very strong or important role that Cabinet secretaries play. But when you have problems that really cut across a swath of agencies, it's very important with respect to the president's priorities to have a strong central place within the White House where people can get on the same strategy and that actions are keyed up and accountability exists. That has proven to be an effective way of doing business in the federal government on security policy, on economic policy."

And now, Podesta says, the administration will be extending it to other realms. Back in imperial Russia, there was only one true czar (a word derived from "caesar"); Washington is about to experience life with a whole kingdom of czars.

But success, as Podesta describes it, requires relentlessly good communication, suppression of egos, presidential support, and agreement on basic issues. None of that is guaranteed. These qualities also don't fit the image of a czar as an autocrat. That, in fact, is one of two models the Obama White House would probably want to avoid.

The Imperial Czar

This is the czar who brooks no challenge and shares no responsibility. Henry Kissinger, when he was national security adviser to President Nixon, probably came closest to the type. The State Department was shut out of foreign policy. "He and Nixon decided the issues and let people know about them when they needed to know about them," says Mac Destler, a foreign-policy expert at the University of Maryland. They had their victories, "but they alienated a large share of the rest of the government." And their way of working reinforced the corrosive atmosphere of suspicion that pervaded the Nixon administration.

Zbigniew Brzezinski, President Carter's national security adviser, tried to wield the same sort of clout, Destler says, but more openly. His failing was that he pushed vigorously, and in public, for policies (such as a harder line against the Soviet Union) that no one else in the administration, including Carter, wanted. It undercut his effort to portray himself as an honest broker, and "that led to very big problems."

Hillary Rodham Clinton directed health reform in 1993 without much input from HHS [Health and Human Services], and the effort ran aground in Congress. The most recent imperial czar was Vice President Cheney, whose office shoved aside at various times the departments of State, Defense, Justice, Interior, and Commerce, not to mention the Environmental Protection Agency [EPA]. History will judge whether his tenure was a success.

The Figurehead Czar

This is the other type to avoid, personified by the various drug czars. William Bennett was the first drug czar, under George H.W. Bush, and he acknowledged being frustrated by a lack of authority. Gen. Barry McCaffrey was drug czar under Bill Clinton, and although by law he had some role in budget-setting, in practice the Office of Management and Budget [OMB] didn't give him a seat at the table, according to Winograd. "If it doesn't include the budget, it doesn't mean anything in Washington,"

Winograd says—and although others say that's not always true, it was nevertheless the case that McCaffrey had no clout. The agencies he was supposed to be coordinating resisted him at every turn.

When, a few years later, the administration and Congress were debating the role of homeland-security adviser, McCaffrey said he worried that Ridge would have the same problems he had had. "Six months from now," McCaffrey warned, "there's a danger that he will turn into little more than the speaker's bureau for homeland defense."

For at least a handful of Obama's czars, that will not be a risk. Carol Browner, Lawrence Summers, and retired Gen. James Jones are formidable players; the new health reform czar, taking the position created for Daschle, may be one, as well. That's not to say that they will have no-drama tenures; but none of them is likely to disappear into irrelevancy.

Look, nonetheless, for "consensus-building" to be more of a mantra than "marching orders." Many applaud the job that Robert Rubin did as head of the National Economic Council [NEC] in the Clinton administration. He organized internal debate while conscientiously keeping the Treasury Department, OMB, and the Council of Economic Advisers in the loop through the NEC. As Maryland's Destler describes it, Rubin then forced presidential decisions on key issues. It was openness and purpose at the same time.

A true czar is something more than an honest broker. The aide who simply presents options to the president, even if he's whispering them in the president's ear, performs a useful service, but it's not what a czar does. A czar has to drive those he's working with toward a plan to present to the president. That was Rubin's strength. Summers, the new head of the NEC, has a dominating personality, coupled with credibility as a thinker. He won't be a neutral figure, and he's likely to see his mandate as Rubinesque. Timothy Geithner, at Treasury, is very much on the same wavelength as Summers, although his tax troubles may have given Summers the opportunity to grab a little more clout early on than he otherwise would have. They both have plenty to do. How they'll get along with Paul Volcker, who has his own panel for thinking about financial reform, is more problematic.

Condoleezza Rice played the role of honest broker, or at least gatekeeper, as national security adviser in Bush's first term and got steamrolled. Her cerebral but understated successor, Stephen Hadley, gained a reputation as someone who lacked the political muscle or strength of personality to force coordinated execution of the president's policies. The result was a Bush administration penchant for grand designs and plans, and poor, disjointed execution.

Obama's pick, Jones, is a former Marine commandant and supreme allied commander of NATO [North Atlantic Treaty Organization] and seems intent on regaining the czarist orb for the national security adviser.

NATO command has taught him how to cajole coordinated action out of a multitude of players, and he has been in close contact with a number of think tanks and experts on the Joint Chiefs of Staff and elsewhere who are pushing reforms designed to repair what is seen as a dysfunctional interagency process that failed miserably in Iraq and Afghanistan.

An empowered adviser is essentially the president's alter ego on matters of national security. By virtue of its longevity and its statutory existence, the job comes with plenty of prestige (although it should be mentioned that the drug czar's position is also long-lived and spelled out by law). The president, as head of state and commander-in-chief, has a personal role to play in foreign affairs, and that adds to the heft of the national security czar's position.

Other Obama czars start with neither a formal council to provide structure nor an institutional history. The administration's health reform project is already under way, even with no one to lead it. Jeanne Lambrew, who was going to be Daschle's deputy at the White House, has been at work, and she knows the subject as well as Daschle does. If she is picked to be health czar, the question will be whether she can succeed without the clout and reputation that he enjoyed.

Carol Browner is the energy and climate-change czar, and her position raises the question of what, exactly, gets left to the departments. The departments have the budgets. They also, in many cases, have responsibilities peripheral to the czar's concern. HHS, for instance, has plenty to take care of, even as a White House health czar is drawing up a reform program, and the delineation should be fairly clear. It's a bit muddier with the AIDS czar. And what about EPA or Interior functions that have to do with pollution but not climate-change pollution? Jeff Ruch, executive director of Public Employees for Environmental Responsibility, worries that Browner will be concerned with trying "to accomplish two or three things, and everything is going to be bent to serve those two or three objectives."

Townsend, the former homeland-security adviser, asks where the accountability will lie. No accountability means no czar, in her book. If the role of these new White House coordinators is to look out across the government, spot gaps, assign responsibility for filling them, set priorities, and keep accountability within departments—then that sounds like their jobs will resemble hers, and that means they're not czars.

"I Guess I Ought to Go to That"

Maybe this is just a matter of definition. Czars, by whatever name you call them, can get it right. A czar whose reign was peaceful and successful was John Koskinen, the Y2K czar. (And no smirking, please—he argues persuasively that there's a reason the year 2000 arrived uneventfully, although the low-level wind detectors at the nation's airports and communications links with defense intelligence satellites did go down. Moreover, he says it was because of the Y2K preparations that stock markets were able to reopen on the Monday after September 11, 2001, with assurances that transactions would be properly handled.)

An element of Koskinen's success was the specific task he faced, and the unmovable deadline. It helped that no agency really wanted to crash on December 31, 1999, if, as feared, computers—old mainframe computers in particular, with which the government was well supplied—misread the date and went haywire. Koskinen was able to direct agencies toward a $2 billion fund that OMB handled, but he succeeded without any real budgetary authority.

"I kind of knew everybody," recalls Koskinen, who recently became chairman of the board at Freddie Mac. He had been a deputy director at OMB and had overseen the two government shutdowns in 1995; as a result he was acquainted with a broad swath of executive branch office-holders. "So that was a big advantage."

Koskinen began his czardom in 1998 with three people working for him. But he presided over a council of about 25 from around the government to coordinate the policy. Koskinen asked each Cabinet secretary, in person, to appoint a representative to the council who would know the full sweep of issues in that department, and who would have the authority to make decisions on the spot.

He had what he calls "convening authority" rather than "dictating authority," but that was no small thing. "If someone says we have a meeting at the White House, you're going to say, 'Well, I guess I ought to go to that.'"

Koskinen knew he wouldn't be effective if he handed out orders to the council. That would elicit mild expressions of interest and little more. Instead, he says, "you have to pull people together around the problem, and make them feel like they're part of the solution. They'll have far more information than you'll ever have. And once people understand what needs to be done, they will work with you to get it done. If you get a group of people, they will always come up with a better answer than any individual can."

The first order of business, Koskinen says, is to sit the participants down and ask, "What are the easiest things to do? Where can we get leverage? What do we need? What's working and not working?" People in the agencies know that sort of thing. Of course there will be recalcitrants, but "once it starts moving, people want to be a part of it." At one point, he says, Vice President Gore chaired a meeting of agency heads at which those who had been a little slow on the year 2000 conversion were asked to explain why. "That was effective." One Cabinet secretary, whom Koskinen declined to identify, remained difficult to the end; Koskinen instead forged a relationship with his deputy.

People knew Koskinen could, if he had to, ask the president to make a call. He never had to.

Another Clinton-era czar who had a well-defined task, and pulled it off, was William Daley, who was the "NAFTA czar" before he became Commerce secretary. That assignment involved riding herd on the departments (including Commerce) with an interest in the agreement and organizing the approach to Congress, where the chief opposition came from organized labor. Once the North American Free Trade Agreement was signed, the job was done.

In one sense, Koskinen's czardom could be seen as a precursor for the technology czardom that Obama has promised to create. Its purview will be arcane but will cut across the whole government. Is there a private-sector model? Companies and universities have chief technology officers to make the organizations' computers, software, and databases blend together, and to help increase transparency, efficiency, and productivity. These CTOs sometimes succeed, especially if the CEO and the company culture are aligned with the technology, and especially if the goals are modest.

But the government is different, because the technology is varied and each department and agency is self-interested. The Defense Department probably poses the biggest challenge for the tech czar; it has its own variety of CTOs, cultures, and needs. But every agency, and every department in every agency, will resist to some degree because none wants to have its central nervous system—with all of its decisions, reports, mistakes, inefficiencies, secrets, and game-playing—displayed to rivals and superiors and even outsiders. Agencies already resist rules requiring them to disclose their goals and performance to the White House and Congress, and a tech czar would be far more intrusive than any congressional panel.

In a different sense—that of the limited, specified mandate—Koskinen's and Daley's tenures could have a parallel in the auto czar. This job, created in December [2008] by Treasury Secretary Henry Paulson Jr., comes with a jurisdiction that cuts across several departments and executive agencies: Treasury, because the money that Detroit receives comes from the TARP funds; Energy, because the czar reviews the automakers' compliance with the advanced vehicle loan program, administered by the Energy Department; Labor, which has to sign off on the compensation reductions called for by the bailout; and EPA and Transportation, which share jurisdiction over fuel-economy standards while EPA administers automotive emissions regulations, both of which are covered by the auto restructuring plans. It's a potential minefield.

But Greg Martin, General Motors' spokesman in Washington, says that there is an advantage to having someone close to the president immersed in the industry's issues. "We genuinely see it as an opportunity to build a constructive working relationship with this position and to create a strong, deep knowledge of our industry within the administration," he says. What frustrates the automakers is the prolonged delay in filling the position.

The car czar structure differs from the nearest precedent: The Chrysler bailout of 1979 was administered not by a czar but by a board, chaired by the Treasury secretary and including the Federal Reserve Board chairman and the U.S. comptroller general, with the secretaries of Labor and Transportation as nonvoting members. Brock says that in a less formal way this sort of council setup, headed by a lead Cabinet officer, was typical in the Reagan administration, and he argues that it often worked well. When Chrysler paid back its loans seven years ahead of time, in 1983, the government made a profit.

The statutory power of the car czar, like the power of the Chrysler board earlier, is mostly directed outward, toward the car companies, suppliers, dealers, and unions. In this, it is an exception to the usual experience of White House czars, who tend to have much more general, and thus much less well-defined, mandates.

* * *

DISCUSSION QUESTIONS

1. One criticism of the widespread use of informal advisors is that they are not subject to Senate consent; therefore very little is known about them. Should there be some formal vetting process for presidential advisors? Would this conflict with the president's constitutional prerogative to organize advisory networks as he or she sees fit?

2. What methods can you think of to make executive branch agencies more responsive to presidential policy preferences?

3. In 1900 there were seven Cabinet agencies and 240,000 civilian federal government employees. In 1940, nine agencies and 1 million employees. In 2010, there are fifteen Cabinet agencies, five agencies or boards with Cabinet status, dozens of other agencies, boards, and commissions, and 2.7 million civilian employees. Are there any limits to the size of government?

CHAPTER 8

The Federal Judiciary

40

The Federalist, No. 78

Alexander Hamilton

The judiciary, Hamilton wrote in The Federalist, No. 78, *"will always be the least dangerous to the political rights of the Constitution; because it will be least in a capacity to annoy or injure them." The lack of danger Hamilton spoke of stems from the courts' lack of enforcement or policy power. Or as Hamilton more eloquently put it, the judiciary has "no influence over either the sword or the purse": it must rely on the executive branch and state governments to enforce its rulings, and depends on the legislature for its appropriations and rules governing its structure. Critics of "judicial activism" would likely disagree about the weakness of the judiciary relative to the other branches of government. But Hamilton saw an independent judiciary as an important check on the other branches' ability to assume too much power (the "bulwarks of a limited Constitution against legislative encroachments"). He also argued that the federal judiciary, as interpreter of the Constitution, would gain its power from the force of its judgments, which were rooted in the will of the people.*

To the People of the State of New York:

We proceed now to an examination of the judiciary department of the proposed government.

In unfolding the defects of the existing Confederation, the utility and necessity of a federal judicature have been clearly pointed out. It is the less necessary to recapitulate the considerations there urged, as the propriety of the institution in the abstract is not disputed; the only questions which have been raised being relative to the manner of constituting it, and to its extent. To these points, therefore, our observations shall be confined.

The manner of constituting it seems to embrace these several objects: 1ST. The mode of appointing the judges. 2D. The tenure by which they are to hold their places. 3D. The partition of the judiciary authority between different courts, and their relations to each other.

First. As to the mode of appointing the judges; this is the same with that of appointing the officers of the Union in general, and has been so fully discussed in the two last numbers, that nothing can be said here which would not be useless repetition.

Second. As to the tenure by which the judges are to hold their places: this chiefly concerns their duration in office; the provisions for their support; the precautions for their responsibility.

According to the plan of the convention, all judges who may be appointed by the United States are to hold their offices *during good behavior*; which is conformable to the most approved of the State constitutions, and among the rest, to that of this State. Its propriety having been drawn into question by the adversaries of that plan, is no light symptom of the rage for objection, which disorders their imaginations and judgments. The standard of good behavior for the continuance in office of the judicial magistracy is certainly one of the most valuable of the modern improvements in the practice of government. In a monarchy it is an excellent barrier to the despotism of the prince; in a republic it is a no less excellent barrier to the encroachments and oppressions of the representative body. And it is the best expedient which can be devised in any government to secure a steady, upright, and impartial administration of the laws.

Whoever attentively considers the different departments of power must perceive, that, in a government in which they are separated from each other, the judiciary, from the nature of its functions, will always be the least dangerous to the political rights of the Constitution; because it will be least in a capacity to annoy or injure them. The Executive not only dispenses the honors, but holds the sword of the community. The legislature not only commands the purse, but prescribes the rules by which the duties and rights of every citizen are to be regulated. The judiciary, on the contrary, has no influence over either the sword or the purse; no direction either of the strength or of the wealth of the society; and can take no active resolution whatever. It may truly be said to have neither FORCE nor WILL, but merely judgment; and must ultimately depend upon the aid of the executive arm even for the efficacy of its judgments.

This simple view of the matter suggests several important consequences. It proves incontestably that the judiciary is beyond comparison the weakest of the three departments of power that it can never attack with success either of the other two; and that all possible care is requisite to enable it to defend itself against their attacks. It equally proves that though individual oppression may now and then proceed from the courts of justice, the general liberty of the people can never be endangered from that quarter; I mean so long as the judiciary remains truly distinct from both the legislature and the Executive. For I agree, that "there is no liberty, if the power of judging be not separated from the legislative and executive powers." And it proves, in the last place, that as liberty can have nothing to fear from the judiciary alone, but would have every thing to fear from its union with either of the other departments; that as all the effects of such a union must ensue from a dependence of the former on the latter, notwithstanding a nominal and apparent separation; that as, from the natural feebleness of the judiciary it is in continual jeopardy of being overpowered, awed, or influenced by its coordinate branches; and that as nothing can contribute so much to its firmness and independence as permanency in office, this quality may therefore be justly regarded as an indispensable ingredient in its constitution, and, in a great measure, as the citadel of the public justice and the public security.

The complete independence of the courts of justice is peculiarly essential in a limited Constitution. By a limited Constitution, I understand one which contains certain specified exceptions to the legislative authority; such, for instance, as that it shall pass no bills of attainder, no *ex-post-facto* laws, and the like. Limitations of this kind can be preserved in practice no other way than through the medium of courts of justice, whose duty it must be to declare all acts contrary to the manifest tenor of the Constitution void. Without this, all the reservations of particular rights or privileges would amount to nothing.

Some perplexity respecting the rights of the courts to pronounce legislative acts void, because contrary to the constitution, has arisen from an imagination that the doctrine would imply a superiority of the judiciary to the legislative power. It is urged that the authority which can declare the acts of another void must necessarily be superior to the one whose acts may be declared void. As this doctrine is of great importance in all the American constitutions, a brief discussion of the ground on which it rests cannot be unacceptable.

There is no position which depends on clearer principles than that every act of a delegated authority, contrary to the tenor of the commission under which it is exercised, is void. No legislative act, therefore, contrary to the Constitution, can be valid. To deny this would be to affirm that the deputy is greater than his principal; that the servant is above his master; that the representatives of the people are superior to the people themselves; that men acting by virtue of powers may do not only what their powers do not authorize, but what they forbid.

If it be said that the legislative body are themselves the constitutional judges of their own powers, and that the construction they put upon them is conclusive upon the other departments, it may be answered that this cannot be the natural presumption where it is not to be collected from any particular provisions in the Constitution. It is not otherwise to be supposed that the Constitution could intend to enable the representatives of the people to substitute their *will* to that of their constituents. It is far more rational to suppose that the courts were designed to be an intermediate body between the people and the legislature, in order, among other things, to keep the latter within the limits assigned to their authority. The interpretation of the laws is the proper and peculiar province of the courts. A constitution is, in fact, and must be regarded by the judges, as a fundamental law. It therefore belongs to them to ascertain its meaning, as well as the meaning of any particular act proceeding from the legislative body. If there should happen to be an irreconcilable variance between the two, that which has the superior obligation and validity ought, of course, to be preferred; or, in other words, the Constitution ought to be preferred to the statute, the intention of the people to the intention of their agents.

Nor does this conclusion by any means suppose a superiority of the judicial to the legislative power. It only supposes that the power of the people is superior to both; and that where the will of the legislature, declared in its statutes, stands in opposition to that of the people, declared in the Constitution, the judges ought to be governed by the latter rather than the former. They ought to regulate their decisions by the fundamental laws, rather than by those which are not fundamental.

This exercise of judicial discretion, in determining between two contradictory laws, is exemplified in a familiar instance. It not uncommonly happens that there are two statutes existing at one time, clashing in whole or in part with each other, and neither of them containing any repealing clause or expression. In such a case, it is the province of the courts to liquidate and fix their meaning and operation. So far as they can, by any fair construction, be reconciled to each other, reason and law conspire to dictate that this should be done; where this is impracticable, it becomes a matter of necessity to give effect to one in exclusion of the other. The rule which has obtained in the courts for determining their relative validity is, that the last in order of time shall be preferred to the first. But this is a mere rule of construction, not derived from any positive law but from the nature and reason of the thing. It is a rule not enjoined upon the courts by legislative provision but adopted by themselves, as consonant to truth and propriety for the direction of their conduct as interpreters of the law. They thought it reasonable, that between the interfering acts of an *equal* authority, that which was the last indication of its will should have the preference.

But in regard to the interfering acts of a superior and subordinate authority, of an original and derivative power, the nature and reason of the thing indicate the converse of that rule as proper to be followed. They teach us that the prior act of a superior ought to be preferred to the subsequent act of an inferior and subordinate authority; and that accordingly, whenever a particular statute contravenes the Constitution, it will be the duty of the judicial tribunals to adhere to the latter and disregard the former.

It can be of no weight to say that the courts, on the pretence of a repugnancy, may substitute their own pleasure to the constitutional intentions of the legislature. This might as well happen in the case of two contradictory statutes; or it might as well happen in every adjudication upon any single statute. The courts must declare the sense of the law; and if they should be disposed to exercise WILL instead of JUDGMENT, the consequence would equally be the substitution of their pleasure to that of the legislative body. The observation, if it prove any thing, would prove that there ought to be no judges distinct from that body.

If, then, the courts of justice are to be considered as the bulwarks of a limited Constitution against legislative encroachments, this consideration will afford a strong argument for the permanent tenure of judicial offices, since nothing will contribute so much as this to that independent spirit in the judges which must be essential to the faithful performance of so arduous a duty.

This independence of the judges is equally requisite to guard the Constitution and the rights of individuals from the effects of those ill humors, which the arts of designing men or the influence of particular conjunctures sometimes disseminate among the people themselves; and which, though they speedily give place to better information and more deliberate reflection, have a tendency, in the meantime, to occasion dangerous innovations in the government, and serious oppressions of the minor party in the community. Though I trust the friends of the proposed Constitution will never concur with its enemies in questioning that fundamental principle of republican government, which admits the right of the people to alter or abolish the established Constitution whenever they find it inconsistent with their happiness; yet it is not to be inferred from this principle that the representatives of the people, whenever a momentary inclination happens to lay hold of a majority of their constituents, incompatible with the provisions in the existing Constitution, would, on that account, be justifiable in a violation of those provisions; or that the courts would be under a greater obligation to connive at infractions in this shape, than when they had proceeded wholly from the cabals of the representative body. Until the people have by some solemn and authoritative act annulled or changed the established form, it is binding upon themselves collectively, as well as individually; and no presumption, or even knowledge, of their sentiments, can warrant their representatives in a departure from it, prior to such an act. But it is easy to see that it would require an uncommon portion of fortitude in the judges to do their duty as faithful guardians of the Constitution, where legislative invasions of it had been instigated by the major voice of the community.

But it is not with a view to infractions of the Constitution only that the independence of the judges may be an essential safeguard against the effects of occasional ill humors in the society. These sometimes extend no farther than to the injury of the private rights of particular classes of citizens by unjust and partial laws. Here also the firmness of the judicial magistracy is of vast importance in mitigating the severity and confining the operation of such laws. It not only serves to moderate the immediate mischiefs of those which may have been passed, but it operates as a check upon the legislative body in passing them; who, perceiving that obstacles to the success of iniquitous intention are to be expected from the scruples of the courts, are in a manner compelled by the very motives of the injustice they meditate to qualify their attempts. This is a circumstance calculated to have more influence upon the character of our governments, than but few may be aware of. The benefits of the integrity and moderation of the judiciary have already been felt in more States than one; and though they may have displeased those whose sinister expectations they may have disappointed, they must have commanded the esteem and applause of all the virtuous and disinterested. Considerate men of every description ought to prize whatever will tend to beget or fortify that temper in the courts; as no man can be sure that he may not be tomorrow the victim of a spirit of injustice by which he may be a gainer today. And every man must now feel that the inevitable tendency of such a spirit is to sap the foundations of public and private confidence, and to introduce in its stead universal distrust and distress.

That inflexible and uniform adherence to the rights of the Constitution and of individuals, which we perceive to be indispensable in the courts of justice, can certainly not be expected from judges who hold their offices by a temporary commission. Periodical appointments, however regulated or by whomsoever made, would, in some way or other, be fatal to their necessary independence. If the power of making them was committed either to the Executive or legislature, there would be danger of an improper complaisance to the branch which possessed it; if to both, there would be an unwillingness to hazard the displeasure of either; if to the people or to persons chosen by them for the special purpose, there would be too great a disposition to consult popularity, to justify a reliance that nothing would be consulted but the Constitution and the laws.

There is yet a further and a weightier reason for the permanency of the judicial offices, which is deducible from the nature of the qualifications they require. It has been frequently remarked, with great propriety, that a voluminous code of laws is one of the inconveniences necessarily connected with the advantages of a free government. To avoid an arbitrary discretion in the courts, it is indispensable that they should be bound down by strict rules and precedents, which serve to define and point out their duty in every particular case that comes before them; and it will readily be conceived from the variety of controversies which grow out of the folly and wickedness of mankind, that the records of those precedents must unavoidably swell to a very considerable bulk, and must demand long and laborious study to acquire a competent knowledge of them. Hence it is, that there can be but few men in the society who will have sufficient skill in the laws to qualify them for the stations of judges. And making the proper deductions for the ordinary depravity of human nature, the number must be still smaller of those who unite the requisite integrity with the requisite knowledge. These considerations apprise us that the government can have no great option between fit character; and that a temporary duration in office, which would naturally discourage such characters from quitting a lucrative line of practice to accept a seat on the bench, would have a tendency to throw the administration of justice into hands less able, and less well qualified, to conduct it with utility and dignity. In the present circumstances of this country and in those in which it is likely to be for a long time to come, the disadvantages on this score would be greater than they may at first sight appear; but it must be confessed that they are far inferior to those which present themselves under the other aspects of the subject.

Upon the whole, there can be no room to doubt that the convention acted wisely in copying from the models of those constitutions which have established *good behavior* as the tenure of their judicial offices, in point of duration; and that so far from being blamable on this account, their plan would have been inexcusably defective if it had wanted this important feature of good government. The experience of Great Britain affords an illustrious comment on the excellence of the institution.

PUBLIUS

DISCUSSION QUESTIONS

1. Was Hamilton correct in arguing that the judiciary is the least dangerous branch of government?

2. Critics of the Supreme Court often charge that it rules on issues that should be properly decided in the legislature, while supporters claim that the Court is often the last check against the tyranny of the majority. Who has the stronger case? Can both sides be correct?

3. Hamilton argues that the "power of the people is superior to both" the legislature and the judiciary, and that judges uphold the power of the people when they support the Constitution over a statute that runs counter to the Constitution. He asserts that the people's will is reflected in the Constitution but refers to statutes as reflecting the will of the legislators. Is it legitimate to argue that the Supreme Court is supporting the will of the people, given that it is an unelected body?

41

"The Court and American Life," from *Storm Center: The Supreme Court in American Politics*

David O'Brien

The "textbook" view of the federal judiciary is one in which judges sit in dispassionate review of complex legal questions, render decisions based on a careful reading of constitutional or statutory language, and expect their rulings to be adhered to strictly; the law is the law. This selection shows how unrealistic that picture is. O'Brien notes that the Supreme Court is very much a political institution, whose members pay more attention to the political cycle and public opinion than one might expect. O'Brien reviews the decision-making process in the famous Brown v. Board of Education of Topeka, Kansas, *in which the Court invalidated segregated public schools, as an example of how the Court fits itself into the political process. Throughout the case, justices delayed their decision, consolidated cases from around the country, and refused to set a firm timetable for implementation, relying instead on the ambiguous standard "with all deliberate speed." Far from being a purely objective arbiter of legal questions, the Court must pay close attention to its own legitimacy, and by extension the likelihood of compliance: it does no good to issue decisions that will be ignored.*

"Why does the Supreme Court pass the school desegregation case?" asked one of Chief Justice Vinson's law clerks in 1952. *Brown v. Board of Education of Topeka, Kansas* had arrived on the Court's docket in 1951, but it was carried over for oral argument the next term and then consolidated with four other cases and reargued in December 1953. The landmark ruling did not come down until May 17, 1954. "Well," Justice Frankfurter explained, "we're holding it for the election"—1952 was a presidential election year. "You're holding it for the election?" The clerk persisted in disbelief. "I thought the Supreme Court was supposed to decide cases without regard to elections." "When you have a major social political issue of this magnitude," timing and public reactions are important considerations, and, Frankfurter continued, "we do not think this is the time to decide it." Similarly, Tom Clark recalled that the Court awaited, over Douglas's dissent, additional cases from the District of Columbia and other regions, so as "to get a national coverage, rather than a sectional one." Such political considerations are by no means unique. "We often delay adjudication. It's not a question of evading at all," Clark concluded. "It's just the practicalities of life—common sense."

Denied the power of the sword or the purse, the Court must cultivate its institutional prestige. The power of the Court lies in the persuasiveness of its rulings and ultimately rests with other political institutions and public opinion. As an independent force, the Court has no chance to resolve great issues of public policy. *Dred Scott v. Sandford* (1857) and *Brown v. Board of Education* (1954) illustrate the limitations of Supreme Court policy-making. The "great folly," as Senator Henry Cabot Lodge characterized *Dred Scott*, was not the Court's interpretation of the Constitution or the unpersuasive moral position that blacks were not persons under the Constitution. Rather, "the attempt of the Court to settle the slavery question by judicial decision was simple madness." As Lodge explained:

> Slavery involved not only the great moral issue of the right of one man to hold another in bondage and to buy and sell him but it involved also the foundations of a social fabric covering half the country and caused men to feel so deeply that it finally brought them beyond the question of nullification to a point where the life of the Union was at stake and a decision could only be reached by war.

A hundred years later, political struggles within the country and, notably, presidential and congressional leadership in enforcing the Court's school desegregation ruling saved the moral appeal of *Brown* from becoming another "great folly."

Because the Court's decisions are not self-executing, public reactions inevitably weigh on the minds of the justices. Justice Stone, for one, was furious at Chief Justice Hughes's rush to hand down *Powell v. Alabama* (1932). Picketers protested the Scottsboro boys' conviction and death sentence. Stone attributed the Court's rush to judgment to Hughes's "wish to put a stop to the [public] demonstrations around the Court." Opposition to the school desegregation ruling in *Brown* led to bitter, sometimes violent confrontations. In Little Rock, Arkansas, Governor Orval Faubus encouraged disobedience by southern segregationists. The federal National Guard had to be called out to maintain order. The school board in Little Rock unsuccessfully pleaded, in *Cooper v. Aaron* (1958), for the Court's postponement of the implementation of *Brown's* mandate. In the midst of the controversy, Frankfurter worried that Chief Justice Warren's attitude had become "more like that of a fighting politician than that of a judicial statesman." In such confrontations between the Court and the country, "the transcending issue," Frankfurter reminded the brethren, remains that of preserving "the Supreme Court as the authoritative organ of what the Constitution requires." When the justices move too far or too fast in their interpretation of the Constitution, they threaten public acceptance of the Court's legitimacy.

* * *

When deciding major issues of public law and policy, justices must consider strategies for getting public acceptance of their rulings. When striking down the doctrine of "separate but equal" facilities in 1954 in *Brown v. Board of Education (Brown I)*, for instance, the Warren Court waited a year before issuing, in *Brown II*, its mandate for "all deliberate speed" in ending racial segregation in public education.

Resistance to the social policy announced in *Brown I* was expected. A rigid timetable for desegregation would only intensify opposition. During oral arguments on *Brown II*, devoted to the question of what kind of decree the Court should issue to enforce *Brown*, Warren confronted the hard fact of southern resistance. The attorney for South Carolina, S. Emory Rogers, pressed for an open-ended decree—one that would not specify when and how desegregation should take place. He boldly proclaimed:

> Mr. Chief Justice, to say we will conform depends on the decree handed down. I am frank to tell you, right now [in] our district I do not think that we will send—[that] the white people of the district will send their children to the Negro schools. It would be unfair to tell the Court that we are going to do that. I do not think it is. But I do think that something can be worked out. We hope so.

"It is not a question of attitude," Warren shot back, "it is a question of conforming to the decree." Their heated exchange continued as follows:

> CHIEF JUSTICE WARREN: But you are not willing to say here that there would be an honest attempt to conform to this decree, if we did leave it to the district court [to implement]?
> MR. ROGERS: No, I am not. Let us get the word "honest" out of there.
> CHIEF JUSTICE WARREN: No, leave it in.
> MR. ROGERS: No, because I would have to tell you that right now we would not conform—we would not send our white children to the Negro schools.

The exchange reinforced Warren's view "that reasonable attempts to start the integration process is [sic] all the court can expect in view of the scope of the problem, and that an order to immediately admit all negroes in white schools would be an absurdity because impossible to obey in many areas. Thus, while total immediate integration might be a reasonable order for Kansas, it would be unreasonable for Virginia, and the district judge might decide that a grade a year or three grades a year is [sic] reasonable compliance in Virginia." Six law clerks were assigned to prepare a segregation research report. They summarized available studies, discussed how school districts in different regions could be desegregated, and projected the effects and reactions to various desegregation plans.

The Court's problem, as one of Reed's law clerks put it, was to frame a decree "so as to allow such divergent results without making it so broad that evasion is encouraged." The clerks agreed that there should be a simple decree but disagreed on whether there should be guidelines for its implementation. One clerk opposed any guidelines. The others thought that their absence "smacks of indecisiveness, and gives the extremists more time to operate." The problem was how precise a guideline should be established. What would constitute "good-faith" compliance? "Although we think a 12-year gradual desegregation plan permissible," they confessed, "we are not certain that the opinion should explicitly sanction it."

At conference, Warren repeated these concerns. Black and Minton thought that a simple decree, without an opinion, was enough. As Black explained, "the less we say the better off we are." The others disagreed. A short, simple opinion seemed advisable for reaffirming *Brown I* and providing guidance for dealing with the inevitable problems of compliance. Harlan wanted *Brown II* expressly to recognize that school desegregation was a local problem to be solved by local authorities. The others also insisted on making clear that school boards and lower courts had flexibility in ending segregation. In Burton's view, "neither this Court nor district courts should act as a school board or formulate the program" for desegregation.

Agreement emerged that the Court should issue a short opinion-decree. In a memorandum, Warren summarized the main points of agreement. The opinion should simply state that *Brown I* held racially segregated public schools to be unconstitutional. *Brown II* should acknowledge that the ruling created various administrative problems, but emphasize that "local school authorities have the primary responsibility for assessing and solving these problems; [and] the courts will have to consider these problems in determining whether the efforts of local school authorities" are in good-faith compliance. The cases, he concluded, should be remanded to the lower courts "for such proceedings and decree necessary and proper to carry out this Court's decision." The justices agreed, and along these lines Warren drafted the Court's short opinion-decree.

The phrase "all deliberate speed" was borrowed from Holmes's opinion in *Virginia v. West Virginia* (1911), a case dealing with how much of the state's public debt, and when, Virginia ought to receive at the time West Virginia broke off and became a state. It was inserted in the final opinion at the suggestion of Frankfurter. Forced integration might lead to a lowering of educational standards. Immediate, court-ordered desegregation, Frankfurter warned, "would make a mockery of the Constitutional adjudication designed to vindicate a claim to equal treatment to achieve 'integrated' but lower educational standards." The Court, he insisted, "does its duty if it gets effectively under way the righting of a wrong. When the wrong is deeply rooted state policy the court does its duty if it decrees measures that reverse the direction of the unconstitutional policy so as to uproot it 'with all deliberate speed.'" As much an apology for not setting precise guidelines as a recognition of the limitations of judicial power, the phrase symbolized the Court's bold moral appeal to the country.

Ten years later, after school closings, massive resistance, and continuing litigation, Black complained. "There has been entirely too much deliberation and not enough speed" in complying with *Brown.* "The time for mere 'deliberate speed' has run out." *Brown*'s moral appeal amounted to little more than an invitation for delay.

* * *

Twenty years after *Brown*, some schools remained segregated. David Mathews, secretary of the Department of Health, Education, and Welfare, reported to President Ford the results of a survey of half of the nation's primary and secondary public schools, enrolling 91 percent of all students: of these, 42 percent had an "appreciable percentage" of minority students, 16 percent had undertaken desegregation plans, while 26 percent had not, and 7 percent of the school districts remained racially segregated.

For over three decades, problems of implementing and achieving compliance with *Brown* persisted. Litigation by civil rights groups forced change, but it was piecemeal, costly, and modest. The judiciary alone could not achieve desegregation. Evasion and resistance were encouraged by the reluctance of Presidents and Congress to enforce the mandate. Refusing publicly to endorse *Brown*, Eisenhower would not take steps to enforce the decision until violence erupted in Little Rock, Arkansas. He then did so "*not* to enforce integration but to prevent opposition by violence to orders of a court." Later the Kennedy and Johnson administrations lacked congressional authorization and resources to take major initiatives in enforcing school desegregation. Not until 1964, when Congress passed the Civil Rights Act, did the executive branch have such authorization.

Enforcement and implementation required the cooperation and coordination of all three branches. Little progress could be made, as Assistant Attorney General Stephen Pollock has explained, "where historically there had been slavery and a long tradition of discrimination [until] all three branches of the federal government [could] be lined up in support of a movement forward or a requirement for change." The election of Nixon in 1968 then brought changes both in the policies of the executive branch and in the composition of the Court. The simplicity and flexibility of *Brown*, moreover, invited evasion. It produced a continuing struggle over measures, such as gerrymandering school district lines and busing in the 1970s and 1980s, because the mandate itself had evolved from one of ending segregation to one of securing integration in public schools. Republican and Democratic administrations in turn differed on the means and ends of their enforcement policies in promoting integration.

Almost forty years after *Brown*, over 500 school desegregation cases remained in the lower federal courts. At issue in most was whether schools had achieved integration and become free of the vestiges of past segregation. Although lower courts split over how much proof school boards had to show to demonstrate that present *de facto* racial isolation was unrelated to past *de jure* segregation, the Court declined to review major desegregation cases from the mid-1970s to the end of the 1980s. During that time the dynamics of segregation in the country changed, as did the composition and direction of the Court.

* * *

"By itself," the political scientist Robert Dahl observed, "the Court is almost powerless to affect the course of national policy." Another political scientist, Gerald Rosenberg, goes much farther in claiming that "courts can *almost never* be effective producers of significant social reform." *Brown*'s failure to achieve immediate and widespread desegregation is instructive, Rosenberg contends, in developing a model of judicial policy-making on the basis of two opposing theories of judicial power. On the theory of a "Constrained Court" three institutional factors limit judicial policy-making: "[t]he limited nature of constitutional rights"; "[t]he lack of judicial independence"; and "[t]he judiciary's lack of powers of implementation." On the other hand, a "Dynamic Court" theory emphasizes the judiciary's freedom "from electoral constraints and [other] institutional arrangements that stymie change," and thus enable the courts to take on issues that other political institutions might not or cannot. But neither theory is completely satisfactory, according to Rosenberg, because occasionally courts do bring about social change. The Court may do so when the three institutional restraints identified with the "Constrained Court" theory are absent and at least one of the following conditions exist to support judicial policy-making: when other political institutions and actors offer either (a) incentives or (b) costs to induce compliance; (c) "when judicial decisions can be implemented by the market"; or (d) when the Court's ruling serves as "a shield, cover, or excuse, for persons crucial to implementation who are *willing to act*." On the historical basis of resistance and forced compliance with *Brown*'s mandate, Rosenberg concludes that "*Brown* and its progeny stand for the proposition that courts are impotent to produce significant social reform."

Brown, nonetheless, dramatically and undeniably altered the course of American life in ways and for reasons that Rosenberg underestimates. Neither Congress nor President Eisenhower would have moved to end segregated schools in the 1950s, as their reluctance for a decade to enforce *Brown* underscores. The Court lent moral force and legitimacy to the civil rights movement and to the eventual move by Congress and President Johnson to enforce compliance with *Brown*. More importantly, to argue that the Court is impotent to bring about social change overstates the case. Neither Congress nor the President, any more than the Court, could have singlehandedly dismantled racially segregated public schools. As political scientist Richard Neustadt has argued, presidential power ultimately turns on a President's power of persuasion, the Court's power depends on the persuasiveness of its rulings and the magnitude of change in social behavior mandated. The Court raises the ante in its bid for compliance when it appeals for massive social change through a prescribed course of action, in contrast to when it simply says "no" when striking down a law. The unanimous but ambiguous ruling in *Brown* reflects the justices' awareness that their decisions are not self-enforcing, especially when they deal with highly controversial issues and their rulings depend heavily on other institutions for implementation. Moreover, the ambiguity of *Brown*'s remedial decree was the price of achieving unanimity. Unanimity appeared necessary if the Court was to preserve its institutional prestige while pursuing revolutionary change in social policy. The justices sacrificed their own policy preferences for more precise guidelines, while the Court tolerated lengthy delays in recognition of the costs of open defiance, building consensus, and gaining public acceptance. But in the ensuing decades *Brown*'s mandate was also transformed from that of a simple decree for putting an end to state-imposed segregation into the more vexing one of achieving integrated public schools. With that transformation of *Brown*'s mandate the political dynamics of the desegregation controversy evolved, along with a changing Court and country.

Discussion Questions

1. In what ways does the Supreme Court take politics and public opinion into account in making decisions? Is this appropriate? What would the alternative be?

2. How does the process of appointment to the Supreme Court shape Court decisions? Should presidents make nominations based on the political views of potential justices?

3. Does O'Brien's argument confirm Hamilton's observations about the power of the Court?

4. In several states, Supreme Courts have ruled that bans on same-sex marriage violated the state's constitution. Did these courts' rulings damage their public standing by ignoring the political context (a majority of the public opposes same-sex marriage and many states passed laws or constitutional amendments following these decisions to prohibit same-sex marriage in their states), or did the courts do the correct thing by supporting the basic rights of a minority group? Is there some way the courts could have finessed the issue, the way the Supreme Court did in *Brown*? Should they have?

42

"Overruling the Court"

Leon Friedman

This article develops another theme that was addressed in Alexander Hamilton's Federalist, No. 78. Hamilton argued that the Supreme Court should be the final interpreter of the Constitution. If Congress passed a law that was clearly unconstitutional, the Court must strike it down. However, as Friedman points out, Congress often disagrees with Supreme Court decisions and will pass legislation that overrules specific decisions, even if the Court claims that it has the final say. These tussles between Congress and the Supreme Court may often go back and forth for several rounds before one of the branches backs down. In general, he writes, Congress should have the upper hand if the question concerns statutory interpretation (that is, what a law passed by Congress really means), while the Supreme Court gets the final word concerning constitutional interpretation. Friedman explores these issues in the context of civil rights legislation. The Supreme Court has favored a narrower conception of civil rights than Congress in a series of decisions across three decades. On several occasions Congress has responded by passing new legislation to clarify the intent of the 1964 Civil Rights Act and other laws. Friedman argues that the time has come for additional corrective legislation. He outlines five Supreme Court decisions on age discrimination, disability discrimination, language discrimination, lawyers' fees for civil rights cases, and remedies for violence against women that, in his view, restrict the scope of civil rights in the United States. Friedman also discusses the types of actions that Congress could take to overturn these decisions. Some changes would be relatively direct, in the case of statutory interpretation; others would be more indirect, when dealing with constitutional issues such as federalism.

One of the myths of our political system is that the Supreme Court has the last word on the scope and meaning of federal law. But time and time again, Congress has shown its dissatisfaction with Supreme Court interpretations of laws it passes—by amending or re-enacting the legislation to clarify its original intent and overrule a contrary Court construction.

The Supreme Court often insists that Congress cannot really "overrule" its decisions on what a law means: The justices' interpretation has to be correct since the Constitution gives final say to the highest court in the land. But Congress certainly has the power to pass a new or revised law that "changes" or "reverses" the meaning or scope of the law as interpreted by the Court, and the legislative history of the new law usually states that it was intended to "overrule" a specific Court decision.

Often the reversal is in highly technical areas, such as the statute of limitations in securities-fraud cases, the jurisdiction of tribal courts on Indian reservations, or the power of state courts to order denaturalization of citizens. But in the last 20 years, a main target of congressional "overruling" has been the Supreme Court's decisions in the area of civil rights. In 1982, for example, Congress amended the Voting Rights Act of 1965 to overrule a narrow Supreme Court holding in *Mobile v. Bolden*, a 1980 decision that addressed whether intentional discrimination must be shown before the act could be invoked. In 1988, Congress overruled another Supreme Court decision (in the 1984 case *Grove City College v. Bell*) by passing the Civil Rights Restoration Act, which broadened the coverage of Title VI of the Civil Rights Act of 1964. The legislative history of that law specifically recited that "certain aspects of recent decisions and opinions of the Supreme Court have unduly narrowed or cast doubt upon" a number of federal civil rights statutes and that "legislative action is necessary to restore the prior consistent and long-standing executive branch interpretations" of those laws.

And in 1991, Congress passed a broad, new Civil Rights Act that specifically reversed no fewer than five Supreme Court cases decided in 1989—decisions that severely restricted and limited workers' rights under federal antidiscrimination laws. Led by Massachusetts Democrat Edward Kennedy in the Senate and New York Republican Hamilton Fish, Jr., in the House, Congress acted to undo those rulings, as well as make other changes to federal law that strengthened the weapons available to workers against discrimination. Despite partisan contention over the language of certain provisions (which led to last-minute-compromise language), President George Bush the elder supported the changes. The new law recited in its preamble that its purpose was "to respond to recent decisions of the Supreme Court by expanding the scope of relevant civil rights statutes in order to provide adequate protection to victims of discrimination."

Given the current Supreme Court's track record in civil rights cases, there can be no doubt that congressional remediation is again necessary. In a series of cases over the past two years, the Court has been giving narrow readings to various federal civil rights laws. And once again, an attentive Congress can and should overrule the Court's decisions if the legislators care about fairness in the operation of government and in the workplace.

The recent cases were decided by identical 5–4 votes: Three conservative justices (William Rehnquist, Antonin Scalia, and Clarence Thomas) were joined by two centrists (Sandra Day O'Connor and Anthony

Kennedy) to narrow the reach of the laws at issue. Four liberal justices (John Paul Stevens, David Souter, Ruth Bader Ginsburg, and Stephen Breyer) dissented in all of the cases, four of which are described below.

- Last year [2000], on the grounds of federalism, the Supreme Court held in *Kimel v. Florida Board of Regents* that persons working for state governments cannot sue in federal court under the Age Discrimination in Employment Act, which Congress adopted in 1967. Such suits, the high court said, were constitutionally barred by the 11th Amendment's prohibition of suits against states in federal court. This ruling removed 3.4 percent of the nation's total workforce from the federal law's protections against age bias—some 5 million state employees across the country.
- On the same basis as the age-discrimination case, the Court held in February of this year that state employees cannot sue in federal court under the Americans with Disabilities Act. In this ruling, *Board of Trustees of the University of Alabama v. Garrett*, state workers who alleged disabilities discrimination were relegated to seeking recourse through state courts, where the available remedies are often much weaker than those provided under federal law.
- In April of this year [2001], the Supreme Court narrowed the reach of Title VI, the 1964 provision that prohibits recipients of federal financial assistance from discriminating on the basis of race, color, or national origin. In *Alexander v. Sandoval*, the Court held that Title VI is violated only if a plaintiff proves that the funded party *intentionally* discriminated on the basis of race—an interpretation that runs contrary to the rule for other civil rights laws (such as Title VII), which require only a showing of a discriminatory impact to trigger enforcement. At the same time, the justices held that neither public nor private recipients of federal financial aid who violate the nation's antidiscrimination regulations can be sued in federal court. Thus the state of Alabama was not vulnerable to suit when it established an "English only" requirement for taking a driver's license exam, even though federal regulations prohibit such restrictions. The only remedy, the Court held, was termination of federal funding to the state entity that violated the regulations (a sanction that entails a complicated administrative process).
- On May 29, the Court decided that civil rights litigants who bring suit against the government or an employer cannot collect attorney fees if the defendant voluntarily ceases the practice complained of or settles the claim before going to trial (the case was *Buckhannon Board and Care Home, Inc., v. West Virginia Department of Health and Human Services*). In 1976, Congress passed the Civil Rights Attorneys Fees Award Act to encourage lawyers to take civil rights cases as "private attorney generals." Such cases "vindicate public policies of the highest order," Congress explained when it passed the law. The act specified that the legal

fees of "prevailing parties" would be paid by the losing party—generally a government that violated the plaintiff's constitutional rights. As Justice Ginsburg pointed out in her dissent in the *Buckhannon* case, Congress enacted the law to "ensure that nonaffluent plaintiffs would have effective access to the Nation's courts to enforce . . . civil rights laws." The effect of the Buckhannon decision is that a government body can tenaciously litigate a case until the last minute, then throw in the towel and evade the requirement of paying attorney fees. Since lawyers can no longer be sure that they'll be paid if they file civil rights suits, this ruling will certainly discourage them from taking on such cases, even those that clearly have merit.

Two of these cases are quite easy to correct. Congress can reverse the Supreme Court's decision about attorney fees by simply amending the civil rights law to provide that a litigant is considered a prevailing party entitled to fees if the lawsuit "was a substantial factor" in remedial action taken by the government and the suit brought by the plaintiff had a "substantial basis in fact and law." That was the rule generally applied by the lower courts before the Supreme Court decision.

The *Sandoval* rule can also be corrected by legislation. Congress could amend Title VI to provide that "any person aggrieved by the violation of any regulation issued pursuant to this act may bring a civil action in an appropriate federal court. Such actions may include suits challenging any discriminatory practice or policy that would be deemed unlawful if it has a disparate impact upon persons protected by this title."

The *Kimel* and *Garrett* decisions are more difficult to attack. The Supreme Court held that the 11th Amendment to the Constitution protects states against suits in federal court for age or disabilities discrimination by their employees. Although Congress cannot overrule a constitutional determination made by the Court, it can condition federal financial assistance on state adherence to federal requirements. In 1987 the Supreme Court held in *South Dakota v. Dole* (a 7–2 decision written by Chief Justice Rehnquist, in which Justice Scalia joined) that Congress could insist that South Dakota increase the minimum drinking age to 21 as a condition of obtaining federal highway funds. In other words, while Congress cannot force states to do its bidding, it in effect may bribe them to follow federal requirements.

Thus Congress could condition federal grants under Medicaid, Medicare, or the Social Security Act on the states' surrendering their 11th Amendment immunity under the federal acts banning discrimination based on age and disability. If a state wished to obtain federal funds under various social-welfare provisions, it would have to accede to the U.S. antidiscrimination laws and waive its immunity from being sued by its employees in federal court. Indeed, the 1986 Civil Rights Remedies Equalization Amendment specifically declared that Congress intended for states to waive their 11th Amendment immunity in order to receive federal financial assistance.

Congress could use the same device to overrule another recent Supreme Court decision: last year's 5–4 holding in *United States v. Morrison* that the civil-remedy provisions of the Violence Against Women Act of 1994 are unconstitutional. The majority held that the law exceeded congressional power under the Constitution's commerce clause—the first time a federal law had been invalidated on that basis since 1936. But Congress can counter the Court's action by ensuring that such civil remedies are available to victims of gender-motivated acts of violence through state courts. How? By making the federal funds that are available through Medicare or Social Security programs contingent on a state's provision of such remedies.

In 1991, Congress and the first President Bush acted courageously to overrule manifestly narrow decisions of the Supreme Court that violated a national consensus against discrimination by government or by employers. Now that the Democrats have control of the Senate, they should make similar corrective legislation one of their first objectives. And who knows? This President Bush might even follow the lead of his father and endorse the changes.

Discussion Questions

1. To what extent should the Supreme Court shape policy in an area such as civil rights, and to what extent should policy be made by Congress or the states?

2. If you think that the Court should play a central role in policy- and lawmaking, how would you answer critics who say that laws should be made by popularly elected institutions and not by unelected judges? If you think that Congress should play a central role, how would you answer those who point to the mid twentieth century and show that Congress was dominated by segregationists who killed civil rights legislation for decades? Do the answers to these questions depend, at least in part, on how you view the policy in question and which branch of government would be more sympathetic to your views?

Debating the Issues: Interpreting the Constitution— Originalism or a Living Constitution?

Debates over the federal judiciary's role in the political process often focus on the question of how judges should interpret the Constitution. Should judges apply the document's original meaning as stated by the Framers, or should they use a framework that incorporates shifting interpretations across time? This debate intensified during Earl Warren's tenure as Chief Justice (1953–69) because of Court decisions that expanded the scope of civil liberties and criminal rights far beyond what "originalists" thought the Constitution's language authorized. The debate continues in the current, more conservative Court. The two readings in this section offer contrasting viewpoints from two sitting Supreme Court justices.

Antonin Scalia, the intellectual force behind the conservative wing of the Court, argues that justices must be bound by the original meaning of the document, because that is the only neutral principle that allows the judiciary to function as a legal body instead of a political one. The alternative is to embrace an evolving or "Living Constitution," which Scalia criticizes as allowing judges to decide cases on the basis of what seems right at the moment. He says that this "evolutionary" approach does not have any overall guiding principle and therefore "is simply not a practicable constitutional philosophy." He provides several examples of how the Living Constitution approach had produced decisions that stray from the meaning of the Constitution in the areas of property rights, the right to bear arms, and the right to confront one's accuser. This last example is especially provocative, given that it concerned the right of an accused child molester to confront the child who accused him of the crime. Scalia also challenges the notion that the Living Constitution approach produces more individual freedoms. Instead, he says, this approach has led to a variety of new restrictions on practices that had previously been allowed in the political process.

Stephen Breyer argues for the Living Constitution approach, and places it within a broader constitutional and theoretical framework. He argues for a "consequentialist" approach that is rooted in basic constitutional purposes, the most important of which is "active liberty," which he defines as "an active and constant participation in collective power." Breyer applies this framework to a range of difficult constitutional issues, including freedom of speech in the context of campaign finance and privacy rights in the context of rapidly evolving technology. He argues that the plain language of the Constitution does not provide enough guidance to answer these difficult questions. He turns the tables on Scalia, arguing that it is the literalist or originalist position that will, ironically, lead justices to rely too heavily on their own personal views, whereas his consequentialist position is actually the view that is more likely to produce judicial restraint. Breyer goes on to criticize the originalist position as fraught with inconsistencies. It is inherently subjective, despite its attempt to emphasize the "objective" words of the Constitution. By relying on the consequentialist perspective, which emphasizes democratic participation and active liberty, justices are more likely to reach limited conclusions that apply to the facts at hand, while maximizing the positive implications for democracy.

Linda Greenhouse, an observer of the Supreme Court, summarized the debate between Scalia and Breyer in these terms: "It is a debate over text versus context. For Justice Scalia, who focuses on text, language is supreme, and the court's job is to derive and apply rules from the words chosen by the Constitution's framers or a statute's drafters. For Justice Breyer, who looks to context, language is only a starting point to an inquiry in which a law's purpose and a decision's likely consequences are the more important elements."

43

"Common-Law Courts in a Civil-Law System: The Role of United States Federal Courts in Interpreting the Constitution and Laws"

ANTONIN SCALIA

I want to say a few words about the distinctive problem of interpreting our Constitution. The problem is distinctive, not because special principles of interpretation apply, but because the usual principles are being applied to an unusual text. Chief Justice Marshall put the point as well as it can be put in *McCulloch* v. *Maryland*:

> A constitution, to contain an accurate detail of all the subdivisions of which its great powers will admit, and of all the means by which they may be carried into execution, would partake of the prolixity of a legal code, and could scarcely be embraced by the human mind. It would probably never be understood by the public. Its nature, therefore, requires, that only its great outlines should be marked, its important objects designated, and the minor ingredients which compose the objects be deduced from the nature of the objects themselves.

In textual interpretation, context is everything, and the context of the Constitution tells us not to expect nit-picking detail, and to give words and phrases an expansive rather than narrow interpretation—though not, of course, an interpretation that the language will not bear.

Take, for example, the provision of the First Amendment that forbids abridgment of "the freedom of speech, or of the press." That phrase does not list the full range of communicative expression. Handwritten letters, for example, are neither speech nor press. Yet surely there is no doubt they cannot be censored. In this constitutional context, speech and press, the two most common forms of communication, stand as a sort of synecdoche for the whole. That is not strict construction, but it is reasonable construction.

It is curious that most of those who insist that the drafter's intent gives meaning to a statute reject the drafter's intent as the criterion for interpretation of the Constitution. I reject it for both. I will consult the writings of some men who happened to be Framers—Hamilton's and Madison's writings in the *Federalist*, for example. I do so, however, not because they were Framers and therefore their intent is authoritative and must be the law; but rather because their writings, like those of other intelligent and informed people of the time, display how the text of the Constitution was originally understood. Thus, I give equal weight to Jay's pieces in the *Federalist*, and to Jefferson's writings, even though neither of them was a Framer. What I look for in the Constitution is precisely what I look for in a statute: the original meaning of the text, not what the original draftsmen intended.

But the Great Divide with regard to constitutional interpretation is not that between Framers' intent and objective meaning; but rather that between *original* meaning (whether derived from Framers' intent or not) and *current* meaning. The ascendant school of constitutional interpretation affirms the existence of what is called the "Living Constitution," a body of law that (unlike normal statutes) grows and changes from age to age, in order to meet the needs of a changing society. And it is the judges who determine those needs and "find" that changing law. Seems familiar, doesn't it? Yes, it is the common law returned, but infinitely more powerful than what the old common law ever pretended to be, for now it trumps even the statutes of democratic legislatures. Recall the words I quoted earlier from the Fourth-of-July speech of the avid codifier Robert Rantoul: "The judge makes law, by extorting from precedents something which they do not contain. He extends his precedents, which were themselves the extension of others, till, by this accommodating principle, a whole system of law is built up without the authority or interference of the legislator." Substitute the word "people" for "legislator," and it is a perfect description of what modern American courts have done with the Constitution.

If you go into a constitutional law class, or study a constitutional-law casebook, or read a brief filed in a constitutional-law case, you will rarely find the discussion addressed to the text of the constitutional provision that is at issue, or to the question of what was the originally understood or even the originally intended meaning of that text. Judges simply ask themselves (as a good common-law judge would) what *ought* the result to be, and then proceed to the task of distinguishing (or, if necessary, overruling) any prior Supreme Court cases that stand in the way. Should there be (to take one of the less controversial examples) a constitutional right to die? If so, there is. Should there be a constitutional right to reclaim a biological child put out for adoption by the other parent? Again, if so, there is. If it is good, it is so. Never mind the text that we are supposedly construing; we will smuggle these in, if all else fails, under the Due Process Clause (which, as I have described, is textually incapable of containing them). Moreover, what the Constitution meant yesterday it does not necessarily mean today. As our opinions say in the context of our Eighth Amendment jurisprudence (the Cruel and Unusual Punishments Clause), its meaning changes to reflect "the evolving standards of decency that mark the progress of a maturing society."

This is preeminently a common-law way of making law, and not the way of construing a democratically adopted text. I mentioned earlier a famous English treatise on statutory construction called *Dwarris on Statutes*. The fourth of Dwarris's Maxims was as follows: "An act of Parliament cannot alter by reason of time; but the common law may, since *cessante ratione cessat lex*." This remains (however much it may sometimes be evaded) the formally enunciated rule for statutory construction: statutes do not change. Proposals for "dynamic statutory construction," such as those of Judge Calabresi and Professor Eskridge that I discussed yesterday, are concededly avant-garde. The Constitution, however, even though a democratically adopted text, we formally treat like the common law. What, it is fair to ask, is our justification for doing so?

One would suppose that the rule that a text does not change would apply *a fortiori* to a constitution. If courts felt too much bound by the democratic process to tinker with statutes, when their tinkering could be adjusted by the legislature, how much more should they feel bound not to tinker with a constitution, when their tinkering is virtually irreparable. It surely cannot be said that a constitution naturally suggests changeability; to the contrary, its whole purpose is to prevent change—to embed certain rights in such a manner that future generations cannot take them away. A society that adopts a bill of rights is skeptical that "evolving standards of decency" always "mark progress," and that societies always "mature," as opposed to rot. Neither the text of such a document nor the intent of its framers (whichever you choose) can possibly lead to the conclusion that its only effect is to take the power of changing rights away from the legislature and give it to the courts.

The argument most frequently made in favor of the Living Constitution is a pragmatic one: Such an evolutionary approach is necessary in order to provide the "flexibility" that a changing society requires; the Constitution would have snapped, if it had not been permitted to bend and grow. This might be a persuasive argument if most of the "growing" that the proponents of this approach have brought upon us in the past, and are determined to bring upon us in the future, were the *elimination* of restrictions upon democratic government. But just the opposite is true. Historically, and particularly in the past thirty-five years, the "evolving" Constitution has imposed a vast array of new constraints—new inflexi-bilities—upon administrative, judicial, and legislative action. To mention only a few things that formerly could be done or not done, as the society desired, but now cannot be done:

> admitting in a state criminal trial evidence of guilt that was obtained by an unlawful search;
> permitting invocation of God at public-school graduations;
> electing one of the two houses of a state legislature the way the United States Senate is elected (i.e., on a basis that does not give all voters nu-merically equal representation);
> terminating welfare payments as soon as evidence of fraud is received, subject to restoration after hearing if the evidence is satisfactorily re-futed;
> imposing property requirements as a condition of voting;
> prohibiting anonymous campaign literature;
> prohibiting pornography.

And the future agenda of constitutional evolutionists is mostly more of the same—the creation of *new* restrictions upon democratic govern-ment, rather than the elimination of old ones. *Less* flexibility in govern-ment, not *more*. As things now stand, the state and federal governments may either apply capital punishment or abolish it, permit suicide or for-bid it—all as the changing times and the changing sentiments of society may demand. But when capital punishment is held to violate the Eighth Amendment, and suicide is held to be protected by the Fourteenth Amendment, all flexibility with regard to those matters will be gone. No, the reality of the matter is that, generally speaking, devotees of the Living Constitution do not seek to faciliate social change but to *prevent* it.

There are, I must admit, a few exceptions to that—a few instances in which, historically, greater flexibility *has been* the result of the process. But those exceptions only serve to refute another argument of the proponents of an evolving Constitution, that evolution will always be in the direction of greater personal liberty. (They consider that a great advantage, for rea-sons that I do not entirely understand. All government represents a bal-ance between individual freedom and social order, and it is not true that every alteration of that balance in the direction of greater individual free-dom is necessarily good.) But in any case, the record of history refutes the proposition that the evolving Constitution will invariably enlarge individual rights. The most obvious refutation is the modern Court's limitation of the constitutional protections afforded to property. The provision prohibiting impairment of the obligation of contracts, for example, has been gutted. I am sure that We the People agree with that development; we value property rights less than the Founders did. So also, we value the right to bear arms less than the Founders (who thought the right of self-defense to be absolutely fundamental), and there will be few tears shed if and when the Second Amendment is held to guarantee nothing more than the State National Guard. But this just shows that the Founders were right when they feared that some (in their view misguided) future generation might wish to abandon liberties that they considered essential, and so sought to protect those liberties in a Bill of Rights. We may *like* the abridgment of property rights, and *like* the elimination of the right to bear arms; but let us not pretend that these are not a *reduction* of *rights*.

Or if property rights are too cold to get your juices flowing, and the right to bear arms too dangerous, let me give another example: Several terms ago a case came before the Supreme Court involving a prosecution for sexual abuse of a young child. The trial court found that the child would be too frightened to testify in the presence of the (presumed) abuser, and so, pursuant to state law, she was permitted to testify with only the prosecutor and defense counsel present, the defendant, the judge, and the jury watching over closed-circuit television. A reasonable enough procedure, and it was held to be constitutional by my Court. I dissented, because the Sixth Amendment provides that "[i]n *all* criminal prosecutions" (let me emphasize the word "all") "the accused shall enjoy the right . . . to be confronted with the witnesses against him." There is no doubt what confrontation meant—or indeed means today. It means face-to-face, not watching from another room. And there is no doubt what one of the major purposes of that provision was: to induce *precisely* that pressure upon the witness which the little girl found it difficult to endure. It is difficult to accuse someone to his face, particularly when you are lying. Now no extrinsic factors have changed since that provision was adopted in 1791. Sexual abuse existed then, as it does now; little children were more easily upset than adults, then as now; a means of placing the defendant out of sight of the witness existed then as now (a screen could easily have been erected that would enable the defendant to see the witness, but not the witness the defendant). But the Sixth Amendment nonetheless gave *all* criminal defendants the right to *confront* the witnesses against them, because that was thought to be an important protection. The only significant thing that *has* changed, I think, is the society's sensitivity to so-called psychic trauma (which is what we are told the child witness in such a situation suffers) and the society's assessment of where the proper balance ought to be struck between the two extremes of a procedure that assures convicting 100 percent of all child abusers, and a procedure that assures acquitting 100 percent of those who have been falsely accused of child abuse. I have no doubt that the society is, as a whole, happy and pleased with what my Court decided. But we should not pretend that the decision did not *eliminate* a liberty that previously existed.

My last remarks may have created the false impression that proponents of the Living Constitution follow the desires of the American people in determining how the Constitution should evolve. They follow nothing so precise; indeed, as a group they follow nothing at all. Perhaps the most glaring defect of Living Constitutionalism, next to its incompatibility with the whole anti-evolutionary purpose of a constitution, is that there is no agreement, and no chance of agreement, upon what is to be the guiding principle of the evolution. *Panta rhei* [all things are in constant flux] is not a sufficiently informative principle of constitutional interpretation. What is it that the judge must consult to determine when, and in what direction, evolution has occurred? Is it the will of the majority, discerned from newspapers, radio talk shows, public opinion polls, and chats at the country club? Is it the philosophy of Hume, or of John Rawls, or of John Stuart Mill, or of Aristotle? As soon as the discussion goes beyond the issue of whether the Constitution is static, the evolutionists divide into as many camps as there are individual views of the good, the true, and the beautiful. I think that is inevitably so, which means that evolutionism is simply not a practicable constitutional philosophy.

I do not suggest, mind you, that originalists always agree upon their answer. There is plenty of room for disagreement as to what original meaning was, and even more as to how that original meaning applies to the situation before the court. But the originalist at least knows what he is looking for: the original meaning of the text. Often, indeed I dare say usually, that is easy to discern and simple to apply. Sometimes (though not very often) there will be disagreement regarding the original meaning; and sometimes there will be disagreement as to how that original meaning applies to new and unforeseen phenomena. How, for example, does the First Amendment guarantee of "the freedom of speech" apply to new technologies that did not exist when the guarantee was created—to sound trucks, or to government-licensed over-the-air television? In such new fields the Court must follow the trajectory of the First Amendment, so to speak, to determine what it requires—and assuredly that enterprise is not entirely cut-and-dried, but requires the exercise of judgment.

But the difficulties and uncertainties of determining original meaning and applying it to modern circumstances are negligible compared with the difficulties and uncertainties of the philosophy which says that the Constitution *changes*; that the very act which it once prohibited it now permits, and which it once permitted it now forbids; and that the key to that change is unknown and unknowable. The originalist, if he does not have all the answers, has many of them. The Confrontation Clause, for example, requires confrontation. For the evolutionist, however, every question is an open question, every day a new day. No fewer than three of the Justices with whom I have served have maintained that the death penalty is unconstitutional, *even though its use is explicitly contemplated in the Constitution*. The Due Process Clause of the Fifth and Fourteenth Amendments say that no person shall be deprived of life without due process of law; and the Grand Jury Clause of the Fifth Amendment says that no person shall be held to answer for a capital crime without grand jury indictment. No matter. Under the Living Constitution the death penalty may have *become* unconstitutional. And it is up to each Justice to decide for himself (under no standard I can discern) when that occurs.

In the last analysis, however, it probably does not matter what principle, among the innumerable possibilities, the evolutionist proposes to determine in what direction the Living Constitution will grow. For unless the evolutionary dogma is kept a closely held secret among us judges and law professors, it will lead to the result that the Constitution evolves the way the majority wishes. The people will be willing to leave interpretation of the Constitution to a committee of nine lawyers so long as the people believe that it is (like the interpretation of a statute) lawyers' work—requiring a close examination of text, history of the text, traditional understanding of the text, judicial precedent, etc. But if the people come to believe that the Constitution is *not* a text like other texts; if it means, not what it says or what it was understood to mean, but what it *should* mean, in light of the "evolving standards of decency that mark the progress of a maturing society," well then, they will look for qualifications other than impartiality, judgment, and lawyerly acumen in those whom they select to interpret it. More specifically, they will look for people who agree with *them* as to what those evolving standards have evolved to; who agree with *them* as to what the Constitution *ought* to be.

It seems to me that that is where we are heading, or perhaps even where we have arrived. Seventy-five years ago, we believed firmly enough in a rock-solid, unchanging Constitution that we felt it necessary to adopt the Nineteenth Amendment to give women the vote. The battle was not fought in the courts, and few thought that it could be, despite the constitutional guarantee of Equal Protection of the Laws; that provision* did not, when it was adopted, and hence did not in 1920, guarantee equal access to the ballot, but permitted distinctions on the basis not only of age, but of property and of sex. Who can doubt that, if the issue had been deferred until today, the Constitution would be (formally) unamended, and the courts would be the chosen instrumentality of change? The American people have been converted to belief in the Living Constitution, a

*Scalia is referring to the "equal protection clause" of the Fourteenth Amendment, which states, "No state shall . . . deny to any person within its jurisdiction the equal protection of the laws" [Editors].

"morphing" document that means, from age to age, what it ought to mean. And with that conversion has inevitably come the new phenomenon of selecting and confirming federal judges, at all levels, on the basis of their views regarding a whole series of proposals for constitutional evolution. If the courts are free to write the Constitution anew, they will, by God, write it the way the majority wants; the appointment and confirmation process will see to that. This, of course, is the end of the Bill of Rights, whose meaning will be committed to the very body it was meant to protect against: the majority. By trying to make the Constitution do everything that needs doing from age to age, we shall have caused it to do nothing at all.

44

"Our Democratic Constitution"

STEPHEN BREYER

I shall focus upon several contemporary problems that call for governmental action and potential judicial reaction. In each instance I shall argue that, when judges interpret the Constitution, they should place greater emphasis upon the "ancient liberty," i.e., the people's right to "an active and constant participation in collective power." I believe that increased emphasis upon this active liberty will lead to better constitutional law, a law that will promote governmental solutions consistent with individual dignity and community need.

At the same time, my discussion will illustrate an approach to constitutional interpretation that places considerable weight upon consequences—consequences valued in terms of basic constitutional purposes. It disavows a contrary constitutional approach, a more "legalistic" approach that places too much weight upon language, history, tradition, and precedent alone while understating the importance of consequences. If the discussion helps to convince you that the more "consequential" approach has virtue, so much the better.

Three basic views underlie my discussion. First, the Constitution, considered as a whole, creates a framework for a certain kind of government. Its general objectives can be described abstractly as including (1) democratic self-government, (2) dispersion of power (avoiding concentration of too much power in too few hands), (3) individual dignity (through protection of individual liberties), (4) equality before the law (through equal protection of the law), and (5) the rule of law itself.

The Constitution embodies these general objectives in particular pro-visions. In respect to self-government, for example, Article IV guarantees a "republican Form of Government;" Article I insists that Congress meet at least once a year, that elections take place every two (or six) years, that a census take place every decade; the Fifteenth, Nineteenth, Twenty-fourth, and Twenty-sixth Amendments secure a virtually universal adult suffrage. But a general constitutional objective such as self-government plays a constitutional role beyond the interpretation of an individual pro-vision that refers to it directly. That is because constitutional courts must consider the relation of one phrase to another. They must consider the document as a whole. And consequently the document's handful of gen-eral purposes will inform judicial interpretation of many individual pro-visions that do not refer directly to the general objective in question. My examples seek to show how that is so. And, as I have said, they will sug-gest a need for judges to pay greater attention to one of those general objectives, namely participatory democratic self-government.

Second, the Court, while always respecting language, tradition, and precedent, nonetheless has emphasized different general constitutional objectives at different periods in its history. Thus one can characterize the early nineteenth century as a period during which the Court helped to establish the authority of the federal government, including the federal judiciary. During the late nineteenth and early twentieth centuries, the Court underemphasized the Constitution's efforts to secure participation by black citizens in representative government—efforts related to the participatory "active" liberty of the ancients. At the same time, it over-emphasized protection of property rights, such as an individual's free-dom to contract without government interference, to the point where President Franklin Roosevelt commented that the Court's Lochner-era decisions had created a legal "no-man's land" that neither state nor fed-eral regulatory authority had the power to enter.

The New Deal Court and the Warren Court in part reemphasized "ac-tive liberty." The former did so by dismantling various Lochner-era dis-tinctions, thereby expanding the scope of democratic self-government. The latter did so by interpreting the Civil War Amendments in light of their purposes and to mean what they say, thereby helping African-Americans become members of the nation's community of self-governing citizens—a community that the Court expanded further in its "one per-son, one vote" decisions.

More recently, in my view, the Court has again underemphasized the importance of the citizen's active liberty. I will argue for a contemporary reemphasis that better combines "the liberty of the ancients" with that "freedom of governmental restraint" that Constant called "modern."

Third, the real-world consequences of a particular interpretive de-cision, valued in terms of basic constitutional purposes, play an impor-tant role in constitutional decision-making. To that extent, my approach differs from that of judges who would place nearly exclusive interpretive weight upon language, history, tradition and precedent. In truth, the difference is one of degree. Virtually all judges, when interpreting a constitution or a statute, refer at one time or another to language, to history, to tradition, to precedent, to purpose, and to consequences. Even those who take a more literal approach to constitutional interpretation sometimes find consequences and general purposes relevant. But the more "literalist" judge tends to ask those who cannot find an interpretive answer in language, history, tradition, and precedent alone to rethink the problem several times, before making consequences determinative. The more literal judges may hope to find in language, history, tradition, and precedent objective interpretive standards; they may seek to avoid an interpretive subjectivity that could confuse a judge's personal idea of what is good for that which the Constitution demands; and they may believe that these more "original" sources will more readily yield rules that can guide other institutions, including lower courts. These objectives are desirable, but I do not think the literal approach will achieve them, and, in any event, the constitutional price is too high. I hope that my examples will help to show you why that is so, as well as to persuade some of you why it is important to place greater weight upon constitutionally-valued consequences, my consequential focus in this lecture being the affect of a court's decisions upon active liberty.

To recall the fate of Socrates is to understand that the "liberty of the ancients" is not a sufficient condition for human liberty. Nor can (or should) we replicate today the ideal represented by the Athenian agora or the New England town meeting. Nonetheless, today's citizen does participate in democratic self-governing processes. And the "active" liberty to which I refer consists of the Constitution's efforts to secure the citizen's right to do so.

To focus upon that active liberty, to understand it as one of the Constitution's handful of general objectives, will lead judges to consider the constitutionality of statutes with a certain modesty. That modesty embodies an understanding of the judges' own expertise compared, for example, with that of a legislature. It reflects the concern that a judiciary too ready to "correct" legislative error may deprive "the people" of "the political experience and the moral education that come from . . . correcting their own errors." It encompasses that doubt, caution, prudence, and concern—that state of not being "too sure" of oneself—that Learned Hand described as the "spirit of liberty." In a word, it argues for traditional "judicial restraint."

But active liberty argues for more than that. I shall suggest that increased recognition of the Constitution's general democratic participatory objectives can help courts deal more effectively with a range of specific constitutional issues. To show this I shall use examples drawn from the areas of free speech, federalism, privacy, equal protection and statutory interpretation. In each instance, I shall refer to an important modern problem of government that calls for a democratic response. I shall then describe related constitutional implications. I want to draw a picture of some of the different ways that increased judicial focus upon the Constitution's participatory objectives can have a positive effect.

* * *

I begin with free speech and campaign finance reform. The campaign finance problem arises out of the recent explosion in campaign costs along with a vast disparity among potential givers. * * * The upshot is a concern by some that the matter is out of hand—that too few individuals contribute too much money and that, even though money is not the only way to obtain influence, those who give large amounts of money do obtain, or appear to obtain, too much influence. The end result is a marked inequality of participation. That is one important reason why legislatures have sought to regulate the size of campaign contributions.

The basic constitutional question, as you all know, is not the desirability of reform legislation but whether, how, or the extent to which, the First Amendment permits the legislature to impose limitations or ceilings on the amounts individuals or organizations or parties can contribute to a campaign or the kinds of contributions they can make. * * *

One cannot (or, at least, I cannot) find an easy answer to the constitutional questions in language, history, or tradition. The First Amendment's language says that Congress shall not abridge "the freedom of speech." But it does not define "the freedom of speech" in any detail. The nation's founders did not speak directly about campaign contributions. Madison, who decried faction, thought that members of Congress would fairly represent all their constituents, in part because the "electors" would not be the "rich" any "more than the poor." But this kind of statement, while modestly helpful to the campaign reform cause, is hardly determinative.

Neither can I find answers in purely conceptual arguments. Some argue, for example, that "money is speech"; others say "money is not speech." But neither contention helps much. Money is not speech, it is money. But the expenditure of money enables speech; and that expenditure is often necessary to communicate a message, particularly in a political context. A law that forbids the expenditure of money to convey a message could effectively suppress that communication.

Nor does it resolve the matter simply to point out that campaign contribution limits inhibit the political "speech opportunities" of those who wish to contribute more. Indeed, that is so. But the question is whether, in context, such a limitation abridges "the freedom of speech." And to announce that this kind of harm could never prove justified in a political context is simply to state an ultimate constitutional conclusion; it is not to explain the underlying reasons.

To refer to the Constitution's general participatory self-government objective, its protection of "active liberty" is far more helpful. That is be-cause that constitutional goal indicates that the First Amendment's constitutional role is not simply one of protecting the individual's "negative" freedom from governmental restraint. The Amendment in context also forms a necessary part of a constitutional system designed to sustain that democratic self-government. The Amendment helps to sustain the democratic process both by encouraging the exchange of ideas needed to make sound electoral decisions and by encouraging an exchange of views among ordinary citizens necessary to encourage their informed participation in the electoral process. It thereby helps to maintain a form of government open to participation (in Constant's words "by all citizens without exception").

The relevance of this conceptual view lies in the fact that the campaign finance laws also seek to further the latter objective. They hope to democratize the influence that money can bring to bear upon the electoral process, thereby building public confidence in that process, broadening the base of a candidate's meaningful financial support, and encouraging greater public participation. They consequently seek to maintain the integrity of the political process—a process that itself translates political speech into governmental action. Seen in this way, campaign finance laws, despite the limits they impose, help to further the kind of open public political discussion that the First Amendment also seeks to encourage, not simply as an end, but also as a means to achieve a workable democracy.

For this reason, I have argued that a court should approach most campaign finance questions with the understanding that important First Amendment-related interests lie on both sides of the constitutional equation and that a First Amendment presumption hostile to government regulation, such as "strict scrutiny" is consequently out of place. Rather, the Court considering the matter without benefit of presumptions, must look realistically at the legislation's impact, both its negative impact on the ability of some to engage in as much communication as they wish and the positive impact upon the public's confidence, and consequent ability to communicate through (and participate in) the electoral process.

The basic question the Court should ask is one of proportionality. Do the statutes strike a reasonable balance between their electoral speech-restricting and speech-enhancing consequences? Or do you instead impose restrictions on that speech that are disproportionate when measured against their corresponding electoral and speech-related benefits, taking into account the kind, the importance, and the extent of those benefits, as well as the need for the restrictions in order to secure them?

The judicial modesty discussed earlier suggests that, in answering these questions, courts should defer to the legislatures' own answers insofar as those answers reflect empirical matters about which the legislature is comparatively expert, for example, the extent of the campaign finance problem, a matter that directly concerns the realities of political life. But courts cannot defer when evaluating the risk that reform legislation will defeat the very objective of participatory self-government itself, for example, where laws would set limits so low that, by elevating the reputation-related or media-related advantages of incumbency to the point where they would insulate incumbents from effective challenge.

I am not saying that focus upon active liberty will automatically answer the constitutional question in particular campaign finance cases. I argue only that such focus will help courts find a proper route for arriving at an answer. The positive constitutional goal implies a systemic role for the First Amendment; and that role, in turn, suggests a legal framework, i.e., a more particular set of questions for the Court to ask. Modesty suggests where, and how, courts should defer to legislatures in doing so. The suggested inquiry is complex. But courts both here and abroad have engaged in similarly complex inquiries where the constitutionality of electoral laws is at issue. That complexity is demanded by a Constitution that provides for judicial review of the constitutionality of electoral rules while granting Congress the effective power to secure a fair electoral system.

I next turn to a different kind of example. It focuses upon current threats to the protection of privacy, defined as "the power to control what others can come to know about you." It seeks to illustrate what active liberty is like in modern America, when we seek to arrive democratically at solutions to important technologically-based problems. And it suggests a need for judicial caution and humility when certain privacy matters, such as the balance between free speech and privacy, are at issue.

First, I must describe the "privacy" problem. That problem is unusually complex. It has clearly become even more so since the terrorist attacks. For one thing, those who agree that privacy is important disagree about why. Some emphasize the need to be left alone, not bothered by others, or that privacy is important because it prevents people from being judged out of context. Some emphasize the way in which relationships of love and friendship depend upon trust, which implies a sharing of information not available to all. Others find connections between privacy and individualism, in that privacy encourages non-conformity. Still others find connections between privacy and equality, in that limitations upon the availability of individualized information lead private businesses to treat all customers alike. For some, or all, of these reasons, legal rules protecting privacy help to assure an individual's dignity.

For another thing, the law protects privacy only because of the way in which technology interacts with different laws. Some laws, such as trespass, wiretapping, eavesdropping, and search-and-seizure laws, protect particular places or sites, such as homes or telephones, from searches and monitoring. Other laws protect not places, but kinds of information, for example laws that forbid the publication of certain personal information even by a person who obtained that information legally. Taken together these laws protect privacy to different degrees depending upon place, individual status, kind of intrusion, and type of information.

Further, technological advances have changed the extent to which present laws can protect privacy. Video cameras now can monitor shopping malls, schools, parks, office buildings, city streets, and other places that present law left unprotected. Scanners and interceptors can overhear virtually any electronic conversation. Thermal imaging devices can detect activities taking place within the home. Computers can record and collate information obtained in any of these ways, or others. This technology means an ability to observe, collate and permanently record a vast amount of information about individuals that the law previously may have made available for collection but which, in practice, could not easily have been recorded and collected. The nature of the current or future privacy threat depends upon how this technological/legal fact will affect differently situated individuals.

These circumstances mean that efforts to revise privacy law to take account of the new technology will involve, in different areas of human activity, the balancing of values in light of prediction about the technological future. If, for example, businesses obtain detailed consumer purchasing information, they may create individualized customer profiles. Those profiles may invade the customer's privacy. But they may also help firms provide publicly desired products at lower cost. If, for example, medical records are placed online, patient privacy may be compromised. But the ready availability of those records may lower insurance costs or help a patient carried unconscious into an operating room. If, for example, all information about an individual's genetic make-up is completely confidential, that individual's privacy is protected, but suppose a close relative, a nephew or cousin, needs the information to assess his own cancer risk?

Nor does a "consent" requirement automatically answer the dilemmas suggested, for consent forms may be signed without understanding and, in any event, a decision by one individual to release or to deny information can affect others as well.

Legal solutions to these problems will be shaped by what is technologically possible. Should video cameras be programmed to turn off? Recorded images to self-destruct? Computers instructed to delete certain kinds of information? Should cell phones be encrypted? Should web technology, making use of an individual's privacy preferences, automatically negotiate privacy rules with distant web sites as a condition of access?

The complex nature of these problems calls for resolution through a form of participatory democracy. Ideally, that participatory process does not involve legislators, administrators, or judges imposing law from above. Rather, it involves law revision that bubbles up from below. Serious complex changes in law are often made in the context of a national conversation involving, among others, scientists, engineers, businessmen and -women, the media, along with legislators, judges, and many ordinary citizens whose lives the new technology will affect. That conversation takes place through many meetings, symposia, and discussions, through journal articles and media reports, through legislative hearings and court cases. Lawyers participate fully in this discussion, translating specialized knowledge into ordinary English, defining issues, creating consensus. Typically, administrators and legislators then make decisions, with courts later resolving any constitutional issues that those decisions raise. This "conversation" is the participatory democratic process itself.

The presence of this kind of problem and this kind of democratic process helps to explain, because it suggests a need for, judicial caution or modesty. That is why, for example, the Court's decisions so far have hesitated to preempt that process. In one recent case the Court considered a cell phone conversation that an unknown private individual had intercepted with a scanner and delivered to a radio station. A statute forbid the broadcast of that conversation, even though the radio station itself had not planned or participated in the intercept. The Court had to determine the scope of the station's First Amendment right to broadcast given the privacy interests that the statute sought to protect. The Court held that the First Amendment trumped the statute, permitting the radio station to broadcast the information. But the holding was narrow. It focused upon the particular circumstances present, explicitly leaving open broadcaster liability in other, less innocent, circumstances.

The narrowness of the holding itself serves a constitutional purpose. The privacy "conversation" is ongoing. Congress could well rewrite the statute, tailoring it more finely to current technological facts, such as the widespread availability of scanners and the possibility of protecting conversations through encryption. A broader constitutional rule might itself limit legislative options in ways now unforeseeable. And doing so is particularly dangerous where statutory protection of an important personal liberty is at issue.

By way of contrast, the Court held unconstitutional police efforts to use, without a warrant, a thermal imaging device placed on a public sidewalk. The device permitted police to identify activities taking place within a private house. The case required the Court simply to ask whether the residents had a reasonable expectation that their activities within the house would not be disclosed to the public in this way—a well established Fourth Amendment principle. Hence the case asked the Court to pour new technological wine into old bottles; it did not suggest that doing so would significantly interfere with an ongoing democratic policy conversation.

The privacy example suggests more by way of caution. It warns against adopting an overly rigid method of interpreting the constitution—placing weight upon eighteenth-century details to the point where it becomes difficult for a twenty-first-century court to apply the document's underlying values. At a minimum it suggests that courts, in determining the breadth of a constitutional holding, should look to the effect of a holding on the ongoing policy process, distinguishing, as I have suggested, between the "eavesdropping" and the "thermal heat" types of cases. And it makes clear that judicial caution in such matters does not reflect the fact that judges are mitigating their legal concerns with practical considerations. Rather, the Constitution itself is a practical document—a document that authorizes the Court to proceed practically when it examines new laws in light of the Constitution's enduring, underlying values.

My fourth example concerns equal protection and voting rights, an area that has led to considerable constitutional controversy. Some believe that the Constitution prohibits virtually any legislative effort to use race as a basis for drawing electoral district boundaries—unless, for example, the effort seeks to undo earlier invidious race-based discrimination. Others believe that the Constitution does not so severely limit the instances in which a legislature can use race to create majority-minority districts. Without describing in detail the basic argument between the two positions, I wish to point out the relevance to that argument of the Constitution's democratic objective.

That objective suggests a simple, but potentially important, constitutional difference in the electoral area between invidious discrimination, penalizing members of a racial minority, and positive discrimination, assisting members of racial minorities. The Constitution's Fifteenth Amendment prohibits the former, not simply because it violates a basic Fourteenth Amendment principle, namely that the government must treat all citizens with equal respect, but also because it denies minority citizens the opportunity to participate in the self-governing democracy that the Constitution creates. By way of contrast, affirmative discrimination ordinarily seeks to enlarge minority participation in that self-governing democracy. To that extent it is consistent with, indeed furthers, the Constitution's basic democratic objective. That consistency, along with its more benign purposes, helps to mitigate whatever lack of equal respect any such discrimination might show to any disadvantaged member of a majority group.

I am not saying that the mitigation will automatically render any particular discriminatory scheme constitutional. But the presence of this mitigating difference supports the view that courts should not apply the strong presumptions of unconstitutionality that are appropriate where invidious discrimination is at issue. My basic purpose, again, is to suggest that reference to the Constitution's "democratic" objective can help us apply a different basic objective, here that of equal protection. And in the electoral context, the reference suggests increased legislative authority to deal with multiracial issues.

The instances I have discussed encompass different areas of law—

speech, federalism, privacy, equal protection, and statutory interpretation. In each instance, the discussion has focused upon a contemporary social problem—campaign finance, workplace regulation, environmental regulation, information-based technological change, race-based electoral districting, and legislative politics. In each instance, the discussion illustrates how increased focus upon the Constitution's basic democratic objective might make a difference—in refining doctrinal rules, in evaluating consequences, in applying practical cautionary principles, in interacting with other constitutional objectives, and in explicating statutory silences. In each instance, the discussion suggests how that increased focus might mean better law. And "better" in this context means both (a) better able to satisfy the Constitution's purposes and (b) better able to cope with contemporary problems. The discussion, while not proving its point purely through logic or empirical demonstration, uses example to create a pattern. The pattern suggests a need for increased judicial emphasis upon the Constitution's democratic objective.

My discussion emphasizes values underlying specific constitutional phrases, sees the Constitution itself as a single document with certain basic related objectives, and assumes that the latter can inform a judge's understanding of the former. Might that discussion persuade those who prefer to believe that the keys to constitutional interpretation instead lie in specific language, history, tradition, and precedent and who fear that a contrary approach would permit judges too often to act too subjectively?

Perhaps so, for several reasons. First, the area of interpretive disagreement is more limited than many believe. Judges can, and should, decide most cases, including constitutional cases, through the use of language, history, tradition, and precedent. Judges will often agree as to how these factors determine a provision's basic purpose and the result in a particular case. And where they differ, their differences are often differences of modest degree. Only a handful of constitutional issues—though an important handful—are as open in respect to language, history, and basic purpose as those that I have described. And even in respect to those issues, judges must find answers within the limits set by the Constitution's language. Moreover, history, tradition, and precedent remain helpful, even if not determinative.

Second, those more literalist judges who emphasize language, history, tradition, and precedent cannot justify their practices by claiming that is what the Framers wanted, for the Framers did not say specifically what factors judges should emphasize when seeking to interpret the Constitution's open language. Nor is it plausible to believe that those who argued about the Bill of Rights, and made clear that it did not contain an exclusive detailed list, had agreed about what school of interpretive thought should prove dominant in the centuries to come. Indeed, the Constitution itself says that the "enumeration" in the Constitution of some rights "shall not be construed to deny or disparage others retained by the people." Professor Bailyn concludes that the Framers added this language to make clear that "rights, like law itself, should never be fixed, frozen, that new dangers and needs will emerge, and that to respond to these dangers and needs, rights must be newly specified to protect the individual's integrity and inherent dignity." Instead, justification for the literalist's practice itself tends to rest upon consequences. Literalist arguments often seek to show that such an approach will have favorable results, for example, controlling judicial subjectivity.

Third, judges who reject a literalist approach deny that their decisions are subjective and point to important safeguards of objectivity. A decision that emphasizes values, no less than any other, is open to criticism based upon (1) the decision's relation to the other legal principles (precedents, rules, standards, practices, institutional understandings) that it modifies and (2) the decision's consequences, i.e., the way in which the entire bloc of decision-affected legal principles subsequently affects the world. The relevant values, by limiting interpretive possibilities and guiding interpretation, themselves constrain subjectivity, indeed the democratic values that I have emphasized themselves suggest the importance of judicial restraint. An individual constitutional judge's need for consistency over time also constrains subjectivity. That is why Justice O'Connor has explained that need in terms of a constitutional judge's initial decisions creating "footprints" that later decisions almost inevitably will follow.

Fourth, the literalist does not escape subjectivity, for his tools, language, history, and tradition, can provide little objective guidance in the comparatively small set of cases about which I have spoken. In such cases, the Constitution's language is almost always nonspecific. History and tradition are open to competing claims and rival interpretations. Nor does an emphasis upon rules embodied in precedent necessarily produce clarity, particularly in borderline areas or where rules are stated abstractly. Indeed, an emphasis upon language, history, tradition, or prior rules in such cases may simply channel subjectivity into a choice about: Which history? Which tradition? Which rules? It will then produce a decision that is no less subjective but which is far less transparent than a decision that directly addresses consequences in constitutional terms.

Finally, my examples point to offsetting consequences—at least if "literalism" tends to produce the legal doctrines (related to the First Amendment, to federalism, to statutory interpretation, to equal protection) that I have criticized. Those doctrines lead to consequences at least as harmful, from a constitutional perspective, as any increased risk of subjectivity. In the ways that I have set out, they undermine the Constitution's efforts to create a framework for democratic government—a government that, while protecting basic individual liberties, permits individual citizens to govern themselves.

To reemphasize the constitutional importance of democratic self-government may carry with it a practical bonus. We are all aware of figures that show that the public knows ever less about, and is ever less interested in, the processes of government. Foundation reports criticize the lack of high school civics education. Comedians claim that more students know the names of the Three Stooges than the three branches of government. Even law school graduates are ever less inclined to work for government—with the percentage of those entering government (or non-government public interest) work declining at one major law school from 12% to 3% over a generation. Indeed, polls show that, over that same period of time, the percentage of the public trusting the government declined at a similar rate.

This trend, however, is not irreversible. Indeed, trust in government has shown a remarkable rebound in response to last month's terrible tragedy [September 11]. Courts cannot maintain this upward momentum by themselves. But courts, as highly trusted government institutions, can help some, in part by explaining in terms the public can understand just what the Constitution is about. It is important that the public, trying to cope with the problems of nation, state, and local community, understand that the Constitution does not resolve, and was not intended to resolve, society's problems. Rather, the Constitution provides a framework for the creation of democratically determined solutions, which protect each individual's basic liberties and assures that individual equal respect by government, while securing a democratic form of government. We judges cannot insist that Americans participate in that government, but we can make clear that our Constitution depends upon it. Indeed, participation reinforces that "positive passion for the public good," that John Adams, like so many others, felt a necessary condition for "Republican Government" and any "real Liberty."

That is the democratic ideal. It is as relevant today as it was 200 or 2000 years ago. Today it is embodied in our Constitution. Two thousand years ago, Thucydides, quoting Pericles, set forth a related ideal—relevant in his own time and, with some modifications, still appropriate to recall today. "We Athenians," said Pericles, "do not say that the man who fails to participate in politics is a man who minds his own business. We say that he is a man who has no business here."

DISCUSSION QUESTIONS

1. Critics of the originalist perspective often point to ambiguities in the language of the Constitution. Justice Breyer outlines several of these in his speech. What are some other examples of ambiguous language in the Constitution? (Look at the Bill of Rights as a start.) What alternative interpretations can you develop?

2. Critics of the Living Constitution, such as Justice Scalia, often argue that judges substitute their own reading of what they think the law

should be for what the law is. Do you think it is possible for justices to avoid having their own views shape their decisions? How could they protect against this happening?

3. Should judges take public opinion or changing societal standards into account when ruling on the constitutionality of a statute or practice? If so, what evidence of public opinion or societal standards should matter? Surveys? Laws enacted in states? If not, what are the risks in doing so?

4. Consider Scalia's list of activities that are no longer allowed by the Court (the list begins with using illegally obtained evidence in a criminal trial). How would Breyer's approach of active liberty decide these cases? Which do you think is the better outcome?

PART III

Political Behavior: Participation

CHAPTER 9

Public Opinion and the Mass Media

45

"Polling the Public,"
from *Public Opinion in a Democracy*

GEORGE GALLUP

Assessing public opinion in a democracy of over 310 million people is no easy task. George Gallup, who is largely responsible for the development of modern opinion polling, argued that public opinion polls enhance the democratic process by providing elected officials with a picture of what Americans think about current events. Despite Gallup's vigorous defense of his polling techniques and the contribution of polling to democracy, the public opinion poll remains controversial. Some critics charge that public officials pay too much attention to polls, making decisions based on fluctuations in public opinion rather than on informed, independent judgment. Others say that by urging respondents to give an opinion, even if they initially respond that they have no opinion on a question, polls may exaggerate the amount of division in American society. And some critics worry that election-related polls may affect public behavior: if a potential voter hears that her candidate is trailing in the polls, perhaps she becomes demoralized, does not vote, and the poll becomes a self-fulfilling prophecy. In effect, rather than reporting on election news, the poll itself becomes the news.

We have a national election every two years only. In a world which moves as rapidly as the modern world does, it is often desirable to know the people's will on basic policies at more frequent intervals. We cannot put issues off and say "let them be decided at the next election." World events do not wait on elections. We need to know the will of the people at all times.

If we know the collective will of the people at all times the efficiency of democracy can be increased, because we can substitute specific knowledge of public opinion for blind groping and guesswork. Statesmen who know the true state of public opinion can then formulate plans with a sure knowledge of what the voting public is thinking. They can know what degree of opposition to any proposed plan exists, and what efforts are necessary to gain public acceptance for it. The responsibility for initiating action should, as always, rest with the political leaders of the country. But the collective will or attitude of the people needs to be learned without delay.

The Will of the People

How is the will of the people to be known at all times?

Before I offer an answer to this question, I would like to examine some of the principal channels by which, at the present time, public opinion is expressed.

The most important is of course a national election. An election is the only official and binding expression of the people's judgment. But, as viewed from a strictly objective point of view, elections are a confusing and imperfect way of registering national opinion. In the first place, they come only at infrequent intervals. In the second place, as [James] Bryce pointed out in *The American Commonwealth*, it is virtually impossible to separate issues from candidates. How can we tell whether the public is voting for the man or for his platform? How can we tell whether all the candidate's views are endorsed, or whether some are favored and others opposed by the voters? Because society grows more and more complex, the tendency is to have more and more issues in an election. Some may be discussed; others not. Suppose a candidate for office takes a position on a great many public issues during the campaign. If elected, he inevitably assumes that the public has endorsed all his planks, whereas this may actually not be the case.

* * *

The Role of the Elected Representative

A second method by which public opinion now expresses itself is through elected representatives. The legislator is, technically speaking, supposed to represent the interests of all voters in his constituency. But under the two-party system there is a strong temptation for him to represent, and be influenced by, only the voters of his own party. He is subject to the pressure of party discipline and of wishes of party leaders back home. His very continuance in office may depend on giving way to such pressure. Under these circumstances his behavior in Congress is likely to be governed not by what he thinks the voters of his State want, but by what he thinks the leaders of his own party in that State want.

* * *

Even in the event that an elected representative does try to perform his duty of representing the whole people, he is confronted with the problem: What is the will of the people? Shall he judge their views by the letters they write him or the telegrams they send him? Too often such expressions of opinion come only from an articulate minority. Shall the congressman judge their views by the visitors or delegations that come to him from his home district?

Pressure Groups and the Whole Nation

Legislators are constantly subject to the influence of organized lobbies and pressure groups. Senator Tydings * * * pointed out recently that the United States is the most fertile soil on earth for the activity of pressure groups. The American people represent a conglomeration of races, all with different cultural backgrounds. Sections and groups struggle with one another to fix national and international policy. And frequently in such struggles, as Senator Tydings pointed out, "self-interest and sectionalism, rather than the promotion of national welfare, dominate the contest." Senator Tydings mentions some twenty important group interests. These include labor, agriculture, veterans, pension plan advocates, chambers of commerce, racial organizations, isolationists and internationalists, high-tariff and low-tariff groups, preparedness and disarmament groups, budget balancers and spending advocates, soft-money associations and hard-money associations, transportation groups and states righters and centralizationists.

The legislator obviously owes a duty to his home district to legislate in its best interests. But he also owes a duty to legislate in the best interests of the whole nation. In order, however, to carry out this second duty he must *know* what the nation thinks. Since he doesn't always know what the voters in his own district think, it is just that much more difficult for him to learn the views of the nation. Yet if he could know those views at all times he could legislate more often in the interest of the whole country.

* * *

The Cross-Section Survey

This effort to discover public opinion has been largely responsible for the introduction of a new instrument for determining public opinion—the cross-section or sampling survey. By means of nationwide studies taken at frequent intervals, research workers are today attempting to measure and give voice to the sentiments of the whole people on vital issues of the day.

Where does this new technique fit into the scheme of things under our form of government? Is it a useful instrument of democracy? Will it prove to be vicious and harmful, or will it contribute to the efficiency of the democratic process?

The sampling referendum is simply a procedure for sounding the opinions of a relatively small number of persons, selected in such manner as to reflect with a high degree of accuracy the views of the whole voting population. In effect such surveys canvass the opinions of a miniature electorate.

Cross-section surveys do not place their chief reliance upon numbers. The technique is based on the fact that a few thousand voters correctly selected will faithfully reflect the views of an electorate of millions of voters. The key to success in this work is the cross section—the proper selection of voters included in the sample. Elaborate precautions must be taken to secure the views of members of all political parties—of rich and poor, old and young, of men and women, farmers and city dwellers, persons of all religious faiths—in short, voters of all types living in every State in the land. And all must be included in correct proportion.

* * *

Reliability of Opinion Surveys

Whether opinion surveys will prove to be a useful contribution to democracy depends largely on their reliability in measuring opinion. During the last four years [1935–39] the sampling procedure, as used in measuring public opinion, has been subjected to many tests. In general these tests indicate that present techniques can attain a high degree of accuracy, and it seems reasonable to assume that with the development of this infant science, the accuracy of its measurements will be constantly improved.

The most practical way at present to measure the accuracy of the sampling referendum is to compare forecasts of elections with election results. Such a test is by no means perfect, because a preelection survey must not only measure opinion in respect to candidates but must also predict just what groups of people will actually take the trouble to cast their ballots. Add to this the problem of measuring the effect of weather on turnout, also the activities of corrupt political machines, and it can easily be seen that election results are by no means a perfect test of the accuracy of this new technique.

* * *

Many thoughtful students of government have asked: Why shouldn't the Government itself, rather than private organizations, conduct these sampling surveys? A few political scientists have even suggested the establishment of a permanent federal bureau for sounding public opinion, arguing that if this new technique is a contribution to democracy, the government has a duty to take it over.

The danger in this proposal, as I see it, lies in the temptation it would place in the way of the party in power to conduct surveys to prove itself right and to suppress those which proved it to be wrong. A private organization, on the other hand, must stand or fall not so much on what it reports or fails to report as on the accuracy of its results, and the impartiality of its interpretations. An important requirement in a democracy is complete and reliable news reports of the activities of all branches of the government and of the views of all leaders and parties. But few persons would argue that, for this reason, the government should take over the press, and all its news gathering associations.

*   *   *

Cloture on Debate?

It is sometimes argued that public opinion surveys impose a cloture on debate. When the advocates of one side of an issue are shown to be in the majority, so the argument runs, the other side will lose hope and abandon their cause believing that further efforts are futile.

Again let me say that there is little evidence to support this view. Every election necessarily produces a minority. In 1936 the Republicans polled less than 40 percent of the vote. Yet the fact that the Republicans were defeated badly wasn't enough to lead them to quit the battle. They continued to fight against the New Deal with as much vigor as before. An even better example is afforded by the Socialist Party. For years the Socialist candidate for President has received but a small fraction of the total popular vote, and could count on sure defeat. Yet the Socialist Party continues as a party, and continues to poll about the same number of votes.

Sampling surveys will never impose a cloture on debate so long as it is the nature of public opinion to change. The will of the people is dynamic; opinions are constantly changing. A year ago an overwhelming majority of voters were skeptical of the prospects of the Republican Party in 1940. Today, half the voters think the G.O.P. will win. If elections themselves do not impose cloture on debate, is it likely that opinion surveys will?

Possible Effect on Representative Government

The form of government we live under is a representative form of government. What will be the effect on representative government if the will of the people is known at all times? Will legislators become mere rubber stamps, mere puppets, and the function of representation be lost?

Under a system of frequent opinion measurement, the function of representation is not lost, for two reasons. First, it is well understood that the people have not the time or the inclination to pass on all the problems that confront their leaders. They cannot be expected to express judgment on technical questions of administration and government. They can pass judgment only on basic general policies. As society grows more complex there is a greater and greater need for experts. Once the voters have indicated their approval of a general policy or plan of action, experts are required to carry it out.

Second, it is not the province of the people to initiate legislation, but to decide which of the programs offered they like best. National policies do not spring full-blown from the common people. Leaders, knowing the general will of the people, must take the initiative in forming policies that will carry out the general will and must put them into effect.

Before the advent of the sampling referendum, legislators were not isolated from their constituencies. They read the local newspapers; they toured their districts and talked with voters; they received letters from their home State; they entertained delegations who claimed to speak for large and important blocs of voters. The change that is brought about by sampling referenda is merely one which provides these legislators with a truer measure of opinion in their districts and in the nation.

* * *

How Wise Are the Common People?

The sampling surveys of recent years have provided much evidence concerning the wisdom of the common people. Anyone is free to examine this evidence. And I think that the person who does examine it will come away believing as I do that, collectively, the American people have a remarkably high degree of common sense. These people may not be brilliant or intellectual or particularly well read, but they possess a quality of good sense which is manifested time and again in their expressions of opinion on present-day issues.

* * *

It is not difficult to understand why the conception of the stupidity of the masses has so many adherents. Talk to the first hundred persons whom you happen to meet in the street about many important issues of the day, and the chances are great that you will be struck by their lack of accurate or complete knowledge on these issues. Few of them will likely have sufficient information in this particular field to express a well founded judgment.

But fortunately a democracy does not require that every voter be well informed on every issue. In fact a democracy does not depend so much on the enlightenment of each individual, as upon the quality of the collective judgment or intelligence of thousands of individuals.

* * *

It would of course be foolish to argue that the collective views of the common people always represent the most intelligent and most accurate answer to any question. But results of sampling referenda on hundreds of issues do indicate, in my opinion, that we can place great faith in the collective judgment or intelligence of the people.

The New England Town Meeting Restored

One of the earliest and purest forms of democracy in this country was the New England town meeting. The people gathered in one room to discuss and to vote on the questions of the community. There was a free exchange of opinions in the presence of all the members. The town meeting was a simple and effective way of articulating public opinion, and the decisions made by the meeting kept close to the public will. When a democracy thus operates on a small scale it is able to express itself swiftly and with certainty.

But as communities grew, the town meeting became unwieldy. As a result the common people became less articulate, less able to debate the vital issues in the manner of their New England forefathers. Interest in politics lagged. Opinion had to express itself by the slow and cumbersome method of election, no longer facilitated by the town meeting with its frequent give and take of ideas. The indifference and apathy of voters made it possible for vicious and corrupt political machines to take over the administration of government in many states and cities.

The New England town meeting was valuable because it provided a forum for the exchange of views among all citizens of the community and for a vote on these views. Today, the New England town meeting idea has, in a sense, been restored. The wide distribution of daily newspapers reporting the views of statesmen on issues of the day, the almost universal ownership of radios which bring the whole nation within the hearing of any voice, and now the advent of the sampling referendum which provides a means of determining quickly the response of the public to debate on issues of the day, have in effect created a town meeting on a national scale.

How nearly the goal has been achieved is indicated in the following data recently gathered by the American Institute of Public Opinion. Of the 45,000,000 persons who voted in the last presidential election [1936], approximately 40,000,000 read a daily newspaper, 40,000,000 have radios, and only 2,250,000 of the entire group of voters in the nation neither have a radio nor take a daily newspaper.

This means that the nation is literally in one great room. The newspapers and the radio conduct the debate on national issues, presenting both information and argument on both sides, just as the townsfolk did in person in the old town meeting. And finally, through the process of the sampling referendum, the people, having heard the debate on both sides of every issue, can express their will. After one hundred and fifty years we return to the town meeting. This time the whole nation is within the doors.

DISCUSSION QUESTIONS

1. What are the advantages and disadvantages of modern public opinion polling for policy making and elections?

2. How would our political system change if polls were banned?

3. Imagine you are an elected official. How would you determine when to pay attention to public opinion polls and when to ignore them? In a representative democracy, should you as an elected official *ever* ignore public opinion as revealed in polls?

46

"Choice Words: If You Can't Understand Our Poll Questions, Then How Can We Understand Your Answers?"

Richard Morin

Although polls play a prominent role in contemporary politics, Richard Morin cautions that polls can be "risky." Morin, director of polling for the Washington Post, *notes that minor differences in question wording can—and, during the impeachment of President Clinton, did—result in dramatically different polling results. Other problems arise because people will answer questions "even if they don't really have an opinion or understand the question that has been asked." Ultimately, argues Morin, pollsters and the politicians who rely on them should be somewhat skeptical of the depth or significance of any particular response in the absence of additional survey data that establish a pattern.*

If his current government job ends abruptly, President Clinton might think about becoming a pollster. Anyone who ponders the meaning of the word *is* has precisely the right turn of mind to track public opinion in these mindless, mindful times.

Never has polling been so risky—or so much in demand. Never have so many of the rules of polling been bent or broken so cleanly, or so often. Pollsters are sampling public reaction just hours—sometimes minutes—after events occur. Interviewing periods, which traditionally last several days to secure a solid sample, have sometimes shrunk to just a few hours on a single night. Pollsters have been asking questions that were taboo until this past year. Is oral sex really sex? (Yes, said 76 percent of those interviewed in a *Newsweek* poll conducted barely a week after the scandal broke back in January.)

"No living pollster has ever had to poll in a situation like this," said Michael Kagay, the editor of news surveys at the *New York Times*. "We're in uncharted territory." After all, Andrew Johnson had to deal with political enemies, but not pollsters. And Richard Nixon's resignation before impeachment meant that pollsters didn't have a chance to ask whether the Senate should give him the boot.

Clinton has it about right: Words do have different meanings for different people, and these differences matter. At the same time, some seemingly common words and phrases have no meaning at all to many Americans; even on the eve of the impeachment vote last month, nearly a third of the country, didn't know or didn't understand what *impeachment* meant.

Every pollster knows that questions with slightly different wording can produce different results. In the past year, survey researchers learned just how big and baffling those differences can be, particularly when words are used to capture public reaction to an arcane process that no living American—not even [then ninety-five-year-old Senator] Strom Thurmond—has witnessed in its entirety.

Fear of getting it wrong—coupled with astonishment over the persistent support for Clinton revealed in poll after poll—spawned a flood of novel tests by pollsters to determine precisely the right words to use in our questions.

Last month, less than a week before Clinton was impeached by the House, *The Washington Post* and its polling partner ABC News asked half of a random sampling of Americans whether Clinton should resign if he were impeached or should "fight the charges in the Senate." The other half of the sample was asked a slightly different question: Should Clinton resign if impeached or should he "remain in office and face trial in the Senate?"

The questions are essentially the same. The results were not. Nearly six in 10—59 percent—said Clinton should quit rather than fight impeachment charges in the Senate. But well under half—43 percent—said he should resign when the alternative was to "remain in office and stand trial in the Senate." What gives?

The difference appears to be the word *fight*. America is a peaceable kingdom; we hate it when our parents squabble and are willing to accept just about any alternative—including Clinton's resignation—to spare the country a partisan fight. But when the alternative is less overtly combative—stand trial in the Senate—Americans are less likely to scurry to the resignation option.

Such a fuss over a few words. But it is just more proof that people do not share the same understanding of terms, and that a pollster who ignores this occupational hazard may wind up looking for a new job.

Think I'm exaggerating? Then let's do another test. A month ago, [December 1998], how would you have answered this question: "If the full House votes to send impeachment articles to the Senate for a trial, then do you think it would be better for the country if Bill Clinton resigned from office, or not?"

And how would you have answered this question: "If the full House votes to impeach Bill Clinton, then do you think it would be better for the country if Bill Clinton resigned from office, or not?"

The questions (asked in a *New York Times*/CBS News poll in mid-December) seem virtually identical. But the differences in results were stunning: Forty-three percent said the president should quit if the House sends "impeachment articles to the Senate" while 60 percent said he should quit if the House "votes to impeach."

What's going on here? Kagay says he doesn't know. Neither do I, but here's a guess: Perhaps "impeach" alone was taken as "found guilty" and the phrase "send impeachment articles to the Senate for a trial" suggests that the case isn't over. If only we could do another wording test. . . .

Language problems have challenged pollsters from the very start of the Monica Lewinsky scandal. Among the first: How to describe Monica herself? *The Washington Post*'s first survey questions referred to her as a "21-year-old intern at the White House," as did questions asked by other news organizations. But noting her age was potentially biasing. Highlighting her youthfulness conjured up visions of innocence and victimhood that appeared inconsistent with her apparently aggressive and explicitly amorous conduct with Clinton. In subsequent *Post* poll questions, she became a "former White House intern" of indeterminate age.

Then came the hard part: How to describe what she and Bill were accused of doing in a way that didn't offend, overly titillate or otherwise stampede people into one position or the other? In these early days, details about who did what to whom and where were sketchy but salacious. It clearly wasn't a classic adulterous love affair; love had apparently little to do with it, at least on Clinton's part. Nor was it a one-night stand. It seemed more like the overheated fantasy of a 16-year-old boy or the musings of the White House's favorite pornographer, *Penthouse* magazine publisher Larry Flynt. Piled on top of the sex were the more complex and less easily understood issues of perjury and obstruction of justice. After various iterations, we and other organizations settled on simply "the Lewinsky matter"—nice and neutral, leaving exactly what that meant to the imaginations (or memories) of survey respondents.

One thing is clear, at least in hindsight: Results of hypothetical questions—those that ask what if?—did not hold up in the past 12 months, said political scientist Michael Traugott of the University of Michigan. Last January, pollsters posed questions asking whether Clinton should resign or be impeached if he lied under oath about having an affair with Lewinsky. Clear majorities said he should quit or be impeached.

Fast forward to the eve of the impeachment vote. Nearly everybody believed Clinton had lied under oath about his relationship with Lewinsky, but now healthy majorities said he should not be impeached—a tribute, perhaps, to the White House strategy of drawing out (dare we say stonewalling?) the investigation to allow the public to get used to the idea that their president was a sleazy weasel.

Fortunately, pollsters had time to work out the kinks in question wording. Demand for polling produced a flood of questions of all shades and flavors, and good wording drove out the bad. At times, it seemed even to pollsters that there may be too many questions about the scandal, said

Kathy Frankovic, director of surveys for CBS News. Through October [1998], more than 1,000 survey questions specifically mentioned Lewinsky's name—double the number of questions that have ever been asked about the Watergate scandal, Frankovic said.

Polling's new popularity has attracted a tonier class of critic. In the past, mostly assistant professors and aggrieved political operatives or their bosses trashed the public polls. Today, one of the fiercest critics of polling is syndicated columnist Arianna Huffington, the onetime Cambridge University debating champ, A-list socialite and New Age acolyte. A few weeks ago, Huffington revealed in her column that lots of people refuse to talk to pollsters, a problem that's not new (except, apparently, to Huffington).

Actually, I think Huffington has it backward. The real problem is that people are too willing to answer poll questions—dutifully responding to poll takers even if they don't really have an opinion or understand the question that has been asked.

A famous polling experiment illustrates the prevalence of pseudo-opinions: More than 20 years ago, a group of researchers at the University of Cincinnati asked a random sample of local residents whether the 1975 Public Affairs Act should be repealed. About half expressed a view one way or another.

Of course there never was a Public Affairs Act of 1975. Researchers made it up to see how willing people were to express opinions on things they knew absolutely nothing about.

I duplicated that experiment a few years ago in a national survey, and obtained about the same result: Forty-three percent expressed an opinion, with 24 percent saying it should be repealed and 19 percent saying it should not.

But enough about the problems. In hindsight, most experts say that the polls have held up remarkably well. Within a month of the first disclosure, the public moved quickly to this consensus, as captured by the polls: Clinton's a good president but a man of ghastly character who can stay in the White House—but stay away from my house, don't touch my daughter and don't pet the dog.

"It is so striking. The public figured this one out early on and stuck with it," said Thomas E. Mann, director of governmental studies at the Brookings Institution. "If anything, the only changes were these upward blips in support for Clinton in the face of some dramatic development that was certain to presage his collapse."

Mann and others argue that public opinion polls may never have played a more important role in American political life. "This last year illustrates the wisdom of George Gallup's optimism about the use of polls in democracy: to discipline the elites, to constrain the activists, to allow ordinary citizens to register sentiments on a matter of the greatest public importance," Mann said.

Well, hooray for us pollsters! Actually, there is evidence suggesting that all the attention in the past year may have improved the public's opinions of opinion polls and pollsters. And why shouldn't they? These polls have had something for everyone: While Democrats revel in Clinton's high job-approval ratings and otherwise bulletproof presidency, Republicans can point to the equally lopsided majority who think Clinton should be censured and formally reprimanded for his behavior.

A few weeks ago, as bombs fell in Baghdad and talk of impeachment roiled Washington, pollster Nancy Belden took a break from business to attend the annual holiday pageant at her 10-year-old son's school. As she left the auditorium, the steadfast Republican mother of one of her son's classmates approached Belden and clapped her on the shoulder. "Thank heavens for you pollsters," she said.

"I was stunned. I was delighted," Belden laughed. "I've spent many years being beat up on by people who complain that public opinion polling is somewhat thwarting the political process, as opposed to helping it. Suddenly, people are coming up to me at parties and saying thanks for doing what you do. What a relief!"

DISCUSSION QUESTIONS

1. Morin presents striking differences in poll results when a word or a few words in a question are changed. Does this diminish the value of public opinion polls in the democratic process?

2. How might Morin respond to the arguments that George Gallup makes in "Polling the Public"?

3. Try to think of an example where subtly different wording might lead to very different polling results. Why do you think it would have that effect? As a consumer of polls, how would you try to determine what the "true" public opinion is on that issue?

47

"News vs. Entertainment: How Increasing Media Choice Widens Gaps in Political Knowledge and Turnout"

Markus Prior

Although everyone has contact with the government nearly every day—attending a public school, driving on public roads, using government-regulated electricity, and so on—few citizens have direct contact with the policymaking process. Because of this distance between the public and policymakers, the behavior of intermediaries between the government and the governed is a significant issue in a democratic polity. The media, in particular the news media, are among the most significant of these intermediaries that tell the people what the government is doing and tell the government what the people want.

In today's media environment, information is more abundant than ever, Markus Prior notes, yet participation and knowledge levels have remained stagnant. Rather than enhancing participatory democracy, as advocates of the new media suggest is the norm, the onset of cable television and the Internet has worsened information and participation gaps between those individuals who like to follow the news and those who are more interested in entertainment. A spread of additional news choices, which sounds democratic, has had nondemocratic effects, Prior argues. Newshounds can dig ever deeper into the news, but other members of the public are increasingly able to ignore the news. Other critics have made a similar argument that new media tend to exacerbate public polarization because readers, viewers, and listeners gravitate to outlets presenting opinions they agree with and ignore those sources that would challenge their views.

The rise of new media has brought the question of audience fragmentation and selective exposure to the forefront of scholarly and popular debate. In one of the most widely discussed contributions to this debate. Sunstein has proposed that people's increasing ability to customize their political information will have a polarizing impact on democracy as media users become less likely to encounter information that challenges their partisan viewpoints. While this debate is far from settled, the issue which precedes it is equally important and often sidestepped: as choice between different media content increases, who continues to access *any type* of political information? Cable television and the Internet have increased media choice so much in recent decades that many Americans now live in a high-choice media environment. As media choice increases, the likelihood of "chance encounters" *with any political content* declines significantly for many people. Greater choice allows politically interested people to access more information and increase their political knowledge. Yet those who prefer nonpolitical content can more easily escape the news and therefore pick up less political information than they used to. In a high-choice environment, lack of motivation, not lack of skills or resources, poses the main obstacle to a widely informed electorate.

As media choice increases, content preferences thus become the key to understanding political learning and participation. In a high-choice environment, politics constantly competes with entertainment. Until recently, the impact of content preferences was limited because media users did not enjoy much choice between different content. Television quickly became the most popular mass medium in history, but for decades the networks' scheduling ruled out situations in which viewers had to choose between entertainment and news. Largely unexposed to entertainment competition, news had its place in the early evening and again before the late-night shows. Today, as both entertainment and news are available around the clock on numerous cable channels and web sites, people's content preferences determine more of what those with cable or Internet access watch, read, and hear.

Distinguishing between people who like news and take advantage of additional information and people who prefer other media content explains a puzzling empirical finding: despite the spectacular rise in available political information, mean levels of political knowledge in the population have essentially remained constant. Yet the fact that average knowledge levels did not change hides important trends: political knowledge has risen in some segments of the electorate, but declined in others. Greater media choice thus widens the "knowledge gap." [N]umerous studies have examined the diffusion of information in the population and the differences that emerge between more and less informed individuals. According to some of these studies, television works as a "knowledge leveler" because it presents information in less cognitively demanding ways. To reconcile this effect with the hypothesis that more television widens the knowledge gap, it is necessary to distinguish the effect of news exposure from the effect of the medium itself. In the low-choice broadcast environment, access to the medium and exposure to news were practically one and the same, as less politically interested television viewers had no choice but to watch the news from time to time. As media choice increases, exposure to the news may continue to work as a "knowledge leveler," but the distribution of news exposure itself has become more unequal. Access to the medium no longer implies exposure to the news. Television news narrows the knowledge gap *among its viewers*. For the population as a whole, more channels widen the gap.

The consequences of increasing media choice reach beyond a less equal distribution of political knowledge. Since political knowledge is an important predictor of turnout and since exposure to political information motivates turnout, the shift from a low-choice to a high-choice media environment implies changes in electoral participation as well. Those with a preference for news not only become more knowledgeable, but also vote at higher rates. Those with a stronger interest in other media content vote less.

This study casts doubt on the view that the socioeconomic dimension of the digital divide is the greatest obstacle to an informed and participating electorate. Many casual observers emphasize the great promise new technologies hold for democracy. They deplore current socioeconomic inequalities in access to new media, but predict increasing political knowledge and participation among currently disadvantaged people once these inequalities have been overcome. This ignores that greater media choice leads to greater *voluntary* segmentation of the electorate. The present study suggests that gaps based on socioeconomic status will be eclipsed by preference-based gaps once access to new media becomes cheaper and more widely available. Gaps created by unequal distribution of resources and skills often emerged due to circumstances outside of people's control. The preference-based gaps documented in this article are self-imposed as many people abandon the news for entertainment simply because they like it better. Inequality in political knowledge and turnout increases as a result of voluntary, not circumstantial, consumption decisions.

* * *

Theory

The basic premise of this analysis is that people's media environment determines the extent to which their media use is governed by content preferences. According to theories of program choice, viewers have preferences over program characteristics or program types and select the program that promises to best satisfy these preferences. The simplest models distinguish between preferences for information and entertainment. In the low-choice broadcast environment, most people watched news and learned about politics because they were reluctant to turn off the set even if the programs offered at the time did not match their preferences. One study conducted in the early 1970s showed that 40% of the respondents reported watching programs because they appeared on the channel they were already watching or because someone else wanted to see them. Audience research has proposed a two-stage model according to which people first decide to watch television and then pick the available program they like best. Klein aptly called this model the "Theory of Least Objectionable Program." If television viewers are routinely "glued to the box" and select the best available program, we can explain why so many Americans watched television news in the 1960s and 70s despite modest political interest. Most television viewing in the broadcast era did not stem from a deliberate choice of a program, but rather was determined by convenience, availability of spare time and the decision to spend that time in front of the TV set. And since broadcast channels offered a solid block of news at the dinner hour and again after primetime, many viewers were routinely exposed to news even though they watched television primarily to be entertained.

Once exposed to television news, people learn about politics. Although a captive news audience does not exhibit the same political interest as a self-selected one and therefore may not learn as much, research on passive learning suggests that even unmotivated exposure can produce learning. Hence, even broadcast viewers who prefer entertainment programs absorb at least basic political knowledge when they happen to tune in when only news is on.

I propose that such accidental exposure should become less likely in a high-choice environment because greater horizontal diversity (the number of genres available at any particular point in time) increases the chance that viewers will find content that matches their preferences. The impact of one's preferences increases, and "indiscriminate viewing" becomes less likely. Cable subscribers' channel repertoire (the number of frequently viewed channels) is not dramatically higher than that of non-subscribers, but their repertoire reflects a set of channels that are more closely related to their genre preferences. Two-stage viewing behavior thus predicts that news audiences should decrease as more alternatives are offered on other channels. Indeed, local news audiences tend to be smaller when competing entertainment programming is scheduled. Baum and Kernell show that cable subscribers, especially the less informed among them, are less likely to watch the presidential debates than otherwise similar individuals who receive only broadcast television. According to my first hypothesis, the advent of cable TV increased the knowledge gap between people with a preference for news and people with a preference for other media content.

Internet access should contribute to an increasing knowledge gap as well. Although the two media are undoubtedly different in many respects, access to the Internet, like cable, makes media choice more efficient. Yet, while they both increase media users' content choice, cable TV and the Internet are not perfect substitutes for each other. Compared at least to dial-up Internet service, cable offers greater immediacy and more visuals. The web offers more detailed information and can be customized to a greater extent. Both media, in other words, have unique features, and access to both of them offers users the greatest flexibility. For instance, people with access to both media can watch a campaign speech on cable and then compare online how different newspapers cover the event. Depending on their needs or the issue that interests them, they can actively search a wealth of political information online or passively consume cable politics. Hence, the effects of cable TV and Internet access should be additive and the knowledge gap largest among people with access to both new media.

There are several reasons why exposure to political information increases the likelihood that an individual will cast a vote on election day. Exposure increases political knowledge, which in turn increases turnout because people know where, how, and for whom to vote. Furthermore, knowledgeable people are more likely to perceive differences between candidates and thus less likely to abstain due to indifference. Independent of learning effects, exposure to political information on cable news and political web sites is likely to increase people's campaign interest. Interest, in turn, affects turnout even when one controls for political knowledge. Entertainment fans with a cable box or Internet connection, on the other hand, will miss both the interest- and the information-based effect of broadcast news on turnout. My second hypothesis thus predicts a widening turnout gap in the current environment, as people who prefer news vote at higher rates and those with other preferences increasingly stay home from the polls.

*   *   *

Conclusion

When speculating about the political implications of new media, pundits and scholars tend to either praise the likely benefits for democracy in the digital age or dwell on the dangers. The optimists claim that the greater availability of political information will lead more people to learn more about politics and increase their involvement in the political process. The pessimists fear that new media will make people apolitical and provide mind-numbing entertainment that keeps citizens from fulfilling their democratic responsibilities. These two predictions are often presented as mutually exclusive. Things will either spiral upwards or spiral downwards; the circle is either virtuous or vicious. The analyses presented here show that both are true. New media do indeed increase political knowledge and involvement in the electoral process among some people, just as the optimists predict. Yet, the evidence supports the pessimists' scenario as well. Other people take advantage of greater choice and tune out of politics completely. Those with a preference for entertainment, once they gain access to new media, become less knowledgeable about politics and less likely to vote. People's media content preferences become the key to understanding the political implications of new media.

* * *

The decline in the size of news audiences over the last three decades has been identified as cause for concern by many observers who have generally interpreted it as a sign of waning political interest and a disappearing sense of civic duty. Yet changes in available content can affect news consumption and learning *even in the absence of preference changes.* People's media use may change in a modified media environment, even if their preferences (or political interest or sense of civic duty) remain constant. By this logic, the decreasing size of the news audience is not necessarily an indication of reduced political interest. Interest in politics may simply never have been as high as audience shares for evening news suggested. A combined market share for the three network newscasts of almost 90% takes on a different meaning if one considers that people had hardly any viewing alternatives. It was "politics by default," not politics by choice. Even the mediocre levels of political knowledge during the broadcast era, in other words, were partly a result of de facto restrictions of people's freedom to choose their preferred media content.

Ironically, we might have to pin our hopes of creating a reasonably evenly informed electorate on that reviled form of communication, political advertising. Large segments of the electorate in a high-choice environment do not voluntarily watch, read, or listen to political information. Their greatest chance for encounters with the political world occurs when commercials are inserted into their regular entertainment diet. And exposure to political ads can increase viewers' political knowledge. At least for the time being, before recording services like TiVo, which automatically skip the commercial breaks, or subscriber-financed premium cable channels without advertising become more widespread, political advertising is more likely than news coverage to reach these viewers.

It might seem counterintuitive that political knowledge has decreased for a substantial portion of the electorate even though the amount of political information has multiplied and is more readily available than ever before. The share of politically uninformed people has risen since we entered the so-called "information age." Television as a medium has often been denigrated as "dumb," but, helped by the features of the broadcast environment, it may have been more successful in reaching less interested segments of the population than the "encyclopedic" Internet. In contrast to the view that politics is simply too difficult and complex to understand, this study shows that motivation, not ability, is the main obstacle that stands between an abundance of political information and a well- and evenly informed public.

When differences in political knowledge and turnout arise from inequality in the distribution of resources and skills, recommendations for how to help the information have-nots are generally uncontroversial. To the extent that knowledge and turnout gaps in the new media environment arise from voluntary consumption decisions, recommendations for how to narrow them, or whether to narrow them at all, become more contestable on normative grounds. As [Anthony] Downs remarked a long time ago, "[t]he loss of freedom involved in forcing people to acquire information would probably far outweigh the benefits to be gained from a better-informed electorate." Even if a consensus emerged to reduce media choice for the public good, it would still be technically impossible, even temporarily, to put the genie back in the bottle. Avoiding politics will never again be as difficult as it was in the "golden age" of television.

* * *

DISCUSSION QUESTIONS

1. Are you concerned by the findings in Prior's study? If not, why not? If you are, can you think of any way to overcome the problem he has identified?

2. What lessons should public officials take from Prior's study? Should they pay less attention to public opinion because of the gaps in information and interest among members of the public?

Debating the Issues: The Future of Political Journalism

From the 1960s through the 1980s, when people thought of media and news, they thought of newspapers and, increasingly, the broadcast television networks. Cable news soon emerged to provide an alternative, but one that for the most part followed the same operating procedure for major nightly newscasts as the big networks. Late in the 1980s, talk radio, which had been around for some time, boomed in popularity and hosts such as Rush Limbaugh became household names. Hosts gleefully tweaked the mainstream media and embraced a much more aggressive, hard-hitting style that was explicitly ideological and partisan. There was, in this new forum, no pretense to being objective but, talk-radio fans would argue, the mainstream media were also not objective—they just pretended to be. News-oriented talk shows on cable followed the same pattern. The rise of the Internet in the 1990s was the most recent dramatic change in communications technology. Today, blogs receive most of the attention, with Twitter gaining ground, and sites such as YouTube make it possible for every misstep by a politician to be easily viewed by millions of viewers.

Major changes in communications technology have produced major changes in the practice of politics and the way people learn about government. Earlier technologies do not necessarily fade away, but their role changes and their dominance diminishes. Pamphlets, then newspapers, then radio, and then television all had their eras of ascendancy. All continued to play important roles when other technologies emerged. Political talk radio in the 1980s and 1990s, for example, gave new life to radio in the age of television, creating another kind of information exchange with which politicians had to become conversant. Inevitably, these technological shifts raise concerns that the new form of information dissemination will drive out some of the positive features of the previous technology.

Does the rise of new media inevitably mean that the old media must fade away? And if so, at what cost to democracy? In the excerpt of his article presented here, Tom Price provides background for analyzing these questions. He focuses particularly on the struggles facing newspapers, long the most significant location for news journalism. Even when Americans relied more on television than newspapers to get their news, newspaper coverage often influenced what was reported on TV. In addition to detailing the difficult environment for newspapers, Price presents concerns that newspaper supporters have raised about news gathering and presentation by new media. Fans of the new media argue that those media have the potential to provide a powerful check on politicians and to allow for a more participatory democracy.

By combining the knowledge, memory, and energy of multitudes of contributors, blogs and new media such as Twitter can reveal faulty or absent reporting by the mainstream media. As Price notes, however, some observers are skeptical this promise will be fulfilled. Critics worry that blogs and other new media may gain increasing sway over politicians and the public while not being held to high journalistic standards and that they are as likely to generate misleading interpretations as uncover truth.

To Paul Starr, the decline of newspapers is a crisis for democracy. In his view, newspapers were uniquely able to hold government accountable and expose corruption. In large part, this was because the financial model that supported newspapers allowed extensive news staffs to be subsidized by advertisers, classified ads, and sections catering to sports and lifestyles. In the new media world, these components have become largely unbundled. News now has to be financially self-sustaining, which has proven to be a difficult task. Starr explores whether the idea that newspapers must make money has to be abandoned in favor of a model in which philanthropy subsidizes the news.

James Fallows discusses ways in which the new media and the old are mutually interdependent. In particular, Fallows focuses on concerns at Google: because it thrives as a search engine when users find quality content, Google is concerned about the problems facing the news media, particularly newspapers. Fallows reports on Google's concerns and the ways in which the company is attempting to assist news organizations. According to company executives, there is no single big thing that will save newspapers, but lots of little things might.

48

"Future of Journalism"

TOM PRICE

Forty-three years ago, *Time* magazine posed a provocative question on its cover: "Is God Dead?" The answer turned out to be: "not so much."

This February, the magazine's cover pondered ways to stave off the death of newspapers. With the industry copiously bleeding red ink, reporters and editors losing jobs by the thousands and online news becoming increasingly popular—and controversial—*Time*'s editors aren't the only people wondering about journalism's future. Certainly the recent news has been grim:

- The *Rocky Mountain News* shut down on Feb. 27 after reporting about the Denver region for 150 years.
- The 146-year-old *Seattle Post-Intelligencer* turned off its presses on March 17, becoming a Web-only publication.
- *The Christian Science Monitor*, a highly regarded national daily newspaper since 1908, plans in April [2010] to become a Web and e-mail publication, offering only a weekly, magazine-like, printed edition.
- Thirty-three newspapers—including the *Los Angeles Times*, *Chicago Tribune* and *Philadelphia Inquirer*—sought Chapter 11 bankruptcy protection from December through February.
- Even the mighty *New York Times*, heavily in debt, in early 2009 borrowed an additional $250 million at 14 percent interest from Mexican billionaire Carlos Slim Helu, once described by *The Times* itself as having a "robber baron reputation."

Newspapers across the country are declining in circulation, advertising and profitability. In 2008 alone, publicly traded newspaper stock prices fell 83 percent. The Fitch credit-rating service forecasts more newspaper closures this year and next, which could leave a growing number of cities with no newspaper at all.

*   *   *

Thomas Jefferson once famously remarked that, if he had to choose between government without newspapers or newspapers without government, he wouldn't hesitate to preserve newspapers. In the subsequent 222 years, Americans have had both, and newspapers have been citizens' primary source of information about government at all levels.

Many journalists, scholars, lobbyists and government officials worry that the decline of newspapers will leave citizens without sufficient information for effective self-government. They also worry that the fragmented nature of Internet and cable television audiences could turn the clock back to the late-18th and early-19th centuries, when a large number of partisan newspapers printed more opinion than news, and many readers read only publications with which they agreed.

As more Americans turn to the Internet and cable television for news, however, others are hopeful that new forms of journalism will fill the gaps. They envision cable news channels, bloggers, other online content providers and newspapers' own Web sites picking up the slack.

Ironically, newspapers' readership appears to be higher now than ever before as more and more readers access their papers online. U.S. daily newspapers sell about 51 million copies a day, while hosting nearly 75 million unique visitors on their Web sites each month. *The New York Times* sells about a million newspapers daily and about 1.4 million on Sunday, while its Web site attracts 20 million unique visitors monthly. Circulation and advertising revenues have been in a steady decline, however, and newspapers have not figured out how to profit from their Web sites. Only about 10 percent of newspaper advertising revenues are earned on the Internet.

Journalists, scholars, entrepreneurs and philanthropists are looking for ways to finance high-quality, comprehensive reporting online. In addition to the traditional for-profit model, they are experimenting with nonprofit news organizations and philanthropic support of journalistic enterprises. Some are discussing government funding.

* * *

* * * [M]ost news online is produced by newspapers or by organizations that are funded substantially by newspapers, such as the Associated Press. Many television organizations field significant newsgathering operations. But most lag far behind their newspaper counterparts—particularly at the local, regional and state levels—and they often follow newspapers' reporting leads.

"The decline of newspapers has a big ripple effect," says Peter Shane, executive director of the Knight Commission on the Information Needs of Communities in a Democracy, "because to a substantial extent television and radio news always has been based on local newspapers' reporting."

Yet, nearly across the board, newspapers are shrinking the government coverage that's most important to informing citizens in a democracy. Papers that remain in business are cutting staff, closing bureaus and reducing the number of reporters who cover public affairs full time.

Even as the United States is involved in an ever more globalized world—fighting wars in Iraq and Afghanistan, guarding against far-flung terrorist organizations, competing in a globalized economy—U.S. news organizations are bringing their foreign correspondents home.

And with a new administration shaking up Washington and the troubled global economy looking to Washington for leadership, newspapers are shrinking or closing their Washington bureaus. More than 40 regional correspondents—those who cover a particular community's interests in the nation's capital—lost their jobs over the last three years. Even major papers—including the *Los Angeles Times, Chicago Tribune* and *Baltimore Sun*—have cut the size of their Washington bureaus. Other publications have eliminated their Washington staffs entirely—notably *The San Diego Union* whose D.C. reporters won a 2006 Pulitzer Prize for exposing corrupt U.S. Rep. Randy "Duke" Cunningham, who now sits in jail. Newspapers in half the states now have no congressional correspondent.

Associated Press Senior Vice President Sue Cross lamented declining coverage of city, county and state governments as well—not just the number of reporters but their expertise. "Seasoned beat reporters are, in many cases, leaving the industry," she said.

Virginia's capital press corps shrank by half during the last decade, according to AP Richmond Correspondent Bob Lewis. Maryland media are sending half as many correspondents to Annapolis to cover state government as they did just two years ago, former AP reporter Tom Stukey said. In Broward County, Fla. (Fort Lauderdale), Commissioner John Rodstrom said, local newspapers have cut their county government coverage in half in a year.

* * *

The reduction in regional correspondents has generated particular concern in Washington. Regional reporters' importance goes beyond uncovering wrongdoing, according to Michael Gessel, a longtime congressional aide who now works as a Washington lobbyist for the Dayton Development Corp. in Ohio. "At least equally important is the day-to-day—and sometimes mundane—coverage of what our elected officials do that isn't scandalous," Gessel says.

Members of Congress often work hardest on matters that get the most coverage by news media in their districts, Gessel explains. Without a hometown reporter tracking the districts' interests in Washington, he says, those interests are likely to get less congressional attention.

Citizens also need to know when government does things well, he adds. "All democracies require consent of the governed. If people only hear about scandals, then that consent is withdrawn. Practically speaking, that means less willingness to have their tax dollars support government."

* * *

A Washington correspondent must know the actors and understand the processes of the federal government, Gessel says. "You can't get that by phone, by Internet or by e-mail."

As journalists, scholars and politicians try to navigate the new media environment, here are some of the questions they are asking about the future of democracy:

Can the Internet Fill the Reporting Gaps Caused by the Decline of Newspapers?

News-reporting sites are popping up on the Internet even faster than newspapers are losing circulation.

On Jan. 12, for instance, *GlobalPost* went online in an ambitious effort to do the kind of international journalism that newspapers and television networks have scaled back. Led by news veterans, the site promises comprehensive, frontline reporting by more than 60 freelance correspondents in more than 40 countries. The new operation hopes to turn a profit by selling advertising, syndicating its reporting to other news organizations and selling $199-a-year subscriptions to a premium service.

Two years earlier, other news veterans launched *Politico*, which quickly became a popular source of political news during the long campaign that carried Barack Obama to the White House. *Politico*—a Web site and a newspaper distributed free in Washington—is performing ahead of its business plan and expects to turn a profit this year, says Editor-in-Chief John Harris, a 21-year veteran of *The Washington Post*.

Across the country, countless sites have been created to cover local and regional communities. They range from highly professional organizations covering major metropolitan areas to primarily volunteer operations serving small communities to professional-amateur collaborations of all sizes.

MinnPost in Minnesota and *Voice of San Diego* have won widespread praise for practicing high-quality, professional journalism, for instance. Smaller, mostly amateur, sites contain little more than announcements from community organizations. *The New York Times* and the *Chicago Tribune* have assigned professionals to oversee networks of volunteers who report for Web sites operated by those papers, focusing on news about specific neighborhoods.

The Internet surpassed newspapers as Americans' favorite source of national and international news in late 2008. Both trailed television by a substantial margin among the population at large. But Americans younger than 30 turned to the Internet as often as to television—and twice as often as to newspapers. Readers still turn to newspapers more than to the Internet for local news.

Most of the news Americans obtain on the Web is not produced by online news organizations, however. On Election Day 2008, for instance, seven of the 10 most-popular Internet news sites belonged to CNN, MSNBC, Fox News, *The New York Times*, Tribune Newspapers, *The Washington Post* and *USA Today*. The others—Yahoo! News, AOL News and Google News—simply aggregate content produced by newsgathering organizations such as newspapers and television networks. Many other Web sites also link to reports produced by traditional news organizations.

* * *

Politico and *GlobalPost* are promising examples of niche sites that might succeed by attracting national or international audiences that advertisers want to reach. *Politico*, for instance, sells most of its ads to organizations that want to influence the federal government, and many of those ads appear in the printed edition, which targets an elite Washington audience.

*   *   *

"There's no sign anywhere of anything replacing the comprehensive metropolitan newspaper, replacing the kind of watchfulness that even a mediocre city newspaper might offer," says Tom Rosenstiel, director of the Project for Excellence in Journalism.

*   *   *

Others worry that online news sites can't serve Americans who don't have Internet access, a group that tends to be older and poorer than the general public. While nearly all young Americans go online, nearly three-quarters of Americans older than 75 do not. That also is true for a majority between 70 and 75, more than a third between 60 and 69, a quarter between 50 and 59 and a fifth between 45 and 49.

Business consultant James Moore—who advises newspapers to shut down their presses and become online-only operations—argues that publications can't afford to worry about those lost readers. "They are not the people advertisers reach out to," Moore says. "The people they're going after are people in the 35-to-45 category. You have to look to the future, and the future is the young."

Are the New Media Bad for Democracy?

On Oct. 3, 2008, CNN's *iReport* Internet site reported, incorrectly, that Apple CEO Steve Jobs had been rushed to the hospital after a heart attack. The account quickly was repeated on other Web sites, and Apple stock fell more than 9 percent in 12 minutes—a total loss of $9 billion in the company's value.

A month earlier, the Bloomberg financial Web site mistakenly posted a six-year-old report about United Airlines' 2002 bankruptcy filing. Thinking the airline was going bankrupt again, investors dumped the stock, which lost three-quarters of its value before the NASDAQ stock exchange halted trading. A financial newsletter had found the old newspaper story while doing a Google search and passed it on to Bloomberg believing it was current.

The credibility of the erroneous reports was enhanced by CNN's and Bloomberg's reputations as legitimate news organizations. But in both cases the reports appeared on the organizations' Web sites without being vetted.

The incidents illustrate some criticisms of Internet-based news operations.

Many bloggers—and even some traditional media—are cavalier about accuracy on the Web, critics complain. Moreover, they say, Internet public-affairs sites tend to publish more opinion than fact, much of it vicious, mean-spirited and profane. And they worry that fragmentation of the online audience can lead many Web surfers to experience a narrow, distorted view of the world in what some call the Internet "echo chamber."

Indeed, the Jobs story was repeated by blogger Henry Blodget on the widely read *Silicon Alley Insider* Web site. Blodget later unapologetically proclaimed he would do it again, noting he had warned readers he didn't know if the report was true.

"You, our readers, are smart enough to know the difference between rumors and facts, and you are smart enough to evaluate what we tell you," Blodget said. Posting unverified information "flushes out the truth," he argued. "We wouldn't want you to not tell us what everyone was talking about because you couldn't verify it."

That's an example of what Rosenstiel and Bill Kovach—former Washington bureau chief of *The New York Times* and former editor of *The Atlanta Journal-Constitution*—have termed "the journalism of assertion." Traditional journalistic ethics require that facts be confirmed before they're published, Rosenstiel and Kovach said. Many figures on talk radio, cable news and the Internet are "less interested in substantiating whether something is true and more interested in getting it into the public discussion." While they coined the phrase a decade ago, Rosenstiel says, it's even more true today.

CNN also defended its unverified *iReports* by noting the Web site carries a disclaimer that "the stories submitted by users are not edited, fact-checked or screened before they post."

CNN says it created *iReports* to extend CNN's newsgathering reach and to increase viewers' personal attachment to the cable network. It checks the accuracy of *iReporters'* contributions only before using them in its telecasts.

A growing number of news organizations are recruiting volunteer, "citizen" journalists, especially online, as a way to compensate for cutbacks in their professional reporting staffs.

* * *

Journalism historian Anthony Fellow at California State University, Fullerton, is among those who worry about the fragmentation of the Internet audience among ideologically oriented sites. "We're back to the party press era" after the Revolutionary War, he says, "the viciousness that went on between the two camps, the name-calling."

* * *

City University of New York journalism Professor Jeff Jarvis rejects the echo-chamber charge. "We have more arguments than ever," he says. "The echo chamber was when there was one newspaper in town."

* * *

Most Americans aren't limiting themselves to partisan sites. Just 5 percent of the general public and 10 percent of conservatives say they listen to Limbaugh regularly, for instance. According to the Project for Excellence in Journalism's 2007 report on the "State of the News Media," two-thirds of Americans prefer to get their news from neutral sources, while just a quarter want sources that share their point of view.

*   *   *

Outlook

Newspapers Doomed?

A consensus is growing among journalists and scholars that newspapers as we've known them are doomed, but journalism always will be in demand.

What they don't know is when the last newspaper will dismantle its presses—or if a few will survive—and what kind of journalism will be preserved. * * *

*   *   *

Jay Smith, who retired last year as president of the Cox Newspapers chain, agrees that "far more important than the future of newspapers is the future of journalism." Smith expects printed newspapers to continue to shrink in size and circulation, while their online presence grows.

*   *   *

[Some observers] argue that newspapers will have to recruit amateur volunteers to provide comprehensive coverage, particularly at the local level. * * *

Others are less comfortable with that model. "So many public-policy stories today require not just going to meetings and listening to what people say but accessing records, acquiring data and analyzing that data," says Peter Shane at the Knight Commission on the Information Needs of Communities. "Amateurs are better than nothing, but they're not better than having trained people with experience and a deep knowledge of the community."

Similarly, Brian Tierney, CEO and publisher of *The Philadelphia Inquirer* and *Daily News*, scoffs: "The idea that citizen journalists are going to replace traditionally trained and paid journalists is like saying citizen surgeons are going to replace people who actually have a degree in medicine."

Niche Web sites with national audiences enjoy the best prospects, many say. So do sites with valuable information that some audiences will pay premium prices for.

*   *   *

But that prospect worries former *Atlanta Journal-Constitution* Editor Kovach and others. If general-circulation newspapers decline and important information is available only from expensive vendors, "the people get less information while the people in power get more information," he said. "If we talk about a government as Abraham Lincoln did—'of the people, by the people, for the people'—then that democracy is in trouble."

*   *   *

For his part, Tierney says the Philadelphia newspapers are exploring how to charge for online content. "We're going to have to find a way to encourage people to pay for quality journalism," he says. "To create great content, we've got to pay people. We just can't give it away."

*   *   *

49

"Goodbye to the Age of Newspapers (Hello to a New Era of Corruption)"

PAUL STARR

I.

We take newspapers for granted. They have been so integral a part of daily life in America, so central to politics and culture and business, and so powerful and profitable in their own right, that it is easy to forget what a remarkable historical invention they are. Public goods are notoriously under-produced in the marketplace, and news is a public good—and yet, since the mid-nineteenth century, newspapers have produced news in abundance at a cheap price to readers and without need of direct subsidy. More than any other medium, newspapers have been our eyes on the state, our check on private abuses, our civic alarm systems. It is true that they have often failed to perform those functions as well as they should have done. But whether they can continue to perform them at all is now in doubt.

*   *   *

II.

These developments raise practical questions for anyone concerned about the future of American democracy. * * * To answer those practical questions, it is necessary first to ponder a more theoretical one. Along with other new technology, the Internet was supposed to bring us a cornucopia of information, and in many respects it has done so. But if one of its effects is to shrink the production of professionally reported news, perhaps we need to understand the emerging framework of post-industrial society and politics somewhat differently.

* * *

III.

Of course, a medium that 40 percent of the public still claim to read should not be pronounced dead yet. The situation is also a bit more complicated, and more hopeful, than these trends suggest. Total readership of news that originates from newspapers has probably at least stabilized. Online, many people read news items on blogs and other sites that take items from the press, and the news junkies among us are reading more news from more papers than they did before the Internet made the sampling of multiple publications so easy. And some newspapers are clearly gaining wider reach online.

* * *

Some critics of the companies wonder why they cannot adjust to lower profits and make do. The trouble is that the declines in print circulation and advertising are virtually certain to continue, and if newspapers try to maintain the size and the scope of their operations, they may not be able [to] make any profit even when the recession is over. Nor is it clear that they can cut deep enough fast enough while retaining enough readers to be profitable.

* * *

Among many journalists as well as investors, the hope has vanished that newspapers as we have known them can make the transition to a world of hybrid print-online publication. Like network TV news and weekly newsmagazines, newspapers have been living off aging audiences that acquired their media habits in earlier decades. A few years ago, it seemed that they could rely on that aging print readership to tide them over until revenue began gushing from the Web. But online ads still account for only 8 percent of ad sales, and their growth has stalled just as earnings from print have tumbled. The result is that newspapers are shrinking not just physically or in labor power, but in the most important dimension of all—their editorial mission.

*   *   *

Besides cutting back foreign, national, and state coverage, newspapers are also reducing space devoted to science and the arts, and laying off science and medical reporters, music critics, and book reviewers. But there is one type of coverage that newspapers have tried to protect, at least in the early phases of cutbacks. According to the 2008 Pew survey of news executives, they have devoted more resources to local news. The case for "hyperlocalism," as it is known, is that newspapers enjoy comparative advantage as sources of information about their immediate communities. But this strategy may not work commercially if it means moving down-market. The less coverage of the wider world and cultural life that newspapers provide, the more they stand to lose readership among the relatively affluent who have those interests, and the less attractive newspapers will be to many advertisers. Hyperlocalism may be just a short step from hollowing out the newsroom to the point where most newspapers come to resemble the free tabloids distributed at supermarkets rather than the newspapers of the past.

*   *   *

* * * Many of the functions that were bundled together in the newspaper are being unbundled online. But if the emerging media environment favors niche journalism, how will public-service journalism be able to reach and influence the broad public that newspapers have had? There is no going back to the way things used to be. If independent news media capable of holding government accountable are going to flourish, they are going to have to do so in the new world of the news, not the one that used to exist.

IV.

After the dot-com bust, the effusive talk about the miracles of the information revolution thankfully went out of style. But the social transformation under way—and there ought to be no doubt that one is indeed underway—is breaking up old monopolies of communication and power and creating new possibilities for free expression and democratic politics. As in any upheaval, some effects are unanticipated, and not all of them are positive, and what is perhaps most confusing, the good and bad are often intertwined.

By vastly increasing the options for diversion as well as information, the Internet has extended a process that had already begun when cable began increasing the number of TV channels. And if the political scientist Markus Prior is right, that expansion of choice is partly responsible for one of the most worrisome trends in American life: diminished attention to the news and reduced engagement in civic life among a significant part of the public.

*   *   *

The decline of newspapers and the growth of the Internet as a source of news may have a similar impact. On the one hand, there is likely to be less incidental learning among those with low political interest. Like the entertainment-oriented TV viewers who learned about the world because they had no alternative except to sit through the national network news, many people who have bought a paper for the sports, the recipes, the comics, or the crossword puzzle have nonetheless learned something about the wider world because they have been likely at least to scan the front page. Online, by contrast, they do not necessarily see what would be front-page news in their city, and so they are likely to become less informed about news and politics as the reading of newspapers drops.

* * *

But there is another side to the story. As Yochai Benkler argues in his brilliant book *The Wealth of Networks: How Social Production Transforms Markets and Freedom*, the new "networked information economy" has some critical advantages for realizing democratic values. The old "industrial model" mass media have required large investments of capital and provided a platform to speak to the public for a relatively small number of people, but now the falling costs of computers and communication have "placed the material means of information and cultural production in the hands of a significant fraction of the world's population—on the order of a billion people around the globe." Instead of being confined to a passive role, ordinary people can talk back to the media or circumvent them entirely and enter the public conversation.

The new public sphere, in Benkler's view, is also developing mechanisms for filtering information for reliability and relevance, organizing it into easily navigated paths, and raising it to higher levels of public debate, contrary to critics who have worried that the Internet would be a chaotic Babel or a polarized system of "echo chambers" (as Cass Sunstein argued in his book *Republic.com*). And, unlike the old mass media, the new digital environment facilitates decentralized individual and cooperative action, often organized on an open and voluntary basis. Benkler invests a great deal of hope in this type of non-market collaborative production—the kind that has generated new social media such as Wikipedia, which, amazingly, despite being an encyclopedia, has also become an important news medium because it is so rapidly updated.

Of course, some of these innovations are mixed blessings: people can now share their misinformation as well as their knowledge. Viral email, Twitter, and social network sites can be used to spread rumors and malice through channels hidden from the wider public and insulated from criticism. Benkler is right about the many important gains from new technology, but he does not adequately balance the gains against the losses that the emerging networked economy is also bringing about—among them the problems that Prior identifies, such as the diminished share of the public following the news, and perhaps most important, the toll on the institutions of professional journalism.

* * *

The non-market collaborative networks on the Web celebrated by Benkler represent an alternative way of producing information as a public good. Before Wikipedia was created, hardly anyone supposed it would work as well as it has. But it has severe limitations as a source of knowledge. Its entries, including news items, are rewritten from other sources, and it does not purport to offer original research or original reporting. The blogosphere and the news aggregators are also largely parasitic: they feed off the conventional news media. Citizen journalists contribute reports from the scene of far-flung events, but the reports may just be the propaganda of self-interested parties.

Voluntary networks cannot easily duplicate certain critical advantages that large-scale and professionally run media have had—the financial wherewithal to invest in trained reporters and editors and to assign them to beats and long projects, and a well-established system of professional norms that has been a source of conscientious motivation and restraint in the reporting of news. The new social media add value when they are a supplement to professional journalism. To the extent that they supplant it, however, the wildfires of rumor and malice will be harder to check.

* * *

V.

And this returns us to the central problem. If newspapers are no longer able to cross-subsidize public-service journalism and if the de-centralized, non-market forms of collaboration cannot provide an adequate substitute, how is that work going to be paid for? The answer, insofar as there is one, is that we are going to need much more philanthropic support for journalism than we have ever had in the United States.

When a society requires public goods, the solution is often to use government to subsidize them or to produce them directly. But if we want a press that is independent of political control, we cannot have government sponsoring or bailing out specific papers. In the late eighteenth and nineteenth centuries, besides using printing contracts to subsidize favored party organs, the federal government supported the press in what First Amendment lawyers today would call a "viewpoint-neutral" way— through cheap postal rates that were available to all newspapers. And since the 1960s, both the federal and state governments have aided public broadcasting, which has enabled public TV and radio stations to become important sources of news.

Public radio has been a particularly notable success. In a period when commercial radio stations have abandoned all but headline news,

National Public Radio has become the last refuge of original reporting on the dial. But as Charles Lewis, a long-time leader in investigative reporting, has pointed out in the *Columbia Journalism Review*, public radio stations, for all their excellent work, have not done a lot of investigative stories. The dependence of many local stations on state government funding makes them vulnerable to political pressure and unlikely to fill the void left by the decline in newspaper coverage of the states. Virtually any proposal for government subsidies of the press today would likely fail on just these grounds: funding by the federal government or the states has too much potential for political manipulation. Elsewhere governments are subsidizing the press. In an effort to aid newspapers in France, President Nicolas Sarkozy recently announced a program to give eighteen-year-olds a free year-long subscription to a daily paper of their choice. In America this would be a joke, though depending on how many teenagers chose one of our racier tabloids, it could give added meaning to the concept of a "stimulus package."

The other standard means of supporting the production of public goods is through private non-profit organization. In fact, non-profit support of journalism has recently been increasing. But much of the discussion about non-profit journalism has failed to recognize that it can mean at least three different things. The first, though not necessarily the most relevant, is the conversion of newspapers from commercial to non-profit status as a way of preserving their public-service role. Florida's *St. Petersburg Times*, which is owned by a journalism school, the Poynter Institute for Media Studies, is often mistakenly cited as a model for this approach. In fact, the *Times* itself has been run at a profit, which has been used to build up the Poynter Institute into a major center for training in journalism. Today, however, the question is not whether to use a money-making newspaper to support philanthropy, but whether non-profit organizations can sustain newspapers that may be losing money. Britain's Guardian Media Group, owned by the Scott Trust, comes closer to present demands. The trust uses profits from its money-making media subsidiaries to ensure the survival of the daily *Guardian*, which has lost money in recent years. But the *Guardian* model depends on having profitable subsidiaries to offset losses in a daily paper.

Before stopping the presses for the last time, the owners of some declining newspapers may try to convert them into non-profits in the hope of raising contributions to keep them in operation. I would not be surprised if some papers do have a devoted core of readers who would be willing to give more in tax-deductible contributions than they currently pay in subscriptions. But no paper has yet tested whether this option could raise enough money to stay in business.

Besides full non-profit operation of a newspaper, a second approach is philanthropic support of specific kinds of journalism, available through multiple outlets, whether they are commercial or non-profit. The best-known example of this solution is ProPublica, which describes itself as "an independent, non-profit newsroom that produces investigative journalism in the public interest." Publishing online as of last June, ProPublica also works in partnership on some stories with newspapers such as the *New York Times*. The partnerships enable newspapers to keep down the costs of investigative stories, and they give ProPublica access to mass distribution as well as a check on quality. Similarly, the Kaiser Family Foundation, which focuses on health policy, announced last fall that it would begin directly employing reporters to create a health policy news service. According to Drew Altman, Kaiser's president, besides making some stories freely available to newspapers and online, the news service will establish partnerships with newspapers for specific stories, which the papers will then have the right to release first. Some other foundations that focus on specific areas of policy may follow this approach as a way to promote public awareness of their concerns.

Both the non-profit operation of newspapers and the philanthropic subsidy of particular types of reporting are aimed at fostering forms of public-service journalism that would otherwise be in jeopardy. But there is yet a third use of non-profits—and it is for underwriting new models of journalism in the online environment. A good example of this approach is the Center for Independent Media, which, according to its director David Bennahum, receives about $4 million annually from seventy funders to support online political news sites in five states as well as one for national news, The Washington Independent. Bennahum says that "the narrative voice of newspapers is not what [online] readers want" and that the sites his center finances are instead doing a kind of journalism that brings readers into dialogue.

The notion that the digital medium requires a more inclusive relationship with the "people formerly called the audience" is a common theme among online journalists. Joshua Micah Marshall, the founder of Talking PointsMemo.com, which runs on a commercial basis, says that many of the stories on his site grow out of ideas and tips supplied by readers in thousands of emails daily. Any news operation has information flowing in and out; an online publication can productively open up this process to anyone who is able and prepared to help. Stories develop online incrementally, often through participation in a collaborative network, rather than being written behind the scenes and released only when checked and finished. This is entirely different from "citizen journalism," and has the potential to be just as rigorous as traditional journalistic practices.

In cities around the country, journalists are experimenting with a variety of strategies for building up Web-only news sites to make up for the shrinking newsrooms of local papers. MinnPost.com in Minneapolis-St. Paul, the most substantial of these ventures, hopes to attract a wide range of readers and sponsors with news coverage of relatively broad scope, according to its CEO and editor Joel Kramer. But its annual budget of $1.3 million cannot support an operation on the scale of a metropolitan daily; with only seven full-time staff, MinnPost.com relies primarily on free-lancers, many of them journalists who have left St. Paul's *Pioneer Press* or Minneapolis's *Star-Tribune* (which in January filed for bankruptcy protection despite having cut its editorial staff by 25 percent). Another non-profit online metropolitan news site, the VoiceofSanDiego.org, developed as a response to scandals in the city and has specialized in investigative stories. Like public radio, these ventures raise money through individual membership contributions and grants from local foundations, though not from government.

Doubtful that they can ever achieve the scale of the big metros, Rosenstiel compares the Web-based city news sites to aggressive city magazines. If one major concern is keeping government accountable, that kind of aggressive reporting is certainly a valuable function and well worth supporting. But owing to their more limited economic basis, the non-profit news sites are unlikely to be able to offer the coverage, or to exert the influence, of a daily newspaper read by half the people in a city. The great metros did not emerge just because cities needed newspapers to inform citizens—after all, cities need lots of things that they are never able to develop. Newspapers flourished at the metropolitan level because their role as local market intermediaries enabled them to generate substantial advertising as well as circulation income and thereby to become strong and independent. Non-profit news sites that lack a strong advertising base depend on donors for their survival and are at risk of being destroyed by a single lawsuit, and so they are unlikely to be able to match the traditional power of the press.

Many people have been expecting the successors of newspapers to emerge on the Web. But there may be no successor, at least none like the papers we have known. The metropolitan daily may be a peculiar historical invention whose time is passing. We may be approaching not the end of newspapers, but the end of the age of newspapers—the long phase in history when newspapers published in major cities throughout the United States have been central to both the production of news and the life of their metropolitan regions.

Metropolitan newspapers have dominated news gathering, set the public agenda, served as the focal point of controversy, and credibly represented themselves as symbolizing and speaking for the cities whose names they have carried. They have tried to be everyone's source of news, appealing across the ideological spectrum, and to be comprehensive, providing their readers with whatever was of daily interest to them. Some newspapers, a smaller number than exist today, will survive the transition to the Web, but they probably will not possess the centrality, the scope, or the authoritative voice—much less the monopolies on metropolitan advertising—that newspapers have had.

* * *

For those with the skills and interest to take advantage of this new world of news, there should be much to be pleased with. Instead of being limited to a local paper, such readers already enjoy access to a broader range of publications and discussions than ever before. But without a local newspaper or even with a shrunken one, many other people will learn less about what is going on in the world. As of now, moreover, no source in any medium seems willing and able to pay for the general-interest reporting that newspapers are abandoning. Philanthropy can help to offset some of these cutbacks, but it is unlikely to make up fully for what we are losing.

News coverage is not all that newspapers have given us. They have lent the public a powerful means of leverage over the state, and this leverage is now at risk. If we take seriously the notion of newspapers as a fourth estate or a fourth branch of government, the end of the age of newspapers implies a change in our political system itself. Newspapers have helped to control corrupt tendencies in both government and business. If we are to avoid a new era of corruption, we are going to have to summon that power in other ways. Our new technologies do not retire our old responsibilities.

50

"How to Save the News"

JAMES FALLOWS

Everyone knows that Google is killing the news business. Few people know how hard Google is trying to bring it back to life, or why the company now considers journalism's survival crucial to its own prospects.

Of course this overstates Google's power to destroy, or create. The company's chief economist, Hal Varian, likes to point out that perhaps the most important measure of the newspaper industry's viability—the number of subscriptions per household—has headed straight down, not just since Google's founding in the late 1990s but ever since World War II. In 1947, each 100 U.S. households bought an average of about 140 newspapers daily. Now they buy fewer than 50, and the number has fallen nonstop through those years. If Google had never been invented, changes in commuting patterns, the coming of 24-hour TV news and online information sites that make a newspaper's information stale before it appears, the general busyness of life, and many other factors would have created major problems for newspapers. Moreover, "Google" is shorthand for an array of other Internet-based pressures on the news business, notably the draining of classified ads to the likes of Craigslist and eBay. On the other side of the balance, Google's efforts to shore up news organizations are extensive and have recently become intense but are not guaranteed to succeed.

*   *   *

Let's start with the diagnosis: If you are looking at the troubled ecology of news from Google's point of view, how do you define the problem to be solved? You would accept from the outset that something "historic," "epochal," "devastating," "unprecedented," "irresistible," and so on was happening to the news business—all terms I heard used in interviews to describe the challenges facing newspapers in particular and the journalism business more broadly.

"There really is no single cause," I was told by Josh Cohen, a former Web-news manager for Reuters who now directs Google's dealings with publishers and broadcasters, at his office in New York. "Rather, you could pick any single cause, and that on its own would be enough to explain the problems—except it's not on its own." The most obvious cause is that classified advertising, traditionally 30 to 40 percent of a newspaper's total revenue, is disappearing in a rush to online sites. "There are a lot of people in the business who think that in the not-too-distant future, the classified share of a paper's revenue will go to zero," Cohen said. "Stop right there. In any business, if you lose a third of your revenue, you're going to be in serious trouble."

You can't stop right there, Cohen said, and he went through the list of the other, related trends weighing on newspapers in particular, each pointing downward and each making the others worse. First, the relentless decline of circulation—"fewer people using your product," as he put it. Then, the consequent defection of advertisers from the lucrative "display" category—the big ads for cars, banks, airlines—as well as from classifieds. The typical newspaper costs much more to print and deliver than a subscriber pays. Its business rationale is as an advertising-delivery vehicle, with 80 percent of the typical paper's total revenue coming from ads. That's what's going away. In hopes of preserving that advertising model, newspapers have decided to defend their hold on the public's attention by giving away, online, the very information they were trying to sell in print. However that decision looks in the long run, for now it has created a rising generation of "customers" who are out of the habit of reading on paper and are conditioned to think that information should be free.

"It's the triple whammy," [Google CEO] Eric Schmidt said when I interviewed him. "Loss of classifieds, loss of circulation, loss of the value of display ads in print, on a per-ad basis. Online advertising is growing but has not caught up."

So far, this may sound familiar. To me, the interesting aspects of the Google diagnosis, which of course sets the stage for the proposed cure, were these:

First, it was strikingly not moralistic or mocking. This was a change, not simply from what I'd grown used to hearing at tech conferences over the past decade—the phrase "dead-tree edition" captures the tone—but also from the way Americans usually talk about distressed industries. Think of the connotations of "Big Auto" or "Rust Belt." * * *

Next in the Google assessment is the emphasis on "unbundling" as an insurmountable business problem for journalism. "Bundling" was the idea that all parts of the paper came literally in one wrapper—news, sports, comics, grocery-store coupons—and that people who bought the paper for one part implicitly subsidized all the rest. This was important not just because it boosted overall revenue but because it kept publishers from having to figure out whether enough people were reading stories from the statehouse or Mexico City to pay the costs of reporters there.

* * * The Internet has been one giant system for stripping away such cross-subsidies. Why look to the newspaper real-estate listings when you can get more up-to-date, searchable info on Zillow—or better travel deals on Orbitz, or a broader range of movie showtimes on Yahoo? Google has been the most powerful unbundling agent of all. It lets users find the one article they are looking for, rather than making them buy the entire paper that paid the reporter. It lets advertisers reach the one customer who is searching for their product, rather than making them advertise to an entire class of readers.

Next, and significantly for the company's vision of the future, nearly everyone at Google emphasized that prospects look bleak for the printed versions of newspapers—but could be bright for the news industry as a whole, including newspaper publishers. This could seem an artificial distinction, but it is fundamental to the company's view of how news organizations will support themselves.

*   *   *

Publishers would be overjoyed to stop buying newsprint—if the new readers they are gaining for their online editions were worth as much to advertisers as the previous ones they are losing in print. Here is a crucial part of the Google analysis: they certainly will be. The news business, in this view, is passing through an agonizing transition—bad enough, but different from dying. The difference lies in the assumption that soon readers will again pay for subscriptions, and online display ads will become valuable.

"Nothing that I see suggests the 'death of newspapers,'" Eric Schmidt told me. The problem was the high cost and plummeting popularity of their print versions. "Today you have a subscription to a print newspaper," he said. "In the future model, you'll have subscriptions to information sources that will have advertisements embedded in them, like a newspaper. You'll just leave out the print part. I am quite sure that this will happen." We'll get to the details in a moment, but the analytical point behind his conviction bears emphasis. "I observe that as print circulation falls, the growth of the online audience is dramatic," Schmidt said. "Newspapers don't have a demand problem; they have a business-model problem." Many of his company's efforts are attempts to solve this, so that newspaper companies can survive, as printed circulation withers away.

Finally, and to me most surprisingly, the Google analysis reveals something about journalism that people inside the business can't easily see about themselves. This involves a kind of inefficiency that a hard-pressed journalistic establishment may no longer be able to afford.

*   *   *

Except for an 18-month period when [Krishna] Bharat founded and ran Google's R&D center in Bangalore, his original hometown, he has been guiding Google News ever since. In this role, he sees more of the world's news coverage daily than practically anyone else on Earth. I asked him what he had learned about the news business.

He hesitated for a minute, as if wanting to be very careful about making a potentially offensive point. Then he said that what astonished him was the predictable and pack-like response of most of the world's news outlets to most stories. Or, more positively, how much opportunity he saw for anyone who was willing to try a different approach.

The Google News front page is a kind of air-traffic-control center for the movement of stories across the world's media, in real time. "Usually, you see essentially the same approach taken by a thousand publications at the same time," he told me. "Once something has been observed, nearly everyone says approximately the same thing." He didn't mean that the publications were linking to one another or syndicating their stories. Rather, their conventions and instincts made them all emphasize the same things. This could be reassuring, in indicating some consensus on what the "important" stories were. But Bharat said it also indicated a faddishness of coverage—when Michael Jackson dies, other things cease to matter—and a redundancy that journalism could no longer afford. "It makes you wonder, is there a better way?" he asked. "Why is it that a thousand people come up with approximately the same reading of matters? Why couldn't there be five readings? And meanwhile use that energy to observe something else, equally important, that is currently being neglected." He said this was not a purely theoretical question. "I believe the news industry is finding that it will not be able to sustain producing highly similar articles."

With the debut of Krishna Bharat's Google News in 2002, Google began its first serious interactions with news organizations. Two years later, it introduced Google Alerts, which sent e-mail or instant-message notifications to users whenever Google's relentless real-time indexing of the world's news sites found a match for a topic the user had flagged. Two years after that, in the fall of 2006, Google began scanning the paper or microfilmed archives of many leading publications so that articles from their pre-digital era could be indexed, searched for, and read online.

*   *   *

"About two years ago, we started hearing more and more talk about the decline of the press," Schmidt told me. "A set of people [inside the company] began looking at what might be the ways we could help newspapers."

Why should the company bother? Until recently, I would have thought that the answer was a combination of PR concerns and Schmidt's personal interest. * * *

Before this year, when I asked Google employees about the health of the news business, their answers often seemed dutiful. During my interviews this year, people sounded as if they meant it. Google is valuable, by the logic I repeatedly heard, because the information people find through it is valuable. If the information is uninteresting, inaccurate, or untimely, people will not want to search for it. How valuable would Google Maps be, if the directions or street listings were wrong?

Nearly everyone I spoke with made this point in some way. Nikesh Arora's version was that Google had a "deeply symbiotic relationship" with serious news organizations. "We help people find content," he told me. "We don't generate content ourselves. As long as there is great content, people will come looking for it. When there's no great content, it's very hard for people to be interested in finding it. That's what we do for a living." * * *

"For the last eight years, we mainly focused on getting the algorithms better," Krishna Bharat said, referring to the automated systems for finding and ranking items in Google News. "But lately, a lot of my time has gone into thinking about the basis on which the product"—news—"is built. A lot of our thinking now is focused on making the news sustainable."

So how can news be made sustainable? The conceptual leap in Google's vision is simply to ignore print. It's not that everyone at the company assumes "dead tree" newspapers and magazines will disappear. * * * No one I spoke with at Google went quite that far. But all of their plans for reinventing a business model for journalism involve attracting money to the Web-based news sites now available on computers, and to the portable information streams that will flow to whatever devices evolve from today's smart phones, iPods and iPads, Nooks and Kindles, and mobile devices of any other sort. This is a natural approach for Google, which is, except for its Nexus One phone, a strictly online company.

The three pillars of the new online business model, as I heard them invariably described, are distribution, engagement, and monetization. That is: getting news to more people, and more people to news-oriented sites; making the presentation of news more interesting, varied, and involving; and converting these larger and more strongly committed audiences into revenue, through both subscription fees and ads. Conveniently, each calls on areas of Google's expertise. "Not knowing as much about the news business as the newspapers do, it is unlikely that we can solve the problems better than they can," Nikesh Arora told me. "But we are willing to support any formal and informal effort that newspapers or journalists more generally want to make" to come up with new sources of money.

In practice this involves projects like the ones I'm about to describe, which share two other traits beyond the "distribution, engagement, monetization" strategy that officially unites them. One is the Google concept of "permanent beta" and continuous experimentation—learning what does work by seeing all the things that don't. "We believe that teams must be nimble and able to fail quickly," Josh Cohen told me. (I resisted making the obvious joke about the contrast with the journalism world, which believes in slow and statesmanlike failure.) "The three most important things any newspaper can do now are experiment, experiment, and experiment," Hal Varian said.

*   *   *

The other implicitly connecting theme is that an accumulation of small steps can together make a surprisingly large difference. The forces weighing down the news industry are titanic. In contrast, some of the proposed solutions may seem disappointingly small-bore. But many people at Google repeated a maxim from Clay Shirley, of New York University, in an essay last year about the future of the news: "Nothing will work, but everything might."

In all, Google teams are working with hundreds of news organizations, which range in scale from the Associated Press, the Public Broadcasting System, and *The New York Times* to local TV stations and papers. The last two efforts I'll mention are obviously different in scale and potential from all the others, but these examples give a sense of what "trying everything" means.

Living Stories

News reporting is usually incremental. Something happens in Kabul today. It's related to what happened there yesterday, plus 20 years ago, and further back. It has a bearing on what will happen a year from now. High-end news organizations reflect this continuous reality in hiring reporters and editors who (ideally) know the background of today's news and in the way they present it, usually with modest additions to the sum of established knowledge day by day.

The modest daily updating of the news—another vote in Congress, another debate among political candidates—matches the cycle of papers and broadcasts very well, but matches the Internet very poorly, in terms of both speed and popularity rankings. *The Financial Times* might have given readers better sustained coverage of European economic troubles than any other paper. But precisely because it has done so many incremental stories, no one of them might rise to the top of a Google Web search, compared with an occasional overview story somewhere else. By the standards that currently generate online revenue, better journalism gets a worse result.

This past winter, the Google News team worked with *The New York Times* and *The Washington Post* to run the Living Stories experiment, essentially a way to rig Google's search results to favor serious, sustained reporting. All articles about a big topic—the war in Afghanistan, health-care reform—were grouped on one page that included links to all aspects of the paper's coverage (history, videos, reader comments, related articles). "It is a repository of information, rather than ephemeral information," Krishna Bharat said, explaining that it was a repository designed to prosper in what he called "today's link economy." In February, Google called off the *Times-Post* experiment—and declared it a success, by making the source code available free online, for any organization that would like to create a Living Stories feature for its site.

*   *   *

Fast Flip

The Internet is a great way to get news but often a poor way to read it. Usually the longer the item, the worse the experience; a screenful is fine, clicking through thousands of words is an ordeal. * * *

The Fast Flip project, which began last summer and has now graduated to "official" status, is an attempt to approximate the inviting aspects of leafing through a magazine. It works by loading magazine pages not as collections of text but as highly detailed photos of pages as a whole, cached in Google's system so they load almost as quickly as a (human) reader can leaf through them. "It was an experiment in giving you a preview of an article that was more than just a link to the title," Krishna Bharat said. "It gives you a sense of the graphics, the emphasis, the quality, the feel. Whether you would like to spend time with it." Spending time with an article, whether in print or online, is of course the definition of "engagement" and the behavior advertisers seek. * * *

"We're not saying we have worked out exactly the right model," Krishna Bharat said when I asked about Fast Flip details. "We just want news to be available, fast, all over the place on the Internet."

YouTube Direct

Projects like Living Stories and Fast Flip are tactical in their potential. Google's hope is that broader use of YouTube videos could substantially boost a news organization's long-term ability to engage an audience. Amateur-produced video is perhaps the most powerful new tool of the Internet era in journalism, making the whole world a potential witness to dramas, tragedies, achievements almost anywhere. The idea behind the various YouTube projects is that the same newspapers that once commanded an audience with printed reports of local news, sports, crime, and weather could re-create their central role by becoming a clearinghouse for video reports.

* * * For instance, Google offers, for free, the source code for YouTube Direct, which any publication can put on its own Web site. Readers can then easily send in their video clips, for the publication to review, censor, combine, or shorten before putting them up on its site. After a blizzard, people could send in clips of what they had seen outside. Same for a local football game, or a train wreck, or a city-council meeting, or any other event when many people would be interested in what their neighbors had seen. The advertising potential might be small, for YouTube and the local paper alike. The point would be engagement. Al Jazeera used YouTube Direct during the elections in Iraq this spring to show footage from around the country.

*   *   *

Another tool extends the lessons of the YouTube Debates during the 2008 presidential campaign, in which [Google] invited YouTube users from around the country to send in clips of brief questions for the candidates. Anderson Cooper of CNN then introduced YouTube clips of the questions CNN had chosen to use. They ranged from serious to silly and included one asking Barack Obama whether he was "black enough." YouTube has added a feature that lets users vote for the questions they want asked and has used the method effectively many times since then. . . .

Whatever comes of these experiments, two other broad initiatives are of unquestionable importance, because they address the two biggest business emergencies today's news companies face: they can no longer make enough money on display ads, and they can no longer get readers to pay. According to the Google view, these are serious situations, but temporary.

Display Ads

The idea for improving display-ad prospects begins with insignificant-sounding adjustments that have great potential payoff. For instance: Neal Mohan of Google pointed out that news organizations now typically sell their online ad space in two very different ways. Premium space—on the home page, facing certain featured articles or authors—is handled by "direct sales," through the publication's own sales staff. "Remnant" space, anything left over, is generally franchised out to a national sales network or "exchange" that digs up whatever advertisers it can. Publications decide on the division of space ahead of time, and hope the real-world results more or less fit.

One of Google's new systems does for online ad space what the airlines' dreaded "yield management" systems do for seats on a plane. Airlines constantly adjust the fares on a route, and the size of the planes that will fly it, toward the goal of making each plane as full as it can be before it takes off. The Google system does the same thing, allowing publishers to adjust the allocation of high- and low-priced space, second by second. "Your top salesperson might just have had dinner with the biggest client, who decides to run a big campaign," Mohan told me. The dynamic allocation system ensures that the publisher doesn't lose a penny of potential ad revenue to avoidable supply/demand glitches. If an advertiser wants to spend more on "premium" ads, the necessary space will be automatically redeployed from lower-value sections. * * * Yield management has allowed airlines to survive; according to Mohan, the advertising equivalent in Google's new system "has generated a lift for publishers of 130 percent, versus what they did when dividing the space themselves."

Mohan suggested a variety of other small but significant operational improvements, which together led to a proposal so revolutionary that it challenges all despairing conclusions about the economic future of the press. * * * Online display ads may not be so valuable now, he said, but that is because we're still in the drawn-out "transition" period. Sooner or later—maybe in two years, certainly in 10—display ads will, per eyeball, be worth more online than they were in print.

How could this be? In part, he said, today's discouraging ad results simply reflect a lag time. The audience has shifted dramatically from print to online. So has the accumulation of minutes people choose to spend each day reading the news. Wherever people choose to spend their time, Mohan said, they can eventually be "monetized"—the principle on which every newspaper and magazine (and television network) has survived until today.

*   *   *

* * * "The online world will be a lot more attuned to who you are and what you care about, and it will be interactive in a way it never has been before." Advertising has been around forever, Mohan said, "but until now it has always been a one-way conversation. Now your users can communicate back to you." His full argument is complex, but his conclusion is: eventually news operations will wonder why they worried so much about print display ads, since online display will be so much more attractive.

*   *   *

Designing the Paywall

The other hugely consequential effort Google is exploring involves reviving the idea of "subscriptions"—the quaint old custom of an audience paying for what it receives. Most Google people I spoke with had zero interest in the paywall question as an abstraction, because it seemed so obvious that different publications in different circumstances with different business models will make different decisions about how customers should pay.

*   *   *

"We don't want to encourage anyone to start charging for content, or not to charge for content," Chris Gaither said. "That is entirely up to them." But Google teams based in Mountain View and New York have been working with newspapers and magazines on the surprisingly complex details of making any kind of payment system work. Paywalls themselves come in a wide variety: absolute barriers to anyone who is not a subscriber, metered approaches that allow nonsubscribers a certain number of free views per day or month, "first click free" schemes to let anyone see the start of an article but reserve the full text for subscribers, and many more. Each involves twists in how the publication's results show up in Google searches and on Google News. For instance: if you are a paid subscriber to the *Financial Times*, any Web search you run should include FT results—and indeed rank them all the higher, since your status as a subscriber means you place extra value on the paper's reports. If you don't subscribe, those FT links should come lower in the search results, since you won't be able to read them—but the results should still appear, in case you decide you want them enough to subscribe. But when you run the search, how can Google tell whether or not you subscribe? How can it know that you are you, whether you're using your computer, or a friend's, or one at an Internet cafe, or an iPhone? And how can its Web crawlers index the FTs stories in the first place, if they're behind the paywall? All these questions have answers, but they're not always obvious.

"We often hear from publishers saying, 'We're thinking of this approach, and we want to understand it fully,'" Josh Cohen told me. "'We want to be sure this works the way we intend it to work. Can you give it a look?' We will tell them how their ideas would turn out with our system." Then, without giving the newspaper's name or the proprietary details of its specific plan, the Google team will also post its findings and advice on its public Web site. And for publications thinking of the "E-ZPass" approach—some automatic way to collect small per-article charges without slowing the user down or involving cumbersome forms—another Google team is working on the practicalities.

As for the very idea of paid subscriptions: How can they have a future in the Google-driven world of atomized spot information? "It is probable that unbundling has a limit," Eric Schmidt said. Something basic in human nature craves surprise and new sources of stimulation. Few people are "so monomaniacal," as he put it, that they will be interested only in a strict, predefined list of subjects. Therefore people will still want to buy subscriptions to sources of information and entertainment—"bundles," the head of the world's most powerful unbundler said—and advertisers will still want to reach them. His example:

"It's obvious that in five or 10 years, most news will be consumed on an electronic device of some sort. Something that is mobile and personal, with a nice color screen. Imagine an iPod or Kindle smart enough to show you stories that are incremental to a story it showed you yesterday, rather than just repetitive. And it knows who your friends are and what they're reading and think is hot. And it has display advertising with lots of nice color, and more personal and targeted, within the limits of creepiness. And it has a GPS and a radio network and knows what is going on around you. If you think about that, you get to an interesting answer very quickly, involving both subscriptions and ads."

This vision, which Schmidt presented as Utopian, helps illustrate the solution Google believes it will find; the problem it knows it can't solve; and another problem that goes well beyond its ambitions.

The solution is simply the idea that there can be a solution. The organization that dominates the online-advertising world says that much more online-ad money can be flowing to news organizations. The company whose standard price to consumers is zero says that subscribers can and will pay for news. The name that has symbolized disruption of established media says it sees direct self-interest in helping the struggling journalism business. In today's devastated news business, these are major and encouraging developments, all the more so for their contrast with what other tech firms are attempting.

The problem Google is aware of involves the disruption still ahead. Ten years from now, a robust and better-funded news business will be thriving. What next year means is harder to say. * * * But this is consistent with the way the news has always worked, rather than a threatening change. Fifteen years ago, Fox News did not exist. A decade ago, Jon Stewart was not known for political commentary. The news business has continually been reinvented by people in their 20s and early 30s. . . .

The challenge Google knows it has not fully coped with is a vast one, which involves the public function of the news in the broadest sense. The company views the survival of "premium content" as important to its own welfare. But Schmidt and his colleagues realize that a modernized news business might conceivably produce "enough" good content for Google's purposes even if no one has fully figured out how to pay for the bureau in Baghdad, or even at the statehouse. This is the next challenge, and a profound one, for a reinvented journalistic culture. The fluid history of the news business, along with today's technological pattern of Google-style continuous experimentation, suggests that there will be no one big solution but a range of partial remedies. Google's efforts may have bought time for a panicked, transitional news business to see a future for itself and begin discovering those new remedies and roles.

DISCUSSION QUESTIONS

1. Which part or parts of the news media—newspapers, television, the Internet, blogs, radio, social networks, Twitter—do you rely on most? Which would you say you trust the most? Should all news-oriented media, whether new or old, use the same standards in determining what to broadcast or publish?

2. Imagine you are a blogger and you have come across some damaging information about a presidential candidate. Do you blog it? On one hand, it might not be true. On the other, if it is true, it is critical information that voters should know. Do you put the information into the blogosphere and trust it will be filtered and proven true or false by other media? Or do you approach it as mainstream media journalists traditionally would, requiring more corroboration for the story—which can take time to obtain—before presenting it to the public? Would your answer depend on how late in the campaign it is? Now imagine the same scenario, except that the office in question is an elected position in your hometown, where people know you. Would you handle this situation differently?

3. All three articles express concerns about the fate of newspapers. What are the key concerns? Do you share them? Why or why not?

4. What do you see as the strengths and weaknesses of the solutions described by Starr and Fallows for the problems facing newspapers?

CHAPTER 10

Elections and Voting

51

"The Voice of the People: An Echo," from *The Responsible Electorate*

V. O. KEY, JR.

The votes are cast, the tallies are in, the winning candidate claims victory and a mandate to govern—the people have spoken! But what exactly have the people said when they cast a plurality of the votes for one candidate? The political scientist V. O. Key, Jr., argued that the voice of the people was nothing more than an echo of the cacophony and hubbub of candidates and parties scrambling for popular support. "Even the most discriminating popular judgment," wrote Key, "can reflect only ambiguity, uncertainty, or even foolishness if those are the qualities of the input into the echo chamber."

So what was the logic of the voting decision? Key argued that the effort among social scientists to develop theories for understanding the voting decision was important because of the ways political candidates and political leaders would respond to them. If research demonstrates that voters are influenced by "images and cultivation of style," rather than the "substance of politics," then that is what candidates will offer the voters. If the people receive only images and style as the input to the echo chamber, then eventually that is all they will come to expect. However, Key argues that contrary to the picture of voters held by many politicians and some academic research of his day, the "voters are not fools" who are easily manipulated by campaign tactics or who vote predictably according to the social groups they are in. Individual voters may behave oddly, he concedes, but "in the large, the electorate behaves about as rationally and responsibly as we should expect." His analysis of presidential elections convinced him that the electorate made decisions based upon a concern for public policy, the performance of government, and the personality of the candidates.

In his reflective moments even the most experienced politician senses a nagging curiosity about why people vote as they do. His power and his position depend upon the outcome of the mysterious rites we perform as opposing candidates harangue the multitudes who finally march to the polls to prolong the rule of their champion, to thrust him, ungratefully, back into the void of private life, or to raise to eminence a new tribune of the people. What kinds of appeals enable a candidate to win the favor of the great god, The People? What circumstances move voters to shift their preferences in this direction or that? What clever propaganda tactic or slogan led to this result? What mannerism of oratory or style of rhetoric produced another outcome? What band of electors rallied to this candidate to save the day for him? What policy of state attracted the devotion of another bloc of voters? What action repelled a third sector of the electorate?

The victorious candidate may claim with assurance that he has the answers to all such questions. He may regard his success as vindication of his beliefs about why voters vote as they do. And he may regard the swing of the vote to him as indubitably a response to the campaign positions he took, as an indication of the acuteness of his intuitive estimates of the mood of the people, and as a ringing manifestation of the esteem in which he is held by a discriminating public. This narcissism assumes its most repulsive form among election winners who have championed intolerance, who have stirred the passions and hatreds of people, or who have advocated causes known by decent men to be outrageous or dangerous in their long-run consequences. No functionary is more repugnant or more arrogant than the unjust man who asserts, with a color of truth, that he speaks from a pedestal of popular approbation.

It thus can be a mischievous error to assume, because a candidate wins, that a majority of the electorate shares his views on public questions, approves his past actions, or has specific expectations about his future conduct. Nor does victory establish that the candidate's campaign strategy, his image, his television style, or his fearless stand against cancer and polio turned the trick. The election returns establish only that the winner attracted a majority of the votes—assuming the existence of a modicum of rectitude in election administration. They tell us precious little about why the plurality was his.

For a glaringly obvious reason, electoral victory cannot be regarded as necessarily a popular ratification of a candidate's outlook. The voice of the people is but an echo. The output of an echo chamber bears an inevitable and invariable relation to the input. As candidates and parties clamor for attention and vie for popular support, the people's verdict can be no more than a selective reflection from among the alternatives and outlooks presented to them. Even the most discriminating popular judgment can reflect only ambiguity, uncertainty, or even foolishness if those are the qualities of the input into the echo chamber. A candidate may win despite his tactics and appeals rather than because of them. If the people can choose only from among rascals, they are certain to choose a rascal.

Scholars, though they have less at stake than do politicians, also have an abiding curiosity about why voters act as they do. In the past quarter of a century [since the 1940s] they have vastly enlarged their capacity to check the hunches born of their curiosities. The invention of the sample survey—the most widely known example of which is the Gallup poll—enabled them to make fairly trustworthy estimates of the characteristics and behaviors of large human populations. This method of mass observation revolutionized the study of politics—as well as the management of political campaigns. The new technique permitted large-scale tests to check the validity of old psychological and sociological theories of human behavior. These tests led to new hunches and new theories about voting behavior, which could, in turn, be checked and which thereby contributed to the extraordinary ferment in the social sciences during recent decades.

The studies of electoral behavior by survey methods cumulate into an imposing body of knowledge which conveys a vivid impression of the variety and subtlety of factors that enter into individual voting decisions. In their first stages in the 1930s the new electoral studies chiefly lent precision and verification to the working maxims of practicing politicians and to some of the crude theories of political speculators. Thus, sample surveys established that people did, indeed, appear to vote their pocketbooks. Yet the demonstration created its embarrassments because it also established that exceptions to the rule were numerous. Not all factory workers, for example, voted alike. How was the behavior of the deviants from "group interest" to be explained? Refinement after refinement of theory and analysis added complexity to the original simple explanation. By introducing a bit of psychological theory it could be demonstrated that factory workers with optimistic expectations tended less to be governed by pocketbook considerations than did those whose outlook was gloomy. When a little social psychology was stirred into the analysis, it could be established that identifications formed early in life, such as attachments to political parties, also reinforced or resisted the pull of the interest of the moment. A sociologist, bringing to play the conceptual tools of his trade, then could show that those factory workers who associate intimately with like-minded persons on the average vote with greater solidarity than do social isolates. Inquiries conducted with great ingenuity along many such lines have enormously broadened our knowledge of the factors associated with the responses of people to the stimuli presented to them by political campaigns.

Yet, by and large, the picture of the voter that emerges from a combination of the folklore of practical politics and the findings of the new electoral studies is not a pretty one. It is not a portrait of citizens moving to considered decision as they play their solemn role of making and unmaking governments. The older tradition from practical politics may regard the voter as an erratic and irrational fellow susceptible to manipulation by skilled humbugs. One need not live through many campaigns to observe politicians, even successful politicians, who act as though they regarded the people as manageable fools. Nor does a heroic conception of the voter emerge from the new analyses of electoral behavior. They can be added up to a conception of voting not as a civic decision but as an almost purely deterministic act. Given knowledge of certain characteristics of a voter—his occupation, his residence, his religion, his national origin, and perhaps certain of his attitudes—one can predict with a high probability the direction of his vote. The actions of persons are made to appear to be only predictable and automatic responses to campaign stimuli.

* * *

Conceptions and theories of the way voters behave do not raise solely arcane problems to be disputed among the democratic and antidemocratic theorists or questions to be settled by the elegant techniques of the analysts of electoral behavior. Rather, they touch upon profound issues at the heart of the problem of the nature and workability of systems of popular government. Obviously the perceptions of the behavior of the electorate held by political leaders, agitators, and activists condition, if they do not fix, the types of appeals politicians employ as they seek popular support. These perceptions—or theories—affect the nature of the input to the echo chamber, if we may revert to our earlier figure, and thereby control its output. They may govern, too, the kinds of actions that governments take as they look forward to the next election. If politicians perceive the electorate as responsive to father images, they will give it father images. If they see voters as most certainly responsive to nonsense, they will give them nonsense. If they see voters as susceptible to delusion, they will delude them. If they see an electorate receptive to the cold, hard realities, they will give it the cold, hard realities.

In short, theories of how voters behave acquire importance not because of their effects on voters, who may proceed blithely unaware of them. They gain significance because of their effects, both potentially and in reality, on candidates and other political leaders. If leaders believe the route to victory is by projection of images and cultivation of styles rather than by advocacy of policies to cope with the problems of the country, they will project images and cultivate styles to the neglect of the substance of politics. They will abdicate their prime function in a democratic system, which amounts, in essence, to the assumption of the risk of trying to persuade us to lift ourselves by our bootstraps.

Among the literary experts on politics there are those who contend that, because of the development of tricks for the manipulation of the masses, practices of political leadership in the management of voters have moved far toward the conversion of election campaigns into obscene parodies of the models set up by democratic idealists. They point to the good old days when politicians were deep thinkers, eloquent orators, and farsighted statesmen. Such estimates of the course of change in social institutions must be regarded with reserve. They may be only manifestations of the inverted optimism of aged and melancholy men who, estopped from hope for the future, see in the past a satisfaction of their yearning for greatness in our political life.

Whatever the trends may have been, the perceptions that leadership elements of democracies hold of the modes of response of the electorate must always be a matter of fundamental significance. Those perceptions determine the nature of the voice of the people, for they determine the character of the input into the echo chamber. While the output may be governed by the nature of the input, over the longer run the properties of the echo chamber may themselves be altered. Fed a steady diet of buncombe [bunkum], the people may come to expect and to respond with highest predictability to buncombe. And those leaders most skilled in the propagation of buncombe may gain lasting advantage in the recurring struggles for popular favor.

The perverse and unorthodox argument of this little book is that voters are not fools. To be sure, many individual voters act in odd ways indeed; yet in the large the electorate behaves about as rationally and responsibly as we should expect, given the clarity of the alternatives presented to it and the character of the information available to it. In American presidential campaigns of recent decades the portrait of the American electorate that develops from the data is not one of an electorate straitjacketed by social determinants or moved by subconscious urges triggered by devilishly skillful propagandists. It is rather one of an electorate moved by concern about central and relevant questions of public policy, of governmental performance, and of executive personality. Propositions so uncompromisingly stated inevitably represent overstatements. Yet to the extent that they can be shown to resemble the reality, they are propositions of basic importance for both the theory and the practice of democracy.

To check the validity of this broad interpretation of the behavior of voters, attention will center on the movements of voters across party lines as they reacted to the issues, events, and candidates of presidential campaigns between 1936 and 1960. Some Democratic voters of one election turned Republican at the next; others stood pat. Some Republicans of one presidential season voted Democratic four years later; others remained loyal Republicans. What motivated these shifts, sometimes large and sometimes small, in voter affection? How did the standpatters differ from the switchers? What led them to stand firmly by their party preference of four years earlier? Were these actions governed by images, moods, and other irrelevancies; or were they expressions of judgments about the sorts of questions that, hopefully, voters will weigh as they responsibly cast their ballots? On these matters evidence is available that is impressive in volume, if not always so complete or so precisely relevant as hindsight would wish. If one perseveres through the analysis of this extensive body of information, the proposition that the voter is not so irrational a fellow after all may become credible.

DISCUSSION QUESTIONS

1. When you cast your vote, how do you decide whom to vote for? Is your decision process affected by the nature of the political campaign that has just been completed?

2. Do the 2008 and 2010 presidential and midterm congressional elections support Key's view of the electoral process? How would he explain such differing results in the two elections?

52

"Power to the Voters"

Richard D. Parker

We live in a republic, not a pure democracy. That is, rather than have citizens make direct choices on questions of public policy, we delegate that responsibility to elected officials. They make decisions on our behalf, and we exercise control over them through periodic elections. To its supporters, one advantage of a republic is that it can thwart popular ideas that might be built on passionate impulses and reactions rather than thoughtful responses to public problems. Critics of this type of system, though they do not challenge its fundamental legitimacy, argue for more direct public participation in the policy process. This might include allowing voters to indicate their preference for specific public policies on election day, as is allowed in many states via the initiative and referendum processes. Or it might mean a system where citizens, perhaps through the Internet, vote for public policies on an ongoing basis.

Richard Parker falls squarely into what we might call the populist camp. In his view, direct public participation has many political benefits: it emphasizes the equality of voters (rather than the distinction between the mass electorate and political elites), transcends the traditional left-right orientation of most political debate, and has a positive impact on communities. Contemporary politics, in his view, focuses on minimizing direct participation by the public—elites view public participation as a good thing only under limited conditions. He calls for a "revitalization through democracy," *i.e., using existing democratic processes and channels to reinvigorate participation. His solution calls for a dramatic effort to increase voting turnout. In his view, this is the only way to create political equality. To accomplish this goal, Parker wants to encourage third parties, impose term limits, and support the ballot initiatives process. The latter two would require constitutional amendments and the first might, depending on the remedy proposed.*

A theme that runs through this article is one of skepticism about the idea of political professionalism. The political process, in Parker's view, should be less friendly to incumbents and public officials in general: "[N]ow is the time to start treating [officials] . . . with a somewhat exaggerated disrespect." On the other hand, Parker has great faith in the virtue of mass participation.

I am, or try to be, a populist democrat. For decades, populism was largely invisible, barely a straw man, in the discourse of the law schools. Well-meaning ideologues of the governing class were accustomed to prescribe—for the people—policies and institutional processes based on an assumption that government of and by the people is—obviously and of course—not to be trusted. Now, that is changing. Populism, today, is a recognized position in legal academia. The ideal is now embraced, its possible implications explored, by a growing band.

Its meaning is, to say the the least, contested. At a minimum, though, my premise is that populism should involve taking popular sovereignty more seriously than has been the practice in legal discourse. More particularly, it ought to involve a renewed emphasis on the value of political equality which—in negotiation with values of political freedom and political community—constitutes the democratic idea. From this it follows that populism ought to involve renewed respect for majority rule as generally the fairest practical guarantor of political equality among persons as well as the most practical way of approximating popular sovereignty over time.

If populism is imagined, above all, in terms of popular sovereignty and political equality, it may acquire a bite that cuts across and shakes up stultified left/right lines of "debate." By the same token, if notions of popular sovereignty and political equality are injected with a populist sensibility—an acceptance and, more, an embrace of ordinariness: ranging from our own ordinariness (and so our deep equality) to the ordinariness of "the people"—these ideas may recover from their torpor of several long decades and acquire, at last, new critical vigor.

What such a re-orientation yields is a back-to-basics approach to the revitalization of democracy. Let me sketch, in three steps, a few fundamental features of this approach.

Mass Political Participation: A Good in Itself

The most potent rationalizations for "governance" of the masses by enlightened elites are, nowadays, packaged as paeans to democracy. Against a backdrop of perfectionist premises, they insist that participation by the mass of real people in the real world of politics has value *only* if other conditions are met—only if reality is radically transformed in one way or another. They deplore the inadequacy (even the "corruption") of democracy as we know it. And they conclude, regretfully of course, that the world is not yet safe for democracy. This line of argument must be rejected at the outset as a barrier, rather than a roadmap, to democratic revitalization.

The most transparently naked rationalization focuses on *outcomes* of political processes. The political empowerment of ordinary people is good, so the argument goes, only insofar as its likely outcomes are good. Today, the argument continues, the masses tend to have "bad values" or, at the very least, a mistaken understanding of their own interests. Hence, bad outcomes. There are, sad to say, some who would call themselves populists who take this line. The assumption of these rationalizers of political elitism is that they know better and, so, that they and their ilk should "lead"—be the "spokesmen" or "advocates" for—ordinary people. For them, political equality is but an "idealistic" fantasy—to be used, if at all, as a cynical smoke screen.

A somewhat more subtle version of the argument focuses on the *quality* of political processes. The participation of the masses in politics is good, it asserts, only so long as the political process is otherwise a good one. Today, it continues, our political process is utterly spoiled—poisoned by a few who, with clever thirty second spots, play on the ignorance, shortsightedness and emotions of the many. Thus, it concludes, the political influence of the many may have to be restricted. Again, there are self-styled populists who make this argument. The assumption is that ordinary people are incompetent dupes in need of enlightened cosseting. Again, political equality is imagined as an "ideal" too fine to flourish as a practice—much less motivate and enable a challenge, even if a messy one, to the few by the many—in the real world.

The most sophisticated version of the argument focuses on *preconditions* of democracy. Mass political participation is good, it claims, only after some level of social and economic empowerment, enlightenment and equality has first been achieved for everyone. Again, there are "populists" who take this line. But at bottom, despite the apparent sophistication, it repeats the other versions of the argument. For it assumes that ordinary people who suffer deprivation and inequality need help from their betters before acting politically on their own. It sees them as victims. It presupposes that they cannot or will not—if and as they choose—help themselves.

In place of these pseudo-democratic rationalizations of elite rule, movement toward a revitalization of democracy requires a different, more positive as well as more realistic, attitude toward mass participation, on a basis of political equality, in democratic rule. It requires an appreciation of such participation in politics as a good in itself. But how so?

The answer, I think, is not to invoke the inherent value of self-government, of autonomy. For in politics there are, after all, going to be winners and losers. The losers do not govern themselves in the same way the winners do. They are governed, instead, by the winners, at least for a time, to a degree and in some respects. The argument from self-government is, as we know, too easily turned by losers in the democratic arena into yet another claim for vindication—and, in the end, a claim for the government of everyone—by an elite of paternalistic protectors.

The answer, rather, lies in an old idea of personal and public hygiene. The idea is that active engagement in political life—win or lose—is good for you and for your community. It is good in the same way that an experience of vitality—regularly summoning and expressing and disciplining your energy (successfully or not) toward a chosen end—is good for you. In an old-fashioned sense, it is good for your "constitution." It is an important way in which you constitute yourself. As participants in the mid-century civil rights movement understood (and as some "civil rights leaders" of the *fin de siècle* seem to have forgotten) political self-help is an indispensable (though not, of course, the exclusive) route to an achievement of respect as well as self-respect.

To be sure, politics can be boring, perverse, even depressing. But physical exercise, too, is often painful. And in a regime of competition among political—if not (yet) social and economic—equals, the gain resulting from the pain is likely all the greater.

Should it be surprising that the prescription for a revitalization of democracy is a promise of revitalization *through* democracy?

The Apex of Political Equality: One Person, One Vote

No one can say, nowadays, that cultural and political elites are uninterested in political equality. In fact, one huge sector of the establishment—the one that nods when it reads editorials in *The New York Times*—talks about no topic more passionately than it does about this one. The focus of its concern, however, is skewed.

The focus is, of course, on equality in the realm of political campaign speech. Indeed, campaign finance reform has surpassed even "minority" rights as *the* cause of the establishment sector I have in mind. But while I support many reform proposals—public financing of campaigns, free television time for candidates, an abolition of "soft money"—I believe we all should be skeptical of claims that such reform would go far toward a goal of political equality.

There is, first, the problem of political advertising "independent" of official campaign organizations. If (as I am convinced) the Supreme Court will never allow a closing of this "loophole"—if wealthy people remain free to spend as much as they want "independently" of the candidate they promote—then it is fatuous to suppose that other reforms will produce anything like political equality in campaign speech. If, on the other hand, "independent" expenditures are somehow shut down—so that the political marketplace is left exclusively to limited spending by campaign organizations—the result would be political *in*equality of another kind. For, then, electoral discourse would be controlled by an even *more* concentrated group: the *coterie* of official campaign managers. Establishment advocates of campaign finance reform tend not to see this as a problem. For their goal is orderly equality among officials of campaign organizations—not among citizens. Nevertheless, as a practical matter, the issue is whether campaign advertising will be dominated by a larger, more fluid and chaotic elite—or a smaller, more tightly organized one, as many reform advocates prefer.

Second, there is the matter of the "free press" exception for media corporations. Plainly, the Court would not permit a limitation (much less a suppression) of speech about candidates by the owners and managers of print and electronic media. They are imagined as "independent" by definition. Indeed, many establishment advocates of campaign finance reform seem surprised that rich people who own newspapers might be regarded as rich people. Their horror at a mixing of "money and politics" tends to disappear abruptly when the money belongs to the owners of *The New York Times*. Nonetheless, so long as the wealthy are free to buy— and then, bluntly or subtly, to support candidates through—such media, participation in campaign debate before a mass audience will be anything but equal.

The problem with focusing our concern about political equality on campaign finance reform is not just the barrier posed by the Supreme Court. Nor is it just that reformers find themselves aspiring to little more than a rearrangement of the elite domination of campaign discourse. There are two deeper problems: On one hand, anything like real equality of *effective* participation in political debate is a chimera. Given the protean nature of "speech," the most that can be imagined (if not hoped for) is a very, very rough equality of opportunity. On the other hand, the assumption underlying the focus on the financing of political advertising is typically an assumption of political inequality—that the mass of ordinary people are passive and rather incompetent consumers (rather than actors), easily duped or swayed (rather than appropriately persuaded) by competing waves of thirty-second spots. If we want to vindicate political equality—as we should if we want to revitalize democracy—we ought to focus, instead, on something that does not, from the very outset, tend to compromise or contradict our goal.

We should focus on the vote. Taking the vote, rather than speech, as the key resource for participation in democratic politics—seeking to promote its use and the effect of using it—is the best way to take political equality seriously. For a focus on voting enables us to begin with a standard of equality that is both strong and established in law: one person, one vote. What's more, equal participation in voting is a practical goal. Not everyone can speak at once or as effectively as everyone else. But everyone can vote at once. And every vote counts as much as every other. Most important, the aspiration to enhance the value of the vote is grounded in a respect for ordinary people—as political actors, indeed as rulers—that is unambiguous.

Strangely, the vote seems now to be out of favor. Across the conventional political spectrum, many denigrate the value of voting and the one person, one vote standard. Some claim voting is irrational. Others purvey a narcissistic notion of "deliberative" democracy to eclipse what they imagine as the tawdry marking of a ballot. Still others claim that "communities"—rather than shifting collections or coalitions of individuals—should somehow express themselves in politics. On the surface, what unites them all is a tendency to idealize democracy and, so, to find its reality disappointing. But what accounts for this idealizing tendency? It is, I think, fear—fear of losing and of trying to win, fear of ordinary people and of their own ordinariness. To them, I would say: Get over it. Get into voting. It will be good for you. And for others as well.

Rock the Vote

How, then, might democracy be revitalized by promoting the use and effect of the vote? The central scandal of American democracy, from my populist point of view, is that most people do not cast a ballot in most elections. To promote use of the vote, the obvious strategy is to promote its effect. If something really significant seems to be at stake, people are more likely to take part. Even if no one believes her own vote will make the difference, she will see value—as have so many, from soldiers to protestors—in doing her part. For the moment, all I can do is gesture toward a few ways of enhancing the effect—and so the value, and so the use—of the vote. With respect to each, I want to encourage not only law reform, but also political action.

First of all, in candidate elections the voters must be presented with a real contest. In 2000, only about 35 seats in the U.S. House of Representatives are said to be in play. In a great many districts, the incumbent faces no (or only nominal) opposition. In other districts—and in many other elections up to and including presidential elections—there frequently seems not much more than a dime's (or perhaps a dollar's) worth of difference between the candidates. Hardly a motivation to cast a ballot.

For this condition, the legal remedy need not go so far as instituting systems of proportional representation. (Such systems tend to funnel power to party elites and, so, should be rejected by populists.) But barriers to entry—from ballot qualification requirements to exclusions from debates—facing "minor" party candidates surely must be lowered. Once a number of "minor" parties gain a foothold, run-off elections should be held. In the run-offs, the two highest vote-getters would be moved to address issues of concern to the others while, at the same time, the principle of popular majority rule would be vindicated. At the same time, the system for drawing legislative districts needs to be transformed. Districting should be taken from the hands of incumbent-friendly politicians and transferred to incumbent-unfriendly commissions. The commissions should be given one overriding instruction: draw and re-draw district lines so as to promote hotly contested elections in as many as possible.

In support of such legal remedies, a political one may now be underway. For the bulk of "alienated" non-voters may now be so huge as to have reached a critical mass. Politicians are more and more likely to take the opportunity to offer the "something different" these non-voters seem to want. In the last decade, candidates ranging from Ross Perot to Jesse Ventura to John McCain to Ralph Nader have done just that and, so, have begun to shake up political business-as-usual. The lesson for democratic populists is: When in doubt, support a maverick.

Second, the suffocating smugness of officialdom must be dispelled. In the last few decades, this pathological condition has become acute. Whether they be elected officials pompously touting "Burkean" notions of representation or civil servants claiming indispensable experience and expertise or judges relying on imagined wisdom and independence, these self-important middlemen—ensconced between voters and lawmaking—now are an incubus, cabining and repressing the political energy essential to popular sovereignty at the ballot box.

The primary legal remedy should be term limits. With respect to elected officials, term limits are an important supplement to the promotion of contested elections. But with respect to unelected officials, they are even more vital. If civil servants and judges (judges!) were limited to no more than fifteen years in office, government in all its nooks and crannies would, to a significant degree, be cracked open to the influence of the voters in periodic elections.

The political remedy, in this case, is largely attitudinal. We must stop acting as the enablers of the inflated arrogance of officialdom. For too long, we have treated officials with exaggerated respect. Now, it is time to start treating them—as they were treated in the early decades of our history—with a somewhat exaggerated disrespect. As reformers of bygone days knew well, regularly exposing the misdeeds, the incompetence, the hypocrisy of officials is not cynicism or nihilism; it is realism, the tonic of democratic lawmaking. (And that goes for lazy Justices and lying Presidents.)

The third and most important way of enhancing the effect, and so the use, of the vote is to eliminate the middlemen entirely. I am referring, of course, to direct democracy, lawmaking by initiative and referendum. What is at stake at the ballot box is, there, about as clear and immediate as can be. Popular support for direct democratic lawmaking, in states that allow it, is strong and consistent. So, however, is elite opposition to it. Today, direct democracy is at a turning point.

The pressing legal challenge, right now, is to resist growing efforts to hem in and hobble the initiative and referendum. That will involve challenges to new infringements on the right to petition, new ballot qualification requirements, and new "interpretations" of arcane rules like the "single subject" standard. Eventually, it is likely also to involve defense against federal constitutional arguments, particularly the claim that direct democracy violates the "republican form of government" clause. (In the 1950s and 1960s, it was exclusively conservatives who insisted that "America is a republic, not a democracy." Now, it is mostly progressives.) While turning back these anti-democratic thrusts, the time is ripe to go on the offensive as well—mending (rather than ending) processes by which proposals for popular lawmaking are drafted and summarized, then extending the initiative and referendum to all fifty states and even experimenting (at first) with "advisory" or "instructive" initiatives and referenda at the federal level.

Politically, beyond exposing elitist assumptions behind the wave of assault on direct democracy, I have one main suggestion: If there is an initiative or referendum proposal that you don't like, oppose it actively. And if it is passed, don't throw up your hands and go to the courts or the newspapers to pontificate about "republican" government. Instead, launch your own initiative campaign to repeal the popularly made law you don't like or to enact one you do like.

My bottom line is this: Democracy will be revitalized when more and more and then more of us give it a try.

DISCUSSION QUESTIONS

1. Do you agree with Parker's argument that increased mass participation is, by definition, a good thing? Is it "elitist" to disagree with him?

2. Is Parker correct in arguing that third parties, term limits, referenda, and increased competitiveness in elections would spur more participation? What positive, and negative, consequences might arise under his proposals?

3. What might the Framers be likely to say about Parker's ideas? Does it matter?

53

"The Unpolitical Animal: How Political Science Understands Voters"

Louis Menand

How well do Americans measure up to the ideal of highly informed, engaged, attentive, involved citizens? V. O. Key argued that Americans, on the whole, do reasonably well in making sound collective judgments. Writing around the same time as Key, another political scientist, Philip Converse, reached a gloomier conclusion. Most Americans couldn't be "ideal" citizens because most had minimal and inconsistent political belief systems. To a large part, he concluded, Americans had a lot of top-of-the-head opinions that had no strong connection to a set of principles. Louis Menand revisits the question addressed by V. O. Key: do elections represent the will of the people? Menand reviews Converse's conclusions and then discusses three theories that attempt to make some sense of Americans' failure to behave as ideal citizens. One theory declares that elections are more or less random events in which a large bloc of voters responds to "slogans, misinformation, 'fire alarms' (sensational news), 'October surprises' (last-minute sensational news), random personal associations, and 'gotchas.'" Another theory posits that voter decisions are guided not simply by random events and information, but by elite opinion. Elites do understand the issues and work within ideological frameworks and they find ways to pitch ideas to voters so they gain a governing majority. Elections are thus primarily about the interests and beliefs of rival elite factions. The third theory in part rescues the voter from these unflattering portraits. Here, voters use information shortcuts, especially but not only political party labels, to render verdicts that are substantively meaningful. "People use shortcuts—the social-scientific term is 'heuristics'—to reach judgments about political candidates, and, on the whole, these shortcuts are as good as the long and winding road of reading party platforms, listening to candidate debates, and all the other elements of civic duty." Menand concludes that voter decisions may be based on shortcuts that make sense to them—like which candidate is more optimistic—rather than the weighing and balancing of principles and policy positions that ideologues would prefer.

In every Presidential-election year, there are news stories about undecided voters, people who say that they are perplexed about which candidate's positions make the most sense. They tell reporters things like

"I'd like to know more about Bush's plan for education," or "I'm worried that Kerry's ideas about Social Security don't add up." They say that they are thinking about issues like "trust," and whether the candidate cares about people like them. To voters who identify strongly with a political party, the undecided voter is almost an alien life form. For them, a vote for Bush is a vote for a whole philosophy of governance and a vote for Kerry is a vote for a distinctly different philosophy. The difference is obvious to them, and they don't understand how others can't see it, or can decide whom to vote for on the basis of a candidate's personal traits or whether his or her position on a particular issue "makes sense." To an undecided voter, on the other hand, the person who always votes for the Democrat or the Republican, no matter what, must seem like a dangerous fanatic. Which voter is behaving more rationally and responsibly?

If you look to the political professionals, the people whose job it is to know what makes the fish bite, it is clear that, in their view, political philosophy is not the fattest worm. *Winning Elections: Political Campaign Management, Strategy & Tactics . . .* is a collection of articles drawn from the pages of *Campaigns & Elections: The Magazine for People in Politics.* The advice [of] the political professionals is: Don't assume that your candidate's positions are going to make the difference. "In a competitive political climate," as one article explains, "informed citizens may vote for a candidate based on issues. However, uninformed or undecided voters will often choose the candidate whose name and packaging are most memorable. To make sure your candidate has that 'top-of-mind' voter awareness, a powerful logo is the best place to start." You want to present your candidate in language that voters will understand. They understand colors. "Blue is a positive color for men, signaling authority and control," another article advises. "But it's a negative color for women, who perceive it as distant, cold and aloof. Red is a warm, sentimental color for women—and a sign of danger or anger to men. If you use the wrong colors to the wrong audience, you're sending a mixed message."

It can't be the case, though, that electoral outcomes turn on things like the color of the buttons. Can it? When citizens stand in the privacy of the booth and contemplate the list of those who bid to serve, do they really think, That's the guy with the red logo. A lot of anger there. I'll take my chances with the other one? In Civics 101, the model voter is a citizen vested with the ability to understand the consequences of his or her choice; when these individual rational choices are added up, we know the will of the people. How accurate is this picture?

Skepticism about the competence of the masses to govern themselves is as old as mass self-government. Even so, when that competence began to be measured statistically, around the end of the Second World War, the numbers startled almost everyone. The data were interpreted most powerfully by the political scientist Philip Converse, in an article on "The

Nature of Belief Systems in Mass Publics," published in 1964. Forty years later, Converse's conclusions are still the bones at which the science of voting behavior picks.

Converse claimed that only around ten per cent of the public has what can be called, even generously, a political belief system. He named these people "ideologues," by which he meant not that they are fanatics but that they have a reasonable grasp of "what goes with what"—of how a set of opinions adds up to a coherent political philosophy. Non-ideologues may use terms like "liberal" and "conservative," but Converse thought that they basically don't know what they're talking about, and that their beliefs are characterized by what he termed a lack of "constraint": they can't see how one opinion (that taxes should be lower, for example) logically ought to rule out other opinions (such as the belief that there should be more government programs). About forty-two per cent of voters, according to Converse's interpretation of surveys of the 1956 electorate, vote on the basis not of ideology but of perceived self-interest. The rest form political preferences either from their sense of whether times are good or bad (about twenty-five per cent) or from factors that have no discernible "issue content" whatever. Converse put twenty-two per cent of the electorate in this last category. In other words, about twice as many people have no political views as have a coherent political belief system.

Just because someone's opinions don't square with what a political scientist recognizes as a political ideology doesn't mean that those opinions aren't coherent by the lights of some more personal system of beliefs. But Converse found reason to doubt this possibility. When pollsters ask people for their opinion about an issue, people generally feel obliged to have one. Their answer is duly recorded, and it becomes a datum in a report on "public opinion." But, after analyzing the results of surveys conducted over time, in which people tended to give different and randomly inconsistent answers to the same questions, Converse concluded that "very substantial portions of the public" hold opinions that are essentially meaningless—off-the-top-of-the-head responses to questions they have never thought about, derived from no underlying set of principles. These people might as well base their political choices on the weather. And, in fact, many of them do.

Findings about the influence of the weather on voter behavior are among the many surveys and studies that confirm Converse's sense of the inattention of the American electorate. In election years from 1952 to 2000, when people were asked whether they cared who won the Presidential election, between twenty-two and forty-four per cent answered "don't care" or "don't know." In 2000, eighteen per cent said that they decided which Presidential candidate to vote for only in the last two weeks of the campaign; five per cent, enough to swing most elections, decided the day they voted.

Seventy per cent of Americans cannot name their senators or their congressman. Forty-nine per cent believe that the President has the power to suspend the Constitution. Only about thirty per cent name an issue when they explain why they voted the way they did, and only a fifth hold consistent opinions on issues over time. Rephrasing poll questions reveals that many people don't understand the issues that they have just offered an opinion on. According to polls conducted in 1987 and 1989, for example, between twenty and twenty-five per cent of the public thinks that too little is being spent on welfare, and between sixty-three and sixty-five per cent feels that too little is being spent on assistance to the poor. And voters apparently do punish politicians for acts of God. In a paper written in 2004, the Princeton political scientists Christopher Achen and Larry Bartels estimate that "2.8 million people voted against Al Gore in 2000 because their states were too dry or too wet" as a consequence of that year's weather patterns. Achen and Bartels think that these voters cost Gore seven states, any one of which would have given him the election.

All political systems make their claim to legitimacy by some theory, whether it's the divine right of kings or the iron law of history. Divine rights and iron laws are not subject to empirical confirmation, which is one reason that democracy's claims have always seemed superior. What polls and surveys suggest, though, is that the belief that elections express the true preferences of the people may be nearly as imaginary. When you move downward through what Converse called the public's "belief strata," candidates are quickly separated from ideology and issues, and they become attached, in voters' minds, to idiosyncratic clusters of ideas and attitudes. The most widely known fact about George H. W. Bush in the 1992 election was that he hated broccoli. Eighty-six per cent of likely voters in that election knew that the Bushes' dog's name was Millie; only fifteen per cent knew that Bush and Clinton both favored the death penalty. It's not that people know nothing. It's just that politics is not what they know.

In the face of this evidence, three theories have arisen. The first is that electoral outcomes, as far as "the will of the people" is concerned, are essentially arbitrary. The fraction of the electorate that responds to substantive political arguments is hugely outweighed by the fraction that responds to slogans, misinformation, "fire alarms" (sensational news), "October surprises" (last-minute sensational news), random personal associations, and "gotchas." Even when people think that they are thinking in political terms, even when they believe that they are analyzing candidates on the basis of their positions on issues, they are usually operating behind a veil of political ignorance. They simply don't understand, as a practical matter, what it means to be "fiscally conservative," or to have "faith in the private sector," or to pursue an "interventionist foreign policy." They can't hook up positions with policies. From the point of view of democratic theory, American political history is just a random walk through a series of electoral options. Some years, things turn up red; some years, they turn up blue.

A second theory is that although people may not be working with a full deck of information and beliefs, their preferences are dictated by something, and that something is elite opinion. Political campaigns, on this theory, are essentially struggles among the elite, the fraction of a fraction of voters who have the knowledge and the ideological chops to understand the substantive differences between the candidates and to argue their policy implications. These voters communicate their preferences to the rest of the electorate by various cues, low-content phrases and images (warm colors, for instance) to which voters can relate, and these cues determine the outcome of the race. Democracies are really oligarchies with a populist face.

The third theory of democratic politics is the theory that the cues to which most voters respond are, in fact, adequate bases on which to form political preferences. People use shortcuts—the social-scientific term is "heuristics"—to reach judgments about political candidates, and, on the whole, these shortcuts are as good as the long and winding road of reading party platforms, listening to candidate debates, and all the other elements of civic duty. Voters use what Samuel Popkin, one of the proponents of this third theory, calls "low-information rationality"—in other words, gut reasoning—to reach political decisions; and this intuitive form of judgment proves a good enough substitute for its high-information counterpart in reflecting what people want.

An analogy (though one that Popkin is careful to dissociate himself from) would be to buying an expensive item like a house or a stereo system. A tiny fraction of consumers has the knowledge to discriminate among the entire range of available stereo components, and to make an informed choice based on assessments of cost and performance. Most of us rely on the advice of two or three friends who have recently made serious stereo-system purchases, possibly some online screen shopping, and the pitch of the salesman at J&R Music World. We eyeball the product, associate idiosyncratically with the brand name, and choose from the gut. When we ask "experts" for their wisdom, mostly we are hoping for an "objective" ratification of our instinctive desire to buy the coolest-looking stuff. Usually, we're O.K. Our tacit calculation is that the marginal utility of more research is smaller than the benefit of immediate ownership.

On the theory of heuristics, it's roughly the same with candidates: voters don't have the time or the inclination to assess them in depth, so they rely on the advice of experts—television commentators, political activists, Uncle Charlie—combined with their own hunches, to reach a decision. Usually (they feel), they're O.K. If they had spent the time needed for a top-to-toe vetting, they would probably not have chosen differently. Some voters might get it wrong in one direction, choosing the liberal candidate when they in fact preferred a conservative one, but their error is cancelled out by the voters who mistakenly choose the conservative. The will of the people may not be terribly articulate, but it comes out in the wash.

This theory is the most attractive of the three, since it does the most to salvage democratic values from the electoral wreckage Converse described. It gives the mass of voters credit for their decisions by suggesting not only that they can interpret the cues given by the campaigns and the elite opinion-makers but that the other heuristics they use—the candidate seems likable, times are not as good as they were—are actually defensible replacements for informed, logical reasoning. Popkin begins his well-regarded book on the subject, *The Reasoning Voter*, with an example from Gerald Ford's primary campaign against Ronald Reagan in 1976. Visiting a Mexican-American community in Texas, Ford (never a gaffe-free politician) made the mistake of trying to eat a tamale with the corn husk, in which it is traditionally served, still on it. This ethnic misprision made the papers, and when he was asked, after losing to Jimmy Carter in the general election, what the lesson of his defeat was, Ford answered, "Always shuck your tamales." Popkin argues that although familiarity with Mexican-American cuisine is not a prerequisite for favoring policies friendly to Mexican-Americans, Mexican-Americans were justified in concluding that a man who did not know how to eat a tamale was not a man predisposed to put their needs high on his list. The reasoning is illogical: Ford was not running for chef, and it was possible to extrapolate, from his positions, the real difference it would make for Mexican-Americans if he were President rather than Reagan or Carter. But Mexican-Americans, and their sympathizers, felt "in their gut" that Ford was not their man, and that was enough.

The principal shortcut that people use in deciding which candidates to vote for is, of course, the political party. The party is the ultimate Uncle Charlie in American politics. Even elite voters use it when they are confronted, in the voting booth, with candidates whose names they have never seen before. There is nothing in the Constitution requiring candidates to be listed on the ballot with their party affiliations, and, if you think about it, the custom of doing so is vaguely undemocratic. It makes elections a monopoly of the major parties, by giving their candidates an enormous advantage—the advantage of an endorsement right there on the ballot—over everyone else who runs. It is easy to imagine a constitutional challenge to the practice of identifying candidates by party, but it is also easy to imagine how wild the effects would be if voters were confronted by a simple list of names with no identifying tags. Every election would be like an election for student-body president: pure name recognition.

Any time information is lacking or uncertain, a shortcut is generally better than nothing. But the shortcut itself is not a faster way of doing the math; it's a way of skipping the math altogether. My hunch that the coolest-looking stereo component is the best value simply does not reflect an intuitive grasp of electronics. My interest in a stereo is best served if I choose the finest sound for the money, as my interest in an election is best served if I choose the candidate whose policies are most likely to benefit me or the people I care about. But almost no one calculates in so abstract a fashion. Even voters who supported Michael Dukakis in 1988 agreed that he looked ridiculous wearing a weird helmet when he went for a ride in a tank, and a lot of those people felt that, taken together with other evidence of his manner and style of self-expression, the image was not irrelevant to the substance of his campaign. George H. W. Bush underwent a similar moment in 1992, when he was caught showing astonishment at the existence of scanners at supermarket checkout counters. Ideologues opposed to Bush were pleased to propose this as what psychologists call a "fast and frugal" means of assessing the likely effects of his economic policies.

When political scientists interpret these seat-of-the-pants responses as signs that voters are choosing rationally, and that representative government therefore really does reflect the will of the people, they are, in effect, making a heuristic of heuristics. They are not doing the math. Doing the math would mean demonstrating that the voters' intuitive judgments are roughly what they would get if they analyzed the likely effects of candidates' policies, and this is a difficult calculation to perform. One shortcut that voters take, and that generally receives approval from the elite, is pocketbook voting. If they are feeling flush, they vote for the incumbent; if they are feeling strapped, they vote for a change. But, as Larry Bartels, the co-author of the paper on Gore and the weather, has pointed out, pocketbook voting would be rational only if it could be shown that replacing the incumbent did lead, on average, to better economic times. Without such a demonstration, a vote based on the condition of one's pocketbook is no more rational than a vote based on the condition of one's lawn. It's a hunch.

Bartels has also found that when people do focus on specific policies they are often unable to distinguish their own interests. His work, which he summed up in a recent article for *The American Prospect*, concerned public opinion about the estate tax. When people are asked whether they favor Bush's policy of repealing the estate tax, two-thirds say yes—even though the estate tax affects only the wealthiest one or two per cent of the population. Ninety-eight per cent of Americans do not leave estates large enough for the tax to kick in. But people have some notion—Bartels refers to it as "unenlightened self-interest"—that they will be better off if the tax is repealed. What is most remarkable about this opinion is that it is unconstrained by other beliefs. Repeal is supported by sixty-six per cent of people who believe that the income gap between the richest and the poorest Americans has increased in recent decades, and that this is a bad thing. And it's supported by sixty-eight per cent of people who say that the rich pay too little in taxes. Most Americans simply do not make a connection between tax policy and the overall economic condition of the country. Whatever heuristic they are using, it is definitely not doing the math for them. This helps make sense of the fact that the world's greatest democracy has an electorate that continually "chooses" to transfer more and more wealth to a smaller and smaller fraction of itself.

But who *ever* does the math? As Popkin points out, everybody uses heuristics, including the elite. Most of the debate among opinion-makers is conducted in shorthand, and even well-informed voters rely on endorsements and party affiliations to make their choices. The very essence of being an ideologue lies in trusting the label—liberal or conservative, Republican or Democrat. Those are "bundling" terms: they pull together a dozen positions on individual issues under a single handy rubric. They do the work of assessment for you.

It is widely assumed that the upcoming [2004] Presidential election will be decided by an electorate that is far more ideological than has historically been the case. Polls indicate much less volatility than usual, supporting the view that the public is divided into starkly antagonistic camps—the "red state-blue state" paradigm. If this is so, it suggests that we have at last moved past Converse's picture of an electoral iceberg, in which ninety per cent of the population is politically underwater. But Morris Fiorina, a political scientist at Stanford, thinks that it is not so, and that the polarized electorate is a product of elite opinion. "The simple truth is that there is no culture war in the United States—no battle for the soul of America rages, at least none that most Americans are aware of," he says in his short book *Culture War? The Myth of a Polarized America*. . . . Public-opinion polls, he argues, show that on most hot-button issues voters in so-called red states do not differ significantly from voters in so-called blue states. Most people identify themselves as moderates, and their responses to survey questions seem to substantiate this self-description. What has become polarized, Fiorina argues, is the elite. The chatter—among political activists, commentators, lobbyists, movie stars, and so on—has become highly ideological. It's a non-stop *Crossfire*, and this means that the candidates themselves come wrapped in more extreme ideological coloring. But Fiorina points out that the ideological position of a candidate is not identical to the position of the people who vote for him or her. He suggests that people generally vote for the candidate whose views strike them as closest to their own, and "closest" is a relative term. With any two candidates, no matter how far out, one will always be "closer" than the other.

Of course, if Converse is correct, and most voters really don't have meaningful political beliefs, even ideological "closeness" is an artifact of survey anxiety, of people's felt need, when they are asked for an opinion, to have one. This absence of "real opinions" is not from lack of brains; it's from lack of interest. "The typical citizen drops down to a lower level of mental performance as soon as he enters the political field," the economic theorist Joseph Schumpeter wrote, in 1942. "He argues and analyzes in a way which he would readily recognize as infantile within the sphere of his real interests. He becomes a primitive again. His thinking is associative and affective." And Fiorina quotes a passage from the political scientist Robert Putnam: "Most men are not political animals. The world of public affairs is not their world. It is alien to them—possibly benevolent, more probably threatening, but nearly always alien. Most men are not interested in politics. Most do not participate in politics."

Man may not be a political animal, but he is certainly a social animal. Voters do respond to the cues of commentators and campaigners, but only when they can match those cues up with the buzz of their own social group. Individual voters are not rational calculators of self-interest (nobody truly is), and may not be very consistent users of heuristic shortcuts, either. But they are not just random particles bouncing off the walls of the voting booth. Voters go into the booth carrying the imprint of the hopes and fears, the prejudices and assumptions of their family, their friends, and their neighbors. For most people, voting may be more meaningful and more understandable as a social act than as a political act.

That it is hard to persuade some people with ideological arguments does not mean that those people cannot be persuaded, but the things that help to convince them are likely to make ideologues sick—things like which candidate is more optimistic. For many liberals, it may have been dismaying to listen to John Kerry and John Edwards, in their speeches at the Democratic National Convention, utter impassioned bromides about how "the sun is rising" and "our best days are still to come." But that is what a very large number of voters want to hear. If they believe it, then Kerry and Edwards will get their votes. The ideas won't matter, and neither will the color of the buttons.

DISCUSSION QUESTIONS

1. What information shortcuts do you think would be reasonable to use when making voting decisions?

2. Menand is concerned that voters' heuristics might not be reliable if voters actually "did the math." What heuristics do you think might be particularly unreliable guides to voting choices?

3. What, if any, risks are posed to the American political system if voters base their decisions on information shortcuts? Which of the three theories discussed by Menand would be the most troubling for democracy, in your view?

DEBATING THE ISSUES: VOTER IDENTIFICATION

The last three national elections have raised many concerns about the voting system and the standards for administering elections in the United States. Charges of impropriety in voting procedures and vote counting as well as complaints that certain voting technologies were systematically likely to produce more voter error or not record voter choices were legion. Massive voter mobilization campaigns on both the political left and right registered millions of new voters. Huge sums were poured into campaign advertising, further stoking the interest of these newly registered voters and the public in general. In such a charged political environment, concerns about the integrity of the process took on a particular urgency. One issue on which battle lines are frequently drawn is voter identification, especially requiring voters to show a photo ID.

One argument, presented here by Chandler Davidson, contends that these complaints about fraud are part of a strategy to discourage or scare away potential voters. Voter ID laws are most likely to restrict turnout among minorities and the elderly, and the threat of fraud is minimal. To Davidson, voter ID laws are intended to promote the fortunes of the Republican party and are little different from other attempts to suppress voter turnout, such as the poll tax.

The opposing argument, presented here by Hans von Spakovsky, is that voter fraud is a reality. He points to voters registered in multiple locations, voting more than once, illegally registered, paid an inducement to vote, and to felons voting as symptomatic of the lack of control over the voting process. Spakovsky supports voter-ID laws and rejects the idea that they will systematically discriminate against minorities or other groups.

Edward Foley argues that conservatives and liberals both have valid points. Even if voting fraud is minimal, he writes, it is real and should be a concern, as conservatives argue. Similarly, liberals are right to be concerned that the cost of obtaining a photo ID might discourage some citizens from voting. Foley suggests the solution is to delink the photo ID from voting. Instead, potential voters would be able to get free digital photos from government offices if they do not have one. They would have to show this photo when they register to vote. When a voter arrives at the polls to vote, poll workers could pull up an electronic file of the photo and match it to the person standing in front of them. This solution, Foley argues, ensures that anyone who wants to register can, while also guaranteeing that the person voting at the polling place is the same person who is registered under that name.

54

"The Historical Context of Voter Photo-ID Laws"

Chandler Davidson

The issue before the U.S. Supreme Court in the *Crawford* case (*Crawford v. Marion County Election Bd.* 2008) was whether a law (Indiana Senate Enrolled Act No. 483) passed by the Indiana legislature requiring most voters to show a photo ID in order to cast a ballot violates the First and Fourteenth Amendments. Plaintiffs argued that it works an unfair hardship on many people who do not have the government-issued documents that count as a legitimate ID. They argued that the law, in effect, constitutes a poll tax, inasmuch as there are costs to obtain the right kind of photo ID, costs that unduly burden many eligible citizens wanting to exercise their right to vote.

Given the long history of legally sanctioned disfranchisement of large and disparate groups of citizens, from the founding of the Republic to the recent past, the case raised important questions to scholars of voting rights. Indeed, Indiana's new law brought to mind events during the half-century following the Civil War, when the language of "progressive reform" cloaked the disfranchisement of blacks and poor whites in the South—those most likely to vote for Republican or Populist candidates. Actually adopted for partisan and racially discriminatory purposes, these laws were often presented as high-minded attacks on fraud—efforts to "purify" the electorate that would only inconvenience "vote sellers" or the ignorant and "shiftless."

To be sure, unlike today, when proponents of voter identification must strain mightily to find the rarest examples of fraud, particularly in-person voter fraud at the polls, in the nineteenth century there was widespread and readily admitted fraud. However, this was often committed against African Americans and the Republican Party to which they then overwhelmingly adhered. Louisiana senator and former governor Samuel D. McEnery stated in 1898 that his state's 1882 election law "was intended to make it the duty of the governor to treat the law as a formality and count in the Democrats." A leader of the 1890 Mississippi constitutional convention admitted that "it is no secret that there has not been a full vote and a fair count in Mississippi since 1875," which was the last year until 1967 in which blacks voted at all freely in the state. Nonetheless, these same Democrats invoked the language of reform in calling for a wide range of restrictions on the suffrage: registration acts, poll taxes, literacy and property tests, "understanding" qualifications, and white primaries, among others.

Between 1889 and 1913, for example, nine states outside the South made the ability to read English a prerequisite for voting. Literacy tests were said to reduce the influence of immigrants or African Americans who supported "bosses" and "demagogues." Moreover, between 1890 and 1908, seven of the 11 ex-Confederate states adopted state constitutional amendments allowing only literate voters or those with a certain amount of property to vote. There were sometimes loopholes like "understanding" qualifications or "grandfather" clauses that allowed some whites to vote who could not meet literacy or property tests. Shortly after passage of these amendments, less than 10% of African Americans managed to register to vote in most states, and no more than 15% in any.

The poll tax was one of the most notorious disfranchising mechanisms of its day. The current debate over the Indiana photo-ID requirement—as well as similar laws in other states—has led to claims that they are a "modern-day poll tax." This implies that the new Indiana law, too, falls within the ignominious American tradition of disfranchising laws passed under the guise of "good government" reform.

Frederick Ogden, perhaps the foremost scholar of the poll tax, wrote in the 1950s: "While critics of legalized restrictions on Negro voting may find it hard to discover any high moral tone in such activities, these restrictions reflected a movement for purifying the electoral process in southern states." Ogden quotes the editor of the *San Antonio Express* writing in 1902: "By requiring a poll tax receipt, secured six months previous to an election, fraudulent elections can be prevented almost entirely."

Other essays in this symposium address the nature and extent of burdens imposed on various subsets of Indiana citizens by the photo-ID law, and I shall forgo discussing them. Suffice it to say that the most accessible photo-ID in Indiana consists either of the state's driver's license or a state-issued ID card. Obtaining one or the other has been shown to be a good deal more difficult for some people than it might seem at first glance. At least 43,000 persons of voting age in Indiana are estimated to have neither.

The demographic characteristics of persons lacking the requisite ID are suggested by a November 2006 telephone survey of 987 randomly selected voting-age American citizens by the independent Opinion Research Corporation conducted for the Brennan Center for Justice at NYU School of Law: 11% did not have valid government-issued photo ID, while 18% of citizens 65 years of age or older lacked it, as did 25% of African Americans. The latter two demographic groups, the elderly and African Americans, are more likely to self-identify as Democrats—African-Americans disproportionately so. Elderly African Americans, who are even more unlikely than members of their ethnic group in general to have a photo ID, would be strongly predisposed to vote Democratic. In close elections, the additional burdens placed on both the elderly and African Americans by the photo-ID law could help elect Republican candidates. There is no reason to believe this national pattern is much different from that in Indiana.

Nonetheless, it is often asserted that such barriers should not prevent a truly motivated citizen from voting. In a classic article by Kelley, Ayres, and Bowen attempting to measure determinants of voter turnout, the authors make the following observation:

> A frequent objection to such efforts [to get out the vote] is that voters not interested enough to vote are not apt to vote wisely and so should be left alone. This view recalls the statement of a New York voter regarding the adequacy of the facilities for registering in New York City in 1964: "I sure do want to vote against that man . . . but I don't think I hate him enough to stand on that line all day long." How much interest should a voter have to qualify him for voting? Enough to stand in line all day? For half a day? For two days? We cannot say, but those who think voting should be limited to the "interested" ought to be prepared to do so.

Their question, posed in terms of the burden of time alone, can also be posed with regard to money: particularly concerning the least well off, how large a monetary imposition should be placed on the right to vote before it becomes the functional equivalent of a poll tax? Regarding these twin burdens, two questions may be posed to help determine whether the Indiana photo-ID law should be interpreted according to the good-government language of its proponents: First, how will the application of the law help shape the Indiana electorate "to a size and composition deemed desirable by those in power," as Kelley, Ayres, and Bowen put it? In other words, to what extent is the law motivated by partisan efforts to disfranchise voters who are undesirable to Republicans and thus increase their chances of winning elections? Second, did supporters of the law demonstrate a significant degree of fraud of the kind the law was fashioned to prevent? Let us consider each question in turn.

While it is impossible to know the motives of those lawmakers who favored the photo-ID bill under consideration by the Indiana legislature in April 2005, we can ascertain whether it was passed by a partisan vote. Significantly, Indiana's photo-ID bill was one of at least 10 bills introduced by Republicans in state legislatures between 2005 and 2007 requiring voters to show a photo ID at the polls. Two of these states' bills were initially enjoined, and a second bill was introduced in one state. (Besides Indiana, the other states included Georgia, Florida, Missouri, Kansas, New Hampshire, Pennsylvania, Texas, and Wisconsin.) If the House and Senate votes for all 10 proposals are combined, *95.3%* of the 1,222 Republicans voting and *2.1%* of the 796 Democrats voting supported the bills. Moreover, in the five cases in which both houses passed a bill and a

Republican was governor, he signed it. In the three cases in which both houses passed a bill and a Democrat was governor, he vetoed it. (In two cases, only one house passed a bill.) The Indiana vote was part of this pattern, although even more extreme. In the vote on Senate Bill 483, 85 Republicans voted for it and none against; 62 Democrats voted against it and none in favor. The Republican governor signed the bill into law.

Did supporters of the law demonstrate that there is a significant degree of fraud of the kind the law was fashioned to prevent? The debate over the extent and kind of vote fraud that exists in the United States today has been widespread and acerbic at least since the 2000 presidential election, and it shows no signs of abating. There are numerous kinds of vote fraud, and distinctions among them—which are necessary to determine the most effective means of their prevention—are often lost in popular debate. As critics of the Indiana law have asserted, the photo-ID requirement was implemented to prevent one type of fraud: voter impersonation at the polls on Election Day. Among the many kinds it does not prevent is that involving mail-in ballots, which some believe to be more common than impersonation at the polls. What makes the statute particularly suspect in the case of Indiana is the fact that there has not been a single prosecution for in-person vote fraud in the history of the state—a fact that Richard Posner, judge on the U.S. Court of Appeals for the Seventh Circuit and author of that court's split decision favoring Indiana, attributed to lax law enforcement.

Recent events in Texas are relevant in this regard. In both 2005 and 2007 Republicans in the legislature introduced photo-ID bills less restrictive than that in Indiana. In 2007, according to a newspaper reporter: "Republicans like the voter ID bill because they believe it will weaken Democrats, but can argue that it is a reasonable requirement" because it would prevent vote fraud. Not all Republicans, however, shared the belief that it would curtail fraud. Royal Masset, former political director of the Texas Republican Party, was one. He told the reporter he agreed that among his fellow Republicans it was "an article of religious faith that voter fraud is causing us to lose elections." He was not convinced. He did believe, however, that requiring photo IDs could cause enough of a drop-off in legitimate Democratic voting to add 3% to the Republican vote.

In January 2006, after his party's first failure to pass a photo-ID bill, Greg Abbott, the Republican attorney general of Texas, announced a "training initiative to identify, prosecute [and] prevent voter fraud." This was the most ambitious and costly effort in recent Texas history—perhaps ever—by the state's government to attack the alleged problem. "Vote fraud has been an epidemic in Texas for years, but it hasn't been treated like one," Abbott said. "It's time for that to change." He promised that his newly created Special Investigations Unit (SIU) would "help police departments, sheriff's offices, and district and county attorneys successfully identify, investigate and prosecute various types of voter fraud offences."

Established with a $1.5 million grant from the governor's office, the SIU would have as one of its prime responsibilities investigating voter-fraud allegations, he said. Abbott targeted 44 counties containing 78% of registered voters in the state. According to the *Austin American-Statesman*, "Complaints originate from voting officials, district attorneys or citizens and are sent to the secretary of state or the attorney general. Each complaint is evaluated by a professional employee to determine whether the complaint is legitimate and warrants further investigation."

Such an initiative would seem to constitute a model of the aggressive, responsible, multi-level law-enforcement effort that Judge Posner seemed to believe had been lacking in Indiana. Moreover, given Republicans' desire to provide evidence of widespread voter fraud in order to justify new statutes criticized by Democrats and some media sources, one would expect Abbott to have conducted the effort with enthusiasm. What has been the result?

Texas is a large state, with thousands of elections occurring in a four-year period in its numerous governmental units. In 2006, there were 16.6 million persons of voting age, and of those, 13.1 million were registered to vote. An anti-immigration organization estimated that 1.7 million Texas inhabitants resided there illegally in 2007. Given these facts, one would expect an aggressive, centralized vote-fraud initiative by the state's highest law-enforcement officer to yield a sizable number of indictments during the more than 21 months of its existence if, in fact, vote fraud had reached "epidemic" proportions.

The data presented by Attorney General Abbot on his Web site told a different story. In the almost two years between the day the initiative was announced in late January 2006 and October 2007, 13 persons had either been indicted, found guilty, or sentenced for vote fraud, six on misdemeanor counts typically involving helping others with mail-in ballots. Of the 13, five were accused of having committed fraud before 2006, the year the initiative was announced, and the remaining eight in 2006. A total of 4.4 million Texans voted in the general elections for governor or U.S. senator that year, in addition to those who voted in primaries and local non-partisan elections. At that point, six of the 13 persons mentioned above had not yet been found guilty. This, then, is the extent of vote fraud in Texas that has been uncovered after the announcement and implementation of the $1.5 million vote-fraud initiative. Moreover, of the seven found guilty and the six remaining under indictment, *none of the types of fraud they had been charged with would have been prevented by the photo-ID requirement advocated by Republicans in the 2007 legislative session.* That is to say, none involved voter impersonation at the polls. Most either involved political officials who were charged with engaging in illegal efforts to affect the election outcome, or persons who helped elderly or disabled friends with their mail-in ballots, apparently unaware of a law passed in 2003 requiring them to sign the envelope containing the friend's ballot before mailing it.

These data do not appear to be anomalous. A survey of the director or deputy director of all 88 Ohio boards of election in June 2005 found that a total of only four votes cast in the state's general elections in 2002 and 2004 (in which over nine million votes were cast) were judged ineligible and thus likely constituted actual voter fraud. Interviews by *New York Times* reporters with election-law-enforcement officials and academic experts suggest that the pattern in Ohio is not anomalous. Professor Richard L. Hasen, an election law expert at Loyola Law School, summed up knowledgeable opinion about vote fraud to the reporters as follows: "what we see is isolated, small-scale activities that often have not shown any kind of criminal intent."

While it is possible, as Judge Posner implied in his Seventh Circuit decision, that aggressive vote-fraud enforcement in Indiana might uncover its existence in the state, the Texas investigation suggests otherwise, and the burden of proof rests on those who allege that vote fraud there is widespread and of the kind that is deterred by a photo-ID requirement. Until that burden is responsibly shouldered by state authorities, the question of whether the Indiana voter-ID law has accomplished its ostensible purpose must be answered in the negative. When this conclusion is placed alongside our earlier findings that the legislative vote for the law was strictly along partisan lines and that the people most likely to be disfranchised by it are Democratic voters—particularly African Americans—Indiana's law appears to fit comfortably within the long and unsavory history of those in positions of power disfranchising blacks and less-well-off whites for partisan gain. Moreover, Indiana's attempt to justify its new law with claims of voter fraud is as dubious as those that justified the now unconstitutional poll tax.

A great deal of progress has been made over the past 50 years in combating racial discrimination in politics, thanks in part to such epochal events as passage of the Twenty-Fourth Amendment and the Voting Rights Act. However, race, class, and partisanship continue to be inextricably intertwined in the United States, just as they were from the end of Reconstruction to the Civil Rights Era. The 2005 Indiana voter-ID law, if the above analysis is correct, is an excellent example of this fact.

55

"Requiring Identification by Voters"

Hans von Spakovsky

Testimony Before the Texas Senate
Delivered March 10, 2009

I appreciate the invitation to be here today to discuss the importance of states such as Texas requiring individuals to authenticate their identity at the polls through photo and other forms of identification.

By way of background, I have extensive experience in voting matters, including both the administration of elections and the enforcement of federal voting rights laws. Prior to becoming a Legal Scholar at the Heritage Foundation, I was a member for two years of the Federal Election Commission. I spent four years at the Department of Justice as a career lawyer, including as Counsel to the Assistant Attorney General for Civil Rights. I also spent five years in Atlanta, Georgia, on the Fulton County Board of Registration and Elections, which is responsible for administering elections in the largest county in Georgia, a county that is almost half African-American. I have published extensively on election and voting issues, including on the subject of voter ID.

Guaranteeing the integrity of elections requires having security throughout the entire election process, from voter registration to the casting of votes to the counting of ballots at the end of the day when the polls have closed. For example, jurisdictions that use paper ballots seal their ballot boxes when all of the ballots have been deposited, and election officials have step-by-step procedures for securing election ballots and other materials throughout the election process.

I doubt any of you think that it would be a good idea for a county to allow world wide Internet access to the computer it uses in its election headquarters to tabulate ballots and count votes—we are today a computer-literate generation and you understand that allowing that kind of outside access to the software used for counting votes would imperil the integrity of the election.

Requiring voters to authenticate their identity at the polling place is part and parcel of the same kind of security necessary to protect the integrity of elections. Every illegal vote steals the vote of a legitimate voter. Voter ID can prevent:

- impersonation fraud at the polls;
- voting under fictitious voter registrations;
- double voting by individuals registered in more than one state or locality; and
- voting by illegal aliens.

As the Commission on Federal Election Reform headed by President Jimmy Carter and Secretary of State James Baker said in 2005:

> The electoral system cannot inspire public confidence if no safeguards exist to deter or detect fraud or to confirm the identity of voters. Photo identification cards currently are needed to board a plane, enter federal buildings, and cash a check. Voting is equally important.

Voter fraud does exist, and criminal penalties imposed after the fact are an insufficient deterrent to protect against it. In the Supreme Court's voter ID case decided last year, the Court said that despite such criminal penalties:

> It remains true, however, that flagrant examples of such fraud in other parts of the country have been documented throughout this Nation's history by respected historians and journalists, that occasional examples have surfaced in recent years, and that [they] demonstrate that not only is the risk of voter fraud real but that it could affect the outcome of a close election.

The relative rarity of voter fraud prosecutions for impersonation fraud at the polls, as the Seventh Circuit Court of Appeals pointed out in the Indiana case, can be explained in part because the fraud cannot be detected without the tools—a voter ID—available to detect it. However, as I pointed out in a paper published by the Heritage Foundation last year, a grand jury in New York released a report in the mid-1980's detailing a widespread voter fraud conspiracy involving impersonation fraud at the polls that operated successfully for 14 years in Brooklyn without detection. That fraud resulted in thousands of fraudulent votes being cast in state and congressional elections and involved not only impersonation of legitimate voters at the polls, but voting under fictitious names that had been successfully registered without detection by local election officials. This fraud could have been easily stopped and detected if New York had required voters to authenticate their identity at the polls. According to the grand jury, the advent of mail-in registration was also a key factor in perpetrating the fraud. In recent elections, thousands of fraudulent voter registration forms have been detected by election officials. But given the minimal to nonexistent screening efforts engaged in by most election jurisdictions, there is no way to know how many others slipped through. In states without identification requirements, election officials have no way to prevent bogus votes from being cast by unscrupulous individuals based on fictitious voter registrations.

The problem of possible double voting by someone who is registered in two states is illustrated by one of the Indiana voters who was high-lighted by the League of Women Voters in their amicus brief before the Supreme Court in the Indiana case. After an Indiana newspaper inter-viewed her, it turned out that the problems she encountered voting in Indiana stemmed from her trying to use a Florida driver's license to vote in Indiana. Not only did she have a Florida driver's license, but she was also registered to vote in Florida where she owned a second home. In fact, she had claimed residency in Florida by claiming a home-stead exemption on her property taxes, which as you know is normally only available to residents. So the Indiana law worked perfectly as in-tended to prevent someone who could have illegally voted twice without detection.

I don't want to single out Texas, but just like Indiana, New York, and Illinois, Texas has a long and unfortunate history of voter fraud. In the late 1800's, for example, Harrison County was so infamous for its mas-sive election fraud that the phrase "Harrison County Methods" became synonymous with election fraud. From Ballot Box 13 in Lyndon Johnson's 1948 Senate race, to recent reports of voting by illegal aliens in Bexar County, Texas does have individuals who are willing to risk criminal prosecution in order to win elections. I do not claim that there is massive voter fraud in Texas or anywhere else. In fact, as a former election official, I think we do a good job overall in administering our elections. But the potential for abuse exists, and there are many close elections that could turn on a very small number of votes. There are enough incidents of voter fraud to make it very clear that we must take the steps necessary to make it hard to commit. Requiring voter ID is just one such common sense step.

Not only does voter ID help prevent fraudulent voting, but where it has been implemented, it has not reduced turnout. There is no evidence that voter ID decreases the turnout of voters or has a disparate impact on minority voters, the poor, or the elderly—the overwhelming majority of Americans have photo ID or can easily obtain one.

Numerous studies have borne this out. A study by a University of Mis-souri professor of turnout in Indiana showed that turnout actually in-creased by about two percentage points overall in Indiana after the voter ID law went into effect. There was no evidence that counties with higher percentages of minority, poor, elderly or less-educated populations suf-fered any reduction in voter turnout. In fact, "the only consistent and statistically significant impact of photo ID in Indiana is to increase voter turnout in counties with a greater percentage of Democrats relative to other counties."

The Heritage Foundation released a study in September of 2007 that analyzed 2004 election turnout data for all states. It found that voter ID laws do not reduce the turnout of voters, including African-Americans and Hispanics—such voters were just as likely to vote in states with ID as in states where just their name was asked at the polling place.

A study by professors at the Universities of Delaware and Nebraska-Lincoln examined data from the 2000, 2002, 2004, and 2006 elections. At both the aggregate and individual levels, the study found that voter ID laws do not affect turnout including across racial/ethnic/socioeconomic lines. The study concluded that "concerns about voter identification laws affecting turnout are much ado about nothing."

In 2007 as part of the MIT/CalTech Voter Project, an MIT professor did an extensive national survey of 36,500 individuals about Election Day practices. The survey found:

• overwhelming support for photo ID requirements across ethnic and racial lines with "over 70% of Whites, Hispanics and Blacks support[ing] the requirement"; and
• Only 23 people out of the entire 36,500 person sample said that they were not allowed to vote because of voter ID, although the survey did not indicate whether they were even eligible to vote or used provisional ballots.

A similar study by John Lott in 2006 also found no effect on voter turnout, and in fact, found an indication that efforts to reduce voter fraud such as voter ID may have a positive impact on voter turnout. That is certainly true in a case study of voter fraud in Greene County, Alabama that I wrote about recently for the Heritage Foundation. In that county, voter turnout went up after several successful voter fraud prosecutions instilled new confidence in local voters in the integrity of the election process.

Recent election results in Georgia and Indiana also confirm that the suppositions that voter ID will hurt minority turnout are incorrect. Turnout in both states went up dramatically in 2008 in both the presidential preference primary and the general election.

In Georgia, there was record turnout in the 2008 presidential primary election—over 2 million voters, more than twice as much as in 2004 when the voter photo ID law was not in effect. The number of African-Americans voting in the 2008 primary also doubled from 2004. In fact, there were 100,000 more votes in the Democratic Primary than in the Republican Primary. And the number of individuals who had to vote with a provisional ballot because they had not gotten the free photo ID available from the state was less that 0.01%.

In the general election, Georgia, with one of the strictest voter ID laws in the nation, had the largest turnout in its history—more than 4 million voters. Democratic turnout was up an astonishing 6.1 percentage points from the 2004 election. Overall turnout in Georgia went up 6.7 percentage points, the second highest increase of any state in the country. The black share of the statewide vote increased from 25% in 2004 to 30% in 2008. By contrast, the Democratic turnout in the nearby state of Mississippi, also a state with a high percentage of black voters but without a voter ID requirement, increased by only 2.35 percentage points.

I should point out that the Georgia voter ID law was upheld in final orders issued by every state and federal court in Georgia that reviewed the law, including most recently by the Eleventh Circuit Court of Appeals. Just as in Texas, various organizations in Georgia made the specious claims that there were hundreds of thousands of Georgians without photo ID. Yet when the federal district court dismissed all of their claims, the court pointed out that after two years of litigation, none of the plaintiff organizations like the NAACP had been able to produce a single individual or member who did not have a photo ID or could not easily obtain one. The district court judge concluded that this "failure to identify those individuals is particularly acute in light of the Plaintiffs' contention that a large number of Georgia voters lack acceptable Photo ID . . . the fact that Plaintiffs, in spite of their efforts, have failed to uncover anyone who can attest to the fact that he/she will be prevented from voting provides significant support for a conclusion that the photo ID requirement does not unduly burden the right to vote."

In Indiana, which the Supreme Court said has the strictest voter ID law in the country, turnout in the Democratic presidential preference primary in 2008 quadrupled from the 2004 election when the photo ID law was not in effect—in fact, there were 862,000 more votes cast in the Democratic primary than the Republican primary. In the general election in November, the turnout of Democratic voters increased by 8.32 percentage points from 2004, the largest increase in Democratic turnout of any state in the nation. The neighboring state of Illinois, with no photo ID requirement and President Obama's home state, had an increase in Democratic turnout of only 4.4 percentage points—nearly half of Indiana's increase.

Just as in the federal case in Georgia, the federal court in Indiana noted the complete inability of the plaintiffs in that case to produce anyone who would not be able to vote because of the photo ID law:

> Despite apocalyptic assertions of wholesale vote disenfranchisement, Plaintiffs have produced not a single piece of evidence of any identifiable registered voter who would be prevented from voting pursuant to [the photo ID law] because of his or her inability to obtain the necessary photo identification.

One final point on the claims that requiring an ID, even when it is free, is a "poll tax" because of the incidental costs like possible travel to a registrar's office or obtaining a birth certificate that may be involved. That claim was also raised in Georgia. The federal court dismissed this claim, pointing out that such an "argument represents a dramatic overstatement of what fairly constitutes a 'poll tax'. Thus, the imposition of tangential burdens does not transform a regulation into a poll tax. Moreover, the cost of time and transportation cannot plausibly qualify as a prohibited poll tax because those same 'costs' also result from voter registration and in-person voting requirements, which one would not reasonably construe as a poll tax."

We are [the only] one of about one hundred democracies that do not uniformly require voters to present photo ID when they vote. All of those countries administer that law without any problems and without any reports that their citizens are in any way unable to vote because of that requirement. In fact, our southern neighbor Mexico, which has a much larger population in poverty than Texas or the United States, requires both a photo ID and a thumbprint to vote—and turnout has increased in their elections since this requirement went into effect in the 1990's.

Requiring voters to authenticate their identity is a perfectly reasonable and easily met requirement. It is supported by the vast majority of voters of all races and ethnic backgrounds. As the Supreme Court said, voter ID protects the integrity and reliability of the electoral process. Texas has a valid and legitimate state interest not only in deterring and detecting voter fraud, but in maintaining the confidence of its citizens in the security of its elections.

56

"Is There a Middle Ground in the Voter ID Debate?"

Edward B. Foley

The left and the right are increasingly trading accusations in the debate over new voter ID laws, and the rhetoric is heating up. Georgia's new law has been called the new "Jim Crow," although similar measures have recently been enacted in non-Southern states like Arizona and Indiana. (Wisconsin's legislature, too, has passed this kind of law, although it has been vetoed by Governor Doyle.) Defenders of such measures say opponents are willfully blind to the possibility of fraud unless a photo ID requirement is imposed.

Given that heels are digging in, it might seem naïve to search for a compromise. Yet it is imperative to do so. Election laws cannot serve their intended function unless they are accepted by both the left and the right as fair means for conducting the competition between these two political camps to win approval from the citizenry. If the right insists that a voter

ID law is necessary to make the electoral process legitimate, while the left simultaneously says that the same ID law makes the electoral process illegitimate, then it becomes impossible for our society to settle upon rules of procedure for a fair contest between opposing political forces.

With that observation in mind, it is worth searching for a middle position on the voter ID issue, even if at the outset a successful conclusion to this endeavor is far from assured.

In principle, some form of identification requirement should not be objectionable to liberals. Voting is an activity that only the eligible are entitled to engage in, and so it is not unreasonable to ask citizens for some information to demonstrate their eligibility. For example, liberals do not generally object to the traditional requirements that voters provide their names, addresses, and signatures before casting their ballots.

Conservatives, however, say that these traditional requirements no longer suffice because an imposter easily could forge a signature and, in contemporary society, poll workers are unlikely to distinguish eligible from ineligible voters simply by looking at their visages. Therefore, according to these conservatives, a photo ID is necessary to show the voter's eligibility. The picture will show that the person standing before the poll worker is the same one who, according to the poll book, is registered to vote under that particular name and address.

Liberals object, however, to a photo ID requirement on the ground that it is burdensome to citizens who do not have a driver's license, passport, or comparable document. Part of the burden is cost, which can be addressed by making a valid photo ID free of charge. Another part of the burden is the difficulty of accessing locations where no-charge IDs may be obtained. That problem could be remedied by making them available at any post office, public library, or public school, as well as other social service agencies (hospitals, police stations, and so forth).

But a remaining concern of liberals is that, even if photo IDs are easily obtained, many voters will fail to bring them to the polls on Election Day. Public reminders may be issued, including public service announcements on TV. Still, some voters are forgetful, perhaps senior citizens more so than younger adults, and thus the obligation to carry an ID to the polls might serve as a barrier for these eligible citizens.

A potential solution to this problem is to break the connection with the photo requirement and the obligation to produce identification at the polls. Eligible citizens could be required to provide a photograph at the time they *register* to vote, and poll workers would match this photograph with the image of the person standing in front of them. Given the availability of digital photography, the photos of registered voters could be stored in electronic poll books and easily "pulled up" with a click of a computer mouse when voters sign in to vote.

These electronic photos should satisfy the anti-fraud concerns of conservatives as much as printed photos that citizens would be required to bring to the polls. After all, the purpose of a *photo* ID requirement—beyond the traditional requirement of providing one's name, address, and signature—is to compare the likeness of the person seeking to vote with the photograph that is linked to the name and address of the registered voter (whom the flesh-and-blood person purports to be). This function can just as easily occur by comparing the likeness of the person with the computerized photo in the electronic poll book, which was linked to the name and address of the registered voter at time of registration.

Of course, to satisfy the concerns of liberals, a requirement to provide a digital photograph at time of registration would have to address the cost and accessibility issues identified earlier. But, again, a system in which citizens could go to a wide variety of public offices (including post offices, libraries, and schools), where clerical officials would be authorized to take a digital photo of the citizen and then email it to the applicable board of election, without any cost to the citizen, would satisfactorily address these concerns. In addition, for those citizens seeking to register by mail, they could be permitted to email their own digital photos of themselves, if they conform to "passport style" specifications. In this way, nursing homes and other senior citizens centers could take "at home" digital photos of their elderly residents and email them to the board of election, without requiring these elderly citizens to travel to a post office, library, or other public building. (Another comparable approach would be to permit individuals to become a kind of "deputized notary public," trained to take the right sort of digital photo, so that other citizens could meet with any of these designated individuals whenever and wherever it would be convenient.) Moreover, as an alternative, those citizens who do not submit a digital photo at time of registration could provide the more conventional form of photo ID (like a driver's license) at time of voting, making either approach an equally available option, depending solely on which the particular citizen prefers.

Liberals might still complain that any form of photo ID requirement is unnecessary to reduce the risk of fraud and, in any event, will be ineffective if inapplicable to absentee voting. The point about absentee voting is surely a valid one. (For this reason, one wonders whether it is wise to expand the availability of at-home voting, as many states are doing.) If individuals sitting at home can vote without providing any form of photo ID, the opportunity for fraud exists even if voters who go to the polls are subject to a photograph requirement. One way around this discrepancy would be to require absentee voters to submit a photocopy of their photo ID when they mail in their absentee ballot. Or, if the digital photo proposal is adopted, absentee voters could mail with their ballot a printed copy of the digital photo they submitted as part of their registration. In the future, absentee voters might simply email a second copy of their digital photo when emailing their absentee ballots.

A liberal objection to any form of photo ID requirement is more difficult to sustain, particularly if the goal is a compromise acceptable to both sides. To be sure, the frequency of fraud at polling places that would be preventable by a photo ID requirement may be fairly low—there is clearly a debate between conservatives and liberals on this factual point—but it is not non-existent. Liberals acknowledge the possibility of fraudulent absentee voting, saying that its risk is greater than polling place voting. But if an imposter can obtain and submit an absentee ballot, he or she can show up at a polling place purporting to be someone else. Even if the latter is more difficult, the lack of a photo ID requirement makes this deceit easier than it otherwise would be.

Thus, an acceptable compromise must take the form of a photo ID requirement that is not unduly onerous. The proposal here, to permit voters to submit an easily obtainable and no-charge digital photo at the time they register, as an alternative to having to produce a driver's license or comparable photo ID when they go to the polls on Election Day, satisfies this objective. Pursuing this proposal would enable both sides to move beyond the vituperative rhetoric that increasingly, and unfortunately, is clouding the policy debate on this topic.

DISCUSSION QUESTIONS

1. Would you approve of a proposal that all voters had to show photo identification at polling places? Do you think that would decrease turnout? If so, is that a reasonable cost?

2. Would you have any concerns with having voting conducted over the Internet or by mail (as is done in Washington and Oregon)? Are there benefits that outweigh these concerns?

3. What might be some possible objections raised against Foley's proposal by the two sides in the voter-ID debate?

4. As a general matter, do you believe there is a tradeoff between maximizing turnout and minimizing fraud? Or are these goals compatible? Why?

CHAPTER 11

Political Parties

57

"The Decline of Collective Responsibility in American Politics"

Morris P. Fiorina

For more than three decades, political scientists have studied the changing status of American political parties. Morris Fiorina, writing in the early 1980s, suggests that political parties provide many benefits for American democracy, in particular by clarifying policy alternatives and letting citizens know whom to hold accountable when they are dissatisfied with government performance. He sees decline in all the key areas of political-party involvement: the electorate, in government, and in party organizations. He argues that the decline eliminates the motivation for elected members of the parties to define broad policy objectives, leading to diminished political participation and a rise in alienation. Policies are aimed at serving the narrow interests of the various single-issue groups that dominate politics rather than the broad constituencies represented by parties. Without strong political parties to provide electoral accountability, American politics has suffered a "decline in collective responsibility" in Fiorina's view. In the effort to reform the often-corrupt political parties of the late 1800s—often referred to as "machines" led by "bosses"—Fiorina asks us to consider whether we have eliminated the best way to hold elected officials accountable at the ballot box.

Though the Founding Fathers believed in the necessity of establishing a genuinely national government, they took great pains to design one that could not lightly do things *to* its citizens; what government might do *for* its citizens was to be limited to the functions of what we know now as the "watchman state."

*   *   *

Given the historical record faced by the Founders, their emphasis on constraining government is understandable. But we face a later historical record, one that shows two hundred years of increasing demands for government to act positively. Moreover, developments unforeseen by the Founders increasingly raise the likelihood that the uncoordinated actions of individuals and groups will inflict serious damage on the nation as a whole. The by-products of the industrial and technological revolutions impose physical risks not only on us, but on future generations as well. Resource shortages and international cartels raise the spectre of economic ruin. And the simple proliferation of special interests with their intense, particularistic demands threatens to render us politically incapable of taking actions that might either advance the state of society or prevent foreseeable deteriorations in that state. None of this is to suggest that we should forget about what government can do *to* us—the contemporary concern with the proper scope and methods of government intervention in the social and economic orders is long overdue. But the modern age demands as well that we worry about our ability to make government work *for* us. The problem is that we are gradually losing that ability, and a principal reason for this loss is the steady erosion of *responsibility* in American politics.

* * *

Unfortunately, the importance of responsibility in a democracy is matched by the difficulty of attaining it. In an autocracy, individual responsibility suffices; the location of power in a single individual locates responsibility in that individual as well. But individual responsibility is insufficient whenever more than one person shares governmental authority. We can hold a particular congressman individually responsible for a personal transgression such as bribe-taking. We can even hold a president individually responsible for military moves where he presents Congress and the citizenry with a *fait accompli*. But on most national issues individual responsibility is difficult to assess. If one were to go to Washington, randomly accost a Democratic congressman, and berate him about a 20-percent rate of inflation, imagine the response. More than likely it would run, "Don't blame me. If 'they' had done what I've advocated for x years, things would be fine today."

* * *

American institutional structure makes this kind of game-playing all too easy. In order to overcome it we must lay the credit or blame for national conditions on all those who had any hand in bringing them about: some form of *collective responsibility* is essential.

The only way collective responsibility has ever existed, and can exist given our institutions, is through the agency of the political party; in American politics, responsibility requires cohesive parties. This is an old claim to be sure, but its age does not detract from its present relevance. In fact, the continuing decline in public esteem for the parties and continuing efforts to "reform" them out of the political process suggest that old arguments for party responsibility have not been made often enough or, at least, convincingly enough, so I will make these arguments once again in this essay.

A strong political party can generate collective responsibility by creating incentive for leaders, followers, and popular supporters to think and act in collective terms. First, by providing party leaders with the capability (e.g., control of institutional patronage, nominations, and so on) to discipline party members, genuine leadership becomes possible. Legislative output is less likely to be a least common denominator—a residue of myriad conflicting proposals—and more likely to consist of a program actually intended to solve a problem or move the nation in a particular direction. Second, the subordination of individual officeholders to the party lessens their ability to separate themselves from party actions. Like it or not, their performance becomes identified with the performance of the collectivity to which they belong. Third, with individual candidate variation greatly reduced, voters have less incentive to support individuals and more incentive to support or oppose the party as a whole. And fourth, the circle closes as party-line voting in the electorate provides party leaders with the incentive to propose policies that will earn the support of a national majority, and party back-benchers* with the personal incentive to cooperate with leaders in the attempt to compile a good record for the party as a whole.

In the American context, strong parties have traditionally clarified politics in two ways. First, they allow citizens to assess responsibility easily, at least when the government is unified, which it more often was in earlier eras when party meant more than it does today. Citizens need only evaluate the social, economic, and international conditions they observe and make a simple decision for or against change. They do not need to decide whether the energy, inflation, urban, and defense policies advocated by their congressman would be superior to those advocated by [the president]—were any of them to be enacted!

The second way in which strong parties clarify American politics follows from the first. When citizens assess responsibility on the party as a whole, party members have personal incentives to see the party evaluated favorably. They have little to gain from gutting their president's program one day and attacking him for lack of leadership the next, since they share in the president's fate when voters do not differentiate within the party. Put simply, party responsibility provides party members with a personal stake in their collective performance.

---

*Back-benchers are junior members of the British Parliament, who sit in the rear benches of the House of Commons. Here, the term refers to junior members of political parties [Editors].

Admittedly, party responsibility is a blunt instrument. The objection immediately arises that party responsibility condemns junior Democratic representatives to suffer electorally for an inflation they could do little to affect. An unhappy situation, true, but unless we accept it, Congress as a whole escapes electoral retribution for an inflation they *could* have done something to affect. Responsibility requires acceptance of both conditions. The choice is between a blunt instrument or none at all.

* * *

In earlier times, when citizens voted for the party, not the person, parties had incentives to nominate good candidates, because poor ones could have harmful fallout on the ticket as a whole. In particular, the existence of presidential coattails (positive and negative) provided an inducement to avoid the nomination of narrowly based candidates, no matter how committed their supporters. And, once in office, the existence of party voting in the electorate provided party members with the incentive to compile a good *party* record. In particular, the tendency of national mid-term elections to serve as referenda on the performance of the president provided a clear inducement for congressmen to do what they could to see that their president was perceived as a solid performer. By stimulating electoral phenomena such as coattail effects and mid-term referenda, party transformed some degree of personal ambition into concern with collective performance.

* * *

The Continuing Decline of Party in the United States

Party Organizations

In the United States, party organization has traditionally meant state and local party organization. The national party generally has been a loose confederacy of subnational units that swings into action for a brief period every four years. This characterization remains true today, despite the somewhat greater influence and augmented functions of the national organizations. Though such things are difficult to measure precisely, there is general agreement that the formal party organizations have undergone a secular decline since their peak at the end of the nineteenth century. The prototype of the old-style organization was the urban machine, a form approximated today only in Chicago.

* * *

[*Fiorina discusses the reforms of the late nineteenth and early twentieth century.*]

In the 1970s two series of reforms further weakened the influence of organized parties in American national politics. The first was a series of legal changes deliberately intended to lessen organized party influence in the presidential nominating process. In the Democratic party, "New Politics" activists captured the national party apparatus and imposed a series of rules changes designed to "open up" the politics of presidential nominations. The Republican party—long more amateur and open than the Democratic party—adopted weaker versions of the Democratic rules changes. In addition, modifications of state electoral laws to conform to the Democratic rules changes (enforced by the federal courts) stimulated Republican rules changes as well.

*   *   *

A second series of 1970s reforms lessened the role of formal party organizations in the conduct of political campaigns. These are financing regulations growing out of the Federal Election Campaign Act of 1971 as amended in 1974 and 1976. In this case the reforms were aimed at cleaning up corruption in the financing of campaigns; their effects on the parties were a by-product, though many individuals accurately predicted its nature. Serious presidential candidates are now publicly financed. Though the law permits the national party to spend two cents per eligible voter on behalf of the nominee, it also obliges the candidate to set up a finance committee separate from the national party. Between this legally mandated separation and fear of violating spending limits or accounting regulations, for example, the law has the effect of encouraging the candidate to keep his party at arm's length.

*   *   *

The ultimate results of such reforms are easy to predict. A lesser party role in the nominating and financing of candidates encourages candidates to organize and conduct independent campaigns, which further weakens the role of parties. . . . [I]f parties do not grant nominations, fund their choices, and work for them, why should those choices feel any commitment to their party?

Party in the Electorate

In the citizenry at large, party takes the form of a psychological attachment. The typical American traditionally has been likely to identify with one or the other of the two major parties. Such identifications are transmitted across generations to some degree, and within the individual they tend to be fairly stable. But there is mounting evidence that the basis of identification lies in the individual's experiences (direct and vicarious, through family and social groups) with the parties in the past. Our current party system, of course, is based on the dislocations of the

Depression period and the New Deal attempts to alleviate them. Though only a small proportion of those who experienced the Depression directly are active voters today, the general outlines of citizen party identifications much resemble those established at that time.

Again, there is reason to believe that the extent of citizen attachments to parties has undergone a long-term decline from a nineteenth-century high. And again, the New Deal appears to have been a period during which the decline was arrested, even temporarily reversed. But again, the decline of party has reasserted itself in the 1970s.

* * *

As the 1960s wore on, the heretofore stable distribution of citizen party identifications began to change in the general direction of weakened attachments to the parties. Between 1960 and 1976, independents, broadly defined, increased from less than a quarter to more than a third of the voting-age population. Strong identifiers declined from slightly more than a third to about a quarter of the population.

* * *

Indisputably, party in the electorate has declined in recent years. Why? To some extent the electoral decline results from the organizational decline. Few party organizations any longer have the tangible incentives to turn out the faithful and assure their loyalty. Candidates run independent campaigns and deemphasize their partisan ties whenever they see any short-term electoral gain in doing so. If party is increasingly less important in the nomination and election of candidates, it is not surprising that such diminished importance is reflected in the attitudes and behavior of the voter.

Certain long-term sociological and technological trends also appear to work against party in the electorate. The population is younger, and younger citizens traditionally are less attached to the parties than their elders. The population is more highly educated; fewer voters need some means of simplifying the choices they face in the political arena, and party, of course, has been the principal means of simplification. And the media revolution has vastly expanded the amount of information easily available to the citizenry. Candidates would have little incentive to operate campaigns independent of the parties if there were no means to apprise the citizenry of their independence. The media provide the means.

Finally, our present party system is an old one. For increasing numbers of citizens, party attachments based on the Great Depression seem lacking in relevance to the problems of the late twentieth century. Beginning with the racial issue in the 1960s, proceeding to the social issue of the 1970s, and to the energy, environment, and inflation issues of today, the parties have been rent by internal dissension. Sometimes they failed to take stands, at other times they took the wrong ones from the standpoint of the rank and file, and at most times they have failed to solve the new problems in any genuine sense. Since 1965 the parties have done little or nothing to earn the loyalties of modern Americans.

Party in Government

If the organizational capabilities of the parties have weakened, and their psychological ties to the voters have loosened, one would expect predictable consequences for the party in government. In particular, one would expect to see an increasing degree of split party control within and across the levels of American government. The evidence on this point is overwhelming.

* * *

The increased fragmentation of the party in government makes it more difficult for government officeholders to work together than in times past (not that it has ever been terribly easy). Voters meanwhile have a more difficult time attributing responsibility for government performance, and this only further fragments party control. The result is lessened collective responsibility in the system.

What has taken up the slack left by the weakening of the traditional [party] determinants of congressional voting? It appears that a variety of personal and local influences now play a major role in citizen evaluations of their representatives. Along with the expansion of the federal presence in American life, the traditional role of the congressman as an all-purpose ombudsman has greatly expanded. Tens of millions of citizens now are directly affected by federal decisions. Myriad programs provide opportunities to profit from government largesse, and myriad regulations impose costs and/or constraints on citizen activities. And, whether seeking to gain profit or avoid costs, citizens seek the aid of their congressmen. When a court imposes a desegregation plan on an urban school board, the congressional offices immediately are contacted for aid in safeguarding existing sources of funding and in determining eligibility for new ones. When a major employer announces plans to quit an area, the congressional offices immediately are contacted to explore possibilities for using federal programs to persuade the employer to reconsider. Contractors appreciate a good congressional word with DOD [Department of Defense] procurement officers. Local artistic groups cannot survive without NEA [National Endowment for the Arts] funding. And, of course, there are the major individual programs such as social security and veterans' benefits that create a steady demand for congressional information and aid services. Such activities are nonpartisan, nonideological, and, most important, noncontroversial. Moreover, the contribution of the congressman in the realm of district service appears considerably greater than the impact of his or her single vote on major national issues. Constituents respond rationally to this modern state of affairs by weighing nonprogrammatic constituency service heavily when casting their congressional votes. And this emphasis on the part of constituents provides the means for incumbents to solidify their hold on the office. Even if elected by a narrow margin, diligent service activities enable a congressman to neutralize or even convert a portion of those who would otherwise oppose him on policy or ideological grounds. Emphasis on local, nonpartisan factors in congressional voting enables the modern congressman to withstand national swings, whereas yesteryear's uninsulated congressmen were more dependent on preventing the occurrence of the swings.

* * *

[*The result is the insulation of the modern congressional member from national forces altogether.*]

The withering away of the party organizations and the weakening of party in the electorate have begun to show up as disarray in the party in government. As the electoral fates of congressmen and the president have diverged, their incentives to cooperate have diverged as well. Congressmen have little personal incentive to bear any risk in their president's behalf, since they no longer expect to gain much from his successes or suffer much from his failures. Only those who personally agree with the president's program and/or those who find that program well suited for their particular district support the president. And there are not enough of these to construct the coalitions necessary for action on the major issues now facing the country. By holding only the president responsible for national conditions, the electorate enables officialdom as a whole to escape responsibility. This situation lies at the root of many of the problems that now plague American public life.

Some Consequences of the Decline of Collective Responsibility

The weakening of party has contributed directly to the severity of several of the important problems the nation faces. For some of these, such as the government's inability to deal with inflation and energy, the connections are obvious. But for other problems, such as the growing importance of single-issue politics and the growing alienation of the American citizenry, the connections are more subtle.

Immobilism

As the electoral interdependence of the party in government declines, its ability to act also declines. If responsibility can be shifted to another level or to another officeholder, there is less incentive to stick one's neck out in an attempt to solve a given problem. Leadership becomes more difficult, the ever-present bias toward the short-term solution becomes more pronounced, and the possibility of solving any given problem lessens.

. . . [P]olitical inability to take actions that entail short-run costs ordinarily will result in much higher costs in the long run—we cannot continually depend on the technological fix. So the present American immobilism cannot be dismissed lightly. The sad thing is that the American people appear to understand the depth of our present problems and, at least in principle, appear prepared to sacrifice in furtherance of the long-run good. But they will not have an opportunity to choose between two or more such long-term plans. Although both parties promise tough, equitable policies, in the present state of our politics, neither can deliver.

Single-Issue Politics

In recent years both political analysts and politicians have decried the increased importance of single-issue groups in American politics. Some in fact would claim that the present immobilism in our politics owes more to the rise of single-issue groups than to the decline of party. A little thought, however, should reveal that the two trends are connected. Is single-issue politics a recent phenomenon? The contention is doubtful; such groups have always been active participants in American politics. The gun lobby already was a classic example at the time of President Kennedy's assassination. And however impressive the antiabortionists appear today, remember the temperance movement, which succeeded in getting its constitutional amendment. American history contains numerous forerunners of today's groups, from anti-Masons to abolitionists to the Klan—singularity of purpose is by no means a modern phenomenon. Why, then, do we hear all the contemporary hoopla about single-issue groups? Probably because politicians fear them now more than before and thus allow them to play a larger role in our politics. Why should this be so? Simply because the parties are too weak to protect their members and thus to contain single-issue politics.

In earlier times single-issue groups were under greater pressures to reach accommodations with the parties. After all, the parties nominated candidates, financed candidates, worked for candidates, and, perhaps most important, party voting protected candidates. When a contemporary single-issue group threatens to "get" an officeholder, the threat must be taken seriously.

* * *

Not only did the party organization have greater ability to resist single-issue pressures at the electoral level, but the party in government had greater ability to control the agenda, and thereby contain single-issue pressures at the policy-making level. Today we seem condemned to go through an annual agony over federal abortion funding. There is little doubt that politicians on both sides would prefer to reach some reasonable compromise at the committee level and settle the issue. But in today's decentralized Congress there is no way to put the lid on. In contrast, historians tell us that in the late nineteenth century a large portion of the Republican constituency was far less interested in the tariff and other questions of national economic development than in whether German immigrants should be permitted to teach their native language in their local schools, and whether Catholics and "liturgical Protestants" should be permitted to consume alcohol. Interestingly, however, the national agenda of the period is devoid of such issues. And when they do show up on the state level, the exceptions prove the rule; they produce party splits and striking defeats for the party that allowed them to surface.

In sum, a strong party that is held accountable for the government of a nation-state has both the ability and the incentive to contain particularistic pressures. It controls nominations, elections, and the agenda, and it collectively realizes that small minorities are small minorities no matter how intense they are. But as the parties decline they lose control over nominations and campaigns, they lose the loyalty of the voters, and they lose control of the agenda. Party officeholders cease to be held collectively accountable for party performance, but they become individually exposed to the political pressure of myriad interest groups. The decline of party permits interest groups to wield greater influence, their success encourages the formation of still more interest groups, politics becomes increasingly fragmented, and collective responsibility becomes still more elusive.

Popular Alienation from Government

For at least a decade political analysts have pondered the significance of survey data indicative of a steady increase in the alienation of the American public from the political process. . . . The American public is in a nasty mood, a cynical, distrusting, and resentful mood. The question is, Why?

If the same national problems not only persist but worsen while ever-greater amounts of revenue are directed at them, why shouldn't the typical citizen conclude that most of the money must be wasted by incompetent officials? If narrowly based interest groups increasingly affect our politics, why shouldn't citizens increasingly conclude that the interests run the government? For fifteen years the citizenry has listened to a steady stream of promises but has seen very little in the way of follow-through. An increasing proportion of the electorate does not believe that elections make a difference, a fact that largely explains the much-discussed post-1960 decline in voting turnout.

Continued public disillusionment with the political process poses several real dangers. For one thing, disillusionment begets further disillusionment. Leadership becomes more difficult if citizens do not trust their leaders and will not give them the benefit of a doubt. Policy failure becomes more likely if citizens expect the policy to fail. Waste increases and government competence decreases as citizens disrespect for politics encourages a lesser breed of person to make careers in government. And "government by a few big interests" becomes more than a cliché if citizens increasingly decide the cliché is true and cease participating for that reason.

Finally, there is the real danger that continued disappointment with particular government officials ultimately metamorphoses into disillusionment with government per se. Increasing numbers of citizens believe that government is not simply overextended but perhaps incapable of any further bettering of the world. Yes, government is overextended, inefficiency is pervasive, and ineffectiveness is all too common. But government is one of the few instruments of collective action we have, and even those committed to selective pruning of government programs cannot blithely allow the concept of an activist government to fall into disrepute.

Of late, however, some political commentators have begun to wonder whether contemporary thought places sufficient emphasis on government *for* the people. In stressing participation have we lost sight of *accountability*? Surely, we should be as concerned with what government produces as with how many participate. What good is participation if the citizenry is unable to determine who merits their support?

Participation and responsibility are not logically incompatible, but there is a degree of tension between the two, and the quest for either may be carried to extremes. Participation maximizers find themselves involved with quotas and virtual representation schemes, while responsibility maximizers can find themselves with a closed shop under boss rule. Moreover, both qualities can weaken the democracy they supposedly underpin. Unfettered participation produces Hyde Amendments* and immobilism. Responsible parties can use agenda power to thwart democratic decision—for more than a century the Democratic party used what power it had to suppress the racial issue. Neither participation nor responsibility should be pursued at the expense of all other values, but that is what has happened with participation over the course of the past two decades, and we now reap the consequences in our politics.

---

*The Hyde Amendment, passed in 1976 (three years after *Roe v. Wade*), prohibited using Medicaid funds for abortion [Editors].

Discussion Questions

1. How do political parties provide "collective responsibility" and improve the quality of democracy? Do you believe the complaints raised by Fiorina thirty years ago remain persuasive?

2. Are strong parties in the interest of individual politicians? What might be some reasons that members of Congress would agree to strong parties or would distance themselves from their party's leadership?

58

"Parliamentary Government in the United States?" from *The State of the Parties*

Gerald M. Pomper

Writing in the late 1990s, Gerald Pomper revisits the issues Fiorina raised and reaches a somewhat more positive assessment of the state of American political parties. Like Fiorina, Pomper believes that political parties should have a strong, prominent place in American politics. Unlike him, he believes that parties have that place. Looking at developments since the 1980s, Pomper argues that parties are today doing nearly everything that political scientists seem to want from them—they are constructing meaningful, coherent policy programs at the congressional level and in the party platforms; they are implementing the promises they make in campaigns; they are strikingly unified in Congress; they present clear, competing visions of the role of government; they are aggressively involved in campaigning, especially through providing campaign funds; and successful presidential candidates are largely those backed by the party rather than outsiders or mavericks. Although the presidency is obviously still a major institution in American government, Pomper wonders whether the U.S. might be evolving toward its own form of parliamentary government, in which the leadership of government clearly rests in the congressional parties. Suggesting that the presidency is a diminished institution, he asserts that "it may well be time to end the fruitless quest for a presidential savior and instead turn our attention, and our support, to the continuing and emerging strengths of our political parties."

In 1996, the important political decision for American political warriors was not the contest between Bill Clinton and Robert Dole. "For virtually all of the powerful groups behind the Republican Party their overriding goal of keeping control of the House stemmed from their view that that was where the real political power—nearand long-term—lay." Moreover, "Sitting in his office on the sixth floor of the AFL-CIO building on 16th Street, political director Steve Rosenthal said that labor, too, saw the House elections as the most important of 1996—more important than the contest for the Presidency."

These informed activists alert us to a major shift in the character of American politics. To baldly summarize my argument, I suggest that the United States is moving toward a system of parliamentary government, a fundamental change in our constitutional regime. This change is not a total revolution in our institutions, and it will remain incomplete, given the drag of historical tradition. Nevertheless, this trend can be seen if we look beyond the formal definition of parliamentary governments, the union of legislature and executive.

The parliamentary model is evident in both empirical and normative political science. Anthony Downs begins his classic work by defining a political party virtually as a parliamentary coalition, "a team of men seeking to control the governing apparatus by gaining office in a duly constituted election." Normatively, for decades, some political scientists have sought to create a "responsible party system," resembling such parliamentary features as binding party programs and legislative cohesion.

Significant developments toward parliamentary government can be seen in contemporary American politics. The evidence of these trends cannot be found in the formal institutions of the written (capital C) Constitution. Institutional stability, however, may disguise basic change. For example, in formal terms, the president is not chosen until the electoral college meets in December, although we know the outcome within hours of the closing of the polls in early November.

Let us go beyond "literary theory" and compare the present reality of U.S. politics with more general characteristics attributed to parliamentary systems. In the ideal parliamentary model, elections are contests between competitive parties presenting alternative programs, under leaders chosen from and by the parties' legislators or activists. Electoral success is interpreted as a popular mandate in support of these platforms. Using their parliamentary powers, the leaders then enforce party discipline to implement the promised programs.

The United States increasingly evidences these characteristics of parliamentary government. This fundamental change is due to the development of stronger political parties. In particular, I will try to demonstrate transformations of American politics evident in the following six characteristics of the parties:

- The parties present meaningful programs;
- They bridge the institutional separations of national government;
- They reasonably fulfill their promises;
- They act cohesively under strong legislative leadership;
- They have assumed a major role in campaigning; and
- They provide the recruitment base for presidential candidates.

Party Programs

A parliamentary system provides the opportunity to enact party programs. By contrast, in the American system, observers often have doubted that there were party programs, and the multiple checks and balances of American government have made it difficult to enact any coherent policies. For evidence, I examine the major party platforms of 1992–1996, the

1994 Republican Contract with America, and the 1996 Democratic Families First Agenda.

In previous research, we argued that party platforms were meaningful statements and that they were good forecasts of government policy. We found, contrary to cynical belief, that platforms were composed of far more than hot air and empty promises. Rather, a majority of the platforms were relevant defenses and criticisms of the parties' past records and reasonably specific promises of future actions. Moreover, the parties delivered: close to 70 percent of their many specific pledges were actually fulfilled to some degree.

Furthermore, parties have differed in their programs. Examining party manifestos in the major industrial democracies over forty years, 1948–1988, Budge concludes, "American Democrats and Republicans . . . consistently differentiate themselves from each other on such matters as support for welfare, government intervention, foreign aid, and defense, individual initiative and freedom. . . . Indeed, they remain as far apart as many European parties on these points, and more so than many."

In recent years, we might expect platforms to be less important. National conventions have become television exercises rather than occasions for party decision making. The expansion of interest groups has made it more difficult to accomplish policy intentions. Candidate-centered campaigning reduces the incentives to achieve collective, party goals and appears to focus more on individual characteristics than on policy issues.

The party platforms of 1992 provide a test. An independent replication confirms our previous research on platform content. Perhaps surprisingly, this new work indicates that the most recent platforms, like those of previous years, provide significant political and policy statements. These manifestos meet one of the tests of a parliamentary system: meaningful party programs.

The 1992 platforms can be divided into three categories: puff pieces of rhetoric and fact, approvals of one's own party policy record and candidates or disapproval of the opposition, and pledges for future action. The pledges, in turn, can be categorized as being simply rhetorical or general promises or more useful statements of future intentions, such as promises to continue existing policies, expressions of party goals, pledges of action, or quite detailed promises.

Much in the platforms induces yawns and cynicism. The Democrats were fond of such rhetorical statements as "It is time to listen to the grassroots of America." (Actually a difficult task, since most plants are speechless.) The Republicans were prone to vague self-congratulation, as when they boasted, "Republicans recognize the importance of having fathers and mothers in the home." (Possibly even more so if these parents are unemployed, not distracted by jobs?)

Nevertheless, these documents—while hardly models of rational discussion—did provide useful guides to party positions. When the

Democrats criticized "the Bush administration's efforts to bankrupt the public school system . . . through private school vouchers," and when the Republicans declared that "American families must be given choice in education," there was an implicit policy debate. Comparison was also facilitated by the similar distributions of platform statements across policy areas. Each party tended to devote about as much attention to particular or related policy areas as its opposition. The only important difference is that Democrats gave far more attention to issues involving women and abortion. Overall, about half of the platforms were potentially useful to the voters in locating the parties on a policy continuum.

The 1994 Contract with America was even more specific. It consisted entirely of promises for the future, potentially focusing attention on public policy. Moreover, the large majority of its fifty-five sentences were reasonably specific promises. Pledges of definite action comprised 42 percent of the total document, and detailed pledges another 27 percent, while less than 4 percent consisted of only vague rhetoric. From the promise of a balanced budget amendment to advocacy of term limits, the Republicans foreshadowed major innovations in American institutions and law. This high degree of specificity can facilitate party accountability to the electorate.

Party as Programmatic Bridge

The great obstacle to party responsibility in the United States has always been the separation of national institutions, the constitutional division between the executive and legislative branches. Party has sometimes been praised as a bridge across this separation, and party reformers have often sought to build stronger institutional ties, even seeking radical constitutional revision to further the goal. Despite these hopes and plans, however, the separation has remained. Presidential parties make promises, but Congress has no institutional responsibility to act on these pledges.

In a parliamentary system, the most current research argues—contrary to Downs—"that office is used as a basis for attaining policy goals, rather than that policy is subordinated to office." In the United States as well, party program rather than institutional discipline may provide the bridge between the legislature and its executive. In previous years, however, we lacked a ready means to compare presidential and congressional programs. Now we have authoritative statements from both institutionalized wings of the parties. The Republican Contract with America marks a major first step toward coherent, interinstitutional programs.

The 1994 contract was far more than a campaign gimmick or an aberrational invention of Newt Gingrich. It was actually a terse condensation of continuing Republican Party doctrine. A majority of these promises had already been anticipated in 1992 and the party endorsed five-sixths of its provisions in 1996.

For example, the 1992 national platform criticized the Democratic Congress for its refusal "to give the President a line-item veto to curb their self-serving porkbarrel projects" and promised adoption of the procedure in a Republican Congress. The 1994 contract repeated the pledge of a "line-item veto to restore fiscal responsibility to an out-of-control Congress," while the 1996 platform reiterated, "A Republican president will fight wasteful spending with the line-item veto which was finally enacted by congressional Republicans this year over bitter Democrat opposition." Republicans built on traditional party doctrine, specified the current party program, and then affirmed accountability for their actions. Building on this achievement in party building, and their claims of legislative "success," the Republicans have already promised to present a new contract for the elections at the turn of the century.

The Democrats imitatively developed a congressional program, the Families First Agenda, for the 1996 election. Intended primarily as a campaign document by the minority party, it is less specific than the Republican contract. Still, 90 of its 204 statements were reasonably precise promises. The legislative Democrats also showed significant and increasing agreement with their presidential wing and platform. By 1996, three-fourths of the congressional agenda was also incorporated into the Clinton program, and the official platform specifically praised the congressional program. The agenda's three sections—"security," "opportunity," and "responsibility"—paralleled those of the national platform (which added "freedom," "peace," and "community"—values presumably shared by congressional Democrats), and many provisions are replicated from one document to another.

The Republican contract with America and the Democratic Families First agenda, then, can be seen as emblems of party responsibility and likely precedents for further development toward parliamentary practice in American politics. Party doctrine has become a bridge across the separation of institutions.

Program Fulfillment

Both Democrats and Republicans, as they held power, followed through on their election promises, as expected in a parliamentary model. Despite the clumsiness of the Clinton administration, and despite the Democrats' loss of their long-term control of Congress in their catastrophic election defeat in 1994, they actually fulfilled most of the 167 reasonably specific pledges in their 1992 manifest.

A few examples illustrate the point. The Democrats promised negative action, in opposing major change in the Clean Air Act—and they stood fast. In their 1993 economic program, the Democrats won action similar to their platform pledge to "make the rich pay their fair share in taxes." Through executive action, the Clinton administration redeemed its promise to reduce U.S. military forces in Europe. The Democrats achieved full action on their promise of "A reasonable waiting period to permit background checks for purchases of handguns."

To be sure, the Democrats have not become latter-day George Washingtons, unable to tell an untruth. There clearly has been no action on the pledge to "limit overall campaign spending and . . . the disproportionate and excessive role of PACs." In other cases, the Democrats did try but were defeated, most notably in their promise of "reform of the health-care system to control costs and make health care affordable." (It is obviously too early to judge fulfillment of 1996 Democratic pledges, made in either the presidential platform or the congressional party Families First Agenda.)

Most impressive are not the failures but the achievements. Altogether, Democrats did accomplish something on nearly 70 percent of their 1992 promises, in contrast to inaction on only 19 percent. In a completely independent analysis, another researcher came to remarkably similar conclusions, calculating Clinton's fulfillment of his campaign promises at the same level, 69 percent. I do not believe this record is the result of the virtues of the Democratic Party, which I use for this analysis simply because it controlled the government, nor can this record be explained by Bill Clinton's personal qualities of steadfast commitment to principle. The explanation is that we now have a system in which parties, whatever their names or leaders, make and keep promises.

This conclusion is strengthened if we examine the Republicans. While the GOP of course did not hold the presidency, it did win control of Congress in 1994. In keeping with the model of parliamentary government, Republicans interpreted their impressive victory as an endorsement of the Contract with America, and then they attempted to implement the program. We must remember that the 1994 election cannot be seen as a popular mandate for the Republican manifesto: two-thirds of the public had not even heard of it in November, and only 19 percent expressed support. The contract expressed party ideology, not voter demands.

Despite its extravagant tone and ideological character, the Republicans delivered on their contract just as Democrats fulfilled much of their 1992 platform. Of the more specific pledges, 69 percent were accomplished in large measure (coincidentally, perhaps, the same success rate as the Democrats). Even if we include the rhetorical and unspecific sentences in our test, more than one-half of this party program was accomplished.

Despite the heroics of vetoes and government shutdown, despite bicameralism and the vaunted autonomy of the Senate, and despite popular disapproval, the reality is that most of the Contract with America was implemented. The Republicans accomplished virtually all that they promised in regard to congressional reform, unfunded mandates and welfare, as well as substantial elements of their program in regard to crime, child support, defense, and the social security earnings limit. Defeated on major economic issues, they later achieved many of these goals, including a balanced budget agreement in place of a constitutional amendment, a children's tax credit, and a reduction in capital gains taxes. On these questions, as indeed on the general range of American government, they won the greatest victory of all: they set the agenda for the United States, and the Democratic president eventually followed their lead. Such initiative is what we would expect in a parliamentary system.

*   *   *

Party Cohesion

Program fulfillment results from party unity. The overall trend in Congress, as expected in a parliamentary system, is toward more party differentiation. One indicator is the proportion of legislative votes in which a majority of one party is opposed to a majority of the other (i.e., "party unity" votes). Not too long ago, in 1969, such party conflict was evident on only about one-third of all roll calls. By 1995, nearly three-fourths of House votes and over two-thirds of Senate roll calls showed these clear party differences. There is another trend—the increasing commitment of representatives and senators to their parties. The average legislator showed party loyalty (expressed as a "party unity score") of less than 60 percent in 1970. In 1996, the degree of loyalty had climbed to 80 percent for Democrats and to an astounding 87 percent for Republicans. Cohesion was still greater on the thirty-three House roll calls in 1995 on final passage of items in the Contract with America. Republicans were unanimous on sixteen of these votes, and the *median* number of Republican dissents was but *one*. Neither the British House of Commons nor the erstwhile Supreme Soviet could rival this record of party unity.

The congressional parties now are ideologically cohesive bodies, even with the occasional but significant split among Democrats on such issues as trade and welfare reform. We need to revise our political language to take account of this ideological cohesion. There are no more "Dixiecrats" or southern conservative Democrats, and therefore there is no meaningful "conservative coalition" in Congress. Supportive evidence is found in the same roll call data: the average southern Democrat supported his or her party 71 percent of the time in 1996, and barely over a tenth of the roll calls found Dixie legislators in opposition to their own party and in alliance with a majority of Republicans. It also seems likely that "liberal Republican" will soon be an oxymoron restricted to that patronized minority holding a pro-choice attitude on abortion, confined to the back of the platform or, so to speak, to the back of the party bus.

Republicans have been acting like a parliamentary party beyond their ideological unity on a party program. The "central leaders efforts during the Contract period were attempts to *impose* a form of party government," which succeeded in winning cooperation from committee chairman and changed roll call behavior as "many Republicans modified their previous preferences in order to accommodate their party colleagues." Beyond programmatic goals, the Republicans have created strong party institutions in Congress, building on previous Democratic reforms.

Even after the Contract with America is completely passed or forgotten, these institutions will likely remain. In their first days in power, as they organized the House, the Republicans centralized power in the hands of the Speaker, abolished institutionalized caucuses of constituency interests, distributed chairmanships on the basis of loyalty to the party program and in disregard of seniority, and changed the ratios of party memberships on committees to foster passage of the party program. Instruments of discipline have become more prevalent and more exercised, including caucus resolutions, committee assignments, aid in securing campaign contributions, and disposition of individual members' bills.

The building of parliamentary party institutions continues. Some of the structural changes in the House have now been adopted by both the Senate and the Democrats, perhaps most significantly the rotation of committee chairmanships, curbing the antiparty influence of seniority. The Republicans have insisted that committees report party bills, even when opposed by the chair, as in the cases of term limits and telecommunications. The party record became the major issue in the 1996 congressional elections, with party leaders Newt Gingrich and Richard Armey doing their best to aid loyalists—but only loyalists—through fund-raising and strong-arming of ideological allies among political action committees.

The party differences and cohesion in Congress partially reflect the enhanced power of legislative leaders. The more fundamental reason for congressional party unity—as in parliamentary systems—is not discipline as much as agreement. Party members vote together because they think the same way. Republicans act as conservatives because they *are* conservatives; Democrats act like liberals or as they now prefer, progressives because they believe in these programs.

* * *

The most recent nominating conventions provide further support for the ideological cohesion of the national parties. The CBS/*New York Times* Poll found massive differences between Republican and Democratic delegates on questions involving the scope of government, social issues, and international affairs. A majority of these partisans opposed each other on *all* of ten questions; they were remotely similar on only one issue—international trade—and were in essentially different political worlds (fifty or more percentage points apart) on issues of governmental regulation, the environment, abortion, assault weapons, civil rights, affirmative action, and immigration.

Party Organization

Party unity has another source, related to the recruitment of individual candidates with a common ideology. Unity is also fostered by the development of strong national party organizations, precisely measured by the dollars of election finance. Amid all of the proper concern over the problems of campaign contributions and spending, we have neglected the increasing importance of the parties in providing money, "the mother's milk of politics."

There are two large sources of party money: the direct subsidies provided by the federal election law, and the "soft money" contributions provided for the parties' organizational work. Together, even in 1992, these funds totaled $213 million for the major candidates and their parties. Underlining the impact of this party spending, the Republican and Democratic presidential campaigns in 1992 each spent twice as much money as did billionaire Ross Perot, whose candidacy is often seen as demonstrating the decline of the parties.

An enhanced party role was also evident in the other national elections of 1992. Beyond direct contributions and expenditures, the parties developed a variety of ingenious devices, such as bundling, coordinated spending, and agency agreements, to again become significant players in the election finance game. Overall, in 1992, the six national party committees spent $290 million. (For comparison, total spending in all House and Senate races was $678 million.) The party role became even more evident in 1994, with the victory of a Republican majority originally recruited and financed by Newt Gingrich's GOPAC, a party body disguised as a political action committee.

The party role expanded hugely in 1996, bolstered by the Supreme Court, in its 1996 *Colorado* decision. The Court approved unlimited "independent" spending by political parties on behalf of its candidates. Moreover, four justices explicitly indicated that they were prepared to approve even direct unlimited expenditures by parties, and three other justices are ready to rule on that issue in a future case.

The parties quickly took advantage of the Court's opening. Together, Republican and Democratic party groups spent close to a billion dollars, conservatively 35 percent of all election spending, without even counting the $160 million in federal campaign subsidies for the presidential race. Despite the commonplace emphasis on "candidate-centered" campaigns, the parties' expenditures were greater than that of all individual House and Senate candidates combined. In discussions of election finance, political action committees receive most of the attention, and condemnation, but the reality is that PACs are of decreasing importance. PACs' money has barely increased since 1988, and they were outspent 2 to 1 by the parties in 1996. The parties now have the muscle to conduct campaigns and present their programs, to act as we would expect of parliamentary contestants.

Party Leadership

Parties need leaders as much as money. In parliamentary governments, leaders achieve power through their party activity. That has always been the case even in America when we look at congressional leadership: a long apprenticeship in the House and Senate has usually been required before one achieves the positions of Speaker, majority and minority leader, and whip. A strong indication of the development of parliamentary politics in the United States is the unrecognized trend toward party recruitment for the presidency, the allegedly separated institution.

*　*　*

Contrary to the fears of many observers, the new presidential nominating system has developed along with new institutions of party cohesion. Front-runners have great advantages in this new system, but that means that prominent party figures—rather than obscure dark horses stabled in smoke-filled rooms—are most likely to win nomination. Contrary to fears of a personalistic presidency, the candidates chosen in the postreform period tackle tough issues, support their party's program, and agree with their congressional party's leaders on policy positions as much, or even more, than in the past.

Contemporary presidential nominations have become comparable—although not identical—to the choice of leadership in a hypothetical U.S. parliamentary system. Is the selection of Reagan in 1980 that different from the British Tories' choice of Margaret Thatcher to lead the party's turn toward ideological free market conservatism? In a parliamentary system, would not Bush and Dole, Reagan's successors, be the ideal analogues to Britain's John Major? Is the selection of Mondale as the liberal standard-bearer of the liberal Democratic Party that different from the lineage of left-wing leaders in the British Labour Party? Is the Democratic turn toward the electoral center with Clinton not analogous to Labour's replacement of Michael Foot by Neil Kinnock, John Smith, and Tony Blair?

To be sure, American political leadership is still quite open, the parties quite permeable. Presidential nominations do depend greatly on personal coalitions, and popular primaries are the decisive points of decision. Yet it is also true that leadership of the parties is still, and perhaps increasingly, related to prominence within the parties.

Toward Parliamentary Government?

Do these changes amount to parliamentary government in the United States? Certainly not in the most basic definitional sense, since we will surely continue to have separated institutions, in which the president is elected differently from the legislature, and the Senate differently from the House. Unlike a formal parliamentary system, the president will hold his office for a fixed term, regardless of the "votes of confidence" he wins or loses in Congress. By using his veto and the bully pulpit of the White House, Bill Clinton has proven that the president is independent and still "relevant." It is also true that we will never have a system in which a single political party can both promise and deliver a complete and coherent ideological program. As Jones correctly maintains, American government remains a "separated system," in which "serious and continuous in-party and cross-party coalition building typifies policy making." These continuing features were strikingly evident in the adoption of welfare reform in the 104th Congress.

But parliaments also evidence coalition building, particularly in multiparty systems. British parliamentarians can be stalemated by factional and party differences on issues such as Northern Ireland just as the Democrats and Republicans were on health care in the 103d Congress. Achieving a consensual policy on the peace process in Israel's multiparty system is as difficult as achieving a consensual policy on abortion among America's two parties.

* * *

The party basis of parliamentary government will continue, because the ideological basis of intraparty coherence and interparty difference will continue and even be increased with the ongoing departure of moderate legislators of both parties. The need for strong party institutions in Congress will also be furthered by new policy problems, more rapid turnover of membership, and the continuation of split-party control of government.

Of course, the presidency will remain relevant, yet it may also come to be seen as almost superfluous. A principal argument on behalf of Bob Dole's candidacy was that he would sign the legislation passed by a Republican Congress—hardly a testament to presidential leadership. President Clinton fostered his reelection by removing himself from partisan leadership, "triangulating" the White House between congressional Democrats and Republicans, and following the model of patriotic chief of state created by George Washington and prescribed in *The Federalist*: "to guard the community against the effects of faction, precipitancy, or of any impulse unfriendly to the public good."

* * *

The absence of presidential initiative is more than a problem of the Clinton administration. Throughout American history, the president has persistently provided the energy of American government, the source of new "regimes" and policy initiatives. Perhaps the lassitude of contemporary politics is only the latest example of the recurrent cycle of presidential initiative, consolidation, and decline. Or, more profoundly, perhaps it marks the decline of the executive office itself as a source of creativity in the government of the United States.

America needs help. It may well be time to end the fruitless quest for a presidential savior and instead turn our attention, and our support, to the continuing and emerging strengths of our political parties. We are developing, almost unnoticed, institutions of semiparliamentary, semiresponsible government. To build a better bridge between the past and the future, perhaps this new form of American government is both inevitable and necessary.

Discussion Questions

1. Does Pomper address the concerns Fiorina raised? Or have some aspects of his argument not been resolved by the changes in political parties identified by Pomper?

2. If the United States is evolving toward a semiparliamentary system, is this a good thing? Pomper suggests that the presidency is weakening. Are there advantages to a weaker-presidency system compared to a system with a stronger presidency?

3. Pomper was writing before the presidency of George W. Bush. Has the evolution toward congressional-party leadership continued under the Bush and Obama presidencies?

Debating the Issues: Red America versus Blue America—Are We Polarized?

In 1992, Patrick Buchanan famously stated at the Republican national convention that the United States was in the midst of a culture war that posited traditional, conservative social values against liberal, secular values. Bill Clinton's defeat of President George H. W. Bush seemed to defuse that idea: Clinton was a southern Democrat who had pushed his party toward the ideological center and, although garnering only 43 percent of the vote, he won states in all regions of the country. His 1996 victory was broader, adding states he had lost in 1992. In the 2000 presidential election, however, a striking regional pattern emerged in the results. Al Gore, the Democratic candidate, did well on the coasts and in the upper Midwest, while George W. Bush, the Republican candidate, picked up the remaining states. Many analysts were struck by this "red state/blue state" pattern—named after the coloring of the states on post-election maps—and suggested that it told us something more fundamental about American politics. Indeed, these analysts argued, Patrick Buchanan was in large measure right: the American public was deeply divided and polarized and in many respects living in two different worlds culturally. This polarization showed up not only in voting, but in presidential approval ratings, with the partisan gap in evaluations of Bill Clinton and George W. Bush being larger than for any previous presidents.

The 2004 presidential election looked very much like 2000: with a few exceptions, the red states stayed red and the blue states stayed blue. Eighty-five percent of conservatives voted for Bush; the same percentage of liberals voted for Kerry; and moderates split 54–45 percent for Kerry.

In 2008, Barack Obama campaigned on the idea of practicing a new kind of politics that set aside red-America/blue-America distinctions. His victory scattered the red/blue map, as he picked up nine states Bush won in 2004. Shortly into his presidency, however, Obama's policy plans became engulfed in deep partisan and ideological strife. Like those of Clinton and Bush before him, President Obama's approval ratings were sharply different among Democrats and Republicans. And like those two presidents, Obama invigorated his opponents. Where the Bush presidency played a major role in galvanizing the liberal blogosphere, Obama's contributed to the rise of the Tea Party, a political movement deeply skeptical about the effectiveness and growing size of American government.

Is America deeply polarized along partisan lines? Is there a culture war? Is the red-America/blue-America split real? Is there division on certain highly charged issues but not on most others? Are the divisions just artifacts of the way that survey questions are worded? In this debate, the political scientists James Q. Wilson and Morris Fiorina agree that the political elite—elected leaders, the news media, and interest groups—are polarized, but they disagree on the answers to the rest of the questions. Wilson argues that the cultural split is deep and is reflected in party competition and the public opinion of partisans within and across the red and blue states. Fiorina counters that the idea of a cultural war is vastly exaggerated—there might be a skirmish, but there is no war.

John Judis aligns more with Wilson. Clearly not a fan of the Tea Party, Judis nonetheless argues that it is a real movement with the potential for lasting influence. Its issues, anxieties, and ideological orientation, he states, draw on a deep populist tradition in American politics. As with other populist movements, supporters see the Tea Party as engaged in a struggle to define America, a struggle between "the people" and "the elites."

59

"*What* Culture Wars? Debunking the Myth of a Polarized America"

MORRIS P. FIORINA

"There is a religious war going on in this country, a cultural war as critical to the kind of nation we shall be as the Cold War itself, for this war is for the soul of America."

With those ringing words insurgent candidate Pat Buchanan fired up his supporters at the 1992 Republican National Convention. To be sure, not all delegates cheered Buchanan's call to arms, which was at odds with the "kinder, gentler" image that George H.W. Bush had attempted to project. Election analysts later included Buchanan's fiery words among the factors contributing to the defeat of President Bush, albeit one of lesser importance than the slow economy and the repudiation of his "Read my lips, no new taxes" pledge.

In the years since Buchanan's declaration of cultural war, the idea of a clash of cultures has become a common theme in discussions of American politics. The culture war metaphor refers to a displacement of the classic economic conflicts that animated twentieth-century politics in the advanced democracies by newly emergent moral and cultural ones. The literature generally attributes Buchanan's inspiration to a 1991 book,

Culture Wars, by sociologist James Davison Hunter, who divided Americans into the culturally "orthodox" and the culturally "progressive" and argued that increasing conflict was inevitable.

No one has embraced the concept of the culture war more enthusiastically than journalists, ever alert for subjects that have "news value." Conflict is high in news value. Disagreement, division, polarization, battles, and war make good copy. Agreement, consensus, moderation, compromise, and peace do not. Thus, the notion of a culture war fits well with the news sense of journalists who cover politics. Their reports tell us that contemporary voters are sharply divided on moral issues. As David Broder wrote in the *Washington Post* in November 2000, "The divide went deeper than politics. It reached into the nation's psyche. . . . It was the moral dimension that kept Bush in the race."

Additionally, it is said that close elections do not reflect indifferent or ambivalent voters; rather, such elections reflect evenly matched blocs of deeply committed partisans. According to a February 2002 report in *USA Today*, "When George W. Bush took office, half the country cheered and the other half seethed"; some months later the *Economist* wrote that "such political divisions cannot easily be shifted by any president, let alone in two years, because they reflect deep demographic divisions. . . . The 50-50 nation appears to be made up of two big, separate voting blocks, with only a small number of swing voters in the middle."

The 2000 election brought us the familiar pictorial representation of the culture war in the form of the "red" and "blue" map of the United States. Vast areas of the heartland appeared as Republican red, while coastal and Great Lakes states took on a Democratic blue hue. Pundits reified the colors on the map, treating them as prima facie evidence of deep cultural divisions: Thus "Bush knew that the landslide he had wished for in 2000 . . . had vanished into the values chasm separating the blue states from the red ones" (John Kenneth White, in *The Values Divide*). In the same vein, the *Boston Herald* reported Clinton adviser Paul Begala as saying, on November 18, 2000, that "tens of millions of good people in Middle America voted Republican. But if you look closely at that map you see a more complex picture. You see the state where James Byrd was lynched—dragged behind a pickup truck until his body came apart—it's red. You see the state where Matthew Shepard was crucified on a split-rail fence for the crime of being gay—it's red. You see the state where right-wing extremists blew up a federal office building and murdered scores of federal employees—it's red."

Claims of bitter national division were standard fare after the 2000 elections, and few commentators publicly challenged them. On the contrary, the belief in a fractured nation was expressed even by high-level political operatives. Republican pollster Bill McInturff commented to the *Economist* in January 2001 that "we have two massive colliding forces. One is rural, Christian, religiously conservative. [The other] is socially tolerant, pro-choice, secular, living in New England and the Pacific Coast." And Matthew Dowd, a Bush reelection strategist, explained to the *Los Angeles Times* why Bush has not tried to expand his electoral base: "You've got 80 to 90 percent of the country that look at each other like they are on separate planets."

The journalistic drumbeat continues unabated. A November 2003 report from the Pew Research Center led E. J. Dionne Jr. of the *Washington Post* to comment: "The red states get redder, the blue states get bluer, and the political map of the United States takes on the coloration of the Civil War."

And as the 2004 election approaches, commentators see a continuation, if not an intensification, of the culture war. *Newsweek*'s Howard Fineman wrote in October 2003, "The culture war between the Red and Blue Nations has erupted again—big time—and will last until Election Day next year. Front lines are all over, from the Senate to the Pentagon to Florida to the Virginia suburbs where, at the Bush-Cheney 2004 headquarters, they are blunt about the shape of the battle: 'The country's split 50-50 again,' a top aide told me, 'just as it was in 2000.' "

In sum, observers of contemporary American politics have apparently reached a new consensus around the proposition that old disagreements about economics now pale in comparison to new divisions based on sexuality, morality, and religion, divisions so deep and bitter as to justify talk of war in describing them.

Yet research indicates otherwise. Publicly available databases show that the culture war script embraced by journalists and politicos lies somewhere between simple exaggeration and sheer nonsense. There is no culture war in the United States; no battle for the soul of America rages, at least none that most Americans are aware of.

Certainly, one can find a few warriors who engage in noisy skirmishes. Many of the activists in the political parties and the various cause groups do hate each other and regard themselves as combatants in a war. But their hatreds and battles are not shared by the great mass of Americans— certainly nowhere near "80–90 percent of the country"—who are for the most part moderate in their views and tolerant in their manner. A case in point: To their embarrassment, some GOP senators recently learned that ordinary Americans view gay marriage in somewhat less apocalyptic terms than do the activists in the Republican base.

If swing voters have disappeared, how did the six blue states in which George Bush ran most poorly in 2000 all elect Republican governors in 2002 (and how did Arnold Schwarzenegger run away with the 2003 recall in blue California)? If almost all voters have already made up their minds about their 2004 votes, then why did John Kerry surge to a 14-point trial-heat lead when polls offered voters the prospect of a Kerry-McCain ticket? If voter partisanship has hardened into concrete, why do virtually identical majorities in both red and blue states favor divided control of the presidency and Congress, rather than unified control by their party? Finally, and ironically, if voter positions have become so uncompromising, why did a recent CBS story titled "Polarization in America" report that 76 percent of Republicans, 87 percent of Democrats, and 86 percent of Independents would like to see elected officials compromise more rather than stick to their principles?

Still, how does one account for reports that have almost 90 percent of Republicans planning to vote for Bush and similarly high numbers of Democrats planning to vote for Kerry? The answer is that while voter *positions* have not polarized, their *choices* have. There is no contradiction here; positions and choices are not the same thing. Voter choices are functions of their positions and the positions and actions of the candidates they choose between.

Republican and Democratic elites unquestionably have polarized. But it is a mistake to assume that such elite polarization is equally present in the broader public. It is not. However much they may claim that they are responding to the public, political elites do not take extreme positions because *voters* make them. Rather, by presenting them with polarizing alternatives, elites make voters appear polarized, but the reality shows through clearly when voters have a choice of more moderate alternatives—as with the aforementioned Republican governors.

Republican strategists have bet the Bush presidency on a high-risk gamble. Reports and observation indicate that they are attempting to win in 2004 by getting out the votes of a few million Republican-leaning evangelicals who did not vote in 2000, rather than by attracting some modest proportion of 95 million other non-voting Americans, most of them moderates, not to mention moderate Democratic voters who could have been persuaded to back a genuinely compassionate conservative. Such a strategy leaves no cushion against a negative turn of events and renders the administration vulnerable to a credible Democratic move toward the center. Whether the Democrats can capitalize on their opportunity remains to be seen.

60

"How Divided Are We?"

JAMES Q. WILSON

The 2004 election left our country deeply divided over whether our country is deeply divided. For some, America is indeed a polarized nation, perhaps more so today than at any time in living memory. In this view, yesterday's split over Bill Clinton has given way to today's even more acrimonious split between Americans who detest George Bush and Americans who detest John Kerry, and similar divisions will persist as long as angry liberals and angry conservatives continue to confront each other across the political abyss. Others, however, believe that most Americans are moderate centrists, who, although disagreeing over partisan issues in 2004, harbor no deep ideological hostility. I take the former view.

By polarization I do not have in mind partisan disagreements alone. These have always been with us. Since popular voting began in the 19th century, scarcely any winning candidate has received more than 60 percent of the vote, and very few losers have received less than 40 percent. Inevitably, Americans will differ over who should be in the White House. But this does not necessarily mean they are polarized.

By polarization I mean something else: an intense commitment to a candidate, a culture, or an ideology that sets people in one group definitively apart from people in another, rival group. Such a condition is revealed when a candidate for public office is regarded by a competitor and his supporters not simply as wrong but as corrupt or wicked; when one way of thinking about the world is assumed to be morally superior to any other way; when one set of political beliefs is considered to be entirely correct and a rival set wholly wrong. In extreme form, as defined by Richard Hofstadter in *The Paranoid Style in American Politics* (1965), polarization can entail the belief that the other side is in thrall to a secret conspiracy that is using devious means to obtain control over society. Today's versions might go like this: "Liberals employ their dominance of the media, the universities, and Hollywood to enforce a radically secular agenda"; or, "conservatives, working through the religious Right and the big corporations, conspired with their hired neocon advisers to invade Iraq for the sake of oil."

Polarization is not new to this country. It is hard to imagine a society more divided than ours was in 1800, when pro-British, pro-commerce New Englanders supported John Adams for the presidency while pro-French, pro-agriculture Southerners backed Thomas Jefferson. One sign of this hostility was the passage of the Alien and Sedition Acts in 1798; another was that in 1800, just as in 2000, an extremely close election was settled by a struggle in one state (New York in 1800, Florida in 2000).

The fierce contest between Abraham Lincoln and George McClellan in 1864 signaled another national division, this one over the conduct of the Civil War. But thereafter, until recently, the nation ceased to be polarized in that sense. Even in the half-century from 1948 to (roughly) 1996, marked as it was by sometimes strong expressions of feeling over whether the presidency should go to Harry Truman or Thomas Dewey, to Dwight Eisenhower or Adlai Stevenson, to John F. Kennedy or Richard Nixon, to

Nixon or Hubert Humphrey, and so forth, opinion surveys do not indicate widespread detestation of one candidate or the other, or of the people who supported him.

Now they do. Today, many Americans and much of the press regularly speak of the President as a dimwit, a charlatan, or a knave. A former Democratic presidential candidate has asserted that Bush "betrayed" America by launching a war designed to benefit his friends and corporate backers. A senior Democratic Senator has characterized administration policy as a series of "lies, lies, and more lies" and has accused Bush of plotting a "mindless, needless, senseless, and reckless" war. From the other direction, similar expressions of popular disdain have been directed at Senator John Kerry (and before him at President Bill Clinton); if you have not heard them, that may be because (unlike many of my relatives) you do not live in Arkansas or Texas or other locales where the *New York Times* is not read. In these places, Kerry is widely spoken of as a scoundrel.

In the 2004 presidential election, over two-thirds of Kerry voters said they were motivated explicitly by the desire to defeat Bush. By early 2005, President Bush's approval rating, which stood at 94 percent among Republicans, was only 18 percent among Democrats—the largest such gap in the history of the Gallup poll. These data, moreover, were said to reflect a mutual revulsion between whole geographical sections of the country, the so-called Red (Republican) states versus the so-called Blue (Democratic) states. As summed up by the distinguished social scientist who writes humor columns under the name of Dave Barry, residents of Red states are "ignorant racist fascist knuckle-dragging NASCAR-obsessed cousin-marrying roadkill-eating tobacco-juice-dribbling gun-fondling religious fanatic rednecks," while Blue-state residents are "godless unpatriotic pierced-nose Volvo-driving France-loving leftwing Communist latte-sucking tofu-chomping holistic-wacko neurotic vegan weenie perverts."

To be sure, other scholars differ with Dr. Barry. To them, polarization, although a real enough phenomenon, is almost entirely confined to a small number of political elites and members of Congress. In *Culture War?*, which bears the subtitle "The Myth of a Polarized America," Morris Fiorina of Stanford argues that policy differences between voters in Red and Blue states are really quite small, and that most are in general agreement even on issues like abortion and homosexuality.

But the extent of polarization cannot properly be measured by the voting results in Red and Blue states. Many of these states are in fact deeply divided internally between liberal and conservative areas, and gave the nod to one candidate or the other by only a narrow margin. Inferring the views of individual citizens from the gross results of presidential balloting is a questionable procedure.

Nor does Fiorina's analysis capture the very real and very deep division over an issue like abortion. Between 1973, when *Roe v. Wade* was decided, and now, he writes, there has been no change in the degree to which people will or will not accept any one of six reasons to justify an abortion: (1) the woman's health is endangered; (2) she became pregnant because of a rape; (3) there is a strong chance of a fetal defect; (4) the family has a low income; (5) the woman is not married; and (6) the woman simply wants no more children. Fiorina may be right about that. Nevertheless, only about 40 percent of all Americans will support abortion for any of the last three reasons in his series, while over 80 percent will support it for one or another of the first three.

In other words, almost all Americans are for abortion in the case of maternal emergency, but fewer than half if it is simply a matter of the mother's preference. That split—a profoundly important one—has remained in place for over three decades, and it affects how people vote. In 2000 and again in 2004, 70 percent of those who thought abortion should always be legal voted for Al Gore or John Kerry, while over 70 percent of those who thought it should always be illegal voted for George Bush.

Division is just as great over other high-profile issues. Polarization over the war in Iraq, for example, is more pronounced than any war-related controversy in at least a half-century. In the fall of 2005, according to Gallup, 81 percent of Democrats but only 20 percent of Republicans thought the war in Iraq was a mistake. During the Vietnam war, by contrast, itself a famously contentious cause, there was more unanimity across party lines, whether for or against: in late 1968 and early 1969, about equal numbers of Democrats and Republicans thought the intervention there was a mistake. Pretty much the same was true of Korea: in early 1951, 44 percent of Democrats and 61 percent of Republicans thought the war was a mistake—a partisan split, but nowhere near as large as the one over our present campaign in Iraq.

Polarization, then, is real. But what explains its growth? And has it spread beyond the political elites to influence the opinions and attitudes of ordinary Americans?

The answer to the first question, I suspect, can be found in the changing politics of Congress, the new competitiveness of the mass media, and the rise of new interest groups.

That Congress is polarized seems beyond question. When, in 1998, the House deliberated whether to impeach President Clinton, all but four Republican members voted for at least one of the impeachment articles, while only five Democrats voted for even one. In the Senate, 91 percent of Republicans voted to convict on at least one article; every single Democrat voted for acquittal.

The impeachment issue was not an isolated case. In 1993, President Clinton's budget passed both the House and the Senate without a single Republican vote in favor. The same deep partisan split occurred over taxes and supplemental appropriations. Nor was this a blip: since 1950, there has been a steady increase in the percentage of votes in Congress pitting most Democrats against most Republicans.

In the midst of the struggle to pacify Iraq, Howard Dean, the chairman of the Democratic National Committee, said the war could not be won and Nancy Pelosi, the leader of the House Democrats, endorsed the view that American forces should be brought home as soon as possible. By contrast, although there was congressional grumbling (mostly by Republicans) about Korea and complaints (mostly by Democrats) about Vietnam, and although Senator George Aiken of Vermont famously proposed that we declare victory and withdraw, I cannot remember party leaders calling for unconditional surrender.

The reasons for the widening fissures in Congress are not far to seek. Each of the political parties was once a coalition of dissimilar forces: liberal Northern Democrats and conservative Southern Democrats, liberal coastal Republicans and conservative Midwestern Republicans. No longer; the realignments of the South (now overwhelmingly Republican) and of New England (now strongly Democratic) have all but eliminated legislators who deviate from the party's leadership. Conservative Democrats and liberal Republicans are endangered species now approaching extinction. At the same time, the ideological gap between the parties is growing: if there was once a large overlap between Democrats and Republicans—remember "Tweedledum and Tweedledee"?—today that congruence has almost disappeared. By the late 1990s, virtually every Democrat was more liberal than virtually every Republican.

The result has been not only intense partisanship but a sharp rise in congressional incivility. In 1995, a Republican-controlled Senate passed a budget that President Clinton proceeded to veto; in the loggerhead that followed, many federal agencies shut down (in a move that backfired on the Republicans). Congressional debates have seen an increase not only in heated exchanges but in the number of times a representative's words are either ruled out of order or "taken down" (that is, written by the clerk and then read aloud, with the offending member being asked if he or she wishes to withdraw them).

It has been suggested that congressional polarization is exacerbated by new districting arrangements that make each House seat safe for either a Democratic or a Republican incumbent. If only these seats were truly competitive, it is said, more centrist legislators would be elected. That seems plausible, but David C. King of Harvard has shown that it is wrong: in the House, the more competitive the district, the more extreme the views of the winner. This odd finding is apparently the consequence of a nomination process dominated by party activists. In primary races, where turnout is low (and seems to be getting lower), the ideologically motivated tend to exercise a preponderance of influence.

All this suggests a situation very unlike the half-century before the

1990s, if perhaps closer to certain periods in the eighteenth and nineteenth centuries. Then, too, incivility was common in Congress, with members not only passing the most scandalous remarks about each other but on occasion striking their rivals with canes or fists. Such partisan feeling ran highest when Congress was deeply divided over slavery before the Civil War and over Reconstruction after it. Today the issues are different, but the emotions are not dissimilar.

Next, the mass media: Not only are they themselves increasingly polarized, but consumers are well aware of it and act on that awareness. Fewer people now subscribe to newspapers or watch the network evening news. Although some of this decline may be explained by a preference for entertainment over news, some undoubtedly reflects the growing conviction that the mainstream press generally does not tell the truth, or at least not the whole truth.

In part, media bias feeds into, and off, an increase in business competition. In the 1950s, television news amounted to a brief 30-minute interlude in the day's programming, and not a very profitable one at that; for the rest of the time, the three networks supplied us with westerns and situation comedies. Today, television news is a vast, growing, and very profitable venture by the many broadcast and cable outlets that supply news twenty-four hours a day, seven days a week.

The news we get is not only more omnipresent, it is also more competitive and hence often more adversarial. When there were only three television networks, and radio stations were forbidden by the fairness doctrine from broadcasting controversial views, the media gravitated toward the middle of the ideological spectrum, where the large markets could be found. But now that technology has created cable news and the Internet, and now that the fairness doctrine has by and large been repealed, many media outlets find their markets at the ideological extremes.

Here is where the sharper antagonism among political leaders and their advisers and associates comes in. As one journalist has remarked about the change in his profession, "We don't deal in facts [any longer], but in attributed opinions." Or, these days, in unattributed opinions. And those opinions are more intensely rivalrous than was once the case.

The result is that, through commercial as well as ideological self-interest, the media contribute heavily to polarization. Broadcasters are eager for stories to fill their round-the-clock schedules, and at the same time reluctant to trust the government as a source for those stories. Many media outlets are clearly liberal in their orientation; with the arrival of Fox News and the growth of talk radio, many are now just as clearly conservative.

The evidence of liberal bias in the mainstream media is very strong. The Center for Media and Public Affairs (CMPA) has been systematically studying television broadcasts for a quarter-century. In the 2004 presidential campaign, John Kerry received more favorable mentions than any presidential candidate in CMPA's history, especially during the month before election day. This is not new: since 1980 (and setting aside the recent advent of Fox News), the Democratic candidate has received more favorable mentions than the Republican candidate in every race except the 1988 contest between Michael Dukakis and George H. W. Bush. A similarly clear orientation characterizes weekly newsmagazines like *Time* and *Newsweek*.

For its part, talk radio is listened to by about one-sixth of the adult public, and that one-sixth is made up mostly of conservatives. National Public Radio has an audience of about the same size; it is disproportionately liberal. The same breakdown affects cable-television news, where the rivalry is between CNN (and MSNBC) and Fox News. Those who watch CNN are more likely to be Democrats than Republicans; the reverse is emphatically true of Fox. As for news and opinion on the Internet, which has become an important source for college graduates in particular, it, too, is largely polarized along political and ideological lines, emphasized even more by the culture that has grown up around news blogs.

At one time, our culture was only weakly affected by the media because news organizations had only a few points of access to us and were largely moderate and audience-maximizing enterprises. Today the media have many lines of access, and reflect both the maximization of controversy and the cultivation of niche markets. Once the media talked to us; now they shout at us.

And then there are the interest groups. In the past, the major ones—the National Association of Manufacturers, the Chamber of Commerce, and labor organizations like the AFL-CIO—were concerned with their own material interests. They are still active, but the loudest messages today come from very different sources and have a very different cast to them. They are issued by groups concerned with social and cultural matters like civil rights, managing the environment, alternatives to the public schools, the role of women, access to firearms, and so forth, and they directly influence the way people view politics.

Interest groups preoccupied with material concerns can readily find ways to arrive at compromise solutions to their differences; interest groups divided by issues of rights or morality find compromise very difficult. The positions taken by many of these groups and their supporters, often operating within the two political parties, profoundly affect the selection of candidates for office. In brief, it is hard to imagine someone opposed to abortion receiving the Democratic nomination for President, or someone in favor of it receiving the Republican nomination.

Outside the realm of party politics, interest groups also file briefs in important court cases and can benefit from decisions that in turn help shape the political debate. Abortion became a hot controversy in the 1970s not because the American people were already polarized on the matter but because their (mainly centrist) views were not consulted;

instead, national policy was determined by the Supreme Court in a decision, *Roe v. Wade,* that itself reflected a definition of "rights" vigorously promoted by certain well-defined interest groups.

Polarization not only is real and has increased, but it has also spread to rank-and-file voters through elite influence.

In *The Nature and Origins of Mass Opinion . . . ,* John R. Zaller of UCLA listed a number of contemporary issues—homosexuality, a nuclear freeze, the war in Vietnam, busing for school integration, the 1990–91 war to expel Iraq from Kuwait—and measured the views held about them by politically aware citizens. (By "politically aware," Zaller meant people who did well answering neutral factual questions about politics.) His findings were illuminating.

Take the Persian Gulf war. Iraq had invaded Kuwait in August 1990. From that point through the congressional elections in November 1990, scarcely any elite voices were raised to warn against anything the United States might contemplate doing in response. Two days after the mid-term elections, however, President George H. W. Bush announced that he was sending many more troops to the Persian Gulf. This provoked strong criticism from some members of Congress, especially Democrats.

As it happens, a major public-opinion survey was under way just as these events were unfolding. Before criticism began to be voiced in Congress, both registered Democrats and registered Republicans had supported Bush's vaguely announced intention of coming to the aid of Kuwait; the more politically aware they were, the greater their support. After the onset of elite criticism, the support of Republican voters went up, but Democratic support flattened out. As Bush became more vigorous in indicating his aims, politically aware voters began to differ sharply, with Democratic support declining and Republican support increasing further.

Much the same pattern can be seen in popular attitudes toward the other issues studied by Zaller. As political awareness increases, attitudes split apart, with, for example, highly aware liberals favoring busing and job guarantees and opposing the war in Vietnam, and highly aware conservatives opposing busing and job guarantees and supporting the war in Vietnam.

But why should this be surprising? To imagine that extremist politics has been confined to the chattering classes is to believe that Congress, the media, and American interest groups operate in an ideological vacuum. I find that assumption implausible.

As for the extent to which these extremist views have spread, that is probably best assessed by looking not at specific issues but at enduring political values and party preferences. In 2004, only 12 percent of Democrats approved of George Bush; at earlier periods, by contrast, three to four times as many Democrats approved of Ronald Reagan, Gerald Ford, Richard Nixon, and Dwight D. Eisenhower. Over the course of about two decades, in other words, party affiliation had come to exercise a critical influence over what people thought about a sitting President.

The same change can be seen in the public's view of military power. Since the late 1980s, Republicans have been more willing than Democrats to say that "the best way to ensure peace is through military strength." By the late 1990s and on into 2003, well over two-thirds of all Republicans agreed with this view, but far fewer than half of all Democrats did. In 2005, three-fourths of all Democrats but fewer than a third of all Republicans told pollsters that good diplomacy was the best way to ensure peace. In the same survey, two-thirds of all Republicans but only one fourth of all Democrats said they would fight for this country "whether it is right or wrong."

Unlike in earlier years, the parties are no longer seen as Tweedledum and Tweedledee. To the contrary, as they sharpen their ideological differences, attentive voters have sharpened their ideological differences. They now like either the Democrats or the Republicans more than they once did, and are less apt to feel neutral toward either one.

How deep does this polarization reach? As measured by opinion polls, the gap between Democrats and Republicans was twice as great in 2004 as in 1972. In fact, rank-and-file Americans disagree more strongly today than did politically active Americans in 1972.

To be sure, this mass polarization involves only a minority of all voters, but the minority is sizable, and a significant part of it is made up of the college-educated. As Marc Hetherington of Vanderbilt puts it: "people with the greatest ability to assimilate new information, those with more formal education, are most affected by elite polarization." And that cohort has undeniably grown.

In 1900, only 10 percent of all young Americans went to high school. My father, in common with many men his age in the early twentieth century, dropped out of school after the eighth grade. Even when I graduated from college, the first in my family to do so, fewer than one-tenth of all Americans over the age of twenty-five had gone that far. Today [2006], 84 percent of adult Americans have graduated from high school and nearly 27 percent have graduated from college. This extraordinary growth in schooling has produced an ever larger audience for political agitation.

Ideologically, an even greater dividing line than undergraduate education is postgraduate education. People who have proceeded beyond college seem to be very different from those who stop with a high-school or college diploma. Thus, about a sixth of all voters describe themselves as liberals, but the figure for those with a postgraduate degree is well over a quarter. In mid-2004, about half of all voters trusted George Bush; less than a third of those with a postgraduate education did. In November of the same year, when over half of all college graduates voted for Bush, well over half of the smaller cohort who had done postgraduate work voted for Kerry. According to the Pew Center for Research on the People and the Press, more than half of all Democrats with a postgraduate education supported the antiwar candidacy of Howard Dean.

The effect of postgraduate education is reinforced by being in a profession. Between 1900 and 1960, write John B. Judis and Ruy Teixeira in *The Emerging Democratic Majority* . . . , professionals voted pretty much the same way as business managers; by 1988, the former began supporting Democrats while the latter supported Republicans. On the other hand, the effect of postgraduate education seems to outweigh the effect of affluence. For most voters, including college graduates, having higher incomes means becoming more conservative; not so for those with a postgraduate education, whose liberal predilections are immune to the wealth effect.

The results of this linkage between ideology, on the one hand, and congressional polarization, media influence, interest-group demands, and education on the other are easily read in the commentary surrounding the 2004 election. In their zeal to denigrate the President, liberals, pronounced one conservative pundit, had "gone quite around the twist." According to liberal spokesmen, conservatives with their "religious intolerance" and their determination to rewrite the Constitution had so befuddled their fellow Americans that a "great nation was felled by a poisonous nut."

If such wholesale slurs are not signs of polarization, then the word has no meaning. To a degree that we cannot precisely measure, and over issues that we cannot exactly list, polarization has seeped down into the public, where it has assumed the form of a culture war. The sociologist James Davison Hunter, who has written about this phenomenon in a mainly religious context, defines culture war as "political and social hostility rooted in different systems of moral understanding." Such conflicts, he writes, which can involve "fundamental ideas about who we are as Americans," are waged both across the religious/secular divide and within religions themselves, where those with an "orthodox" view of moral authority square off against those with a "progressive" view.

To some degree, this terminology is appropriate to today's political situation as well. We are indeed in a culture war in Hunter's sense, though I believe this war is itself but another component, or another symptom, of the larger ideological polarization that has us in its grip. Conservative thinking on political issues has religious roots, but it also has roots that are fully as secular as anything on the Left. By the same token, the liberal attack on conservatives derives in part from an explicitly "progressive" religious orientation—liberal Protestantism or Catholicism, or Reform Judaism—but in part from the same secular sources shared by many conservatives.

But what, one might ask, is wrong with having well-defined parties arguing vigorously about the issues that matter? Is it possible that polarized politics is a good thing, encouraging sharp debate and clear positions? Perhaps that is true on those issues where reasonable compromises can be devised. But there are two limits to such an arrangement.

First, many Americans believe that unbridgeable political differences have prevented leaders from addressing the problems they were elected to address. As a result, distrust of government mounts, leading to an alienation from politics altogether. The steep decline in popular approval of our national officials has many causes, but surely one of them is that ordinary voters agree among themselves more than political elites agree with each other—and the elites are far more numerous than they once were.

In the 1950s, a committee of the American Political Science Association (APSA) argued the case for a "responsible" two-party system. The model the APSA had in mind was the more ideological and therefore more "coherent" party system of Great Britain. At the time, scarcely anyone thought our parties could be transformed in such a supposedly salutary direction. Instead, as Governor George Wallace of Alabama put it in his failed third-party bid for the presidency, there was not a "dime's worth of difference" between Democrats and Republicans.

What Wallace forgot was that, however alike the parties were, the public liked them that way. A half-century ago, Tweedledum and Tweedledee enjoyed the support of the American people; the more different they have become, the greater has been the drop in popular confidence in both them and the federal government.

A final drawback of polarization is more profound. Sharpened debate is arguably helpful with respect to domestic issues, but not for the management of important foreign and military matters. The United States, an unrivaled superpower with unparalleled responsibilities for protecting the peace and defeating terrorists, is now forced to discharge those duties with its own political house in disarray.

We fought World War II as a united nation, even against two enemies (Germany and Italy) that had not attacked us. We began the wars in Korea and Vietnam with some degree of unity, too, although it was eventually whittled away. By the early 1990s, when we expelled Iraq from Kuwait, we had to do so over the objections of congressional critics; the first President Bush avoided putting the issue to Congress altogether. In 2003 we toppled Saddam Hussein in the face of catcalls from many domestic leaders and opinion-makers. Now, in stabilizing Iraq and helping that country create a new free government, we have proceeded despite intense and mounting criticism, much of it voiced by politicians who before the war agreed that Saddam Hussein was an evil menace in possession of weapons of mass destruction and that we had to remove him.

Denmark or Luxembourg can afford to exhibit domestic anguish and uncertainty over military policy; the United States cannot. A divided America encourages our enemies, disheartens our allies, and saps our resolve—potentially to fatal effect. What General Giap of North Vietnam once said of us is even truer today. America cannot be defeated on the battlefield, but it can be defeated at home. Polarization is a force that can defeat us.

"Polarized America?"

February 21, 2006

To the editor:

James Q. Wilson (February) takes issue with my demonstration in *Culture War? The Myth of a Polarized America* (with Samuel Abrams and Jeremy Pope) that the polarization evident among the members of the American political class has only a faint reflection in the American public. As a long-time admirer of Wilson's work I am naturally concerned when his take on some aspect of American politics differs from mine. But I believe that his criticisms are a result of misunderstanding. I would like to address two of them.

First, Wilson discounts our red state-blue state comparisons with the comment that "Inferring the views of individual citizens from the gross results of presidential balloting is a questionable procedure." Indeed it is, which is why we did not do that. As we wrote in the book, inferring polarization from close elections is precisely what pundits have done and why their conclusions have been wrong. In contrast, we report detailed analyses of the policy views expressed by voters in 2000 and 2004 and contrary to the claims of Garry Wills, Maureen Dowd, and other op-ed columnists, we find surprisingly small differences between the denizens of the blue states and the red states. As we show in the book and emphasize repeatedly, people's *choices* (as expressed, say, in presidential balloting) can be polarized while their *positions* are not, and the evidence strongly indicates that this is the case.

Moreover, we report that not only are red and blue state citizens surprisingly similar in their views, but other studies find little evidence of growing polarization no matter how one slices and dices the population—affluent v. poor, white v. black v. brown, old v. young, well educated v. the less educated, men v. women, and so on. Like many before him, Wilson confuses partisan *sorting* with polarization—the Democrats have largely shed their conservative southern wing while Republicans have largely shed their liberal Rockefeller wing, resulting in more distinct parties, even while the aggregate distribution of ideology and issue stances among the citizenry remains much the same as in the past.

Second, Wilson criticizes our analysis of Americans' views on the specific issue of abortion, contending that the small numerical differences expressed by people on a General Social Survey scale constitute a significantly larger substantive difference. Although we disagree, even if one accepted Wilson's contention, it would not apply to our supporting analysis of a differently-worded Gallup survey item that yields the same conclusions, or to numerous other survey items that clearly show that most Americans are "pro-choice, buts."

For example, Wilson notes that "70 percent of those who thought abortion should always be legal voted for Al Gore or John Kerry, while over 70 percent of those who thought it should always be illegal voted for George Bush." True enough, but he does not mention that Gallup repeatedly finds that a majority of the American people place themselves between those polar categories—they think abortion should be "legal only under certain circumstances." Even limiting the analysis to avowed partisans, in 2005 only 30 percent of Democrats thought abortion should always be legal, and fewer than 30 percent of Republicans thought it should always be illegal. One can raise questions about every survey item that has ever been asked, but the cumulative weight of the evidence on Americans' abortion views is overwhelming. Contrary to the wishes of the activists on both sides, the American people prefer a middle ground on abortion, period.

Wilson approvingly cites James Davison Hunter, whose book, *Culture War*, inspired Patrick Buchanan's 1992 speech at the Republican National Convention. In a forthcoming Brookings Institution volume, Hunter now limits his thesis to "somewhere between 10 and 15 percent who occupy these opposing moral and ideological universes." That leaves more than 80 percent of the American public not engaged in the moral and ideological battles reveled in by the political class. Note that Wilson's examples of incivil discourse reference "the press," "a former Democratic presidential candidate," "a senior Democratic Senator," "liberal spokesmen," and "one conservative pundit." Absent from this list are well-intentioned, ordinary working Americans not given to the kind of incendiary remarks that get quoted by journalists.

I share Wilson's concern with the potentially harmful consequences of polarization. But the first step in addressing those concerns is to get the facts correct. I remain convinced that we have done that. If Americans are offered competent, pragmatic candidates with a problem-solving orientation, the shallow popular roots of political polarization will be exposed for all to see.

Morris P. Fiorina
Stanford, California

61

"Tea Minus Zero"

John B. Judis

Liberals have responded to the Tea Party movement by reaching a comforting conclusion: that there is no way these guys can possibly be for real. The movement has variously been described as a "front group for the Republican party" and a "media creation"; Paul Krugman has called Tea Party rallies "AstroTurf (fake grass roots) events, manufactured by the usual suspects."

I can understand why liberals would want to dismiss the Tea Party movement as an inauthentic phenomenon; it would certainly be welcome news if it were. The sentiments on display at Tea Party rallies go beyond run-of-the-mill anti-tax, anti-spending conservatism and into territory that rightly strikes liberals as truly disturbing. Among the signs I saw at an April 15 protest in Washington: "IF IT SOUNDS LIKE MARX AND ACTS LIKE STALIN IT MUST BE OBAMA," "STOP OBAMA'S BROWN-SHIRT INFILTRAITORS," and "OBAMA BIN LYIN," which was accompanied by an illustration of the president looking like a monkey.

But the Tea Party movement is not inauthentic, and—contrary to the impression its rallies give off—it isn't a fringe faction either. It is a genuine popular movement, one that has managed to unite a number of ideological strains from U.S. history—some recent, some older. These strains can be described as many things, but they cannot be dismissed as passing phenomena. Much as liberals would like to believe otherwise, there is good reason to think the Tea Party movement could exercise considerable influence over our politics in the coming years.

The movement essentially began on February 19, 2009, when CNBC commentator Rick Santelli, speaking from the floor of the Chicago Mercantile Exchange, let loose against the Obama administration's plan to help homeowners who could no longer pay their mortgages. "This is America!" Santelli exclaimed. "How many of you people want to pay for your neighbors' mortgage that has an extra bathroom and can't pay their bills?" Santelli called for a "Chicago Tea Party" to protest the administration's plan.

Santelli's appeal was answered by a small group of bloggers, policy wonks, and Washington politicos who were primarily drawn from the libertarian wing of the conservative movement. They included John O'Hara from the Illinois Policy Institute (who has written a history of the movement, titled *A New American Tea Party*); Brendan Steinhauser of Free-domWorks, a Washington lobbying group run by former Representative Dick Armey; and blogger Michael Patrick Leahy, a founder of Top Conservatives on Twitter. The initial round of Tea Party protests took place at the end of February in over 30 cities. There were more protests in April, and, by the time of the massive September 12 protest last year, the Tea Party movement had officially arrived as a political force.

Like many American movements, the Tea Parties are not tightly organized from above. They are a network of local groups and national ones (Tea Party Patriots, Tea Party Express, Tea Party Nation), Washington lobbies and quasi-think tanks (FreedomWorks, Americans for Prosperity), bloggers, and talk-show hosts. There are no national membership lists, but extensive polls done by Quinnipiac, the Winston Group, and Economist/YouGov suggest that the movement commands the active allegiance of between 13 percent and 15 percent of the electorate. That is a formidable number, and, judging from other polls that ask whether someone has a "favorable" view of the Tea Parties, the movement gets a sympathetic hearing from as much as 40 percent of the electorate.

Tea Partiers' favorite politician is undoubtedly Sarah Palin—according to the Economist/YouGov poll, 71 percent of Tea Partiers think Palin "is more qualified to be president than Barack Obama" (and another 15 percent are "not sure")—but, more than anyone else, the movement takes its cues from Glenn Beck. Unlike fellow talkers Rush Limbaugh and Sean Hannity, Beck has never been a conventional Republican; he calls himself a conservative rather than a member of the GOP. While Limbaugh has attempted to soft-pedal his personal failings, the baby-faced Beck makes his into a story of redemption. He is, in his own words, an "average, everyday person." You need to have followed Beck's conspiratorial meanderings to understand what preoccupies many members of the Tea Party movement. At the Washington demonstration in April, for instance, there were people holding signs attacking Frances Fox Piven and Richard Cloward, two 1960s-era Columbia University sociologists who, Beck claims, were the brains behind both the community group ACORN and Obama's attempt to destroy capitalism by bankrupting the government through national health care reform.

In the last year, the movement's focus has shifted from demonstrations to elections. Currently, Tea Party groups are backing Republican Senate candidates in Kentucky, Utah, and Florida, while trying to knock off Democratic Senators Harry Reid in Nevada and Arlen Specter in Pennsylvania. In some places, Tea Party organizations have begun to displace the state GOP. Last month, Action is Brewing, the northern Nevada Tea Party affiliate, hosted a televised debate for the Republican gubernatorial and senatorial candidates. In addition, numerous candidates are running for Congress as Tea Party supporters.

The Tea Parties are the descendants of a number of conservative insurgencies from the past two generations: the anti-tax rebellion of the late '70s, the Moral Majority and Christian Coalition of the '80s and '90s, and Pat Buchanan's presidential runs. Like the Tea Partiers I saw in Washington—and the picture of the Tea Partiers put forward by the Winston and Quinnipiac polls—these movements have been almost entirely white, disproportionately middle-aged or older, and more male than female (though parts of the Christian right are an exception on this count). A majority of their adherents generally are not college-educated, with incomes in the middle range—attributes that also closely match the Tea Party movement's demographic profile. (A misleading picture of Tea Partiers as college-educated and affluent came from a *New York Times*/CBS poll of people who merely "support," but don't necessarily have anything to do with, the Tea Party movement. The other polls surveyed people who say they are "part of" the movement.)

Sociologists who have studied these earlier movements describe their followers as coming from the "marginal segments of the middle class." That's a sociological, but also a political, fact. These men and women look uneasily upward at corporate CEOs and investment bankers, and downward at low-wage service workers and laborers, many of whom are minorities. And their political outlook is defined by whether they primarily blame those below or above for the social and economic anxieties they feel. In the late nineteenth and early twentieth century, the marginal middle class was the breeding ground for left-wing attacks against Wall Street. For the last half-century, it has nourished right-wing complaints about blacks, illegal immigrants, and the poor.

It isn't just demography that the Tea Parties have in common with recent conservative movements; it's also politics. To be sure, some of the original Tea Party organizers were young libertarians, many of whom, like Brendan Steinhauser, voted for Ron Paul in 2008 and have rediscovered Ayn Rand's ethic of rational selfishness. They remain part of the movement—one sign I saw at the Washington rally read, "WE ARE JOHN GALT," referring to the hero of *Atlas Shrugged*—but, as the movement has grown, its adherents have become more conventionally conservative. As Grover Norquist likes to point out, what distinguishes one conservative group from another is not their members' overall views, but what "moves" them to demonstrate or to vote. The Christian right, for instance, went to the barricades over abortion and gay marriage, yet most members also hold conservative economic views. Likewise, the Tea Partiers have been moved to action by economic issues, but they share the outlook of social conservatives. According to the Economist/YouGov poll, 74 percent of Tea Party members think abortion is "murder," and 81 percent are against gay marriage. Sixty-three percent are in favor of public school students learning that "the Book of Genesis in the Bible explains how God created the world"; 62 percent think that "the only way to Heaven is through Jesus Christ." These beliefs are on display at rallies: In

Washington, one demonstrator in clerical garb held a sign saying, "GOD HATES TAXES." Moreover, aside from the followers of Ron Paul, Tea Party members also share the post-September 11 national security views of the GOP. When Tea Partiers were asked to name the "most important issue" to them, terrorism came in third out of ten, behind only the economy and the budget deficit.

If you look at the people who are running as pro–Tea Party candidates, you discover that some of them have simply graduated from one stage of the conservative movement to another. Jason Meade, who is running for Congress in Ohio, was just out of school, working in his father's business and playing music, when he "returned to the church and left the music world behind." Now 38, he sees his participation in Tea Party politics as a continuation of his twelve subsequent years in ministry school. "I decided to try and minister in a new way; by trying to be involved in the protection of the freedoms and liberty that God has given us and that have been woven into the fabric of our country," he wrote on his website. Jason Sager, 36, who is running in a Republican congressional primary northeast of Tampa, got into conservative politics in the wake of September 11. A Navy veteran, he joined a group called Protest Warrior that staged counter-demonstrations at antiwar rallies, and he was a volunteer in George W. Bush's 2004 campaign. After Obama's election, he got involved with Glenn Beck's 912 Project and, then, with the local Tea Parties.

But the Tea Parties' roots in U.S. history go back much further than the conservative movements of recent decades. The Tea Parties are defined by three general ideas that have played a key role in U.S. politics since the country's early days. The first is an obsession with decline. This idea, which traces back to the outlook of New England Puritans during the seventeenth century, consists of a belief that a golden age occurred some time ago; that we are now in a period of severe social, economic, or moral decay; that evil forces and individuals are the cause of this situation; that the goal of politics is to restore the earlier period; and that the key to doing so is heeding a special text that can serve as a guidebook for the journey backward. (The main difference between the far right and far left is that the left locates the golden age in the future.) The Puritans were trying to reproduce the circumstances of early Christianity in New England, using the Bible as their guiding text. Their enemies were Catholics and the Church of England, who they believed had corrupted the religion. For the Tea Partiers, the golden age is the time of the Founders, and adherence to the Constitution is the means to restore this period in the face of challenges from secular humanism, radical Islam, and especially socialism.

Beck has been instrumental in sacralizing the Constitution. He has touted the works of the late W. Cleon Skousen, a John Birch Society defender who projected his ultraconservative views back onto the Founding

Fathers. In *The 5000 Year Leap*, which has been reissued with a foreword by Beck, Skousen claimed that the Founders "warned against the 'welfare state'" and against "the drift toward the collectivist left."

In Arizona, Tea Party members hand out copies of the Constitution at political meetings the way a missionary group might hand out Bibles. The San Antonio Tea Party group has demanded that politicians sign a "contract with the Constitution." In speeches, Tea Partiers cite articles and amendments from the Constitution the same way that clerics cite Biblical verses. Speaking at the Lakeland Tea Party rally on tax day, Jason Sager said, "You are now able to see the most pressing issue that faces our nation and our society. Do you know what that issue is? We are now witnessing the fundamental breakdown of the republican form of government that we are guaranteed in Article Four, Section Four of our Constitution." In typical fashion, Sager did not go on to explain what Article Four, Section Four was. (You can look it up. I had to.)

Just as the Puritans believed Catholics and the Church of England were undermining Christianity, the Tea Partiers have fixated on nefarious individuals and groups—Saul Alinsky, ACORN, and, of course, Obama himself—who they believe are destroying the country. (According to the Economist/YouGov poll, 52 percent of Tea Party members think ACORN stole the 2008 election from John McCain; another 24 percent are still not sure.) "America has let thieves into her home," writes Beck, "and that nagging in your gut is a final warning that our country is about to be stolen." Their determination to locate the threat outside the United States accounts for their emphasis on Obama being a socialist, Marxist, communist, or even fascist—all of which are foreign faiths—rather than what he is: a conventional American liberal. It also helps explain the repeated references to Obama's African father. And it explains why some Tea Partiers continue to believe, in the face of incontrovertible evidence, that Obama was born outside the United States. The Economist/YouGov poll found that 34 percent of Tea Party members think he was not born in the United States, and another 34 percent are not sure.

But how could a movement that cultivates such crazy, conspiratorial views be regarded favorably by as much as 40 percent of the electorate? That is where the Tea Party movement's second link to early U.S. history comes in. The Tea Partiers may share the Puritans' fear of decline, but it is what they share with Thomas Jefferson that has far broader appeal: a staunch anti-statism. What began as a sentiment of the left—a rejection of state monopolies—became, after the industrial revolution and the rise of the labor movement, a weapon against progressive reforms. The basic idea—that government is a "necessary evil"—has retained its power, and, when the economy has faltered, Americans have been quick to blame Washington, perhaps even before they looked at Wall Street or big corporations. It happened in the late '70s under Jimmy Carter and in the early

'90s under George H. W. Bush; and it has happened again during Obama's first 18 months in office. According to a Pew poll, the percentage of Americans "angry" with government has risen from 10 percent in February 2000 to 21 percent today, while another 56 percent are "frustrated" with government.

Of course, during Franklin Roosevelt's first term, most voters didn't blame the incumbent administration for the Great Depression. Roosevelt was able to deflect blame for the depression back onto the Hoover administration and the "economic royalists" of Wall Street and corporate America. But Roosevelt took office at the nadir of the Great Depression, and his policies achieved dramatic improvements in unemployment and economic growth during his first term. Obama took office barely four months after the financial crisis visibly hit, and he has had to preside over growing unemployment.

Simmering economic frustration also accounts for the final historical strain that defines the Tea Parties: They are part of a tradition of producerism that dates to Andrew Jackson. Jacksonian Democrats believed that workers should enjoy the fruits of what they produce and not have to share them with the merchants and bankers who didn't actually create anything. The Populists of the late nineteenth century invoked this ethic in denouncing the Eastern bankers who held their farms hostage. Producerism also underlay Roosevelt's broadsides against economic royalists and Bill Clinton's promise to give priority to those who "work hard and play by the rules."

During the 1970s, conservatives began invoking producerism to justify their attacks on the welfare state, and it was at the core of the conservative tax revolt. While the Jacksonians and Populists had largely directed their anger upward, conservatives directed their ire at the people below who were beneficiaries of state programs—from the "welfare queens" of the ghetto to the "illegal aliens" of the barrio. Like the attack against "big government," this conservative producerism has most deeply resonated during economic downturns. And the Tea Parties have clearly built their movement around it.

Producerism was at the heart of Santelli's rant against government forcing the responsible middle class to subsidize those who bought homes they couldn't afford. In his history of the Tea Party movement, O'Hara described an America divided between "moochers, big and small, corporate and individual, trampling over themselves with their hands out demanding endless bailouts" and "disgusted, hardworking citizens getting sick of being played for chumps and punished for practicing personal responsibility." The same theme recurs in the Tea Partiers' rejection of liberal legislation. Beck dismissed Obama's health care reform plan as "good old socialism . . . raping the pocketbooks of the rich to give to the poor." Speaking to cheers at the April 15 rally in Washington, Armey denounced the progressive income tax in the same terms. "I can't steal your money and give it to this guy," he declared. "Therefore, I shouldn't use the power of the state to steal your money and give it to this guy."

The Tea Parties are not managed by the Republican National Committee, and they are not really a wing of the GOP. It is telling that Beck devoted his February speech at the Conservative Political Action Conference to bashing Republicans—and that, in a survey of 50 Tea Party leaders, the Sam Adams Alliance found that 28 percent identify themselves as Independents and 11 percent as Tea Party members rather than Republicans. Still, the Tea Partiers' political objective is clearly to push the GOP to the right. They agitated last summer for a Republican party-line vote against health care reform and are now arguing that states have a constitutional right to refuse to comply with it. They have been calling the offices of Republican senators to demand that they oppose a bipartisan compromise on financial regulatory reform. In South Carolina, they have attacked Senator Lindsey Graham, who is also a favorite Beck target, for backing a cap-and-trade [environmental] bill. The Arizona Tea Party pressured Governor Jan Brewer to sign the now-infamous bill targeting illegal immigrants. And Tea Party Nation has issued a "Red Alert" to prevent Congress from adopting "amnesty" legislation.

If the GOP wins back at least one house of Congress in November, the Tea Parties will be able to claim victory and demand a say in Republican congressional policies. That could lead to a replay of the Newt Gingrich Congress of 1995–1996, from which the country was lucky to escape relatively unscathed. But, beyond this, it's hard to say what will become of the movement. If the economy improves in a significant way next year, it is likely to fade. That is what happened to the tax revolt, which peaked from 1978 to 1982 and then subsided. But, if the economy limps along— say, in the manner of Japan over the last 15 years—then the Tea Parties will likely remain strong, and may even become a bigger force in U.S. politics than they are now.

For all of its similarities to previous insurgencies, the Tea Party movement differs in one key respect from the most prominent conservative movement of recent years, the Christian right: The Tea Parties do not have the same built-in impediments to growth. The Christian right looked like it was going to expand in the early '90s, but it ran up against the limit of its politics, which were grounded ultimately in an esoteric theology and a network of churches. If it strayed too far from the implications of that theology, it risked splitting its membership. But, if it articulated it— as Pat Robertson and others did at various inopportune moments—then it risked alienating the bulk of Americans. The Tea Parties do not have the same problem. They have their own crazy conspiracy theories, but even the wackiest Tea Partiers wouldn't demand that a candidate seeking their endorsement agree that ACORN fixed the election or that Obama is foreign-born. And their core appeal on government and spending will continue to resonate as long as the economy sputters. None of this is what liberals want to hear, but we might as well face reality: The Tea Party movement—firmly grounded in a number of durable U.S. political traditions and well-positioned for a time of economic uncertainty—could be around for a while.

Discussion Questions

1. According to Wilson and Judis, what are the chief factors contributing to polarization and cultural division in the United States? Are these factors likely to change anytime soon? What part, if any, of Wilson's and Judis's arguments would Fiorina agree with?

2. Based on the articles and other information you might have, do you think Fiorina is right that the American public is not deeply split on a range of issues and that they tend to favor more moderate solutions to problems? Can you think of issues for which this would be true?

3. If you were an adviser for one of the two major parties, how would you advise them to address the issue of polarization or culture war? Should they emphasize issues where broader consensus might be possible? Or is it the job of political parties to emphasize precisely those issues that might be the most divisive in order to appeal to their strongest supporters? Which is better for voters—a focus on consensus or on contrasts?

4. Party strategists often talk about changing a party's public image. In your view, what would a party have to do to change its public image significantly? What would convince you that a party had changed?

CHAPTER 12

Groups and Interests

62

"Political Association in the United States," from *Democracy in America*

ALEXIS DE TOCQUEVILLE

The right of political association has long been a cornerstone of American democracy. Alexis de Tocqueville, a French citizen who studied early nineteenth-century American society, argued that the right to associate provides an important check on a majority's power to suppress a political minority. Tocqueville pointed out that allowing citizens to associate in a variety of groups with a variety of crosscutting interests provides a political outlet for all types of political interests. It also enables compromises to be reached as each interest group attempts to build support among shifting coalitions. "There is a place for individual independence," Tocqueville argued, in the American system of government. "[A]s in society, all the members are advancing at the same time toward the same goal, but they are not obliged to follow exactly the same path."

Better use has been made of association and this powerful instrument of action has been applied to more varied aims in America than anywhere else in the world.

* * *

The inhabitant of the United States learns from birth that he must rely on himself to combat the ills and trials of life; he is restless and defiant in his outlook toward the authority of society and appeals to its power only when he cannot do without it. The beginnings of this attitude first appear at school, where the children, even in their games, submit to rules settled by themselves and punish offenses which they have defined themselves. The same attitude turns up again in all the affairs of social life. If some obstacle blocks the public road halting the circulation of traffic, the neighbors at once form a deliberative body; this improvised assembly produces an executive authority which remedies the trouble before anyone has thought of the possibility of some previously constituted authority beyond that of those concerned. Where enjoyment is concerned, people associate to make festivities grander and more orderly. Finally, associations are formed to combat exclusively moral troubles: intemperance is fought in common. Public security, trade and industry, and morals and religion all provide the aims for associations in the United States. There is no end which the human will despairs of attaining by the free action of the collective power of individuals.

* * *

The right of association being recognized, citizens can use it in different ways. An association simply consists in the public and formal support of specific doctrines by a certain number of individuals who have undertaken to cooperate in a stated way in order to make these doctrines prevail. Thus the right of association can almost be identified with freedom to write, but already associations are more powerful than the press. When some view is represented by an association, it must take clearer and more precise shape. It counts its supporters and involves them in its cause; these supporters get to know one another, and numbers increase zeal. An association unites the energies of divergent minds and vigorously directs them toward a clearly indicated goal.

Freedom of assembly marks the second stage in the use made of the right of association. When a political association is allowed to form centers of action at certain important places in the country, its activity becomes greater and its influence more widespread. There men meet, active measures are planned, and opinions are expressed with that strength and warmth which the written word can never attain.

But the final stage is the use of association in the sphere of politics. The supporters of an agreed view may meet in electoral colleges and appoint mandatories to represent them in a central assembly. That is, properly speaking, the application of the representative system to one party.

* * *

In our own day freedom of association has become a necessary guarantee against the tyranny of the majority. In the United States, once a party has become predominant, all public power passes into its hands; its close supporters occupy all offices and have control of all organized forces. The most distinguished men of the opposite party, unable to cross the barrier keeping them from power, must be able to establish themselves outside it; the minority must use the whole of its moral authority to oppose the physical power oppressing it. Thus the one danger has to be balanced against a more formidable one.

The omnipotence of the majority seems to me such a danger to the

American republics that the dangerous expedient used to curb it is actually something good.

Here I would repeat something which I have put in other words when speaking of municipal freedom: no countries need associations more—to prevent either despotism of parties or the arbitrary rule of a prince—than those with a democratic social state. In aristocratic nations secondary bodies form natural associations which hold abuses of power in check. In countries where such associations do not exist, if private people did not artificially and temporarily create something like them, I see no other dike to hold back tyranny of whatever sort, and a great nation might with impunity be oppressed by some tiny faction or by a single man.

* * *

In America the citizens who form the minority associate in the first place to show their numbers and to lessen the moral authority of the majority, and secondly, by stimulating competition, to discover the arguments most likely to make an impression on the majority, for they always hope to draw the majority over to their side and then to exercise power in its name.

Political associations in the United States are therefore peaceful in their objects and legal in the means used; and when they say that they only wish to prevail legally, in general they are telling the truth.

* * *

The Americans * * * have provided a form of government within their associations, but it is, if I may put it so, a civil government. There is a place for individual independence there; as in society, all the members are advancing at the same time toward the same goal, but they are not obliged to follow exactly the same path. There has been no sacrifice of will or of reason, but rather will and reason are applied to bring success to a common enterprise.

DISCUSSION QUESTIONS

1. Tocqueville argues that "freedom of association has become a necessary guarantee against the tyranny of the majority." Although freedom of association is a central part of any free society, would you place limits on this freedom? What if an American sought to offer nonviolent assistance to a foreign terrorist group? What activities would be acceptable and which would be unacceptable, in your view?

2. Placing restrictions on interest-group activities is difficult because of the constitutional protections afforded to these groups. The Constitution guarantees the people the right to assemble and to petition government regarding their grievances, and it also guarantees

freedom of speech. All these are the essence of interest-group activity. Nonetheless, many Americans are uneasy with the influence wielded by organized interest groups. What, if any, restrictions on interest-group activity would you be comfortable with? Would you support limits on what interest groups could spend to lobby government officials? To communicate with the public? To run advertisements that support or criticize candidates? How are these restrictions, if any, consistent with the constitutional guarantee of freedom to associate, organize, and petition government?

63

"The Logic of Collective Action," from *Rise and Decline of Nations*

Mancur Olson

Americans organize at a tremendous rate to pursue common interests in the political arena. Yet not all groups are created equal, and some types of political organizations are much more common than others. In particular, it is far easier to organize groups around narrow economic interests than it is to organize around broad "public goods" interests. Why do some groups organize while others do not?

The nature of collective goods, according to the economist Mancur Olson, explains this phenomenon. When a collective good is provided to a group, no member of the group can be denied the benefits of the good. For example, if Congress passes a law that offers subsidies for a new kind of energy technology, any company that produces that technology will benefit from the subsidy. The catch is, any company will benefit even if they did not participate in the collective effort to win the subsidy. Olson argues that "the larger the number of individuals or firms that would benefit from a collective good, the smaller the share of the gains . . . that will accrue to the individual or firm." Hence, the less likely any one member of the group will contribute to the collective effort to secure the collective benefit. For smaller groups, any one member's share of the collective good is larger and more meaningful; thus it is more likely any one member of the group will be willing to make an individual sacrifice to provide a benefit shared by the entire group. An additional distinction is that in a large group, there is often a tendency to assume someone else will take care of the problem—this is known as the "free rider" problem or, as Olson puts it, "let George do it." This is less likely to happen in smaller groups.

The logic helps to explain the greater difficulty "public interest groups" have in organizing and staying organized to provide such collective goods as clean air, consumer product safety, and banking regulations aimed at promoting inner-city investments by banks. These goods benefit very large numbers of people, but the benefit to any one person, Olson would argue, is not sufficient for them to sacrifice time or money for the effort to succeed, especially if the individual believes that he or she will benefit from the collective good, even if they do not contribute. Olson identifies "selective incentives" as one way in which these larger groups are able to overcome the incentive to free ride.

The Logic

The argument of this book begins with a paradox in the behavior of groups. It has often been taken for granted that if everyone in a group of individuals or firms had some interest in common, then there would be a tendency for the group to seek to further this interest. Thus many students of politics in the United States for a long time supposed that citizens with a common political interest would organize and lobby to serve that interest. Each individual in the population would be in one or more groups and the vector of pressures of these competing groups explained the outcomes of the political process. Similarly, it was often supposed that if workers, farmers, or consumers faced monopolies harmful to their interests, they would eventually attain countervailing power through organizations such as labor unions or farm organizations that obtained market power and protective government action. On a larger scale, huge social classes are often expected to act in the interest of their members; the unalloyed form of this belief is, of course, the Marxian contention that in capitalist societies the bourgeois class runs the government to serve its own interests, and that once the exploitation of the proletariat goes far enough and "false consciousness" has disappeared, the working class will in its own interest revolt and establish a dictatorship of the proletariat. In general, if the individuals in some category or class had a sufficient degree of self-interest and if they all agreed on some common interest, then the group would to some extent also act in a self-interested or group-interested manner.

If we ponder the logic of the familiar assumption described in the preceding paragraph, we can see that it is fundamentally and indisputably faulty. Consider those consumers who agree that they pay higher prices for a product because of some objectionable monopoly or tariff, or those workers who agree that their skill deserves a higher wage. Let us now ask what would be the expedient course of action for an individual consumer who would like to see a boycott to combat a monopoly or a lobby to repeal the tariff, or for an individual worker who would like a strike threat or a minimum wage law that could bring higher wages. If the consumer or worker contributes a few days and a few dollars to organize a boycott or a union or to lobby for favorable legislation, he or she will have sacrificed time and money. What will this sacrifice obtain? The individual will at best succeed in advancing the cause to a small (often imperceptible) degree. In any case he will get only a minute share of the gain from his action. The very fact that the objective or interest is common to or shared by the group entails that the gain from any sacrifice an individual makes to serve this common purpose is shared with everyone in the group. The successful boycott or strike or lobbying action will bring the better price or wage for everyone in the relevant category, so the individual in any large group with a common interest will reap only a minute share of the gains from whatever sacrifices the individual makes to achieve this common interest. Since any gain goes to everyone in the group, those who contribute nothing to the effort will get just as much as those who made a contribution. It pays to "let George do it," but George has little or no incentive to do anything in the group interest either, so (in the absence of factors that are completely left out of the conceptions mentioned in the first paragraph) there will be little, if any, group action. The paradox, then, is that (in the absence of special arrangements or circumstances to which we shall turn later) large groups, at least if they are composed of rational individuals, will *not* act in their group interest.

This paradox is elaborated and set out in a way that lets the reader check every step of the logic in a book I wrote entitled *The Logic of Collective Action*.

*   *   *

Organizations that provide collective goods to their client groups through political or market action * * * are * * * not supported because of the collective goods they provide, but rather because they have been fortunate enough to find what I have called *selective incentives*. A selective incentive is one that applies selectively to the individuals depending on whether they do or do not contribute to the provision of the collective good.

A selective incentive can be either negative or positive; it can, for example, be a loss or punishment imposed only on those who do *not* help provide the collective good. Tax payments are, of course, obtained with the help of negative selective incentives, since those who are found not to have paid their taxes must then suffer both taxes and penalties. The best-known type of organized interest group in modern democratic societies, the labor union, is also usually supported, in part, through negative selective incentives. Most of the dues in strong unions are obtained through union shop, closed shop, or agency shop arrangements which make dues paying more or less compulsory and automatic. There are often also informal arrangements with the same effect; David McDonald, former president of the United Steel Workers of America, describes one of these arrangements used in the early history of that union. It was, he writes, a technique

> which we called . . . visual education, which was a high-sounding label for a practice much more accurately described as dues picketing. It worked very simply. A group of dues-paying members, selected by the district director (usually more for their size than their tact) would stand at the plant gate with pick handles or baseball bats in hand and confront each worker as he arrived for his shift.

As McDonald's "dues picketing" analogy suggests, picketing during strikes is another negative selective incentive that unions sometimes need; although picketing in industries with established and stable unions is usually peaceful, this is because the union's capacity to close down an enterprise against which it has called a strike is clear to all; the early phase of unionization often involves a great deal of violence on the part of both unions and anti-union employers and scabs.

* * *

Positive selective incentives, although easily overlooked, are also commonplace, as diverse examples in *The Logic* demonstrate. American farm organizations offer prototypical examples. Many of the members of the stronger American farm organizations are members because their dues payments are automatically deducted from the "patronage dividends" of farm cooperatives or are included in the insurance premiums paid to mutual insurance companies associated with the farm organizations. Any number of organizations with urban clients also provide similar positive selective incentives in the form of insurance policies, publications, group air fares, and other private goods made available only to members. The grievance procedures of labor unions usually also offer selective incentives, since the grievances of active members often get most of the attention. The symbiosis between the political power of a lobbying organization and the business institutions associated with it often yields tax or other advantages for the business institution, and the publicity and other information flowing out of the political arm of a movement often generates patterns of preference or trust that make the business activities of the movement more remunerative. The surpluses obtained in such ways in turn provide positive selective incentives that recruit participants for the lobbying efforts.

Small groups, or occasionally large "federal" groups that are made up of many small groups of socially interactive members, have an additional source of both negative and positive selective incentives. Clearly most people value the companionship and respect of those with whom they interact. In modern societies solitary confinement is, apart from the rare death penalty, the harshest legal punishment. The censure or even ostracism of those who fail to bear a share of the burdens of collective action can sometimes be an important selective incentive. An extreme example of this occurs when British unionists refuse to speak to uncooperative colleagues, that is, "send them to Coventry." Similarly, those in a socially interactive group seeking a collective good can give special respect or honor to those who distinguish themselves by their sacrifices in the interest of the group and thereby offer them a positive selective incentive. Since most people apparently prefer relatively like-minded or agreeable and respectable company, and often prefer to associate with those whom they especially admire, they may find it costless to shun those who shirk the collective action and to favor those who over-subscribe.

Social selective incentives can be powerful and inexpensive, but they are available only in certain situations. As I have already indicated, they have little applicability to large groups, except in those cases in which the large groups can be federations of small groups that are capable of social interaction. It also is not possible to organize most large groups in need of a collective good into small, socially interactive subgroups, since most individuals do not have the time needed to maintain a huge number of friends and acquaintances.

The availability of social selective incentives is also limited by the social heterogeneity of some of the groups or categories that would benefit from a collective good. Everyday observation reveals that most socially interactive groups are fairly homogeneous and that many people resist extensive social interaction with those they deem to have lower status or greatly different tastes. Even Bohemian or other nonconformist groups often are made up of individuals who are similar to one another, however much they differ from the rest of society. Since some of the categories of individuals who would benefit from a collective good are socially heterogeneous, the social interaction needed for selective incentives sometimes cannot be arranged even when the number of individuals involved is small.

* * *

In short, the political entrepreneurs who attempt to organize collective action will accordingly be more likely to succeed if they strive to organize relatively homogeneous groups. The political managers whose task it is to maintain organized or collusive action similarly will be motivated to use indoctrination and selective recruitment to increase the homogeneity of their client groups. This is true in part because social selective incentives are more likely to be available to the more nearly homogeneous groups, and in part because homogeneity will help achieve consensus.

Information and calculation about a collective good is often itself a collective good. Consider a typical member of a large organization who is deciding how much time to devote to studying the policies or leadership of the organization. The more time the member devotes to this matter, the greater the likelihood that his or her voting and advocacy will favor effective policies and leadership for the organization. This typical member will, however, get only a small share of the gain from the more effective policies and leadership: in the aggregate, the other members will get almost all the gains, so that the individual member does not have an incentive to devote nearly as much time to fact-finding and thinking about the organization as would be in the group interest. Each of the members of the group would be better off if they all could be coerced into spending more time finding out how to vote to make the organization best further their interests. This is dramatically evident in the case of the typical voter in a national election in a large country. The gain to such a voter from studying issues and candidates until it is clear what vote is truly in his or her interest is given by the difference in the value to the individual of the "right" election outcome as compared with the "wrong" outcome, *multiplied by the probability a change in the individual's vote will alter the outcome of the election*. Since the probability that a typical voter will change the outcome of the election is vanishingly small, the typical citizen is usually "rationally ignorant" about public affairs. Often, information about public affairs is so interesting or entertaining that it pays to acquire it for these reasons alone—this appears to be the single most important source of exceptions to the generalization that *typical* citizens are rationally ignorant about public affairs.

Individuals in a few special vocations can receive considerable rewards in private goods if they acquire exceptional knowledge of public goods. Politicians, lobbyists, journalists, and social scientists, for example, may earn more money, power, or prestige from knowledge of this or that public business. Occasionally, exceptional knowledge of public policy can generate exceptional profits in stock exchanges or other markets. Withal, the typical citizen will find that his or her income and life chances will not be improved by zealous study of public affairs, or even of any single collective good.

The limited knowledge of public affairs is in turn necessary to explain the effectiveness of lobbying. If all citizens had obtained and digested all pertinent information, they could not then be swayed by advertising or other persuasion. With perfectly informed citizens, elected officials would not be subject to the blandishments of lobbyists, since the constituents would then know if their interests were betrayed and defeat the unfaithful representative at the next election. Just as lobbies provide collective goods to special-interest groups, so their effectiveness is explained by the imperfect knowledge of citizens, and this in turn is due mainly to the fact that information and calculation about collective goods is also a collective good.

*   *   *

The fact that the typical individual does not have an incentive to spend much time studying many of his choices concerning collective goods also helps to explain some otherwise inexplicable individual contributions toward the provision of collective goods. The logic of collective action that has been described in this chapter is not immediately apparent to those who have never studied it; if it were, there would be nothing paradoxical in the argument with which this chapter opened, and students to whom the argument is explained would not react with initial skepticism. No doubt the practical implications of this logic for the individual's own choices were often discerned before the logic was ever set out in print, but this does not mean that they were always understood even at the intuitive and practical level. In particular, when the costs of individual contributions to collective action are very small, the individual has little incentive to investigate whether or not to make a contribution or even to exercise intuition. If the individual knows the costs of a contribution to collective action in the interest of a group of which he is a part are trivially small, he may rationally not take the trouble to consider whether the gains are smaller still. This is particularly the case since the size of these gains and the policies that would maximize them are matters about which it is usually not rational for him to investigate.

This consideration of the costs and benefits of calculation about public goods leads to the testable prediction that voluntary contributions toward the provision of collective goods for large groups without selective incentives will often occur when the costs of the individual contributions are negligible, but that they will *not* often occur when the costs of the individual contributions are considerable. In other words, when the costs of individual action to help to obtain a desired collective good are small enough, the result is indeterminate and sometimes goes one way and sometimes the other, but when the costs get larger this indeterminacy disappears. We should accordingly find that more than a few people are willing to take the moment of time needed to sign petitions for causes they support, or to express their opinions in the course of discussion, or to vote for the candidate or party they prefer. Similarly, if the argument here is correct, we should not find many instances where individuals voluntarily contribute substantial sums of resources year after year for the purpose of obtaining some collective good for some large group of which they are a part. Before parting with a large amount of money or time, and particularly before doing so repeatedly, the rational individual will reflect on what this considerable sacrifice will accomplish. If the individual is a typical individual in a large group that would benefit from a collective good, his contribution will not make a perceptible difference in the amount that is provided. The theory here predicts that such contributions become less likely the larger the contribution at issue.

Even when contributions are costly enough to elicit rational calculation, there is still one set of circumstances in which collective action can occur without selective incentives. This set of circumstances becomes evident the moment we think of situations in which there are only a few individuals or firms that would benefit from collective action. Suppose there are two firms of equal size in an industry and no other firms can enter the industry. It still will be the case that a higher price for the industry's product will benefit both firms and that legislation favorable to the industry will help both firms. The higher price and the favorable legislation are then collective goods to this "oligopolistic" industry, even though there are only two in the group that benefit from the collective goods. Obviously, each of the oligopolists is in a situation in which if it restricts output to raise the industry price, or lobbies for favorable legislation for the industry, it will tend to get half of the benefit. And the cost-benefit ratio of action in the common interest easily could be so favorable that, even though a firm bears the whole cost of its action and gets only half the benefit of this action, it could still profit from acting in the common interest. Thus if the group that would benefit from collective action is sufficiently small and the cost-benefit ratio of collective action for the group sufficiently favorable, there may well be calculated action in the collective interest even without selective incentives.

* * *

Untypical as my example of equal-sized firms may be, it makes the general point intuitively obvious: other things being equal, *the larger the number of individuals or firms that would benefit from a collective good, the smaller the share of the gains from action in the group interest that will accrue to the individual or firm that undertakes the action. Thus, in the absence of selective incentives, the incentive for group action diminishes as group size increases, so that large groups are less able to act in their common interest than small ones.* If an additional individual or firm that would value the collective good enters the scene, then the share of the gains from group-oriented action that anyone already in the group might take must diminish. This holds true whatever the relative sizes or valuations of the collective good in the group.

* * *

The significance of the logic that has just been set out can best be seen by comparing groups that would have the same net gain from collective action, if they could engage in it, but that vary in size. Suppose there are a million individuals who would gain a thousand dollars each, or a billion in the aggregate, if they were to organize effectively and engage in collective action that had a total cost of a hundred million. If the logic set out above is right, they could not organize or engage in effective collective action without selective incentives. Now suppose that, although the total gain of a billion dollars from collective action and the aggregate cost of a hundred million remain the same, the group is composed instead of five big corporations or five organized municipalities, each of which would gain two hundred million. Collective action is not an absolute certainty even in this case, since each of the five could conceivably expect others to put up the hundred million and hope to gain the collective good worth two hundred million at no cost at all. Yet collective action, perhaps after some delays due to bargaining, seems very likely indeed. In this case any one of the five would gain a hundred million from providing the collective good even if it had to pay the whole cost itself; and the costs of bargaining among five would not be great, so they would sooner or later probably work out an agreement providing for the collective action. The numbers in this example are arbitrary, but roughly similar situations occur often in reality, and the contrast between "small" and "large" groups could be illustrated with an infinite number of diverse examples.

The significance of this argument shows up in a second way if one compares the operations of lobbies or cartels within jurisdictions of vastly different scale, such as a modest municipality on the one hand and a big country on the other. Within the town, the mayor or city council may be influenced by, say, a score of petitioners or a lobbying budget of a thousand dollars. A particular line of business may be in the hands of only a few firms, and if the town is distant enough from other markets only these few would need to agree to create a cartel. In a big country, the resources needed to influence the national government are likely to be much more substantial, and unless the firms are (as they sometimes are) gigantic, many of them would have to cooperate to create an effective cartel. Now suppose that the million individuals in our large group in the previous paragraph were spread out over a hundred thousand towns or jurisdictions, so that each jurisdiction had ten of them, along with the same proportion of citizens in other categories as before. Suppose also that the cost-benefit ratios remained the same, so that there was still a billion dollars to gain across all jurisdictions or ten thousand in each, and that it would still cost a hundred million dollars across all jurisdictions or a thousand in each. It no longer seems out of the question that in many jurisdictions the groups of ten, or subsets of them, would put up the thousand-dollar total needed to get the thousand for each individual. Thus we see that, if all else were equal, small jurisdictions would have more collective action per capita than large ones.

Differences in intensities of preference generate a third type of illustration of the logic at issue. A small number of zealots anxious for a particular collective good are more likely to act collectively to obtain that good than a larger number with the same aggregate willingness to pay. Suppose there are twenty-five individuals, each of whom finds a given collective good worth a thousand dollars in one case, whereas in another there are five thousand, each of whom finds the collective good worth five dollars. Obviously, the argument indicates that there would be a greater likelihood of collective action in the former case than in the latter, even though the aggregate demand for the collective good is the same in both. The great historical significance of small groups of fanatics no doubt owes something to this consideration.

The argument in this chapter predicts that those groups that have access to selective incentives will be more likely to act collectively to obtain collective goods than those that do not, and that smaller groups will have a greater likelihood of engaging in collective action than larger ones. The empirical portions of *The Logic* show that this prediction has been correct for the United States.

*   *   *

DISCUSSION QUESTIONS

1. Besides the size of a group, what other considerations do you think would play a role in people's decision to join a collective endeavor? Are you convinced that the size of a group is as important as Olson argues?

2. Think of your own decisions to join or not join a group. Have you ever been a "free rider?" For example, have there been protests against tuition increases at your school that you supported but did not participate in? If so, what would it have taken to get you to join?

3. If Olson is right, would Tocqueville's view about the role of groups in overcoming the potential tyranny of majority need to be modified?

64

"Associations Without Members"

Theda Skocpol

One of the hot topics in social science research since the mid-1990s has been the idea of "social capital." Put simply, social capital suggests that involvement in group and social activities generates side benefits that promote the health of the political system. Involvement in these groups tends to contribute to trust, efficacy, and a broader interest and involvement in public affairs. The idea emerged as scholars noted that several measures of public participation in politics— voting turnout, for example—had declined markedly since the early 1960s. At the same time, measures of public disaffection, mistrust, and alienation from politics were growing. Analysts such as the political scientist Robert Putnam noted that, in fact, not only were measures like voting turnout on the downswing, but many indicators of social involvement were drooping. As Putnam famously pointed out, it seemed that even bowling league memberships were dropping and that Americans were increasingly "bowling alone." If in fact involvement broadly speaking was on the decline, then the positive effects of involvement ("social capital") would also be on the decline, with significant impacts on social and political life.

These ideas generated a mountain of research, ranging from studies questioning the thesis of participatory decline, to those trying to explain the decline, to those evaluating the effects of the decline. Theda Skocpol steps into this debate by offering an analysis of how Americans have changed not so much the quantity, but the quality, of their participation. Once, Americans were group members who participated in group activities and group decision making. These associations, in many senses, reflected America's democratic political system, both in terms of their decision making and in terms of their often federal structure. Increasingly, however, the civic world is filled with "associations without members" centered not in communities but in Washington, D.C., led not by ordinary members, but by elite professionals. "Membership" in these organizations usually means little more than writing a check which entitles the check-writer to receive a monthly publication. Meetings and local involvement are absent. Of course, not all associations operate this way, but Skocpol suggests that this is increasingly becoming the norm and that it has had deleterious effects for the political system. She identifies a range of reasons for this transformation, including "racial and gender change; shifts in the political opportunity structure; new techniques and models for building organizations; and recent transformations in U.S. class relations."

In just a third of a century, Americans have dramatically changed their style of civic and political association. A civic world once centered in locally rooted and nationally active membership associations is a relic. Today, Americans volunteer for causes and projects, but only rarely as ongoing members. They send checks to service and advocacy groups run by professionals, often funded by foundations or professional fundraisers. Prime-time airways echo with debates among their spokespersons: the National Abortion Rights Action League debates the National Right to Life Committee; the Concord Coalition takes on the American Association of Retired Persons; and the Environmental Defense Fund counters business groups. Entertained or bemused, disengaged viewers watch as polarized advocates debate.

The largest membership groups of the 1950s were old-line and well-established, with founding dates ranging from 1733 for the Masons to 1939 for the Woman's Division of Christian Service (a Methodist women's association formed from "missionary" societies with nineteenth-century roots). Like most large membership associations throughout American history, most 1950s associations recruited members across class lines. They held regular local meetings and convened periodic assemblies of elected leaders and delegates at the state, regional, or national levels. Engaged in multiple rather than narrowly specialized pursuits, many associations combined social or ritual activities with community service, mutual aid, and involvement in national affairs. Patriotism was a leitmotif; during and after World War II, a passionate and victorious national endeavor, these associations sharply expanded their memberships and renewed the vigor of their local and national activities.

To be sure, very large associations were not the only membership federations that mattered in postwar America. Also prominent were somewhat smaller, elite-dominated civic groups—including male service groups like Rotary, Lions, and Kiwanis, and longstanding female groups like the American Association of University Women and the League of Women Voters. Dozens of ethnically based fraternal and cultural associations flourished, as did African-American fraternal groups like the Prince Hall Masons and the Improved Benevolent and Protective Order of Elks of the World.

For many membership federations, this was a golden era of national as well as community impact. Popularly rooted membership federations rivaled professional and business associations for influence in policy debates. The AFL-CIO was in the thick of struggles about economic and social policies; the American Legion and the Veterans of Foreign Wars advanced veterans' programs; the American Farm Bureau Federation (AFBF) joined other farmers' associations to influence national and state agricultural policies; and the National Congress of Parents and Teachers (PTA) and the General Federation of Women's Clubs were influential on educational, health, and family issues. The results could be decisive, as exemplified by the pivotal role of the American Legion in drafting and lobbying for the GI Bill of 1944.

Then, suddenly, old-line membership federations seemed passé. Upheavals shook America during "the long 1960s," stretching from the mid-1950s through the mid-1970s. The southern Civil Rights movement challenged white racial domination and spurred legislation to enforce legal equality and voting rights for African Americans. Inspired by Civil Rights achievements, additional "rights" movements exploded, promoting equality for women, dignity for homosexuals, the unionization of farm workers, and the mobilization of other nonwhite ethnic minorities. Movements arose to oppose U.S. involvement in the war in Vietnam, champion a new environmentalism, and further other public causes. At the forefront of these groundswells were younger Americans, especially from the growing ranks of college students and university graduates.

The great social movements of the long 1960s were propelled by combinations of grassroots protest, activist radicalism, and professionally led efforts to lobby government and educate the public. Some older membership associations ended up participating and expanding their bases of support, yet the groups that sparked movements were more agile and flexibly structured than pre-existing membership federations.

The upheavals of the 1960s could have left behind a reconfigured civic world, in which some old-line membership associations had declined but others had reoriented and reenergized themselves. Within each great social movement, memberships could have consolidated and groups coalesced into new omnibus federations able to link the grass roots to state, regional, and national leaderships, allowing longstanding American civic traditions to continue in new ways.

But this is not what happened. Instead, the 1960s, 1970s, and 1980s brought extraordinary organizational proliferation and professionalization. At the national level alone, the *Encyclopedia of Associations* listed approximately 6,500 associations in 1958. This total grew by 1990 to almost 23,000. Within the expanding group universe, moreover, new kinds of associations came to the fore: relatively centralized and professionally led organizations focused on policy lobbying and public education.

Another wave of the advocacy explosion involved "public interest" or "citizens" groups seeking to shape public opinion and influence legislation. Citizens' advocacy groups espouse "causes" ranging from environmental protection (for example, the Sierra Club and the Environmental Defense Fund), to the well-being of poor children (the Children's Defense Fund), to reforming politics (Common Cause) and cutting public entitlements (the Concord Coalition).

The Fortunes of Membership Associations

As the associational explosions of 1960 to 1990 took off, America's once large and confident membership federations were not only bypassed in national politics; they also dwindled as locally rooted participant groups. To be sure, some membership associations have been founded or expanded in recent decades. By far the largest is the American Association of Retired Persons (AARP), which now boasts more than 33 million adherents, about one-half of all Americans aged 50 or older. But AARP is not a democratically controlled organization. Launched in 1958 with backing from a teachers' retirement group and an insurance company, the AARP grew rapidly in the 1970s and 1980s by offering commercial discounts to members and establishing a Washington headquarters to monitor and lobby about federal legislation affecting seniors. The AARP has a legislative and policy staff of 165 people, 28 registered lobbyists, and more than 1,200 staff members in the field. After recent efforts to expand its regional and local infrastructure, the AARP involves about 5 o 10 percent of its members in (undemocratic) membership chapters. But for the most part, the AARP national office—covering an entire city block with its own zip code—deals with masses of individual adherents through the mail.

Four additional recently expanded membership associations use modern mass recruitment methods, yet are also rooted in local and state units. Interestingly, these groups are heavily involved in partisan electoral politics. Two recently launched groups are the National Right to Life Committee (founded in 1973) and the Christian Coalition (founded in 1989). They bridge from church congregations, through which they recruit members and activists, to the conservative wing of the Republican Party, through which they exercise political influence. Two old-line membership federations—the National Education Association (founded in 1857) and the National Rifle Association (founded in 1871)—experienced explosive growth after reorienting themselves to take part in partisan politics. The NRA expanded in the 1970s, when right-wing activists opposed to gun control changed what had traditionally been a network of marksmen's clubs into a conservative, Republican-leaning advocacy group fiercely opposed to gun control legislation. During the same period, the NEA burgeoned from a relatively elitist association of public educators into a quasi-union for public school teachers and a stalwart in local, state, and national Democratic Party politics.

Although they fall short of enrolling 1 percent of the adult population, some additional chapter-based membership associations were fueled by the social movements of the 1960s and 1970s. From 1960 to 1990, the Sierra Club (originally created in 1892) ballooned from some 15,000 members to 565,000 members meeting in 378 "local groups." And the National Audubon Society (founded in 1905) went from 30,000 members and 330 chapters in 1958 to about 600,000 members and more than 500 chapters in the 1990s. The National Organization for Women (NOW) reached 1,122 members and 14 chapters within a year of its founding in 1966, and spread across all 50 states with some 125,000 members meeting in 700 chapters by 1978. But notice that these "1960s" movement associations do not match the organizational scope of old-line membership federations. At its post–World War II high point in 1955, for example, the General Federation of Women's Clubs boasted more than 826,000 members meeting in 15,168 local clubs, themselves divided into representative networks within each of the 50 states plus the District of Columbia. By contrast, at its high point in 1993, NOW reported some 280,000 members and 800 chapters, with no intermediate tier of representative governance between the national center and local chapters. These membership associations certainly matter, but mainly as counterexamples to dominant associational trends—of organizations without members.

After nearly a century of civic life rooted in nation-spanning membership federations, why was America's associational universe so transformed? A variety of factors have contributed, including racial and gender change; shifts in the political opportunity structure; new techniques and models for building organizations; and recent transformations in U.S. class relations. Taken together, I suggest, these account for civic America's abrupt and momentous transition from membership to advocacy.

Society Decompartmentalized

Until recent times, most American membership associations enrolled business and professional people together with white-collar folks, farmers, and craft or industrial workers. There was a degree of fellowship across class lines—yet at the price of other kinds of exclusions. With only a few exceptions, old-line associations enrolled either men or women, not both together (although male-only fraternal and veterans' groups often had ties to ladies' auxiliaries). Racial separation was also the rule. Although African Americans did manage to create and greatly expand fraternal associations of their own, they unquestionably resented exclusion by the parallel white fraternals.

Given the pervasiveness of gender and racial separation in classic civic America, established voluntary associations were bound to be shaken after the 1950s. Moreover, changing gender roles and identities blended with other changing values to undercut not just membership appeals but long-standing routes to associational leadership. For example, values of patriotism, brotherhood, and sacrifice had been celebrated by all fraternal groups. During and after each war, the Masons, Knights of Pythias, Elks, Knights of Columbus, Moose, Eagles, and scores of other fraternal groups celebrated and memorialized the contributions of their soldier-members. So did women's auxiliaries, not to mention men's service clubs and trade union "brotherhoods." But "manly" ideals of military service faded after the early 1960s as America's bitter experiences during the war in Vietnam disrupted the intergenerational continuity of male identification with martial brotherliness.

In the past third of a century, female civic leadership has changed as much or more than male leadership. Historically, U.S. women's associations—ranging from female auxiliaries of male groups to independent groups like the General Federation of Women's Clubs, the PTA, and church-connected associations—benefited from the activism of educated wives and mothers. Although a tiny fraction of all U.S. females, higher-educated women were a surprisingly substantial and widespread presence—because the United States was a pioneer in the schooling of girls and the higher education of women. By 1880, some 40,000 American women constituted a third of all students in U.S. institutions of higher learning; women's share rose to nearly half at the early twentieth-century peak in 1920, when some 283,000 women were enrolled in institutions of higher learning. Many higher-educated women of the late 1800s and early 1900s married immediately and stayed out of the paid labor force. Others taught for a time in primary and secondary schools, then got married and stopped teaching (either voluntarily or because school systems would not employ married women). Former teachers accumulated in every community. With skills to make connections within and across communities—and some time on their hands as their children grew older—former teachers and other educated women became mainstays of classic U.S. voluntary life.

Of course, more American women than ever before are now college-educated. But contemporary educated women face new opportunities and constraints. Paid work and family responsibilities are no longer separate spheres, and the occupational structure is less sex-segregated at all levels. Today, even married women with children are very likely to be employed, at least part-time. Despite new time pressures, educated and employed women have certainly not dropped out of civic life. Women employed part-time are more likely to be members of groups or volunteers than housewives; and fully employed women are often drawn into associations or civic projects through work. Yet styles of civic involvement have changed—much to the disadvantage of broad-gauged associations trying to hold regular meetings.

The Lure of Washington, D.C.

The centralization of political change in Washington, D.C. also affected the associational universe. Consider the odyssey of civil rights lawyer Marian Wright Edelman. Fresh from grassroots struggles in Mississippi, she arrived in Washington, D.C. in the late 1960s to lobby for Mississippi's Head Start program. She soon realized that arguing on behalf of children might be the best way to influence legislation and sway public sympathy in favor of the poor, including African Americans. So between 1968 and 1973 Edelman obtained funding from major foundations and developed a new advocacy and policy research association, the Children's Defense Fund (CDF). With a skillful staff, a small national network of individual supporters, ties to social service agencies and foundations, and excellent relationships with the national media, the CDF has been a determined proponent of federal antipoverty programs ever since. The CDF has also worked with Democrats and other liberal advocacy groups to expand such efforts; and during periods of conservative Republican ascendancy, the CDF has been a fierce (if not always successful) defender of federal social programs.

Activists, in short, have gone where the action is. In this same period, congressional committees and their staffs subdivided and multiplied. During the later 1970s and 1980s, the process of group formation became self-reinforcing—not only because groups arose to counter other groups, but also because groups begot more groups. Because businesses and citizens use advocacy groups to influence government outside of parties and between elections, it is not surprising that the contemporary group explosion coincides with waning voter loyalty to the two major political parties. As late as the 1950s, U.S. political parties were networks of local and state organizations through which party officials often brokered nominations, cooperated with locally rooted membership associations, and sometimes directly mobilized voters. The party structure and the associational structure were mutually reinforcing.

Then, demographic shifts, reapportionment struggles, and the social upheavals of the 1960s disrupted old party organizations; and changes in party rules led to nomination elections that favored activists and candidate-centered efforts over backroom brokering by party insiders. Such "reforms" were meant to enhance grassroots participation, but in practice have furthered oligarchical ways of running elections. No longer the preserve of party organizations, U.S. campaigns are now managed by coteries of media consultants, pollsters, direct mail specialists, and—above all—fundraisers. In this revamped electoral arena, advocacy groups have much to offer, hoping to get access to elected officials in return for helping candidates. In low-turnout battles to win party nominations, even groups with modest mail memberships may be able to field enough (paid or unpaid) activists to make a difference. At all stages of the electoral process, advocacy groups with or without members can provide endorsements that may be useful in media or direct mail efforts. And PACs pushing business interests or public interests causes can help candidates raise the huge amounts of money they need to compete.

A New Model of Association-Building

Classic American association-builders took it for granted that the best way to gain national influence, moral or political, was to knit together national, state, and local groups that met regularly and engaged in a degree of representative governance. Leaders who desired to speak on behalf of masses of Americans found it natural to proceed by recruiting self-renewing mass memberships and spreading a network of interactive groups. After the start-up phase, associational budgets usually depended heavily on membership dues and on sales of newsletters or supplies to members and local groups. Supporters had to be continuously recruited through social networks and person-to-person contacts. And if leverage over government was desired, an association had to be able influence legislators, citizens, and newspapers across many districts. For all of these reasons, classic civic entrepreneurs with national ambitions moved quickly to recruit activists and members in every state and across as many towns and cities as possible within each state.

Today, nationally ambitious civic entrepreneurs proceed in quite different ways. When Marian Wright Edelman launched a new advocacy and research group to lobby for the needs of children and the poor, she turned to private foundations for funding and then recruited an expert staff of researchers and lobbyists. In the early 1970s, when John Gardner launched Common Cause as a "national citizens lobby" demanding governmental reforms, he arranged for start-up contributions from several wealthy friends, contacted reporters in the national media, and purchased mailing lists to solicit masses of members giving modest monetary contributions. Patron grants, direct mail techniques, and the capacity to convey images and messages through the mass media have changed the realities of organization building and maintenance.

The very model of civic effectiveness has been up-ended since the 1960s. No longer do civic entrepreneurs think of constructing vast federations and recruiting interactive citizen-members. When a new cause (or tactic) arises, activists envisage opening a national office and managing association-building as well as national projects from the center. Even a group aiming to speak for large numbers of Americans does not absolutely need members. And if mass adherents are recruited through the mail, why hold meetings? From a managerial point of view, interactions with groups of members may be downright inefficient. In the old-time membership federations, annual elections of leaders and a modicum of representative governance went hand in hand with membership dues and interactive meetings. But for the professional executives of today's advocacy organizations, direct mail members can be more appealing because, as Kenneth Godwin and Robert Cameron Mitchell explain, "they contribute without 'meddling'" and "do not take part in leadership selection or policy discussions." This does not mean the new advocacy groups are malevolent; they are just responding rationally to the environment in which they find themselves.

Associational Change and Democracy

This brings us, finally, to what may be the most civically consequential change in late-twentieth-century America: the rise of a very large, highly educated upper middle class in which "expert" professionals are prominent along with businesspeople and managers. When U.S. professionals were a tiny, geographically dispersed stratum, they understood themselves as "trustees of community," in the terminology of Stephen Brint. Working closely with and for nonprofessional fellow citizens in thousands of towns and cities, lawyers, doctors, ministers, and teachers once found it quite natural to join—and eventually help to lead—locally rooted, cross-class voluntary associations. But today's professionals are more likely to see themselves as expert individuals who can best contribute to national well-being by working with other specialists to tackle complex technical or social problems.

Cause-oriented advocacy groups offer busy, privileged Americans a rich menu of opportunities to, in effect, hire other professionals and managers to represent their values and interests in public life. Why should highly trained and economically well-off elites spend years working their way up the leadership ladders of traditional membership federations when they can take leading staff roles at the top, or express their preferences by writing a check?

If America has experienced a great civic transformation from membership to advocacy—so what? Most traditional associations were racially exclusive and gender segregated; and their policy efforts were not always broad-minded. More than a few observers suggest that recent civic reorganizations may be for the best. American public life has been rejuvenated, say the optimists, by social movements and advocacy groups fighting for social rights and an enlarged understanding of the public good.

Local community organizations, neighborhood groups, and grassroots protest movements nowadays tap popular energies and involve people otherwise left out of organized politics. And social interchanges live on in small support groups and occasional volunteering. According to the research of Robert Wuthnow, about 75 million men and women, a remarkable 40 percent of the adult population, report taking part in "a small group that meets regularly and provides caring and support for those who participate in it." Wuthnow estimates that there may be some 3 million such groups, including Bible study groups, 12-step self-help groups, book discussion clubs, singles groups, hobby groups, and disease support groups. Individuals find community, spiritual connection, introspection, and personal gratification in small support groups. Meanwhile, people reach out through volunteering. As many as half of all Americans give time to the community this way, their efforts often coordinated by paid social service professionals. Contemporary volunteering can be intermittent and flexibly structured, an intense one-shot effort or spending "an evening a week on an activity for a few months as time permits, rather than having to make a long-term commitment to an organization."

In the optimistic view, the good civic things Americans once did are still being done—in new ways and in new settings. But if we look at U.S. democracy in its entirety and bring issues of power and social leverage to the fore, then optimists are surely overlooking the downsides of our recently reorganized civic life. Too many valuable aspects of the old civic America are not being reproduced or reinvented in the new public world of memberless organizations.

Despite the multiplicity of voices raised within it, America's new civic universe is remarkably oligarchical. Because today's advocacy groups are staff-heavy and focused on lobbying, research, and media projects, they are managed from the top with few opportunities for member leverage from below. Even when they have hundreds of thousands of adherents, contemporary associations are heavily tilted toward upper-middle-class constituencies. Whether we are talking about memberless advocacy groups, advocacy groups with some chapters, mailing-list associations, or nonprofit institutions, it is hard to escape the conclusion that the wealthiest and best-educated Americans are much more privileged in the new civic world than their (less numerous) counterparts were in the pre-1960s civic world of cross-class membership federations.

Mostly, they involve people in "doing for" others—feeding the needy at a church soup kitchen; tutoring children at an after-school clinic; or guiding visitors at a museum exhibit—rather than in "doing with" fellow citizens. Important as such volunteering may be, it cannot substitute for the central citizenship functions that membership federations performed.

A top-heavy civic world not only encourages "doing for" rather than "doing with." It also distorts national politics and public policymaking. Imagine for a moment what might have happened if the GI Bill of 1944 had been debated and legislated in a civic world configured more like the one that prevailed during the 1993–1994 debates over the national health insurance proposal put forward by the first administration of President Bill Clinton. This is not an entirely fanciful comparison, because goals supported by the vast majority of Americans were at issue in both periods: in the 1940s, care and opportunity for millions of military veterans returning from World War II; in the 1990s, access for all Americans to a modicum of health insurance coverage. Back in the 1940s, moreover, there were elite actors—university presidents, liberal intellectuals, and conservative congressmen—who could have condemned the GI Bill to the same fate as the 1990s health security plan. University presidents and liberal New Dealers initially favored versions of the GI Bill that would have been bureaucratically complicated, niggardly with public expenditures, and extraordinarily limited in veterans' access to subsidized higher education.

But in the actual civic circumstances of the 1940s, elites did not retain control of public debates or legislative initiatives. Instead, a vast voluntary membership federation, the American Legion, stepped in and drafted a bill to guarantee every one of the returning veterans up to four years of post-high school education, along with family and employment benefits, business loans, and home mortgages. Not only did the Legion draft one of the most generous pieces of social legislation in American history, thousands of local Legion posts and dozens of state organizations mounted a massive public education and lobbying campaign to ensure that even conservative congressional representatives would vote for the new legislation.

Half a century later, the 1990s health security episode played out in a transformed civic universe dominated by advocacy groups, pollsters, and big-money media campaigns. Top-heavy advocacy groups did not mobilize mass support for a sensible reform plan. Hundreds of business and professional groups influenced the Clinton administration's complex policy schemes, and then used a combination of congressional lobbying and media campaigns to block new legislation. Both the artificial polarization and the elitism of today's organized civic universe may help to explain why increasing numbers of Americans are turned off by and pulling back from public life. Large majorities say that wealthy "special interests" dominate the federal government, and many Americans express cynicism about the chances for regular people to make a difference. People may be entertained by advocacy clashes on television, but they are also ignoring many public debates and withdrawing into privatism. Voting less and less, American citizens increasingly act—and claim to feel—like mere spectators in a polity where all the significant action seems to go on above their heads, with their views ignored by pundits and clashing partisans.

From the nineteenth through the mid-twentieth century, American democracy flourished within a unique matrix of state and society. Not only was America the world's first manhood democracy and the first nation in the world to establish mass public education. It also had a uniquely balanced civic life, in which markets expanded but could not subsume civil society, in which governments at multiple levels deliberately and indirectly encouraged federated voluntary associations. National elites had to pay attention to the values and interests of millions of ordinary Americans.

Over the past third of a century, the old civic America has been bypassed and shoved to the side by a gaggle of professionally dominated advocacy groups and nonprofit institutions rarely attached to memberships worthy of the name. Ideals of shared citizenship and possibilities for democratic leverage have been compromised in the process. Since the 1960s, many good things have happened in America. New voices are now heard, and there have been invaluable gains in equality and liberty. But vital links in the nation's associational life have frayed, and we may need to find creative ways to repair those links if America is to avoid becoming a country of detached spectators. There is no going back to the civic world we have lost. But we Americans can and should look for ways to re-create the best of our civic past in new forms suited to a renewed democratic future.

Discussion Questions

1. What does Skocpol mean by "shifts in the political opportunity structure"?

2. Skocpol is obviously alarmed by the shift in organizational style over the latter half of the twentieth century. What are her concerns? Do you share her concerns? Can you see any advantages to the new model over the old?

3. Do you belong to any national associations that have local group meetings? If so, do you agree that this involvement might generate social capital? What about campus groups? Do you think your involvement in these groups has any "spillover" effect that makes you more likely to be involved elsewhere or increases your sense that your involvement makes a difference?

4. Has the rise of social networking reduced the importance of Skocpol's argument? Does this networking provide the kind of "in-person" participation Skocpol desires, but in another form?

Debating the Issues: Was Madison Right?

In his famous essay *Federalist* 10, the future president James Madison expressed concern about the "mischief of factions." It was natural, he argued, for people to organize around a principle or interest they held in common, and the most common motivation for organizing such factions was property—those who had it versus those who did not, creditors versus lenders. The danger in such efforts, however, was that a majority faction might usurp the rights of a minority. In a small direct democracy, where a majority of the people could share a "common passion," the threat was very real. Expand the geographic size of the country, however, and replace direct democracy with a system of elected representatives, separation of powers, and checks and balances, and the threat diminished. The likelihood of any one faction appealing to a majority of citizens in a large republic governed by representatives from diverse geographic regions was remote. To Madison, factions were a natural outgrowth of the differences between people, and the only way to eliminate factions would be to eliminate liberty. Eliminating factions might not be possible or desirable, but the mischief of factions could be controlled with a system of representation based upon varied constituencies that embraced multiple, diverse interests. From the competition of diverse interests would arise compromise and balanced public policy.

Madison's concerns about interests and particularly organized interests have resonated throughout American history. At various times in U.S. history, the public has seemed to become especially concerned with the power of interests in politics. One political scientist refers to this as the "ideals vs. institutions" gap: there are times when "what is" is so different from what Americans believe "should be" that pressure mounts to reform lobbying laws, campaign regulations, business practices, and so on. Positions on these issues do not always neatly sort out into the typical liberal and conservative categories. For example, in the early 2000s, a Democratic senator (Russ Feingold) and a Republican senator (John McCain) joined forces to lead the effort for campaign finance reform, but since then liberal and conservative interest groups have frequently joined forces to challenge the constitutionality of some of the new law's limits on interest-group campaign advertising as well as the constitutionality of other campaign-finance laws and regulations.

Was Madison right about the benefits that would emerge from the competition of interests? In the following excerpt from *The Governmental Process*, David Truman answers with an emphatic Yes! Despite the popular criticism of "special" interests that seem to taint the political process with their dominant influence, Truman argues that such groups have been a common and inevitable feature of American government.

Groups form to give individuals a means of self-expression and to help individuals find security in an uncertain world. In fact, the uncertainty of the social environment, and the resulting threat to one's interests, is a chief motivation for groups to form, and "taming" this environment is a central concern for group members. Truman suggests that rather than leading to a system ruled by a few dominant powers, the reality is much more fluid. What the critics of group influence fail to recognize is that people have "multiple or overlapping membership" in groups so that "no tolerable normal person is totally absorbed in any group in which he participates." There is balance, in other words, to the views any one member brings to the organization and ultimately to the political process. Further, the potential for a group to form is always present, and "[s]ometimes it may be this possibility of organization that alone gives the potential group a minimum of influence in the political process." Just because someone is not a member of an organized group does not obviate the influence he or she can bring to bear on the political process. The result, as Madison argued, is a balanced approach to the diverse interests that must compromise to form public policy.

Writing in 1960, about a decade after Truman, E. E. Schattschneider finds much to lament in Truman's group-oriented theory of politics. That approach, Schattschneider argues, attributes almost all of the outcomes in politics to the actions of groups. Thus, group-oriented theory misses much that is important in politics. First, Schattschneider writes, the political process matters. The relative advantages that one group has over another can be lost as opinions and options change. You cannot simply determine the relative power advantage of one group over another and believe you have either explained past outcomes or can predict future ones. Second, by omitting the political process, the group theory ignores the majority by focusing on the narrow interests that are battling over an issue. But the fact that an issue is now on the public agenda is itself highly significant. Politics is the "socialization of conflict," Schattschneider writes. Because they are dominant, powerful interests would be content to leave conflicts private. Seemingly weaker groups aim to widen (i.e., socialize) conflict by bringing it into the political process, where the fight is no longer limited to two relatively narrow interests. And last, the relationships among interest groups and political parties are interdependent. Using the example of the Republican party and business, Schattschneider analyzes how each finds the other useful. He also notes that once an interest group such as business enters into activity with a political party, it loses some control, because the party has to satisfy a majority of the population if it is to win elections. To Schattschneider, strong political parties are a crucial element of a properly working American political system. To weaken parties is to strengthen the influences of narrow special interests.

Jonathan Rauch views with pessimism the ever-expanding number of interest groups in the political process. Whether groups claim to represent narrow economic interests or a broader public interest, Rauch does not see balance and compromise as the result of their competition in the political arena. Rather, he sees a nation suffering from "hyper-pluralism," or the explosion of groups making claims on government power and resources. When elected officials attempt to reduce budget deficits or to establish new priorities and refocus expenditures, they are overwhelmed by the pressures of a wide range of groups. As a result, government programs are not terminated or restructured; tough budget cuts or tax changes are rarely made; and a very rich democratic country and its government becomes immobilized. Rather than the dynamic system of change and compromise Truman envisioned, Rauch sees a system characterized primarily by inertia because of the power of groups to prevent government action.

65

"The Alleged Mischiefs of Faction," from *The Governmental Process*

David B. Truman

Most accounts of American legislative sessions—national, state, or local—are full of references to the maneuverings and iniquities of various organized groups. Newspaper stories report that a legislative proposal is being promoted by groups of business men or school teachers or farmers or consumers or labor unions or other aggregations of citizens. Cartoonists picture the legislature as completely under the control of sinister, portly, cigar-smoking individuals labeled "special interests," while a diminutive John Q. Public is pushed aside to sulk in futile anger and pathetic frustrations. A member of the legislature rises in righteous anger on the floor of the house or in a press conference to declare that the bill under discussion is being forced through by the "interests," by the most unscrupulous high-pressure "lobby" he has seen in all his years of public life. An investigating committee denounces the activities of a group as deceptive, immoral, and destructive of our constitutional methods and ideals. A chief executive attacks a "lobby" or "pressure group" as the agency responsible for obstructing or emasculating a piece of legislation that he has recommended "in the public interest."

* * *

Such events are familiar even to the casual student of day-to-day politics, if only because they make diverting reading and appear to give the citizen the "low-down" on his government. He tends, along with many of his more sophisticated fellow citizens, to take these things more or less for granted, possibly because they merely confirm his conviction that "as everybody knows, politics is a dirty business." Yet at the same time he is likely to regard the activities of organized groups in political life as somehow outside the proper and normal processes of government, as the lapses of his weak contemporaries whose moral fiber is insufficient to prevent their defaulting on the great traditions of the Founding Fathers. These events appear to be a modern pathology.

Group Pressure and the Founding Fathers

Group pressures, whatever we may wish to call them, are not new in America. One of the earliest pieces of testimony to this effect is essay number 10 of *The Federalist*, which contains James Madison's classic statement of the impact of divergent groups upon government and the reasons for their development. He was arguing the virtues of the proposed Union as a means to "break and control the violence of faction," having in mind, no doubt, the groups involved in such actions of the debtor or propertyless segment of the population as Shays's Rebellion. He defined faction in broader terms, however, as "a number of citizens, whether amounting to a majority or minority of the whole, who are united and actuated by some common impulse of passion, or of interest. . . ."

* * *

[Madison's] analysis is not just the brilliant generalization of an armchair philosopher or pamphleteer; it represents as well the distillation from Madison's years of acquaintance with contemporary politics as a member of the Virginia Assembly and of [the Continental] Congress. Using the words "party" and "faction" almost interchangeably, since the political party as we know it had not yet developed, he saw the struggles of such groups as the essence of the political process. One need not concur in all his judgments to agree that the process he described had strong similarities to that of our own day.

The entire effort of which *The Federalist* was a part was one of the most skillful and important examples of pressure group activity in American history. The State ratifying conventions were handled by the Federalists with a skill that might well be the envy of a modern lobbyist. It is easy to overlook the fact that "unless the Federalists had been shrewd in manipulation as they were sound in theory, their arguments could not have prevailed."

* * *

Alexis de Tocqueville, perhaps the keenest foreign student ever to write on American institutions, noted as one of the most striking characteristics of the nation the penchant for promoting a bewildering array of projects through organized societies, among them those using political means. "In no country in the world," he observed, "has the principle of association been more successfully used or applied to a greater multitude of objects than in America." De Tocqueville [sic] was impressed by the organization of such groups and by their tendency to operate sometimes upon and sometimes parallel to the formal institutions of government. Speaking of the similarity between the representatives of such groups and the members of legislatures, he stated: "It is true that they [delegates of these societies] have not the right, like the others, of making the laws; but they have the power of attacking those which are in force and of drawing up beforehand those which ought to be enacted."

Since the modern political party was, in the Jackson period, just taking the form that we would recognize today, De Tocqueville does not always distinguish sharply between it and other types of political interest groups. In his discussion of "political associations," however, he gives an account of the antitariff convention held in Philadelphia in October of 1831, the form of which might well have come from the proceedings of a group meeting in an American city today:

> Its debates were public, and they at once assumed a legislative character; the extent of the powers of Congress, the theories of free trade, and the different provisions of the tariff were discussed. At the end of ten days the Convention broke up, having drawn up an address to the American people in which it declared: (1) that Congress had not the right of making a tariff, and that the existing tariff was unconstitutional; (2) that the prohibition of free trade was prejudicial to the interests of any nation, and to those of the American people especially.

Additional evidence might be cited from many quarters to illustrate the long history of group politics in this country. Organized pressures supporting or attacking the charter of the Bank of the United States in Jackson's administration, the peculations surrounding Pendleton's "Palace of Fortune" in the pre–Civil War period, the operations of the railroads and other interests in both national and state legislatures in the latter half of the last century, the political activities of farm groups such as the Grange in the same period—these and others indicate that at no time have the activities of organized political interests not been a part of American politics. Whether they indicate pathology or not, they are certainly not new.

* * *

The political interest group is neither a fleeting, transitory newcomer to the political arena nor a localized phenomenon peculiar to one member of the family of nations. The persistence and the dispersion of such organizations indicate rather that we are dealing with a characteristic aspect of our society. That such groups are receiving an increasing measure of popular and technical attention suggests the hypothesis that they are appreciably more significant in the complex and interdependent society of our own day than they were in the simpler, less highly developed community for which our constitutional arrangements were originally designed.

Many people are quite willing to acknowledge the accuracy of these propositions about political groups, but they are worried nevertheless. They are still concerned over the meaning of what they see and read of the activities of such organizations. They observe, for example, that certain farm groups apparently can induce the Government to spend hundreds of millions of dollars to maintain the price of food and to take "surplus" agricultural produce off the market while any urban residents are encountering painful difficulty in stretching their food budgets to provide adequately for their families. They observe that various labor organizations seem to be able to prevent the introduction of cheaper methods into building codes, although the cost of new housing is already beyond the reach of many. Real estate and contractors' trade associations apparently have the power to obstruct various governmental projects for slum clearance and low-cost housing. Veterans' organizations seem able to secure and protect increases in pensions and other benefits almost at will. A church apparently can prevent the appropriation of Federal funds to public schools unless such funds are also given to the schools it operates in competition with the public systems. The Government has declared that stable and friendly European governments cannot be maintained unless Americans buy more goods and services abroad. Yet American shipowners and seamen's unions can secure a statutory requirement that a large proportion of the goods purchased by European countries under the Marshall Plan* must be carried in American ships. Other industries and trade associations can prevent the revision of tariff rates and customs regulations that restrict imports from abroad.

In all these situations the fairly observant citizen sees various groups slugging it out with one another in pursuit of advantages from the Government. Or he sees some of them co-operating with one another to their mutual benefit. He reads of "swarms" of lobbyists "putting pressure on" congressmen and administrators. He has the impression that any group can get what it wants in Washington by deluging officials with mail and telegrams. He may then begin to wonder whether a governmental system like this can survive, whether it can carry its responsibilities in the world and meet the challenges presented by a ruthless dictatorship. He wants to see these external threats effectively met. The sentimental nonsense of the commercial advertisements aside, he values free speech, free

*The Marshall Plan was the U.S. European Recovery Plan after World War II [Editors].

elections, representative government, and all that these imply. He fears and resents practices and privileges that seem to place these values in jeopardy.

A common reaction to revelations concerning the more lurid activities of political groups is one of righteous indignation. Such indignation is entirely natural. It is likely, however, to be more comforting than constructive. What we seek are correctives, protections, or controls that will strengthen the practices essential in what we call democracy and that will weaken or eliminate those that really threaten that system. Uncritical anger may do little to achieve that objective, largely because it is likely to be based upon a picture of the governmental process that is a composite of myth and fiction as well as of fact. We shall not begin to achieve control until we have arrived at a conception of politics that adequately accounts for the operations of political groups. We need to know what regular patterns are shown by group politics before we can predict its consequences and prescribe for its lapses. We need to re-examine our notions of how representative government operates in the United States before we can be confident of our statements about the effects of group activities upon it. Just as we should not know how to protect a farm house from lightning unless we knew something of the behavior of electricity, so we cannot hope to protect a governmental system from the results of group organization unless we have an adequate understanding of the political process of which these groups are a part.

*   *   *

There are two elements in this conception of the political process in the United States that are of crucial significance and that require special emphasis. These are, first, the notion of multiple or overlapping membership and, second, the function of unorganized interests, or potential interest groups.

The idea of overlapping membership stems from the conception of a group as a standardized pattern of interactions rather than as a collection of human units. Although the former may appear to be a rather misty abstraction, it is actually far closer to complex reality than the latter notion. he view of a group as an aggregation of individuals abstracts from the observable fact that in any society, and especially a complex one, no single group affiliation accounts for all of the attitudes or interests of any individual except a fanatic or a compulsive neurotic. No tolerably normal person is totally absorbed in any group in which he participates. The diversity of an individual's activities and his attendant interests involve him in a variety of actual and potential groups. Moreover, the fact that the genetic experiences of no two individuals are identical and the consequent fact that the spectra of their attitudes are in varying degrees dissimilar means that the members of a single group will perceive the group's claims in terms of a diversity of frames of reference. Such heterogeneity may be of little significance until such time as these multiple memberships conflict. Then the cohesion and influence of the affected group depend upon the incorporation or accommodation of the conflicting loyalties of any significant segment of the group, an accommodation that may result in altering the original claims. Thus the leaders of a Parent-Teacher Association must take some account of the fact that their proposals must be acceptable to members who also belong to the local taxpayers' league, to the local chamber of commerce, and to the Catholic Church.

* * *

We cannot account of an established American political system without the second crucial element in our conception of the political process, the concept of the unorganized interest, or potential interest group. Despite the tremendous number of interest groups existing in the United States, not all interests are organized. If we recall the definition of an interest as a shared attitude, it becomes obvious that continuing interaction resulting in claims upon other groups does not take place on the basis of all such attitudes. One of the commonest interest groups forms, the association, emerges out of severe or prolonged disturbances in the expected relationships of individuals in similar institutionalized groups. As association continues to function as long as it succeeds in ordering these disturbed relationships, as a labor union orders the relationships between management and workers. Not all such expected relationships are simultaneously or in a given short period sufficiently disturbed to produce organization. Therefore only a portion of the interests or attitudes involved in such expectations are represented by organized groups. Similarly, many organized groups—families, businesses, or churches, for example—do not operate continuously as interest groups or as political interest groups.

Any mutual interest, however, any shared attitude, is a potential group. A disturbance in established relationships and expectations anywhere in the society may produce new patterns of interaction aimed at restricting or eliminating he disturbance. Sometimes it may be this possibility of organization that alone gives the potential group a minimum of influence in the political process. Thus . . . the Delta planters in Mississippi "must speak for their Negroes in such programs as health and education," although the latter are virtually unorganized and are denied the means of active political participation.*

* * *

Obstacles to the development of organized groups from potential ones may be presented by inertia or by the activities of opposed groups, but the possibility that severe disturbances will be created if these submerged, potential interests should organize necessitates some recognition

---

*Until the 1960s, most Southern black people were denied the right to vote [Editors].

of the existence of these interests and gives them at least a minimum of influence.

More important for present purposes than the potential groups representing separate minority elements are those interests or expectations that are so widely held in the society and are so reflected in the behavior of almost all citizens that they are, so to speak, taken for granted. Such "majority" interests are significant not only because they may become the basis for organized interest groups overlaps extensively the memberships of the various organized interest groups. The resolution of conflicts between the claims of such unorganized interests and those of organized interest groups must grant recognition to the former not only because affected individuals may feel strongly attached to them but even more certainly because these interests are widely shared and are a part of many established patterns of behavior the disturbance of which would be difficult and painful. They are likely to be highly valued.

* * *

It is thus multiple memberships in potential groups based on widely held and accepted interests that serve as a balance wheel in a going political system like that of the United States. To some people this observation may appear to be a truism and to others a somewhat mystical notion. It is neither. In the first place, neglect of this function of multiple memberships in most discussions of organized interest groups indicates that the observation is not altogether commonplace. Secondly, the statement has no mystical quality; the effective operation of these widely held interests is to be inferred directly from verbal and other behavior in the political sphere. Without the notion of multiple memberships in potential groups it is literally impossible to account for the existence of a viable polity such as that in the United States or to develop a coherent conception of the political process. The strength of these widely held but largely unorganized interests explains the vigor with which propagandists for organized groups attempt to change other attitudes by invoking such interests. Their importance is further evidenced in the recognized function of the means of mass communication, notably the press, in reinforcing widely accepted norms of "public morality."

* * *

Thus it is only as the effects of overlapping memberships and the functions of unorganized interests and potential groups are included in the equation that it is accurate to speak of governmental activity as the product or resultant of interest group activity. As [political scientist Arthur F.] Bentley has put it:

> There are limits to the technique of the struggle, this involving also limits to the group demands, all of which is solely a matter of empirical observation. . . . Or, in other words, when the struggle proceeds too harshly at any point

there will become insistent in the society a group more powerful than either of those involved which tends to suppress the extreme and annoying methods of the groups in the primary struggle. It is within the embrace of these great lines of activity that the smaller struggles proceed, and the very word struggle has meaning only with reference to its limitations.

To assert that the organization and activity of powerful interest groups constitutes a threat to representative government without measuring their relation to and effects upon the widespread potential groups is to generalize from insufficient data and upon an incomplete conception of the political process. Such an analysis would be as faulty as one that ignoring differences in national systems, predicted identical responses to a given technological change in the United States, Japan, and the Soviet Union.

66

"The Scope and Bias of the Pressure System," from *The Semisovereign People*

E. E. Schattschneider

A Critique of Group Theories of Politics

It is extremely unlikely that the vogue of group theories of politics would have attained its present status if its basic assumptions had not been first established by some concept of economic determinism. The economic interpretation of politics has always appealed to those political philosophers who have sought a single prime mover, a sort of philosopher's stone of political science around which to organize their ideas. The search for a single, ultimate cause has something to do with the attempt to explain *everything* about politics in terms of group concepts. The logic of economic determinism is to *identify the origins of conflict and to assume the conclusion.* This kind of thought has some of the earmarks of an illusion. The somnambulatory quality of thinking in this field appears also in the tendency of research to deal only with successful pressure campaigns or the willingness of scholars to be satisfied with having placed pressure groups on the scene of the crime without following through to see if the effect can really be attributed to the cause. What makes this kind of thinking remarkable is the fact that in political contests there are as many failures as there are successes. Where in the literature of pressure politics are the failures?

Students of special-interest politics need a more sophisticated set of intellectual tools than they have developed thus far. The theoretical problem involved in the search for a single cause is that all power relations in a democracy are reciprocal. Trying to find the original cause is like trying to find the first wave of the ocean.

Can we really assume that we know all that is to be known about a conflict if we understand its *origins?* Everything we know about politics suggests that a conflict is likely to change profoundly as it becomes political. It is a rare individual who can confront his antagonists without changing his opinions to some degree. Everything changes once a conflict gets into the political arena—*who* is involved, *what* the conflict is about, the resources available, etc. It is extremely difficult to predict the outcome of a fight by watching its beginning because we do not even know who else is going to get into the conflict. The logical consequence of the exclusive emphasis on the determinism of the private origins of conflict is to assign zero value to the political process.

The very expression "pressure politics" invites us to misconceive the role of special-interest groups in politics. The word "pressure" implies the use of some kind of force, a form of intimidation, something other than reason and information, to induce public authorities to act against their own best judgment. In Latham's famous statement already quoted the legislature is described as a "referee" who "ratifies" and "records" the "balance of power" among the contending groups.

It is hard to imagine a more effective way of saying that Congress has no mind or force of its own or that Congress is unable to invoke new forces that might alter the equation.

Actually the outcome of political conflict is not like the "resultant" of opposing forces in physics. To assume that the forces in a political situation could be diagrammed as a physicist might diagram the resultant of opposing physical forces is to wipe the slate clean of all remote, general and public considerations for the protection of which civil societies have been instituted.

* * *

Moreover, the notion of "pressure" distorts the image of the power relations involved. *Private conflicts are taken into the public arena precisely because someone wants to make certain that the power ratio among the private interests most immediately involved shall not prevail. To treat a conflict as a mere test of the strength of the private interests is to leave out of the most significant factors.* This is so true that it might indeed be said that the only way to preserve private power ratios is to keep conflicts out of the public arena.

The assumption that it is only the "interested" who count ought to be re-examined in view of the foregoing discussion. The tendency of the literature of pressure politics has been to neglect the low-tension force of large numbers because it *assumes that the equation of forces is fixed at the outset.*

Given the assumptions made by the group theorists, the attack on the idea of the majority is completely logical. The assumption is that conflict is monopolized narrowly by the parties immediately concerned. There is no room for a majority when conflict is defined so narrowly. It is a great deficiency of the group theory that it has found no place in the political system for the majority. The force of the majority is of an entirely different order of magnitude something not to be measured by pressure-group standards.

Instead of attempting to exterminate all political forms, organizations and alignments that do not qualify as pressure groups, would it not be better to attempt to make a synthesis, covering the whole political system and finding a place for all kinds of political life?

One possible synthesis of pressure politics and party politics might be produced by *describing politics as the socialization of conflict.* That is to say, the political process is a sequence; conflicts are initiated by highly motivated, high-tension groups so directly and immediately involved that it is difficult for them to see the justice of competing claims. As long as the conflicts of these groups remain *private* (carried on in terms of economic competition, reciprocal denial of goods and services, private negotiations and bargaining, struggles for corporate control or competition for membership), no political process is initiated. Conflicts become political only when an attempt is made to involve the wider public. Pressure politics might be described as a stage in the socialization of conflict. This analysis makes pressure politics an integral part of all politics, including party politics.

One of the characteristic points of origin of pressure politics is a breakdown of the discipline of the business community. The flight to government is perpetual. Something like this is likely to happen wherever there is a point of contact between competing power systems. It is the *losers in intrabusiness conflict who seek redress from public authority. The dominant business interests resist appeals to the government.* The role of the government as the patron of the defeated private interest sheds light on its function as the critic of private power relations.

Since the contestants in private conflicts are apt to be unequal in strength, it follows that *the most powerful special interests want private settlements* because they are able to dictate the outcome as long as the conflict remains private. If A is a hundred times as strong as B he does not welcome the intervention of a third party because he expects to impose his own terms on B; he wants to isolate B. He is especially opposed to the intervention of public authority, because public authority represents the most overwhelming form of outside intervention. Thus, if $\frac{A}{B} = \frac{1}{100}$, it is obviously not to A's advantage to involve a third party a million times as strong as A and B combined. Therefore, it is the weak, not the strong, who appeal to public authority for relief. It is the weak who want to socialize conflict, i.e., to involve more and more people in the conflict until the balance of forces is changed. In the school yard it is not the bully, but the defenseless smaller boys who "tell the teacher." When the teacher intervenes the balance of power in the school yard is apt to change drastically. It is the function of public authority to *modify private power relations by enlarging the scope of conflict.* Nothing could be more mistaken than to suppose that public authority merely registers the dominance of the strong over the weak. The mere existence of public order has already ruled out a great variety of forms of private pressure. Nothing could be more confusing than to suppose that the refugees from the business community who come to Congress for relief and protection *force* Congress to do their bidding.

Evidence of the truth of this analysis may be seen in the fact that the big private interests do not necessarily win if they are involved in public conflicts with petty interests. The image of the lobbyists as primarily the agents of big business is not easy to support on the face of the record of congressional hearings, for example. The biggest corporations in the country tend to avoid the arena in which pressure groups and lobbyists fight it out before congressional committees. To describe this process exclusively in terms of an effort of business to intimidate congressmen is to misconceive what is actually going on.

It is probably a mistake to assume that pressure politics is the typical or even the most important relation between government and business. The pressure group is by no means the perfect instrument of the business community. What does big business want? The *winners* in intrabusiness strife want (1) to be let alone (they want autonomy) and (2) to preserve the solidarity of the business community. For these purposes pressure politics is not a wholly satisfactory device. The most elementary considerations of strategy call for the business community to develop some kind of common policy more broadly based than any special-interest group is likely to be.

The political influence of business depends on the kind of solidarity that, on the one hand, leads all business to rally to the support of *any* businessman in trouble with the government, and on the other hand, keeps internal business disputes out of the public arena. In this system businessmen resist the impulse to attack each other in public and discourage the efforts of individual members of the business community to take intrabusiness conflicts into politics.

The attempt to mobilize a united front of the whole business community does not resemble the classical concept of pressure politics. The logic of business politics is to keep peace within the business community by supporting as far as possible all claims that business groups make for themselves. The tendency is to support all businessmen who have conflicts with the government and support all businessmen in conflict with labor. In this way *special-interest politics can be converted into party policy.* The search is for a broad base of political mobilization grounded on the strategic need for political organization on a wider scale than is possible in the case of the historical pressure group. Once the business community begins to think in terms of a larger scale of political organization the Republican party looms large in business politics.

It is a great achievement of American democracy that business has been forced to form a political organization designed to win elections, i.e., has been forced to compete for power in the widest arena in the political system. On the other hand, *the power of the Republican party to make terms with business rests on the fact that business cannot afford to be isolated.*

The Republican party has played a major role in *the political organization of the business community*, a far greater role than many students of politics seem to have realized. The influence of business in the Republican party is great, but it is never absolute because business is remarkably dependent on the party. The business community is too small, it arouses too much antagonism, and its aims are too narrow to win the support of a popular majority. The political education of business is a function of the Republican party that can never be done so well by anyone else.

In the management of the political relations of the business community, the Republican party is much more important than any combination of pressure groups ever could be. The success of special interests in Congress is due less to the "pressure" exerted by these groups than it is due to the fact that Republican members of Congress are committed in advance to a general probusiness attitude. The notion that business groups coerce Republican congressmen into voting for their bills underestimates the whole Republican posture in American politics.

It is not easy to manage the political interests of the business community because there is a perpetual stream of losers in intrabusiness conflicts who go to the government for relief and protection. It has not been possible therefore to maintain perfect solidarity, and when solidarity is breached the government is involved almost automatically. The fact that business has not become hopelessly divided and that it has retained great influence in American politics has been due chiefly to the over-all mediating role played by the Republican party. There has never been a pressure group or a combination of pressure groups capable of performing this function.

67

"The Hyperpluralism Trap"

Jonathan Rauch

Anyone who believes Washington needs to get closer to the people ought to spend a little time with Senator Richard Lugar, the Indiana Republican. "Take a look at the people coming into my office on a normal Tuesday and Wednesday," Lugar said in a speech not long ago [1994]. "Almost every organization in our society has a national conference. The typical way of handling this is to come in on a Monday, rev up the troops, give them the bill number and send them up to the Hill. If they can't get in on Tuesday, strike again on Wednesday. I regularly have on Tuesday as many as fifteen constituent groups from Indiana, all of whom have been revved up by some skillful person to cite bills that they don't understand, have never heard of prior to that time, but with a score sheet to report back to headquarters whether I am for or against. It is so routine, it is so fierce, that at some point you [can't be] immune to it."

This is the reality of modern government. The rhetoric of modern politics, alas, is a little different. Take today's standard-issue political stemwinder, which goes something like this: "I think perhaps the most important thing that we understand here in the heartland . . . is the need to reform the political system, to reduce the influence of special interests and give more influence back to the kind of people that are in this crowd tonight by the tens of thousands." That stream of boilerplate is from Bill Clinton (from his election-night speech), but it could have come from almost any politician. It's pitched in a dominant key of political rhetoric today: *standard populism*—that is, someone has taken over the government and "we" must take it back, restore government to the people, etc. But who, exactly, are those thousands of citizens who troop weekly through Senator Lugar's suite, clutching briefing packets and waving scorecards? Standard populism says they are the "special interests," those boils on the skin of democracy, forever interposing themselves between the American people and the people's servants in Washington.

Well, fifty years ago that analysis may have been useful, but not anymore. In America today, the special interests and "the people" have become objectively indistinguishable. Groups are us. As a result, the populist impulse to blame special interests, big corporations and political careerists for our problems—once a tonic—has become Americans' leading political narcotic. Worse, it actually abets the lobbying it so righteously denounces.

Begin with one of the best known yet most underappreciated facts of our time: over the past three or four decades we have busily organized ourselves into interest groups—lobbies, loosely speaking—at an astonishing rate. Interest groups were still fairly sparse in America until about the time of World War II. Then they started proliferating, and in the 1960s the pace of organizing picked up dramatically.

Consider, for instance, the numbers of groups listed in Gale Research's *Encyclopedia of Associations*. The listings have grown from fewer than 5,000 in 1956 to well over 20,000 today. They represent, of course, only a small fraction of America's universe of interest groups. Environmental organizations alone number an estimated 7,000, once you count local clean-up groups and the like; the Washington *Blade*'s resource directory lists more than 400 gay groups, up from 300 at the end of 1990. Between 1961 and 1982 the number of corporate offices in Washington increased tenfold. Even more dramatic was the explosion in the number of public-interest organizations and grass-roots groups. These barely existed at all before the 1960s; today they number in the tens of thousands and collect more than $4 billion per year from 40 million individuals, according to political scientist Ronald Shaiko of American University.

Well, so what? Groups do many good things—provide companionship for the like-minded, collect and disseminate information, sponsor contests, keep the catering industry solvent. Indeed, conventional political theory for much of the postwar period was dominated by a strain known as pluralism, which holds that more groups equals more representation equals better democracy. Yet pluralism missed something. It assumed that the group-forming process was self-balancing and stable, as opposed to self-feeding and unstable. Which is to say, it failed to grasp the danger of what American University political scientist James Thurber aptly calls hyperpluralism.

In economics, inflation is a gradual increase in the price level. Up to a point, if the inflation rate is stable, people can plan around it. But if the rate starts to speed up, people start expecting more inflation. They hoard goods and dump cash, driving the inflation still faster. Eventually, an invisible threshold is crossed: the inflation now feeds on its own growth and undermines the stability of the whole economic system.

What the pluralists missed is that something analogous can happen with interest groups. People see that it pays to organize into groups and angle for benefits, so they do it. But as more groups make more demands, and as even more hungry groups form to compete with all the other groups, the process begins to feed on itself and pick up momentum. At some point there might be so many groups that they choke the political system, sow contention and conflict, even erode society's governability.

That's hyperpluralism. And if it is less destabilizing than hyperinflation, it may be more insidious.

The pattern is most visible in smaller social units, such as local school districts, where groups colonize the curriculum—sex education for liberals, values instruction for conservatives, recycling lessons for environmentalists, voluntary silent prayer for Christians. But even among the general population the same forces are at work. Fifty years ago the phrase "the elderly" denoted a demographic category; today, thanks largely to federal pension programs and the American Association of Retired Persons (AARP), it denotes a giant and voracious lobby. In the 1930s the government set up farm-subsidy programs, one per commodity; inevitably, lobbies sprang up to defend each program, so that today American agriculture is fundamentally a collection of interest groups. With the help of group organizers and race-based benefits, loose ethnic distinctions coalesce into hard ethnic lobbies. And so on.

Even more depressing, any attempt to fight back against the proliferating mass of subdivision is foiled by the rhetoric of standard populism and its useful stooge: the special interest. The concept of a "special interest" is at the very core of standard populism—the "them" without which there can be no "us." So widely accepted is this notion, and so useful is it in casual political speech, that most of us talk routinely about special interests without a second thought. We all feel we know a special interest when we see one, if only because it is a group of which we are not a member. Yet buried in the special interest idea is an assumption that is no longer true.

The concept of the special interest is not based on nothing. It is, rather, out of date, an increasingly empty relic of the time of machine politics and political bosses, when special interests were, quite literally, special. Simply because of who they were, they enjoyed access that was available to no one else. But the process of everyone's organizing into more and more groups can go only so far before the very idea of a special interest loses any clear meaning. At some point one must throw up one's hands and concede that the hoary dichotomy between special interests and "us" has become merely rhetoric.

According to a 1990 survey conducted for the American Society of Association Executives, seven out of ten Americans belong to at least one association, and one in four Americans belongs to four or more. Practically everyone who reads these words is a member of an interest group, probably several. Moreover, formal membership tallies omit many people whom we ordinarily think of as being represented by lobbies. For example, the powerful veterans' lobbies enroll only perhaps one-seventh of American veterans, yet the groups lobby on behalf of veterans as a class, and all 27 million veterans share in the benefits. Thus the old era of lobbying by special interests—by a well-connected, plutocratic few—is as dead now as slavery and Prohibition. We Americans have achieved the full democratization of lobbying: influence-peddling for the masses.

The appeal of standard populism today comes precisely from the phony reassurance afforded by its real message: "Other people's groups are the special interests. Less for them—more for you!" Spread that sweet manure around and the natural outgrowth is today's tendency, so evident in the Clinton style, to pander to interest groups frantically while denouncing them furiously. It is the public's style, too: sending ever more checks to the AARP and the National Rifle Association and the National Federation of Independent Business and the National Wildlife Federation and a million others, while railing against special interests. Join and join, blame and blame.

So hyperpluralism makes a hash of the usual sort of standard populist prescription, which calls for "the people" to be given more access to the system, at the expense of powerful Beltway figures who are alleged to have grown arrogant or corrupt or out of touch. Activists and reformers who think the answer to democracy's problems is more access for more of the people need to wake up. Uncontrolled access only breeds more lobbies. It is axiomatic that "the people" (whatever that now means) do not organize to seek government benefits; lobbies do. Every new door to the federal treasury is an opportunity for new groups to queue up for more goodies.

Populists resolutely refuse to confront this truth. Last year, for example, Republicans and the editors of *The Wall Street Journal* campaigned fiercely—and successfully—for new congressional rules making it easier for legislators and groups to demand that bottled-up bills be discharged from committee. The idea was to bring Congress closer to "the people" by weakening the supposedly high-handed barons who rule the Hill. But burying the Free Christmas Tree for Every American Act (or whatever) in committee—while letting members of Congress say they *would* have voted for it—was one of the few remaining ways to hold the door against hungry lobbies clamoring for gifts.

A second brand of populism, *left-populism*, is even more clueless than the standard brand, if that's possible. Many liberals believe the problem is that the wrong groups—the rich, the elites, the giant corporations, etc.—have managed to out-organize the good guys and take control of the system. One version of this model was elaborated by William Greider in his book *Who Will Tell the People*. The New Deal legacy, he writes, "rests upon an idea of interest group bargaining that has gradually been transformed into the random deal-making and permissiveness of the present. The alterations in the system are decisive and . . . the ultimate effects are anti-democratic. People with limited resources, with no real representation in the higher levels of politics, are bound to lose in this environment." So elaborate is the Washington machine of lobbyists, consultants,

P.R. experts, political action committees and for-hire think tanks, says Greider, that "powerful economic interests," notably corporations and private wealth, inevitably dominate.

What's appealing about this view is the truism from which it springs: the wealthy enjoy a natural advantage in lobbying, as in almost everything else. Thus many lobbies—even liberal lobbies—are dominated by the comfortable and the wealthy. Consider the case of environmental groups. Anyone who doubts they are major players in Washington today need only look at the massive 1990 Clean Air Act, a piece of legislation that business gladly would have done without. Yet these groups are hardly battalions of the disfranchised. "Readers of *Sierra*, the magazine of the Sierra Club, have household incomes twice that of the average American," notes Senior Economist Terry L. Anderson of the Political Economy Research Center. And *The Economist* notes that "in 1993 the Nature Conservancy, with $915 million in assets, drew 73 percent of its income from rich individuals." When such groups push for emissions controls or pesticide rules, they may be reflecting the priorities of people who buy BMWs and brie more than the priorities of people who buy used Chevies and hamburger. So left-populism's claim to speak for "the people" is often suspect, to say the least.

The larger problem with left-populism, however, is its refusal to see that it is feeding the very problem it decries. Left-populism was supposed to fix the wealth-buys-power problem by organizing the politically disadvantaged into groups: unions, consumer groups, rainbow coalitions and so on. But the strategy has failed. As the left (the unions, the environmentalists) has organized ever more groups, the right (the bosses, the polluters) has followed suit. The group-forming has simply spiralled. This makes a joke of the left-populist prescription, which is to form more "citizens' groups" on the Naderite model, supposedly reinvigorating representative democracy and giving voice to the weak and the silenced. Greider proposes giving people subsidies to spend on political activism: "Giving individual citizens the capacity to deploy political money would inevitably shift power from existing structures and disperse it among the ordinary millions who now feel excluded."

Inevitably, it would do no such thing. Subsidies for activism would perforce go straight into the waiting coffers of (what else?) interest groups, new and old. That just makes matters worse, for if one side organizes more groups, the other side simply redoubles its own mobilization ad infinitum. That escalating cycle is the story of the last three decades. The only winner is the lobbying class. Curiously, then, left-populism has come to serve the very lobbying elites—the Washington lawyers and lobby shops and P.R. pros and interest group execs—whom leftists ought, by rights, to loathe.

The realization that the lobbying class is, to a large extent, both entrepreneurial and in business for itself has fed the third brand of populism, *right-populism*. In the right-populist model, self-serving political careerists have hijacked government and learned to manipulate it for profit. In refreshing contrast to the other two brands of populism, however, this one is in touch with reality. Washington *is* in business for itself, though not only for itself. Legislators and lobbies have an interest in using the tax code to please their constituents, but they also have an interest in churning the tax code to generate campaign contributions and lobbying fees. Luckily for them, those two imperatives generally coincide: the more everyone hunts for tax breaks, the more lobbying jobs there are. Right-populism has tumbled to the fact that so-called public interest and citizens' groups are no more immune to this self-serving logic of lobbying—create conflict, reap rewards—than is any other sort of professional lobby.

Yet right-populism fails to see to the bottom of the problem. It looks into the abyss but flinches. This is not to say that term limits and other procedural fine-tunes may not help; such reforms are no doubt worth trying. But even if noodling with procedures succeeded in diluting the culture of political careerism, it would help (or hurt) mainly at the margins. No, tinkering with the process isn't the answer. What we must do is go straight at the beast itself. We must attack and weaken the lobbies—that is, the *people*'s lobbies.

It sounds so simple: weaken the lobbies! Shove them aside, reclaim the government! "It's just that simple," twinkles Ross Perot. But it's not that simple. Lobbies in Washington have clout because the people who scream when "special interests" are attacked are Medicare recipients defending benefits, farmers defending price supports, small businesses defending subsidized loans, racial groups defending set-asides and so on. Inherently, challenging these groups is no one's idea of fun, which is why politicians so rarely propose to do it. The solution is to strip away lobbies' protections and let competition hammer them. In practice, that means:

Balance the federal budget. It is a hackneyed prescription, but it is the very first thing we should do to curtail the lobbies' ability to rob the future. Deficits empower lobbies by allowing them to raid the nation's scarce reserves of investment capital. Deprived of that ability, they will be forced to compete more fiercely for money, and they'll be unable to steal from the future.

Cut the lobbies' lifelines. Eliminate subsidies and programs, including tax loopholes, by the hundreds. Killing a program here or there is a loser's game; it creates a political uproar without actually making a noticeable difference. The model, rather, should be the 1986 tax reform measure, which proved that a wholesale housecleaning really is possible. Back then, tax loopholes were cleared away by the truckload. The trick was—and is—to do the job with a big package of reforms that politicians can tout back home as real change. That means ditching whole Cabinet departments and abolishing virtually all industry-specific subsidies. Then go after subsidies for the non-needy—wholesale, not retail.

*Promote domestic perestroika.** Lobbies live to lock benefits in and competition out, so government restraints on competition should be removed—not indiscriminately, but determinedly. President Carter's deregulation of transportation industries and interest rates, though imperfectly executed, were good examples. Air travel, trucking and rail shipping are cheaper *and* safer. The affected industries have been more turbulent, but that's exactly the point. Domestic competition shakes up interest groups that settle cozily into Washington.

Encourage foreign competition. This is most important of all. The forces that breed interest groups never abate, and so fighting them requires a constant counterforce. Foreign competition is such a counterforce. Protection invariably benefits the industries and groups with the sharpest lobbyists and the fattest political action committees; stripping away protection forces them to focus more on modernizing and less on lobbying.

No good deed, they say, goes unpunished. We sought to solve pressing social problems, so we gave government vast power to reassign resources. We also sought to look out for ourselves and bring voices to all of our many natures and needs, so we built countless new groups to seek government's resources. What we did not create was a way to control the chain reaction we set off. Swarming interest groups excited government to perpetual activism, and government activism drew new groups to Washington by the thousands. Before we knew it, society itself was turning into a collection of ravenous lobbies.

Why was this not always a problem? Because there used to be control rods containing the chain reaction. Smoke-filled rooms, they were called. On Capitol Hill or in Tammany Hall, you needed to see one of about six people to have any hope of getting what you wanted, and those six people dispensed (and conserved) favors with parsimonious finesse. Seen from today's vantage, smoke-filled rooms and political machines did a creditable job of keeping a lid on the interest group frenzy—they just didn't do it particularly fairly. That's why we opened up access to anyone who wants to organize and lobby, and opened up power to subcommittee chairs and caucus heads and even junior legislators. In doing so, we abolished the venal gatekeepers. But that was only the good news. The bad news was that we also abolished the gate.

No, we shouldn't go back to smoke-filled rooms. But the way forward is harder than it ever was before. The maladies that now afflict government are ones in which the public is wholly, enthusiastically implicated. Still, there are sprigs and shoots of encouragement all around. There was the surprisingly strong presidential bid of former Senator Paul Tsongas,

---

*1980s Soviet Union program of political and economic reform [*Editors*].

which built something of a constituency for straight talk. There's the rise of a school of Democrats in Congress—among them Senator Bob Kerrey and retiring Representative Tim Penny—who are willing to drag the White House toward sterner fiscal measures. There was the Clinton-led triumph of NAFTA [North American Free Trade Agreement] last year. Those developments show promise of a political movement that is counterpopulist yet also popular. Maybe—is it too much to hope?—they point beyond the desert of populism.

DISCUSSION QUESTIONS

1. Can you think of any examples of overlapping group memberships—that is, situations where members of a group are also likely to be members of other groups that may have different public policy positions? How about an example of a new organization that had a significant impact on a recent policy debate? Can you think of instances in which, counter to Truman, a new organization surprisingly did not emerge, leaving a group unrepresented?

2. Rauch complains that interest groups slow down the policy-making process, but isn't this what the Framers of the Constitution intended? Is the interest-group system as portrayed by Rauch a danger to democracy? Or is it in fact implementing the principles implicit in the Constitution?

3. Think of two examples of recent policy debates where one side or the other attempted to socialize conflict. That is, one side sought to widen the issue, to bring in more participants, to have the debates be about a broader rather than a narrower set of concerns. Would you agree with Schattschneider that this tactic was adopted by the side that seemed to be in a weaker position?

4. Does Rauch's analysis conform or argue against Schattschneider's points about the benefits of political parties in the interest-group process?

PART IV

Public Policy

CHAPTER 13

Politics and Policy

68

"The Science of Muddling Through"

CHARLES E. LINDBLOM

Today's national government plays a role in virtually every aspect of our lives. It provides health insurance for the elderly and the poor, welfare assistance, veterans' benefits, student loans, and a tax break for home owners paying a mortgage. It regulates the activities of the stock markets, polluting industries, worker safety and worker rights, the quality of our food, and air traffic. These programs and regulatory policies are all designed and implemented by the government to achieve particular goals—such as an expanding economy, healthy citizens, college education, and home ownership. It is important that we know just how the government goes about formulating and implementing public policy, and the consequences of those efforts. Who plays a role in the making of public policy besides elected officials, and what motivates their decision making? Who are the beneficiaries of various public policies, and is the "public interest" being served?

In the article below, the economist and political scientist Charles Lindblom argues that the efforts of scholars to study and improve on the policy process were flawed because they were based on the assumption that public policy could be made in a "rational" manner. The problem, according to Lindblom, is that decision making for public policy normally proceeds incrementally: policy makers are incapable of defining and developing alternatives that encompass all possible means of achieving explicitly defined goals. Rather, decision makers start with what already exists, goals defined in part by what is known to work and by the interests that are the most vocal and powerful, and changes are made at the margin to achieve these various ends. Further, the way we evaluate any given policy is heavily dependent upon our values and beliefs about what government ought to do and how it ought to be achieved. There is rarely, according to Lindblom, a clear objective standard of a "good" policy that all policy makers and analysts can agree upon. Lindblom's article, originally published in 1959, was groundbreaking in that it challenged conventional wisdom among analysts that rational comprehensive analysis was possible for purposes of formulating public policy.

Suppose an administrator is given responsibility for formulating policy with respect to inflation. He might start by trying to list all related values in order of importance, e.g., full employment, reasonable business profit, protection of small savings, prevention of a stock market crash. Then all possible policy outcomes could be rated as more or less efficient in attaining a maximum of these values. This would of course require a prodigious inquiry into values held by members of society and an equally prodigious set of calculations on how much each value is equal to how much of each other value. He could then proceed to outline all possible policy alternatives. In a third step, he could undertake systematic comparison of his multitude of alternatives to determine which attains the greatest amount of values.

In comparing policies, he would take advantage of any theory available that generalized about classes of policies. In considering inflation, for example, he would compare all policies in the light of the theory of prices. Since no alternatives are beyond his investigation, he would consider strict central control and the abolition of all prices and markets on the one hand and elimination of all public controls with reliance completely on the free market on the other, both in the light of whatever theoretical generalizations he could find on such hypothetical economies.

Finally, he would try to make the choice that would in fact maximize his values.

An alternative line of attack would be to set as his principal objective, either explicitly or without conscious thought, the relatively simple goal of keeping prices level. This objective might be compromised or complicated by only a few other goals, such as full employment. He would in fact disregard most other social values as beyond his present interest, and he would for the moment not even attempt to rank the few values that he regarded as immediately relevant. Were he pressed, he would quickly admit that he was ignoring many related values and many possible important consequences of his policies.

As a second step, he would outline those relatively few policy alternatives that occurred to him. He would then compare them. In comparing his limited number of alternatives, most of them familiar from past controversies, he would not ordinarily find a body of theory precise enough to carry him through a comparison of their respective consequences. Instead he would rely heavily on the record of past experience with small policy steps to predict the consequences of similar steps extended into the future.

Moreover, he would find that the policy alternatives combined objectives or values in different ways. For example, one policy might offer price level stability at the cost of some risk of unemployment; another might offer less price stability but also less risk of unemployment. Hence, the next step in his approach—the final selection—would combine into one the choice among values and the choice among instruments for reaching values. It would not, as in the first method of policy-making, approximate a more mechanical process of choosing the means that best satisfied goals that were previously clarified and ranked. Because practitioners of the second approach expect to achieve their goals only partially, they would expect to repeat endlessly the sequence just described, as conditions and aspirations changed and as accuracy of prediction improved.

By Root or by Branch

For complex problems, the first of these two approaches is of course impossible. Although such an approach can be described, it cannot be practiced except for relatively simple problems and even then only in a somewhat modified form. It assumes intellectual capacities and sources of information that men simply do not possess, and it is even more absurd as an approach to policy when the time and money that can be allocated to a policy problem is limited, as is always the case. Of particular importance to public administrators is the fact that public agencies are in effect usually instructed not to practice the first method. That is to say, their prescribed functions and constraints—the politically or legally possible—restrict their attention to relatively few values and relatively few alternative policies among the countless alternatives that might be imagined. It is the second method that is practiced.

Curiously, however, the literatures of decision-making, policy formulation, planning, and public administration formalize the first approach rather than the second, leaving public administrators who handle complex decisions in the position of practicing what few preach. For emphasis I run some risk of overstatement. True enough, the literature is well aware of limits on man's capacities and of the inevitability that policies will be approached in some such style as the second. But attempts to formalize rational policy formulation—to lay out explicitly the necessary steps in the process—usually describe the first approach and not the second.

The common tendency to describe policy formulation even for complex problems as though it followed the first approach has been strengthened by the attention given to, and success enjoyed by, operations research,* statistical decision theory,† and systems analysis.‡ The hallmarks of these procedures, typical of the first approach, are clarity of

---

* *Operations research:* type of analysis, based on mathematical models, used to determine the most efficient use of resources for a set of goals [*Editors*].

† *Statistical decision theory:* theory that allows one to make choices between alternatives by objectifying problems and analyzing them quantitatively. Also called Bayesian decision theory after Thomas Bayes (1702–1761), who developed the mathematical foundation of inference, the method of using information on a sample to infer characteristics about a population [*Editors*].

‡ *Systems analysis:* analysis of systemic data by means of advanced quantitative techniques to aid in selecting the most appropriate course of action among a series of alternatives [*Editors*].

objective, explicitness of evaluation, a high degree of comprehensiveness of overview, and, wherever possible, quantification of values for mathematical analysis. But these advanced procedures remain largely the appropriate techniques of relatively small-scale problem-solving where the total number of variables to be considered is small and value problems restricted. Charles Hitch, head of the Economics Division of RAND Corporation, one of the leading centers for application of these techniques, has written:

> I would make the empirical generalization from my experience at RAND and elsewhere that operations research is the art of sub-optimizing, i.e., of solving some lower-level problems, and that difficulties increase and our special competence diminishes by an order of magnitude with every level of decision making we attempt to ascend. The sort of simple explicit model which operations researchers are so proficient in using can certainly reflect most of the significant factors influencing traffic control on the George Washington Bridge, but the proportion of the relevant reality which we can represent by any such model or models in studying, say, a major foreign-policy decision, appears to be almost trivial.

Accordingly, I propose in this paper to clarify and formalize the second method, much neglected in the literature. This might be described as the method of *successive limited comparisons*. I will contrast it with the first approach, which might be called the rational-comprehensive method. More impressionistically and briefly—and therefore generally used in this article—they could be characterized as the branch method and root method, the former continually building out from the current situation, step-by-step and by small degrees; the latter starting from fundamentals anew each time, building on the past only as experience is embodied in a theory, and always prepared to start completely from the ground up.

Let us put the characteristics of the two methods side by side in simplest terms.

Rational-Comprehensive (Root)

1a. Clarification of values or objectives distinct from and usually prerequisite to empirical analysis of alternative policies.
2a. Policy-formulation is therefore approached through means-end analysis: First the ends are isolated, then the means to achieve them are sought.
3a. The test of a "good" policy is that it can be shown to be the most appropriate means to desired ends.
4a. Analysis is comprehensive; every important relevant factor is taken into account.
5a. Theory is often heavily relied upon.

Assuming that the root method is familiar and understandable, we proceed directly to clarification of its alternative by contrast. In explaining the second, we shall be describing how most administrators do in fact approach complex questions, for the root method, the "best" way as a blueprint or model, is in fact not workable for complex policy questions, and administrators are forced to use the method of successive limited comparisons.

Intertwining Evaluation and Empirical Analysis (1B)

The quickest way to understand how values are handled in the method of successive limited comparisons is to see how the root method often breaks down in *its* handling of values or objectives. The idea that values should be clarified, and in advance of the examination of alternative policies, is appealing. But what happens when we attempt it for complex social problems? The first difficulty is that on many critical values or objectives, citizens disagree, congressmen disagree, and public administrators disagree. Even where a fairly specific objective is prescribed for the administrator, there remains considerable room for disagreement on sub-objectives. Consider, for example, the conflict with respect to locating public housing, described in Meyerson and Banfield's study of the Chicago Housing Authority—disagreement which occurred despite the clear objective of providing a certain number of public housing units in the city. Similarly conflicting are objectives in highway location, traffic control, minimum wage administration, development of tourist facilities in national parks, or insect control.

Successive Limited Comparisons (Branch)

1b. Selection of value goals and empirical analysis of the needed action are not distinct from one another but are closely intertwined.
2b. Since means and ends are not distinct, means-end analysis is often inappropriate or limited.
3b. The test of a "good" policy is typically that various analysts find themselves directly agreeing on a policy (without their agreeing that it is the most appropriate means to an agreed objective).
4b. Analysis is drastically limited: i) Important possible outcomes are neglected. ii) Important alternative potential policies are neglected. iii) Important affected values are neglected.
5b. A succession of comparisons greatly reduces or eliminates reliance on theory.

Administrators cannot escape these conflicts by ascertaining the majority's preference, for preferences have not been registered on most issues; indeed, there often *are* no preferences in the absence of public discussion sufficient to bring an issue to the attention of the electorate. Furthermore, there is a question of whether intensity of feeling should be considered as well as the number of persons preferring each alternative.

By the impossibility of doing otherwise, administrators often are reduced to deciding policy without clarifying objectives first.

Even when an administrator resolves to follow his own values as a criterion for decisions, he often will not know how to rank them when they conflict with one another, as they usually do. Suppose, for example, that an administrator must relocate tenants living in tenements scheduled for destruction. One objective is to empty the buildings fairly promptly, another is to find suitable accommodation for persons displaced, another is to avoid friction with residents in other areas in which a large influx would be unwelcome, another is to deal with all concerned through persuasion if possible, and so on.

How does one state even to himself the relative importance of these partially conflicting values? A simple ranking of them is not enough; one needs ideally to know how much of one value is worth sacrificing for some of another value. The answer is that typically the administrator chooses—and must choose—directly among policies in which these values are combined in different ways. He cannot first clarify his values and then choose among policies.

A more subtle third point underlies both the first two. Social objectives do not always have the same relative values. One objective may be highly prized in one circumstance, another in another circumstance. If, for example, an administrator values highly both the dispatch with which his agency can carry through its projects *and* good public relations, it matters little which of the two possibly conflicting values he favors in some abstract or general sense. Policy questions arise in forms which put to administrators such a question as: Given the degree to which we are or are not already achieving the values of dispatch and the values of good public relations, is it worth sacrificing a little speed for a happier clientele, or is it better to risk offending the clientele so that we can get on with our work? The answer to such a question varies with circumstances.

The value problem is, as the example shows, always a problem of adjustments at a margin. But there is no practicable way to state marginal objectives or values except in terms of particular policies. That one value is preferred to another in one decision situation does not mean that it will be preferred in another decision situation in which it can be had only at great sacrifice of another value. Attempts to rank or order values in general and abstract terms so that they do not shift from decision to decision end up by ignoring the relevant marginal preferences. The significance of this third point thus goes very far. Even if all administrators had at hand an agreed set of values, objectives, and constraints, and an agreed ranking of these values, objectives, and constraints, their marginal values in actual choice situations would be impossible to formulate.

Unable consequently to formulate the relevant values first and then choose among policies to achieve them, administrators must choose directly among alternative policies that offer different marginal combinations of values. Somewhat paradoxically, the only practicable way to disclose one's relevant marginal values even to oneself is to describe the policy one chooses to achieve them. Except roughly and vaguely, I know of no way to describe—or even to understand—what my relative evaluations are for, say, freedom and security, speed and accuracy in governmental decisions, or low taxes and better schools than to describe my preferences among specific policy choices that might be made between the alternatives in each of the pairs.

In summary, two aspects of the process by which values are actually handled can be distinguished. The first is clear: evaluation and empirical analysis are intertwined; that is, one chooses among values and among policies at one and the same time. Put a little more elaborately, one simultaneously chooses a policy to attain certain objectives and chooses the objectives themselves. The second aspect is related but distinct: the administrator focuses his attention on marginal or incremental values. Whether he is aware of it or not, he does not find general formulations of objectives very helpful and in fact makes specific marginal or incremental comparisons. Two policies, X and Y, confront him. Both promise the same degree of attainment of objectives a, b, c, d, and e. But X promises him somewhat more of f than does Y, while Y promises him somewhat more of g than does X. In choosing between them, he is in fact offered the alternative of a marginal or incremental amount of f at the expense of a marginal or incremental amount of g. The only values that are relevant to his choice are these increments by which the two policies differ; and, when he finally chooses between the two marginal values, he does so by making a choice between policies.

As to whether the attempt to clarify objectives in advance of policy selection is more or less rational than the close intertwining of marginal evaluation and empirical analysis, the principal difference established is that for complex problems the first is impossible and irrelevant, and the second is both possible and relevant. The second is possible because the administrator need not try to analyze any values except the values by which alternative policies differ and need not be concerned with them except as they differ marginally. His need for information on values or objectives is drastically reduced as compared with the root method; and his capacity for grasping, comprehending, and relating values to one another is not strained beyond the breaking point.

* * *

Successive Comparison as a System

Successive limited comparisons is, then, indeed a method or system; it is not a failure of method for which administrators ought to apologize. None the less, its imperfections, which have not been explored in this paper, are many. For example, the method is without a built-in safeguard for all relevant values, and it also may lead the decision-maker to over-look excellent policies for no other reason than that they are not suggested by the chain of successive policy steps leading up to the present. Hence, it ought to be said that under this method, as well as under some of the most sophisticated variants of the root method—operations research, for example—policies will continue to be as foolish as they are wise.

Why then bother to describe the method in all the above detail? Because it is in fact a common method of policy formulation, and is, for complex problems, the principal reliance of administrators as well as of other policy analysts. And because it will be superior to any other decision-making method available for complex problems in many circumstances, certainly superior to a futile attempt at superhuman comprehensiveness. The reaction of the public administrator to the exposition of method doubtless will be less a discovery of a new method than a better acquaintance with an old. But by becoming more conscious of their practice of this method, administrators might practice it with more skill and know when to extend or constrict its use. (That they sometimes practice it effectively and sometimes not may explain the extremes of opinion on "muddling through," which is both praised as a highly sophisticated form of problem-solving and denounced as no method at all. For I suspect that in so far as there is a system in what is known as "muddling through," this method is it).

One of the noteworthy incidental consequences of clarification of the method is the light it throws on the suspicion an administrator sometimes entertains that a consultant or adviser is not speaking relevantly and responsibly when in fact by all ordinary objective evidence he is. The trouble lies in the fact that most of us approach policy problems within a framework given by our view of a chain of successive policy choices made up to the present. One's thinking about appropriate policies with respect, say, to urban traffic control is greatly influenced by one's knowledge of the incremental steps taken up to the present. An administrator enjoys an intimate knowledge of his past sequences that "outsiders" do not share, and his thinking and that of the "outsider" will consequently be different in ways that may puzzle both. Both may appear to be talking intelligently, yet each may find the other unsatisfactory. The relevance of the policy chain of succession is even more clear when an American tries to discuss, say, antitrust policy with a Swiss, for the chains of policy in the two countries are strikingly different and the two individuals consequently have organized their knowledge in quite different ways.

If this phenomenon is a barrier to communication, an understanding of it promises an enrichment of intellectual interaction in policy formulation. Once the source of difference is understood, it will sometimes be stimulating for an administrator to seek out a policy analyst whose recent experience is with a policy chain different from his own.

This raises again a question only briefly discussed above on the merits of like-mindedness among government administrators. While much of organization theory argues the virtues of common values and agreed organizational objectives, for complex problems in which the root method is inapplicable, agencies will want among their own personnel two types of diversification: administrators whose thinking is organized by reference to policy chains other than those familiar to most members of the organization and, even more commonly, administrators whose professional or personal values or interests create diversity of view (perhaps coming from different specialties, social classes, geographical areas) so that, even within a single agency, decision-making can be fragmented and parts of the agency can serve as watchdogs for other parts.

DISCUSSION QUESTIONS

1. When you decide what you will have for dinner this evening do you use the "root" or "branch" method of decision making? How about when you decided which college to attend or which career you might choose?

2. Do you see any problems with incremental decision making? What types of decisions does it tend to favor? Is this a good or a bad thing?

3. Is the comprehensive method of decision making possible, or is it too taxing for the human brain, as Lindblom suggests?

69

"American Business, Public Policy, Case Studies, and Political Theory"

Theodore J. Lowi

Before Lowi's article appeared in 1964, many social scientists analyzed public policy through case studies that focused on one particular policy and its implementation. Lowi argued that what the social sciences lacked was a means to cumulate, compare, and contrast the diverse findings of these studies. We needed, in other words, a typology of policy making. In the article below, Lowi argues that different types of public policies produce different patterns of participation. Public policies can be classified as distributive, regulatory, or redistributive, each with its own distinctive "arena of power." For example, public policies that provide benefits to a single congressional district, group, or company can be classified as distributive. In the distributive arena of power, policy beneficiaries are active in seeking to expand or extend their benefits, but there is no real opposition. Rather, legislators build coalitions premised upon "mutual non-interference" interests, and their representatives seek particular benefits, such as a research and development contract, a new highway, or a farm subsidy, but they do not oppose the similar requests of others. The regulatory and redistributive policy arenas also display distinctive dynamics and roles that participants in the process play. Lowi's work was important not only for providing a classification scheme by which social scientists could think more systematically about different public policies, but for proposing that we study "politics" as a consequence of different types of public policy. Traditionally, social scientists have studied politics to see what kinds of policies are produced.

What is needed is a basis for cumulating, comparing, and contrasting diverse findings. Such a framework or interpretative scheme would bring the diverse cases and findings into a more consistent relation to each other and would begin to suggest generalizations sufficiently close to the data to be relevant and sufficiently abstract to be subject to more broadly theoretical treatment.

* * *

The scheme is based upon the following argument: (1) The types of relationships to be found among people are determined by their expectations—by what they hope to achieve or get from relating to others. (2) In politics, expectations are determined by governmental outputs or policies. (3) Therefore, a political relationship is determined by the type of policy at stake, so that for every type of policy there is likely to be a distinctive type of political relationship. If power is defined as a share in the making of policy, or authoritative allocations, then the political relationship in question is a power relationship or, over time, a power structure.

*   *   *

There are three major categories of public policies in the scheme: distribution, regulation, and redistribution. These types are historically as well as functionally distinct, distribution being almost the exclusive type of national domestic policy from 1789 until virtually 1890. Agitation for regulatory and redistributive policies began at about the same time, but regulation had become an established fact before any headway at all was made in redistribution.

These categories are not mere contrivances for purposes of simplification. They are meant to correspond to real phenomena—so much so that the major hypotheses of the scheme follow directly from the categories and their definitions. Thus, *these areas of policy or government activity constitute real arenas of power.* Each arena tends to develop its own characteristic political structure, political process, elites, and group relations. What remains is to identify these arenas, to formulate hypotheses about the attributes of each, and to test the scheme by how many empirical relationships it can anticipate and explain.

Areas of Policy Defined

(1) In the long run, all governmental policies may be considered redistributive, because in the long run some people pay in taxes more than they receive in services. Or, all may be thought regulatory because, in the long run, a governmental decision on the use of resources can only displace a private decision about the same resource or at least reduce private alternatives about the resource. But politics works in the short run, and in the short run certain kinds of government decisions can be made without regard to limited resources. Policies of this kind are called "distributive," a term first coined for nineteenth-century land policies, but easily extended to include most contemporary public land and resource policies; rivers and harbors ("pork barrel") programs; defense procurement and R & D [research and development]; labor, business, and agricultural "clientele" services; and the traditional tariff. Distributive policies are characterized by the ease with which they can be disaggregated and dispensed unit by small unit, each unit more or less in isolation from other units and from any general rule. "Patronage" in the fullest meaning of the word can be taken as a synonym for "distributive." These are policies that are virtually not policies at all but are highly individualized decisions that

only by accumulation can be called a policy. They are policies in which the indulged and the deprived, the loser and the recipient, need never come into direct confrontation. Indeed, in many instances of distributive policy, the deprived cannot as a class be identified, because the most influential among them can be accommodated by further disaggregation of the stakes.

(2) Regulatory policies are also specific and individual in their impact, but they are not capable of the almost infinite amount of disaggregation typical of distributive policies. Although the laws are stated in general terms ("Arrange the transportation system artistically." "Thou shalt not show favoritism in pricing."), the impact of regulatory decisions is clearly one of directly raising costs and/or reducing or expanding the alternatives of private individuals ("Get off the grass!" "Produce kosher if you advertise kosher!"). Regulatory policies are distinguishable from distributive in that in the short run the regulatory decision involves a direct choice as to who will be indulged and who deprived. Not all applicants for a single television channel or an overseas air route can be propitiated. Enforcement of an unfair labor practice on the part of management weakens management in its dealings with labor. So, while implementation is firm-by-firm and case-by-case, policies cannot be disaggregated to the level of the individual or the single firm (as in distribution), because individual decisions must be made by application of a general rule and therefore become interrelated within the broader standards of law. Decisions cumulate among all individuals affected by the law in roughly the same way. Since the most stable lines of perceived common impact are the basic sectors of the economy, regulatory decisions are cumulative largely along sectoral lines; regulatory policies are usually disaggregable only down to the sector level.

(3) Redistributive policies are like regulatory policies in the sense that relations among broad categories of private individuals are involved and, hence, individual decisions must be interrelated. But on all other counts there are great differences in the nature of impact. The categories of impact are much broader, approaching social classes. They are, crudely speaking, haves and have-nots, bigness and smallness, bourgeoisie and proletariat. The aim involved is not use of property but property itself, not equal treatment but equal possession, not behavior but being. The fact that our income tax is in reality only mildly redistributive does not alter the fact of the aims and the stakes involved in income tax policies. The same goes for our various "welfare state" programs, which are redistributive only for those who entered retirement or unemployment rolls without having contributed at all. The nature of a redistributive issue is not determined by the outcome of a battle over how redistributive a policy is going to be. Expectations about what it *can* be, what it threatens to be, are determinative.

Arenas of Power

Once one posits the general tendency of these areas of policy or governmental activity to develop characteristic political structures, a number of
hypotheses become compelling. And when the various hypotheses are
accumulated, the general contours of each of the three arenas begin
quickly to resemble, respectively, the three "general" theories of political
process identified earlier. The arena that develops around distributive
policies is best characterized in the terms of [E. E.] Schattschneider's findings. The regulatory arena corresponds to the pluralist school, and the
school's general notions are found to be limited pretty much to this one
arena. The redistributive arena most closely approximates, with some adaptation, an elitist view of the political process.

(1) The distributive arena can be identified in considerable detail from
Schattschneider's case-study alone. What he and his pluralist successors
did not see was that the traditional structure of tariff politics is also in
largest part the structure of politics of all those diverse policies identified
earlier as distributive. The arena is "pluralistic" only in the sense that a
large number of small, intensely organized interests are operating. In fact,
there is even greater multiplicity of participants here than the pressure-
group model can account for, because essentially it is a politics of every
man for himself. The single person and the single firm are the major
activists.

*   *   *

When a billion-dollar issue can be disaggregated into many millions of
nickel-dime items and each item can be dealt with without regard to
the others, multiplication of interests and of access is inevitable, and so is
reduction of conflict. All of this has the greatest of bearing on the relations among participants and, therefore, the "power structure." Indeed,
coalitions must be built to pass legislation and "make policy," but what
of the nature and basis of the coalitions? In the distributive arena, political relationships approximate what Schattschneider called "mutual non-
interference"—"a mutuality under which it is proper for each to seek
duties [indulgences] for himself but improper and unfair to oppose duties [indulgences] sought by others." In the area of rivers and harbors,
references are made to "pork barrel" and "log-rolling," but these collo-
quialisms have not been taken sufficiently seriously. A log-rolling coalition is not one forged of conflict, compromise, and tangential interest but,
on the contrary, one composed of members who have absolutely nothing
in common; and this is possible because the "pork barrel" is a container
for unrelated items. This is the typical form of relationship in the distributive arena.

The structure of these log-rolling relationships leads typically, though not always, to Congress; and the structure is relatively stable because all who have access of any sort usually support whoever are the leaders. And there tend to be "elites" of a peculiar sort in the Congressional committees whose jurisdictions include the subject-matter in question. Until recently, for instance, on tariff matters the House Ways and Means Committee was virtually the government. Much the same can be said for Public Works on rivers and harbors. It is a broker leadership, but "policy" is best understood as cooptation rather than conflict and compromise.

*   *   *

(2) The regulatory arena could hardly be better identified than in the thousands of pages written for the whole polity by the pluralists. But, unfortunately, some translation is necessary to accommodate pluralism to its more limited universe. The regulatory arena appears to be composed of a multiplicity of groups organized around tangential relations. . . . Within this narrower context of regulatory decisions, one can even go so far as to accept the most extreme pluralist statement that policy tends to be a residue of the interplay of group conflict. This statement can be severely criticized only by use of examples drawn from non-regulatory decisions.

As I argued before, there is no way for regulatory policies to be disaggregated into very large numbers of unrelated items. Because individual regulatory decisions involve direct confrontations of indulged and deprived, the typical political coalition is born of conflict and compromise among tangential interests that usually involve a total sector of the economy. Thus, while the typical basis for coalition in distributive politics is uncommon interests (log-rolling), an entirely different basis is typical in regulatory politics. The pluralist went wrong only in assuming the regulatory type of coalition is *the* coalition.

*   *   *

What this suggests is that the typical power structure in regulatory politics is far less stable than that in the distributive arena. Since coalitions form around shared interests, the coalitions will shift as the interests change or as conflicts of interest emerge. With such group-based and shifting patterns of conflict built into every regulatory issue, it is in most cases impossible for a Congressional committee, an administrative agency, a peak association governing board, or a social elite to contain all the participants long enough to establish a stable power elite. Policy outcomes seem inevitably to be the residue remaining after all the reductions of demands by all participants have been made in order to extend support to majority size. But a majority-sized coalition of shared interests on one issue could not possibly be entirely appropriate for some other issue. In regulatory decision-making, relationships among group leadership elements and between them on any one or more points of governmental access are too unstable to form a single policy-making elite. As a consequence, decision-making tends to pass from administrative agencies and Congressional committees to Congress, the place where uncertainties in the policy process have always been settled. Congress as an institution is the last resort for breakdowns in bargaining over policy, just as in the case of parties the primary is a last resort for breakdowns in bargaining over nominations. No one leadership group can contain the conflict by an almost infinite subdivision and distribution of the stakes. In the regulatory political process, Congress and the "balance of power" seem to play the classic role attributed to them by the pluralists.

* * *

(3) Issues that involve redistribution cut closer than any others along class lines and activate interests in what are roughly class terms. If there is ever any cohesion within the peak associations, it occurs on redistributive issues, and their rhetoric suggests that they occupy themselves most of the time with these. In a ten-year period just before and after, but not including, the war years [World War II], the Manufacturers' Association of Connecticut, for example, expressed itself overwhelmingly more often on redistributive than on any other types of issues.

* * *

Where the peak associations, led by elements of Mr. Mills's power elite,* have reality, their resources and access are bound to affect power relations. Owing to their stability and the impasse (or equilibrium) in relations among broad classes of the entire society, the political structure of the redistributive arena seems to be highly stabilized, virtually institutionalized. Its stability, unlike that of the distributive arena, derives from shared interests. But in contrast to the regulatory arena, these shared interests are sufficiently stable and clear and consistent to provide the foundation for ideologies.

* * *

. . . Finally, just as the nature of redistributive policies influences politics towards the centralization and stabilization of conflict, so does it further influence the removal of decision-making from Congress. A decentralized and bargaining Congress can cumulate but it cannot balance, and redistributive policies require complex balancing on a very large scale. What [William] Riker has said of budget-making applies here: ". . . legislative governments cannot endure a budget. Its finances must be totted up by party leaders in the legislature itself. In a complex fiscal system, however, haphazard legislative judgments cannot bring revenue

---

* According to C. Wright Mills, a small network of individuals, which he called the "power elite," controls the economy, the political system, and the military [Editors].

into even rough alignment with supply. So budgeting is introduced—which transfers financial control to the budget maker. . . ." Congress can provide exceptions to principles and it can implement those principles with elaborate standards of implementation as a condition for the concessions that money-providers will make. But the makers of principles of redistribution seem to be the holders of the "command posts."

None of this suggests a power elite such as Mills would have had us believe existed, but it does suggest a type of stable and continual conflict that can only be understood in class terms. The foundation upon which the social-stratification and power-elite school rested, especially when dealing with national power, was so conceptually weak and empirically unsupported that its critics were led to err in the opposite direction by denying the direct relevance of social and institutional positions and the probability of stable decision-making elites. But the relevance of that approach becomes stronger as the scope of its application is reduced and as the standards for identifying the scope are clarified. But this is equally true of the pluralist school and of those approaches based on a "politics of this-or-that policy."

* * *

DISCUSSION QUESTIONS

1. Provide examples of each type of policy that Lowi discusses (distributive, regulatory, and redistributive).

2. If you were a member of Congress, which type of policy would you try to emphasize if your main interest was in getting reelected?

3. Are there any types of policies that do not seem to fit Lowi's framework? Do some policies fit more than one category?

70

"The Human Factor: Should the Government Put a Price on Your Life?"

Jim Holt

At the core of cost-benefit analysis is the ability to put a dollar value—a price—on the different results and burdens of any government action or policy. Obviously, there are limits to what we are willing to spend to save or preserve life or safety: to dispute this means that you support the expenditure of infinite resources to save even a single life. But if we are not willing to make infinite expenditures, we must then decide how much we will spend. That forces us to put a value on human life, because otherwise we will never know how much is enough, or what risks are worth taking. Even if money is not the issue, we still face trade-offs: drugs that can treat life-threatening diseases can themselves have fatal side effects, for example, and we must balance lives saved against the risk that some might also be lost.

How much is enough? As Holt notes, this is an "idiotic question," since most of us would give everything we have to save our own life, or the life of someone close to us. And even an infinite amount of money does us no good personally if we're dead. But we return to the problem that we must decide how much a life is worth when we are considering the effectiveness of policy choices. The federal government uses different methods to determine the monetary value of a life in its cost-benefit models, producing estimates in the $3- to $4-million range.

How much is your life worth to you? On the face of it, that's an idiotic question. No amount of money could compensate you for the loss of your life, for the simple reason that the money would be no good to you if you were dead. And you might feel, for different reasons, that the dollar value of the lives of your spouse or children—or even a stranger living on the other side of the country—is also infinite. No one should be knowingly sacrificed for a sum of money: that's what we mean when we say that human life is priceless.

But the government set a price for it four years ago: $6.1 million. That's the figure the Environmental Protection Agency came up with when it was trying to decide how far to go in removing arsenic from drinking water. Arsenic can cause diseases, like bladder cancer, that will predictably kill a certain number of people. But reducing the arsenic in water gets more and more expensive as the poison levels approach zero. How many dollars should be spent to save one "statistical life"? The answer, reasoned the people at the E.P.A., depends on how much that life is worth. And they're not the only ones doing such calculations. The Department of Transportation also puts a price tag on a human life when deciding which road improvements are worth making, although it's the rather more modest one of $3 million.

Presumably, losing your life in a highway smashup is less unpleasant than slowly dying of bladder cancer.

The advantage of this kind of cost-benefit analysis, its proponents declare, is that it promises to make our public policies more rational. But critics find the idea of putting a dollar value on human life preposterous. Part of their case is ethical: it is simply wrong, they say, to count death as a "cost"; no public action that involves lost lives should be evaluated in monetary terms. But they also object to the ways in which the price of life is calculated.

How, exactly, did the E.P.A. arrive at its figure of $6.1 million?

Economists looked at the salaries paid to workers in riskier jobs like mining. They figured out that such workers received, on average, an additional $61 a year for facing an extra 1-in-100,000 risk of accidental death. Evidently, these workers valued their own lives at 100,000 times $61, or $6.1 million. (In 2002, the E.P.A. revised the price of a life downward, to $3.7 million—or if you're older than 70, $2.3 million.)

Ingeniously simple, no? But on closer inspection, you begin to have misgivings about this methodology. In the first place, it is not at all obvious that workers really understand the risks they face in the workplace. Women seem to be much less willing to accept such risks than men. Does that mean their lives should be priced higher? Blacks and nonunionized workers demand little or no risk premium for taking dangerous jobs. Does that mean their lives should be priced lower? Poorer people, for whom an extra dollar is highly valuable, will take less compensation for facing danger. Thus, cost-benefit analysis tells us it is more efficient to locate toxic waste dumps near poorer neighborhoods.

Perhaps the strangest thing about the life-pricing business is the way the lives of future generations become discounted—quite literally. Regulators begin with the assumption that it's better to have $200 in your pocket today—when you can earn interest on it—than a promise of $200 in the future. Equating money with human life, they conclude that a life saved today should count twice as much, in dollar terms, as a life saved 10 years from now; a life saved a century from now scarcely counts at all. That is why cost-benefit analysis might sanction, say, nuclear reactors that provide you and me with cheap energy at the expense of lives lost to cancer decades down the road. But as Frank Ackerman and Lisa Heinzerling point out in their recent book, "Priceless: On Knowing the Price of Everything and the Value of Nothing," it is hardly clear why the same logic should apply to the value of our great-grandchildren. (On the other hand, those future generations may well have developed a cure for cancer, so perhaps we are justified in worrying about them less.)

Champions of cost-benefit analysis—from the controversial [George W.] Bush administration regulatory guru John D. Graham to the more circumspect liberal law professor Cass Sunstein—maintain that the government is always valuing human life implicitly anyway, so we might as well be forthright about it. Only then, they say, will we be able to stop spending excessively large sums to protect against small risks and vice versa. Most of us, after all, are deficient in rationality: we are excessively fearful of unlikely hazards when those hazards are shockingly unfamiliar or disturbingly involuntary (like dying in a terrorist attack or from something in the drinking water). And we are far too cavalier about much more immediate risks like dying on the highway (which we do at a rate of 117 fatalities per day).

But are ordinary people really being irrational when they seem to "price" their lives differently at different times? Some people even put a *negative* price on their lives—when, for instance, they pay money to engage in a risky activity like mountain climbing. The economist E. J. Mishan, an early authority on cost-benefit analysis, has argued that the value of a human life has no meaning apart from the nature of the risk that is being measured. To say that a human life is "priceless" does not necessarily mean that it is worth more than any amount of money. It may just mean that money is the wrong yardstick to use when our decisions involve the loss of life. Even the most ardent cost-benefit analyst would spend more money to rescue a single actual child than to save 10 "statistical lives."

DISCUSSION QUESTIONS

1. Not even Holt really answers the question of how much a life is worth. What factors should go into this evaluation? Age? Income? Future-earnings capacity? What are the implications of concluding that some lives might be "worth" more than others?

2. Is it correct to say that we're not willing to spend an infinite amount to save a life? In an actual life-threatening emergency—a child trapped in a well, people on a sinking ship, a collapsed building, coal miners trapped underground—we probably would spend without limit until we either completed the rescue or knew that the victims were dead. Why aren't we willing to do this in the case of saving potential lives?

3. We could come close to eliminating 34,000 automotive fatalities each year by imposing a nationwide 20-mile-per-hour speed limit, but such a step is inconceivable. Does this mean we are willing to trade lives for time and convenience? What are the implications of this decision?

534

Debating the Issues: How Should We Address Global Warming?

Policy analysts often make distinctions between what are called Type I and Type II errors. Type I errors occur when a problem exists and policy makers fail to respond. Type II errors occur when there is no problem, but policy makers still respond as if there were.

If ever there was a policy for which we had to have the right policy response, it would be global warming. The question is whether emissions of carbon dioxide, which result primarily from the burning of fossil fuels, are contributing to a rise in global temperature. There is little doubt the earth is warming (a conclusion not substantially affected by the 2009 controversy over leaked e-mails from climate researchers at Britain's East Anglia University, suggesting that climate scientists were suppressing dissenting scientific views and had tinkered with temperature readings to get the desired results). If human-caused (anthropogenic) global warming is real, and if the threat is as serious as some claim, failure to act could have catastrophic worldwide consequences: mass extinction, permanent expansion of deserts, massive shifts in the distribution of arable land, rising sea levels that could wipe out coastal cities. Some of the scenarios are nearly apocalyptic. And yet, if the threat is *not* so bad as claimed—if the recent increase in global temperatures is due to natural variation in climate or the result of poor measurements, or if nothing we do will have much effect on temperature change—and we still impose the sorts of draconian solutions that some insist are necessary, then we will have invested hundreds of billions of dollars, perhaps trillions, with nothing to show for it. We will be poorer, but still warmer.

The debate is acrimonious; Al Gore, who won an Academy Award for his documentary *An Inconvenient Truth* and the 2007 Nobel Peace Prize for his environmental work, declares the science "settled" and says questioning anthropogenic global warming is no different from insisting that the earth is flat. Skeptics argue that models of global climate are far too complex and poorly understood to allow accurate forecasts fifty or one hundred years into the future. A nonexpert has little chance of truly assessing the evidence, because the science is complicated and often poorly communicated. Efforts to take collective action, such as the 2009 Copenhagen Conference, have failed, mostly because of disagreements between the industrialized world and developing nations. Developing nations say it is unfair to ask them to reduce their carbon emissions (which are a byproduct of economic growth) when the wealthy nations have already benefitted from cheap energy and unrestrained carbon emissions.

In this section we offer competing perspectives on how to handle global warming. Bill McKibben, who also calls the science settled, addresses arguments against global warming. He declares that we are out of time, and that it indeed may be too late to stop significant temperature increases. He notes that it will be expensive to shift toward a green-energy economy but claims that the costs are bearable. Some of the changes, he argues, would even save money, though he concedes nobody is sure of the total costs. But, he insists, doing nothing would impose unbearable costs; he cites several potentially catastrophic consequences, including famine, wars, droughts, floods, and disease.

Bjørn Lomborg, a Danish scholar, takes a pure cost-benefit approach to the problem. He begins by dismissing the apocalyptic visions promoted by (among others) Al Gore, and claims that most of the solutions proposed will produce minimal benefit at enormous cost. Using Gore's main proposals as his examples—setting global targets for carbon dioxide emissions, raising the costs of fossil fuels—Lomborg estimates that they would cost $800 billion over the next ninety years but reduce temperatures by only a fraction of a degree over the same period. We will have spent an enormous amount of money to little avail.

Instead of forcing reductions in fossil fuel use, Lomborg urges much higher spending on research and development. Research into alternative renewable energy will produce far more benefits that setting arbitrary caps on carbon emissions.

Finally, Lomborg argues that global warming is far from the greatest threat to the globe. Millions of people die from indoor air pollution, malaria, malnutrition, and accidents. We would be better off, Lomborg argues, by spending that $800 billion on those problems.

71

"Climate Change"

Bill McKibben

"Scientists Are Divided"

No, they're not. In the early years of the global warming debate, there was great controversy over whether the planet was warming, whether humans were the cause, and whether it would be a significant problem. That debate is long since over. Although the details of future forecasts remain unclear, there's no serious question about the general shape of what's to come.

Every national academy of science, long lists of Nobel laureates, and in recent years even the science advisors of President George W. Bush have agreed that we are heating the planet. Indeed, there is a more thorough scientific process here than on almost any other issue: Two decades ago, the United Nations formed the Intergovernmental Panel on Climate Change (IPCC) and charged its scientists with synthesizing the peer-reviewed science and developing broad-based conclusions. The reports have found since 1995 that warming is dangerous and caused by humans. The panel's most recent report, in November 2007, found it is "very likely" (defined as more than 90 percent certain, or about as certain as science gets) that heat-trapping emissions from human activities have caused "most of the observed increase in global average temperatures since the mid-20th century."

If anything, many scientists now think that the IPCC has been too conservative—both because member countries must sign off on the conclusions and because there's a time lag. Its last report synthesized data from the early part of the decade, not the latest scary results, such as what we're now seeing in the Arctic.

In the summer of 2007, ice in the Arctic Ocean melted. It melts a little every summer, of course, but this time was different—by late September, there was 25 percent less ice than ever measured before. And it wasn't a one-time accident. By the end of the summer season in 2008, so much ice had melted that both the Northwest and Northeast passages were open. In other words, you could circumnavigate the Arctic on open water. The computer models, which are just a few years old, said this shouldn't have happened until sometime late in the 21st century. Even skeptics can't dispute such alarming events.

"We Have Time"

Wrong. Time might be the toughest part of the equation. That melting Arctic ice is unsettling not only because it proves the planet is warming rapidly, but also because it will help speed up the warming. That old white ice reflected 80 percent of incoming solar radiation back to space; the new blue water left behind absorbs 80 percent of that sunshine. The process amps up. And there are many other such feedback loops. Another occurs as northern permafrost thaws. Huge amounts of methane long trapped below the ice begin to escape into the atmosphere; methane is an even more potent greenhouse gas than carbon dioxide.

Such examples are the biggest reason why many experts are now fast-forwarding their estimates of how quickly we must shift away from fossil fuel. Indian economist Rajendra Pachauri, who accepted the 2007 Nobel Peace Prize alongside Al Gore on behalf of the IPCC, said recently that we must begin to make fundamental reforms by 2012 or watch the climate system spin out of control; NASA scientist James Hansen, who was the first to blow the whistle on climate change in the late 1980s, has said that we must stop burning coal by 2030. Period.

All of which makes the Copenhagen climate change talks that are set to take place in December 2009 more urgent than they appeared a few years ago. At issue is a seemingly small number: the level of carbon dioxide in the air. Hansen argues that 350 parts per million is the highest level we can maintain "if humanity wishes to preserve a planet similar to that on which civilization developed and to which life on Earth is adapted." But because we're already past that mark—the air outside is currently about 387 parts per million and growing by about 2 parts annually—global warming suddenly feels less like a huge problem, and more like an Oh-My-God Emergency.

"Climate Change Will Help as Many Places as It Hurts"

Wishful thinking. For a long time, the winners-and-losers calculus was pretty standard: Though climate change will cause some parts of the planet to flood or shrivel up, other frigid, rainy regions would at least get some warmer days every year. Or so the thinking went. But more recently, models have begun to show that after a certain point almost everyone on the planet will suffer. Crops might be easier to grow in some places for a few decades as the danger of frost recedes, but over time the threat of heat stress and drought will almost certainly be stronger.

A 2003 report commissioned by the Pentagon forecasts the possibility of violent storms across Europe, megadroughts across the Southwest United States and Mexico, and unpredictable monsoons causing food shortages in China. "Envision Pakistan, India, and China—all armed with nuclear weapons—skirmishing at their borders over refugees, access to shared rivers, and arable land," the report warned. Or Spain and Portugal "fighting over fishing rights—leading to conflicts at sea."

Of course, there are a few places we used to think of as possible winners—mostly the far north, where Canada and Russia could theoretically produce more grain with longer growing seasons, or perhaps explore for oil beneath the newly melted Arctic ice cap. But even those places will have to deal with expensive consequences—a real military race across the high Arctic, for instance.

Want more bad news? Here's how that Pentagon report's scenario played out: As the planet's carrying capacity shrinks, an ancient pattern of desperate, all-out wars over food, water, and energy supplies would reemerge. The report refers to the work of Harvard archaeologist Steven LeBlanc, who notes that wars over resources were the norm until about three centuries ago. When such conflicts broke out, 25 percent of a population's adult males usually died. As abrupt climate change hits home, warfare may again come to define human life. Set against that bleak backdrop, the potential upside of a few longer growing seasons in Vladivostok doesn't seem like an even trade.

"It's China's Fault"

Not so much. China is an easy target to blame for the climate crisis. In the midst of its industrial revolution, China has overtaken the United States as the world's biggest carbon dioxide producer. And everyone has read about the one-a-week pace of power plant construction there. But those numbers are misleading, and not just because a lot of that carbon dioxide was emitted to build products for the West to consume. Rather, it's because China has four times the population of the United States, and per capita is really the only way to think about these emissions. And by that standard, each Chinese person now emits just over a quarter of the carbon dioxide that each American does. Not only that, but carbon dioxide lives in the atmosphere for more than a century. China has been at it in a big way less than 20 years, so it will be many, many years before the Chinese are as responsible for global warming as Americans.

What's more, unlike many of their counterparts in the United States, Chinese officials have begun a concerted effort to reduce emissions in the midst of their country's staggering growth. China now leads the world in the deployment of renewable energy, and there's barely a car made in the United States that can meet China's much tougher fuel-economy standards.

For its part, the United States must develop a plan to cut emissions—something that has eluded Americans for the entire two-decade history of the problem. Although the U.S. Senate voted down the last such attempt, Barack Obama has promised that it will be a priority in his administration. He favors some variation of a "cap and trade" plan that would limit the total amount of carbon dioxide the United States could release, thus putting a price on what has until now been free.

Despite the rapid industrialization of countries such as China and India, and the careless neglect of rich ones such as the United States, climate change is neither any one country's fault, nor any one country's responsibility. It will require sacrifice from everyone. Just as the Chinese might have to use somewhat more expensive power to protect the global environment, Americans will have to pay some of the difference in price, even if just in technology. Call it a Marshall Plan for the environment. Such a plan makes eminent moral and practical sense and could probably be structured so as to bolster emerging green energy industries in the West. But asking Americans to pay to put up windmills in China will be a hard political sell in a country that already thinks China is prospering at its expense. It could be the biggest test of the country's political maturity in many years.

"Climate Change Is an Environmental Problem"

Not really. Environmentalists were the first to sound the alarm. But carbon dioxide is not like traditional pollution. There's no Clean Air Act that can solve it. We must make a fundamental transformation in the most important part of our economies, shifting away from fossil fuels and on to something else. That means, for the United States, it's at least as much a problem for the Commerce and Treasury departments as it is for the Environmental Protection Agency.

And because every country on Earth will have to coordinate, it's far and away the biggest foreign-policy issue we face. (You were thinking terrorism? It's hard to figure out a scenario in which Osama bin Laden destroys Western civilization. It's easy to figure out how it happens with a rising sea level and a wrecked hydrological cycle.)

Expecting the environmental movement to lead this fight is like asking the USDA to wage the war in Iraq. It's not equipped for this kind of battle. It may be ready to save Alaska's Arctic National Wildlife Refuge, which is a noble undertaking but on a far smaller scale. Unless climate change is quickly de-ghettoized, the chances of making a real difference are small.

"Solving It Will Be Painful"

It depends. What's your definition of painful? On the one hand, you're talking about transforming the backbone of the world's industrial and consumer system. That's certainly expensive. On the other hand, say you manage to convert a lot of it to solar or wind power—think of the money you'd save on fuel.

And then there's the growing realization that we don't have many other possible sources for the economic growth we'll need to pull ourselves out of our current economic crisis. Luckily, green energy should be bigger than IT and biotech combined.

Almost from the moment scientists began studying the problem of climate change, people have been trying to estimate the costs of solving it. The real answer, though, is that it's such a huge transformation that no one really knows for sure. The bottom line is, the growth rate in energy use worldwide could be cut in half during the next 15 years and the steps would, net, save more money than they cost. The IPCC included a cost estimate in its latest five-year update on climate change and looked a little further into the future. It found that an attempt to keep carbon levels below about 500 parts per million would shave a little bit off the world's economic growth—but only a little. As in, the world would have to wait until Thanksgiving 2030 to be as rich as it would have been on January 1 of that year. And in return, it would have a much-transformed energy system.

Unfortunately though, those estimates are probably too optimistic. For one thing, in the years since they were published, the science has grown darker. Deeper and quicker cuts now seem mandatory.

But so far we've just been counting the costs of fixing the system. What about the cost of doing nothing? Nicholas Stern, a renowned economist commissioned by the British government to study the question, concluded that the costs of climate change could eventually reach the combined costs of both world wars and the Great Depression. In 2003, Swiss Re, the world's biggest reinsurance company, and Harvard Medical School explained why global warming would be so expensive. It's not just the infrastructure, such as sea walls against rising oceans, for example. It's also that the increased costs of natural disasters begin to compound. The diminishing time between monster storms in places such as the U.S. Gulf Coast could eventually mean that parts of "developed countries would experience developing nation conditions for prolonged periods." Quite simply, we've already done too much damage and waited too long to have any easy options left.

"We Can Reverse Climate Change"

If only. Solving this crisis is no longer an option. Human beings have already raised the temperature of the planet about a degree Fahrenheit. When people first began to focus on global warming (which is, remember, only 20 years ago), the general consensus was that at this point we'd just be standing on the threshold of realizing its consequences—that the big changes would be a degree or two and hence several decades down the road. But scientists seem to have systematically underestimated just how delicate the balance of the planet's physical systems really is.

The warming is happening faster than we expected, and the results are more widespread and more disturbing. Even that rise of 1 degree has seriously perturbed hydrological cycles: Because warm air holds more water vapor than cold air does, both droughts and floods are increasing dramatically. Just look at the record levels of insurance payouts, for instance. Mosquitoes, able to survive in new places, are spreading more malaria and dengue. Coral reefs are dying, and so are vast stretches of forest.

None of that is going to stop, even if we do everything right from here on out. Given the time lag between when we emit carbon and when the air heats up, we're already guaranteed at least another degree of warming.

The only question now is whether we're going to hold off catastrophe. It won't be easy, because the scientific consensus calls for roughly 5 degrees more warming this century unless we do just about everything right. And if our behavior up until now is any indication, we won't.

72

"Mr. Gore, Your Solution to Global Warming Is Wrong"

Bjørn Lomborg

I. A False Choice

On a family visit to Kenya long before he became president of the United States, Barack Obama declared that he wanted to go on safari. His Kenyan half sister, Auma, chided him for being a neocolonialist.

"Why should all that land be set aside for tourists," she asked, "when it could be used for farming? These wazungu [white people] care more about one dead elephant than they do for a hundred black children." Obama had no answer to her question, he would later write in *Dreams from My Father*. Why are rich countries more concerned about poor nations' nature reserves than about farms that would ward off starvation?

The safari story calls to mind the current preoccupation with global warming in the Western world. The financial crisis notwithstanding, many people—including President Obama—believe that global warming is among the most urgent issues of our time, and that cutting CO_2 emissions is the most virtuous thing we can do about it. In fact, many say that doing so is perhaps the greatest moral obligation of the current inhabitants of planet earth. And they frame any discussion on warming by telling us that if we don't radically alter the way we live, the worst problems of humanity—chiefly disease and hunger—will become devastatingly worse. Before long, they say—perhaps a decade if we do not act immediately—it will be too late for us.

These apocalyptic visions are not at all supported by the available evidence. And to me, the solutions prescribed by those leading the charge are akin to building more safari parks instead of farms to feed the hungry. Campaigners in rich countries are pushing politicians to spend a great fortune on an ineffective solution to climate change instead of tackling the real problems of today—or looking for better responses to warming.

President Obama and other world leaders face a clear choice. They can continue on their current path—what we might call the "Gore solution" to climate change, given that the former vice-president is the fiercest advocate of cutting CO_2 emissions, whether through a carbon tax or a cap-and-trade scheme.

Or, here's the truth: There are better, more cost-effective ways to fight global warming. And if we want to fight the problems that will be made worse by global warming, the solutions have very little to do with cutting CO_2 emissions.

II. The Real Moral Imperative

The effort to cut carbon emissions is generally cast as a moral imperative necessary to avert the human consequences of warming. In reality, however, it does very little at very high cost. It is also politically complicated, because it requires every nation on earth to agree to reduction targets and then reach them. Even if this were somehow achievable, the plan's meager effects on global temperatures are simply not worth all the pain: If we spent $800 billion over the next ninety years solely on the Gore solution of mitigating carbon emissions, we would rein in temperature increases by just 0.3 degrees by the end of this century. That was the finding reached recently by some of the world's top climate economists at a gathering called the Copenhagen Consensus, where the ramifications of this response to climate change were calculated.

In addition to calculating the effect on temperature of reducing carbon emissions, these economists calculated the environmental and humanitarian benefits that would accrue from this reduction in the rate of warming. Through models, they have estimated the benefits of a wide range of effects, from fewer heat deaths and less malaria to fewer floods and more preserved wetlands. Converting all these benefits into monetary terms—i.e., What would societies be willing to pay for such benefits?—means that we don't have to guess; we can actually compare the costs of climate policies with the benefits.

And, simply put, when we count up all the expected benefits from this ever-so-slight reduction in temperature, they are significantly less than the costs. In fact, it turns out that—at best—each dollar spent on the Gore solution would achieve just ninety cents' worth of good. And this assumes that every cent of the $800 billion is maximized. If we factor in more realistic expectations—allowing, say, for some of the money to be used in less efficient ways, as is the case with the EU's new climate policies—every dollar of the hypothetical $800 billion spent on the Gore solution to global warming could achieve as little as four cents of good.

Worse than that, it means there's much less money available to respond to the big problems facing developing countries today.

There is another way to respond to climate change. Instead of putting arbitrary, expensive caps on carbon emissions, we can and should immediately spend more money on researching and developing alternative energy. This means renewable sources of energy like wind, solar, geothermal, and wave. These are all promising but in their current forms are incredibly inefficient compared with fossil fuels. It also means developing second-generation biofuel from biomass. It also means investing in energy efficiency, fission and fusion, and carbon capture and storage. Unless we make a much bigger investment in these areas right now, fossil fuels are going to maintain their stranglehold on all the economies of the world.

Spending more on research will mean that we can shift away from carbon-heavy energy much faster. It gives us the possibility of a low-carbon, high-wealth future—something the Gore solution rules out because of its primary focus on trying to make fossil fuels more expensive. We will never succeed in making fossil fuels so expensive that they become unappealing by following the Gore approach—but we can succeed if we focus on making alternative energy sources so cheap that they become competitive.

When we calculate the costs and benefits of this alternative solution, we discover that each time we invest a dollar, we create benefits worth sixteen dollars—at least eighteen times and possibly four hundred times better than the Gore approach. This is because the money spent on research and development will make alternatives to fossil fuels cheaper sooner, and make for a genuine transition to a low-carbon future, with all its benefits accruing sooner and at lower costs.

So where does President Obama stand on the choice between these two paths? He has promised to spend $150 billion over the next decade on clean technology. This could do a lot of good, if he uses it primarily to invest in creating new technologies, rather than simply subsidizing existing ones (which is much easier politically). Investing in current-day solar panels costs a lot for little benefit. Germany is the leading consumer of solar panels and will end up spending about $150 billion on them, yet the effect will be to delay global warming by one hour by the end of the century. However, investing in the creation of an entirely new way to harness the energy of the sun that can become competitive with fossil fuels will mean that everyone, including China and India, can shift to a low-carbon economy sooner rather than later.

Unfortunately, it looks like much of the $150 billion proposed by the president will be going to the existing technologies with the loudest lobbyists. Likewise, the Obama administration seems more inclined to go for the Gore-like solution of fixing climate change through an ambitious cap-and-trade policy. This will do little for the climate, and it will cost Americans dearly.

It is a very good thing that President Obama accepts that global warming is real and man-made; his predecessor's reluctance or inability to recognize the issue was an embarrassment. However, making rational decisions on global warming has become incredibly difficult. Discussion has been warped by politics and by a polarizing, irrelevant debate between those who believe that the problem is not real and those who believe that it is the worst problem humanity has ever faced. So we must both ignore the blithe deniers of science and overthrow the regime of hysterical solutions on the other side—and consider this simple truth: For once, the sensible approach and the most moral approach are one and the same.

III. A Matter of Simple Economics

Malaria will claim more than one million lives this year. It undermines entire societies, making them less productive and even poorer. The economic toll runs to tens of billions of dollars.

Campaigners for drastic CO_2 emission cuts will tell President Obama and other world leaders that the Gore solution is especially critical because global warming will mean more malaria. In warmer, wetter conditions, mosquitoes can expand their range. Models reveal that global warming will put 3 percent more of the earth's population at risk of catching malaria by the end of the century.

But this is a perfect demonstration of the problem with the Gore solution. Even if we continued with worldwide Kyoto Protocol–style CO_2 emission cuts for the rest of this century, with its inconsequential 0.3 degree reduction in temperatures by the year 2100, we would cut the malaria risk by only 0.2 percent. On the other hand, for $3 billion—2 percent of the annual cost of the Kyoto Protocol—we could invest in mosquito nets and medicine today and cut malaria cases by half within one decade.

Put another way: Every time the Gore solution of CO_2 reduction saves one person from dying from malaria in the future, the same money could save thirty-six thousand people today.

Tell me, which approach makes the most sense?

Of course, an increase in malaria is not the only result of global warming. Malnutrition is another issue that has prompted calls for drastic CO_2 emission cuts. In isolation, global warming will probably cause the number of malnourished people to increase by twenty-eight million by the end of the century. Yet the much more important point is that there are more than nine hundred million malnourished people on earth right now.

Tackling hunger through climate-change policy would be amazingly inefficient. For $180 billion each year, Kyoto Protocol–style CO_2 emission cuts would reduce the number of hungry people globally by two million by the end of the century. Alternatively, just $10 billion spent on direct malnutrition-reduction programs would save 229 million people now.

President Obama has a stark choice to make. Whatever is spent on climate policies to save one person from hunger in one hundred years could instead save five thousand people today.

Often I hear the argument that if so little is achieved by cutting CO_2, then obviously we just need to make bigger cuts. Unfortunately, this would only transform an implausible solution into a ridiculous one. Even Kyoto was overly ambitious; by 2010, the world will probably end up implementing less than 5 percent of the originally envisioned cuts. If we decided to increase the size of the reductions tenfold, the costs would increase much more than ten times, whereas the benefits would increase much less. This is because we do not have cost-effective replacements for burning carbon. Using carbon, particularly coal, is helping lift millions of people from poverty in India and China. Massive carbon cuts just now are not a smart solution, and not at all plausible. And that is not a matter of political opinion; it is a matter of simple economics.

IV. Sometimes, We Need to Burn More Fossil Fuels

I did not always look at the world this way. There was a time when I would have eagerly climbed onto the bandwagon calling for CO_2 emission cuts.

Twenty years ago, I took it for granted that the world was in a terrible environmental state. I supported Greenpeace and lobbied my friends on environmental issues. I am from Denmark, and was particularly upset during the 1980s when our government allowed ocean die-off zones to expand because of agricultural runoff. I thought that political leaders were criminal for not prioritizing longer-term environmental concerns. Later, when I was a university lecturer, my students and I set out to counter what we believed were far-fetched arguments that global environmental conditions were actually improving.

My thinking started to change when I analyzed the data. It was clear that many things were indeed getting better, not worse. It is obvious, for instance, that air pollution in most developed countries is much better than it was thirty or forty years ago.

Another important lesson I learned was that when poor countries battle to raise their living standards, they give very little priority to environmental concerns. In these circumstances, pollution rises. But once a country achieves a certain standard of living, with their kids healthy and educated, citizens invariably begin to shift their focus toward the environment, and pollution starts to fall.

This effect is called the Kuznets curve, named after the Nobel-prize-winning [sic] economist who developed it, and it tells us that one of the pivotal things we can do to help the environment is to help poor countries get richer.

And so it is a paradox that today rich countries care more about global warming than about virtually any other global problem, whereas in the developing world, the biggest environmental challenge is simply the pollution caused by too many people trying to survive in one small space.

There is a lack of public awareness of sustainable agricultural practices. There is illegal logging, soil erosion, habitat loss for animals and plants, and disruption of water flow.

When we look across poor nations, the biggest environmental issue is actually indoor air pollution. In developing countries, 2.5 billion people rely on biomass such as wood, waste, and dung to cook and keep warm. Each year, indoor air pollution kills about 1.3 million people, most of them women and children. In this case, a switch from biomass to fossil fuels would dramatically improve the lives of almost half the world's population.

There are plenty of other major global problems that have reasonably cheap solutions. One billion people lack clean drinking water. Two billion lack sanitation. Three billion lack basic micronutrients. One quarter of all deaths each year are caused by infectious diseases that we could easily combat.

The Gore solution will do nothing to reduce those stunning numbers. In fact, the Global Fund to Fight AIDS, Tuberculosis and Malaria has acknowledged that billions of dollars could potentially be redirected to global warming at the expense of diseases that are the biggest killers in poor countries.

V. The Debate Starts Now

The Copenhagen Consensus Center, which we started in 2004, put my conclusion about the Gore solution to the severest test. First, we commissioned independent research on solutions to ten of the planet's biggest challenges: problems like hunger, conflict, global warming, and barriers to education. World experts were asked to identify the best ways to spend $50 billion in their field. The findings, published in academic papers, were reviewed by a second team of specialists.

The point of the project wasn't simply to identify good ways to spend money—it was to promote prioritization between competing options. We gathered a team of the best economists in the world, including several Nobel laureates. We asked this group to consider, test, and debate all the research and identify the best and worst ways that a limited pool of money could be spent.

Economists are experts in prioritization. The massive media hype about certain problems is irrelevant to them; they focus simply on where limited funds could achieve the most good.

In 2004—and again last year, when we repeated the global project—the world's top minds did not select CO_2 emission cuts as the best use of money. In fact, both times, CO_2 emission reductions came out at the bottom of their lists. In 2008, the top priority the Nobel-laureate economists identified was providing micronutrients to developing countries.

Three billion people—about half the world's population—lack one or more micronutrients, such as vitamin A, iron, iodine, or zinc. About two billion—or almost one third of the world's population—lack iron, a deficiency that causes physical and mental impairment. On average, a person with iron deficiency is 17 percent weaker and loses 8 IQ points.

We could so easily right this wrong. At a cost of less than $400 million a year, we could permanently help almost half the world get stronger and smarter. In monetary terms, for every dollar we spend, we could do more than twenty dollars' worth of good in the world.

Interestingly, also in 2008, the assembled experts heard from a lead author for the Intergovernmental Panel on Climate Change, the very group that shared the Nobel Peace Prize with Al Gore, that the Gore approach of spending even $800 billion on carbon cuts would slow the pace of global warming—and this bears repeating—by just 0.3 degrees over the next ninety years.

It is vital that decision makers pay heed to these facts, so that better responses to global warming can be more seriously considered immediately. But the atmosphere has become one in which the "good guys" fight for more money for global warming against foes real and imagined. And this polarization stops us from seeing that we need to tackle climate change the same way that we tackle most public-policy problems—by weighing benefits and costs.

Let me offer this analogy: Just as we know that global warming is real and serious, we also know that speed kills. Globally, 1.2 million people die in traffic accidents and 50 million are injured every year. By 2020, the World Health Organization estimates that traffic deaths will be the second-biggest killer in the world. About 90 percent of traffic deaths occur in Third World countries. Politicians could instantly save all these lives and eliminate $500 billion worth of damage by simply lowering global speed limits to five miles per hour. Of course, that won't happen, because the benefits from driving moderately fast vastly outweigh the costs. Traffic interconnects our societies, brings people together, and delivers goods at competitive prices to wherever we happen to live. A world trudging along at five miles per hour is a world gone medieval.

Just like traffic fatalities, global warming is caused by man. Just like traffic fatalities, we have the technology to effectively eliminate the problem—in this case by making massive cuts in CO_2 emissions. But this is not sensible. The benefits from moderate use of fossil fuels vastly outweigh the costs. Fossil fuels give us low-cost light, heat, food, communication, and travel. We can eat fruits and vegetables year-round, and air-conditioning means that people in the United States no longer die in droves during heat waves. Communication and cheap flights give ever more people the opportunity to experience other cultures and forge global friendships. Carbon has powered growth in China and India, allowing millions of workers to escape poverty.

To stretch the traffic analogy slightly further: We don't ignore the impact of speed, nor should we disregard global warming. Countries set speed limits at a sensible level. We should do the same thing with taxes on CO_2 emissions. When it comes to reducing carbon emissions, President Obama should talk realistically about setting a price on carbon that reflects its damage. Economic estimates show that the cost is about seven dollars per ton of CO_2—or about six cents on the gallon of gas. Yet, though such a tax can be used to raise funds to tackle global warming smartly, we should not have any illusions that it will in itself reduce global warming. As we have shown above, it will have virtually no impact, even a hundred years from now.

Underlying these economic arguments is a basic moral one: With limited resources, carbon cuts shouldn't be our top priority. I hope that President Obama will not be swayed by the loud, well-meaning, but mistaken appeals from climate-change activists, and instead identify the obvious areas that need more urgent attention. It would be grossly immoral to knowingly squander colossal sums of money achieving almost nothing, while comparatively tiny sums could save millions of lives right now.

But the United States should not go it alone. Every country should agree to spend 0.05 percent of its GDP on low-carbon energy R&D. The total global cost would be ten times greater than current spending on this research, yet ten times less than the cost of the Kyoto Protocol. Such an agreement could be the new Kyoto treaty for the world—only this protocol would actually make a difference.

President Obama stands at the juncture of two very different paths. One would be enormously expensive and is destined to end in failure. The other would recapture a vision that has become lost amid pessimistic, alarmist rhetoric: that of a world that is both low-carbon and high-income. Debate about the science is over.

But the debate over a sensible solution starts now.

DISCUSSION QUESTIONS

1. "I'll believe it's a crisis when the people who say it's a crisis act as if it's a crisis. Al Gore tells us that we have to drastically cut our energy use, but he flies around the world in a private jet and has a mansion 10 times the size of the average American house. He's a hypocrite, and he's not the only one." Is this a valid argument? Can we draw any inferences about the nature of the evidence from the behavior of global warming proponents? What if the proponents of curbing global warming would benefit from the policies that they are urging, such as carbon offsets or particular technologies in which they have a stake?

2. What level of certainty should be required before major international action is taken? Is it enough to be 75 percent sure that anthropogenic global warming is real? 80 percent? 95 percent? Is there a

way to assess these uncertainties reasonably? Or is too much at stake?

3. Is Lomborg right that global warming must be addressed in the context of other issues of global health and safety? Where would you rank global warming on the list of most important problems?

4. What is your view of global warming? How did you come to your view? How well do you think you understand the science? How certain are you that you are right? What would change your mind?

CHAPTER 14

Government and the Economy

73

"Call for Federal Responsibility"

FRANKLIN ROOSEVELT

The national government has always played a role in the economy. Since the late 1700s, the government has provided property for private development, enforced contracts and prohibited the theft of private property, provided subsidies to encourage the growth of particular industries, developed the infrastructure of the growing country, and regulated trade. The question that commands the attention of political leaders and citizens alike today is what the limits of government involvement in the economy ought to be. To what extent should the free market make most economic decisions to maximize efficiency and productivity? Should the government regulate markets in the pursuit of other goals, such as equality, and to address market failures, such as monopolies and public goods that are underprovided by the market (such as education and environmental protection)?

This debate reached a peak during the Great Depression, as the nation struggled to define the government's role in reviving the economy, and played a critical role in the 1932 presidential election between the Democratic candidate, Franklin Roosevelt, and the Republican president, Herbert Hoover. In the campaign speech printed here, FDR argued that the federal government should play a role in unemployment insurance, housing for the poor, and public-works programs to compensate for the hardship of the Great Depression. Hoover, on the other hand, was very much opposed to altering the relationship between government and the private sector, which was "builded up by 150 years of toil of our fathers." It was the extension of freedom and the exercise of individual initiative, Hoover claimed, that made the American economic system strong and that would gradually bring about economic recovery. Roosevelt prevailed, and the resulting New Deal changed the face of government. Although the federal government adopted a much more active role in regulating the economy and providing social safety, the central issues discussed by Roosevelt and Hoover are still being debated today.

The first principle I would lay down is that the primary duty rests on the community, through local government and private agencies, to take care of the relief of unemployment. But we then come to a situation where there are so many people out of work that local funds are insufficient.

It seems clear to me that the organized society known as the State comes into the picture at this point. In other words, the obligation of government is extended to the next higher unit.

I [practice] what I preach. In 1930 the state of New York greatly increased its employment service and kept in close touch with the ability of localities to take care of their own unemployed. But by the summer of 1931 it became apparent to me that actual state funds and a state-supervised system were imperative.

I called a special session of the legislature, and they appropriated a fund of $20 million for unemployment relief, this fund to be reimbursed to the state through the doubling of our income taxes. Thus the state of New York became the first among all the states to accept the definite obligation of supplementing local funds where these local funds were insufficient.

The administration of this great work has become a model for the rest of the country. Without setting up any complex machinery or any large overhead, the state of New York is working successfully through local agencies, and, in spite of the fact that over a million people are out of work and in need of aid in this one state alone, we have so far met at least the bare necessities of the case.

This past spring the legislature appropriated another $5 million, and on November 8 the voters will pass on a $30 million bond issue to tide us over this winter and at least up to next summer.

*   *   *

I am very certain that the obligation extends beyond the states and to the federal government itself, if and when it becomes apparent that states and communities are unable to take care of the necessary relief work.

It may interest you to have me read a short quotation from my message to the legislature in 1931:

> What is the State? It is the duly constituted representative of an organized society of human beings, created by them for their mutual protection and well-being. One of the duties of the State is that of caring for those of its citizens who find themselves the victims of such adverse circumstances as make them unable to obtain even the necessities of mere existence without the aid of others.
>
> In broad terms, I assert that modern society, acting through its government, owes the definite obligation to prevent the starvation or the dire want of any of its fellowmen and women who try to maintain themselves but cannot. To these unfortunate citizens aid must be extended by the government, not as a matter of charity but as a matter of social duty.

That principle which I laid down in 1931, I reaffirm. I not only reaffirm it, I go a step further and say that where the State itself is unable success-fully to fulfill this obligation which lies upon it, it then becomes the posi-tive duty of the federal government to step in to help.

In the words of our Democratic national platform, the federal govern-ment has a "continuous responsibility for human welfare, especially for the protection of children." That duty and responsibility the federal gov-ernment should carry out promptly, fearlessly, and generously.

It took the present Republican administration in Washington almost three years to recognize this principle. I have recounted to you in other speeches, and it is a matter of general information, that for at least two years after the crash, the only efforts made by the national administration to cope with the distress of unemployment were to deny its existence.

When, finally, this year, after attempts at concealment and minimizing had failed, it was at last forced to recognize the fact of suffering among millions of unemployed, appropriations of federal funds for assistance to states were finally made.

I think it is fair to point out that a complete program of unemployment relief was on my recommendation actually under way in the state of New York over a year ago; and that in Washington relief funds in any large volume were not provided until this summer, and at that they were pushed through at the demand of Congress rather than through the lead-ership of the President of the United States.

At the same time, I have constantly reiterated my conviction that the expenditures of cities, states, and the federal government must be re-duced in the interest of the nation as a whole. I believe that there are many ways in which such reduction of expenditures can take place, but I am utterly unwilling that economy should be practised at the expense of starving people.

We must economize in other ways, but it shall never be said that the American people have refused to provide the necessities of life for those who, through no fault of their own, are unable to feed, clothe, and house themselves. The first obligation of government is the protection of the welfare and well-being, indeed the very existence, of its citizens.

*   *   *

The next question asks my attitude toward appropriations for public works as an aid to unemployment. I am perfectly clear as to the princi-ples involved in this case also.

From the long-range point of view it would be advisable for govern-ments of all kinds to set up in times of prosperity what might be called a nest egg to be used for public works in times of depression. That is a policy which we should initiate when we get back to good times.

But there is the immediate possibility of helping the emergency through appropriations for public works. One question, however, must be answered first because of the simple fact that these public works cost money.

We all know that government treasuries, whether local or state or federal, are hard put to it to keep their budgets balanced; and, in the case of the federal Treasury, thoroughly unsound financial policies have made its situation not exactly desperate but at least threatening to future stability if the policies of the present administration are continued.

All public works, including federal, must be considered from the point of view of the ability of the government Treasury to pay for them. There are two ways of paying for public works. One is by the sale of bonds. In principle, such bonds should be issued only to pay for self-sustaining projects or for structures which will without question have a useful life over a long period of years. The other method of payment is from current revenues, which in these days means in most cases added taxes. We all know that there is a very definite limit to the increase of taxes above the present level.

From this point, therefore, I can go on and say that, if funds can be properly provided by the federal government for increased appropriations for public works, we must examine the character of these public works. I have already spoken of that type which is self-sustaining. These should be greatly encouraged. The other type is that of public works which are honestly essential to the community. Each case must rest on its own merits.

It is impossible, for example, to say that all parks or all playgrounds are essential. One may be and another may not be. If a school, for instance, has no playground, it is obvious that the furnishing of a playground is a necessity to the community. But if the school already has a playground and some people seek merely to enlarge it, there may be a very definite question as to how necessary that enlargement is.

Let me cite another example. I am much interested in providing better housing accommodations for the poor in our great cities. If a slum area can be torn down and new modern buildings put up, I should call that almost a human necessity; but, on the other hand, the mere erection of new buildings in some other part of the city while allowing the slums to remain raises at once a question of necessity. I am confident that the federal government working in cooperation with states and cities can do much to carry on increased public works and along lines which are sound from the economic and financial point of view.

Now I come to another question. I am asked whether I favor a system of unemployment insurance reserves made compulsory by the states, supplemented by a system of federally coordinated state employment offices to facilitate the reemployment of jobless workers.

The first part of the question is directly answered by the Democratic platform which advocates unemployment insurance under state laws.

This is no new policy for me. I have advocated unemployment insurance in my own state for some time, and, indeed, last year six Eastern governors were my guests at a conference which resulted in the drawing up of what might be called an idea plan of unemployment insurance.

This type of insurance is not a cure-all but it provides at least a cushion to mitigate unemployment in times of depression. It is sound if, after starting it, we stick to the principle of sound insurance financing. It is only where governments, as in some European countries, have failed to live up to these sound principles that unemployment insurance has been an economic failure.

As to the coordinated employment offices, I can only tell you that I was for the bills sponsored by Senator Wagner of my own state and passed by the Congress. They created a nationally coordinated system of employment offices operated by the individual states with the advisory cooperation of joint boards of employers and employees.

To my very great regret this measure was vetoed by the President of the United States. I am certain that the federal government can, by furnishing leadership, stimulate the various states to set up and coordinate practical, useful systems.

DISCUSSION QUESTIONS

1. Franklin Roosevelt's call for a New Deal and the importance of government investment in "public works" as a way of helping the economy get out of the Great Depression and get people back to work sounds very similar to President Obama's call for more investment in the nation's infrastructure. What is the proper role of the government in helping people get jobs? Should this be left to the private sector, or should the national government invest more in building highways, bridges, and airports to get more people back to work?

2. FDR's famous line from this speech is, "The first obligation of every government is the protection of the welfare and well-being, indeed the very existence, of its citizens." Do you agree? If so, how do you define the limits of that obligation?

74

"Against the Proposed New Deal"

Herbert Hoover

This campaign is more than a contest between two men. It is more than a contest between two parties. It is a contest between two philosophies of government.

We are told by the opposition that we must have a change, that we must have a new deal. It is not the change that comes from normal development of national life to which I object but the proposal to alter the whole foundations of our national life which have been builded through generations of testing and struggle, and of the principles upon which we have builded the nation. The expressions our opponents use must refer to important changes in our economic and social system and our system of government, otherwise they are nothing but vacuous words. And I realize that in this time of distress many of our people are asking whether our social and economic system is incapable of that great primary function of providing security and comfort of life to all of the firesides of our 25 million homes in America, whether our social system provides for the fundamental development and progress of our people, whether our form of government is capable of originating and sustaining that security and progress.

This question is the basis upon which our opponents are appealing to the people in their fears and distress. They are proposing changes and so-called new deals which would destroy the very foundations of our American system.

Our people should consider the primary facts before they come to the judgment—not merely through political agitation, the glitter of promise, and the discouragement of temporary hardships—whether they will support changes which radically affect the whole system which has been builded up by 150 years of the toil of our fathers. They should not approach the question in the despair with which our opponents would clothe it.

Our economic system has received abnormal shocks during the past three years, which temporarily dislocated its normal functioning. These shocks have in a large sense come from without our borders, but I say to you that our system of government has enabled us to take such strong action as to prevent the disaster which would otherwise have come to our nation. It has enabled us further to develop measures and programs which are now demonstrating their ability to bring about restoration and progress.

We must go deeper than platitudes and emotional appeals of the public platform in the campaign if we will penetrate to the full significance of the changes which our opponents are attempting to float upon the wave of distress and discontent from the difficulties we are passing through. We can find what our opponents would do after searching the record of their appeals to discontent, group and sectional interest. We must search for them in the legislative acts which they sponsored and passed in the Democratic-controlled House of Representatives in the last session of Congress. We must look into measures for which they voted and which were defeated. We must inquire whether or not the presidential and vice-presidential candidates have disavowed these acts. If they have not, we must conclude that they form a portion and are a substantial indication of the profound changes proposed.

And we must look still further than this as to what revolutionary changes have been proposed by the candidates themselves.

We must look into the type of leaders who are campaigning for the Democratic ticket, whose philosophies have been well known all their lives, whose demands for a change in the American system are frank and forceful. I can respect the sincerity of these men in their desire to change our form of government and our social and economic system, though I shall do my best tonight to prove they are wrong. I refer particularly to Senator Norris, Senator La Follette, Senator Cutting, Senator Huey Long, Senator Wheeler, William R. Hearst and other exponents of a social philosophy different from the traditional American one. Unless these men feel assurance of support to their ideas, they certainly would not be supporting these candidates and the Democratic Party. The seal of these men indicates that they have sure confidence that they will have voice in the administration of our government.

I may say at once that the changes proposed from all these Democratic principals and allies are of the most profound and penetrating character. If they are brought about, this will not be the America which we have known in the past.

Let us pause for a moment and examine the American system of government, of social and economic life, which it is now proposed that we should alter. Our system is the product of our race and of our experience in building a nation to heights unparalleled in the whole history of the world. It is a system peculiar to the American people. It differs essentially from all others in the world. It is an American system.

It is founded on the conception that only through ordered liberty, through freedom to the individual, and equal opportunity to the individual will his initiative and enterprise be summoned to spur the march of progress.

It is by the maintenance of equality of opportunity and therefore of a society absolutely fluid in freedom of the movement of its human particles that our individualism departs from the individualism of Europe. We resent class distinction because there can be no rise for the individual through the frozen strata of classes, and no stratification of classes can take place in a mass livened by the free rise of its particles. Thus in our ideals the able and ambitious are able to rise constantly from the bottom to leadership in the community.

This freedom of the individual creates of itself the necessity and the cheerful willingness of men to act cooperatively in a thousand ways and for every purpose as occasion arises; and it permits such voluntary cooperations to be dissolved as soon as they have served their purpose, to be replaced by new voluntary associations for new purposes.

There has thus grown within us, to gigantic importance, a new conception. That is, this voluntary cooperation within the community. Cooperation to perfect the social organization; cooperation for the care of those in distress; cooperation for the advancement of knowledge, of scientific research, of education; for cooperative action in the advancement of many phases of economic life. This is self-government by the people outside of government; it is the most powerful development of individual freedom and equal opportunity that has taken place in the century and a half since our fundamental institutions were founded.

It is in the further development of this cooperation and a sense of its responsibility that we should find solution for many of our complex problems, and not by the extension of government into our economic and social life. The greatest function of government is to build up that cooperation, and its most resolute action should be to deny the extension of bureaucracy. We have developed great agencies of cooperation by the assistance of the government which promote and protect the interests of individuals and the smaller units of business. The Federal Reserve System, in its strengthening and support of the smaller banks; the Farm Board, in its strengthening and support of the farm cooperatives; the Home Loan Banks, in the mobilizing of building and loan associations and savings banks; the Federal Land Banks, in giving independence and strength to land mortgage associations; the great mobilization of relief to distress, the mobilization of business and industry in measures of recovery, and a score of other activities are not socialism—they are the essence of protection to the development of free men.

The primary conception of this whole American system is not the regimentation of men but the cooperation of free men. It is founded upon the conception of responsibility of the individual to the community, of the responsibility of local government to the state, of the state to the national government.

It is founded on a peculiar conception of self-government designed to maintain this equal opportunity to the individual, and through decentralization it brings about and maintains these responsibilities. The centralization of government will undermine responsibilities and will destroy the system.

Our government differs from all previous conceptions, not only in this decentralization but also in the separation of functions between the legislative, executive, and judicial arms of government, in which the independence of the judicial arm is the keystone of the whole structure.

It is founded on a conception that in times of emergency, when forces are running beyond control of individuals or other cooperative action, beyond the control of local communities and of states, then the great reserve powers of the federal government shall be brought into action to protect the community. But when these forces have ceased, there must be a return of state, local, and individual responsibility.

The implacable march of scientific discovery with its train of new inventions presents every year new problems to government and new problems to the social order. Questions often arise whether, in the face of the growth of these new and gigantic tools, democracy can remain master in its own house, can preserve the fundamentals of our American system. I contend that it can; and I contend that this American system of ours has demonstrated its validity and superiority over any other system yet invented by human mind.

It has demonstrated it in the face of the greatest test of our history— that is the emergency which we have faced in the past three years.

When the political and economic weakness of many nations of Europe, the result of the World War and its aftermath, finally culminated in collapse of their institutions, the delicate adjustment of our economic and social life received a shock unparalleled in our history. No one knows that better than you of New York. No one knows its causes better than you. That the crisis was so great that many of the leading banks sought directly or indirectly to convert their assets into gold or its equivalent with the result that they practically ceased to function as credit institutions; that many of our citizens sought flight for their capital to other countries; that many of them attempted to hoard gold in large amounts. These were but indications of the flight of confidence and of the belief that our government could not overcome these forces.

Yet these forces were overcome—perhaps by narrow margins—and this action demonstrates what the courage of a nation can accomplish under the resolute leadership in the Republican Party. And I say the Republican Party, because our opponents before and during the crisis, proposed no constructive program; though some of their members patriotically supported ours. Later on the Democratic House of Representatives did develop the real thought and ideas of the Democratic Party, but it was so destructive that it had to be defeated, for it would have destroyed, not healed.

In spite of all these obstructions, we did succeed. Our form of government did prove itself equal to the task. We saved this nation from a quarter of a century of chaos and degeneration, and we preserved the savings, the insurance policies, gave a fighting chance to men to hold their homes. We saved the integrity of our government and the honesty of the American dollar. And we installed measures which today are bringing back recovery. Employment, agriculture, business—all of these show the steady, if slow, healing of our enormous wound.

I therefore contend that the problem of today is to continue these measures and policies to restore this American system to its normal functioning, to repair the wounds it has received, to correct the weaknesses and evils which would defeat that system. To enter upon a series of deep changes, to embark upon this inchoate new deal which has been propounded in this campaign, would be to undermine and destroy our American system.

DISCUSSION QUESTIONS

1. State governments have always played a role in regulating the economy, from consumer protection to using tax breaks as a way to attract business investment within a state's borders. What kind of economic activities are best regulated at the state level? When should the federal government play a role?

2. Which of the activities that the government performs do you consider essential? Why?

3. Hoover's arguments against government bureaucracy and in favor of individual and community responsibility resonate today with the Tea Party supporters. What similarities do you see between Hoover's arguments and the current opponents of big government?

75

"The Rise and Fall of the GDP"

Jon Gertner

"Gross Domestic Product," or GDP, is a familiar economic term: It is a standard measure of overall economic activity, the amount of money that is spent during a particular period of time. Politicians are quick to take credit when the GDP grows, for growth is a sign of economic expansion. And when communities are concerned about the environmental or quality-of-life impact of a new development or industrial site, community and business leaders reassure them by pointing to the economic growth that will result.

But is all growth good growth? Jon Gertner argues that GDP is an inaccurate measure of overall economic well-being. Higher GDP does not necessarily mean we are better off, because it includes all types of spending—even spending that results from waste (gasoline burned by cars sitting in traffic jams), unhealthy activities (consumption of cholesterol-laden foods and the cardiologists' bills that often result), or high-spending consumerism (buying a new car every few years or the newest electricity-hog appliances). By comparing "high GDP man" and "low GDP man," Gertner makes it clear that the person spending more and contributing more to the economy may not be acting in the nation's best interests. He also uses the analogy of a car dashboard that tells the driver only how fast she is going and conveys no other information about how the car is functioning. Political leaders would be better served by a "human development index" that would reveal the nation's performance according to measures of health, education, the environment, employment, material well-being, interpersonal connectedness, and political engagement, rather than simply growth.

Whatever you may think progress looks like—a rebounding stock market, a new house, a good raise—the governments of the world have long held the view that only one statistic, the measure of gross domestic product, can really show whether things seem to be getting better or getting worse. GDP is an index of a country's entire economic output—a tally of, among many other things, manufacturers' shipments, farmers' harvests, retail sales and construction spending. It's a figure that compresses the immensity of a national economy into a single data point of surpassing density. The conventional feeling about GDP is that the more it grows, the better a country and its citizens are doing. In the U.S., economic activity plummeted at the start of 2009 and only started moving up during the second half of the year. Apparently things are moving in that direction still. In the first quarter of this year, the economy again expanded, this time by an annual rate of about 3.2 percent.

All the same, it has been a difficult few years for GDP. For decades, academics and gadflies have been critical of the measure, suggesting that it is an inaccurate and misleading gauge of prosperity. What has changed more recently is that GDP has been actively challenged by a variety of world leaders, especially in Europe, as well as by a number of international groups, like the Organization for Economic Cooperation and Development. The GDP, according to arguments I heard from economists as far afield as Italy, France and Canada, has not only failed to capture the well-being of a 21st-century society but has also skewed global political objectives toward the single-minded pursuit of economic growth. "The economists messed everything up," Alex Michalos, a former chancellor at the University of Northern British Columbia, told me recently when I was in Toronto to hear his presentation on the Canadian Index of Well-Being. The index is making its debut this year as a counterweight to the monolithic gross domestic product numbers. "The main barrier to getting progress has been that statistical agencies around the world are run by economists and statisticians," Michalos said. "And they are not people who are comfortable with human beings." The fundamental national measure they employ, he added, tells us a good deal about the economy but almost nothing about the specific things in our lives that really matter.

In the U.S., one challenge to the GDP is coming not from a single new index, or even a dozen new measures, but from several hundred new measures—accessible free online for anyone to see, all updated regularly. Such a system of national measurements, known as State of the USA, will go live online this summer [see www.stateoftheusa.org]. Its arrival comes at an opportune moment, but it has been a long time in the works. In 2003, a government official named Chris Hoenig was working at the U.S. Government Accountability Office, the investigative arm of Congress, and running a group that was researching ways to evaluate national progress. Since 2007, when the project became independent and took the name State of the USA, Hoenig has been guided by the advice of the National Academy of Sciences, an all-star board from the academic and business worlds and a number of former leaders of federal statistical agencies. Some of the country's elite philanthropies—including the Hewlett, MacArthur and Rockefeller foundations—have provided grants to help get the project started.

* * *

Those involved with the self-defined indicators movement—people like Hoenig, as well as supporters around the world who would like to dethrone GDP—argue that achieving a sustainable economy, and a sustainable society, may prove impossible without new ways to evaluate national progress. Left unanswered, however, is the question of which indicators are the most suitable replacements for, or most suitable enhancements to, GDP. Should they measure educational attainment or employment? Should they account for carbon emissions or happiness? As Hoenig himself is inclined to say, and not without some enthusiasm, a new panel of national measures won't necessarily settle such arguments. On the contrary, it will have a tendency to start them.

High-GDP Man vs. Low-GDP Man

For now at least, GDP holds almost unassailable sway, not only as the key national indicator for the economic health of the United States but also for that of the rest of the world's developed countries, which employ a standardized methodology—there's actually a handbook—to calculate their economic outputs. And, as it happens, there are some good reasons that everyone has depended on it for so long. "If you want to know why GDP matters, you can just put yourself back in the 1930 period, where we had no idea what was happening to our economy," William Nordhaus, a Yale economist who has spent a distinguished career thinking about economic measurement, told me recently. "There were people then who said things were fine and others who said things weren't fine. But we had no comprehensive measures, so we looked at things like boxcar loadings." If you compare the crisis of 1930 with the crisis of 2008, Nordhaus added, it has made an enormous difference to track what's happening in the economy through indexes like GDP. Such knowledge can enable a quick and informed policy response, which in the past year took shape as a big stimulus package, for example. To Nordhaus, in fact, the GDP—the antecedents of which were developed in the early 1930s by an economist named Simon Kuznets at the federal government's request—is one of the greatest inventions of the 20th century. "It's not a machine or a computer," he says, "and it's not the way you usually think of an invention. But it's an awesome thing."

* * *

* * * For years, economists critical of the measure have enjoyed spinning narratives to illustrate its logical flaws and limitations. Consider, for example, the lives of two people—let's call them High-GDP Man and Low-GDP Man. High-GDP Man has a long commute to work and drives an automobile that gets poor gas mileage, forcing him to spend a lot on fuel. The morning traffic and its stresses aren't too good for his car (which he replaces every few years) or his cardiovascular health (which he treats with expensive pharmaceuticals and medical procedures). High-GDP Man works hard, spends hard. He loves going to bars and restaurants, likes his flat-screen televisions and adores his big house, which he keeps at 71 degrees year round and protects with a state-of-the-art security system. High-GDP Man and his wife pay for a sitter (for their kids) and a nursing home (for their aging parents). They don't have time for housework, so they employ a full-time housekeeper. They don't have time to cook much, so they usually order in. They're too busy to take long vacations.

As it happens, all those things—cooking, cleaning, home care, three-week vacations and so forth—are the kind of activity that keep Low-GDP Man and his wife busy. High-GDP Man likes his washer and dryer; Low-GDP Man doesn't mind hanging his laundry on the clothesline. High-GDP Man buys bags of prewashed salad at the grocery store; Low-GDP Man grows vegetables in his garden. When High-GDP Man wants a book, he buys it; Low-GDP Man checks it out of the library. When High-GDP Man wants to get in shape, he joins a gym; Low-GDP Man digs out an old pair of Nikes and runs through the neighborhood. On his morning commute, High-GDP Man drives past Low-GDP Man, who is walking to work in wrinkled khakis.

By economic measures, there's no doubt High-GDP Man is superior to Low-GDP Man. His salary is higher, his expenditures are greater, his economic activity is more robust. You can even say that by modern standards High-GDP Man is a bigger boon to his country. What we can't really say for sure is whether his life is any better. In fact, there seem to be subtle indications that various "goods" that High-GDP Man consumes should, as some economists put it, be characterized as "bads." His alarm system at home probably isn't such a good indicator of his personal security; given all the medical tests, his health care expenditures seem to be excessive. Moreover, the pollution from the traffic jams near his home, which signals that business is good at the local gas stations and auto shops, is very likely contributing to social and environmental ills. And we don't know if High-GDP Man is living beyond his means, so we can't predict his future quality of life. For all we know, he could be living on borrowed time, just like a wildly overleveraged bank.

GDP vs. Human Development Index

* * *

Most criticisms of GDP have tended to fall into two distinct camps. The first group maintains that GDP itself needs to be fixed. High-GDP Man and Low-GDP Man have to become one, in effect. This might entail, for starters, placing an economic value on work done in the home, like housekeeping and child care. Activities that are currently unaccounted for, like cooking dinner at your own stove, could also be treated the same as activities that are now factored into GDP, like food prepared in a restaurant. Another fix might be to cease giving only positive values to events that actually detract from a country's well-being, like hurricanes and floods; both boost GDP through construction costs.

The second group of critics, meanwhile, has sought to recast the criticism of GDP from an accounting debate to a philosophical one. Here things get far more complicated. The argument goes like this: Even if GDP was revised as a more modern, logical GDP 2.0, our reliance on such a measure suggests that we may still be equating economic growth with progress on a planet that is possibly overburdened already by human consumption and pollution. The only way to repair such an imbalance would be to institutionalize other national indicators (environmental, say, or health-related) to reflect the true complexity of human progress. Just how many indicators are required to assess societal health—3? 30? 300, à la State of the USA?—is something economists have been struggling with for years as well.

So far only one measure has succeeded in challenging the hegemony of growth-centric thinking. This is known as the Human Development Index, which turns 20 this year. The HDI is a ranking that incorporates a nation's GDP and two other modifying factors: its citizens' education, based on adult literacy and school-enrollment data, and its citizens' health, based on life-expectancy statistics. The HDI, which happens to be used by the United Nations, has plenty of critics. For example, its three-part weightings are frequently criticized for being arbitrary; another problem is that minor variations in the literacy rates of developed nations, for example, can yield significant differences in how countries rank.

One economist who helped create the Human Development Index was Amartya Sen, a Nobel laureate in economics who teaches at Harvard.

* * *

* * * Sen joined the Nobel laureate Joseph Stiglitz and the French economist Jean-Paul Fitoussi on a commission established by President Nicolas Sarkozy of France to consider alternatives to GDP.

* * *

* * * [T]he commission endorsed both main criticisms of the GDP: the economic measure itself should be fixed to better represent individuals' circumstances today, and every country should also apply other indicators to capture what is happening economically, socially and environmentally. The commission sought a metaphor to explain what it meant. Eventually it settled on an automobile.

Suppose you're driving, Stiglitz told me. You would like to know how the vehicle is functioning, but when you check the dashboard there is only one gauge. (It's a peculiar car.) That single dial conveys one piece of important information: how fast you're moving. It's not a bad comparison to the current GDP, but it doesn't tell you many other things: How much fuel do you have left? How far can you go? How many miles have you gone already? So what you want is a car, or a country, with a big dashboard—but not so big that you can't take in all of its information.

The question is: How many measures beyond GDP—how many dials on a new dashboard—will you need? Stiglitz and his fellow academics ultimately concluded that assessing a population's quality of life will require metrics from at least seven categories: health, education, environment, employment, material well-being, interpersonal connectedness and political engagement. They also decided that any nation that was serious about progress should start measuring its "equity"—that is, the distribution of material wealth and other social goods—as well as its economic and environmental sustainability. "Too often, particularly I think in an American context, everybody says, 'We want policies that reflect our values,' but nobody says what those values are," Stiglitz told me. The opportunity to choose a new set of indicators, he added, is tantamount to saying that we should not only have a conversation about recasting GDP We should also, in the aftermath of an extraordinary economic collapse, talk about what the goals of a society really are.

Taking the Environment Into Account

The report from the Stiglitz-Sen-Fitoussi commission isn't a blueprint, exactly—it's more like open-source software, posted online for anyone to download, discuss and modify. It doesn't tell countries how they should measure progress. It tells them how they should think about measuring progress. One challenge here—something that the commission's members well understood—is that recommending new indicators and actually implementing them are very different endeavors. Almost everyone I spoke with in the indicators movement, including Chris Hoenig at State of the USA, seems to agree that at the moment our reach exceeds our grasp. When I met with Rebecca Blank, the under secretary of commerce for economic affairs, whose job it is to oversee the data agencies that put together GDP, she noted that new national measures depend on more than a government's willingness; they also necessitate additional financing, interagency cooperation and great leaps in the science of statistical analysis. Blank wasn't averse to some of the commission's recommendations—indeed, she recently endorsed the idea, proposed by Steve Landefeld at the Bureau of Economic Analysis, that our national accounts add a "household perspective" that represents individuals' economic circumstances better than GDP. "But some of the constraint is we don't have the money to do it," she told me, referring to various new measures. "Some of the constraint is we know how to do it, but we need to collect additional data that we don't currently have. And some of the constraint is that we don't really know how to do it quite yet."

Environmental and sustainability indicators offer a few good examples of how big the challenge is. A relatively easy first step, several members of the Stiglitz commission told me, would be to build in a "depletion charge" to GDP for the natural resources—oil, gas, timber and even fisheries—that a country transforms into dollars. At the moment, we don't do this; it's as if these commodities have no value until they are extracted and sold. A charge for resource depletion might not affect GDP in the United States all that much; the country is too big and too thoroughly based on knowledge and technology industries for the depletion costs of things like coal mining and oil drilling to make much of an impact. On the other hand, in countries like Saudi Arabia and China, GDP might look different (that is to say, lower) if such a charge were subtracted from their economic outputs. Geoffrey Heal, a professor at Columbia who worked on the environmental aspects of the commission's report, told me that including resource depletion in the national accounts—something the U.S. considered in the early 1990s and then abandoned for political reasons—could be implemented within a year if the world's developed nations agreed to do it. After that, he suggests, a next step might be to subtract from GDP the cost of the health problems—asthma and early deaths, for instance—caused by air pollutants like sulfur dioxide.

But environmental accounting gets more difficult. "We can put monetary values on mineral stocks, fisheries and even forests, perhaps," Heal says. "But it's hard to put a monetary value on alteration of the climate system, loss of species and the consequences that might come from those." On the other hand, Heal points out, you have to decide to measure something difficult before you can come up with a technique for measuring it. That was the case when the U.S. decided to create national accounts on economic production during the Great Depression. What the Stiglitz commission ultimately concluded was that it's necessary to make a few sustainability dials on the dashboard simply raw data—registering things like a country's carbon footprint or species extinctions—until we figure out how to give the effects approximate monetary values. Maybe in 10 years, Heal guesses, economists would be able to do that.

To Heal, making a real and rapid effort at calculating these costs and then posting the information is imperative. According to Heal, we have no sense of how much "natural capital"—our stocks of clean air and water and our various ecosystems—we need to conserve to maintain our economy and our quality of life. "If you push the world's natural capital below a certain level," Heal asks, "do you so radically alter the system that it has a long-term impact on human welfare?" He doesn't know the answer. Yet, he adds, if we were to pass that point—and at present we have no dials to indicate whether we have—then we couldn't compensate for our error through technological innovation or energy breakthroughs. Because by then it would be too late.

Putting a Number on Happiness

As difficult as it might be to compile sustainability indicators, it's equally challenging to create measures that describe our social and emotional lives. In this area, there's a fair amount of skepticism from the academic establishment about putting happiness onto a national dashboard of well-being. William Nordhaus of Yale told me that some of the measurements are "absurd." Amartya Sen, too, told me that he has reservations about the worth of statistics that purport to describe human happiness.

Stiglitz and his colleagues nevertheless concluded that such research was becoming sufficiently rigorous to warrant its possible inclusion. At first the connection to GDP can be puzzling. One explanation, however, is that while our current economic measures can't capture the larger effects of unemployment or chronic depression, providing policy makers with that information may influence their actions. "You might say, If we have unemployment, don't worry, we'll just compensate the person," Stiglitz told me. "But that doesn't fully compensate them." Stiglitz pointed to the work of the Harvard professor Robert Putnam, who served on the Stiglitz-Sen-Fitoussi commission, which suggests that losing a job can have repercussions that affect a person's social connections (one main driver of human happiness, regardless of country) for many years afterward.

When I caught up with Putnam, he said that the "damage to this country's social fabric from this economic crisis must have been huge, huge, huge." And yet, he noted, "We have plenty of numbers about the economic consequences but none of the numbers about the social consequences." Over the past decade, Putnam has been working on measures—having to do with church attendance, community involvement and the like—to quantify our various social links; just recently, the U.S. Census Bureau agreed to include questions of his in some of its monthly surveys. Still, his efforts are a work in progress. When I asked Putnam whether government should be in the business of fostering social connections, he replied, "I don't think we should have a government Department of Friendship that introduces people to one another." But he argued that just as registering the social toll of joblessness would add a dimension of urgency to the unemployment issue, it seemed possible that measuring social connections, and putting those measures on a national dashboard, could be in society's best interests. As it happens, the Canadian Index of Well-Being will contain precisely such a measure; and it's very likely that a related measure of "social capital," as it's often called, will become a State of the USA indicator too. "People will get sick and die, because they don't know their neighbors," Putnam told me. "And the health effects of social isolation are of the same magnitude as people smoking. If we can care about people smoking, because that reduces their life expectancy, then why not think about social isolation too?"

It seems conceivable, in fact, that including various measures of emotional well-being on a national dashboard could lead to policies quite different from what we have now. "There's an enormous inequality of suffering in society," Daniel Kahneman told me recently. By his estimate, "if you look at the 10 percent of people who spend the most time suffering, they account for almost half of the total amount of suffering." Kahneman suggested that tremendous social and economic gains could therefore be made by dealing with the mental-health problems—depression, say—of a relatively small fraction of the population. At the same time, he added, new measures of emotional well-being that he has been working on might soon give us a more enlightened perspective on the complex relationship between money and happiness.

Currently, research suggests that increased wealth leads us to report increased feelings of satisfaction with our lives—a validation, in effect, that higher GDP increases the well-being in a country. But Kahneman told me that his most recent studies, conducted with the Princeton economist Angus Deaton, suggest that money doesn't necessarily make much of a difference in our moment-to-moment happiness, which is distinct from our feelings of satisfaction. According to their work, income over about $70,000 does nothing to improve how much we enjoy our activities on a typical day. And that raises some intriguing questions. Do we want government to help us increase our sense of satisfaction? Or do we want it to help us get through our days without feeling misery? The two questions lead toward two very different policy options. Is national progress a matter of making an increasing number of people very rich? Or is it about getting as many people as possible into the middle class?

The Political Resistance

* * *

As for the effects of such changes, Stiglitz told me, "What we measure affects what we do, and better measurement will lead to better decisions, or at least different decisions." But until the developed nations of the world actually move beyond GDP—a big if—this remains a reasoned hypothesis only. A lingering question is whether some government officials, perceiving dangers in a new measurement system, might conclude that such an overhaul would wreak political havoc and therefore ought to be avoided. A heightened focus on environmental indicators, for starters, could give environmental legislation a far greater urgency. And a revision of economic measures presents other potential policy complications.

It has long been the case, for example, that the GDP of the United States outpaces that of European countries with higher taxes and greater government spending; it has thus seemed reasonable to view our economic growth as a vindication of a national emphasis on free markets and entrepreneurship. But things look different if you see the measure itself as flawed or inadequate. We take shorter vacations than Europeans, for instance, which is one reason their GDP is lower than ours—but that could change if our indicators start putting a value on leisure time. Some of the disparity, meanwhile, between the U.S. and various European countries, Stiglitz argued, is a statistical bias resulting from the way GDP formulas account for public-sector benefits. In other words, the services received from the government in a country like Sweden—in public education, health care and child care, among other things—are likely undervalued. Rejiggering the measures of prosperity would almost certainly challenge our self-perceptions, Stiglitz said, perhaps so much so that in the U.S. we might begin to ask, Is our system working as well for most people as we think it has been?

* * *

DISCUSSION QUESTIONS

1. If all growth (increases in spending) is not necessarily good growth, how can we distinguish between "good" growth and "bad" growth? Of the criteria mentioned for the "human development index," which would be the most difficult to measure? Do you think other things should be included in the measure?

2. In public policy debates, analysts often distinguish "economic" indicators—inflation, unemployment, consumer spending—from "social" indicators, such as crime, divorce, school dropout rates, and teen pregnancies. In light of Gertner's argument, is this separation appropriate? Why or why not?

3. Do you think the Stiglitz-Sen-Fitoussi Commission will make any headway with political leaders (in terms of getting their index implemented)? What political obstacles would they face?

Debating the Issues: Bailing Out Wall Street

The economic meltdown of 2008–2009 resulted in the deepest economic recession since the Great Depression. As the housing market collapsed, financial mainstays such as Bear Stearns, Lehman Brothers, Merrill Lynch, Washington Mutual, and Wachovia went bankrupt or were acquired in fire sales by other institutions. Other troubled institutions such as American International Group (AIG), which was at the center of the financial crisis, and the mortgage-lending giants Fannie Mae and Freddie Mac were deemed "too big to fail" and were essentially taken over by the federal government. Stock markets collapsed and the United States and European banks lost more than $1 trillion on toxic assets from the subprime mortgage market and from other bad loans. Since peaking in the second quarter of 2007, household wealth in the United States was down a staggering $14 trillion due to a 25-percent plunge in the value of homes, as well as shrunken savings and retirement accounts.

In the face of this economic crisis, Congress, the Federal Reserve, and the U.S. Treasury took unprecedented actions to shore up the financial system. Congress created the Troubled Asset Relief Program (TARP), which authorized the Treasury to invest $700 billion to shore up the financial system. The Federal Reserve (the Fed) intervened in the short-term "commercial paper" market (which supplies short-term loans to businesses), shored up money market funds, and provided emergency loans to troubled banks. Was this unprecedented set of measures necessary to thaw out the frozen credit markets and get the financial system working again? Or was it a "bailout hustle" that rewarded Wall Street insiders' risky behavior?

Matt Taibbi is clearly outraged at what he sees as the unjustified bailout of Wall Street. Especially galling were the $16.2 billion in salaries and bonuses that Goldman Sachs employees received in 2009 (and the $140 billion for executive compensation at the nation's six largest banks) as the rest of the country was just starting to climb out of the recession and nearly 10 percent of Americans remained unemployed. Taibbi sees this compensation as troubling because it would not have been possible without the help of the federal government. Even worse, financial institutions seem not to have learned from the experience of 2008–2009 and have gone right back to their same risky behavior. Taibbi compares the Wall Street bailout with con men's old-fashioned hustles with colorful names such as the "swoop and squat" and the "pig in the poke." The clear winners of this hustle are the big financial institutions of Wall Street. The bag holders are the American taxpayers and the little investors.

Treasury Secretary Timothy Geithner obviously has a different take on the situation. In his testimony before the Congressional Oversight

Panel that monitors the expenditure of the TARP funds, Geithner had an upbeat assessment of the impact that the government's actions had on averting a worse economic crisis. Geithner is in a difficult spot because the main success is something that *didn't* happen: as bad as things got in 2008–2009, it could have been much worse if more financial institutions had been allowed to fail. Geithner makes two central points: first, the programs worked just as expected to stabilize financial markets and promote economic growth. Second, TARP will cost the taxpayers far less than the $700 billion that was authorized. As of the Treasury's last statement in November 2010, only $389 billion had been paid out and nearly all of that money will be recovered. Some of the Fed's programs, such as the rescue of money market funds, have actually turned a profit. Although Geithner does not directly address some of Taibbi's criticisms, his response in part would be, "Yes, the banks came out very nicely after all of our initiatives. *That was the point—to stabilize the financial sector.*"

76

"Wall Street's Bailout Hustle"

Matt Taibbi

On January 21st, Lloyd Blankfein left a peculiar voicemail message on the work phones of his employees at Goldman Sachs. * * * In his message, Blankfein addressed his plan to pay out gigantic year-end bonuses amid widespread controversy over Goldman's role in precipitating the global financial crisis.

The bank had already set aside a tidy $16.2 billion for salaries and bonuses—meaning that Goldman employees were each set to take home an average of $498,246, a number roughly commensurate with what they received during the bubble years. Still, the troops were worried: There were rumors that [Blankfein], bowing to political pressure, might be forced to scale the number back. After all, the country was broke, 14.8 million Americans were stranded on the unemployment line, and Barack Obama and the Democrats were trying to recover the populist high ground after their whipping in Massachusetts by calling for a "bailout tax" on banks. Maybe this wasn't the right time for Goldman to be throwing its annual Roman bonus orgy.

Not to worry, Blankfein reassured employees. "In a year that proved to have no shortage of story lines," he said, "I believe very strongly that performance is the ultimate narrative."

Translation: We made a [s***load] of money last year because we're so amazing at our jobs, so [f***] all those people who want us to reduce our bonuses.

Goldman wasn't alone. The nation's six largest banks—all committed to this balls-out, I drink your milkshake! strategy of flagrantly gorging themselves as America goes hungry—set aside a whopping $140 billion for executive compensation last year, a sum only slightly less than the $164 billion they paid themselves in the pre-crash year of 2007. In a gesture of self-sacrifice, Blankfein himself took a humiliatingly low bonus of $9 million, less than the 2009 pay of elephantine New York Knicks washout Eddy Curry. But in reality, not much had changed. "What is the state of our moral being when Lloyd Blankfein taking a $9 million bonus is viewed as this great act of contrition, when every penny of it was a direct transfer from the taxpayer?" asks Eliot Spitzer, who tried to hold Wall Street accountable during his own ill-fated stint as governor of New York.

Beyond a few such bleats of outrage, however, the huge payout was met, by and large, with a collective sigh of resignation. Because beneath America's populist veneer, on a more subtle strata of the national psyche, there remains a strong temptation to not really give a s***. The rich, after all, have always made way too much money; what's the difference if some fat cat in New York pockets $20 million instead of $10 million?

The only reason such apathy exists, however, is because there's still a widespread misunderstanding of how exactly Wall Street "earns" its money, with emphasis on the quotation marks around "earns." The question everyone should be asking, as one bailout recipient after another posts massive profits—Goldman reported $13.4 billion in profits last year, after paying out that $16.2 billion in bonuses and compensation—is this: In an economy as horrible as ours, with every factory town between New York and Los Angeles looking like those hollowed-out ghost ships we see on History Channel documentaries like *Shipwrecks of the Great Lakes*, where in the hell did Wall Street's eye-popping profits come from, exactly? Did Goldman go from bailout city to $13.4 billion in the black because, as Blankfein suggests, its "performance" was just that awesome? A year and a half after they were minutes away from bankruptcy, how are these ***holes not only back on their feet again, but hauling in bonuses at the same rate they were during the bubble?

The answer to that question is basically twofold: They raped the taxpayer, and they raped their clients.

The bottom line is that banks like Goldman have learned absolutely nothing from the global economic meltdown. In fact, they're back conniving and playing speculative long shots in force—only this time with the full financial support of the U.S. government. In the process, they're rapidly re-creating the conditions for another crash, with the same actors once again playing the same crazy games of financial chicken with the same toxic assets as before.

That's why this bonus business isn't merely a matter of getting upset whether or not Lloyd Blankfein buys himself one tropical island or two on his next birthday. The reality is that the post-bailout era in which Goldman thrived has turned out to be a chaotic frenzy of high-stakes con-artistry, with taxpayers and clients bilked out of billions using a dizzying array of old-school hustles that, but for their ponderous complexity, would have fit well in slick grifter movies like *The Sting* and *Matchstick Men*. There's even a term in con-man lingo for what some of the banks are doing right now, with all their cosmetic gestures of scaling back bonuses and giving to charities. In the grifter world, calming down a mark so he doesn't call the cops is known as the "Cool Off."

To appreciate how all of these (sometimes brilliant) schemes work is to understand the difference between earning money and taking scores, and to realize that the profits these banks are posting don't so much represent national growth and recovery, but something closer to the losses one would report after a theft or a car crash. Many Americans instinctively understand this to be true. * * * In that spirit, a brief history of the best 18 months of grifting this country has ever seen:

Con #1: The Swoop and Squat

By now, most people who have followed the financial crisis know that the bailout of AIG was actually a bailout of AIG's "counterparties"—the big banks like Goldman to whom the insurance giant owed billions when it went belly up.

What is less understood is that the bailout of AIG counterparties like Goldman and Société Générale, a French bank, actually began before the collapse of AIG, before the Federal Reserve paid them so much as a dollar. Nor is it understood that these counterparties actually accelerated the wreck of AIG in what was, ironically, something very like the old insurance scam known as "Swoop and Squat," in which a target car is trapped between two perpetrator vehicles and wrecked, with the mark in the game being the target's insurance company—in this case, the government.

This may sound far-fetched, but the financial crisis of 2008 was very much caused by a perverse series of legal incentives that often made failed investments worth more than thriving ones. Our economy was like a town where everyone has juicy insurance policies on their neighbors' cars and houses. In such a town, the driving will be suspiciously bad, and there will be a lot of fires.

AIG was the ultimate example of this dynamic. At the height of the housing boom, Goldman was selling billions in bundled mortgage-backed securities—often toxic crap of the no-money-down, no-identification-needed variety of home loan—to various institutional suckers like pensions and insurance companies, who frequently thought they were buying investment-grade instruments. At the same time, in a glaring example of the perverse incentives that existed and still exist, Goldman was also betting against those same sorts of securities—a practice that one government investigator compared to "selling a car with faulty brakes and then buying an insurance policy on the buyer of those cars."

Goldman often "insured" some of this garbage with AIG, using a virtually unregulated form of pseudoinsurance called credit-default swaps. Thanks in large part to deregulation pushed by Bob Rubin, former chairman of Goldman, and Treasury secretary under Bill Clinton, AIG wasn't required to actually have the capital to pay off the deals. As a result, banks like Goldman bought more than $440 billion worth of this bogus insurance from AIG, a huge blind bet that the taxpayer ended up having to eat.

Thus, when the housing bubble went crazy, Goldman made money coming and going. They made money selling the crap mortgages, and they made money by collecting on the bogus insurance from AIG when the crap mortgages flopped.

Still, the trick for Goldman was: how to collect the insurance money. As AIG headed into a tailspin that fateful summer of 2008, it looked like the beleaguered firm wasn't going to have the money to pay off the bogus insurance. So Goldman and other banks began demanding that AIG provide them with cash collateral. In the 15 months leading up to the collapse of AIG, Goldman received $5.9 billion in collateral. Société Générale, a bank holding lots of mortgage-backed crap originally underwritten by Goldman, received $5.5 billion. These collateral demands squeezing AIG from two sides were the "Swoop and Squat" that ultimately crashed the firm. "It put the company into a liquidity crisis," says Eric Dinallo, who was intimately involved in the AIG bailout as head of the New York State Insurance Department.

It was a brilliant move. When a company like AIG is about to die, it isn't supposed to hand over big hunks of assets to a single creditor like Goldman; it's supposed to equitably distribute whatever assets it has left among all its creditors. Had AIG gone bankrupt, Goldman would have likely lost much of the $5.9 billion that it pocketed as collateral. "Any bankruptcy court that saw those collateral payments would have declined that transaction as a fraudulent conveyance," says Barry Ritholtz, the author of *Bailout Nation*. Instead, Goldman and the other counterparties got their money out in advance—putting a torch to what was left of AIG. Fans of the movie *Goodfellas* will recall Henry Hill and Tommy De-Vito taking the same approach to the Bamboo Lounge nightclub they'd been gouging. Roll the Ray Liotta narration: "Finally, when there's nothing left, when you can't borrow another buck . . . you bust the joint out. You light a match."

And why not? After all, according to the terms of the bailout deal struck when AIG was taken over by the state in September 2008, Goldman was paid 100 cents on the dollar on an additional $12.9 billion it was owed by AIG—again, money it almost certainly would not have seen a fraction of had AIG proceeded to a normal bankruptcy. Along with the collateral it pocketed, that's $19 billion in pure cash that Goldman would not have "earned" without massive state intervention. How's that $13.4 billion in 2009 profits looking now? And that doesn't even include the direct bailouts of Goldman Sachs and other big banks, which began in earnest after the collapse of AIG.

Con #2: The Dollar Store

In the usual "Dollar Store" or "Big Store" scam—popularized in movies like *The Sting*—a huge cast of con artists is hired to create a whole fake environment into which the unsuspecting mark walks and gets robbed over and over again. A warehouse is converted into a makeshift casino or off-track betting parlor, the fool walks in with money, leaves without it.

The two key elements to the Dollar Store scam are the whiz-bang theatrical redecorating job and the fact that everyone is in on it except the mark. In this case, a pair of investment banks were dressed up to look like commercial banks overnight, and it was the taxpayer who walked in and lost his shirt, confused by the appearance of what looked like real Federal Reserve officials minding the store.

Less than a week after the AIG bailout, Goldman and another investment bank, Morgan Stanley, applied for, and received, federal permission to become bank holding companies—a move that would make them eligible for much greater federal support. The stock prices of both firms were cratering, and there was talk that either or both might go the way of Lehman Brothers, another once-mighty investment bank that just a week earlier had disappeared from the face of the earth under the weight of its toxic assets. By law, a five-day waiting period was required for such a conversion—but the two banks got them overnight, with final approval actually coming only five days after the AIG bailout.

Why did they need those federal bank charters? This question is the key to understanding the entire bailout era—because this Dollar Store scam was the big one. Institutions that were, in reality, high-risk gambling houses were allowed to masquerade as conservative commercial banks. As a result of this new designation, they were given access to a virtually endless tap of "free money" by unsuspecting taxpayers. The $10 billion that Goldman received under the better-known TARP bailout was chump change in comparison to the smorgasbord of direct and indirect aid it qualified for as a commercial bank.

When Goldman Sachs and Morgan Stanley got their federal bank charters, they joined Bank of America, Citigroup, J.R Morgan Chase and the other banking titans who could go to the Fed and borrow massive amounts of money at interest rates that, thanks to the aggressive rate-cutting policies of Fed chief Ben Bernanke during the crisis, soon sank to zero percent. The ability to go to the Fed and borrow big at next to no interest was what saved Goldman, Morgan Stanley and other banks from death in the fall of 2008. "They had no other way to raise capital at that moment, meaning they were on the brink of insolvency," says Nomi Prins, a former managing director at Goldman Sachs. "The Fed was the only shot."

In fact, the Fed became not just a source of emergency borrowing that enabled Goldman and Morgan Stanley to stave off disaster—it became a source of long-term guaranteed income. Borrowing at zero percent interest, banks like Goldman now had virtually infinite ways to make money. In one of the most common maneuvers, they simply took the money they borrowed from the government at zero percent and lent it back to the government by buying Treasury bills that paid interest of three or four percent. It was basically a license to print money—no different than attaching an ATM to the side of the Federal Reserve.

"You're borrowing at zero, putting it out there at two or three percent, with hundreds of billions of dollars—man, you can make a lot of money that way," says the manager of one prominent hedge fund. "It's free money."

Which goes a long way to explaining Goldman's enormous profits last year. But all that free money was amplified by another scam:

Con #3: The Pig in the Poke

At one point or another, pretty much everyone who takes drugs has been burned by this one, also known as the "Rocks in the Box" scam or, in its more elaborate variations, the "Jamaican Switch." Someone sells you what looks like an eightball of coke in a baggie, you get home and, you dumbass, it's baby powder.

The scam's name comes from the Middle Ages, when some fool would be sold a bound and gagged pig that he would see being put into a bag; he'd miss the switch, then get home and find a tied-up cat in there instead. Hence the expression "Don't let the cat out of the bag."

The "Pig in the Poke" scam is another key to the entire bailout era. After the crash of the housing bubble—the largest asset bubble in history—the economy was suddenly flooded with securities backed by failing or near-failing home loans. In the cleanup phase after that bubble burst, the whole game was to get taxpayers, clients and shareholders to buy these worthless cats, but at pig prices.

One of the first times we saw the scam appear was in September 2008, right around the time that AIG was imploding. That was when the Fed changed some of its collateral rules, meaning banks that could once borrow only against sound collateral, like Treasury bills or AAA-rated corporate bonds, could now borrow against pretty much anything—including some of the mortgage-backed sewage that got us into this mess in the first place. In other words, banks that once had to show a real pig to borrow from the Fed could now show up with a cat and get pig money. "All of a sudden, banks were allowed to post absolute s*** to the Fed's balance sheet," says the manager of the prominent hedge fund.

The Fed spelled it out on September 14th, 2008, when it changed the collateral rules for one of its first bailout facilities—the Primary Dealer Credit Facility, or PDCF. The Fed's own write-up described the changes: "With the Fed's action, all the kinds of collateral then in use . . . including non-investment-grade securities and equities . . . became eligible for pledge in the PDCF."

Translation: We now accept cats.

The Pig in the Poke also came into play in April of last year, when Congress pushed a little-known agency called the Financial Accounting Standards Board, or FASB, to change the so-called "mark-to-market" accounting rules. Until this rule change, banks had to assign a real-market price to all of their assets. If they had a balance sheet full of securities they had bought at $3 that were now only worth $1, they had to figure their year-end accounting using that $1 value. In other words, if you were the dope who bought a cat instead of a pig, you couldn't invite your shareholders to a slate of pork dinners come year-end accounting time.

But last April, FASB changed all that. From now on, it announced, banks could avoid reporting losses on some of their crappy cat investments simply by declaring that they would "more likely than not" hold on to them until they recovered their pig value. In short, the banks didn't even have to actually hold on to the toxic s*** they owned—they just had to sort of promise to hold on to it.

That's why the "profit" numbers of a lot of these banks are really a joke. In many cases, we have absolutely no idea how many cats are in their proverbial bag. What they call "profits" might really be profits, only minus undeclared millions or billions in losses.

"They're hiding all this stuff from their shareholders," says Ritholtz, who was disgusted that the banks lobbied for the rule changes. "Now, suddenly banks that were happy to mark to market on the way up don't have to mark to market on the way down."

Con #4: The Rumanian Box

One of the great innovations of Victor Lustig, the legendary Depression-era con man who wrote the famous "Ten Commandments for Con Men," was a thing called the "Rumanian Box." This was a little machine that a mark would put a blank piece of paper into, only to see real currency come out the other side. The brilliant Lustig sold this Rumanian Box over and over again for vast sums—but he's been outdone by the modern barons of Wall Street, who managed to get themselves a real Rumanian Box.

How they accomplished this is a story that by itself highlights the challenge of placing this era in any kind of historical context of known financial crime. What the banks did was something that was never—and never could have been—thought of before. They took so much money from the government, and then did so little with it, that the state was forced to start printing new cash to throw at them. Even the great Lustig in his wildest, horniest dreams could never have dreamed up this one.

The setup: By early 2009, the banks had already replenished themselves with billions if not trillions in bailout money. It wasn't just the $700 billion in TARP cash, the free money provided by the Fed, and the untold losses obscured by accounting tricks. Another new rule allowed banks to collect interest on the cash they were required by law to keep in reserve accounts at the Fed—meaning the state was now compensating the banks simply for guaranteeing their own solvency. And a new federal operation called the Temporary Liquidity Guarantee Program let insolvent and near-insolvent banks dispense with their deservedly ruined credit profiles and borrow on a clean slate, with FDIC backing. Goldman borrowed $29 billion on the government's good name, J.P. Morgan Chase $38 billion, and Bank of America $44 billion. "TLGP," says Prins, the former Goldman manager, "was a big one."

Collectively, all this largesse was worth trillions. The idea behind the flood of money, from the government's standpoint, was to spark a national recovery: We refill the banks' balance sheets, and they, in turn, start to lend money again, recharging the economy and producing jobs. "The banks were fast approaching insolvency," says Rep. Paul Kanjorski, a vocal critic of Wall Street who nevertheless defends the initial decision to bail out the banks. "It was vitally important that we recapitalize these institutions."

But here's the thing. Despite all these trillions in government rescues, despite the Fed slashing interest rates down to nothing and showering the banks with mountains of guarantees, Goldman and its friends had still not jump-started lending again by the first quarter of 2009. That's where those [bonuses] of Lloyd Blankfein came into play, as Goldman and other banks basically threatened to pick up their bailout billions and go home if the government didn't fork over more cash—a lot more. "Even if the Fed could make interest rates negative, that wouldn't necessarily help," warned Goldman's chief domestic economist, Jan Hatzius. "We're in a deep recession mainly because the private sector, for a variety of reasons, has decided to save a lot more."

Translation: You can lower interest rates all you want, but we're still not f****** lending the bailout money to anyone in this economy. Until the government agreed to hand over even more goodies, the banks opted to join the rest of the "private sector" and "save" the taxpayer aid they had received—in the form of bonuses and compensation.

The ploy worked. In March of last year, the Fed sharply expanded a radical new program called quantitative easing, which effectively operated as a real-live Rumanian Box. The government put stacks of paper in one side, and out came $1.2 trillion "real" dollars.

The government used some of that freshly printed money to prop itself up by purchasing Treasury bonds—a desperation move, since Washington's demand for cash was so great post-Clusterf*** '08 that even the Chinese couldn't buy U.S. debt fast enough to keep America afloat. But the Fed used most of the new cash to buy mortgage-backed securities in an effort to spur home lending—instantly creating a massive market for major banks.

And what did the banks do with the proceeds? Among other things, they bought Treasury bonds, essentially lending the money back to the government, at interest. The money that came out of the magic Rumanian Box went from the government back to the government, with Wall Street stepping into the circle just long enough to get paid. And once quantitative easing ends, as it is scheduled to do in March, the flow of money for home loans will once again grind to a halt. The Mortgage Bankers Association expects the number of new residential mortgages to plunge by 40 percent this year.

Con #5: The Big Mitt

All of that Rumanian Box paper was made even more valuable by running it through the next stage of the grift. Michael Masters, one of the country's leading experts on commodities trading, compares this part of the scam to the poker game in the Bill Murray comedy *Stripes*. "It's like that scene where John Candy leans over to the guy who's new at poker and says, 'Let me see your cards,' then starts giving him advice," Masters says. "He looks at the hand, and the guy has bad cards, and he's like, 'Bluff me, come on! If it were me, I'd bet everything!' That's what it's like. It's like they're looking at your cards as they give you advice."

In more ways than one can count, the economy in the bailout era turned into a "Big Mitt," the con man's name for a rigged poker game. Everybody was indeed looking at everyone else's cards, in many cases with state sanction. Only taxpayers and clients were left out of the loop.

At the same time the Fed and the Treasury were making massive, earthshaking moves like quantitative easing and TARP, they were also consulting regularly with private advisory boards that include every major player on Wall Street. The Treasury Borrowing Advisory Committee has a J.P. Morgan executive as its chairman and a Goldman executive as its vice chairman, while the board advising the Fed includes bankers from

Capital One and Bank of New York Mellon. That means that, in addition to getting great gobs of free money, the banks were also getting clear signals about when they were getting that money, making it possible to position themselves to make the appropriate investments.

One of the best examples of the banks blatantly gambling, and winning, on government moves was the Public-Private Investment Program, or PPIP. In this bizarre scheme cooked up by goofball-geek Treasury Secretary Tim Geithner, the government loaned money to hedge funds and other private investors to buy up the absolutely most toxic horses*** on the market—the same kind of high-risk, high-yield mortgages that were most responsible for triggering the financial chain reaction in the fall of 2008. These satanic deals were the basic currency of the bubble: Jobless dope fiends bought houses with no money down, and the big banks wrapped those mortgages into securities and then sold them off to pensions and other suckers as investment-grade deals. The whole point of the PPIP was to get private investors to relieve the banks of these dangerous assets before they hurt any more innocent bystanders.

But what did the banks do instead, once they got wind of the PPIP? They started buying that worthless crap again, presumably to sell back to the government at inflated prices! In the third quarter of last year, Goldman, Morgan Stanley, Citigroup and Bank of America combined to add $3.36 billion of exactly this horses*** to their balance sheets.

This brazen decision to gouge the taxpayer startled even hardened market observers. According to Michael Schlachter of the investment firm Wilshire Associates, it was "absolutely ridiculous" that the banks that were supposed to be reducing their exposure to these volatile instruments were instead loading up on them in order to make a quick buck. "Some of them created this mess," he said, "and they are making a killing undoing it."

* * *

Con artists have a word for the inability of their victims to accept that they've been scammed. They call it the "True Believer Syndrome." That's sort of where we are, in a state of nagging disbelief about the real problem on Wall Street. It isn't so much that we have inadequate rules or incompetent regulators, although both of these things are certainly true. The real problem is that it doesn't matter what regulations are in place if the people running the economy are rip-off artists. The system assumes a certain minimum level of ethical behavior and civic instinct over and above what is spelled out by the regulations. If those ethics are absent— well, this thing isn't going to work, no matter what we do. Sure, mugging old ladies is against the law, but it's also easy. To prevent it, we depend, for the most part, not on cops but on people making the conscious decision not to do it.

That's why the biggest gift the bankers got in the bailout was not fiscal but psychological. "The most valuable part of the bailout," says Rep. Sherman, "was the implicit guarantee that they're Too Big to Fail." Instead of liquidating and prosecuting the insolvent institutions that took us all down with them in a giant Ponzi scheme, we have showered them with money and guarantees and all sorts of other enabling gestures. And what should really freak everyone out is the fact that Wall Street immediately started skimming off its own rescue money. If the bailouts validated anew the crooked psychology of the bubble, the recent profit and bonus numbers show that the same psychology is back, thriving, and looking for new disasters to create. "It's evidence," says Rep. Kanjorski, "that they still don't get it."

More to the point, the fact that we haven't done much of anything to change the rules and behavior of Wall Street shows that we still don't get it. Instituting a bailout policy that stressed recapitalizing bad banks was like the addict coming back to the con man to get his lost money back. Ask yourself how well that ever works out. And then get ready for the reload.

77

Written Testimony before the Congressional Oversight Panel

Timothy F. Geithner

Introduction

Chair Warren, Representative Hensarling, and members Neiman, Silvers and Atkins, thank you for the opportunity to testify before you again.

Since I last appeared before this panel, U.S. financial and economic conditions have continued to improve. Borrowing costs have fallen, and businesses have raised substantial capital from private sources. The contraction in bank lending has moderated. Residential mortgage lending by banks actually expanded last month. The economy started growing again in the third quarter, a trend that private economists predict will continue. And the pace of deterioration in the labor market has moderated.

These improvements are remarkable. One year ago, we faced one of the most severe financial crises of the past century, and the economy was contracting sharply. Fear of a possible depression froze markets and spurred businesses to lay off workers and pull back from investment.

A coordinated government response turned this around. Action taken last fall by the Department of the Treasury, the Federal Reserve, the FDIC, and other government agencies averted a catastrophic collapse of our financial system. As your latest report states, the Troubled Asset Relief Program (TARP), which was established by Congress in the Emergency Economic Stabilization Act of 2008 (EESA), played a significant role in that success. But when the Obama Administration took office, the financial system was still extremely fragile, and the economy was shrinking rapidly. The Administration swiftly initiated financial and fiscal policies to address both challenges. In particular, the Financial Stability Plan helped to shore up confidence in our financial institutions and markets, while mobilizing private capital. The Administration also redirected public support from large financial institutions to households, small banks, and small businesses.

As a result of these policies, confidence in our financial system has improved, credit is flowing, and the economy is growing. Moreover, the government is exiting from its emergency financial policies and taxpayers are being repaid. Indeed, the ultimate cost of those policies is likely to be significantly lower than previously expected. In particular, while EESA provided the Secretary of the Treasury with the authority to invest $700 billion, it is clear today that TARP will not cost taxpayers $700 billion. Banks have already repaid nearly half of TARP funds they received over the past year, and we now expect a positive return from the government's investments in banks. We also plan to use significantly less than the full $700 billion in EESA authority. As a result, we now expect that TARP will cost taxpayers at least $200 billion less than was projected in the August Mid-Session Review of the President's Budget.

This week, Treasury published the first annual financial statements for the Office of Financial Stability, which implements TARP. Audited by the GAO, these statements discuss the impact of the program and provide cost estimates for it. Today, I will provide highlights from these statements.

I will also discuss the significant financial and economic challenges that remain and what the Administration is doing to address them. We need to continue to find ways to help mitigate foreclosures for responsible homeowners and to get credit to small businesses. We also must maintain the capacity to address potential threats to our financial system, which could undermine the recovery we have seen to date. Further, we need to reform our laws to provide stronger, more effective regulation of our financial system and to protect consumers. Doing so will decrease the need for future intervention.

In this context, I will lay out an exit strategy for TARP. There are four broad elements to that strategy:

1. terminating and winding down programs that have supported large financial institutions;
2. limiting new investments to housing, small business, and securitization markets that facilitate consumer and small business loans;
3. maintaining the capacity to respond to potential financial threats; and
4. continuing to manage equity investments acquired through TARP in a commercial manner, while protecting taxpayers and unwinding those investments as soon as practicable.

Extending TARP authority is necessary for this strategy to succeed. Therefore, earlier this week I extended that authority until October 3, 2010. While we work to return taxpayer dollars, this Administration will not waver in its commitment to preserve the stability of our financial system and to help restore economic opportunity for American families and small businesses.

TARP Performance

The primary purpose of TARP was to restore the liquidity and stability of our financial system. That system plays a critical role in our economy, for example, by helping businesses raise funds and pay employees, providing consumers with convenient forms of credit, financing education, and allowing millions of Americans to own homes. The success or failure of TARP must be evaluated first and foremost on whether it has achieved that primary purpose.

Second, EESA required that TARP be used in a manner that maximized overall returns to taxpayers, while preserving home ownership and promoting jobs and economic growth.

As I will discuss, TARP has been successful by each measure, although challenges remain that require us to refocus initiatives, particularly toward mitigating foreclosure and getting credit to small businesses.

Impact on the Financial System

Measuring the impact of TARP in isolation is challenging. The health of the overall system and its impact on the U.S. economy are the most important metrics by which we can measure the effectiveness of these policies. However, the cost of the financial system collapse that was averted by TARP and the other government actions taken in the fall of 2008 and since then will never be known. Moreover, it is difficult to measure separately the impact of TARP, as it was part of a coordinated government response to restore confidence in our financial system. Nevertheless, a few TARP programs were uniquely targeted to specific markets and institutions. In those instances, we can measure performance more directly.

At a broad level, confidence in the stability of our financial markets and institutions has improved dramatically over the past year. Interbank lending rates, which reflect stress in the banking system, have returned to levels associated with more stable times. Credit-default swap spreads for financial institutions, which measure investor confidence in their health, have also fallen significantly.

At the same time, borrowing costs have declined for many businesses, homeowners, and municipalities, allowing them to raise substantial capital from private sources. Corporations, for example, have raised over $1 trillion from bond issuance this year. While much of the issuance early this year was supported by government guarantees, private investors have funded most new corporate debt without public support in recent months. Importantly, banks have raised substantial funds from private sources since federal regulators released the results of their "stress test" of major U.S. financial institutions. As a result, the U.S. banking system is better capitalized today. TARP investments provided our financial institutions with an important bridge to critical access to private capital.

More narrowly targeted programs have also had a significant impact. Securitization markets that provide important channels of credit for consumers and small businesses have improved, in large part because of the government's Term Asset-Backed Securities Loan Facility (TALF). Spreads in these markets have narrowed considerably in response to announcements and actions through the program. New issuance has picked up and is shifting from public support to purely private financing. Prices for impaired securities on bank balance sheets have improved significantly this year. Announcements for the Public-Private Investment Program have contributed to these improvements, and the recently-formed Public-Private Investment Funds have started to purchase troubled assets from banks. Meanwhile, housing markets are showing some signs of stabilizing. Thanks in part to federal government financial policies, mortgage rates remain near historic lows, and home prices and sales are increasing. Millions of Americans have refinanced their mortgages since we announced the Making Home Affordable program, and over 650,000 trial modifications have been initiated under the Home Affordable Modification Program, which is largely funded by TARP.

As credit conditions have improved, the U.S. economy has started to grow again, and job losses have slowed. These are significant improvements from where we were last year.

However, the financial and economic recovery still faces significant headwinds. Unemployment remains very high, along with foreclosure and delinquency rates, and housing markets are still overwhelmingly dependent on government support. Lending standards are tight and bank lending continues to contract overall, although the pace of contraction has moderated and residential mortgage lending by banks has stabilized. Commercial real estate losses weigh heavily on many small banks, impairing their ability to extend new loans. Further, although securitization markets have improved, parts of those markets are still impaired, especially for securities backed by commercial mortgages. These conditions place enormous pressure on American families, homeowners, and small businesses, which rely heavily on bank lending. Later, I will describe how we are refocusing EESA-funded programs to mitigate this pressure.

In sum, TARP has largely succeeded in achieving its primary goal, and we are winding down many initiatives established under the program. However, four tasks remain for TARP: preserving financial stability, which is essential for long-term economic growth; mitigating foreclosure for responsible American homeowners; getting credit to small businesses; and supporting securitization markets that facilitate consumer and small business loans.

Financial Returns and Expected Cost

The expected cost of using TARP to stabilize our financial system has fallen dramatically. While EESA provided the Secretary of the Treasury with the authority to invest $700 billion, the ultimate cost for taxpayers will undoubtedly be far less.

One way of evaluating the program's cost is its impact on the Federal deficit. We now expect that TARP's contribution to Federal deficits will be at least $200 billion less than was projected in the August Mid-Session Review of the President's Budget, which assumed a $341 billion cost. And the expected budgetary impact of $364 billion in funds disbursed in Fiscal Year 2009 has fallen from $151 billion to $42 billion.

This improvement is driven by two factors: (1) investments are generating higher returns than previously anticipated, and (2) we do not anticipate using the full spending authority granted by EESA. We now expect to make—not lose—money on $245 billion of investments in banks. We estimate that in the aggregate, major bank stabilization programs funded through TARP will yield a positive net return of over $19 billion, thanks to dividends, interest, early repayments, and the sale of warrants.* In short, taxpayers are being repaid at a substantial profit by banks.

Repayments are already substantial. To date, banks have returned $116 billion in taxpayer investments—nearly one-third of all TARP disbursements to date. Further, we anticipate that total repayments could reach $175 billion by the end of next year; that is, nearly half of TARP disbursements to date.

These early repayments are testaments to the success of the government's efforts to stabilize and rehabilitate our financial system. Private

---

*Warrants are a financial instrument that allows the holder to buy stock in the future at a fixed price. Banks provided the government warrants (basically an equity stake in the bank) in exchange for financial support.

investors now have much greater confidence in the prospects of our major financial institutions. This is reflected in the significant private fundraising by banks this year. Just last week, Bank of America raised $19.3 billion in common equity—after it announced that it would repay $45 billion of government investments. More broadly, the largest U.S. banks have raised over $110 billion in common equity and other regulatory capital since we announced the results of the "stress test" in May. That nearly matches the $116 billion in repayments we have received.

TARP programs have already generated significant income—roughly $15 billion—which has been used to pay down the debt. Our outstanding equity investments continue to generate substantial income through dividends. And we are adding to the taxpayer's return by auctioning warrants. Last week, for example, we raised nearly $150 million from the sale of Capital One warrants. We expect substantial income from additional warrant sales over the next few weeks.

However, we do not expect all TARP investments to generate positive returns. There is a significant likelihood that we will not be repaid for the full value of our investments in AIG, GM, and Chrysler. But here too the outlook has improved. We now expect these institutions to repay $14 billion more than was originally projected.

Furthermore, expenditures through the Home Affordable Modification Program were never intended to generate revenue. Consistent with the mandate of EESA, this program was created to help mitigate foreclosure for responsible but at-risk homeowners. The program requires mortgage lenders to share the financial burden of meeting that goal.

In sum, the ultimate return on TARP investments will depend on how the economy and financial markets evolve, and whether we can reform financial regulation and consumer protection in meaningful, efficient ways. But the bottom line is as follows. In combination with other government programs, TARP helped prevent a financial collapse that would likely have plunged this country into a much deeper recession, led to staggering job losses, and further reduced tax revenue. The financial system continues to improve, private capital is replacing public support, and the economy is growing again. Taxpayers should get back the vast majority of funds invested through TARP. And the ultimate fiscal cost of the program will be substantially less than originally expected, thereby reducing the burden on current and future taxpayers.

Exit Strategy for TARP

Next, I will lay out our exit strategy for TARP. There are four broad elements to that strategy.

First, we will continue terminating and winding down many of the government programs put in place to address the crisis. That process is already well underway. In September, Treasury ended its Money Market

Fund Guarantee Program, which guaranteed at its peak over $3 trillion of assets. The program incurred no losses, and generated $1.2 billion in fees. New issuance under the FDIC's Temporary Liquidity Guarantee Program (TLGP) ended in October. Credit extended through Federal Reserve liquidity programs has declined substantially as market conditions have improved, and most of these programs are scheduled to expire at the beginning of February.

With respect to TARP, support for large financial institutions is coming to an end. The Capital Purchase Program, under which the bulk of support to banks has been provided, is effectively closed. Before this Administration took office, nearly $240 billion in TARP funds had been committed to banks. Since January 20, we have committed approximately $7 billion to banks, much of which went to small institutions. Major U.S. banks subject to the "stress test" conducted last spring have raised over $110 billion in high-quality capital from the private sector. And banks have repaid $116 billion of TARP funds.

Second, we must fulfill EESA's mandate to preserve home ownership, stimulate liquidity for small businesses, and promote jobs and economic growth. To do so, we will limit new commitments in 2010 to three areas.

- We will continue to mitigate foreclosure for responsible American homeowners as we take the steps necessary to stabilize our housing market.
- We recently launched initiatives to provide capital to small and community banks, which are important sources of credit for small businesses. We are also reserving funds for additional efforts to facilitate small business lending.
- Finally, we may increase our commitment to the Term Asset-Backed Securities Loan Facility (TALF), which is improving securitization markets that facilitate consumer and small business loans, as well as commercial mortgage loans. We expect that increasing our commitment to TALF would not result in additional cost to taxpayers.

Third, beyond these limited new commitments, we will not use remaining EESA funds unless necessary to respond to an immediate and substantial threat to the economy stemming from financial instability. As a nation we must maintain capacity to respond to such a threat. Banks are still experiencing significant new credit losses, and the pace of bank failures, which tend to lag economic cycles, remains elevated. At the same time, many of the Federal Reserve and FDIC programs that have complemented TARP investments are ending. This creates a financial environment in which new shocks could have an outsized effect—especially if an adequate financial stability reserve is not maintained. As we wind down many of the government programs launched initially to address the crisis, it is imperative that we maintain this capacity to respond if financial conditions worsen and threaten our economy. However, before using

EESA funds to respond to new financial threats, I would consult with the President and Chairman of the Federal Reserve Board and submit written notification to Congress. This capacity will bolster confidence and improve financial stability, thereby decreasing the probability that it will need to be used.

* * *

By stabilizing our financial system, assisting responsible homeowners, and getting credit to small businesses, EESA authority will continue to improve the outlook for our economy and American workers. And it will do so within the limits established by Congress in EESA. Further, while we are extending the $700 billion program, we do not expect to deploy more than $550 billion. We also expect up to $175 billion in repayments by the end of next year, and substantial additional repayments thereafter. The combination of the reduced scale of TARP commitments and substantial repayments should allow us to commit significant resources to pay down the federal debt over time.

Fourth, we will continue to manage the equity investments acquired through EESA in a commercial manner, while protecting taxpayers and unwinding those investments as soon as practicable. We will exercise our voting rights only on core issues such as election of directors, and not interfere in the day to day management of individual companies. In addition, as the steward of taxpayers' funds, Treasury will manage investments in a manner that ensures accountability, transparency and oversight. And we will work with recipients of EESA funds and their supervisors to accelerate repayment where appropriate. We want to see the capital base of our financial system return to private hands as quickly as possible, while preserving financial stability and promoting economic recovery.

Conclusion

In conclusion, I can report significant improvements in our financial markets and economy, as well as the positive financial results of our TARP programs. However, our job is far from finished. History suggests that exiting too soon from policies designed to contain a financial crisis can significantly prolong an economic downturn. While we exit our emergency financial policies, we must not waver in our resolve to ensure the stability of the financial system and to support the nascent recovery that the Administration and Congress have worked so hard to achieve. Improvements in the financial performance of TARP programs put us in a better position to address the financial and economic challenges that many Americans still face. The Department of the Treasury looks forward to continuing to work with you and the Congress to achieve these goals.

* * *

DISCUSSION QUESTIONS

1. Which of the "hustles" Taibbi describes strike you as the most outrageous? Which seem as if they may have been necessary to stabilize the financial sector?

2. Imagine a debate between Secretary Geithner and Taibbi on a Sunday morning talk show. How do you think Geithner would defend the various "hustles"?

3. How could Congress reform the financial system to prevent the type of crisis the economy suffered in 2008–2009? What could have been done differently to get us out of the crisis?

CHAPTER 15

Government and Society

78

"Growing American Inequality: Sources and Remedies"

GARY BURTLESS

How much, if anything, should the federal government do to promote greater income equality among its citizens? Ignoring the increasing income gap between the richest and poorest Americans, argues Gary Burtless, is a mistake. When more and more Americans see themselves as falling behind, they will show less confidence in political leaders and in government. In addition, income inequalities threaten public health, with larger gaps between rich and poor associated with higher mortality rates and higher incidence of disease. Burtless dismisses the argument that income inequality provides an incentive for the poorest Americans to work harder and earn more, citing evidence that the income of poor Americans has declined in recent years. Public policies that target the working poor—such as the 1986 Tax Reform Act, which eliminated taxes for many low-income Americans and increased the Earned Income Tax Credit—have elevated income levels. But there has been no comparable political support for the "nonworking" poor, and critics charge that the EITC program is riddled with fraud. The 1996 welfare reform, moreover, has been particularly harsh, in Burtless's view. To begin the process of bridging the wage gap, he proposes efforts to bring the nonworking poor into the workforce, and publicly subsidized health care to ease the difficulties of poverty and provide the means for individual families to work their way out of poverty.

Over the past two decades the United States has experienced a startling increase in inequality. The incomes of poor Americans shrank and those of the middle class stagnated while the incomes of the richest families continued to grow. The well-being of families up and down the income scale has increased over the past five years, but the average income of the poorest Americans remains well below where it was at the end of the 1970s.

From the end of World War II until the 1970s, the percentage difference in average cash income between well-to-do and middle-class American families generally declined. In the 1980s, the gap began to widen noticeably. Better measurement of rich families' incomes accounts for some of the apparent jump in the early 1990s, but the gap between middle- and high-income families almost certainly increased after 1992. The cash income difference between middle-income and poor families followed a similar trend. After narrowing for several decades after World War II, largely because of increased wages and improved Social Security and welfare benefits for the poor, the gap began widening in the early 1970s. * * * [T]he trend in inequality has not been driven solely by worsening poverty among the poor or by spectacular income gains among the wealthy. It has been produced by growing disparities between Americans at every level of the income ladder.

Soaring inequality has not been confined to the United States. Rich nations around the world have seen inequality grow since the late 1970s. But the jump in income inequality has been particularly rapid in the United States—and it came on top of a higher initial level of inequality.

Should We Care?

Many Americans are not terribly concerned about income inequality or about the need for public policies to temper inequality. Although public opinion polls find that large majorities of residents in five European countries and Japan believe the government should guarantee each citizen a minimum standard of living, only about a quarter of Americans agree. By and large, Americans tend to believe that people bear primary responsibility for supporting themselves. U.S. citizens are also more likely to believe their society offers an equal opportunity for people who work hard to get ahead. Given these views, why should Americans be concerned about mounting inequality?

One reason for concern is that growing income disparities may undermine Americans' sense of social cohesion. Even if they are indifferent about the abstract principle of economic equality, most Americans probably believe in the ideals of political and legal equality. But greater inequality has almost certainly produced wider discrepancies in political influence and legal bargaining power. In 1979 the income of an American at the 95th percentile of the income distribution was three times the median income and thirteen times the income of an American at the 5th percentile. By 1996 an American at the 95th percentile had an income almost four times the median income and twenty-three times the income of the person at the 5th percentile. The growing income gap between rich, middle-class, and poor and its consequences for the distribution of political influence may contribute to Americans' dwindling confidence that their elected officials care very much about the views of ordinary citizens. According to polling experts Karlyn Bowman and Everett Ladd, in 1960 only a quarter of U.S. respondents agreed with the statement, "I don't think public officials care much about what people like me think." By 1996, the share who agreed had climbed to 60 percent.

Inequality may also affect public health. Demographers and public health researchers have found mounting though controversial evidence that greater inequality can boost mortality rates and contribute to poor health. Countries and communities with above-average inequality have higher mortality rates than countries or communities with comparable incomes and poverty rates but lower inequality. According to one public health researcher, low-income Americans have death rates comparable to those in Bangladesh, one of the world's poorest countries, even though absolute incomes, average consumption, and health care spending are much higher among America's poor than they are in Bangladesh. The possible link between public health and inequality may help explain why the United States, one of the world's wealthiest countries, does not have the longest average life span or the lowest infant mortality rate. If the benefits of U.S. income growth after 1979 had been more equally shared, the average health and life spans of Americans, especially poor Americans, might have improved faster than they did.

Defenders of American economic and political institutions correctly point out that inequality plays a crucial role in creating incentives for people to improve their situations through saving, hard work, and additional schooling. They argue that wage and income disparities must sometimes widen to send correct signals to people to save more, work harder, change jobs, or get a better education. In the long run, poor people might enjoy higher absolute incomes in a society where income disparities are permitted to widen than one where law and social convention keep income differentials small. According to this argument, widening inequality is in the best long-term interest of the poor themselves.

For poor people in the United States, however, the theoretical advantages of greater inequality have proved elusive over the past two decades. Their absolute incomes have not improved; they have declined. Their absolute incomes do not exceed those of low-income residents in countries with less inequality; typically they are lower than those of people in a comparable position in other rich countries. The efficiency advantages, if any, of growing U.S. inequality have not been enjoyed by the poor, at least so far. They have flowed to people much further up the income scale.

Why Has Inequality Increased?

Researchers on income inequality agree on two key facts. Greater family income inequality is closely connected to wider disparities in worker pay—disparities that in turn are associated with rising pay premiums for education, job experience, and occupational skills. In addition, shifts in family composition, specifically the continuing growth of single-parent families and the shrinking fraction of married-couple families, have reinforced the effects of widening wage inequality.

How much of the increase in family income inequality is attributable to rising wage disparities? Both male and female workers saw hourly pay disparities increase over the past two decades, though on average men saw their real earnings fall, while women got a raise. The hourly wage of workers at the 10th percentile fell 16 percent between 1979 and 1997. At the upper end of the pay ladder, wages at the 90th percentile rose 2 percent for men and 24 percent for women. Changes in annual earnings mirrored this pattern. Workers at the bottom of the pay scale saw their yearly labor incomes sink while workers at the top saw their annual pay increase. The gains were especially large among highly paid women.

One way to assess the impact of rising wage disparities on overall income inequality is to calculate how much overall inequality would have changed if wage disparities had remained unchanged. My calculation, using a standard statistical measure of income inequality known as the Gini coefficient, suggests that if male annual earnings disparities had remained unchanged between 1979 and 1996, personal income inequality would have increased about 72 percent of the actual jump. This means that the increase in men's earnings inequality explains about 28 percent of the overall increase in inequality. A similar calculation implies that despite the large increase in pay disparities among women, only about 5 percent of the increase in income inequality can be explained by growing earnings disparities among women. We can combine these two calculations to see what would have happened if male and female earnings inequality had both remained constant after 1979. This third set of calculations suggests that two-thirds of the increase in personal income inequality would have occurred, even without a change in pay disparities. An implication of this finding is that just one-third of the increase in personal income inequality was due to the growth of male and female earnings disparities. Most of the growth was due to some other set of factors.

One factor was the changing American household. In 1979, 74 percent of adults and children lived in married-couple households. By 1996, this share had fallen to 65 percent. Inequality and the incidence of poverty are much lower in married-couple households than in single-adult households. If the percentage of Americans living in married-couple families had remained unchanged after 1979, about one-fifth of the 1979–96 jump in inequality would have been avoided.

Another trend has pushed up income disparities. Women who are married to high-income husbands are increasingly likely to hold year-round jobs and earn high incomes themselves. The increased correlation between husbands' and wives' earnings has widened the income gap between affluent dual-earner families and the rest of the population. If the husband-wife earnings correlation had remained unchanged, about one-eighth of the rise in overall inequality since 1979 would have been avoided. In other words, roughly 13 percent of the increase in income inequality can be traced to the growing correlation between husbands' and wives' earned income.

Policy Response

Though critics of U.S. social policy often overlook the fact, policymakers have not stood still in the face of momentous changes in the income distribution. The direction of policy has shifted noticeably since the early 1980s.

The shift began under President Reagan, who attempted to scale back and reorient welfare programs targeted on the working-age poor. His goal was to make the programs less attractive to potential applicants by cutting benefits or making benefits harder to get. One important policy change, later reversed, was to scale back payments to poor families with a working adult. Reagan thought welfare benefits should be focused on the nonworking poor. He expected working adults to support themselves.

The steep decline in hourly wages of low-skill workers made this view increasingly untenable. Measured in inflation-adjusted dollars, the minimum wage fell more than 30 percent over the 1980s, and wages paid to unskilled young men fell almost as fast. Few breadwinners can support families on wages of $5 or $6 an hour.

Congress and the president responded by reforming tax policy toward low-income families and broadening eligibility for publicly financed health benefits. The Tax Reform Act of 1986 removed millions of low-income Americans from the income tax rolls and boosted the tax rebates low-income workers receive under the Earned Income Tax Credit. The EITC was further liberalized in 1990 and 1993, greatly increasing the credits flowing to low-income breadwinners and their children. Spending on the credit increased elevenfold in the decade after 1986, reaching more than $21 billion by 1996. The credit, payable to breadwinners even if they owe no federal income taxes, has raised the incomes of millions of families with extremely low earnings.

The EITC is the most distinctive American policy innovation on behalf of the working poor, and several European countries may eventually adopt a variant of it. While most cash assistance goes to people who do not work, the EITC goes only to low-income people who do work. In 1997 the credit provided as much as $3,656 to a breadwinner with two or more dependents. For a parent working full time in a minimum-wage job, the EITC can increase net earnings nearly 40 percent.

The idea behind the credit is to encourage work by increasing the incomes available to low-wage breadwinners who have dependent children. Instead of shrinking as a recipient's earnings grow, the credit rises, at least up to a limit. At low earnings levels the credit increases by 34¢ or 40¢ for each extra dollar earned. Most labor economists who have examined the credit conclude that it has contributed to the sudden and sizable increase in job holding among unmarried mothers.

Congress has also liberalized the eligibility requirements for Medicaid health insurance to include a broad population of low-income children with working parents. Until the late 1980s, working-age families with children were usually eligible for health protection only if the families were collecting public assistance. Children typically lost their eligibility for free health insurance when the family breadwinner returned to work. The Medicaid liberalizations of the late 1980s and early 1990s meant that many children were enrolled in the program even if their parents had modest earnings and were not collecting public assistance.

Some state governments have established new programs to provide subsidized health insurance to members of working-poor families, including the adult breadwinners. Congress passed legislation in 1997 offering states generous federal subsidies to establish or enlarge health insurance programs for the working poor and near-poor.

As U.S. policy has expanded tax and health benefits for the working poor, state and federal policymakers have slashed cash assistance to the nonworking poor. General assistance, which provides cash aid to childless adults, has been scaled back or eliminated in several states. Aid to Families with Dependent Children was eliminated in 1996 and replaced with Temporary Assistance to Needy Families (TANF). The new federal program pressures all states to curtail cash benefits to poor parents who are capable of working. The head of each family on welfare is required to work within two years after assistance payments begin. Work-hour requirements are stringent, and states face increasingly harsh penalties for failing to meet them. The law stipulates that the great majority of families may receive benefits for no longer than five years and permits states to impose even shorter time limits. Over a dozen states have already done so.

The new welfare law—and the new state welfare policies that preceded it—helped produce an unprecedented drop in the nation's child welfare rolls. Since peaking in 1994, the number of families collecting public assistance for children has dropped more than 2 million, or 40 percent.

In sum, U.S. policy has become much less generous to the nonworking (but working-age) poor, while it has become much more generous to working-poor adults with children. For many low-wage breadwinners with children, the recent policy changes—the increased generosity of the EITC, Medicaid, state-supported health plans, and child care subsidies—have offset the loss of potential earnings due to shrinking hourly wages.

The reforms are having other economic effects. Poor breadwinners with children have been induced to enter the work force—and stay there. Their entry contributes to the downward pressure on the wages of the least skilled. In effect, public subsidies to the working poor and cuts in welfare benefits to the nonworking poor have helped keep employers' costs low and thus helped fuel employers' creation of poorly paid jobs.

Future Directions

U.S. policies toward low-income, working-age families are not so callous that struggling families have been left wholly on their own to cope with declining wages. But they are not so generous that poor, working-age Americans have shared equally in the prosperity of the past two decades.

Different policies, such as those adopted in Western Europe, would have yielded different results. Some differences, including lower poverty rates and higher wages, make Western Europe a more pleasant place to live, especially for the poor. But others, including high unemployment, are unwelcome. It is not obvious that most Americans, even liberals, would prefer the European approach or approve the policies needed to achieve it.

While the current U.S. policy mix broadly reflects the preferences of U.S. voters, it is haphazard and fails to reach some of those who most need help. Two new policies could aid working-age people who have suffered the worst cuts in hourly pay. The first would assure some of the long-term unemployed a job at a modest wage. The second would make work subsidies more uniformly available and would provide them in a form that most voters approve.

Because public assistance to the nonworking but able-bodied poor is being drastically curtailed, it makes sense to assure at least some poor adults that they will be able to find jobs at a modest wage, however bad the local job market. In some cases this may involve creating publicly subsidized jobs that pay a little less than the minimum wage. It seems particularly important to extend this offer to parents who face the loss of cash public assistance. If voters and policymakers want unskilled parents to begin supporting themselves through jobs, they should assure these parents that some jobs will be available, at least eventually, even when unemployment is high.

For poorly paid breadwinners, it is essential to improve the rewards from working. One possibility is to make a basic package of subsidized health insurance available to all children and young adults. Many Americans regard health insurance for children as a fair and acceptable way to help those in need.

Most health insurance for children is either publicly subsidized through Medicaid or privately provided through employer health plans. When insurance is financed by employers, most of the cost to employers shows up as lower money wages paid to workers. By publicly assuming some or all of the cost of paying for a basic health package for children, we could push employers to boost the wages they pay to insured workers who have child dependents. Such a move would have a greater impact on the pay of low-wage workers, for whom health insurance represents a big fraction of compensation, than on the pay of high-wage workers.

About 15 percent of all children (and nearly a quarter of poor children) have no health insurance. For these children and their working parents, publicly subsidized child health insurance would directly improve well-being and reduce out-of-pocket spending on medical care. It would also greatly increase the reward to work. Parents who do not work qualify for free medical insurance for themselves and for their children under Medicaid. Some lose this insurance when they accept a job that pays modest but above-poverty-level wages. A public health insurance package for all children would reduce or eliminate this penalty for accepting a job.

American economic progress over the past two decades has been quite uneven. Families and workers at the top of the economic ladder have enjoyed rising incomes. Families in the middle have made much smaller income gains. Workers at the bottom have suffered a sharp erosion in their relative income position. For some low-income workers, new public policies have helped offset the loss of wages with larger earnings supplements and better health insurance. But many low-wage workers have not benefited from these policies. Humane public policy should try to assure that the most vulnerable Americans share at least modestly in the nation's prosperity.

DISCUSSION QUESTIONS

1. According to the AFL-CIO, the average pay of working Americans grew by 68 percent over a recent twenty-year period. The pay of an average major-company CEO, by contrast, grew by 1,600 percent during the same period, and was more than 420 times higher than the wage of an average worker. These statistics seem to confirm Burtless's assessment that any "efficiency advantages . . . of growing U.S. inequality . . . have flowed to people much further up the income scale." Similarly, people often bemoan the fact that a top movie or sports star will earn in one movie or one season more than a teacher or nurse might earn in a lifetime. Are these differences in income simply the sign of a highly competitive free-market economy? Should government be concerned with these differentials? If so, what kind of government policy might address the concern?

2. To some, "reducing wage inequalities" is simply another way of saying "income redistribution." How would a policy geared toward reducing wage inequalities affect the economic incentives faced by individuals? Might we reduce the incentive for people to work hard, invest in their education, and take risks?

3. Will the health care reform passed in 2010 and discussed later in this chapter address some of Burtless's concerns?

79

"Objections to These Unions"

Jonathan Rauch

One of the most controversial and politically significant issues in the past few years is same-sex marriage. Jonathan Rauch is less interested in the electoral impact of the same-sex marriage issue than in trying to understand why people are opposed to this form of marriage. He suggests two reasons: the simple antihomosexual position and the not-so-simple view based on tradition. The latter is rooted in the gut-level feeling that marriage between two men or two women is simply wrong because marriage has always been between a man and a woman: no law can change this basic institution because it has roots that are deeper and older than any government or law. Rauch situates this argument within the political thought of F. A. Hayek, one of the great conservative thinkers of the twentieth century. Hayek warns that changing traditions and customs may lead to social chaos. This is precisely one of the arguments made against same-sex marriage: it will undermine the institution of marriage. Rauch replies that other changes have had a far greater impact on undermining the institution of marriage, such as allowing women to own property, the abolition of arranged marriages, legalized contraception, and "no-fault" divorce law. While recognizing the legitimacy of the concerns about same-sex marriage, Rauch concludes that the fears of its negative impact are overstated and the benefits of same-sex marriage for gays and lesbians outweigh the costs for heterosexuals.

There are only two objections to same-sex marriage that are intellectually honest and internally consistent. One is the simple anti-gay position: "It is the law's job to stigmatize and disadvantage homosexuals, and the marriage ban is a means to that end." The other is the argument from tradition—which turns out, on inspection, not to be so simple.

Many Americans may agree that there are plausible, even compelling, reasons to allow same-sex marriage, and that many of the objections to such unions are overwrought, unfair, or misguided. And yet they draw back. They have reservations that are hard to pin down but that seem not a whit less powerful for that. They may cite religion or culture, but the roots of their misgivings go even deeper. Press them, and they might say something like this:

"I understand how hard it must be to live a marriageless life, or at least I try to understand. I see that some of the objections to same-sex marriage are more about excluding gays than about defending marriage.

Believe me, I am no homophobe; I want gay people to have joy and comfort. I respect their relationships and their love, even if they are not what I would want for myself.

"But look. No matter how I come at this question, I keep bumping into the same wall. For the entire history of civilization, marriage has been between men and women. In every religion, every culture, every society—maybe with some minor and rare exceptions, none of them part of our own heritage—marriage has been reserved for the union of male and female. All the words in the world cannot change that. Same-sex marriage would not be an incremental tweak but a radical reform, a break with all of Western history.

"I'm sorry. I am not prepared to take that step, not when we are talking about civilization's bedrock institution. I don't know that I can even give you good reasons. It is just that what you are asking for is too much."

Perhaps it doesn't matter what marriage is for, or perhaps we can't know exactly what marriage is for. Perhaps it is enough simply to say that marriage is as it is, and you can't just make it something else. I call this the Hayekian argument, for Friedrich August von Hayek, one of the 20th century's great economists and philosophers.

Hayek the Conservative?

Hayek—Austrian by birth, British by adoption, winner of the 1974 Nobel Memorial Prize in Economic Sciences—is generally known as one of the leading theoreticians of free market economics and, more broadly, of libertarian (he always said "liberal") social thought. He was eloquent in his defense of the dynamic change that markets bring, but many people are less aware of a deeply traditionalist, conservative strand in his thinking, a strand that traces its lineage back at least to Edmund Burke, the 18th-century English philosopher and politician. Burke famously poured scorn on the French Revolution and its claims to be inventing a new and enlightened social order. The attempt to reinvent society on abstract principles would result not in Utopia, he contended, but in tyranny. For Burke, the existing order might be flawed, even in some respects evil, but it had an organic sense to it; throwing the whole system out the window would bring greater flaws and larger evils.

Outside Britain and America, few people listened. The French Revolution inspired generations of reformers to propose their own Utopian social experiments. Communism was one such, fascism another; today, radical Islamism (the political philosophy, not the religion) is yet one more. "The attempt to make heaven on earth invariably produces hell," wrote Karl Popper, another great Austrian-British philosopher, in 1945, when the totalitarian night looked darkest. He and Hayek came of age in the same intellectual climate, when not only Marxists and fascists but many mainstream Western intellectuals took for granted that a handful of smart people could make better social decisions than could chaotic markets, blind traditions, or crude majorities.

It was in opposition to this "fatal conceit," as he called it, that Hayek organized much of his career. He vigorously argued the case for the dynamism and "spontaneous order" of free markets, but he asserted just as vigorously that the dynamism and freedom of constant change were possible only within a restraining framework of rules and customs and institutions that, for the most part, do not change, or change at a speed they themselves set. No expert or political leader can possibly have enough knowledge to get up every morning and order the world from scratch; decide whether to wear clothing, which side of the street to drive on, what counts as mine and what as yours. "Every man growing up in a given culture will find in himself rules, or may discover that he acts in accordance with rules and will similarly recognize the actions of others as conforming or not conforming to various rules," Hayek wrote in *Law, Legislation, and Liberty*. The rules, he added, are not necessarily innate or unchangeable, but "they are part of a cultural heritage which is likely to be fairly constant, especially so long as they are not articulated in words and therefore also are not discussed or consciously examined."

Tradition Over Reason

Hayek the economist is famous for the insight that, in a market system, the prices generated by impersonal forces may not make sense from any one person's point of view, but they encode far more economic information than even the cleverest person or the most powerful computer could ever hope to organize. In a similar fashion, Hayek the social philosopher wrote that human societies' complicated web of culture, traditions, and institutions embodies far more cultural knowledge than anyone person could master. Like prices, the customs generated by societies over time may seem irrational or arbitrary. But the very fact that these customs have evolved and survived to come down to us implies that a practical logic may be embedded in them that might not be apparent from even a sophisticated analysis. And the web of custom cannot be torn apart and reordered at will, because once its internal logic is violated it may fall apart.

It was on this point that Hayek was particularly outspoken: Intellectuals and visionaries who seek to deconstruct and rationally rebuild social traditions will produce not a better order but chaos. In his 1952 book *The Counter-Revolution of Science: Studies in the Abuse of Reason*, Hayek made a statement that demands to be quoted in full and read at least twice:

> It may indeed prove to be far the most difficult and not the least important task for human reason rationally to comprehend its own limitations. It is essential for the growth of reason that as individuals we should bow to forces and obey principles which we cannot hope fully to understand, yet on which

the advance and even the preservation of civilization depends. Historically this has been achieved by the influence of the various religious creeds and by traditions and superstitions which made man submit to those forces by an appeal to his emotions rather than to his reason. The most dangerous stage in the growth of civilization may well be that in which man has come to regard all these beliefs as superstitions and refuses to accept or to submit to anything which he does not rationally understand. The rationalist whose reason is not sufficient to teach him those limitations of the powers of conscious reason, and who despises all the institutions and customs which have not been consciously designed, would thus become the destroyer of the civilization built upon them. This may well prove a hurdle which man will repeatedly reach, only to be thrown back into barbarism.

For secular intellectuals who are unhappy with the evolved framework of marriage and who are excluded from it—in other words, for people like me—the Hayekian argument is very challenging. The age-old stigmas attached to illegitimacy and out-of-wedlock pregnancy were crude and unfair to women and children. On the male side, shotgun marriages were coercive and intrusive and often made poor matches. The shame associated with divorce seemed to make no sense at all. But when modern societies abolished the stigmas on illegitimacy, divorce, and all the rest, whole portions of the social structure just caved in.

Not long ago I had dinner with a friend who is a devout Christian. He has a heart of gold, knows and likes gay people, and has warmed to the idea of civil unions. But when I asked him about gay marriage, he replied with a firm no. I asked if he imagined there was anything I could say that might budge him. He thought for a moment and then said no again. Why? Because, he said, male-female marriage is a sacrament from God. It predates the Constitution and every other law of man. We could not, in that sense, change it even if we wanted to. I asked if it might alter his conclusion to reflect that legal marriage is a secular institution, that the separation of church and state requires us to distinguish God's law from civil law, and that we must refrain from using law to impose one group's religious precepts on the rest of society. He shook his head. No, he said. This is bigger than that.

I felt he had not answered my argument. His God is not mine, and in a secular country, law can and should be influenced by religious teachings but must not enforce them. Yet in a deeper way, it was I who had not answered his argument. No doubt the government has the right to set the law of marriage without kowtowing to, say the Vatican. But that does not make it wise for the government to disregard the centuries of tradition—of accumulated social knowledge—that the teachings of the world's great religions embody. None of those religions sanctions same-sex marriage.

My friend understood the church-state distinction perfectly well. He was saying there are traditions and traditions. Male-female marriage is one of the most hallowed. Whether you call it a sacrament from God or part of Western civilization's cultural DNA, you are saying essentially the same thing: that for many people a same-sex union, whatever else it may be, can never be a marriage, and that no judge or legislature can change this fact.

Here the advocates of same-sex marriage face peril coming from two directions. On the one side, the Hayekian argument warns of unintended and perhaps grave social consequences if, thinking we're smarter than our customs, we decide to rearrange the core elements of marriage. The current rules for marriage may not be the best ones, and they may even be unfair. But they are all we have, and you cannot reengineer the formula without causing unforeseen results, possibly including the implosion of the institution itself. On the other side, political realism warns that we could do serious damage to the legitimacy of marital law if we rewrote it with disregard for what a large share of Americans recognize as marriage.

If some state passed a law allowing you to marry a Volkswagen, the result would be to make a joke of the law. Certainly legal gay marriage would not seem so silly, but people who found it offensive or illegitimate might just ignore it or, in effect, boycott it. Civil and social marriage would fall out of step. That might not be the end of the world—the vast majority of marriages would be just as they were before—but it could not do marriage, or the law any good either. In such an environment, same-sex marriage would offer little beyond legal arrangements that could be provided just as well through civil unions, and it would come at a price in diminished respect for the law.

Call those, then, the problem of unintended consequences and the problem of legitimacy. They are the toughest problems same-sex marriage has to contend with. But they are not intractable.

The Decoy of Traditional Marriage

The Hayekian position really comes in two quite different versions, one much more sweeping than the other. In its strong version, the Hayekian argument implies that no reforms of longstanding institutions or customs should ever be undertaken, because any legal or political meddling would interfere with the natural evolution of social mores. One would thus have had to say, a century and a half ago, that slavery should not be abolished, because it was customary in almost all human societies. More recently, one would have had to say that the federal government was wrong to step in and end racial segregation instead of letting it evolve at its own pace.

Obviously, neither Hayek nor any reputable follower of his would defend every cultural practice simply on the grounds that it must exist for a reason. Hayekians would point out that slavery violated a fundamental tenet of justice and was intolerably cruel. In calling for slavery's abolition, they would do what they must do to be human: They would establish a moral standpoint from which to judge social rules and reforms. They thus would acknowledge that sometimes society must make changes in the name of fairness or decency, even if there are bound to be hidden costs.

If the ban on same-sex marriage were only mildly unfair or if the costs of lifting it were certain to be catastrophic, then the ban could stand on Hayekian grounds. But if there is any social policy today that has a claim to being scaldingly inhumane, it is the ban on gay marriage. Marriage, after all, is the most fundamental institution of society and, for most people, an indispensable element of the pursuit of happiness. For the same reason that tinkering with marriage should not be undertaken lightly (marriage is important to personal and social well-being), barring a whole class of people from marrying imposes an extraordinary deprivation. Not so long ago, it was illegal in certain parts of the United States for blacks to marry whites; no one would call this a trivial disfranchisement. For many years, the champions of women's suffrage were patted on the head and told, "Your rallies and petitions are all very charming, but you don't really need to vote, do you?" It didn't wash. The strong Hayekian argument has traction only against a weak moral claim.

To rule out a moral and emotional claim as powerful as the right to marry for love, saying that bad things might happen is not enough. Bad things always might happen. People predicted that bad things would happen if contraception became legal and widespread, and indeed bad things did happen, but that did not make legalizing contraception the wrong thing to do; and, in any case, good things happened too. Unintended consequences can also be positive, after all.

Besides, by now the traditional understanding of marriage, however you define it, has been tampered with in all kinds of ways, some of them more consequential than gay marriage is likely to be. No-fault divorce dealt a severe blow to, "till death do us part," which was certainly an essential element of the traditional meaning of marriage.

It is hard to think of a bigger affront to tradition than allowing married women to own property independently of their husbands. In *What Is Marriage For?*, her history of marriage, the journalist E. J. Graff quotes a 19th-century New York legislator as saying that allowing wives to own property would affront both God and nature, "degrading the holy bonds of matrimony [and] striking at the root of those divinely ordained principles upon which is built the superstructure of our society." In 1844 a New York legislative committee said that permitting married women to control their own property would lead to "infidelity in the marriage bed, a high rate of divorce, and increased female criminality" and would turn marriage "from its high and holy purpose" into something arranged for "convenience and sensuality." A British parliamentarian denounced the proposal as "contrary not only to the law of England but to the law of God."

Graff assembles other quotations in the same vein, and goes on to add, wryly, "The funny thing, of course, is that those jeremiads were right."

Allowing married women to control their economic destinies did indeed open the door to today's high divorce rates; but it also transformed marriage into something less like servitude for women and more in keeping with liberal principles of equality in personhood and citizenship.

An off-the-cuff list of fundamental changes to marriage would include not only divorce and property reform but also the abolition of polygamy, the fading of dowries, the abolition of childhood betrothals, the elimination of parents' right to choose mates for their children or to veto their children's choices, the legalization of interracial marriage, the legalization of contraception, the criminalization of marital rape (an offense that wasn't even recognized until recently), and of course the very concept of civil marriage. Surely it is unfair to say that marriage may be reformed for the sake of anyone and everyone except homosexuals, who must respect the dictates of tradition.

Some people will argue that permitting same-sex marriage would be a more fundamental change than any of the earlier ones. Perhaps so; but equally possible is that we forget today just how unnatural and destabilizing and contrary to the meaning of marriage it once seemed, for example, to put the wife on a par, legally, with the husband. Anyway, even if it is true that gay marriage constitutes a more radical definitional change than earlier innovations, in an important respect it stands out as one of the narrowest of reforms. All the earlier alterations directly affected many or all married couples, whereas same-sex marriage would directly pertain to only a small minority. It isn't certain that allowing same-sex couples to marry would have any noticeable effect on heterosexual marriage at all.

True, you never know what might happen when you tinker with tradition. A catastrophe cannot be ruled out. It is worth bearing in mind, though, that predictions of disaster if open homosexuals are integrated into traditionally straight institutions have a perfect track record: They are always wrong. When openly gay couples began making homes together in suburban neighborhoods, the result was not Sodom on every street corner; when openly gay executives began turning up in corporate jobs, stud collars did not replace neckties. I vividly remember, when I lived in London in 1995, the forecasts of morale and unit cohesion crumbling if open homosexuals were allowed to serve in the British armed forces. But when integration came (under court order), the whole thing turned out to be a nonevent. Again and again, the homosexual threat turns out to be imaginary; straights have far less to fear from gay inclusion than gays do from exclusion.

Jeopardizing Marriage's Universality

So the extreme Hayekian position—never reform anything—is untenable. And that point was made resoundingly by no less an authority than F. A. Hayek himself. In a 1960 essay called "Why I Am Not a Conservative," he took pains to argue that his position was as far from that of reactionary traditionalists as from that of utopian rationalists. "Though there is a need for a 'brake on the vehicle of progress,'" he said, "I personally cannot be content with simply helping to apply the brake." Classical liberalism, he writes, "has never been a backward-looking doctrine." To the contrary, it recognizes, as reactionary conservatism often fails to, that change is a constant and the world cannot be stopped in its tracks.

His own liberalism, Hayek wrote, "shares with conservatism a distrust of reason to the extent that the liberal is very much aware that we do not know all the answers," but the liberal, unlike the reactionary conservative, does not imagine that simply clinging to the past or "claiming the authority of supernatural sources of knowledge" is any kind of answer. We must move ahead, but humbly and with respect for our own fallibility.

And there are times, Hayek said (in *Law, Legislation, and Liberty*), when what he called "grown law" requires correction by legislation. "It may be due simply to the recognition that some past development was based on error or that it produced consequences later recognized as unjust," he wrote. "But the most frequent cause is probably that the development of the law has lain in the hands of members of a particular class whose traditional views made them regard as just what could not meet the more general requirements of justice . . . Such occasions when it is recognized that some hereto accepted rules are unjust in the light of more general principles of justice may well require the revision not only of single rules but of whole sections of the established system of case law."

That passage, I think, could have been written with gay marriage in mind. The old view that homosexuals were heterosexuals who needed punishment or prayer or treatment has been exposed as an error. What homosexuals need is the love of another homosexual. The ban on same-sex marriage, hallowed though it is, no longer accords with liberal justice or the meaning of marriage as it is practiced today. Something has to give. Standing still is not an option.

Hayek himself, then, was a partisan of the milder version of Hayekianism. This version is not so much a prescription as an attitude. Respect tradition. Reject utopianism. Plan for mistakes rather than for perfection. If reform is needed, look for paths that follow the terrain of custom, if possible. If someone promises to remake society on rational or supernatural or theological principles, run in the opposite direction. In sum: Move ahead, but be careful.

Good advice. But not advice, particularly, against gay marriage. Remember Hayek's admonition against dogmatic conservatism. In a shifting current, holding your course can be just as dangerous as oversteering. Conservatives, in their panic to stop same-sex marriage, jeopardize marriage's universality and ultimately its legitimacy. They are taking risks, and big ones, and unnecessary ones. The liberal tradition and the *Declaration of Independence* are not currents you want to set marriage against.

It is worth recalling that Burke, the patron saint of social conservatism and the scourge of the French Revolution, supported the American Revolution. He distinguished between a revolt that aimed to overthrow established rights and principles and a revolt that aimed to restore them. Many of the American founders, incidentally, made exactly the same distinction. Whatever else they may have been, they were not Utopian social engineers. Whether a modern-day Burke or Jefferson would support gay marriage, I cannot begin to say; but I am confident they would, at least, have understood and carefully weighed the possibility that to preserve the liberal foundation of civil marriage, we may find it necessary to adjust its boundaries.

DISCUSSION QUESTIONS

1. The idea that same-sex marriage radically redefines the institution of marriage is a key premise of the traditional argument. If you find this premise persuasive, why so? If not, explain why not.

2. Is protecting the institution of marriage an important societal goal? If so, how could that be accomplished? Is this an appropriate area for government involvement? In a society where individualism and equality are said to be important values, should marriage convey any legal benefits or advantages that are not available to single people?

3. Should the strong public opposition to same-sex marriage be a factor in whether states allow this form of marriage? Or is this an issue where public opinion should be less relevant? If so, why?

80

"Providing Social Security Benefits in the Future: A Review of the Social Security System and Plans to Reform It"

David C. John

There is wide agreement that Social Security requires major reforms if it is to continue to provide economic security to retirees. The baby boom generation will be retiring soon and the amount of money paid in benefits will exceed payroll taxes that are used to fund the system by 2016. The program has been running a surplus for the past two decades, but the government has been spending this money and giving the Social Security trust fund special Treasury bonds that will be repaid with general revenue between 2016 and 2038, when the bonds will be gone. By 2030 there will be only 2.2 workers for every retiree, which means that this "pay as you go" program will be facing a series of increasingly difficult choices about how to meet its obligations.

At the heart of the debate are two contrasting perspective of what the Social Security system should accomplish, both deeply rooted in American political culture: Should we view Social Security as a national guarantee of basic income for all individuals in their retirement, no matter what? Or should Social Security be an individualistic program that permits people to succeed—or fail—based on the choices that they make? To put it another way, is Social Security a social welfare program or an investment program? David John weighs into this controversy by outlining some principles for Social Security reform, providing an overview of five plans for reform, and then discussing the central characteristics of the Social Security program that are necessary for understanding the debate over reform. John is a strong supporter of personal retirement accounts (PRA), which would allow workers to invest a portion of their Social Security taxes. However, as John notes, none of these plans addresses the "transition problem." That is, because Social Security is a "pay as you go" program—today's workers pay for the Social Security benefits of today's retirees—if today's workers are allowed to take a portion of their Social Security taxes and put them in a PRA, this means that there will be even less money to pay for the current obligations to retirees than under the current system, at least for the next several decades. John writes, "Neither the current system nor any of the proposed reform plans comes close to closing the gap."

Social Security is the best-loved American government program, but how it works and is financed is almost completely unknown. Most Americans have a vague idea that they pay taxes for their benefits and that their benefits are linked somehow to their earnings. Many also know that the program is in trouble and needs to be "fixed" sometime soon to deal with the retirement of the baby boomers. Beyond this, their knowledge of the facts is severely limited and often colored by rumors and stories.

Most politicians exploit this lack of knowledge and limit their statements on Social Security to platitudes and vague promises. To make matters worse, reformers tend either to be content with similar platitudes or to speak in such detail that few outside the policy world can understand what they are saying. The simple fact is that today's Social Security is extremely complex, and any reform plan that is more than fine words will be similarly complex.

This paper attempts to simplify the reform debate by comparing various plans (including the current system) side by side. Each of the six sections of this paper compares how the current system and the reform plans handle a specific subject. Only reform plans that have been scored by Social Security's Office of the Chief Actuary are included in this comparison, using numbers contained in the 2003 Report of the Social Security Trustees. * * *

While looking at just one or two sections of special interest may be tempting, this approach would probably be misleading. For the best effect, each section should be considered together with the other sections in order to form a complete picture of the plan. Using simply one section by itself to judge an entire plan will not yield an accurate result.

Seven Important Rules for Real Social Security Reform

Information in this side-by-side comparison is based on Social Security's scoring memos for each plan and conclusions that can be drawn from information contained in those memos. While there are many good points in the reform plans examined in this analysis, this is not an endorsement of any proposal by the author or The Heritage Foundation. Instead, this comparison provides details of specific plans. However, it would be wise for reformers to follow a set of general principles to ensure that any Social Security reform both resolves Social Security's problems and provides workers with greater retirement security. Those principles are listed below.

This comparison of plans makes no effort to examine whether the Social Security reform plans included in it meet or violate any or all of the principles.

Principles for Social Security Reform

- **The benefits of current retirees and those close to retirement must not be reduced.** The government has a moral contract with those who currently receive Social Security retirement benefits, as well as with those who are so close to retirement, that they have no other options for building a retirement nest egg. If the benefits of younger workers cannot be maintained given the need to curb the burgeoning cost of the program, then they should have the opportunity to make up the difference by investing a portion of their Social Security taxes in a personal retirement account.
- **The rate of return on a worker's Social Security taxes must be improved.** Today's workers receive very poor returns on their Social Security payroll taxes. As a general rule, the younger a worker is or the lower his or her income, the lower his or her rate of return will be. Reform must provide a better retirement income to future retirees without increasing Social Security taxes. The best way to do this is to allow workers to divert a portion of their existing Social Security taxes into a personal retirement account that can earn significantly more than Social Security can pay.
- **Americans must be able to use Social Security to build a nest egg for the future.** A well-designed retirement system includes three elements: regular monthly retirement income, dependent's insurance, and the ability to save for retirement. Today's Social Security system provides a stable level of retirement income and does provide benefits for dependents. But it does not allow workers to accumulate cash savings to fulfill their own retirement goals or to pass on to their heirs. Workers should be able to use Social Security to build a cash nest egg that can be used to increase their retirement income or to build a better economic future for their families. The best way to do this is to establish, within the framework of Social Security, a system of personal retirement accounts.
- **Personal retirement accounts must guarantee an adequate minimum income.** Seniors must be able to count on a reasonable and predictable minimum level of monthly income, regardless of what happens in the investment markets.
- **Workers should be allowed to fund their Social Security personal retirement accounts by allocating some of their existing payroll tax dollars to them.** Workers should not be required to pay twice for their benefits—once through existing payroll taxes and again through additional income taxes or contributions used to fund a personal retirement account. Moreover, many working Americans can save little after paying

existing payroll taxes and so cannot be expected to make additional contributions to a personal account. Thus Congress should allow Americans to divert a portion of the taxes that they currently pay for Social Security retirement benefits into personal retirement accounts.

- **For currently employed workers, participation in the new accounts must be voluntary.** No one should be forced into a system of personal retirement accounts. Instead, currently employed workers must be allowed to choose between today's Social Security and one that offers personal retirement accounts.
- **Any Social Security reform plan must be realistic, cost-effective and reduce the unfunded liabilities of the current system.** True Social Security reform will provide an improved total retirement benefit. But it should also reduce Social Security's huge unfunded liabilities by a greater level than the "transition" cost needed to finance benefits for retirees during the reform. Like paying points to obtain a better mortgage, Social Security reform should lead to a net reduction in liabilities.

The Social Security System and Plans for Reform

The Current System

Social Security currently pays an inflation-indexed monthly retirement and survivors' benefit, based on a worker's highest 35 years of earnings. Past earnings are indexed for average wage growth in the economy before calculating the benefit. The benefit formula is progressive, meaning that lower-income workers receive a benefit equal to a higher proportion of their average income than upper-income workers receive. The program is expected to continue to collect more in payroll taxes than it pays out in benefits until about 2018.

Unused payroll taxes are borrowed by the federal government and replaced by special-issue Treasury bonds. After the system begins to pay out more than it receives, the federal government will cover the resulting cash flow deficits by repaying the special-issue Treasury bonds out of general revenues. When the bonds run out in about 2042, Social Security benefits will automatically be reduced to a level equal to incoming revenue. This is projected to require a 27 percent reduction in 2042, with greater reductions after that.

The DeMint Plan

Representative Jim DeMint (R-SC) has introduced a voluntary personal retirement account (PRA) plan that would establish progressively funded voluntary individual accounts for workers under age 55 on January 1, 2005. The amount that goes into each worker's account would vary according to income, with lower-income workers able to save a higher percentage. For average-income workers, the account would equal about 5.1 percent of income.

The government would pay the difference between the monthly benefit that can be financed from an annuity paid for by using all or some of the PRA and the amount that the current system promises. The sum of the annuity and the government-paid portion of Social Security would be guaranteed at least to equal benefits promised under the current system, and 35 percent of PRA assets would be invested in government bonds to help pay for any Social Security cash flow deficits. This proportion would be reduced gradually in the future. General revenue money would be used to pay for additional cash flow deficits.

The Graham Plan

Senator Lindsay Graham (R-SC) has proposed a plan that would give workers under age 55 (in 2004) three options. (Workers above the age of 55 would be required to remain in the current system and would receive full benefits.)

Under *Option 1*, workers would establish PRAs funded with part of their existing payroll taxes, equal to 4 percent of pay up to a maximum of $1,300 per year. Workers' benefits would be reduced by changing the benefit indexing formula from the current wage growth index to one based on consumer prices. Over time, this change would reduce benefits for workers at all income levels, but the effect on lower-income workers would be eased by a mandated minimum benefit of at least 120 percent of the poverty level for workers with a 35-year work history. The government-paid monthly benefit would be further reduced to reflect the value of the PRA. This reduction would be calculated using the average earnings of government bonds so that, if the PRA earned more than government bonds, the total monthly benefit would be higher. Option 1 also raises survivor benefits to 75 percent of the couple's benefit for many survivors.

Option 2 is essentially the same as Option 1, but without PRAs. The government would pay all benefits for workers who choose this option. Option 2 includes both the basic benefit reduction and the minimum benefit requirement.

Option 3 pays the same level of benefits promised under current law, but workers who select this option would pay higher payroll taxes in return. Initially, the payroll tax rate for retirement and survivors benefits would increase from 12.4 percent of income to 14.4 percent of income (counting both the worker's and the employer's shares of the tax). In subsequent years, the tax rate would continue to climb in 0.25 percent increments.

The Smith Plan

Representative Nick Smith (R–MI) has proposed a voluntary PRA plan that would create personal retirement savings accounts funded with an amount equal to 2.5 percent of income, paid out of existing payroll taxes. This would increase to 2.75 percent of income in 2025 and could become larger after 2038 if Social Security has surplus cash flows. Retirement and survivors' benefits would be reduced by an amount equal to the value of lifetime account contributions plus a specified interest rate.

The Smith plan would also make many changes in Social Security's benefit formula, mainly affecting middle-income and upper-income workers. These changes would eventually result in most workers receiving a flat monthly benefit of about $550 in 2004 dollars. It would also gradually increase the retirement age for full benefits and require that all newly hired local and state workers be covered by Social Security. The Smith plan transfers $866 billion from general revenues to Social Security between 2007 and 2013 to help cover cash flow deficits and allows additional general revenue transfers when needed after that.

The Ferrara Plan

Peter Ferrara, Director of the International Center for Law and Economics, has proposed a plan that would create voluntary PRAs that would be funded according to a progressive formula that allows lower-income workers to save a higher proportion of their payroll taxes than upper-income workers. Average-income workers could save about 6.4 percent of their income. Workers would be guaranteed that the total of their PRA-generated benefits and government-paid monthly benefits would at least equal the benefits promised under the current system.

Any Social Security cash flow deficits that remain would be financed through general revenue transfers equal to a 1 percent reduction in the growth rate of all government spending for eight years, the corporate income taxes deemed to result from the investment of personal account contributions, and issuing about $1.4 trillion in "off-budget" bonds. Under the Ferrara plan, these bonds would be considered a replacement for the existing system's unfunded liability and thus would not increase the federal debt.

The Orszag-Diamond Plan

Peter Orszag, Senior Fellow at the Brookings Institution,* and Peter Diamond, Institute Professor of Economics at the Massachusetts Institute of Technology, have developed a plan that does not include any form of PRA or government investment of Social Security trust fund money in private markets. Instead, it gradually changes the benefit formula to reduce benefits for moderate-income and upper-income workers and requires that all

*Peter Orszag was President Obama's Budget Director at the Office of Management and Budget until July 2010. He now is at the Council on Foreign Relations [Editors].

state and local government workers come under Social Security. It would also gradually reduce benefits by raising the age at which workers could receive full benefits. Workers could still retire earlier, but at lower benefits. Benefits would increase for lower-income workers, widows, and the disabled.

In addition, the plan would gradually increase the payroll tax for all workers from the current 12.4 percent of income to 15.36 percent of income in 2078. It would also raise the earnings threshold on Social Security taxes—thus requiring higher-income workers to pay additional payroll taxes—and impose a new 3 percent tax on income above the earnings threshold. Workers would not receive any credit toward benefits for income covered by this new tax.

* * *

1. Personal Retirement Accounts

What Is This, and Why Is It Important?

Allowing workers to invest a portion of their Social Security taxes is the only alternative to raising Social Security taxes or reducing Social Security benefits. However, personal retirement accounts are not all equal. The money that goes into the PRAs could come from diverting a portion of existing Social Security taxes or from some other source.

Similarly, the size of the accounts (usually expressed as a percentage of the worker's pay) is important. While larger accounts would temporarily increase the amount of additional funds required to pay benefits to retirees, they would also accumulate a pool of money faster than smaller accounts and finance a greater portion of benefits in future years. This can reduce the amount of additional tax dollars needed in future decades.

Finally, how the PRAs are invested is important. Even though they show steady growth over time stocks and commercial bonds are generally more volatile than government bonds. Investing a portion of the PRAs in government bonds makes the accounts slightly less volatile while providing some of the additional dollars needed to pay benefits to current retirees.

2. Retirement and Survivors Benefits

What Is This, and Why Is It Important?

Other than creating personal retirement accounts that allow workers to self-fund all or a portion of their Social Security retirement benefits, most reform plans deal with the program's coming deficits by either changing the level of retirement benefits promised or finding ways to increase program revenues. This section examines how various reform plans treat promised retirement benefits.

Social Security uses a complex formula to calculate an individual worker's retirement benefits. Subtle changes in this formula can cause a large change in benefits over time. For instance, changing how past income is indexed to a constant purchasing power will have only a minor impact for the first several years. However, the effect is cumulative and after several decades will result in major changes in benefits.

Similarly, seemingly minor changes in "bend points" or other aspects of the benefit formula can, over the long term, cause major changes in benefits for upper-income and/or moderate-income workers. It is even possible to use the benefit formula to approximate an increase in the full retirement age without actually raising it. Thus, a plan could still allow workers to quality for "full retirement benefits" at 65, 66, or 67 but award them full retirement benefits (as defined under the current system) only if they wait to retire until a later age.

The first question that any plan must answer is whether it would pay the full level of benefits promised under the current system. If so, it must deal with how to pay the cost, since the current system cannot afford to pay for all of the promised benefits. Other important questions include whether the plan proposes benefit changes (usually reductions) if workers do not choose to have a personal retirement account, protects lower-income workers (who more often have an interrupted work history) by instituting some sort of minimum benefit level, and/or addresses the low benefits for certain lower-income, widowed, and disabled workers under the current system.

3. Payroll Taxes

What Is This, and Why Is It Important?

Increasing Social Security payroll taxes would be one way to pay projected cash flow deficits. This method is closer to the self-funding that has characterized the system so far, but raising payroll taxes has significant drawbacks. Alternatives to payroll tax increases include instituting some form of personal retirement account to increase the return on taxes, reducing benefits, and using significant amounts of general revenue money to cover Social Security's cash flow deficits.

Currently, all workers pay 5.3 percent of their income to pay for Social Security retirement and survivors benefits. In 2004, this tax will be paid on the first $87,700 of an employee's income.* Employers match this tax for a total of 10.6 percent of each worker's income. In addition, both employer and employee pay an additional 0.9 percent of the worker's income (1.8

*This threshold is indexed and changes every year. It was $110,800 in 2010 [*Editors*].

percent total) for Social Security disability benefits. Thus, the employer and employee pay a total Social Security payroll tax of 12.4 percent.

Additional payroll taxes could be collected in three ways:

- The overall tax rate could be increased. However, this imposes higher taxes on all income groups and could reduce employment in the economy by making it more expensive to hire additional workers.
- The tax could be imposed on income levels above the threshold, currently at $87,700. In the short run, this would increase revenues, but since retirement benefits are paid on all income taxed for Social Security, it would also eventually increase the amount of benefits the system would have to pay each year and offset the amount raised through the higher taxes.
- Payroll taxes could be disconnected from the benefit formula. This could take the form of a new tax paid on income above the current $87,700 earnings threshold, collecting taxes on income up to the $87,700 level but counting only income up to $60,000 or some other level toward benefits, or some combination of the two. In either case, this type of tax would break the link between taxes and income that has existed since Social Security began in 1935. To date, neither the right nor the left has been willing to break this link for fear that it would be the first step toward turning Social Security into a welfare system. Both sides have worried that such a move—or even the perception of such a move—would undermine the program's widespread support among the American people.

4. Social Security's Unfunded Liability

What Is This, and Why Is It Important?

Both the current Social Security system and every plan to reform it will require significant amounts of general revenue money in addition to the amount collected through payroll taxes. This additional money is necessary to reduce the difference between what Social Security currently owes and what it will be able to pay.

In the reform plans, the transition cost represents a major reduction from the unfunded liability of the current program. Even though the reform plans are expensive, all of them would require less additional money than the current system. However, both the amount and the timing of this additional money would vary depending on the plan.

The amount of additional money that is needed can be measured according to two different systems. Both measurements give valuable information.

Present value reflects the idea that a dollar today has more value to a person than that same dollar has sometime in the future. It gives an idea of when the additional money is needed by giving greater weight to money needed in the near future than to an equal amount needed further in the future. In addition to showing the amount of money needed, a higher present value number indicates that money is needed sooner rather than later. [The present value of the unfunded liability ranges from $929 billion in the Orszag-Diamond plan to $7.6 trillion in the Ferrara plan.]

The *sum of the deficits* indicates the total amount of additional money that will be needed. This measure gives $100 needed today the same weight as $100 needed in 15 years. This measure adds up only the future cash flow deficits; it does not include cash flow surpluses because the government does not have any way to save or invest that money for future use. Using both of these measurements gives a better picture of the situation than using just one. [The sum of the deficits of the unfunded liability ranges from $7.1 trillion in the Graham plan to $16.4 trillion in the Ferrara plan.]

Paying for the current system or any of the reform plans will require Congress to balance Social Security's needs against those of the rest of the economy. In general, as more additional dollars are needed for the current system or a reform plan, less money will be available for other government programs and the private sector.

As this burden on the general federal budget increases and persists, Congress would find it increasingly more difficult to come up with that money, and it would become increasingly less likely that such a plan would really be paid for on schedule. This is especially true for the current system, which will incur the massive deficits to pay all of the promised benefits.

* * *

5. Paying for Social Security's Unfunded Liability

What Is This, and Why Is It Important?

Both the current Social Security program and all of the proposed reform plans will require large amounts of general revenue money to cover the annual cash flow deficits. Exactly when that money is first needed, how many years it will be needed, and the total amount that will be needed varies from plan to plan. Avoiding use of general revenue money would require either reducing Social Security benefits enough to eliminate the annual deficits or imposing new taxes to generate sufficient revenue. Neither the current system nor any of the proposed reform plans comes close to closing the gap.

Some plans do specify sources for the needed general revenues, but these are handicapped by the fact that no Congress can bind the hands of a future Congress. Thus, even if Congress did pass a plan that specified the source of the needed general revenues, a future Congress could change the plan by a majority vote. The only way to avoid this uncertainty would be for Congress to pass and the states to ratify the plan as a constitutional amendment—which would be prohibitively difficult.

In short, both the current system and all known reform plans would have to find the necessary general revenues from some combination of four sources: borrowing additional money collecting more taxes than needed to fund the rest of the government, reducing other government spending, or reducing Social Security benefits more than is called for under either current law or any of the reform plans.

The most important thing to remember is that the existing Social Security system and the reform plans all face this problem. This is not a weakness that is limited to PRA plans or any other reform plan. The only question is when the cash flow deficits begin and how large they will be.

Current Law

Current law makes no provision for funding Social Security's unfunded liability. The program has no credit line with the U.S. Treasury, and when its trust fund promises are exhausted, current law will require it to reduce benefits.

The DeMint Plan

While some press releases connected with Representative DeMint's plan suggest that some of its general revenue needs could be generated by reducing the growth of federal spending, no language specifying where the general revenues would come from is included in his legislation.

The Graham Plan

Senator Graham's plan includes a commission that would recommend reductions in corporate welfare and redirect the savings to reduce his plans unfunded liability. At best, a reduction in corporate welfare would generate only part of the needed general revenue. The commission would produce a legislative proposal that would then be considered by Congress.

Because the commission would be created by the same legislation that implements Graham's Social Security reforms, its recommendations could not even be considered until after the plan is enacted. As a result, passage of the Graham plan does not guarantee that these revenues would be available. Regardless of what the commission recommended, a future Congress could reject the proposed cuts in corporate welfare. In that case, Congress would have to come up with another method to raise the needed revenue.

The Smith Plan

Other than the proposed benefit changes that would partially reduce Social Security's unfunded liability, the Smith plan does not specify how it would pay cash flow deficits.

The Ferrara Plan

The Ferrara plan includes three mechanisms designed to create the needed general revenues.

First, it would mandate a 1 percent reduction in the growth of all federal spending (including entitlements such as Social Security) for at least 8 years and redirect that revenue to Social Security. Since Congress cannot legally force a subsequent Congress to follow a set course of action, the only enforcement mechanism available is a constitutional amendment. As a result, the Ferrara plan simply appropriates to Social Security the amount of revenue that would result if Congress were to reduce spending growth. In practice, a future Congress could choose not to reduce spending growth and, instead, just let the deficit grow larger or generate the necessary revenue in some other way.

Second, the Ferrara plan would transfer to Social Security the amount of corporate income taxes that could potentially result from the investment of personal accounts in corporate stocks and bonds. This is not a new or higher tax. This transfer is intended to reflect the taxes that would be paid at the current 35 percent corporate tax rate. Since SSA does not conduct dynamic scoring, this transfer is based on the static assumption that two-thirds of the stocks and bonds held through personal accounts reflect domestic corporate investment.

Third, the Ferrara plan would borrow about $1.4 trillion in special off-budget bonds. However, there is no practical way to create off-budget bonds that would not count against the federal debt. Even if there were, such a move would reduce the amount of transparency in the federal budget.

The Orszag-Diamond Plan

While the Orszag-Diamond plan includes both some benefit reductions and benefit increases for widows, the disabled, and low-income workers, the two elements of the plan are roughly equal. It reduces Social Security's unfunded liability using tax increases contained in the plan, including an increase in the payroll tax rate, a gradual increase in the amount of income subject to Social Security taxes, and a new 3 percent tax on any salary income not subject to Social Security taxes.

6. Making Social Security a Better Deal for Workers

What Is This, and Why Is It Important?

In the long run, a reform plan should do more than just preserve the current Social Security system with its many flaws. While a key requirement of any reform plan is to provide a stable, guaranteed, and adequate level of benefits at an affordable cost, it should do more.

The current system fails to allow workers to build any form of nest egg for the future. Instead, it is the highest single tax for about 80 percent of workers. In return, each worker receives a life annuity that ends with the death(s) of the worker, the surviving spouse (if there is one), or young children (if any). In today's world, where two-earner families are increasingly the norm, the current system even limits survivor benefits to the higher of either the deceased spouses benefits or the surviving spouses benefits. Whichever account is lower, no matter how long that spouse worked, is marked paid in full and extinguished.

At a minimum, a reform plan should allow workers to pass on some of what they earned and paid in Social Security taxes to improve their spouse's retirement benefits. It should also allow workers the flexibility to use their entire account for retirement benefits or take a smaller retirement benefit and use the balance to pay for a grandchild's college education, start a small business, or pass on money to a later generation.

In judging whether each proposed reform would be better for America's workers, readers may differ sharply. However, while most summaries and studies examine Social Security reform from the viewpoint of federal budget impact, tax rates, and the survivability of the system, few consider the overall impact of reform on the workers it was designed to benefit in the first place. Social Security should not be reformed or "saved" for its own sake, but only if it more effectively provides the benefits workers need at a price they can afford.

DISCUSSION QUESTIONS

1. The only plan that does not include partial privatization is the Orszag-Diamond plan. This could be called the "tough medicine" plan because the solvency of Social Security is accomplished through benefit reductions and tax increases. It is the only one of the plans that is funded through cuts and tax increases. Is the tough medicine worth it? Or do you agree with John that PRAs must be part of the overall reform?

2. One alternative to partial privatization that is not mentioned here is to have the federal government invest the Social Security surplus in the stock market or corporate bonds (as every state retirement system in the country does). This would, in theory, provide a high investment return, but critics claim it would also give the government too much leverage (as a large shareholder) over the activities of private corporations. Would this be a legitimate role for the government to play in the economy? Can you think of other ways in which the existing system could be reformed, other than turning portions of the fund over to individuals?

3. Are the broad objectives initially established for Social Security—income security for old age, income redistribution, and risk sharing across the population and across generations—still appropriate today? Are individuals more able to plan for and manage their retirement income today than in the 1930s or even the 1980s? Why or why not? What do you see as the major advantages and disadvantages of the current Social Security system and the plan for partial privatization?

Debating the Issues: Health Care Reform

Every president since Theodore Roosevelt who attempted comprehensive health care reform failed until Barack Obama's success in 2010. Most recently, Bill Clinton's attempt at reform in 1993–94 was unable to win support in Congress even when Democrats controlled both the House and the Senate. Obama faced an uphill battle as well, with unified opposition from Republicans and splits within his own party about the direction of reform. Through the first eight months in office, Obama remained out of the legislative fray in an effort to avoid the centralized micromanaging that had doomed President Clinton's attempt. After poll numbers showed the public turning against health care reform and a series of angry town-hall meetings in August 2009, in which members of Congress faced questions about "death panels" and a government takeover of health care, Obama decided he needed to regain control of the debate. In a nationally televised speech before a joint session of Congress, Obama outlined his priorities, answered his critics, and urged Congress to action. Obama said, "I am not the first President to take up this cause, but I am determined to be the last."

The priorities outlined in this speech—achieving as close to universal coverage as possible; a set of programs that would not "add a dime to the federal deficit;" preventing health insurance companies from denying coverage to people with preexisting health conditions or dropping policy holders when they get ill; and holding down health care costs by adopting "best practices," encouraging competition between health care providers and insurers, and computerizing health records—all became part of the final legislation.

Health care experts surveyed by the nonpartisan *National Journal* gave the law a mixed report card. Marilyn Werber Serfani tried to "craft survey questions to elicit objective assessments rather than partisan or ideological views." Overall, the experts were most impressed with its progress toward universal coverage, with 31 million of the 47 million uninsured Americans gaining health insurance by the time the law is fully implemented. They were less impressed with the impact the law will have on the quality of care, with the greatest hope for improvement coming from computerized records. The lowest scores came on cost control; many experts were disappointed with the delay (until 2018) in and reduction of the "Cadillac tax" that could have had a bigger impact on expensive and unnecessary medical procedures.

Although the *National Journal*'s experts were measured in their critiques, opponents of the bill promised to repeal the law and used this pledge as a central part of their campaign strategy in the 2010 midterm elections. Yuval Levin writes, "Because Obamacare embodies a rejection of incrementalism, it cannot be improved in small steps. Fixing our health care systems in the wake of the program's enactment will require a big step—repeal of the law before most of it takes hold—followed by incremental reforms addressing the public's real concerns." Levin argues that the health care plan will not control costs, will require people to buy insurance they cannot afford, and will bankrupt the country. Given the law's comprehensive scope, affecting one-sixth of the economy, things are bound to go wrong that will produce a host of unanticipated problems. He believes that more market-based solutions would provide the competition to hold down costs.

81

Address to Congress on Health Care Reform

Barack Obama

Madame Speaker, Vice President Biden, Members of Congress, and the American people:

*   *   *

* * * We came to build a future. So tonight, I return to speak to all of you about an issue that is central to that future—and that is the issue of health care.

I am not the first President to take up this cause, but I am determined to be the last. It has now been nearly a century since Theodore Roosevelt first called for health care reform. And ever since, nearly every President and Congress, whether Democrat or Republican, has attempted to meet this challenge in some way. A bill for comprehensive health reform was first introduced by John Dingell Sr. in 1943. Sixty-five years later, his son continues to introduce that same bill at the beginning of each session.

Our collective failure to meet this challenge—year after year, decade after decade—has led us to a breaking point. Everyone understands the extraordinary hardships that are placed on the uninsured, who live every day just one accident or illness away from bankruptcy. These are not primarily people on welfare. These are middle-class Americans. Some can't get insurance on the job. Others are self-employed, and can't afford it, since buying insurance on your own costs you three times as much as the coverage you get from your employer. Many other Americans who are willing and able to pay are still denied insurance due to previous illnesses or conditions that insurance companies decide are too risky or expensive to cover.

We are the only advanced democracy on earth—the only wealthy nation—that allows such hardships for millions of its people. There are now more than thirty million American citizens who cannot get coverage. In just a two year period, one in every three Americans goes without health care coverage at some point. And every day, 14,000 Americans lose their coverage. In other words, it can happen to anyone.

But the problem that plagues the health care system is not just a problem of the uninsured. Those who do have insurance have never had less security and stability than they do today. More and more Americans worry that if you move, lose your job, or change your job, you'll lose your health insurance too. More and more Americans pay their premiums, only to discover that their insurance company has dropped their coverage when they get sick, or won't pay the full cost of care. It happens every day.

One man from Illinois lost his coverage in the middle of chemotherapy because his insurer found that he hadn't reported gallstones that he didn't even know about. They delayed his treatment, and he died because of it. Another woman from Texas was about to get a double mastectomy when her insurance company canceled her policy because she forgot to declare a case of acne. By the time she had her insurance reinstated, her breast cancer more than doubled in size. That is heart-breaking, it is wrong, and no one should be treated that way in the United States of America.

Then there's the problem of rising costs. We spend one-and-a-half times more per person on health care than any other country, but we aren't any healthier for it. This is one of the reasons that insurance premiums have gone up three times faster than wages. It's why so many employers—especially small businesses—are forcing their employees to pay more for insurance, or are dropping their coverage entirely. It's why so many aspiring entrepreneurs cannot afford to open a business in the first place, and why American businesses that compete internationally—like our automakers—are at a huge disadvantage. And it's why those of us with health insurance are also paying a hidden and growing tax for those without it—about $1000 per year that pays for somebody else's emergency room and charitable care.

Finally, our health care system is placing an unsustainable burden on taxpayers. When health care costs grow at the rate they have, it puts greater pressure on programs like Medicare and Medicaid. If we do nothing to slow these skyrocketing costs, we will eventually be spending more on Medicare and Medicaid than every other government program combined. Put simply, our health care problem is our deficit problem. Nothing else even comes close.

These are the facts. Nobody disputes them. We know we must reform this system. The question is how.

There are those on the left who believe that the only way to fix the system is through a single-payer system like Canada's, where we would severely restrict the private insurance market and have the government provide coverage for everyone. On the right, there are those who argue that we should end the employer-based system and leave individuals to buy health insurance on their own.

I have to say that there are arguments to be made for both approaches. But either one would represent a radical shift that would disrupt the health care most people currently have. Since health care represents one-sixth of our economy, I believe it makes more sense to build on what works and fix what doesn't, rather than try to build an entirely new system from scratch. And that is precisely what those of you in Congress have tried to do over the past several months.

*   *   *

The plan I'm announcing tonight would meet three basic goals:

It will provide more security and stability to those who have health insurance. It will provide insurance to those who don't. And it will slow the growth of health care costs for our families, our businesses, and our government. It's a plan that asks everyone to take responsibility for meeting this challenge—not just government and insurance companies, but employers and individuals. And it's a plan that incorporates ideas from Senators and Congressmen; from Democrats and Republicans—and yes, from some of my opponents in both the primary and general election.

Here are the details that every American needs to know about this plan:

First, if you are among the hundreds of millions of Americans who already have health insurance through your job, Medicare, Medicaid, or the VA, nothing in this plan will require you or your employer to change the coverage or the doctor you have. Let me repeat this: nothing in our plan requires you to change what you have.

What this plan will do is to make the insurance you have work better for you. Under this plan, it will be against the law for insurance companies to deny you coverage because of a pre-existing condition. As soon as I sign this bill, it will be against the law for insurance companies to drop your coverage when you get sick or water it down when you need it most. They will no longer be able to place some arbitrary cap on the amount of coverage you can receive in a given year or a lifetime. We will place a limit on how much you can be charged for out-of-pocket expenses, because in the United States of America, no one should go broke because they get sick. And insurance companies will be required to cover, with no extra charge, routine checkups and preventive care, like mammograms and colonoscopies—because there's no reason we shouldn't be catching diseases like breast cancer and colon cancer before they get worse. That makes sense, it saves money, and it saves lives.

That's what Americans who have health insurance can expect from this plan—more security and stability.

Now, if you're one of the tens of millions of Americans who don't currently have health insurance, the second part of this plan will finally offer you quality, affordable choices. If you lose your job or change your job, you will be able to get coverage. If you strike out on your own and start a small business, you will be able to get coverage. We will do this by creating a new insurance exchange—a marketplace where individuals and small businesses will be able to shop for health insurance at competitive prices. Insurance companies will have an incentive to participate in this exchange because it lets them compete for millions of new customers. As one big group, these customers will have greater leverage to bargain with the insurance companies for better prices and quality coverage. This is how large companies and government employees get affordable insurance. It's how everyone in this Congress gets affordable insurance. And it's time to give every American the same opportunity that we've given ourselves.

For those individuals and small businesses who still cannot afford the lower-priced insurance available in the exchange, we will provide tax credits, the size of which will be based on your need. And all insurance companies that want access to this new marketplace will have to abide by the consumer protections I already mentioned. This exchange will take effect in four years, which will give us time to do it right. In the meantime, for those Americans who can't get insurance today because they have pre-existing medical conditions, we will immediately offer low-cost coverage that will protect you against financial ruin if you become seriously ill. This was a good idea when Senator John McCain proposed it in the campaign, it's a good idea now, and we should embrace it.

Now, even if we provide these affordable options, there may be those—particularly the young and healthy—who still want to take the risk and go without coverage. There may still be companies that refuse to do right by their workers. The problem is, such irresponsible behavior costs all the rest of us money. If there are affordable options and people still don't sign up for health insurance, it means we pay for those people's expensive emergency room visits. If some businesses don't provide workers health care, it forces the rest of us to pick up the tab when their workers get sick, and gives those businesses an unfair advantage over their competitors. And unless everybody does their part, many of the insurance reforms we seek—especially requiring insurance companies to cover pre-existing conditions—just can't be achieved.

That's why under my plan, individuals will be required to carry basic health insurance—just as most states require you to carry auto insurance. Likewise, businesses will be required to either offer their workers health care, or chip in to help cover the cost of their workers. There will be a hardship waiver for those individuals who still cannot afford coverage, and 95% of all small businesses, because of their size and narrow profit margin, would be exempt from these requirements. But we cannot have large businesses and individuals who can afford coverage game the system by avoiding responsibility to themselves or their employees. Improving our health care system only works if everybody does their part.

While there remain some significant details to be ironed out, I believe a broad consensus exists for the aspects of the plan I just outlined: consumer protections for those with insurance, an exchange that allows individuals and small businesses to purchase affordable coverage, and a requirement that people who can afford insurance get insurance.

And I have no doubt that these reforms would greatly benefit Americans from all walks of life, as well as the economy as a whole. Still, given all the misinformation that's been spread over the past few months, I realize that many Americans have grown nervous about reform. So tonight I'd like to address some of the key controversies that are still out there.

Some of people's concerns have grown out of bogus claims spread by those whose only agenda is to kill reform at any cost. The best example is the claim, made not just by radio and cable talk show hosts, but prominent politicians, that we plan to set up panels of bureaucrats with the power to kill off senior citizens. Such a charge would be laughable if it weren't so cynical and irresponsible. It is a lie, plain and simple.

There are also those who claim that our reform effort will insure illegal immigrants. This, too, is false—the reforms I'm proposing would not apply to those who are here illegally. And one more misunderstanding I want to clear up—under our plan, no federal dollars will be used to fund abortions, and federal conscience laws will remain in place.

*   *   *

[*Here President Obama discusses the "public option"—a Medicare-type health insurance plan that would have been available to those without insurance. However, the public option was not included as part of the final law*—Editors.]

Finally, let me discuss an issue that is a great concern to me, to members of this chamber, and to the public—and that is how we pay for this plan.

Here's what you need to know. First, I will not sign a plan that adds one dime to our deficits—either now or in the future. Period. And to prove that I'm serious, there will be a provision in this plan that requires us to come forward with more spending cuts if the savings we promised don't materialize. Part of the reason I faced a trillion dollar deficit when I walked in the door of the White House is because too many initiatives over the last decade were not paid for—from the Iraq War to tax breaks for the wealthy. I will not make that same mistake with health care.

Second, we've estimated that most of this plan can be paid for by finding savings within the existing health care system—a system that is currently full of waste and abuse. Right now, too much of the hard-earned savings and tax dollars we spend on health care doesn't make us healthier. That's not my judgment—it's the judgment of medical professionals across this country. And this is also true when it comes to Medicare and Medicaid.

In fact, I want to speak directly to America's seniors for a moment, because Medicare is another issue that's been subjected to demagoguery and distortion during the course of this debate.

More than four decades ago, this nation stood up for the principle that after a lifetime of hard work, our seniors should not be left to struggle with a pile of medical bills in their later years. That is how Medicare was born. And it remains a sacred trust that must be passed down from one generation to the next. That is why not a dollar of the Medicare trust fund will be used to pay for this plan.

The only thing this plan would eliminate is the hundreds of billions of dollars in waste and fraud, as well as unwarranted subsidies in Medicare that go to insurance companies—subsidies that do everything to pad their profits and nothing to improve your care. And we will also create an independent commission of doctors and medical experts charged with identifying more waste in the years ahead.

These steps will ensure that you—America's seniors—get the benefits you've been promised. They will ensure that Medicare is there for future generations. And we can use some of the savings to fill the gap in coverage that forces too many seniors to pay thousands of dollars a year out of their own pocket for prescription drugs. That's what this plan will do for you. So don't pay attention to those scary stories about how your benefits will be cut—especially since some of the same folks who are spreading these tall tales have fought against Medicare in the past, and just this year supported a budget that would have essentially turned Medicare into a privatized voucher program. That will never happen on my watch. I will protect Medicare.

Now, because Medicare is such a big part of the health care system, making the program more efficient can help usher in changes in the way we deliver health care that can reduce costs for everybody. We have long known that some places, like the Intermountain Healthcare in Utah or the Geisinger Health System in rural Pennsylvania, offer high-quality care at costs below average. The commission can help encourage the adoption of these common-sense best practices by doctors and medical professionals throughout the system—everything from reducing hospital infection rates to encouraging better coordination between teams of doctors.

Reducing the waste and inefficiency in Medicare and Medicaid will pay for most of this plan. Much of the rest would be paid for with revenues from the very same drug and insurance companies that stand to benefit from tens of millions of new customers. This reform will charge insurance companies a fee for their most expensive policies, which will encourage them to provide greater value for the money—an idea which has the support of Democratic and Republican experts. And according to these same experts, this modest change could help hold down the cost of health care for all of us in the long-run.

Finally, many in this chamber—particularly on the Republican side of the aisle—have long insisted that reforming our medical malpractice laws can help bring down the cost of health care. I don't believe malpractice reform is a silver bullet, but I have talked to enough doctors to know that defensive medicine may be contributing to unnecessary costs. So I am proposing that we move forward on a range of ideas about how to put patient safety first and let doctors focus on practicing medicine. I know that the Bush Administration considered authorizing demonstration projects in individual states to test these issues. It's a good idea, and I am directing my Secretary of Health and Human Services to move forward on this initiative today.

Add it all up, and the plan I'm proposing will cost around $900 billion over ten years—less than we have spent on the Iraq and Afghanistan wars, and less than the tax cuts for the wealthiest few Americans that Congress passed at the beginning of the previous administration. Most of these costs will be paid for with money already being spent—but spent badly—in the existing health care system. The plan will not add to our deficit. The middle-class will realize greater security, not higher taxes. And if we are able to slow the growth of health care costs by just one-tenth of one percent each year, it will actually reduce the deficit by $4 trillion over the long term.

This is the plan I'm proposing. It's a plan that incorporates ideas from many of the people in this room tonight—Democrats and Republicans. And I will continue to seek common ground in the weeks ahead. If you come to me with a serious set of proposals, I will be there to listen. My door is always open.

*   *   *

[Here President Obama talks about Ted Kennedy and his role in health care reform—Editors.]

That large-heartedness—that concern and regard for the plight of others—is not a partisan feeling. It is not a Republican or a Democratic feeling. It, too, is part of the American character. Our ability to stand in other people's shoes. A recognition that we are all in this together; that when fortune turns against one of us, others are there to lend a helping hand. A belief that in this country, hard work and responsibility should be rewarded by some measure of security and fair play; and an acknowledgement that sometimes government has to step in to help deliver on that promise.

This has always been the history of our progress. In 1933, when over half of our seniors could not support themselves and millions had seen their savings wiped away, there were those who argued that Social Security would lead to socialism. But the men and women of Congress stood fast, and we are all the better for it. In 1965, when some argued that Medicare represented a government takeover of health care, members of Congress, Democrats and Republicans, did not back down. They joined together so that all of us could enter our golden years with some basic peace of mind.

You see, our predecessors understood that government could not, and should not, solve every problem. They understood that there are instances when the gains in security from government action are not worth the added constraints on our freedom. But they also understood that the danger of too much government is matched by the perils of too little; that without the leavening hand of wise policy, markets can crash, monopolies can stifle competition, and the vulnerable can be exploited. And they knew that when any government measure, no matter how carefully crafted or beneficial, is subject to scorn; when any efforts to help people in need are attacked as un-American; when facts and reason are thrown overboard and only timidity passes for wisdom, and we can no longer even engage in a civil conversation with each other over the things that truly matter—that at that point we don't merely lose our capacity to solve big challenges. We lose something essential about ourselves.

What was true then remains true today. I understand how difficult this health care debate has been. I know that many in this country are deeply skeptical that government is looking out for them. I understand that the politically safe move would be to kick the can further down the road—to defer reform one more year, or one more election, or one more term.

But that's not what the moment calls for. That's not what we came here to do. We did not come to fear the future. We came here to shape it. I still believe we can act even when it's hard. I still believe we can replace acrimony with civility, and gridlock with progress. I still believe we can do great things, and that here and now we will meet history's test.

Because that is who we are. That is our calling. That is our character. Thank you, God Bless You, and may God Bless the United States of America.

82

"Grading Health Reform: Experts Assess Whether the Bill Delivers on Its Promises"

Marilyn Werber Serafini

The primary objectives of health care reform were clear long before Congress took up the issue last year: slow the growth of health care spending, insure more people, improve the quality of care—and do it all without busting the federal budget. *National Journal* this week asked 20 health care experts across the political spectrum how the bill that President Obama signed into law on Tuesday measures up against those yardsticks.

The experts generally agreed that the new law comes close to achieving the objective of providing insurance to all Americans and does a fairly good job of making coverage affordable and available to consumers. But the experts also said that the law falls short of promises to lower skyrocketing health care spending, and they concluded that it doesn't do enough to improve the quality of health care.

* * *

Our judges gave each candidate's plan a series of numerical grades, from 1 to 10, depending on how close they thought it would come to achieving a given goal, such as covering the uninsured. A score of 10 indicated that the plan would come extremely close to reaching the goal, while a score of 1 meant that it would not come at all close.

National Journal tried to craft the survey questions to elicit objective assessments rather than partisan or ideological views. Regarding the uninsured, for example, we asked the judges how close each proposal would come to providing health insurance for all Americans. *NJ* did not want answers that reflected the judges' political leanings or personal views about whether a given plan was the best—or even a good—approach.

* * *

A Big Step Toward Universal Coverage

The Congressional Budget Office estimates that the health care reform law will provide coverage to 31 million of the 47 million Americans currently uninsured. Many of the people who won't be covered are illegal immigrants who are ineligible for federal assistance in obtaining insurance.

None of the 20 experts gave the law a perfect score of 10 for providing coverage, although all but two gave it high marks. Indeed, in this category, President Obama received the same grade that he did as a candidate.

During the campaign Obama recommended a narrower mandate requiring only that parents purchase insurance for their children; in contrast, the new law requires many adults to also get coverage. Most people without health insurance will have to pay one of two penalties, whichever is greater: either a fixed fine, starting at $95 in 2014, rising to $325 in 2015, and to $695 in 2016; or a percentage of taxable income, starting at 1.0 percent in 2014 and rising to 2.5 percent in 2016.

People with annual incomes below 100 percent of the federal poverty line ($10,830 for an individual and $22,050 for a family of four) are exempt from the penalties.

The law will significantly expand Medicaid, the federal-state health care program for the poor, to as many as 13 million additional beneficiaries. Beginning in 2014, Medicaid eligibility will extend to people with annual earnings lower than 133 percent of the federal poverty line ($14,440 for an individual).

Some judges took 1 or 2 points off their scores in this category because they advocated tougher penalties for failure to purchase insurance. Paul Ginsburg, president of the Center for Studying Health System Change, said, "I expect that the mandate will be refined in response to experience."

Ed Howard, executive vice president of the Alliance for Health Reform, called the law "a good start," and Jeffrey Levi, executive director of the Trust for America's Health, agreed. "Clearly, a significant group of people will be left out of this reform," he said. "But the addition of over 30 million Americans to the insurance roll is a monumental step of major proportions. But those who are left out will continue to need a safety net—hence the importance of the provisions expanding funding for community health centers and public health."

Gail Wilensky, a senior fellow at Project Hope who was Medicare administrator during the presidency of George H. W. Bush, noted that according to CBO estimates, "the percentage of people without insurance would drop from the current 15 percent to 5 percent, which is two-thirds of the way to universal coverage."

Elizabeth McGlynn, associate director of the health program at Rand, said that based on her think tank's microsimulation modeling, the percentage of uninsured would be reduced by 53 to 57 percent. She called that "a substantial improvement," although she added that it "would not achieve universal coverage." McGlynn concluded, "A large portion of the uninsured would be eligible for, but not enrolled in, Medicaid."

The Lewin Group actuary, John Sheils, said that his firm's model indicates that the law covers 60 percent of the uninsured population but only 43 percent of care that is currently uncompensated. "Very-low-income people exempt from the mandate account for much of this," he said.

According to Joe Antos, an American Enterprise Institute scholar, the goal shouldn't be reducing the number of uninsured but increasing the number of people who have access to appropriate care. "There is nothing in the bill that assures this," he said. Over time, Heritage Foundation Vice President Stuart Butler cautioned, although almost all citizens and legal residents will get coverage, "it may not be of the type, cost, and quality that they would like."

Some conservative opponents argue that an insurance mandate is unconstitutional and sets a worrisome precedent for government power. More than a dozen states have already filed lawsuits challenging the constitutionality of the requirement.

Many health reform advocates are also concerned, but for different reasons. They worry that some people will ignore the mandate—especially those who are young and healthy and see little need for health insurance. America's Health Insurance Plans, which represents insurers, shares this apprehension. Insurers agreed early on to stop denying policies to people with pre-existing conditions and in poor health in exchange for universal coverage.

Minor Impact on Quality of Care

Many of National Journal's health care experts are disappointed that the new law won't do more to improve the quality of health care. "The main focus of the legislation is on coverage expansion, not on improving quality or consumer decision-making," said Elizabeth McGlynn, associate director of the health program at Rand. "The bill contains provisions that would increase the information available to consumers; however, there are no direct incentives for consumers to use that information or to change the decisions they would have otherwise made."

The key, said Paul Ginsburg, president of the Center for Studying Health System Change, is implementing research into medical effectiveness. The new law funds research on so-called comparative effectiveness to evaluate the success of various medical treatments.

But American Enterprise Institute scholar Joe Antos worries that even the most-sophisticated [sic] consumers will have trouble interpreting and applying comparative-effectiveness results. "Sensible consumers will continue to rely on the advice of their doctors, which depends on the community standard of practice, the patient's specific circumstances, how services are paid for, and other factors. Patients are increasingly also seeking information on the Internet, which can lead some to demand inappropriate treatments."

Jeffrey Levi, executive director of Trust for America's Health, shares Antos's concern. "It's one thing to do the comparative-effectiveness research and quality assessment; it's another for consumers to take that information to heart and apply it to their own situations."

Quality may also differ for those getting insurance through an exchange and those in employer-sponsored plans, said Heritage Foundation Vice President Stuart Butler. Those in exchanges will have "a lot more choice and information," he said, predicting that employers will react to extra fees by restricting coverage and shifting costs.

Few experts were optimistic that doctors, hospitals, and other medical providers will gain the tools to improve care using best practices. "The bill promotes comparative-effectiveness research but does nothing to increase adherence to guidelines," said Lewin Group actuary John Sheils. "Adherence is the problem. There is overwhelming evidence in the literature showing that doctors do not follow guidelines."

Former Senate Majority Leader Tom Daschle noted that changes resulting from the research will not come "for some time." And even when the results of comparative-effectiveness research are more readily available, "probably past the 10-year mark," according to Antos, "their appropriate application depends critically on the specific patient's circumstances. Judgment will remain the driving factor, unless future Congresses attempt to impose uniform standards on medical practice."

Grace-Marie Turner, president of the Galen Institute, worries that comparative-effectiveness studies "are historically out of date long before the studies are finalized." What may have a greater effect on quality of care is the funding that President Obama included in last year's economic stimulus law to encourage doctors to adopt electronic medical records. "Considerable work must be done to help physicians who are in solo and small group practice use emerging tools," she said.

Although former Medicare Administrator Gail Wilensky called the law's direction positive, she stressed that much depends on what happens with pilot and demonstration projects that the law establishes for Medicare. The law authorizes pilot projects to test so-called accountable care organizations and the bundling of payments to medical providers. The idea is to get medical providers to better coordinate patient care. The government and private insurers, in turn, could then more effectively base payments on performance.

The experts were somewhat skeptical that the reforms will encourage medical providers to compete for patients based on quality and price. Conservatives were especially critical, but liberals didn't give high scores either.

Competition will change, Butler said, but not to meet that goal. "In Medicaid, Medicare, and in the more regulated private system, the incentive will increase to compete by cutting costs and avoiding certain patients to achieve a reasonable return amid tighter fee schedules," he said.

Bill Gets Low Score For Cost Control

Bringing health care spending in line with the economy's growth rate has been a priority since Washington began talking about health reform decades ago. During the 2008 presidential campaign, judges gave Barack Obama's proposal a score of only 3 for controlling costs.

In rating the newly passed reforms, the scores were nearly as low. Former Medicare Administrator Gail Wilensky noted that the law will institute some "promising" pilot projects for coordinating medical care in Medicare and for testing ways to pay doctors and hospitals. Still, Heritage Foundation Vice President Stuart Butler said that the law will increase, not decrease, the growth rate of total health spending.

"While the bill contains provisions that may ultimately lead to reductions," Elizabeth McGlynn, Rand health program associate director said, her think tank's projections indicate that, "with the exception of payment reform options, most would have a relatively small effect on the growth rate in health spending."

The actuary for the Centers for Medicare and Medicaid Services "reports that health spending will continue to grow faster than the economy, even assuming that future Congresses cut Medicare spending as prescribed in the bill," American Enterprise Institute scholar Joe Antos contended, adding, "This objective is probably impossible to meet even over the long term given the aging populace."

Brookings Institution senior fellow Henry Aaron is more optimistic about the long-term forecast; and Ed Howard, executive vice president of the Alliance for Health Reform, said that "most of what is possible is at least put in place, but will take time to have impact."

Many health care economists had high hopes for a so-called Cadillac tax to discourage employers from offering overly generous benefits. With less coverage, the theory goes, people will have to pay more out of their own pockets and thus become thriftier about purchasing medical services. But the final law watered down the tax and delayed its implementation. The tax on high-end insurance plans will apply to health plan premiums greater than $10,200 for individual coverage and $27,500 for families; it won't kick in until 2018.

Scores were somewhat higher, although mixed, when National Journal asked whether the federal government will get its money's worth from the law. "In terms of government spending per net newly insured individual, the expected value of the services obtained should exceed the cost to the federal government," McGlynn responded.

Butler, however, argued that the law is based on a "very high taxpayer cost for coverage expansions that could have been achieved at much lower cost." In scoring the law on its cost, Butler wanted to know whether zero was an option. "It has been 'funded' with new taxes and 'savings' that will not materialize. It is thus actually being funded with debt obligations on future generations."

Grace-Marie Turner, president of the Galen Institute, particularly worries about Medicare savings, which mostly come from decreasing payments to the Medicare Advantage program.

One-quarter of Medicare recipients get their insurance coverage from health maintenance organizations, preferred provider groups, and even some private fee-for-service plans as part of Medicare Advantage. But the program has been controversial because the government pays participating insurers about 14 percent more per beneficiary than it pays for the care of seniors in Medicare's traditional fee-for-service program.

"Richard Foster, Medicare's chief actuary, warned Congress that making the deep cuts to Medicare contained in the Senate bill 'represent an exceedingly difficult challenge' and, if sustained, would cause one out of five hospitals and nursing homes to become unprofitable," Turner said. "Congress is highly unlikely to allow this to happen, requiring even more tax dollars and deficit spending. This legislation is not paid for, even with half a trillion dollars in cuts to Medicare and half a trillion in new taxes. Political pressures will intensify to provide ever larger subsidies to more and more people and to impose strict price controls on providers. Coverage restrictions inevitably will follow. So, no, reform is not funded with existing health care dollars."

Paul Ginsburg, president of the Center for Studying Health System Change, countered that the government would have cut Medicare Advantage costs even if reform legislation had not passed, "although perhaps less sharply."

83

"Repeal: Why and How Obamacare Must Be Undone"

YUVAL LEVIN

In the days since the enactment of their health care plan, Democrats in Washington have been desperately seeking to lodge the new program in the pantheon of American public-policy achievements. House

Democratic whip James Clyburn compared the bill to the Civil Rights Act of 1964. Vice President Biden argued it vindicates a century of health reform efforts by Democrats and Republicans alike. House speaker Nancy Pelosi said "health insurance reform will stand alongside Social Security and Medicare in the annals of American history."

Even putting aside the fact that Social Security and Medicare are going broke and taking the rest of the government with them, these frantic forced analogies are preposterous. The new law is a ghastly mess, which began as a badly misguided technocratic pipe dream and was then degraded into ruinous incoherence by the madcap process of its enactment.

The appeals to history are understandable, however, because the Democrats know that the law is also exceedingly vulnerable to a wholesale repeal effort: Its major provisions do not take effect for four years, yet in the interim it is likely to begin wreaking havoc with the health care sector—raising insurance premiums, health care costs, and public anxieties. If those major provisions do take effect, moreover, the true costs of the program will soon become clear, and its unsustainable structure will grow painfully obvious. So, to protect it from an angry public and from Republicans armed with alternatives, the new law must be made to seem thoroughly established and utterly irrevocable—a fact on the ground that must be lived with; tweaked, if necessary, at the edges, but at its core politically untouchable.

But it is no such thing. Obamacare starts life strikingly unpopular and looks likely to grow more so as we get to know it in the coming months and years. The entire House of Representatives, two-thirds of the Senate, and the president will be up for election before the law's most significant provisions become fully active. The American public is concerned about spending, deficits, debt, taxes, and overactive government to an extent seldom seen in American history. The excesses of the plan seem likely to make the case for alternative gradual and incremental reforms only stronger.

And the repeal of Obamacare is essential to any meaningful effort to bring down health care costs, provide greater stability and security of coverage to more Americans, and address our entitlement crisis. Both the program's original design and its contorted final form make repairs at the edges unworkable. The only solution is to repeal it and pursue genuine health care reform in its stead.

From Bad to Worse

To see why nothing short of repeal could suffice, we should begin at the core of our health care dilemma.

Conservative and liberal experts generally agree on the nature of the problem with American health care financing: There is a shortage of incentives for efficiency in our methods of paying for coverage and care, and therefore costs are rising much too quickly, leaving too many people unable to afford insurance. We have neither a fully public nor quite a private system of insurance, and three key federal policies—the fee-for-service structure of Medicare, the disjointed financing of Medicaid, and the open-ended tax exclusion for employer-provided insurance—drive spending and costs ever upward.

The disagreement about just how to fix that problem has tended to break down along a familiar dispute between left and right: whether economic efficiency is best achieved by the rational control of expert management or by the lawful chaos of open competition.

Liberals argue that the efficiency we lack would be achieved by putting as much as possible of the health care sector into one big "system" in which the various irregularities could be evened and managed out of existence by the orderly arrangement of rules and incentives. The problem now, they say, is that health care is too chaotic and answers only to the needs of the insurance companies. If it were made more orderly, and answered to the needs of the public as a whole, costs could be controlled more effectively.

Conservatives argue that the efficiency we lack would be achieved by allowing price signals to shape the behavior of both providers and consumers, creating more savings than we could hope to produce on purpose, and allowing competition and informed consumer choices to exercise a downward pressure on prices. The problem now, they say, is that third-party insurance (in which employers buy coverage or the government provides it, and consumers almost never pay doctors directly) makes health care too opaque, hiding the cost of everything from everyone and so making real pricing and therefore real economic efficiency impossible. If it were made more transparent and answered to the wishes of consumers, prices could be controlled more effectively.

That means that liberals and conservatives want to pursue health care reform in roughly opposite directions. Conservatives propose ways of introducing genuine market forces into the insurance system—to remove obstacles to choice and competition, pool risk more effectively, and reduce the inefficiency in government health care entitlements while helping those for whom entry to the market is too expensive (like Americans with preexisting conditions) gain access to the same high quality care. Such targeted efforts would build on what is best about the system we have in order to address what needs fixing.

Liberals, meanwhile, propose ways of moving Americans to a more fully public system, by arranging conditions in the health care sector (through a mix of mandates, regulations, taxes, and subsidies) to nudge people toward public coverage, which could be more effectively managed. This is the approach the Democrats originally proposed last year. The idea was to end risk-based insurance by making it essentially illegal for insurers to charge people different prices based on their health, age, or other factors; to force everyone to participate in the system so that the healthy do not wait until they're sick to buy insurance; to align various insurance reforms in a way that would raise premium costs in the private market; and then to introduce a government-run insurer that, whether through Medicare's negotiating leverage or through various exemptions from market pressures, could undersell private insurers and so offer an attractive "public option" to people being pushed out of employer plans into an increasingly expensive individual market.

Conservatives opposed this scheme because they believed a public insurer could not introduce efficiencies that would lower prices without brutal rationing of services. Liberals supported it because they thought a public insurer would be fairer and more effective.

But in order to gain 60 votes in the Senate last winter, the Democrats were forced to give up on that public insurer, while leaving the other components of their scheme in place. The result is not even a liberal approach to escalating costs but a ticking time bomb: a scheme that will build up pressure in our private insurance system while offering no escape. Rather than reform a system that everyone agrees is unsustainable, it will subsidize that system and compel participation in it—requiring all Americans to pay ever-growing premiums to insurance companies while doing essentially nothing about the underlying causes of those rising costs.

Liberal health care mavens understand this. When the public option was removed from the health care bill in the Senate, Howard Dean argued in the *Washington Post* that the bill had become merely a subsidy for insurance companies, and failed completely to control costs. Liberal health care blogger Jon Walker said, "The Senate bill will fail to stop the rapidly approaching meltdown of our health care system, and anyone is a fool for thinking otherwise." Markos Moulitsas of the Daily Kos called the bill "unconscionable" and said it lacked "any mechanisms to control costs."

Indeed, many conservatives, for all their justified opposition to a government takeover of health care, have not yet quite seen the full extent to which this bill will exacerbate the cost problem. It is designed to push people into a system that will not exist—a health care bridge to nowhere—and so will cause premiums to rise and encourage significant dislocation and then will initiate a program of subsidies whose only real answer to the mounting costs of coverage will be to pay them with public dollars and so increase them further. It aims to spend a trillion dollars on subsidies to large insurance companies and the expansion of Medicaid, to micromanage the insurance industry in ways likely only to raise premiums further, to cut Medicare benefits without using the money to shore up the program or reduce the deficit, and to raise taxes on employment, investment, and medical research.

The case for averting all of that could hardly be stronger. And the nature of the new law means that it must be undone—not trimmed at the edges. Once implemented fully, it would fairly quickly force a crisis that would require another significant reform. Liberals would seek to use that crisis, or the prospect of it, to move the system toward the approach they wanted in the first place: arguing that the only solution to the rising costs they have created is a public insurer they imagine could outlaw the economics of health care. A look at the fiscal collapse of the Medicare system should rid us of the notion that any such approach would work, but it remains the left's preferred solution, and it is their only plausible next move—indeed, some Democrats led by Iowa senator Tom Harkin have already begun talking about adding a public insurance option to the plan next year.

Because Obamacare embodies a rejection of incrementalism, it cannot be improved in small steps. Fixing our health care system in the wake of the program's enactment will require a big step—repeal of the law before most of it takes hold—followed by incremental reforms addressing the public's real concerns.

The Case for Repeal

That big step will not be easy to take. The Democratic party has invested its identity and its future in the fate of this new program, and Democrats control the White House and both houses of Congress. That is why the conservative health care agenda must now also be an electoral agenda—an effort to refine, inform, and build on public opposition to the new program and to the broader trend toward larger and more intrusive, expensive, and fiscally reckless government in the age of Obama. Obamacare is the most prominent emblem of that larger trend, and its repeal must be at the center of the conservative case to voters in the coming two election cycles.

The design of the new law offers some assistance. In an effort to manipulate the program's Congressional Budget Office score so as to meet President Obama's goal of spending less than $1 trillion in its first decade, the Democrats' plan will roll out along a very peculiar trajectory. No significant entitlement benefits will be made available for four years, but some significant taxes and Medicare cuts—as well as regulatory reforms that may begin to push premium prices up, especially in the individual market—will begin before then. And the jockeying and jostling in the insurance sector in preparation for the more dramatic changes that begin in 2014 will begin to be felt very soon.

To blunt the effects of all this, the Democrats have worked mightily to give the impression that some attractive benefits, especially regarding the rules governing insurance companies, will begin immediately. This year, they say, insurance companies will be prevented from using the preexisting medical condition of a child to exclude that child's parents from insurance coverage, and a risk-pool program will be established to help a small number of adults who are excluded too. Additionally, insurance policies cannot be cancelled retroactively when someone becomes sick, some annual and lifetime limits on coverage are prohibited, and "children" may stay on their parents' insurance until they turn 26. Obamacare's champions hope these reforms might build a constituency for the program.

But these benefits are far too small to have that effect. The preexisting condition exclusion prohibits only the refusal to cover treatment for a specific disease, not the exclusion of a family from coverage altogether, and applies only in the individual market, and so affects almost no one. More than half the states already have laws allowing parents to keep adult children on their policies—through ages varying from 24 to 31. And the other new benefits, too, may touch a small number of people (again, mostly in the individual market, where premiums will be rising all the while), but will do nothing to affect the overall picture of American health care financing. CBO scored these immediate reforms as having no effect on the number of uninsured or on national health expenditures.

The bill will also have the government send a $250 check to seniors who reach the "donut hole" gap in Medicare prescription drug coverage this year—and the checks will go out in September, just in time for the fall elections. But the checks will hardly make up for the significant cuts in Medicare Advantage plans that allow seniors to choose among private insurers for their coverage. Those cuts begin in 2011, but the millions of seniors who use the program will start learning about them this year— again, before the election—as insurance companies start notifying their beneficiaries of higher premiums or cancelled coverage.

We are also likely to see some major players in health insurance, including both large employers and large insurers, begin to take steps to prepare for the new system in ways that employees and beneficiaries will find disconcerting. Verizon, for instance, has already informed its employees that insurance premiums will need to rise in the coming years and retiree benefits may be cut. Caterpillar has said new taxes and rules will cost the company $100 million in just the next year, and tractor maker John Deere has said much the same. Such announcements are likely to be common this year, and many insurers active in the individual market are expected to begin curtailing their offerings as that market looks to grow increasingly unprofitable under new rules.

These early indications will help opponents of the new law make their case. But the case will certainly need to focus most heavily on what is to come in the years after this congressional election: spending, taxes, rising health care costs, cuts in Medicare that don't help save the program or reduce the deficit, and a growing government role in the management of the insurance sector.

The numbers are gargantuan and grim—even as laid out by the Congressional Budget Office, which has to accept as fact all of the legislation's dubious premises and promises. If the law remains in place, a new entitlement will begin in 2014 that will cost more than $2.4 trillion in its first 10 years, and will grow faster than either Medicare or private-sector health care spending has in the past decade.

Rather than reducing costs, Obamacare will increase national health expenditures by more than $200 billion, according to the Obama administration's own HHS actuary. Premiums in the individual market will increase by more than 10 percent very quickly, and middle-class families in the new exchanges (where large numbers of Americans who now receive coverage through their employers will find themselves dumped) will be forced to choose from a very limited menu of government-approved plans, the cheapest of which, CBO estimates, will cost more than $12,000. Some Americans—those earning up to four times the federal poverty level—will get subsidies to help with some of that cost, but these subsidies will grow more slowly than the premiums, and those above the threshold will not receive them at all. Many middle-class families will quickly find themselves spending a quarter of their net income on health insurance, according to a calculation by Scott Gottlieb of the American Enterprise Institute.

Through the rules governing the exchanges and other mechanisms (including individual and employer insurance mandates, strict regulation of plan benefit packages, rating rules, and the like), the federal government will begin micromanaging the insurance sector in an effort to extend coverage and control costs. But even CBO's assessment does not foresee a reduction in costs and therefore an easing of the fundamental source of our health care woes.

To help pay for the subsidies, and for a massive expansion of Medicaid, taxes will rise by about half a trillion dollars in the program's first 10 years—hitting employers and investors especially hard, but quickly being passed down to consumers and workers. And the law also cuts Medicare, especially by reducing physician and hospital payment rates, by another half a trillion dollars—cuts that will drastically undermine the program's operation as, according to the Medicare actuary, about 20 percent of doctors and other providers who participate in the program "could find it difficult to remain profitable and, absent legislative intervention, might end their participation." And all of this, CBO says, to increase the portion of Americans who have health insurance from just under 85 percent today to about 95 percent in 10 years.

Of course, this scenario—for all the dark prospects it lays out—assumes things will go more or less as planned. CBO is required to assume as much. But in a program so complex and enormous, which seeks to take control of a sixth of our economy but is profoundly incoherent even in its own terms, things will surely not always go as planned. The

Medicare cuts so essential to funding the new entitlement, for instance, are unlikely to occur. Congress has shown itself thoroughly unwilling to impose such cuts in the past, and if it fails to follow through on them in this case, Obamacare will add hundreds of billions of additional dollars to the deficit. By the 2012 election, we will have certainly begun to see whether the program's proposed funding mechanism is a total sham, or is so unpopular as to make Obamacare toxic with seniors. Neither option bodes well for the program's future.

Some of the taxes envisioned in the plan, especially the so-called Cadillac tax on high-cost insurance, are also unlikely to materialize quite as proposed, adding further to the long-term costs of the program. And meanwhile, the bizarre incentive structures created by the law (resulting in part from the elimination of the public insurance plan which was to have been its focus) are likely to cause massive distortions in the insurance market that will further increase costs. The individual market will quickly collapse, since new regulations will put it at an immense disadvantage against the new exchanges. We are likely to see significant consolidation in the insurance sector, as smaller insurers go out of business and the larger ones become the equivalent of subsidized and highly regulated public utilities. And the fact that the exchanges will offer subsidies not available to workers with employer-based coverage will mean either that employers will be strongly inclined to stop offering insurance, or that Congress will be pressured to make subsidies available to employer-based coverage. In either case, the program's costs will quickly balloon.

Perhaps worst of all, the law not only shirks the obligation to be fiscally responsible, it will also make it much more difficult for future policymakers to do something about our entitlement and deficit crisis. Obamacare constructs a new entitlement that will grow more and more expensive even more quickly than Medicare itself. Even if the program were actually deficit neutral, which it surely won't be, that would just mean that it would keep us on the same budget trajectory we are on now—with something approaching trillion-dollar deficits in each of the next 10 years and a national debt of more than $20 trillion by 2020—but leave us with much less money and far fewer options for doing anything about it.

In other words, Obamacare is an unmitigated disaster—for our health care system, for our fiscal future, and for any notion of limited government. But it is a disaster that will not truly get under way for four years, and therefore a disaster we can avert.

This is the core of the case the program's opponents must make to voters this year and beyond. If opponents succeed in gaining a firmer foothold in Congress in the fall, they should work to begin dismantling and delaying the program where they can: denying funding to key provisions and pushing back implementation at every opportunity. But a true repeal will almost certainly require yet another election cycle, and another president.

The American public is clearly open to the kind of case Obamacare's opponents will need to make. But keeping voters focused on the problems with the program, and with the reckless growth of government beyond it, will require a concerted, informed, impassioned, and empirical case. This is the kind of case opponents of Obamacare have made over the past year, of course, and it persuaded much of the public—but the Democrats acted before the public could have its say at the polls. The case must therefore be sustained until that happens. The health care debate is far from over.

Toward Real Reform

Making and sustaining that case will also require a clear sense of what the alternatives to Obamacare might be—and how repeal could be followed by sensible incremental steps toward controlling health care costs and thereby increasing access and improving care.

Without a doubt, the Democrats' program is worse than doing nothing. But the choice should not be that program or nothing. The problems with our health care system are real, and conservatives must show the public how repealing Obamacare will open the way to a variety of options for more sensible reforms—reforms that will lower costs and help those with preexisting conditions or without affordable coverage options, but in ways that do not bankrupt the country, or undermine the quality of care or the freedom of patients and doctors to make choices for themselves.

Republicans this past year offered a variety of such approaches, which varied in their ambitions, costs, and forms. A group led by representatives Paul Ryan and Devin Nunes and senators Tom Coburn and Richard Burr proposed a broad measures that included reforms of Medicare, Medicaid, the employer-based coverage tax exclusion, and malpractice liability and would cover nearly all of the uninsured. The House Republican caucus backed a more modest first step to make high-risk pools available to those with preexisting conditions, enable insurance purchases across state lines, pursue tort reform, and encourage states to experiment with innovative insurance regulation. Former Bush administration official Jeffrey Anderson has offered an approach somewhere between the two, which pursues incremental reforms through a "small bill." Other conservatives have offered numerous other proposals, including ways of allowing small businesses to pool together for coverage, the expansion of Health Savings Accounts and consumer-driven health care (which Obamacare would thoroughly gut), and various reforms of our entitlement system.

All share a basic commitment to the proposition that our health care dilemmas should be addressed through a series of discrete, modest, incremental solutions to specific problems that concern the American public, and all agree that the underlying cause of these problems is the cost of health coverage and care, which would be best dealt with by using market forces to improve efficiency and bring down prices.

The approach to health care just adopted by President Obama and the Democratic Congress thoroughly fails to deal with efficiency and cost, and stands in the way of any meaningful effort to do so. It is built on a fundamental conceptual error, suffers from a profound incoherence of design, and would make a bad situation far worse. It cannot be improved by tinkering. It must be removed before our health care crisis can be addressed.

If we are going to meet the nation's foremost challenges—ballooning debt, exploding entitlements, out of control health care costs, and the task of keeping America strong and competitive—we must begin by making Obamacare history. We must repeal it, and then pursue real reform.

DISCUSSION QUESTIONS

1. Do you think that President Obama was effective in laying out the case for comprehensive reform and in answering his critics? If you were his speechwriter, what would you have changed?

2. The health care experts surveyed by *National Journal* were most impressed with the law's progress on universal coverage and most concerned about costs. What do you see as the strengths and weaknesses of the law?

3. Do you agree with Yuval Levin that repeal is the only answer? One practical point that Levin does not address is that many popular parts of the law are already in effect, such as allowing young adults to stay on their parents' policies until they are twenty-six, fixing the Medicare drug plan "donut hole," prohibiting insurers from charging copayments or deductibles for preventive care on all new insurance plans, and preventing insurers from dropping policyholders when they get sick. Could these popular parts of the law be kept without a more comprehensive approach?

CHAPTER 16

Foreign Policy and World Politics

84

"The Age of Open Society"

GEORGE SOROS

"Globalization" refers, generally speaking, to the diffusion of interests and ide-ologies across national borders. Proponents of globalization point to the hope that it will encourage global economic development, and foster universal human rights that are not dependent on where someone happens to live. Critics fall into two camps. One consists of those who fear that globalization will undermine national sovereignty and lead to a "one world" government that leaves everyone at the mercy of distant bureaucrats and officials. The other camp consists of those who see globalization as a smokescreen for corporate hegemony, where multina-tional corporations exploit workers in countries with low wages, few job protec-tions, and lax environmental regulation, all in the name of higher profits.

George Soros, an investor who made billions of dollars in currency specula-tion and is now a philanthropist who promotes democracy, believes that economic globalization and political globalization are out of sync: although capital and markets move freely across national boundaries, political institutions do not. A global "open society" would, in his view, insure that the political and social needs of all countries are met (not simply the needs of industrialized nations, whose interests tend to dominate international markets), and would foster the development of stable political and financial institutions. This would require a broad international organization, either as part of the United Nations or as an independent institution. It would have to be based on the idea that certain inter-ests transcend questions of national sovereignty.

Global politics and global economics are dangerously out of sync. Al-though we live in a global economy characterized by free trade and the free movement of capital, our politics are still based on the sover-eignty of the state. International institutions exist, but their powers are limited by how much authority states are willing to confer on them. At the same time, the powers of the state are limited by the freedom of capital to escape taxation and regulation by moving elsewhere. This is particularly true of the countries at the periphery of the global capitalist system, whose economic destiny depends on what happens at the center.

This state of affairs would be sustainable if the market mechanism could be trusted to satisfy social needs. But that is not the case.

We need to find international political arrangements that can meet the requirements of an increasingly interdependent world. These arrangements ought to be built on the principles of open society. A perfect society is beyond our reach. We must content ourselves with the next best thing: a society that holds itself open to improvement. We need institutions that allow people of different views, interests, and backgrounds to live together in peace. These institutions should assure the greatest degree of freedom compatible with the common interest. Many mature democracies come close to qualifying as open societies. But they refuse to accept openness as a universal principle.

How could this principle of openness be translated into practice? By the open societies of the world forming an alliance for this purpose. The alliance would have two distinct but interrelated goals: to foster the development of open society within individual countries; and to establish international laws, rules of conduct, and institutions to implement these norms.

It is contrary to the principles of open society to dictate from the outside how a society should govern itself. Yet the matter cannot be left entirely to the state, either. The state can be an instrument of oppression. To the extent possible, outside help should take the form of incentives; the evolution of open society requires aid for economic and institutional development. Punitive measures, though sometimes unavoidable, tend to be counterproductive.

Unfortunately, positive intervention is out of favor because of an excessive faith in the magic of the marketplace. There is an alliance of democratic countries, NATO, capable of military intervention, but there is no similar alliance to engage in constructive intervention. This open-society alliance ought to have a much broader membership than NATO, and it must include nongovernmental members as well as heads of state. As former U.S. Secretary of State Henry Kissinger points out, states have interests but no principles; we cannot rely on them to implement the principle of openness.

Democratic governments are, however, responsive to the wishes of their electorates. Therefore, the impulse for the alliance has to come from the people, not from their leaders. Citizens living in open societies must recognize a global open society as something worth sacrifice. This responsibility rests in particular with the United States, the sole surviving superpower and the dominant force in the global capitalist system.

There can be no global open society without its leadership. But the United States has become carried away by its success and fails to see why it should subordinate its self-interest to some nebulous common principle. The United States jealously guards its sovereignty and behaves as if it ought to be the sole arbiter of right and wrong. Washington will have to undergo a significant change of heart before it is ready to lead an open-society alliance.

The alliance, if it comes to pass, must not lose sight of its own fallibity. Foreign aid, though very valuable, is notoriously inefficient. Rule-based incentives are more promising. The international financial architecture needs to be redesigned to help give underdeveloped countries a leg up. Incentives would be conditional on each country's success in establishing open political and financial institutions.

The alliance could act within the United Nations, or it could go it alone. But a commitment to such an alliance would offer an opportunity to reform the United Nations. The noble intentions annunciated in the preamble of the U.N. Charter can never be attained as long as the United Nations remains a rigid association of sovereign states. But there is ample room for improvement, and an open-society alliance would be a start. Perhaps one day, then, historians will look back at these years to come as the Age of Open Society.

DISCUSSION QUESTIONS

1. Is Soros's suggestion about an open society practical? Do you think there are circumstances under which nations would agree to such a proposal?

2. How, if at all, will globalization change notions about national identity? Do you think that, twenty-five or fifty years from now, being a U.S. citizen—or a citizen of any other country—will have the same meaning as it does now?

85

"Reality Check"

Peter D. Sutherland

Peter Sutherland confronts the arguments against globalization. Over the past few years, protesters have disrupted meetings of international economic organizations (especially the World Trade Organization, an institution created to foster global free trade). Susan George, a critic of the World Trade Organization, gave the flavor of the arguments against globalization in a recent article in the journal The Nation: *"'Free trade' as managed by the World Trade Organization and reinvigorated at the recent negotiations in Doha is largely the freedom of the fox in the henhouse. Despite the advance on generic drugs for pandemics such as AIDS, tuberculosis and malaria, the South's needs are shelved and the transnationals continue to run the show according to their own preferred rules." Sutherland has little patience with such protests, and believes that protesters are motivated by a simplistic and inaccurate view of what globalization is about: "The notion that globalization is an international conspiracy on the part of industrial-country governments and large firms to marginalize the poorest nations, to exploit low wages and social costs wherever they may be found . . . and even to undermine human rights and cut away democratic processes that stand in the way of ever more open markets is, of course, utter nonsense." He disagrees that international trade organizations ignore the needs of poor countries, and argues that increased global trade is (and has been) the most effective mechanism of economic development. At the same time, he offers some suggestions on how to ensure that existing institutions are strengthened.*

The Seattle Ministerial Conference of the World Trade Organization (WTO) demonstrated with disturbing force the huge confusions that haunt the public mind and much of global politics about the nature of trade and the process now known as globalization. The notion that globalization is an international conspiracy on the part of industrial-country governments and large firms to marginalize the poorest nations, to exploit low wages and social costs wherever they may be found, to diminish cultures in the interests of an Anglo-Saxon model of lifestyle and language, and even to undermine human rights and cut away democratic processes that stand in the way of ever more open markets is, of course, utter nonsense. Yet the Seattle demonstrations vividly exhibited the worrying tendency to equate these concerns and others to the existence and potential development of the World Trade Organization, the institutional and legal face of the world trade system.

This outpouring of misconceived, ill-understood propaganda against a system that has brought vast gains to most nations over the past few decades is extraordinarily dangerous. It is a threat to the prospects of a better life for many millions, perhaps billions, of people at the start of the new millennium. If left unquestioned and unchallenged in the interests of political correctness or political advantage, this sentiment could set the cause of economic and social development back 20 years. This threat is made all the more serious by the difficult new challenges facing governments today. Still, Seattle showed more clearly some of the institutional difficulties of managing effective decision-making processes, with over 100 countries truly interested and involved in managing the geopolitical realities of the 21st century.

The Biggest Straw Man

In order to understand the dangers implied by attacks on the WTO, one must first distinguish between "globalization" and the World Trade Organization. Neither as a body of international law nor as a governmental institution can the WTO be regarded as synonymous with globalization. The WTO, like its predecessor the General Agreement on Tariffs and Trade (GATT), is a collection of rules and undertakings voluntarily entered into and implemented by governments on the basis of consensus among those governments to provide a predictable, stable, and secure environment in which all types of firms can trade and invest. A small transfer of national sovereignty (insofar as any purely intergovernmental structure can affect sovereignty) in the interest of internationally enforceable disciplines brings economic gains for all and prevents economic muscle from being the sole arbiter of commercial advantage. It is easy to argue that in a period when business is as likely to be conducted at the global level as at the national, the WTO recovers a degree of sovereignty for governments that otherwise find themselves no longer able to influence significant aspects of their economic future.

Of course, open and secure markets have encouraged global trade and investment. They have provided jobs, consumer choice, and rising personal wealth in large parts of the world, including many developing countries. Governments everywhere want to see their firms able to trade, and they actively seek inward investment by foreign firms. But that is not the whole story of globalization. The WTO has had only a marginal effect on other significant elements, most of which relate to the mobility of people, information, culture, technology and capital. Air transport, telecommunications, the media, and now the internet are four of the most crucial drivers of globalization. While they are not without their dangers or inadequacies, few would seriously argue that they have not brought widespread benefits. These innovations represent the positive face of the global economy.

Are the more troublesome aspects of globalization really a reflection of the trading system, or do they represent quite different policy failures, including poor education and training, misplaced and inefficient government intervention in industry, corruption in both the public and private sectors, poor governance, crime, lack of transparency in regulatory systems, inadequate or inappropriate social security and pensions systems, and so on? Admittedly, the trading system has not always provided the right results; for instance, it ought to be able to deliver more for the least-developed countries, even if it cannot solve all their problems. However, equating the WTO with the difficulties of the global economy risks damaging a system which has given much and still has more to offer. Such thinking also neglects the importance of the WTO's fundamental role in simply facilitating trade and investment. The tendency to turn to the trade rules to resolve every challenge facing mankind—the environment, human rights, and labor standards—is almost as dangerous as the desire to dismantle the system in order to halt a process of globalization that is beyond the realm of any institution.

Fruits of the Uruguay Round

The first thing governments need to do in the current atmosphere of sometimes dubiously motivated protest and fear is to stop apologizing for the WTO and start defending it. The GATT helped create three decades of remarkably healthy economic growth. It succeeded in a low-profile manner because, in the 1950s and 1960s, high customs duties could be brought down steadily without attracting much political controversy. By the time the Uruguay Round was launched in 1986, the world was left with the hard cases of international trade. Negotiators finally had to face up to protectionism in the most sensitive industries of the developed countries, particularly in textiles, clothing, footwear, agriculture, steel, and automobiles. They also came to realize that the next stages of reducing protection and opening markets, and thus reestablishing the kind of trade growth spurred by the GATT, would mean moving some of the focus of negotiation from conditions at the border (such as tariffs and quota restrictions) to the heart of domestic regulation and sectoral support.

Immense political effort was required at the highest levels of government, but the Uruguay Round succeeded and established the WTO in the process. The advances made on all fronts cannot be underestimated. Policies in agriculture underwent a revolution: all market-access restrictions were translated into transparent tariffs, and the process of winding back the most distorting features of domestic support and export subsidies was initiated. A higher level of practical liberalization for farm goods might have been preferred, but the fundamental policy changes are irreversible and provide the basis to go further next time. Similarly, in textiles and clothing all the countries maintaining heavy quantitative controls on imports are committed to phasing them out. It will take nearly ten years, but the agreement at Uruguay marked a fundamental change of heart and direction.

Many other trade rules were amended, clarified, or added to the system. The practice of "negotiating" so-called "voluntary export restraints" affecting automobiles, steel, cutlery, and many other products for which consumers were forced to pay far more than was reasonable was outlawed. Some of the most damaging features of anti-dumping practices were cut back. Modern rules on technical barriers to trade and health and safety regulation were also put in place.

An agreement requiring intellectual property rights to be available and enforceable in all WTO countries was concluded for the first time, despite doubts and difficulties in some industrial and developing countries. There were two final jewels in the crown. First, an agreement on trade in services brought GATT-like disciplines and concessions in sectors as diverse as banking, telecommunications, professional services, travel, tourism, and the audio-visual industry. Financial services and telecommunications were the subject of additional valuable packages of concessions in the past three years, and the new negotiations, beginning this year, will take the process of progressive liberalization in the services sector much further. Second, the entire body of WTO disciplines and concessions was made enforceable through a tough dispute-settlement procedure that has now been used in nearly 200 cases.

It has become almost an article of faith that while all of these developments were good for the industrialized countries and some of the more advanced developing countries, many poorer countries lost out. Some critics suggest that these countries did not benefit from the results of the round, and that they were, in fact, further marginalized and impoverished. According to these critics, such marginalization is not surprising because developing countries had little or no voice in the negotiations that culminated in agreement at the end of 1993.

Such a position is an insult to the abilities of the many developing country trade negotiators who participated fully in the Uruguay Round. Although I took responsibility at a comparatively late stage, I can attest to the effectiveness and strength of purpose of these officials and ministers from poorer nations. They had considerable influence on the original development of the Uruguay Round agenda; worked assiduously through the eight-year process of examination and elucidation of issues, and negotiation of texts; and were in the foreground during the tough final months of bargaining. Certainly the United States, the European Union, and Japan were more influential, and many of the Uruguay Round texts pay particular attention to their interests. But the developing countries succeeded for the first time in any trade round in melding an influence on the final outcome quite disproportionate to their share of world trade. The WTO is very much their institution and the rules of world trade are as much their rules as those of the industrial countries.

Myths and Realities

So, if it is untrue that developing countries were ignored in the establishment of the WTO, is it at least true that they saw few practical benefits in terms of trade and investment? Again, the answer is no. A few measures demonstrating the long-term trends rather than the short-term aberrations bolster the point. Are developing countries benefiting from more open industrial-country markets? The answer is yes; despite the fall in trade during 1997 because of the drop in commodity prices and the Asian financial crisis, the share of developing countries and the transition economies in the imports of developed countries increased to 25 percent in 1998 from 22.8 percent in 1994. Has the developing countries' share in world trade grown? Again, yes. Despite the setbacks of 1997–1998, the latest WTO figures show that the share of developing countries in world exports of manufactures in 1998 was one percent higher than in 1994, and 6.4 percent higher than in 1990. The same overall growth trend can be observed for merchandise exports generally as well as agricultural products.

What about investment? Have developing countries seen an inward flow of productive investment, as they should if they offer more open markets with stable trade regimes based upon WTO disciplines? As with trade, the picture is mixed, with considerable variations in performance. However, figures from the UN Conference on Trade and Development show that overall inward foreign direct investment (FDI) flows to the developing world rose steadily and consistently from an average of US$35 billion a year in the period 1987–92 to US$166 billion in 1998. Taken as a percentage of gross fixed capital formation, FDI inflows to developing countries rose from an average of 3.9 percent in the period 1987–92 to 10.3 percent in 1998.

There is nothing fundamentally wrong with the system that calls for a wholesale rethinking on behalf of the developing countries. It is accepted that some developing countries have had difficulty in implementing some Uruguay Round commitments. Political and conceptual difficulties have hampered the implementation of certain intellectual property commitments in countries like India. In some of the poorest economies, the absence of solid institutional and technological infrastructure has made the implementation of agreements such as those on customs valuation and health and safety standards difficult. But patience and the right kind of technical assistance can resolve such problems over time. They are not evidence of a systemic failure in the WTO.

Indeed, many developing countries are successfully integrating themselves into the global economy through their commitment to WTO obligations. The failure of the Seattle meeting effectively blocked the continuation of that process or, at the very least, reduced opportunities for further progress. Essentially all that remains is the potential for negotiations on trade in services and agriculture that were mandated in the Uruguay Round agreements. This is not a small agenda, and any successful conclusion in the near future remains in question.

What has been lost or suspended is a larger and, in some respects more urgent, agenda. Developing countries have clearly been denied much that they rightly expected in the implementation of Uruguay Round commitments. They had reasonable demands that industrial countries implement in better faith the agreement to phase out textiles and clothing quotas. The agricultural agreement should have brought them more commercial advantage than has been the case. Antidumping legislation has continued to operate too stringently to the disadvantage of poorer countries. On the other hand, these countries have sometimes had difficulties in meeting their own obligations. That is hardly surprising since they have been required to go much further, much faster than was ever expected of industrial countries. In most cases, additional time needed for implementation of commitments should willingly be provided along with generous technical assistance efforts and the necessary funding for institutional capacity-building.

The least developed countries have been denied the duty-free treatment in market access that has long been promised and discussed in the context of a new round. The entire world has lost the commercial opportunities that would have sprung from global tariff and non-tariff-barrier negotiations covering industrial products. It is estimated that a 50 percent reduction in industrial tariffs would raise some US$270 billion in global income per year, and that developing countries could benefit from as much as 95 percent of the gains from liberalizing trade in manufactures.

Before the Next Round

Perhaps those opportunities will re-emerge, but the immediate priority is not to rush to launch a new round. Governments need to learn the lessons of the Seattle meeting and prepare the ground for the multilateral trading system to move forward on the basis of willing consensus among governments. I would propose four major areas as needing profound reconsideration.

First, coherence in trade policymaking is needed. Until now, this has tended to mean cooperation between the secretariats of the WTO and other major international institutions like the World Bank and the International Monetary Fund. Coherence should now take on a different meaning. It should ensure that the stances of WTO member governments in trade negotiations reflect a domestic consensus. Government departments must coordinate effectively among themselves so that, for instance, environmental, public health, or development concerns are factored into trade-policy decision-making early on. Governments must listen to and work with many different constituencies in an open and transparent manner. Only then can the WTO be clear of the foolish charge that it is some form of government-business conspiracy.

Second, negotiations and decision-making within the WTO itself need to become more coherent and effective. This may require a high level management structure in Geneva, perhaps based upon a restricted constituency-based management or advisory board. Senior policymakers should come to Geneva regularly to set the body's business in the fullest context, including financial development, environmental concerns, and other considerations. Moreover, both the preparatory process and the Seattle ministerial meeting demonstrated that while full transparency is vital—and the institution will have to steel itself to become yet more open—efficient and effective decision-making is necessary if continued paralysis is to be avoided. Of course, negotiating positions may often be so far apart that compromise is simply not possible. Recent history suggests, however, that the techniques of negotiating in a multilateral environment are either inoperable or have been forgotten.

Third, careful consideration must now be given to the speed and intensity with which a new round or any other effort to extend the trading system is pursued. There can be little doubt that the Seattle meeting was both premature and over-burdened with proposals that were poorly thought-out, unnecessary, or premature. Is there really an urgent need to launch a broad-based new trade round in the immediate future? If one believes that neither agriculture nor services negotiations can progress outside such a round, then perhaps the answer is a qualified "yes." But, if the reality is such that an early start would be unlikely to move forward with any conviction, then perhaps governments should take a deep breath and await a more propitious time. Nothing would damage the WTO's image further than another failed attempt to initiate a round.

Fourth, regardless of a new round, governments must now live up to their responsibilities and start energetically defending the principles on which the WTO is based. A "human face" for the trading system is appropriate if it does not serve to undermine the foundations of the system and the huge gains it has provided humanity over the past 50 years. It is perfectly possible to understand and respond to the concerns of those who doubt the value of the system without holding it hostage to local politics. The critics must understand that however justified their causes, the world would not be a better place without the WTO and without continued efforts to make it still more effective for all its members.

This is a turning point for the global trading system. How governments respond to the challenges raised by the Seattle Ministerial Conference could have an overwhelming influence on the contribution that the institution can have on the creation of a better society in the future. Globalization remains a fact and an opportunity. The WTO is one of the most effective instruments at our disposal for translating the opportunity into the reality of improved welfare for billions of citizens. There is no question that it could be a better instrument. But it is the best that we have at our disposal and are likely to have in the future. Governments must learn to use it wisely, change it carefully, and support it convincingly.

DISCUSSION QUESTIONS

1. Many critics of globalization argue that allowing goods and capital to move freely across borders only moves jobs to countries with the cheapest (and most exploitable) labor forces. Supporters argue that these jobs, even though they might not pay much by Western standards, still provide much better opportunities for people in developing nations than would otherwise be available. Who do you think has the better case?

2. Does your campus have organizations active in "anti-sweatshop" organizations? (These groups, among other things, have encouraged universities to insure that clothing and other gear with university symbols are not made by child labor or in dangerous factories). What impact have these organizations had on student opinion?

3. What is the alternative to globalization? What costs are associated with, for example, protecting domestic jobs from being exported? What are the benefits of such protection?

DEBATING THE ISSUES: THE NATIONAL SECURITY STRATEGY OF THE UNITED STATES

Writing down a "National Security Strategy" may seem like an obvious exercise—what is there to say after, "We will respond to attacks on our homeland or allies; we will defend our interests?"—but the obvious parts are merely the starting points. What are our interests? What do we see as the major threats? How will we respond? When will we use military force, and when will we rely on softer forms of power, such as economic sanctions or diplomatic negotiations? When will we act unilaterally, and when will we act only in concert with other nations? The documents state for the public record how the United States defines its national security interests and how it will protect them. The documents do not have any legal force.

The two readings in this section are selections from the national security strategy documents issued by the George W. Bush administration in September 2002 and by the Obama administration in May 2010. Both contain "boilerplate" language—neutral, content-light language that says the obvious. But when read closely, the documents reveal the differences between the approaches each administration took in its effort to safeguard American security. The most provocative aspect of the Bush strategy was its use of "preemptive war." International law has long held that nations do not have to wait until they are attacked to use military force against a threat. But nations are required, under the doctrine of preemptive war, to act only when a threat is immediate—as in the case of a country within days or hours of attacking the United States. The Bush strategy expanded the scope of preemptive war, stating that the United States would use military force to prevent a threat from emerging. (International relations scholars would call this a doctrine of "preventive war," a subtle but important distinction.) This expansion of the circumstances in which the United States would resort to war alarmed the administration's critics, who saw in that language an aggressive unilateralism. The administration's defenders responded that it was a necessary change in an environment in which a single attack, say a nuclear device in a city, could result in millions of deaths.

In his campaign, Obama promised a less unilateral and aggressive national security posture. These themes are reflected in the selection from his administration's national security strategy. It emphasizes collective action and makes far fewer mentions of war or the use of military force. Indeed, the policy on military force is in a separate text box, rather than worked into the language of the strategy document itself.

86

The National Security Strategy
of the United States:
V. Prevent Our Enemies from Threatening Us, Our Allies, and Our Friends with Weapons of Mass Destruction

George W. Bush

The nature of the Cold War threat required the United States—with our allies and friends—to emphasize deterrence of the enemy's use of force, producing a grim strategy of mutual assured destruction. With the collapse of the Soviet Union and the end of the Cold War, our security environment has undergone profound transformation.

Having moved from confrontation to cooperation as the hallmark of our relationship with Russia, the dividends are evident: an end to the balance of terror that divided us; an historic reduction in the nuclear arsenals on both sides; and cooperation in areas such as counterterrorism and missile defense that until recently were inconceivable.

But new deadly challenges have emerged from rogue states and terrorists. None of these contemporary threats rival the sheer destructive power that was arrayed against us by the Soviet Union. However, the nature and motivations of these new adversaries, their determination to obtain destructive powers hitherto available only to the world's strongest states, and the greater likelihood that they will use weapons of mass destruction against us, make today's security environment more complex and dangerous.

In the 1990s we witnessed the emergence of a small number of rogue states that, while different in important ways, share a number of attributes. These states:

- brutalize their own people and squander their national resources for the personal gain of the rulers;
- display no regard for international law, threaten their neighbors, and callously violate international treaties to which they are party;
- are determined to acquire weapons of mass destruction, along with other advanced military technology, to be used as threats or offensively to achieve the aggressive designs of these regimes;

- sponsor terrorism around the globe; and
- reject basic human values and hate the United States and everything for which it stands.

At the time of the Gulf War, we acquired irrefutable proof that Iraq's designs were not limited to the chemical weapons it had used against Iran and its own people, but also extended to the acquisition of nuclear weapons and biological agents. In the past decade North Korea has become the world's principal purveyor of ballistic missiles, and has tested increasingly capable missiles while developing its own WMD arsenal. Other rogue regimes seek nuclear, biological, and chemical weapons as well. These states' pursuit of, and global trade in, such weapons has become a looming threat to all nations.

We must be prepared to stop rogue states and their terrorist clients before they are able to threaten or use weapons of mass destruction against the United States and our allies and friends. Our response must take full advantage of strengthened alliances, the establishment of new partnerships with former adversaries, innovation in the use of military forces, modern technologies, including the development of an effective missile defense system, and increased emphasis on intelligence collection and analysis.

Our comprehensive strategy to combat WMD includes:

- *Proactive counterproliferation efforts.* We must deter and defend against the threat before it is unleashed. We must ensure that key capabilities— detection, active and passive defenses, and counterforce capabilities— are integrated into our defense transformation and our homeland security systems. Counterproliferation must also be integrated into the doctrine, training, and equipping of our forces and those of our allies to ensure that we can prevail in any conflict with WMD-armed adversaries.
- *Strengthened nonproliferation efforts to prevent rogue states and terrorists from acquiring the materials, technologies, and expertise necessary for weapons of mass destruction.* We will enhance diplomacy, arms control, multilateral export controls, and threat reduction assistance that impede states and terrorists seeking WMD, and when necessary, interdict enabling technologies and materials. We will continue to build coalitions to support these efforts, encouraging their increased political and financial support for nonproliferation and threat reduction programs. The recent G-8 agreement to commit up to $20 billion to a global partnership against proliferation marks a major step forward.
- *Effective consequence management to respond to the effects of WMD use, whether by terrorists or hostile states.* Minimizing the effects of WMD use against our people will help deter those who possess such weapons and dissuade those who seek to acquire them by persuading enemies that they cannot attain their desired ends. The United States must also

be prepared to respond to the effects of WMD use against our forces abroad, and to help friends and allies if they are attacked.

It has taken almost a decade for us to comprehend the true nature of this new threat. Given the goals of rogue states and terrorists, the United States can no longer solely rely on a reactive posture as we have in the past. The inability to deter a potential attacker, the immediacy of today's threats, and the magnitude of potential harm that could be caused by our adversaries' choice of weapons, do not permit that option. We cannot let our enemies strike first.

- In the Cold War, especially following the Cuban missile crisis, we faced a generally status quo, risk-averse adversary. Deterrence was an effective defense. But deterrence based only upon the threat of retaliation is less likely to work against leaders of rogue states more willing to take risks, gambling with the lives of their people, and the wealth of their nations.
- In the Cold War, weapons of mass destruction were considered weapons of last resort whose use risked the destruction of those who used them. Today, our enemies see weapons of mass destruction as weapons of choice. For rogue states these weapons are tools of intimidation and military aggression against their neighbors. These weapons may also allow these states to attempt to blackmail the United States and our allies to prevent us from deterring or repelling the aggressive behavior of rogue states. Such states also see these weapons as their best means of overcoming the conventional superiority of the United States.
- Traditional concepts of deterrence will not work against a terrorist enemy whose avowed tactics are wanton destruction and the targeting of innocents; whose so-called soldiers seek martyrdom in death and whose most potent protection is statelessness. The overlap between states that sponsor terror and those that pursue WMD compels us to action.

For centuries, international law recognized that nations need not suffer an attack before they can lawfully take action to defend themselves against forces that present an imminent danger of attack. Legal scholars and international jurists often conditioned the legitimacy of preemption on the existence of an imminent threat—most often a visible mobilization of armies, navies, and air forces preparing to attack.

We must adapt the concept of imminent threat to the capabilities and objectives of today's adversaries. Rogue states and terrorists do not seek to attack us using conventional means. They know such attacks would fail. Instead, they rely on acts of terror and, potentially, the use of weapons of mass destruction—weapons that can be easily concealed, delivered covertly, and used without warning.

The targets of these attacks are our military forces and our civilian population, in direct violation of one of the principal norms of the law of warfare. As was demonstrated by the losses on September 11, 2001, mass civilian casualties is the specific objective of terrorists and these losses would be exponentially more severe if terrorists acquired and used weapons of mass destruction.

The United States has long maintained the option of preemptive actions to counter a sufficient threat to our national security. The greater the threat, the greater is the risk of inaction—and the more compelling the case for taking anticipatory action to defend ourselves, even if uncertainty remains as to the time and place of the enemy's attack. To forestall or prevent such hostile acts by our adversaries, the United States will, if necessary, act preemptively.

The United States will not use force in all cases to preempt emerging threats, nor should nations use preemption as a pretext for aggression. Yet in an age where the enemies of civilization openly and actively seek the world's most destructive technologies, the United States cannot remain idle while dangers gather.

We will always proceed deliberately, weighing the consequences of our actions. To support preemptive options, we will:

• build better, more integrated intelligence capabilities to provide timely, accurate information on threats, wherever they may emerge;
• coordinate closely with allies to form a common assessment of the most dangerous threats; and
• continue to transform our military forces to ensure our ability to conduct rapid and precise operations to achieve decisive results.

The purpose of our actions will always be to eliminate a specific threat to the United States or our allies and friends. The reasons for our actions will be clear, the force measured, and the cause just.

87

The National Security Strategy of the United States: III. Advancing Our Interests

Barack Obama

* * *

Security

* * *

The threats to our people, our homeland, and our interests have shifted dramatically in the last 20 years. Competition among states endures, but instead of a single nuclear adversary, the United States is now threatened by the potential spread of nuclear weapons to extremists who may not be deterred from using them. Instead of a hostile expansionist empire, we now face a diverse array of challenges, from a loose network of violent extremists to states that flout international norms or face internal collapse. In addition to facing enemies on traditional battlefields, the United States must now be prepared for asymmetric threats, such as those that target our reliance on space and cyberspace.

This Administration has no greater responsibility than protecting the American people. Furthermore, we embrace America's unique responsibility to promote international security—a responsibility that flows from our commitments to allies, our leading role in supporting a just and sustainable international order, and our unmatched military capabilities.

The United States remains the only nation able to project and sustain large-scale military operations over extended distances. We maintain superior capabilities to deter and defeat adaptive enemies and to ensure the credibility of security partnerships that are fundamental to regional and global security. In this way, our military continues to underpin our national security and global leadership, and when we use it appropriately, our security and leadership is reinforced. But when we overuse our military might, or fail to invest in or deploy complementary tools, or act without partners, then our military is overstretched, Americans bear a greater burden, and our leadership around the world is too narrowly identified with military force. And we know that our enemies aim to overextend our Armed Forces and to drive wedges between us and those who share our interests.

Therefore, we must continue to adapt and rebalance our instruments of statecraft. At home, we are integrating our homeland security efforts seamlessly with other aspects of our national security approach, and strengthening our preparedness and resilience. Abroad, we are strengthening alliances, forging new partnerships, and using every tool of American power to advance our objectives—including enhanced diplomatic and development capabilities with the ability both to prevent conflict and to work alongside our military. We are strengthening international norms to isolate governments that flout them and to marshal cooperation against nongovernmental actors who endanger our common security.

Strengthen Security and Resilience at Home

At home, the United States is pursuing a strategy capable of meeting the full range of threats and hazards to our communities. These threats and hazards include terrorism, natural disasters, large-scale cyber attacks, and pandemics. As we do everything within our power to prevent these dangers, we also recognize that we will not be able to deter or prevent every single threat. That is why we must also enhance our resilience—the ability to adapt to changing conditions and prepare for, withstand, and rapidly recover from disruption. To keep Americans safe and secure at home, we are working to:

Enhance Security at Home: Security at home relies on our shared efforts to prevent and deter attacks by identifying and interdicting threats, denying hostile actors the ability to operate within our borders, protecting the nation's critical infrastructure and key resources, and securing cyberspace. That is why we are pursuing initiatives to protect and reduce vulnerabilities in critical infrastructure, at our borders, ports, and airports, and to enhance overall air, maritime, transportation, and space and cyber security. Building on this foundation, we recognize that the global systems that carry people, goods, and data around the globe also facilitate the movement of dangerous people, goods, and data. Within these systems of transportation and transaction, there are key nodes—for example, points of origin and transfer, or border crossings—that represent opportunities for exploitation and interdiction. Thus, we are working with partners abroad to confront threats that often begin beyond our borders. And we are developing lines of coordination at home across Federal, state, local, tribal, territorial, nongovernmental, and private-sector partners, as well as individuals and communities.

Effectively Manage Emergencies: We are building our capability to prepare for disasters to reduce or eliminate long-term effects to people and their property from hazards and to respond to and recover from major incidents. To improve our preparedness, we are integrating hazard planning at all levels of government and building key capabilities to respond to emergencies. We continue to collaborate with communities to ensure preparedness efforts are integrated at all levels of government with the private and nonprofit sectors. We are investing in operational capabilities and equipment, and improving the reliability and interoperability of communications systems for first responders. We are encouraging domestic regional planning and integrated preparedness programs and will encourage government at all levels to engage in long-term recovery planning. It is critical that we continually test and improve plans using exercises that are realistic in scenario and consequences.

Empowering Communities to Counter Radicalization: Several recent incidences of violent extremists in the United States who are committed to fighting here and abroad have underscored the threat to the United States and our interests posed by individuals radicalized at home. Our best defenses against this threat are well informed and equipped families, local communities, and institutions. The Federal Government will invest in intelligence to understand this threat and expand community engagement and development programs to empower local communities. And the Federal Government, drawing on the expertise and resources from all relevant agencies, will clearly communicate our policies and intentions, listening to local concerns, tailoring policies to address regional concerns, and making clear that our diversity is part of our strength—not a source of division or insecurity.

Improve Resilience Through Increased Public-Private Partnerships: When incidents occur, we must show resilience by maintaining critical operations and functions, returning to our normal life, and learning from disasters so that their lessons can be translated into pragmatic changes when necessary. The private sector, which owns and operates most of the nation's critical infrastructure, plays a vital role in preparing for and recovering from disasters. We must, therefore, strengthen public-private partnerships by developing incentives for government and the private sector to design structures and systems that can withstand disruptions and mitigate associated consequences, ensure redundant systems where necessary to maintain the ability to operate, decentralize critical operations to reduce our vulnerability to single points of disruption, develop and test continuity plans to ensure the ability to restore critical capabilities, and invest in improvements and maintenance of existing infrastructure.

Engage with Communities and Citizens: We will emphasize individual and community preparedness and resilience through frequent engagement that provides clear and reliable risk and emergency information to the public. A key part of this effort is providing practical steps that all Americans can take to protect themselves, their families, and their neighbors. This includes transmitting information through multiple pathways and to those with special needs. In addition, we support efforts to develop a nationwide public safety broadband network. Our efforts to inform and empower Americans and their communities recognize that resilience has always been at the heart of the American spirit.

Disrupt, Dismantle, and Defeat Al-Qa'ida and Its Violent Extremist Affiliates in Afghanistan, Pakistan, and Around the World

The United States is waging a global campaign against al-Qa'ida and its terrorist affiliates. To disrupt, dismantle and defeat al-Qa'ida and its affiliates, we are pursuing a strategy that protects our homeland, secures the world's most dangerous weapons and material, denies al-Qa'ida safe haven, and builds positive partnerships with Muslim communities around the world. Success requires a broad, sustained, and integrated campaign that judiciously applies every tool of American power—both military and civilian—as well as the concerted efforts of like-minded states and multilateral institutions.

We will always seek to delegitimize the use of terrorism and to isolate those who carry it out. Yet this is not a global war against Islam. We are at war with a specific network, al-Qa'ida, and its terrorist affiliates who support efforts to attack the United States, our allies, and partners.

Prevent Attacks on and in the Homeland: To prevent acts of terrorism on American soil, we must enlist all of our intelligence, law enforcement, and homeland security capabilities. We will continue to integrate and leverage state and major urban area fusion centers that have the capability to share classified information; establish a nationwide framework for reporting suspicious activity; and implement an integrated approach to our counterterrorism information systems to ensure that the analysts, agents, and officers who protect us have access to all relevant intelligence throughout the government. We are improving information sharing and cooperation by linking networks to facilitate Federal, state, and local capabilities to seamlessly exchange messages and information, conduct searches, and collaborate. We are coordinating better with foreign partners to identify, track, limit access to funding, and prevent terrorist travel. Recognizing the inextricable link between domestic and transnational security, we will collaborate bilaterally, regionally, and through international institutions to promote global efforts to prevent terrorist attacks.

Strengthen Aviation Security: We know that the aviation system has been a particular target of al-Qa'ida and its affiliates. We must continue to bolster aviation security worldwide through a focus on increased information collection and sharing, stronger passenger vetting and screening measures, the development of advanced screening technologies, and cooperation with the international community to strengthen aviation security standards and efforts around the world.

Deny Terrorists Weapons of Mass Destruction: To prevent acts of terrorism with the world's most dangerous weapons, we are dramatically accelerating and intensifying efforts to secure all vulnerable nuclear materials by the end of 2013, and to prevent the spread of nuclear weapons. We will also take actions to safeguard knowledge and capabilities in the life and chemical sciences that could be vulnerable to misuse.

Deny Al-Qa'ida the Ability to Threaten the American People, Our Allies, Our Partners and Our Interests Overseas: Al-Qa'ida and its allies must not be permitted to gain or retain any capacity to plan and launch international terrorist attacks, especially against the U.S. homeland. Al Qa'ida's core in Pakistan remains the most dangerous component of the larger network, but we also face a growing threat from the group's allies worldwide. We must deny these groups the ability to conduct operational plotting from any locale, or to recruit, train, and position operatives, including those from Europe and North America.

Afghanistan and Pakistan: This is the epicenter of the violent extremism practiced by al Qa'ida. The danger from this region will only grow if its security slides backward, the Taliban controls large swaths of Afghanistan, and al-Qa'ida is allowed to operate with impunity. To prevent future attacks on the United States, our allies, and partners, we must work with others to keep the pressure on al-Qa'ida and increase the security and capacity of our partners in this region.

In Afghanistan, we must deny al-Qa'ida a safe haven, deny the Taliban the ability to overthrow the government, and strengthen the capacity of Afghanistan's security forces and government so that they can take lead responsibility for Afghanistan's future. Within Pakistan, we are working with the government to address the local, regional, and global threat from violent extremists.

We will achieve these objectives with a strategy comprised of three components.

- First, our military and International Security Assistance Force (ISAF) partners within Afghanistan are targeting the insurgency, working to secure key population centers, and increasing efforts to train Afghan security forces. These military resources will allow us to create the conditions to transition to Afghan responsibly. In July 2011, we will begin reducing our troops' responsibility, taking into account conditions on the ground. We will continue to advise and assist Afghanistan's Security Forces so that they can succeed over the long term.

- Second, we will continue to work with our partners, the United Nations, and the Afghan Government to improve accountable and effective governance. As we work to advance our strategic partnership with the Afghan Government, we are focusing assistance on supporting the President of Afghanistan and those ministries, governors, and local leaders who combat corruption and deliver for the people. Our efforts will be based upon performance, and we will measure progress. We will also target our assistance to areas that can make an immediate and enduring impact in the lives of the Afghan people, such as agriculture, while supporting the human rights of all of Afghanistan's people—women and men. This will support our long-term commitment to a relationship between our two countries that supports a strong, stable, and prosperous Afghanistan.

- Third, we will foster a relationship with Pakistan founded upon mutual interests and mutual respect. To defeat violent extremists who threaten both of our countries, we will strengthen Pakistan's capacity to target violent extremists within its borders, and continue to provide security assistance to support those efforts. To strengthen Pakistan's democracy and development, we will provide substantial assistance responsive to the needs of the Pakistani people, and sustain a long-term partnership committed to Pakistan's future. The strategic partnership that we are developing with Pakistan includes deepening cooperation in a broad range of areas, addressing both security and civilian challenges, and we will continue to expand those ties through our engagement with Pakistan in the years to come.

Deny Safe Havens and Strengthen At-Risk States: Wherever al-Qa'ida or its terrorist affiliates attempt to establish a safe haven—as they have in Yemen, Somalia, the Maghreb, and the Sahel—we will meet them with growing pressure. We also will strengthen our own network of partners to disable al-Qa'ida's financial, human, and planning networks; disrupt terrorist operations before they mature; and address potential safe-havens before al-Qa'ida and its terrorist affiliates can take root. These efforts will focus on information-sharing, law enforcement cooperation, and establishing new practices to counter evolving adversaries. We will also help states avoid becoming terrorist safe havens by helping them build their capacity for responsible governance and security through development and security sector assistance.

Deliver Swift and Sure Justice: To effectively detain, interrogate, and prosecute terrorists, we need durable legal approaches consistent with our security and our values. We adhere to several principles: we will leverage all available information and intelligence to disrupt attacks and dismantle al-Qa'ida and affiliated terrorist organizations; we will bring terrorists to justice; we will act in line with the rule of law and due process; we will submit decisions to checks and balances and accountability; and we will insist that matters of detention and secrecy are addressed in a manner consistent with our Constitution and laws. To deny violent extremists one of their most potent recruitment tools, we will close the prison at Guantanamo Bay.

Resist Fear and Overreaction: The goal of those who perpetrate terrorist attacks is in part to sow fear. If we respond with fear, we allow violent extremists to succeed far beyond the initial impact of their attacks, or attempted attacks—altering our society and enlarging the standing of al-Qa'ida and its terrorist affiliates far beyond its actual reach. Similarly, overreacting in a way that creates fissures between America and certain regions or religions will undercut our leadership and make us less safe.

Contrast Al-Qa'ida's Intent to Destroy with Our Constructive Vision: While violent extremists seek to destroy, we will make clear our intent to build. We are striving to build bridges among people of different faiths and religions. We will continue to work to resolve the Arab-Israeli conflict, which has long been a source of tension. We will continue to stand up for the universal rights of all people, even for those with whom we disagree. We are developing new partnerships in Muslim communities around the world on behalf of health, education, science, employment, and innovation. And through our broader emphasis on Muslim engagement, we will communicate our commitment to support the aspirations of all people for security and opportunity. Finally, we reject the notion that al-Qa'ida represents any religious authority. They are not religious leaders, they are killers; and neither Islam nor any other religion condones the slaughter of innocents.

Use of Force

Military force, at times, may be necessary to defend our country and allies or to preserve broader peace and security, including by protecting civilians facing a grave humanitarian crisis. We will draw on diplomacy, development, and international norms and institutions to help resolve disagreements, prevent conflict, and maintain peace, mitigating where possible the need for the use of force. This means credibly underwriting U.S. defense commitments with tailored approaches to deterrence and ensuring the U.S. military continues to have the necessary capabilities across all domains—land, air, sea, space, and cyber. It also includes helping our allies and partners build capacity to fulfill their responsibilities to contribute to regional and global security.

While the use of force is sometimes necessary, we will exhaust other options before war whenever we can, and carefully weigh the costs and risks of action against the costs and risks of inaction. When force is necessary, we will continue to do so in a way that reflects our values and strengthens our legitimacy, and we will seek broad international support, working with such institutions as NATO and the U.N. Security Council.

The United States must reserve the right to act unilaterally if necessary to defend our nation and our interests, yet we will also seek to adhere to standards that govern the use of force. Doing so strengthens those who act in line with international standards, while isolating and weakening those who do not. We will also outline a clear mandate and specific objectives and thoroughly consider the consequences—intended and unintended—of our actions. And the United States will take care when sending the men and women of our Armed Forces into harm's way to ensure they have the leadership, training, and equipment they require to accomplish their mission.

Discussion Questions

1. Who do you think is the intended audience for these documents? Is it the U.S. electorate? The international community? Potential adversaries?

2. What other differences can you find between the documents? How would you connect them to what you know about the other characteristics of the George W. Bush and the Obama administrations?

3. Critics of the Bush strategy argued that it was too aggressive and unilateral. Critics of the Obama strategy say it places too much emphasis on diplomacy and subordinating U.S. interests to international opinion. What do you see as the strengths and weaknesses of these documents?

4. Is there an ideal national security strategy? Is it possible to construct a strategy that everyone would agree with?

Appendix

Marbury v. Madison (1803)

The power of judicial review—the authority of the federal courts to determine the constitutionality of state and federal legislative acts—was established early in the nation's history in the case of Marbury v. Madison *(1803). While the doctrine of judicial review is now firmly entrenched in the American judicial process, the outcome of* Marbury *was by no means a sure thing. The doctrine had been outlined in* The Federalist, No. 78, *and had been relied on implicitly in earlier, lower federal court cases, but there were certainly sentiments among some of the Founders to suggest that only Congress ought to be able to judge the constitutionality of its acts.*

The facts leading up to the decision in Marbury v. Madison *tell an intensely political story. Efforts to reform the federal judiciary had been ongoing with the Federalist administration of President Adams. Following the defeat of the Federalist party in 1800 and the election of Thomas Jefferson as president, the Federalist Congress passed an act reforming the judiciary. The act gave the outgoing president Adams authority to appoint several Federalist justices of the peace before Jefferson's term as president began. This would have enabled the Federalist party to retain a large measure of power.*

Marbury was appointed to be a justice of the peace by President Adams, but his commission, signed by the president and sealed by the secretary of state, without which he could not assume office, was not delivered to him before President Jefferson took office March 4, 1803. Jefferson refused to order James Madison, his secretary of state, to deliver the commission. Marbury, in turn, filed an action in the U.S. Supreme Court seeking an order—called a writ of mandamus—directing the secretary of state to compel the delivery of the commission.

The Constitution grants the Supreme Court original jurisdiction in only a limited number of cases—those involving ambassadors, public ministers, and those in which a state is a party; in the remaining cases, the Court has authority only as an appellate court. When it acts according to its original jurisdiction, the Court exercises initial authority over a controversy, just like a trial court, as distinguished from the more limited authority it exercises when a case is presented as an appeal from a lower court's decision.

In 1789, Congress passed legislation setting up the federal courts, called the Judiciary Act of 1789. That legislation gave the Supreme Court the original authority to "issue writs of mandamus in cases warranted by the principles and usage of law. . . ." Thus, the ultimate question in Marbury v. Madison *was whether Congress could, by statute, enlarge the original jurisdiction of the Court.*

The Court first considered whether Marbury's appointment was complete— and therefore irrevocable—before Jefferson took office. Under the law, the appointment was deemed complete when the president signed the commission and the secretary of state sealed it; the appointment was a completed fact at that time, and was not dependent upon delivery. Therefore, the Court found that Marbury was entitled to his commission. The Court then decided that by withholding the commission, Secretary of State Madison was violating Marbury's legal rights. The remaining question was whether the Supreme Court could issue an order compelling the delivery of the commission.

CHIEF JUSTICE MARSHALL delivered the opinion of the Court.

. . . It is, then, the opinion of the Court,

1st. That by signing the commission of Mr. Marbury, the President of the United States appointed him a justice of peace for the county of Washington, in the District of Columbia; and that the seal of the United States, affixed thereto by the Secretary of State, is conclusive testimony of the verity of the signature, and of the completion of the appointment, and that the appointment conferred on him a legal right to the office for the space of five years.

2d. That, having this legal title to the office, he has a consequent right to the commission; a refusal to deliver which is a plain violation of that right, for which the laws of his country afford him a remedy.

It remains to be inquired whether,

3d. He is entitled to the remedy for which he applies. This depends on,

1st. The nature of the writ applied for; and,

2d. The power of this court.

* * *

This . . . is a plain case for a mandamus, either to deliver the commission, or a copy of it from the record; and it only remains to be inquired,

Whether it can issue from this court.

The act to establish the judicial courts of the United States authorizes the Supreme Court "to issue writs of mandamus in cases warranted by the principles and usages of law, to any courts appointed, or persons holding office, under the authority of the United States."

The Secretary of State, being a person holding an office under the authority of the United States, is precisely within the letter of the description, and if this court is not authorized to issue a writ of mandamus to such an officer, it must be because the law is unconstitutional, and therefore absolutely incapable of conferring the authority, and assigning the duties which its words purport to confer and assign.

The constitution vests the whole judicial power of the United States in one Supreme Court, and such inferior courts as congress shall, from time to time, ordain and establish. This power is expressly extended to all cases arising under the laws of the United States; and, consequently, in some form, may be exercised over the present case; because the right claimed is given by a law of the United States.

In the distribution of this power it is declared that "the Supreme Court shall have original jurisdiction in all cases affecting ambassadors, other public ministers and consuls, and those in which a state shall be a party. In all other cases, the Supreme Court shall have appellate jurisdiction."

* * *

To enable this court, then, to issue a mandamus, it must be shown to be an exercise of appellate jurisdiction, or to be necessary to enable them to exercise appellate jurisdiction.

* * *

It is the essential criterion of appellate jurisdiction, that it revises and corrects the proceedings in a cause already instituted, and does not create that cause. . . . [Y]et to issue such a writ to an officer for the delivery of a paper, is in effect the same as to sustain an original action for that paper, and, therefore, seems not to belong to appellate, but to original jurisdiction.

The authority, therefore, given to the Supreme Court, by the act establishing the judicial courts of the United States, to issue writs of mandamus to public officers, appears not to be warranted by the constitution; and it becomes necessary to inquire whether a jurisdiction so conferred can be exercised.

The question, whether an act, repugnant to the constitution, can become the law of the land, is a question deeply interesting to the United States; but, happily, not of an intricacy proportioned to its interest. It seems only necessary to recognize certain principles, supposed to have been long and well established, to decide it.

That the people have an original right to establish, for their future government, such principles, as, in their opinion, shall most conduce to their own happiness is the basis on which the whole American fabric has been erected. The exercise of this original right is a very great exertion; nor can it, nor ought it, to be frequently repeated. The principles, therefore, so established, are deemed fundamental. And as the authority from which they proceed is supreme, and can seldom act, they are designed to be permanent.

This original and supreme will organizes the government, and assigns to different departments their respective powers. It may either stop here, or establish certain limits not to be transcended by those departments.

The government of the United States is of the latter description. The powers of the legislature are defined and limited; and that those limits may not be mistaken, or forgotten, the constitution is written. To what purpose are powers limited, and to what purpose is that limitation committed to writing, if these limits may, at any time, be passed by those intended to be restrained? The distinction between a government with limited and unlimited powers is abolished, if those limits do not confine the persons on whom they are imposed, and if acts prohibited and acts allowed, are of equal obligation. It is a proposition too plain to be contested, that the constitution controls any legislative act repugnant to it; or, that the legislature may alter the constitution by an ordinary act.

Between these alternatives there is no middle ground. The constitution is either a superior paramount law, unchangeable by ordinary means, or it is on a level with ordinary legislative acts, and, like other acts, is alterable when the legislature shall please to alter it.

If the former part of the alternative be true, then a legislative act contrary to the constitution is not law: if the latter part be true, then written constitutions are absurd attempts, on the part of the people, to limit a power in its own nature illimitable.

Certainly all those who have framed written constitutions contemplate them as forming the fundamental and paramount law of the nation, and, consequently, the theory of every such government must be, that an act of the legislature, repugnant to the constitution, is void.

This theory is essentially attached to a written constitution, and, is consequently, to be considered, by this court, as one of the fundamental principles of our society. It is not therefore to be lost sight of in the further consideration of this subject.

If an act of the legislature, repugnant to the constitution, is void, does it, notwithstanding its invalidity, bind the courts, and oblige them to give it effect? Or, in other words, though it be not law, does it constitute a rule as operative as if it was a law? This would be to overthrow in fact what was established in theory; and would seem, at first view, an absurdity too gross to be insisted on.

* * *

It is emphatically the province and duty of the judicial department to say what the law is. Those who apply the rule to particular cases, must of necessity expound and interpret that rule. If two laws conflict with each other, the courts must decide on the operation of each.

So if a law be in opposition to the constitution; if both the law and the constitution apply to a particular case, so that the court must either decide that case conformably to the law, disregarding the constitution; or conformably to the constitution, disregarding the law; the court must determine which of these conflicting rules governs the case. This is of the very essence of judicial duty.

If, then, the courts are to regard the constitution, and the constitution is superior to any ordinary act of the legislature, the constitution, and not such ordinary act, must govern the case to which they both apply.

Those, then, who controvert the principle that the constitution is to be considered, in court, as a paramount law, are reduced to the necessity of maintaining that courts must close their eyes on the constitution, and see only the law.

This doctrine would subvert the very foundation of all written constitutions. It would declare that an act which, according to the principles and theory of our government, is entirely void, is yet, in practice, completely obligatory. It would declare that if the legislature shall do what is expressly forbidden, such act, notwithstanding the express prohibition, is in reality effectual. It would be giving to the legislature a practical and real omnipotence, with the same breath which professes to restrict their powers within narrow limits. It is prescribing limits, and declaring that those limits may be passed at pleasure.

That it thus reduces to nothing what we have deemed the greatest improvement on political institutions, a written constitution, would of itself be sufficient, in America, where written constitutions have been viewed with so much reverence, for rejecting the construction. But the peculiar expressions of the constitution of the United States furnish additional arguments in favour of its rejection.

The judicial power of the United States is extended to all cases arising under the constitution.

Could it be the intention of those who gave this power, to say that in using it the constitution should not be looked into? That a case arising under the constitution should be decided without examining the instrument under which it arises?

This is too extravagant to be maintained.

In some cases, then, the constitution must be looked into by the judges.

. . . [I]t is apparent, that the framers of the constitution contemplated that instrument as a rule for the government of courts, as well as of the legislature.

Why otherwise does it direct the judges to take an oath to support it? This oath certainly applies in an especial manner, to their conduct in their official character. How immoral to impose it on them, if they were to be used as the instruments, and the knowing instruments, for violating what they swear to support!

The oath of office, too, imposed by the legislature, is completely demonstrative of the legislative opinion on this subject.

*   *   *

Why does a judge swear to discharge his duties agreeably to the constitution of the United States, if that constitution forms no rule for his government? If it is closed upon him, and cannot be inspected by him?

If such be the real state of things, this is worse than solemn mockery. To prescribe, or to take this oath, becomes equally a crime.

It is also not entirely unworthy of observation, that in declaring what shall be the supreme law of the land, the constitution itself is first mentioned; and not the laws of the United States generally, but those only which shall be made in pursuance of the constitution, have that rank.

Thus, the particular phraseology of the constitution of the United States confirms and strengthens the principle, supposed to be essential to all written constitutions, that a law repugnant to the constitution is void; and that courts, as well as other departments, are bound by that instrument.

McCulloch v. Maryland (1819)

Early in the nation's history, the U.S. Supreme Court interpreted the powers of the national government expansively. The first Supreme Court case to directly address the scope of federal authority under the Constitution was McCulloch v. Maryland *(1819). The facts were straightforward: Congress created the Bank of the United States—to the dismay of many states that viewed the creation of a national bank as a threat to the operation of banks within their own state borders. As a result, when a branch of the Bank of the United States was opened in Maryland, that state attempted to limit the bank's ability to do business under a law that imposed taxes on all banks not chartered by the state.*

In an opinion authored by Chief Justice Marshall, the Court considered two questions: whether Congress had the authority to create a national bank; and whether Maryland could in turn tax it. Marshall's answer to these two questions defends an expansive theory of implied powers for the national government and propounds the principle of national supremacy with an eloquence rarely found in judicial decisions.

CHIEF JUSTICE JOHN MARSHALL delivered the opinion of the Court.

The first question made in the cause is, has Congress power to incorporate a bank? The power now contested was exercised by the first Congress elected under the present constitution. The bill for incorporating the Bank of the United States did not steal upon an unsuspecting legislature, and pass unobserved. Its principle was completely understood, and was opposed with equal zeal and ability. . . . In discussing this question, the counsel for the state of Maryland have deemed it of some importance, in the construction of the constitution, to consider that instrument not as emanating from the people, but as the act of sovereign and independent states. The powers of the general government, it has been said, are delegated by the states, who alone are truly sovereign; and must be exercised in subordination to the states, who alone possess supreme dominion. . . . No political dreamer was ever wild enough to think of breaking down the lines which separate the states, and of compounding the American people into one common mass. Of consequence, when they act, they act in their states. But the measures they adopt do not, on that account, cease to be the measures of the people themselves, or become the measures of the state governments.

From these conventions the constitution derives its whole authority. The government proceeds directly from the people; is "ordained and established" in the name of the people; and is declared to be ordained, "in order to form a more perfect union, establish justice, insure domestic tranquility, and secure the blessings of liberty to themselves and to their posterity." The assent of the states, in their sovereign capacity, is implied in calling a convention, and thus submitting that instrument to the people. But the people were at perfect liberty to accept or reject it; and their act was final. It required not the affirmance, and could not be negatived, by the state governments. The constitution, when thus adopted, was of complete obligation, and bound the state sovereignties.

The government of the Union, then (whatever may be the influence of this fact on the case), is, emphatically, and truly, a government of the people. In form and in substance it emanates from them. Its powers are granted by them, and are to be exercised directly on them, and for their benefit.

This government is acknowledged by all to be one of enumerated powers. The principle, that it can exercise only the powers granted to it, is now universally admitted. But the question respecting the extent of the powers actually granted, is perpetually arising, and will probably continue to arise, as long as our system shall exist. The government of the United States though limited in its powers, is supreme; and its laws, when made in pursuance of the constitution, form the supreme law of the land, "anything in the constitution or laws of any state to the contrary notwithstanding."

* * *

A constitution, to contain an accurate detail of all the subdivisions of which its great powers will admit, and of all the means by which they may be carried into execution, would partake of the prolixity of a legal code, and could scarcely be embraced by the human mind. It would probably never be understood by the public. Its nature, therefore, requires, that only its great outlines should be marked, its important objects designated, and the minor ingredients which compose those objects be deduced from the nature of the objects themselves. . . . in considering this question, then, we must never forget, that it is a constitution we are expounding.

Although, among the enumerated powers of government, we do not find the word "bank" or "incorporation," we find the great powers to lay and collect taxes; to borrow money; to regulate commerce; to declare and conduct a war; and to raise and support armies and navies. The sword and the purse, all the external relations, and no inconsiderable portion of the industry of the nation, are entrusted to its government. . . . [I]t may with great reason be contended, that a government, entrusted with such ample powers, on the due execution of which the happiness and prosperity of the nation so vitally depends, must also be entrusted with ample means for their execution. The power being given, it is the interest of the nation to facilitate its execution. It can never be their interest, and cannot be presumed to have been their intention, to clog and embarrass its execution by withholding the most appropriate means. . . . It is, then, the subject of fair inquiry, how far such means may be employed.

The government which has a right to do an act, and has imposed on it the duty of performing that act, must, according to the dictates of reason, be allowed to select the means.

* * *

But the constitution of the United States has not left the right of Congress to employ the necessary means, for the execution of the powers conferred on the government, to general reasoning. To its enumeration of powers is added that of making "all laws which shall be necessary and proper, for carrying into execution the foregoing powers, and all other powers vested by this constitution, in the government of the United States, or in any department [or officer] thereof."

The counsel for the state of Maryland have urged various arguments, to prove that this clause . . . is really restrictive of the general right, which might otherwise be implied, of selecting means for executing the enumerated powers.

. . . [Maryland argues that] Congress is not empowered by it to make all laws, which may have relation to the powers conferred on the government, but such only as may be "necessary and proper" for carrying them into execution. The word "necessary" is considered as controlling the whole sentence, and as limiting the right to pass laws for the execution of the granted powers, to such as are indispensable, and without which the power would be nugatory. That it excludes the choice of means, and leaves to Congress, in each case, that only which is most direct and simple.

Is it true, that this is the sense in which the word "necessary" is always used? . . . We think it does not. If reference be had to its use, in the common affairs of the world, or in approved authors, we find that it frequently imports no more than that one thing is convenient, or useful, or essential to another. To employ the means necessary to an end, is generally understood as employing any means calculated to produce the end, and not as being confined to those single means, without which the end would be entirely unattainable.

Let this be done in the case under consideration. The subject is the execution of those great powers on which the welfare of a nation essentially depends. It must have been the intention of those who gave these powers, to insure, as far as human prudence could insure, their beneficial execution. This could not be done by confiding the choice of means to such narrow limits as not to leave it in the power of Congress to adopt any which might be appropriate, and which were conducive to the end. This provision is made in a constitution intended to endure for ages to come, and consequently, to be adapted to the various crises of human affairs. To have prescribed the means by which government should, in all future time, execute its powers, would have been to change, entirely, the character of the instrument, and give it the properties of a legal code. It would have been an unwise attempt to provide, by immutable rules, for exigencies which, if foreseen at all, must have been seen dimly, and which can be best provided for as they occur. To have declared that the best means shall not be used, but those alone without which the power given would be nugatory, would have been to deprive the legislature of the capacity to avail itself of experience, to exercise its reason, and to accommodate its legislation to circumstances. If we apply this principle of construction to any of the powers of the government, we shall find it so pernicious in its operation that we shall be compelled to discard it.

* * *

We admit, as all must admit, that the powers of the government are limited, and that its limits are not to be transcended. But we think the sound construction of the constitution must allow to the national legislature that discretion, with respect to the means by which the powers it confers are to be carried into execution, which will enable that body to perform the high duties assigned to it, in the manner most beneficial to the people. Let the end be legitimate, let it be within the scope of the constitution, and all means which are appropriate, which are plainly adapted to that end, which are not prohibited, but consist with the letter and spirit of the constitution, are constitutional.

* * *

It being the opinion of the court that the act incorporating the bank is constitutional, and that the power of establishing a branch in the state of Maryland might be properly exercised by the bank itself, we proceed to inquire: Whether the state of Maryland may, without violating the constitution, tax that branch?

That the power of taxation is one of vital importance; that it is retained by the states; that it is not abridged by the grant of a similar power to the government of the Union; that it is to be concurrently exercised by the two governments; are truths which have never been denied. But, such is the paramount character of the constitution that its capacity to withdraw any subject from the action of even this power, is admitted. . . . [T]he paramount character [of the Constitution] would seem to restrain, as it certainly may restrain, a state from such other exercise of this power as is in its nature incompatible with, and repugnant to, the constitutional laws of the Union. A law, absolutely repugnant to another, as entirely repeals that other as if express terms of repeal were used.

* * *

This great principle is, that the constitution and the laws made in pursuance thereof are supreme; that they control the constitution and laws of the respective states, and cannot be controlled by them. From this, which may be almost termed an axiom, other propositions are adduced as corollaries, on the truth or error of which, and on their application to this case, the cause has been supposed to depend. These are, 1st. That a power to create implies a power to preserve. 2d. That a power to destroy, if wielded by a different hand, is hostile to, and incompatible with, these powers to create and to preserve. 3d. That where this repugnance exists, that authority which is supreme must control, not yield to that over which it is supreme.

. . . [T]axation is said to be an absolute power, which acknowledges no other limits than those expressly prescribed in the constitution, and like sovereign powers of every other description, is trusted to the discretion of those who use it. But the very terms of this argument admit that the sovereignty of the state, in the article of taxation itself, is subordinate to, and may be controlled by the constitution of the United States. How far it has been controlled by that instrument must be a question of construction. In making this construction, no principle not declared can be admissible, which would defeat the legitimate operations of a supreme government.

* * *

All subjects over which the sovereign power of a state extends, are objects of taxation; but those over which it does not extend, are, upon the soundest principles, exempt from taxation. . . . The sovereignty of a state extends to everything which exists by its own authority, or is introduced by its permission; but does it extend to those means which are employed by Congress to carry into execution—powers conferred on that body by the people of the United States? We think it demonstrable that it does not. Those powers are not given by the people of a single state. They are given by the people of the United States, to a government whose laws, made in pursuance of the constitution, are declared to be supreme. Consequently, the people of a single state cannot confer a sovereignty which will extend over them.

If we apply the principle for which the state of Maryland contends, to the constitution generally, we shall find it capable of changing totally the character of that instrument. We shall find it capable of arresting all the measures of the government, and of prostrating it at the foot of the states. The American people have declared their constitution, and the laws made in pursuance thereof, to be supreme; but this principle would transfer the supremacy, in fact, to the states. If the controlling power of the states be established; if their supremacy as to taxation be acknowledged; what is to restrain their exercising this control in any shape they may please to give it? Their sovereignty is not confined to taxation. That is not the only mode in which it might be displayed. The question is, in truth, a question of supremacy; and if the right of the states to tax the means employed by the general government be conceded, the declaration that the constitution, and the laws made in pursuance thereof, shall be the supreme law of the land, is empty and unmeaning declamation.

* * *

We are unanimously of opinion, that the law passed by the legislature of Maryland, imposing a tax on the Bank of the United States, is unconstitutional and void. This opinion does not deprive the states of any resources which they originally possessed. It does not extend to a tax paid by the real property of the bank, in common with other real property within the state, nor to a tax imposed on the interest which the citizens of Maryland may hold in this institution, in common with other property of the same description throughout the state. But this is a tax on the operations of the bank, and is, consequently, a tax on the operation of an instrument employed by the government of the Union to carry its powers into execution. Such a tax must be unconstitutional.

Reversed.

Barron v. Baltimore (1833)

The declaration made in **Barron v. Baltimore** *(1833) that citizenship had a dual aspect—state and national—set the terms of the Supreme Court's interpretation of the Bill of Rights for nearly a century. The reasoning of the case proved persuasive even after the adoption of the Fourteenth Amendment, as the federal courts refused to extend the protections of the federal Constitution to citizens aggrieved by the actions of state or local governments.*

Barron brought suit in a federal court claiming that the city of Baltimore had appropriated his property for a public purpose without paying him just compensation. He asserted that the Fifth Amendment to the Constitution operated as a constraint upon both state and federal governments.

CHIEF JUSTICE JOHN MARSHALL delivered the opinion of the Court.

. . . The question presented is, we think, of great importance, but not of much difficulty. The constitution was ordained and established by the people of the United States for themselves, for their own government, and not for the government of the individual states. Each state established a constitution for itself, and in that constitution, provided such limitations and restrictions on the powers of its particular government, as its judgment dictated. The people of the United States framed such a government for the United States as they supposed best adapted to their situation and best calculated to promote their interests. The powers they conferred on this government were to be exercised by itself; and the limitations on power, if expressed in general terms, are naturally, and, we think, necessarily, applicable to the government created by the instrument. They are limitations of power granted in the instrument itself; not of distinct governments, framed by different persons and for different purposes.

If these propositions be correct, the fifth amendment must be understood as restraining the power of the general government, not as applicable to the states. In their several constitutions, they have imposed such restrictions on their respective governments, as their own wisdom suggested; such as they deemed most proper for themselves. It is a subject on which they judge exclusively, and with which others interfere no further than they are supposed to have a common interest.

* * *

Had the people of the several states, or any of them, required changes in their constitutions; had they required additional safe-guards to liberty from the apprehended encroachments of their particular governments; the remedy was in their own hands, and could have been applied by themselves. A convention could have been assembled by the discontented state, and the required improvements could have been made by itself.

. . . Had Congress engaged in the extraordinary occupation of improving the constitutions of the several states, by affording the people additional protection from the exercise of power by their own governments, in matters which concerned themselves alone, they would have declared this purpose in plain and intelligible language.

But it is universally understood, it is a part of the history of the day, that the great revolution which established the constitution of the United States, was not effected without immense opposition. Serious fears were extensively entertained, that those powers which the patriot statesmen, who then watched over the interests of our country, deemed essential to union, and to the attainment of those unvaluable objects for which union was sought, might be exercised in a manner dangerous to liberty. In almost every convention by which the constitution was adopted, amendments to guard against the abuse of power were recommended. These amendments demanded security against the apprehended encroachments of the general government—not against those of the local governments. In compliance with a sentiment thus generally expressed, to quiet fears thus extensively entertained, amendments were proposed by the required majority in congress, and adopted by the states. These amendments contain no expression indicating an intention to apply them to the state governments. This court cannot so apply them.

We are of opinion, that the provision in the fifth amendment to the constitution, declaring that private property shall not be taken for public use, without just compensation, is intended solely as a limitation on the exercise of power by the government of the United States, and is not applicable to the legislation of the states. We are, therefore, of opinion, that there is no repugnancy between the several acts of the general assembly of Maryland, given in evidence by the defendants at the trial of this cause, in the court of that state, and the constitution of the United States. This court, therefore, has no jurisdiction of the cause, and it is dismissed.

This cause came on to be heard, on the transcript of the record from the court of appeals for the western shore of the state of Maryland, and was argued by counsel: On consideration whereof, it is the opinion of this court, that there is no repugnancy between the several acts of the general assembly of Maryland, given in evidence by the defendants at the trial of this cause in the court of that state, and the constitution of the United States; whereupon, it is ordered and adjudged by this court, that this writ of error be and the same is hereby dismissed, for the want of jurisdiction.

Roe v. Wade (1973)

One of the most significant changes in constitutional interpretation in the last three decades has been the Court's willingness to look beyond the explicit language of the Bill of Rights to find unenumerated rights, such as the right to privacy. In discovering such rights, the Court has engaged in what is known as substantive due process analysis—defining and articulating fundamental rights—distinct from its efforts to define the scope of procedural due process, when it decides what procedures the state and federal governments must follow to be fair in their treatment of citizens. The Court's move into the substantive due process area has generated much of the political discussion over the proper role of the Court in constitutional interpretation.

The case that has been the focal point for this debate is Roe v. Wade, *the 1973 case that held that a woman's right to privacy protected her decision to have an abortion. The right to privacy in matters relating to contraception and childbearing had been recognized in the 1965 decision of* Griswold v. Connecticut, *and was extended in subsequent decisions culminating in* Roe. *The theoretical issue of concern here relates back to the incorporation issue: Should the Supreme Court be able to prohibit the states not only from violating the express guarantees contained in the Bill of Rights, but its implied guarantees as well?*

Texas law prohibited abortions except for "the purpose of saving the life of the mother." The plaintiff challenged the constitutionality of the statute, claiming that it infringed upon her substantive due process right to privacy.

JUSTICE BLACKMUN delivered the opinion of the Court.

. . . [We] forthwith acknowledge our awareness of the sensitive and emotional nature of the abortion controversy, of the vigorous opposing views, and the deep and seemingly absolute convictions that the subject inspires. One's philosophy, one's experiences, one's exposure to the raw edges of human existence, one's religious training, one's attitudes toward life and family and their values, and the moral standards one establishes and seeks to observe, are all likely to affect one's thinking [about] abortion. In addition, population growth, pollution, poverty, and racial overtones tend to complicate and not to simplify the problem. Our task, of course, is to resolve the issue by constitutional measurement, free of emotion and of predilection. We seek earnestly to do this, and, because we do, we have inquired into, and in this opinion place some emphasis upon, medical and medical-legal history and what that history reveals about man's attitudes toward the abortion procedure over the centuries.

* * *

[*The Court here reviewed ancient and contemporary attitudes toward abortion, observing that restrictive laws date primarily from the late nineteenth century. The Court also reviewed the possible state interests in restricting abortions, including discouraging illicit sexual conduct, limiting access to a hazardous medical procedure, and the states' general interests in protecting fetal life. The Court addressed only the third interest as a current legitimate interest of the state.*]

. . . The Constitution does not explicitly mention any right of privacy. In a line of decisions, however, . . . the Court has recognized that a right of personal privacy, or a guarantee of certain areas or zones of privacy, does exist under the Constitution. . . . This right of privacy, whether it be founded in the Fourteenth Amendment's concept of personal liberty and restrictions upon state action, as we feel it is, or, as the District Court determined, in the Ninth Amendment's reservation of rights to the people, is broad enough to encompass a woman's decision whether or not to terminate her pregnancy. The detriment that the State would impose upon the pregnant woman by denying this choice altogether is apparent. Specific and direct harm medically diagnosable even in early pregnancy may be involved. Maternity, or additional offspring, may force upon the woman a distressful life and future. Psychological harm may be imminent. Mental and physical health may be taxed by child care. There is also the distress, for all concerned, associated with the unwanted child, and there is the problem of bringing a child into a family already unable, psychologically and otherwise, to care for it. In other cases, as in this one, the additional difficulties and continuing stigma of unwed motherhood may be involved. All these are factors the woman and her responsible physician necessarily will consider in consultation.

On the basis of elements such as these, appellants and some amici [friends of the Court] argue that the woman's right is absolute and that she is entitled to terminate her pregnancy at whatever time, in whatever way, and for whatever reason she alone chooses. With this we do not agree. Appellants' arguments that Texas either has no valid interest at all in regulating the abortion decision, or no interest strong enough to support any limitation upon the woman's sole determination, is unpersuasive. The Court's decisions recognizing a right of privacy also acknowledge that some state regulation in areas protected by that right is appropriate. As noted above, a State may properly assert important interests in safeguarding health, in maintaining medical standards, and in protecting potential life. At some point in pregnancy, these respective interests become sufficiently compelling to sustain regulation of the factors that govern the abortion decision. The privacy right involved, therefore, cannot be said to be absolute. In fact, it is not clear to us that the claim asserted by some amici that one has an unlimited right to do with one's body as one pleases bears a close relationship to the right of privacy previously articulated in the Court's decisions.

* * *

We therefore conclude that the right of personal privacy includes the abortion decision, but that this right is not unqualified and must be considered against state interests in regulation.

Where certain "fundamental rights" are involved, the Court has held that regulation limiting these rights may be justified only by a "compelling state interest," and that legislative enactments must be narrowly drawn to express only the legitimate state interests at stake.

. . . The District Court held that the appellee failed to meet his burden of demonstrating that the Texas statute's infringement upon Roe's rights was necessary to support a compelling state interest. . . . Appellee argues that the State's determination to recognize and protect prenatal life from and after conception constitutes a compelling state interest. As noted above, we do not agree fully with either formulation.

The appellee and certain amici argue that the fetus is a "person" within the language and meaning of the Fourteenth Amendment. In support of this they outline at length and in detail the well-known facts of fetal development. If this suggestion of personhood is established, the appellant's case, of course, collapses, for the fetus' right to life is then guaranteed specifically by the Amendment. The appellant conceded as much on reargument. On the other hand, the appellee conceded on reargument that no case could be cited that holds that a fetus is a person within the meaning of the Fourteenth Amendment.

The Constitution does not define "person" in so many words. Section 1 of the Fourteenth Amendment contains three references to "person." The first, in defining "citizens," speaks of "persons born or naturalized in the United States." The word also appears both in the Due Process Clause and in the Equal Protection Clause. "Person" is used in other places in the Constitution. . . . But in nearly all these instances, the use of the word is such that it has application only postnatally. None indicates, with any assurance, that it has any possible pre-natal application.

All this, together with our observation, that throughout the major portion of the 19th century prevailing legal abortion practices were far freer than they are today, persuades us that the word "person," as used in the Fourteenth Amendment, does not include the unborn.

. . . The pregnant woman cannot be isolated in her privacy. She carries an embryo and, later, a fetus, if one accepts the medical definitions of the developing young in the human uterus. . . . The situation therefore is inherently different from marital intimacy, or bedroom possession of obscene material, or marriage, or procreation, or education, with which [earlier cases defining the right to privacy] were concerned. As we have intimated above, it is reasonable and appropriate for a State to decide that at some point in time another interest, that of health of the mother or that of potential human life, becomes significantly involved. The woman's privacy is no longer sole and any right of privacy she possesses must be measured accordingly.

Texas urges that, apart from the Fourteenth Amendment, life begins at conception and is present throughout pregnancy, and that, therefore, the State has a compelling interest in protecting that life from and after conception. We need not resolve the difficult question of when life begins. When those trained in the respective disciplines of medicine, philosophy, and theology are unable to arrive at any consensus, the judiciary, at this point in the development of man's knowledge, is not in a position to speculate as to the answer.

. . . In view of all this, we do not agree that, by adopting one theory of life, Texas may override the rights of the pregnant woman that are at stake. We repeat, however, that the State does have an important and legitimate interest in preserving and protecting the health of the pregnant woman, whether she be a resident of the State or a nonresident who seeks medical consultation and treatment there, and that it has still *another* important and legitimate interest in protecting the potentiality of human life. These interests are separate and distinct. Each grows in substantiality as the woman approaches term and, at a point during pregnancy, each becomes "compelling."

With respect to the State's important and legitimate interest in the health of the mother, the "compelling" point, in the light of present medical knowledge, is at approximately the end of the first trimester. This is so because of the now established medical fact . . . that until the end of the first trimester mortality in abortion is less than mortality in normal childbirth. It follows that, from and after this point, a State may regulate the abortion procedure to the extent that the regulation reasonably relates to the preservation and protection of maternal health. Examples of permissible state regulation in this area are requirements as to the qualifications of the person who is to perform the abortion; as to the licensure of that person; as to the facility in which the procedure is to be performed, that is, whether it must be a hospital or may be a clinic or some other place of less-than-hospital status; as to the licensing of the facility; and the like.

This means, on the other hand, that, for the period of pregnancy prior to this "compelling" point, the attending physician, in consultation with his patient, is free to determine, without regulation by the State, that in his medical judgment the patient's pregnancy should be terminated. If that decision is reached, the judgment may be effectuated by an abortion free of interference by the State.

With respect to the State's important and legitimate interest in potential life, the "compelling" point is at viability. This is so because the fetus then presumably has the capability of meaningful life outside the mother's womb. State regulation protective of fetal life after viability thus has both logical and biological justifications. If the State is interested in protecting fetal life after viability, it may go so far as to proscribe abortion during that period except when it is necessary to preserve the life or health of the mother.

Measured against these standards, the Texas Penal Code, in restricting legal abortions to those "procured or attempted by medical advice for the purpose of saving the life of the mother," sweeps too broadly. The statute makes no distinction between abortions performed early in pregnancy and those performed later, and it limits to a single reason, "saving" the mother's life, the legal justification for the procedure. The statute, therefore, cannot survive the constitutional attack made upon it here.

*   *   *

Reversed.

Brown v. Board of Education
of Topeka, Kansas (1954)

Brown v. Board of Education (1954) was a momentous opinion, invalidating the system of segregation that had been established under Plessy v. Ferguson (1896). However, the constitutional pronouncement only marked the beginning of the struggle for racial equality, as federal courts got more and more deeply involved in trying to prod recalcitrant state and local governments into taking steps to end racial inequalities.

The Brown case involved appeals from several states. In each case, the plaintiffs had been denied access to public schools designated only for white children under a variety of state laws. They challenged the Plessy v. Ferguson (1896) "separate but equal" doctrine, contending that segregated schools were by their nature unequal.

Chief Justice Warren first discussed the history of the Fourteenth Amendment's equal protection clause, finding it too inconclusive to be of assistance in determining how the Fourteenth Amendment should be applied to the question of public education.

CHIEF JUSTICE WARREN writing for the majority.

. . . The doctrine of "separate but equal" did not make its appearance in this Court until 1896, in the case of Plessy v. Ferguson, involving not education but transportation. American courts have since labored with the doctrine for over a half a century. In this Court, there have been six cases involving the "separate but equal" doctrine in the field of public education.

* * *

In the instant cases, [the question of the application of the separate but equal doctrine to public education] is directly presented. Here, . . . there are findings below that the Negro and white schools involved have been equalized, or are being equalized, with respect to buildings, curricula, qualifications and salaries of teachers, and other "tangible" factors. Our decision, therefore, cannot turn on merely a comparison of these tangible factors in the Negro and white schools involved in each of the cases. We must look instead to the effect of segregation itself on public education.

In approaching this problem, we cannot turn the clock back to 1868 when the [Fourteenth] Amendment was adopted, or even to 1896 when Plessy v. Ferguson was written. We must consider public education in the light of its full development and its present place in American life throughout the Nation. Only in this way can it be determined if segregation in public schools deprives these plaintiffs of the equal protection of the laws.

Today, education is perhaps the most important function of state and local governments. Compulsory school attendance laws and the great expenditures for education both demonstrate our recognition of the importance of education to our democratic society. It is required in the performance of our most basic responsibilities, even service in the armed forces. It is the very foundation of good citizenship. Today it is a principal instrument in awakening the child to cultural values, in preparing him for later professional training, and in helping him to adjust normally to his environment. In these days, it is doubtful that any child may reasonably be expected to succeed in life if he is denied the opportunity of an education. Such an opportunity, where the state has undertaken to provide it, is a right which must be made available to all on equal terms.

We come then to the question presented: Does segregation of children in public schools solely on the basis of race, even though the physical facilities and other "tangible" factors may be equal, deprive the children of the minority group of equal educational opportunities? We believe that it does.

In *Sweatt v. Painter*, in finding that a segregated law school for Negroes could not provide them equal educational opportunities, this Court relied in large part on "those qualities which are incapable of objective measurement but which make for greatness in a law school." In McLaurin v. Oklahoma State Regents, the Court, in requiring that a Negro admitted to a white graduate school be treated like all other students, again resorted to intangible considerations: ". . . his ability to study, to engage in discussions and exchange views with other students, and, in general, to learn his profession." Such considerations apply with added force to children in grade and high schools. To separate them from others of similar age and qualifications solely because of their race generates a feeling of inferiority as to their status in the community that may affect their hearts and minds in a way unlikely ever to be undone. The effect of this separation on their educational opportunities was well stated by a finding in the Kansas case by a court which nevertheless felt compelled to rule against the Negro plaintiffs:

"Segregation of white and colored children in public schools has a detrimental effect upon the colored children. The impact is greater when it has the sanction of the law; for the policy of separating the races is usually interpreted as denoting the inferiority of the Negro group. A sense of inferiority affects the motivation of a child to learn. Segregation with the sanction of law, therefore, has a tendency to [retard] the educational and mental development of Negro children and to deprive them of some of the benefits they would receive in a racial[ly] integrated school system." Whatever may have been the extent of psychological knowledge at the time of Plessy v. Ferguson, this finding is amply supported by modern authority. Any language in Plessy v. Ferguson contrary to this finding is rejected.

We conclude that in the field of public education the doctrine of "separate but equal" has no place. Separate educational facilities are inherently unequal. Therefore, we hold that the plaintiffs and others similarly situated for whom the actions have been brought are, by reason of the segregation complained of, deprived of the equal protection of the laws guaranteed by the Fourteenth Amendment. This disposition makes unnecessary any discussion whether such segregation also violates the Due Process Clause of the Fourteenth Amendment.

Because these are class actions, because of the wide applicability of this decision, and because of the great variety of local conditions, the formulation of decrees in these cases presents problems of considerable complexity. On reargument, the consideration of appropriate relief was necessarily subordinated to the primary question—the constitutionality of segregation in public education. We have now announced that such segregation is a denial of the equal protection of the laws.

United States v. Nixon (1974)

The Supreme Court has had few occasions to rule on the constitutional limits of executive authority. The Court is understandably reluctant to articulate the boundaries of presidential and legislative power, given the Court's own somewhat ambiguous institutional authority. In the case that follows, however, the Court looked at one of the ways in which the Constitution circumscribes the exercise of presidential prerogative.

United States v. Nixon (1974) involves claims to executive authority. President Richard Nixon was implicated in a conspiracy to cover up a burglary of the Democratic Party Headquarters at the Watergate Hotel in Washington, D.C., during the 1972 reelection campaign. The Special Prosecutor assigned to investigate the break-in and file appropriate criminal charges asked the trial court to order the President to disclose a number of documents and tapes related to the cover-up in order to determine the scope of the President's involvement. The President produced edited versions of some of the materials, but refused to comply with most of the trial court's order, asserting that he was entitled to withhold the information under a claim of "executive privilege."

CHIEF JUSTICE BURGER delivered the opinion of the Court.

In the District Court, the President's counsel argued that the court lacked jurisdiction to issue the subpoena because the matter was an intra-branch dispute between a subordinate and superior officer of the Executive Branch and hence not subject to judicial resolution. That argument has been renewed in this Court with emphasis on the contention that the dispute does not present a "case" or "controversy" which can be adjudicated in the federal courts. The President's counsel argues that the federal courts should not intrude into areas committed to the other branches of Government. He views the present dispute as essentially a "jurisdictional" dispute within the Executive Branch which he analogizes to a dispute between two congressional committees. Since the Executive Branch has exclusive authority and absolute discretion to decide whether to prosecute a case, it is contended that a President's decision is final in determining what evidence is to be used in a given criminal case.

. . . Although his counsel concedes the President has delegated certain specific powers to the Special Prosecutor, he has not "waived nor delegated to the Special Prosecutor the President's duty to claim privilege as to all materials which fall within the President's inherent authority to refuse to disclose to any executive officer." The Special Prosecutor's demand for the items therefore presents, in the view of the President's counsel, a political question since it involves a "textually demonstrable" grant of power under Art. II. . . .

The demands of and the resistance to the subpoena present an obvious controversy in the ordinary sense, but that alone is not sufficient to meet constitutional standards. In the constitutional sense, controversy means more than disagreement and conflict; rather it means the kind of controversy courts traditionally resolve. Here at issue is the production or nonproduction of specified evidence deemed by the Special Prosecutor to be relevant and admissible in a pending criminal case. It is sought by one official of the Government within the scope of his express authority; it is resisted by the Chief Executive on the ground of his duty to preserve the confidentiality of the communications of the President. Whatever the correct answer on the merits, these issues are "of a type which are traditionally justiciable."

* * *

. . . We turn to the claim that the subpoena should be quashed because it demands "confidential conversations between a President and his close advisors that it would be inconsistent with the public interest to produce." The first contention is a broad claim that the separation of powers doctrine precludes judicial review of a President's claim of privilege. The second contention is that if he does not prevail on the claim of absolute privilege, the court should hold as a matter of constitutional law that the privilege prevails over the subpoena. . . .

* * *

[*The Court discussed its authority to interpret the Constitution, concluding that it had full power to adjudicate a claim of executive privilege.*]

In support of his claim of absolute privilege, the President's counsel urges two grounds one of which is common to all governments and one of which is peculiar to our system of separation of powers. The first ground is the valid need for protection of communications between high government officials and those who advise and assist them in the performance of their manifold duties; the importance of this confidentiality is too plain to require further discussion. Human experience teaches that those who expect public dissemination of their remarks may well temper candor with a concern for appearances and for their own interests to the detriment of the decisionmaking process. Whatever the nature of the privilege of confidentiality of presidential communications in the exercise of Art. II powers the privilege can be said to derive from the supremacy of each branch within its own assigned area of constitutional duties. Certain powers and privileges flow from the nature of enumerated powers; the protection of the confidentiality of presidential communications has similar constitutional underpinnings.

The second ground asserted by the President's counsel in support of the claim of absolute privilege rests on the doctrine of separation of powers. Here it is argued that the independence of the Executive Branch within its own sphere, insulates a president from a judicial subpoena in an ongoing criminal prosecution, and thereby protects confidential presidential communications.

However, neither the doctrine of separation of powers, nor the need for confidentiality of high level communications, without more, can sustain an absolute, unqualified presidential privilege of immunity from judicial process under all circumstances. The President's need for complete candor and objectivity from advisers calls for great deference from the courts. However, when the privilege depends solely on the broad, undifferentiated claim of public interest in the confidentiality of such conversations, a confrontation with other values arises. Absent a claim of need to protect military, diplomatic or sensitive national security secrets, we find it difficult to accept the argument that even the very important interest in confidentiality of presidential communications is significantly diminished by production of such material for *in camera* inspection with all the protection that a district court will be obliged to provide.

The impediment that an absolute, unqualified privilege would place in the way of the primary constitutional duty of the judicial branch to do justice in criminal prosecutions would plainly conflict with the function of the courts under Art. III. In designing the structure of our Government and dividing and allocating the sovereign power among three coequal branches, the Framers of the Constitution sought to provide a comprehensive system, but the separate powers were not intended to operate with absolute independence. To read the Art. II powers of the President as providing an absolute privilege as against a subpoena essential to enforcement of criminal statutes on no more than a generalized claim of the public interest in confidentiality of nonmilitary and nondiplomatic discussions would upset the constitutional balance of "a workable government" and gravely impair the role of the court under Art. III.

Since we conclude that the legitimate needs of the judicial process may outweigh presidential privilege, it is necessary to resolve those competing interests in a manner that preserves the essential functions of each branch. The rights and indeed the duty to resolve that question does not free the judiciary from according high respect to the representations made on behalf of the President. The expectation of a President to the confidentiality of his conversations and correspondence, like the claim of confidentiality of judicial deliberations, for example, has all the values to which we accord deference for the privacy of all citizens and added to those values the necessity for protection of the public interest in his responsibilities against the inroads of such a privilege on the fair administration of criminal justice. The interest in preserving confidentiality is weighty indeed and entitled to great respect. However we cannot conclude that advisers will be moved to temper the candor of their remarks by the infrequent occasions of disclosure because of the possibility that such conversations will be called for in the context of a criminal prosecution.

On the other hand, the allowance of the privilege to withhold evidence that is demonstrably relevant in a criminal trial would cut deeply into the guarantee of due process of law and gravely impair the basic function of the courts. A President's acknowleged need for confidentiality in the communications of his office is general in nature, whereas the constitutional need for production of relevant evidence in a criminal proceeding is specific and central to the fair adjudication of a particular criminal case in the administration of justice. Without access to specific facts a criminal prosecution may be totally frustrated. The President's broad interest in confidentiality of communications will not be vitiated by disclosure of a limited number of conversations preliminarily shown to have some bearing on the pending criminal cases.

We conclude that when the ground for asserting privilege as to subpoenaed materials sought for use in a criminal trial is based only on the generalized interest in confidentiality, it cannot prevail over the fundamental demand of due process of law in the fair administration of criminal justice. The generalized assertion of privilege must yield to the demonstrated, specific need for evidence in a pending criminal trial.

* * *

In this case the President challenges a subpoena served on him as a third party requiring the production of materials for use in a criminal prosecution on the claim that he has a privilege against disclosure of confidential communications. He does not place his claim of privilege on the ground they are military or diplomatic secrets. As to these areas of Art. II duties the courts have traditionally shown the utmost deference to presidential responsibilities. No case of the Court, however, has extended this high degree of deference to a President's generalized interest in confidentiality. Nowhere in the Constitution, as we have noted earlier, is there any explicit reference to a privilege of confidentiality; yet to the extent this interest relates to the effective discharge of a President's powers, it is constitutionally based.

* * *

[*The Court distinguished this case from cases involving claims against the president while acting in an official capacity.*]

Mr. Chief Justice Marshall sitting as a trial judge in the *Burr* case was extraordinarily careful to point out that: "[I]n no case of this kind would a Court be required to proceed against the President as against an ordinary individual." Marshall's statement cannot be read to mean in any sense that a President is above the law, but relates to the singularly unique role under Art. II of a President's communications and activities, related to the performance of duties under that Article. Moreover, a President's communications and activities encompass a vastly wider range of sensitive material than would be true of any "ordinary individual." It is therefore necessary in the public interest to afford presidential confidentiality the greatest protection consistent with the fair administration of justice. The need for confidentiality even as to idle conversations with associates in which casual reference might be made concerning political leaders within the country or foreign statesmen is too obvious to call for further treatment. We have no doubt that the District Judge will at all times accord the presidential records that high degree of deference suggested in *United States v. Burr*, and will discharge his responsibility to see to it that until released to the Special Prosecutor no *in camera* [private] material is revealed to anyone. This burden applies with even greater force to excised material; once the decision is made to excise, the material is restored to its privileged status and should be returned under seal to its lawful custodian.

Affirmed.

United States v. Lopez (1995)

How far does Congress's authority extend with respect to the states? Since the 1930s, when a liberalization of Supreme Court doctrine cleared the way for an expansion of federal authority, Congress has relied on a loose interpretation of the Commerce Clause to justify extensive involvement in state and local affairs.

(Congress can also shape what states do, for example, by placing conditions upon the receipt of federal funds). In 1990, Congress enacted the Gun-Free School Zones Act, making possession of a firearm in designated school zones a federal crime. When Alfonso Lopez, Jr., was convicted of violating the act, his lawyer challenged the constitutionality of the law, arguing that it was "invalid as beyond the power of Congress under the Commerce Clause." In a striking reversal of interpretation, the Supreme Court agreed and declared the law invalid, holding that banning guns in schools was too far removed from any effect on interstate commerce to warrant federal intervention. Critics of the decision argued that the Court's reasoning might invalidate a large body of federal crime and drug legislation that relies on the connection between regulated activity and interstate commerce. Supporters maintained that the decision marked a new era of judicial respect for federalism and state autonomy.

CHIEF JUSTICE REHNQUIST delivered the opinion of the Court.

In the Gun-Free School Zones Act of 1990, Congress made it a federal offense "for any individual knowingly to possess a firearm at a place that the individual knows, or has reasonable cause to believe, is a school zone." The Act neither regulates a commercial activity nor contains a requirement that the possession be connected in any way to interstate commerce. We hold that the Act exceeds the authority of "Congress to regulate Commerce . . . among the several States. . . ." (U.S. Constitution Art. I, 8, cl. 3).

On March 10, 1992, respondent, who was then a 12th-grade student, arrived at Edison High School in San Antonio, Texas, carrying a concealed .38 caliber handgun and five bullets. Acting upon an anonymous tip, school authorities confronted respondent, who admitted that he was carrying the weapon. He was arrested and charged under Texas law with firearm possession on school premises. The next day, the state charges were dismissed after federal agents charged respondent by complaint with violating the Gun-Free School Zones Act of 1990.

A federal grand jury indicted respondent on one count of knowing possession of a firearm at a school zone, in violation of 922(q) [the relevant section of the Act of 1990]. Respondent moved to dismiss his federal indictment on the ground that 922(q) "is unconstitutional as it is beyond the power of Congress to legislate control over our public schools." The District Court denied the motion, concluding that 922(q) "is a constitutional exercise of Congress' well-defined power to regulate activities in and affecting commerce, and the 'business' of elementary, middle and high schools . . . affects interstate commerce." Respondent waived his right to a jury trial. The District Court conducted a bench trial, found him guilty of violating 922(q), and sentenced him to six months' imprisonment and two years' supervised release.

On appeal, respondent challenged his conviction based on his claim that 922(q) exceeded Congress' power to legislate under the Commerce Clause. The Court of Appeals for the Fifth Circuit agreed and reversed respondent's conviction. It held that, in light of what it characterized as insufficient congressional findings and legislative history, "in the full reach of its terms, is invalid as beyond the power of Congress under the Commerce Clause." Because of the importance of the issue, we granted *certiorari* and we now affirm.

We start with first principles. The Constitution creates a Federal Government of enumerated powers. As James Madison wrote, "[t]he powers delegated by the proposed Constitution to the federal government are few and defined. Those which are to remain in the State governments are numerous and indefinite." (*The Federalist*, No. 45). This constitutionally mandated division of authority was adopted by the Framers to ensure protection of our fundamental liberties. Just as the separation and independence of the coordinate branches of the Federal Government serves to prevent the accumulation of excessive power in any one branch, a healthy balance of power between the States and the Federal Government will reduce the risk of tyranny and abuse from either front.

[*For the next several pages Rehnquist reviews the evolution of interpretations of the Commerce Clause, starting with* Gibbons v. Ogden *(1824). This case established the relatively narrow interpretation of the Commerce Clause in which the Court prevented* states *from interfering with interstate commerce. Very rarely did cases concern Congress's power. The 1887 Interstate Commerce Act and the 1890 Sherman Antitrust Act expanded Congress's power to regulate intrastate commerce "where the interstate and intrastate aspects of commerce were so mingled together that full regulation of interstate commerce required incidental regulation of intrastate commerce," arguing that the Commerce Clause authorized such regulation. Several New Deal era cases,* NLRB v. Jones & Laughlin Steel Corp. *(1937),* United States v. Darby *(1941), and* Wickard v. Filburn *(1942) broadened the interpretation of the Commerce Clause.*]

Jones & Laughlin Steel, Darby, and *Wickard* ushered in an era of Commerce Clause jurisprudence that greatly expanded the previously defined authority of Congress under that Clause. In part, this was a recognition of the great changes that had occurred in the way business was carried on in this country. Enterprises that had once been local or at most regional in nature had become national in scope. But the doctrinal change also reflected a view that earlier Commerce Clause cases artificially had constrained the authority of Congress to regulate interstate commerce.

But even these modern-era precedents which have expanded congressional power under the Commerce Clause confirm that this power is subject to outer limits. In *Jones & Laughlin Steel,* the Court warned that the scope of the interstate commerce power "must be considered in the light of our dual system of government and may not be extended so as to embrace effects upon interstate commerce so indirect and remote that to embrace them, in view of our complex society, would effectually obliterate the distinction between what is national and what is local and create a completely centralized government." Since that time, the Court has heeded that warning and undertaken to decide whether a rational basis existed for concluding that a regulated activity sufficiently affected interstate commerce.

* * *

Consistent with this structure, we have identified three broad categories of activity that Congress may regulate under its commerce power. First, Congress may regulate the use of the channels of interstate commerce. Second, Congress is empowered to regulate and protect the instrumentalities of interstate commerce, or persons or things in interstate commerce, even though the threat may come only from intrastate activities. Finally, Congress' commerce authority includes the power to regulate those activities having a substantial relation to interstate commerce, those activities that substantially affect interstate commerce.

Within this final category, admittedly, our case law has not been clear whether an activity must *affect* or *substantially affect* interstate commerce in order to be within Congress' power to regulate it under the Commerce Clause. We conclude, consistent with the great weight of our case law, that the proper test requires an analysis of whether the regulated activity *substantially affects* interstate commerce.

We now turn to consider the power of Congress, in the light of this framework, to enact 922(q) [The Gun-Free School Zones Act]. The first two categories of authority may be quickly disposed of: 922(q) is not a regulation of the use of the channels of interstate commerce, nor is it an attempt to prohibit the interstate transportation of a commodity through the channels of commerce; nor can 922(q) be justified as a regulation by which Congress has sought to protect an instrumentality of interstate commerce or a thing in interstate commerce. Thus, if 922(q) is to be sustained, it must be under the third category as a regulation of an activity that substantially affects interstate commerce.

First, we have upheld a wide variety of congressional Acts regulating intrastate economic activity where we have concluded that the activity substantially affected interstate commerce. Examples include the regulation of intrastate coal mining; intrastate extortionate credit transactions, restaurants utilizing substantial interstate supplies, inns and hotels catering to interstate guests, and production and consumption of home-grown wheat. These examples are by no means exhaustive, but the pattern is clear. Where economic activity substantially affects interstate commerce, legislation regulating that activity will be sustained.

Even *Wickard*, which is perhaps the most far reaching example of Commerce Clause authority over intrastate activity, involved economic activity in a way that the possession of a gun in a school zone does not. Roscoe Filburn operated a small farm in Ohio, on which, in the year involved, he raised 23 acres of wheat. It was his practice to sow winter wheat in the fall, and after harvesting it in July to sell a portion of the crop, to feed part of it to poultry and livestock on the farm, to use some in making flour for home consumption, and to keep the remainder for seeding future crops. The Secretary of Agriculture assessed a penalty against him under the Agricultural Adjustment Act of 1938 because he harvested about 12 acres more wheat than his allotment under the Act permitted. The Act was designed to regulate the volume of wheat moving in interstate and foreign commerce in order to avoid surpluses and shortages, and concomitant fluctuation in wheat prices, which had previously obtained. The Court said, in an opinion sustaining the application of the Act to Filburn's activity, "One of the primary purposes of the Act in question was to increase the market price of wheat and to that end to limit the volume thereof that could affect the market. It can hardly be denied that a factor of such volume and variability as home-consumed wheat would have a substantial influence on price and market conditions. This may arise because being in marketable condition such wheat overhangs the market and, if induced by rising prices, tends to flow into the market and check price increases. But if we assume that it is never marketed, it supplies a need of the man who grew it which would otherwise be reflected by purchases in the open market. Home-grown wheat in this sense competes with wheat in commerce" (317 U.S., at 128).

Section 922(q) is a criminal statute that by its terms has nothing to do with *commerce* or any sort of economic enterprise, however broadly one might define those terms. Section 922(q) is not an essential part of a larger regulation of economic activity, in which the regulatory scheme could be undercut unless the intra-state activity were regulated. It cannot, therefore, be sustained under our cases upholding regulations of activities that arise out of or are connected with a commercial transaction, which viewed in the aggregate, substantially affects interstate commerce.

Second, 922(q) contains no jurisdictional element which would ensure, through case-by-case inquiry, that the firearm possession in question affects interstate commerce. . . . 922(q) has no express jurisdictional element which might limit its reach to a discrete set of firearm possessions that additionally have an explicit connection with or effect on interstate commerce.

*   *   *

The Government's essential contention, in fine, is that we may determine here that 922(q) is valid because possession of a firearm in a local school zone does indeed substantially affect interstate commerce. The Government argues that possession of a firearm in a school zone may result in violent crime and that violent crime can be expected to affect the functioning of the national economy in two ways. First, the costs of violent crime are substantial, and, through the mechanism of insurance, those costs are spread throughout the population. Second, violent crime reduces the willingness of individuals to travel to areas within the country that are perceived to be unsafe. The Government also argues that the presence of guns in schools poses a substantial threat to the educational process by threatening the learning environment. A handicapped educational process, in turn, will result in a less productive citizenry. That, in turn, would have an adverse effect on the Nation's economic well-being. As a result, the Government argues that Congress could rationally have concluded that 922(q) substantially affects interstate commerce.

We pause to consider the implications of the Government's arguments. The Government admits, under its "costs of crime" reasoning, that Congress could regulate not only all violent crime, but all activities that might lead to violent crime, regardless of how tenuously they relate to interstate commerce. Similarly, under the Government's "national productivity" reasoning, Congress could regulate any activity that it found was related to the economic productivity of individual citizens: family law (including marriage, divorce, and child custody), for example. Under the theories that the Government presents in support of 922(q), it is difficult to perceive any limitation on federal power, even in areas such as criminal law enforcement or education where States historically have been sovereign. Thus, if we were to accept the Government's arguments, we are hard-pressed to posit any activity by an individual that Congress is without power to regulate.

Although Justice Breyer argues that acceptance of the Government's rationales would not authorize a general federal police power, he is unable to identify any activity that the States may regulate but Congress may not. Justice Breyer posits that there might be some limitations on Congress' commerce power such as family law or certain aspects of education. These suggested limitations, when viewed in light of the dissent's expansive analysis, are devoid of substance.

Justice Breyer focuses, for the most part, on the threat that firearm possession in and near schools poses to the educational process and the potential economic consequences flowing from that threat. Specifically, the dissent reasons that (1) gun-related violence is a serious problem; (2) that problem, in turn, has an adverse effect on classroom learning; and (3) that adverse effect on classroom learning, in turn, represents a substantial threat to trade and commerce. This analysis would be equally applicable, if not more so, to subjects such as family law and direct regulation of education.

For instance, if Congress can, pursuant to its Commerce Clause power, regulate activities that adversely affect the learning environment, then, a fortiori, it also can regulate the educational process directly. Congress could determine that a school's curriculum has a "significant" effect on the extent of classroom learning. As a result, Congress could mandate a federal curriculum for local elementary and secondary schools because what is taught in local schools has a significant "effect on classroom learning," and that, in turn, has a substantial effect on interstate commerce.

Justice Breyer rejects our reading of precedent and argues that "Congress . . . could rationally conclude that schools fall on the commercial side of the line." Again, Justice Breyer's rationale lacks any real limits because, depending on the level of generality, any activity can be looked upon as commercial. Under the dissent's rationale, Congress could just as easily look at child rearing as "fall[ing] on the commercial side of the line" because it provides a "valuable service" namely, to equip [children] with the skills they need to survive in life and, more specifically, in the workplace. We do not doubt that Congress has authority under the Commerce Clause to regulate numerous commercial activities that substantially affect interstate commerce and also affect the educational process. That authority, though broad, does not include the authority to regulate each and every aspect of local schools.

Admittedly, a determination whether an intrastate activity is commercial or noncommercial may in some cases result in legal uncertainty. But, so long as Congress' authority is limited to those powers enumerated in the Constitution, and so long as those enumerated powers are interpreted as having judicially enforceable outer limits, congressional legislation under the Commerce Clause always will engender "legal uncertainty." As Chief Justice Marshall stated in *McCulloch v. Maryland*, (1819), "The [federal] government is acknowledged by all to be one of enumerated powers. The principle, that it can exercise only the powers granted to it . . . is now universally admitted. But the question respecting the extent of the powers actually granted, is perpetually arising, and will probably continue to arise, as long as our system shall exist." The Constitution mandates this uncertainty by withholding from Congress a plenary police power that would authorize enactment of every type of legislation. Congress has operated within this framework of legal uncertainty ever since this Court determined that it was the judiciary's duty "to say what the law is." Any possible benefit from eliminating this "legal uncertainty" would be at the expense of the Constitution's system of enumerated powers.

* * *

These are not precise formulations, and in the nature of things they cannot be. But we think they point the way to a correct decision of this case. The possession of a gun in a local school zone is in no sense an economic activity that might, through repetition elsewhere, substantially affect any sort of interstate commerce. Respondent was a local student at a local school; there is no indication that he had recently moved in interstate commerce, and there is no requirement that his possession of the firearm have any concrete tie to interstate commerce.

To uphold the Government's contentions here, we would have to pile inference upon inference in a manner that would bid fair to convert congressional authority under the Commerce Clause to a general police power of the sort retained by the States. Admittedly, some of our prior cases have taken long steps down that road, giving great deference to congressional action. The broad language in these opinions has suggested the possibility of additional expansion, but we decline here to proceed any further. To do so would require us to conclude that the Constitution's enumeration of powers does not presuppose something not enumerated, and that there never will be a distinction between what is truly national and what is truly local. This we are unwilling to do.

For the foregoing reasons the judgment of the Court of Appeals is Affirmed.

The Declaration of Independence

In Congress, July 4, 1776

When in the course of human events, it becomes necessary for one people to dissolve the political bands which have connected them with another, and to assume among the Powers of the earth, the separate and equal station to which the Laws of Nature and of Nature's God entitle them, a decent respect to the opinions of mankind requires that they should declare the causes which impel them to the separation.

We hold these truths to be self-evident, that all men are created equal, that they are endowed by their Creator with certain unalienable rights, that among these are Life, Liberty and the pursuit of Happiness. That to secure these rights, Governments are instituted among Men, deriving their just powers from the consent of the governed. That whenever any Form of Government becomes destructive of these ends, it is the Right of the People to alter or to abolish it, and to institute new Government, laying its foundation on such principles and organizing its powers in such form, as to them shall seem most likely to effect their Safety and Happiness. Prudence, indeed, will dictate that Governments long established should not be changed for light and transient causes; and accordingly all experience hath shown, that mankind are more disposed to suffer, while evils are sufferable, than to right themselves by abolishing the forms to which they are accustomed. But when a long train of abuses and usurpations, pursuing invariably the same Object evinces a design to reduce them under absolute Despotism, it is their right, it is their duty, to throw off such Government, and to provide new Guards for their future security.—Such has been the patient sufferance of these Colonies; and such is now the necessity which constrains them to alter their former Systems of Government. The history of the present King of Great Britain is a history of repeated injuries and usurpations, all having in direct object the establishment of an absolute Tyranny over these States. To prove this, let Facts be submitted to a candid world.

He has refused his Assent to Laws, the most wholesome and necessary for the public good.

He has forbidden his Governors to pass Laws of immediate and pressing importance, unless suspended in their operation till his Assent should be obtained; and when so suspended, he has utterly neglected to attend to them.

He has refused to pass other Laws for the accommodation of large districts of people, unless those people would relinquish the right of Representation in the Legislature, a right inestimable to them and formidable to tyrants only.

He has called together legislative bodies at places unusual, uncomfortable, and distant from the depository of their public Records, for the sole purpose of fatiguing them into compliance with his measures.

He has dissolved Representative Houses repeatedly, for opposing with manly firmness his invasions on the rights of the people.

He has refused for a long time, after such dissolutions, to cause others to be elected; whereby the Legislative powers, incapable of Annihilation, have returned to the People at large for their exercise; the State remaining in the mean time exposed to all the dangers of invasion from without, and convulsions within.

He has endeavoured to prevent the population of these States; for that purpose obstructing the Laws for Naturalization of Foreigners; refusing to pass others to encourage their migrations hither, and raising the conditions of new Appropriations of Lands.

He has obstructed the Administration of Justice, by refusing his Assent to Laws for establishing Judiciary Powers.

He has made Judges dependent on his Will alone, for the tenure of their offices, and the amount and payment of their salaries.

He has erected a multitude of New Offices, and sent hither swarms of Officers to harrass our People, and eat out their substance.

He has kept among us, in times of peace, Standing Armies without the Consent of our legislature.

He has affected to render the Military independent of and superior to the Civil Power.

He has combined with others to subject us to a jurisdiction foreign to our constitution, and unacknowledged by our laws; giving his Assent to their Acts of pretended Legislation:

For quartering large bodies of armed troops among us:

For protecting them, by a mock Trial, from Punishment for any Murders which they should commit on the Inhabitants of these States:

For cutting off our Trade with all parts of the world:

For imposing Taxes on us without our Consent:

For depriving us in many cases, of the benefits of Trial by jury:

For transporting us beyond Seas to be tried for pretended offences:

For abolishing the free System of English Laws in a neighbouring Province, establishing therein an Arbitrary government, and enlarging its Boundaries so as to render it at once an example and fit instrument for introducing the same absolute rule into these Colonies:

For taking away our Charters, abolishing our most valuable Laws, and altering fundamentally the Forms of our Governments:

For suspending our own Legislatures, and declaring themselves invested with Power to legislate for us in all cases whatsoever.

He has abdicated Government here, by declaring us out of his Protection and waging War against us.

He has plundered our seas, ravaged our Coasts, burnt our towns, and destroyed the lives of our people.

He is at this time transporting large armies of foreign mercenaries to compleat the works of death, desolation and tyranny, already begun with circumstances of Cruelty & perfidy scarcely paralleled in the most barbarous ages, and totally unworthy the Head of a civilized nation.

He has constrained our fellow Citizens taken Captive on the high Seas to bear Arms against their Country, to become the executioners of their friends and Brethren, or to fall themselves by their Hands.

He has excited domestic insurrections amongst us, and has endeavored to bring on the inhabitants of our frontiers, the merciless Indian Savages, whose known rule of warfare, is an undistinguished destruction of all ages, sexes, and conditions.

In every stage of these Oppressions we have Petitioned for Redress in the most humble terms: Our repeated Petitions have been answered only by repeated injury. A Prince, whose character is thus marked by every act which may define a Tyrant, is unfit to be the ruler of a free people.

Nor have we been wanting in attention to our British brethren. We have warned them from time to time of attempts by their legislature to extend an unwarrantable jurisdiction over us. We have reminded them of the circumstances of our emigration and settlement here. We have appealed to their native justice and magnanimity, and we have conjured them by the ties of our common kindred to disavow these usurpations, which, would inevitably interrupt our connections and correspondence. They too must have been deaf to the voice of justice and of consanguinity. We must, therefore, acquiesce in the necessity, which denounces our Separation, and hold them, as we hold the rest of mankind, Enemies in War, in Peace Friends.

WE, THEREFORE, the Representatives of the UNITED STATES OF AMERICA, in General Congress, Assembled, appealing to the Supreme Judge of the world for the rectitude of our intentions, do, in the Name, and by Authority of the good People of these Colonies, solemnly publish and declare, That these United Colonies are, and of Right ought to be FREE AND INDEPENDENT STATES; that they are Absolved from all Allegiance to the British Crown, and that all political connection between them and the State of Great Britain, is and ought to be totally dissolved; and that as Free and Independent States, they have full Power to levy War, conclude Peace, contract Alliances, establish Commerce, and to do all other Acts and Things which Independent States may of right do. And for the support of this Declaration, with a firm reliance on the protection of Divine Providence, we mutually pledge to each other our Lives, our Fortunes and our sacred Honor.

The foregoing Declaration was, by order of Congress, engrossed, and signed by the following members:

John Hancock

NEW HAMPSHIRE
Josiah Bartlett
William Whipple
Matthew Thornton

MASSACHUSETTS BAY
Samuel Adams
John Adams
Robert Treat Paine
Elbridge Gerry

RHODE ISLAND
Stephen Hopkins
William Ellery

CONNECTICUT
Roger Sherman
Samuel Huntington
William Williams
Oliver Wolcott

NEW YORK
William Floyd
Philip Livingston
Francis Lewis
Lewis Morris

NEW JERSEY
Richard Stockton
John Witherspoon
Francis Hopkinson
John Hart
Abraham Clark

PENNSYLVANIA
Robert Morris
Benjamin Rush
Benjamin Franklin
John Morton
George Clymer
James Smith
George Taylor
James Wilson
George Ross

DELAWARE
Caesar Rodney
George Read
Thomas M'Kean

MARYLAND
Samuel Chase
William Paca

Thomas Stone
Charles Carroll,
  of Carrollton

VIRGINIA
George Wythe
Richard Henry Lee
Thomas Jefferson
Benjamin Harrison
Thomas Nelson, Jr.
Francis Lightfoot Lee
Carter Braxton

NORTH CAROLINA
William Hooper
Joseph Hewes
John Penn

SOUTH CAROLINA
Edward Rutledge
Thomas Heyward, Jr.
Thomas Lynch, Jr.
Arthur Middleton

GEORGIA
Button Gwinnett
Lyman Hall
George Walton

Resolved, That copies of the Declaration be sent to the several assemblies, conventions, and committees, or councils of safety, and to the several commanding officers of the continental troops; that it be proclaimed in each of the United States, at the head of the army.

The Federalist, No. 10

James Madison

To the People of the State of New York:

Among the numerous advantages promised by a well-constructed Union, none deserves to be more accurately developed than its tendency to break and control the violence of faction. The friend of popular governments never finds himself so much alarmed for their character and fate, as when he contemplates their propensity to this dangerous vice. He will not fail, therefore, to set a due value on any plan which, without violating the principles to which he is attached, provides a proper cure for it. The instability, injustice, and confusion introduced into the public councils, have, in truth, been the mortal diseases under which popular governments have everywhere perished; as they continue to be the favorite and fruitful topics from which the adversaries to liberty derive their most specious declamations. The valuable improvements made by the American constitutions on the popular models, both ancient and modern, cannot certainly be too much admired; but it would be an unwarrantable partiality, to contend that they have as effectually obviated the danger on this side, as was wished and expected. Complaints are everywhere heard from our most considerate and virtuous citizens, equally the friends of public and private faith, and of public and personal liberty, that our governments are too unstable; that the public good is disregarded in the conflicts of rival parties; and that measures are too often decided, not according to the rules of justice and the rights of the minor party, but by the superior force of an interested and overbearing majority. However anxiously we may wish that these complaints had no foundation, the evidence of known facts will not permit us to deny that they are in some degree true. It will be found, indeed, on a candid review of our situation, that some of the distresses under which we labor have been erroneously charged on the operation of our governments; but it will be found, at the same time, that other causes will not alone account for many of our heaviest misfortunes; and, particularly, for that prevailing and increasing distrust of public engagements, and alarm for private rights, which are echoed from one end of the continent to the other. These must be chiefly, if not wholly, effects of the unsteadiness and injustice with which a factious spirit has tainted our public administrations.

By a faction, I understand a number of citizens, whether amounting to a majority or minority of the whole, who are united and actuated by some common impulse of passion, or of interest, adverse to the rights of other citizens, or to the permanent and aggregate interests of the community.

There are two methods of curing the mischiefs of faction: the one, by removing its causes; the other, by controlling its effects.

There are again two methods of removing the causes of faction: the one, by destroying the liberty which is essential to its existence; the other, by giving to every citizen the same opinions, the same passions, and the same interests.

It could never be more truly said than of the first remedy, that it is worse than the disease. Liberty is to faction what air is to fire, an aliment without which it instantly expires. But it could not be less folly to abolish liberty, which is essential to political life, because it nourishes faction, than it would be to wish the annihilation of air, which is essential to animal life, because it imparts to fire its destructive agency.

The second expedient is as impracticable as the first would be unwise. As long as the reason of man continues fallible, and he is at liberty to exercise it, different opinions will be formed. As long as the connection subsits between his reason and his self-love, his opinions and his passions will have a reciprocal influence on each other; and the former will be objects to which the latter will attach themselves. The diversity in the faculties of men, from which the rights of property originate, is not less an insuperable obstacle to a uniformity of interests. The protection of these faculties is the first object of government. From the protection of different and unequal faculties of acquiring property, the possession of different degrees and kinds of property immediately results; and from the influence of these on the sentiments and views of the respective proprietors, ensues a division of the society into different interests and parties.

The latent causes of faction are thus sown in the nature of man; and we see them everywhere brought into different degrees of activity, according to the different circumstances of civil society. A zeal for different opinions concerning religion, concerning government, and many other points, as well of speculation as of practice; an attachment to different leaders ambitiously contending for pre-eminence and power; or to persons of other descriptions whose fortunes have been interesting to the human passions, have, in turn, divided mankind into parties, inflamed them with mutual animosity, and rendered them much more disposed to vex and oppress each other than to co-operate for their common good. So strong is this propensity of mankind to fall into mutual animosities, that where no substantial occasion presents itself, the most frivolous and fanciful distinctions have been sufficient to kindle their unfriendly passions and excite their most violent conflicts. But the most common

and durable source of factions has been the various and unequal distribution of property. Those who hold and those who are without property
have ever formed distinct interests in society. Those who are creditors,
and those who are debtors, fall under a like discrimination. A landed
interest, a manufacturing interest, a mercantile interest, a moneyed interest, with many lesser interests, grow up of necessity in civilized nations,
and divide them into different classes, actuated by different sentiments
and views. The regulation of these various and interfering interests forms
the principal task of modern legislation, and involves the spirit of party
and faction in the necessary and ordinary operations of the government.

No man is allowed to be a judge in his own cause, because his interest
would certainly bias his judgment, and, not improbably, corrupt his integrity. With equal, nay with greater reason, a body of men are unfit to
be both judges and parties at the same time; yet what are many of the
most important acts of legislation, but so many judicial determinations,
not indeed concerning the rights of single persons, but concerning the
rights of large bodies of citizens? and what are the different classes of
legislators but advocates and parties to the causes which they determine?
Is a law proposed concerning private debts? It is a question to which the
creditors are parties on one side and the debtors on the other. Justice
ought to hold the balance between them. Yet the parties are, and must
be, themselves the judges; and the most numerous party, or, in other
words, the most powerful faction must be expected to prevail. Shall domestic manufactures be encouraged, and in what degree, by restrictions
on foreign manufactures? are questions which would be differently decided by the landed and the manufacturing classes, and probably by
neither with a sole regard to justice and the public good. The apportionment of taxes on the various descriptions of property is an act which
seems to require the most exact impartiality; yet there is, perhaps, no
legislative act in which greater opportunity and temptation are given to
a predominant party to trample on the rules of justice. Every shilling with
which they overburden the inferior number is a shilling saved to their
own pockets.

It is in vain to say that enlightened statesmen will be able to adjust
these clashing interests and render them all subservient to the public
good. Enlightened statesmen will not always be at the helm. Nor, in many
cases, can such an adjustment be made at all without taking into view
indirect and remote considerations, which will rarely prevail over the immediate interest which one party may find in disregarding the rights of
another or the good of the whole.

The inference to which we are brought is, that the *causes* of faction
cannot be removed, and that relief is only to be sought in the means of
controlling its *effects*.

If a faction consists of less than a majority, relief is supplied by the
republican principle, which enables the majority to defeat its sinister

views by regular vote. It may clog the administration, it may convulse the society; but it will be unable to execute and mask its violence under the forms of the Constitution. When a majority is included in a faction, the form of popular government, on the other hand, enables it to sacrifice to its ruling passion or interest both the public good and the rights of other citizens. To secure the public good and private rights against the danger of such a faction, and at the same time to preserve the spirit and the form of popular government, is then the great object to which our inquiries are directed. Let me add that it is the great desideratum [desire] by which this form of government can be rescued from the opprobrium under which it has so long labored, and be recommended to the esteem and adoption of mankind.

By what means is this object attainable? Evidently by one of two only. Either the existence of the same passion or interest in a majority at the same time must be prevented, or the majority, having such coexistent passion or interest, must be rendered by their number and local situation unable to concert and carry into effect schemes of oppression. If the impulse and the opportunity be suffered to coincide, we well know that neither moral nor religious motives can be relied on as an adequate control. They are not found to be such on the injustice and violence of individuals, and lose their efficacy in proportion to the number combined together, that is, in proportion as their efficacy becomes needful.

From this view of the subject it may be concluded that a pure democracy, by which I mean a society consisting of a small number of citizens, who assemble and administer the government in person, can admit of no cure for the mischiefs of faction. A common passion or interest will, in almost every case, be felt by a majority of the whole; a communication and concert result from the form of government itself; and there is nothing to check the inducements to sacrifice the weaker party or an obnoxious individual. Hence it is that such democracies have ever been spectacles of turbulence and contention; have ever been found incompatible with personal security or the rights of property; and have in general been as short in their lives as they have been violent in their deaths. Theoretic politicians, who have patronized this species of government, have erroneously supposed that by reducing mankind to a perfect equality in their political rights, they would, at the same time, be perfectly equalized and assimilated in their possessions, their opinions, and their passions.

A republic, by which I mean a government in which the scheme of representation takes place, opens a different prospect, and promises the cure for which we are seeking. Let us examine the points in which it varies from pure democracy, and we shall comprehend both the nature of the cure and the efficacy which it must derive from the Union.

The two great points of difference between a democracy and a republic are: first, the delegation of the government in the latter to a small number of citizens elected by the rest; secondly, the greater number of citizens and greater sphere of country over which the latter may be extended.

The effect of the first difference is, on the one hand, to refine and enlarge the public views, by passing them through the medium of a chosen body of citizens, whose wisdom may best discern the true interest of their country, and whose patriotism and love of justice will be least likely to sacrifice it to temporary or partial considerations. Under such a regulation, it may well happen that the public voice, pronounced by the representatives of the people, will be more consonant to the public good than if pronounced by the people themselves, convened for the purpose. On the other hand, the effect may be inverted. Men of factious tempers, of local prejudices, or of sinister designs, may by intrigue, by corruption, or by other means, first obtain the suffrages, and then betray the interests of the people. The question resulting is, whether small or extensive republics are more favorable to the election of proper guardians of the public weal; and it is clearly decided in favor of the latter by two obvious considerations.

In the first place, it is to be remarked that, however small the republic may be, the representatives must be raised to a certain number in order to guard against the cabals of a few; and that, however large it may be, they must be limited to a certain number in order to guard against the confusion of a multitude. Hence, the number of representatives in the two cases not being in proportion to that of the two constituents, and being proportionally greater in the small republic, it follows that, if the proportion of fit characters be not less in the large than in the small republic, the former will present a greater option and consequently a greater probability of a fit choice.

In the next place, as each representative will be chosen by a greater number of citizens in the large than in the small republic, it will be more difficult for unworthy candidates to practise with success the vicious arts by which elections are too often carried; and the suffrages of the people being more free, will be more likely to centre in men who possess the most attractive merit and the most diffusive and established characters.

It must be confessed that in this, as in most other cases, there is a mean, on both sides of which inconveniences will be found to lie. By enlarging too much the number of electors, you render the representative too little acquainted with all their local circumstances and lesser interests: as by reducing it too much, you render him unduly attached to these, and too little fit to comprehend and pursue great and national objects. The federal Constitution forms a happy combination in this respect; the great and aggregate interests being referred to the national, the local and particular to the State legislatures.

The other point of difference is, the greater number of citizens and extent of territory which may be brought within the compass of republican than of democratic government; and it is this circumstance principally which renders factious combinations less to be dreaded in the former than in the latter. The smaller the society, the fewer probably will be the distinct parties and interests composing it; the fewer the distinct parties and interests, the more frequently will a majority be found of the same party; and the smaller the number of individuals composing a majority, and the smaller the compass within which they are placed, the more easily will they concert and execute their plans of oppression. Extend the sphere, and you take in a greater variety of parties and interests; you make it less probable that a majority of the whole will have a common motive to invade the rights of other citizens; or if such a common motive exists, it will be more difficult for all who feel it to discover their own strength and to act in unison with each other. Besides other impediments, it may be remarked that, where there is a consciousness of unjust or dishonorable purposes, communication is always checked by distrust in proportion to the number whose concurrence is necessary.

Hence, it clearly appears that the same advantage which a republic has over a democracy in controlling the effects of faction is enjoyed by a large over a small republic,—is enjoyed by the Union over the States composing it. Does the advantage consist in the substitution of representatives whose enlightened views and virtuous sentiments render them superior to local prejudices and to schemes of injustice? It will not be denied that the representation of the Union will be most likely to possess these requisite endowments. Does it consist in the greater security afforded by a greater variety of parties, against the event of any one party being able to outnumber and oppress the rest? In an equal degree does the increased variety of parties comprised within the Union, increase this security. Does it, in fine, consist in the greater obstacles opposed to the concert and accomplishment of the secret wishes of an unjust and interested majority? Here, again, the extent of the Union gives it the most palpable advantage.

The influence of factious leaders may kindle a flame within their particular States, but will be unable to spread a general conflagration through the other States. A religious sect may degenerate into a political faction in a part of the Confederacy; but the variety of sects dispersed over the entire face of it must secure the national councils against any danger from that source. A rage for paper money, for an abolition of debts, for an equal division of property, or for any other improper or wicked project, will be less apt to pervade the whole body of the Union than a particular member of it; in the same proportion as such a malady is more likely to taint a particular county or district, than an entire State.

In the extent and proper structure of the Union, therefore, we behold a republican remedy for the diseases most incident to republican government. And according to the degree of pleasure and pride we feel in being republicans, ought to be our zeal in cherishing the spirit and supporting the character of Federalists.

PUBLIUS

The Constitution of the United States of America

Federalist
Paper
Number
and Author

Annotated with references to the Federalist Papers;
bracketed material is by the editors of this volume.

[PREAMBLE]

84
(Hamilton)

We the People of the United States, in Order to form a more perfect Union, establish Justice, insure domestic Tranquility, provide
for the common defence, promote the general Welfare, and secure the Blessings of Liberty to ourselves and our Posterity, do
ordain and establish this Constitution for the United States of
America.

ARTICLE I

Section 1

[LEGISLATURE POWERS]

10, 45
(Madison)

All legislative Powers herein granted shall be vested in a Congress of the United States, which shall consist of a Senate and
House of Representatives.

Section 2

[HOUSE OF REPRESENTATIVES, HOW
CONSTITUTED, POWER OF IMPEACHMENT]

39
(Madison)
45
(Madison)
52–53, 57
(Madison)

The House of Representatives shall be composed of Members
chosen every second Year by the People of the several States,
and the Electors in each State shall have the Qualifications requisite for Electors of the most numerous Branch of the State
Legislature.

52
(Madison),
60
(Hamilton)

No Person shall be a Representative who shall not have attained to the Age of twenty five Years, and been seven Years a
Citizen of the United States, and who shall not, when elected, be
an Inhabitant of that State in which he shall be chosen.

54
(Madison)

Representatives and *direct Taxes** shall be apportioned among

* [Modified by Sixteenth Amendment.]

714 THE CONSTITUTION

the several States which may be included within this Union, according to their respective Numbers, *which shall be determined by adding to the whole Number of free Persons, including those bound to Service for a Term of Years,* and excluding Indians not taxed, *three-fifths of all other Persons.* * The actual Enumeration shall be made within three Years after the first Meeting of the Congress of the United States, and within every subsequent Term of ten Years, in such Manner as they shall by Law direct. The Number of Representatives shall not exceed one for every thirty Thousand, but each State shall have at Least one Representative; *and until such enumeration shall be made, the State of New Hampshire shall be entitled to chuse three, Massachusetts eight, Rhode Island and Providence Plantations one, Connecticut five, New-York six, New Jersey four, Pennsylvania eight, Delaware one, Maryland six, Virginia ten, North Carolina five, South Carolina five and Georgia three.*†

When vacancies happen in the Representation from any State, the Executive Authority thereof shall issue Writs of Election to fill such Vacancies.

The House of Representatives shall chuse their Speaker and other Officers; and shall have the sole Power of Impeachment.

Section 3

[THE SENATE, HOW CONSTITUTED, IMPEACHMENT TRIALS]

The Senate of the United States shall be composed of two Senators from each State, *chosen by the Legislature thereof,*‡ for six Years; and each Senator shall have one Vote.

Immediately after they shall be assembled in Consequence of the first Election, they shall be divided as equally as may be into three Classes. The Seats of the Senators of the first Class shall be vacated at the Expiration of the second Year, of the second Class at the Expiration of the fourth Year, and of the third Class at the Expiration of the sixth Year, so that one third may be chosen every second Year: *and if Vacancies happen by Resignation, or otherwise, during the Recess of the Legislature of any State, the Executive thereof may make temporary Appointments until the next Meeting of the Legislature, which shall then fill such Vacancies.*§

No person shall be a Senator who shall not have attained to the Age of thirty Years, and been nine Years a Citizen of the

Margin notes: 54 (Madison), 58 (Madison), 55–56 (Madison), 79 (Hamilton), 39, 45 (Madison), 60 (Hamilton), 62–63 (Madison), 59 (Hamilton), 68 (Hamilton), 62 (Madison), 64 (Jay)

* [Modified by Fourteenth Amendment.]
† [Temporary provision.]
‡ [Modified by Seventeenth Amendment.]
§ [Modified by Seventeenth Amendment.]

United States, and who shall not, when elected, be an Inhabitant of that State for which he shall be chosen.

The Vice-President of the United States shall be President of the Senate, but shall have no Vote, unless they be equally divided.

39 (Madison), 65–67, 79 (Hamilton) 65 (Hamilton) 84 (Hamilton) The Senate shall chuse their other Officers, and also a President pro tempore, in the Absence of the Vice-President, or when he shall exercise the Office of President of the United States.

The Senate shall have the sole Power to try all Impeachments. When sitting for that Purpose, they shall be on Oath or Affirmation. When the President of the United States is tried, the Chief Justice shall preside: And no Person shall be convicted without the Concurrence of two thirds of the Members present.

Judgment in Cases of Impeachment shall not extend further than to removal from Office, and disqualification to hold and enjoy any Office of honor, Trust or Profit under the United States: but the Party convicted shall nevertheless be liable and subject to Indictment, Trial, Judgment and Punishment, according to Law.

Section 4

[ELECTION OF SENATORS AND REPRESENTATIVES]

59–61 (Hamilton) The Times, Places and Manner of holding Elections for Senators and Representatives, shall be prescribed in each State by the Legislature thereof; but the Congress may at any time by Law make or alter such Regulations, except as to the Place of Chusing Senators.

*The Congress shall assemble at least once in every Year, and such Meeting shall be on the first Monday in December, unless they shall by Law appoint a different Day.**

Section 5

[QUORUM, JOURNALS, MEETINGS, ADJOURNMENTS]

Each House shall be the Judge of the Elections, Returns and Qualifications of its own Members, and a Majority of each shall constitute a Quorum to do Business; but a smaller Number may adjourn from day to day, and may be authorized to compel the Attendance of absent Members, in such Manner, and under such Penalties as each House may provide.

Each House may determine the Rules of its Proceedings, punish its Members for disorderly Behavior, and, with the Concurrence of two-thirds, expel a Member.

* [Modified by Twentieth Amendment.]

Each House shall keep a Journal of its Proceedings, and from time to time publish the same, excepting such Parts as may in their Judgment require Secrecy; and the Yeas and Nays of the Members of either House on any question shall, at the Desire of one-fifth of those Present, be entered on the Journal.

Neither House, during the Session of Congress, shall, without the Consent of the other, adjourn for more than three days, nor to any other Place than that in which the two Houses shall be sitting.

Section 6

[COMPENSATION, PRIVILEGES, DISABILITIES]

The Senators and Representatives shall receive a Compensation for their Services, to be ascertained by Law, and paid out of the Treasury of the United States. They shall in all Cases, except Treason, Felony and Breach of the Peace, be privileged from Arrest during their Attendance at the Session of their respective Houses, and in going to and returning from the same; and for any Speech or Debate in either House, they shall not be questioned in any other Place.

55 (Madison), 76 (Hamilton) No Senator or Representative shall, during the Time for which he was elected, be appointed to any civil Office under the authority of the United States, which shall have been created, or the Emoluments whereof shall have been increased during such time; and no Person holding any Office under the United States, shall be a Member of either House during his Continuance in Office.

Section 7

[PROCEDURE IN PASSING BILLS AND RESOLUTIONS]

66 (Hamilton) All bills for raising Revenue shall originate in the House of Representatives; but the Senate may propose or concur with Amendments as on other Bills.

69, 73 (Hamilton) Every Bill which shall have passed the House of Representatives and the Senate, shall, before it become a Law, be presented to the President of the United States; If he approve he shall sign it, but if not he shall return it, with his Objections to that House in which it shall have originated, who shall enter the Objections at large on their Journal, and proceed to reconsider it. If after such Reconsideration two-thirds of that House shall agree to pass the Bill, it shall be sent, together with the Objections, to the other House, by which it shall likewise be reconsidered, and if approved by two thirds of that House it shall become a Law. But in all such Cases the Votes of both Houses shall be determined by Yeas and Nays, and the Names of the Persons voting for and against the Bill shall be entered on the Journal of each House respectively. If any Bill shall not be returned by the President within ten Days (Sundays excepted) after it shall have been presented to him, the Same shall be a Law, in like Manner as if he had signed it, unless the Congress by their Adjournment prevent its Return, in which Case it shall not be a Law.

69, 73 (Hamilton)

Every Order, Resolution, or Vote to which the Concurrence of the Senate and House of Representatives may be necessary (except on a question of Adjournment) shall be presented to the President of the United States; and before the Same shall take Effect, shall be approved by him, or being disapproved by him, shall be repassed by two-thirds of the Senate and House of Representatives, according to the Rules and Limitations prescribed in the Case of a Bill.

Section 8

[POWERS OF CONGRESS]

The Congress shall have Power

30–36 (Hamilton),

To lay and collect Taxes, Duties, Imposts and Excises, to pay the Debts and provide for the common Defence and general Welfare of the United States; but all Duties, Imposts and Excises shall be uniform throughout the United States;

41 (Madison)

56 (Madison)

To borrow money on the Credit of the United States;

42, 45, 56 (Madison)

To regulate Commerce with foreign Nations, and among the several States, and with the Indian Tribes;

32 (Hamilton),

To establish an uniform Rule of Naturalization, and uniform Laws on the subject of Bankruptcies throughout the United States;

42 (Madison)

To coin Money, regulate the Value thereof, and of foreign Coin, and fix the Standard of Weights and Measures;

42 (Madison)

42 (Madison)

To provide for the Punishment of counterfeiting the Securities and current Coin of the United States;

To establish Post Offices and Post Roads;

42 (Madison)

43 (Madison)

To promote the Progress of Science and useful Arts, by securing for limited Times to Authors and Inventors the exclusive Right to their respective Writings and Discoveries;

81 (Hamilton)

To constitute Tribunals inferior to the supreme Court;

42 (Madison)

To define and Punish Piracies and Felonies committed on the high Seas, and Offenses against the Law of Nations;

41
(Madison)   To declare War, grant Letters of Marque and Reprisal, and make Rules concerning Captures on Land and Water;

23, 24, 26
(Hamilton),   To raise and support Armies, but no Appropriation of Money to that Use shall be for a longer Term than two Years;

41
(Madison)   To provide and maintain a Navy;

To make Rules for the Government and Regulation of the land and naval forces;

29
(Hamilton)   To provide for calling forth the Militia to execute the Laws of the Union, suppress Insurrections and repel Invasions;

29
(Hamilton),   To provide for organizing, arming, and disciplining the Militia, and for governing such Part of them as may be employed in

56
(Madison)   the Service of the United States, reserving to the States respectively, the Appointment of the Officers, and the Authority of training the Militia according to the discipline prescribed by Congress;

32
(Hamilton),
43
(Madison)   To exercise exclusive Legislation in all Cases whatsoever, over such District (not exceeding ten Miles square) as may, by Cession of particular States, and the Acceptance of Congress, become the Seat of the Government of the United States, and to exercise like Authority over all Places purchased by the Consent of the Leg-

43
(Madison)   islature of the State in which the Same shall be, for the Erection of Forts, Magazines, Arsenals, dock-Yards, and other needful Buildings;—And

29, 33
(Hamilton)   To make all Laws which shall be necessary and proper for carrying into Execution the foregoing Powers, and all other Powers

44
(Madison)   vested by this Constitution in the Government of the United States, or in any Department or Officer thereof.

Section 9

[SOME RESTRICTIONS ON FEDERAL POWER]

42
(Madison)   *The Migration or Importation of such Persons as any of the States now existing shall think proper to admit, shall not be prohibited by the Congress prior to the Year one thousand eight hundred and eight, but a tax or duty may be imposed on such Importation, not exceeding ten dollars for each Person.**

83, 84
(Hamilton)   The privilege of the Writ of *Habeas Corpus* shall not be suspended, unless when in Cases of Rebellion or Invasion the public Safety may require it.

84
(Hamilton)   No Bill of Attainder or ex post facto Law shall be passed.

No Capitation, or other direct, Tax shall be laid, unless in Proportion to the Census or Enumeration herein before directed to be taken.†

* [Temporary provision.]
† [Modified by Sixteenth Amendment.]

No Tax or Duty shall be laid on Articles exported from any State.

32 (Hamilton)

No Preference shall be given by any Regulation of Commerce or Revenue to the Ports of one State over those of another: nor shall Vessels bound to, or from, one State, be obliged to enter, clear, or pay Duties in another.

No Money shall be drawn from the Treasury, but in Consequence of Appropriations made by Law; and a regular Statement and Account of the Receipts and Expenditures of all public Money shall be published from time to time.

39 (Madison), 84 (Hamilton)

No Title of Nobility shall be granted by the United States: And no Person holding any Office of Profit or Trust under them, shall, without the Consent of the Congress, accept of any present, Emolument, Office, or Title, of any kind whatever, from any King, Prince or foreign State.

Section 10

[RESTRICTIONS UPON POWERS OF STATES]

33 (Hamilton), 44 (Madison)

No State shall enter into any Treaty, Alliance, or Confederation; grant Letters of Marque and Reprisal; coin Money; emit Bills of Credit; make any Thing but gold and silver Coin a Tender in Payment of Debts; pass any Bill of Attainder, ex post facto Law, or Law impairing the Obligation of Contracts, or grant any Title of Nobility.

32 (Hamilton), 44 (Madison)

No State shall, without the Consent of the Congress, lay any Imposts or Duties on Imports or Exports, except what may be absolutely necessary for executing its inspection Laws: and the net Produce of all Duties and Imposts, laid by any State on Imports or Exports, shall be for the Use of the Treasury of the United States; and all such Laws shall be subject to the Revision and Controul of the Congress.

No State shall, without the Consent of Congress, lay any duty of Tonnage, keep Troops, or Ships of War in time of Peace, enter into any Agreement or Compact with another State, or with a foreign Power, or engage in War, unless actually invaded, or in such imminent Danger as will not admit of Delay.

ARTICLE II

Section 1

[EXECUTIVE POWER, ELECTION, QUALIFICATIONS OF THE PRESIDENT]

39 (Madison), 70, 71, 84 (Hamilton)

The executive Power shall be vested in a President of the United States of America. *He shall hold his Office during the Term of* *four years, and, together with the Vice-President, chosen for the same Term, be elected, as follows:**

69, 71
(Hamilton)

Each State shall appoint, in such Manner as the Legislature thereof may direct, a Number of Electors, equal to the whole Number of Senators and Representatives to which the State may

39, 45
(Madison),

be entitled in the Congress: but no Senator or Representative, or Person holding an Office of Trust or Profit under the United

68, 77
(Hamilton)

States, shall be appointed an Elector.

The electors shall meet in their respective States, and vote by ballot for two Persons, of whom one at least shall not be an Inhabitant of the same State with themselves. And they shall make a List of all the Persons voted for, and of the Number of Votes for each; which List they shall sign and certify, and transmit sealed to the Seat of the Government of the United States, directed to the President of the Senate. The

66
(Hamilton)

President of the Senate shall, in the Presence of the Senate and House of Representatives, open all the Certificates, and the Votes shall then be counted. The Person having the greatest Number of Votes shall be the President, if such Number be a Majority of the whole Number of Electors appointed; and if there be more than one who have such Majority, and have an equal Number of Votes, then the House of Representatives shall immediately chuse by Ballot one of them for President; and if no Person have a Majority, then from the five highest on the List the said House shall in like Manner chuse the President. But in chusing the President, the Votes shall be taken by States, the Representation from each State having one Vote; a quorum for this Purpose shall consist of a Member or Members from two-thirds of the States, and a Majority of all the States shall be necessary to a Choice. In every Case, after the Choice of the President, the Person having the greatest Number of Votes of the Electors shall be the Vice-President. But if there should remain two or more who have equal Votes, the Senate shall chuse from them by Ballot the Vice-President.†

The Congress may determine the Time of chusing the Electors, and the Day on which they shall give their Votes; which Day shall be the same throughout the United States.

No Person except a natural born Citizen, or a Citizen of the United States, at the time of the Adoption of this Constitution, shall be eligible to the Office of President; neither shall any Person be eligible to that Office who shall not have attained to

64 (Jay)

the Age of thirty-five Years, and been fourteen Years a Resident within the United States.

In Case of the Removal of the President from Office, or his Death, Resignation, or Inability to discharge the Powers and

---

* [Number of terms limited to two by Twenty-second Amendment.]
† [Modified by Twelfth and Twentieth Amendment.]

Duties of the said Office, the same shall devolve on the Vice-President, and the Congress may by Law provide for the Case of Removal, Death, Resignation or Inability, both of the President and Vice-President, declaring what Officer shall then act as President, and such Officer shall act accordingly, until the Disability be removed, or a President shall be elected.

73, 79
(Hamilton)

The President shall, at stated Times, receive for his Services, a Compensation, which shall neither be encreased nor diminished during the Period for which he shall have been elected, and he shall not receive within that Period any other Emolument from the United States, or any of them.

Before he enter on the Execution of his Office, he shall take the following Oath or Affirmation:—"I do solemnly swear (or affirm) that I will faithfully execute the Office of President of the United States, and will to the best of my Ability, preserve, protect and defend the Constitution of the United States."

Section 2

[POWERS OF THE PRESIDENT]

69, 74
(Hamilton)

The President shall be Commander in Chief of the Army and Navy of the United States, and of the Militia of the several States, when called into the actual Service of the United States; he may require the Opinion, in writing, of the principal Officer in each of the executive Departments, upon any Subject relating to the Du-

74
(Hamilton)
69
(Hamilton)
74
(Hamilton)

ties of their respective Offices, and he shall have Power to Grant Reprieves and Pardons for Offenses against the United States, except in Cases of Impeachment.

He shall have Power, by and with the Advice and Consent of

42
(Madison)
64 (Jay),
66
(Hamilton)

the Senate, to make Treaties, provided two thirds of the Senators present concur; and he shall nominate, and by and with the Advice and Consent of the Senate, shall appoint Ambassadors, other public Ministers and Consuls, Judges of the Supreme Court, and

42
(Madison),

all other Officers of the United States, whose Appointments are not herein otherwise provided for, and which shall be established

66, 69,
76, 77
(Hamilton)

by Law: but the Congress may by Law vest the Appointment of such inferior Officers, as they think proper, in the President alone, in the Courts of Law, or in the Heads of Departments.

67, 76
(Hamilton)

The President shall have Power to fill up all Vacancies that may happen during the Recess of the Senate, by granting Commissions which shall expire at the End of their next Session.

Section 3

[POWERS AND DUTIES OF THE PRESIDENT]

77
(Hamilton)
69, 77
(Hamilton)
77
(Hamilton)
69, 77
(Hamilton)
42
(Madison),
69, 77
(Hamilton)
78
(Hamilton)

He shall from time to time give to the Congress Information of the State of the Union, and recommend to their Consideration such Measures as he shall judge necessary and expedient; he may, on extraordinary Occasions, convene both Houses, or either of them, and in Case of Disagreement between them, with Respect to the Time of Adjournment, he may adjourn them to such Time as he shall think proper; he shall receive Ambassadors and other public Ministers; he shall take Care that the Laws be faithfully executed, and shall Commission all the Officers of the United States.

Section 4

[IMPEACHMENT]

39
(Madison),

69
(Hamilton)

The President, Vice-President and all civil Officers of the United States, shall be removed from Office on Impeachment for, and Conviction of, Treason, Bribery, or other high Crimes and Misdemeanors.

ARTICLE III

Section 1

[JUDICIAL POWER, TENURE OR OFFICE]

81, 82
(Hamilton)
65
(Hamilton)
78, 79
(Hamilton)

The judicial Power of the United States, shall be vested in one Supreme Court, and in such inferior Courts as the Congress may from time to time ordain and establish. The Judges, both of the supreme and inferior Courts, shall hold their Offices during good Behavior, and shall, at stated Times, receive for their Services a Compensation, which shall not be diminished during their Continuance in Office.

Section 2

[JURISDICTION]

80
(Hamilton)

The judicial Power shall extend to all Cases, in Law and Equity, arising under this Constitution, the Laws of the United States, and Treaties made, or which shall be made, under their Authority;—to all Cases affecting Ambassadors, other public Ministers and Consuls;—to all Cases of admiralty and maritime Jurisdiction;—to Controversies to which the United States shall be a party;—to Controversies between two or more States;— *between a State and Citizens of another State;*—between Citizens of different States,—between Citizens of the same State claiming

Lands under Grants of different States, *and between a State*, or the Citizens thereof, *and foreign States, Citizens or Subjects.**

81
(Hamilton)

In all Cases affecting Ambassadors, other public Ministers and Consuls, and those in which a State shall be Party, the supreme Court shall have original Jurisdiction. In all the other Cases before mentioned, the Supreme Court shall have appellate Jurisdiction, both as to Law and Fact, with such Exceptions, and under such Regulations as the Congress shall make.

83, 84
(Hamilton)

The Trial of all Crimes, except in Cases of Impeachment, shall be by Jury; and such Trial shall be held in the State where the said Crimes shall have been committed; but when not committed within any State, the Trial shall be at such Place or Places as the Congress may by Law have directed.

Section 3

[TREASON, PROOF, AND PUNISHMENT]

43
(Madison),

98
(Hamilton)

Treason against the United States, shall consist only in levying War against them, or in adhering to their Enemies, giving them Aid and Comfort. No Person shall be convicted of Treason unless on the Testimony of two Witnesses to the same overt Act, or on Confession in open Court.

43
(Madison),
84
(Hamilton)

The Congress shall have Power to declare the Punishment of Treason, but no Attainder of Treason shall work Corruption of Blood, or Forfeiture except during the Life of the Person attained.

ARTICLE IV

Section 1

[FAITH AND CREDIT AMONG STATES]

42
(Madison)

Full Faith and Credit shall be given in each State to the public Acts, Records, and judicial Proceedings of every other State. And the Congress may by general Laws prescribe the Manner in which such Acts, Records and Proceedings shall be proved, and the Effect thereof.

Section 2

[PRIVILEGES AND IMMUNITIES, FUGITIVES]

80
(Hamilton)

The Citizens of each State shall be entitled to all Privileges and Immunities of Citizens in the several States.

A Person charged in any State with Treason, Felony, or other Crime, who shall flee from Justice, and be found in another State, shall on demand of the executive Authority of the State from

---

* [Modified by the Eleventh Amendment.]

which he fled, be delivered up, to be removed to the State having Jurisdiction of the Crime.

No Person held to Service or Labour in one State, under the Laws thereof, escaping into another, shall, in Consequence of any Law or Regulation therein, be discharged from such Service or Labour, but shall be delivered up on Claim of the Party to whom such Service or Labour may be due.*

Section 3

[ADMISSION OF NEW STATES]

43
(Madison)
New States may be admitted by the Congress into this Union; but no new States shall be formed or erected within the Jurisdiction of any other State; nor any State be formed by the Junction of two or more States, or Parts of States, without the Consent of the Legislatures of the States concerned as well as of the Congress.

43
(Madison)
The Congress shall have Power to dispose of and make all needful Rules and Regulations respecting the Territory or other Property belonging to the United States; and nothing in this Constitution shall be so construed as to Prejudice any Claims of the United States, or of any particular State.

Section 4

[GUARANTEE OF REPUBLICAN GOVERNMENT]

39, 43
(Madison)
The United States shall guarantee to every State in this Union a Republican Form of Government, and shall protect each of them against Invasion; and on Application of the Legislature, or of the Executive (when the Legislature cannot be convened) against domestic Violence.

ARTICLE V

[AMENDMENT OF THE CONSTITUTION]

39, 43
(Madison)
85
(Hamilton)
The Congress, whenever two-thirds of both Houses shall deem it necessary, shall propose Amendments to this Constitution, or, on the Application of the Legislatures of two-thirds of the several States, shall call a Convention for proposing Amendments, which, in either Case, shall be valid to all Intents and Purposes, as Part of this Constitution, when ratified by the Legislatures of three-fourths of the several States, or by Conventions in three-fourths thereof, as the one or the other Mode of Ratification may be proposed by the Congress; *Provided that no Amendment which may be*

---

* [Repealed by the Thirteenth Amendment.]

43
(Madison)

made prior to the Year One thousand eight hundred and eight shall in any Manner affect the first and fourth Clauses in the Ninth Section of the first Article;* and that no State, without its Consent, shall be deprived of its equal Suffrage in the Senate.

ARTICLE VI

[DEBTS, SUPREMACY, OATH]

43
(Madison)

All Debts contracted and Engagements entered into, before the Adoption of this Constitution, shall be as valid against the United States under this Constitution, as under the Confederation.

27, 33
(Hamilton),
39, 44
(Madison)

This Constitution, and the Laws of the United States which shall be made in Pursuance thereof; and all Treaties made, or which shall be made, under the Authority of the United States, shall be the supreme Law of the Land; and the Judges in every State shall be bound thereby, any Thing in the Constitution or Laws of any State to the Contrary notwithstanding.

27
(Hamilton),
44
(Madison)

The Senators and Representatives before mentioned, and the Members of the several State Legislatures, and all executive and judicial Officers, both of the United States and of the several States, shall be bound by Oath or Affirmation, to support this Constitution; but no religious Test shall ever be required as a Qualification to any Office or public Trust under the United States.

ARTICLE VII

[RATIFICATION AND ESTABLISHMENT]

39, 40, 43
(Madison)

The Ratification of the Conventions of nine States, shall be sufficient for the Establishment of this Constitution between the States so ratifying the Same.†

Done in Convention by the Unanimous Consent of the States present the Seventeenth Day of September in the Year of our Lord one thousand seven hundred and Eighty seven and of the Independence of the United States of America the Twelfth. *In Witness* whereof We have hereunto subscribed our Names,

G:⁰ WASHINGTON—
*Presidt, and Deputy
from Virginia*

* [Temporary provision.]
† [The Constitution was submitted on September 17, 1787, by the Constitutional Convention, was ratified by the conventions of several states at various dates up to May 29, 1790, and became effective on March 4, 1789.]

New Hampshire	JOHN LANGDON NICHOLAS GILMAN	Delaware	GEO READ GUNNING BEDFOR JUN JOHN DICKINSON
Massachusetts	NATHANIEL GORHAM RUFUS KING		RICHARD BASSETT JACO: BROOM
Connecticut	WM SAML JOHNSON ROGER SHERMAN	Maryland	JAMES MCHENRY DAN OF ST THOS. JENIFER
New York	ALEXANDER HAMILTON		DANL CARROLL
New Jersey	WIL: LIVINGSTON DAVID BREARLEY WM PATERSON JONA: DAYTON	Virginia	JOHN BLAIR— JAMES MADISON JR.
		North Carolina	WM BLOUNT RICHD DOBBS SPAIGHT HU WILLIAMSON
Pennsylvania	B FRANKLIN THOMAS MIFFLIN ROBT MORRIS GEO. CLYMER THOS. FITZSIMONS JARED INGERSOLL JAMES WILSON GOUV MORRIS	South Carolina	J. RUTLEDGE CHARLES COTESWORTH PINCKNEY CHARLES PINCKNEY PIERCE BUTLER
		Georgia	WILLIAM FEW ABR BALDWIN

Amendments to the Constitution

*Proposed by Congress and Ratified
by the Legislatures of the Several States,
Pursuant to Article V of the Original Constitution.*

*Amendments I–X, known as the Bill of Rights, were proposed by Congress on
September 25, 1789, and ratified on December 15, 1791. Federalist Papers comments, mainly in opposition to a Bill of Rights, can be found in #84 (Hamilton).*

AMENDMENT I

[FREEDOM OF RELIGION, OF SPEECH, AND OF THE PRESS]
Congress shall make no law respecting an establishment of religion, or
prohibiting the free exercise thereof; or abridging the freedom of speech,
or of the press; or the right of the people peaceably to assemble, and to
petition the Government for a redress of grievances.

AMENDMENT II

[RIGHT TO KEEP AND BEAR ARMS]
A well regulated Militia, being necessary to the security of a free State,
the right of the people to keep and bear Arms, shall not be infringed.

AMENDMENT III

[QUARTERING OF SOLDIERS]
No Soldier shall, in time of peace be quartered in any house, without
the consent of the Owner, nor in time of war, but in a manner to be prescribed by law.

AMENDMENT IV

[SECURITY FROM UNWARRANTABLE SEARCH AND SEIZURE]

The right of the people to be secure in their persons, houses, papers, and effects, against unreasonable searches and seizures, shall not be violated, and no Warrants shall issue, but upon probable cause, supported by Oath or affirmation, and particularly describing the place to be searched, and the persons or things to be seized.

AMENDMENT V

[RIGHTS OF ACCUSED PERSONS IN CRIMINAL PROCEEDINGS]

No person shall be held to answer for a capital, or otherwise infamous crime, unless on a presentment or indictment of a Grand Jury, except in cases arising in the land or naval forces, or in the Militia, when in actual service in time of War or public danger; nor shall any person be subject for the same offence to be twice put in jeopardy of life or limb; nor shall be compelled in any Criminal Case to be a witness against himself, nor be deprived of life, liberty, or property, without due process of law; nor shall private property be taken for public use, without just compensation.

AMENDMENT VI

[RIGHT TO SPEEDY TRIAL, WITNESSES, ETC.]

In all criminal prosecutions, the accused shall enjoy the right to a speedy and public trial, by an impartial jury of the State and district wherein the crime shall have been committed, which district shall have been previously ascertained by law, and to be informed of the nature and cause of the accusation; to be confronted with the witnesses against him; to have compulsory process for obtaining Witnesses in his favor, and to have the Assistance of Counsel for his defence.

AMENDMENT VII

[TRIAL BY JURY IN CIVIL CASES]

In suits at common law, where the value in controversy shall exceed twenty dollars, the right of trial by jury shall be preserved, and no fact tried by a jury shall be otherwise re-examined in any Court of the United States, than according to the rules of the common law.

AMENDMENT VIII

[BAILS, FINES, PUNISHMENTS]

Excessive bail shall not be required, nor excessive fines imposed, nor cruel and unusual punishments inflicted.

AMENDMENT IX

[RESERVATION OF RIGHTS OF PEOPLE]

The enumeration in the Constitution, of certain rights, shall not be construed to deny or disparage others retained by the people.

AMENDMENT X

[POWERS RESERVED TO STATES OR PEOPLE]

The powers not delegated to the United States by the Constitution, nor prohibited by it to the States, are reserved to the States respectively, or to the people.

AMENDMENT XI

[Proposed by Congress on March 4, 1794; declared ratified on January 8, 1798.]

[RESTRICTION OF JUDICIAL POWER]

The Judicial power of the United States shall not be construed to extend to any suit in law or equity, commenced or prosecuted against one of the United States by Citizens of another State, or by Citizens or Subjects of any foreign State.

AMENDMENT XII

[Proposed by Congress on December 9, 1803; declared ratified on September 25, 1804.]

[ELECTION OF PRESIDENT AND VICE-PRESIDENT]

The Electors shall meet in their respective states, and vote by ballot for President and Vice-President, one of whom, at least, shall not be an inhabitant of the same state with themselves; they shall name in their ballots the person voted for as President, and in distinct ballots the person voted for as Vice-President, and they shall make distinct lists of all persons voted for as President, and of all persons voted for as Vice-President, and of the number of votes for each, which lists they shall sign and certify, and transmit sealed to the seat of the government of the United States, directed to the President of the Senate;—The President of the Senate shall, in presence of the Senate and House of Representatives, open all the certificates and the votes shall then be counted;—The person having the greatest number of votes for President, shall be the President, if such number be a majority of the whole number of Electors appointed; and if no person have such majority, then from the persons having the highest numbers not exceeding three on the list of those voted for as President, the House of Representatives shall choose immediately, by ballot, the President. But in choosing the President, the votes shall be taken by states, the representation from each state having one vote; a quorum for this purpose shall consist of a member or members from two-thirds of the states, and a majority of all the states shall be necessary to a choice. And if the House of Representatives shall not choose a President whenever the right of choice shall devolve upon them, before the fourth day of March next following, then the Vice-President shall act as President, as in the case of the death or other constitutional disability of the President. The person having the greatest number of votes as Vice-President, shall be the Vice-President, if such number be a majority of the whole number of Electors appointed, and if no person have a majority, then from the two highest numbers on the list, the Senate shall choose the Vice-President; a quorum for the purpose shall consist of two-thirds of the whole number of Senators, and a majority of the whole number shall be necessary to a choice. But no person constitutionally ineligible to the office of President shall be eligible to that of Vice-President of the United States.

AMENDMENT XIII

[Proposed by Congress on January 31, 1865; declared ratified on December 18, 1865.]

Section 1

[ABOLITION OF SLAVERY]

Neither slavery nor involuntary servitude, except as a punishment for crime whereof the party shall have been duly convicted, shall exist within the United States, or any place subject to their jurisdiction.

Section 2

[POWER TO ENFORCE THIS ARTICLE]

Congress shall have power to enforce this article by appropriate legislation.

AMENDMENT XIV

[Proposed by Congress on June 13, 1866, declared ratified on July 28, 1868.]

Section 1

[CITIZENSHIP RIGHTS NOT TO BE ABRIDGED BY STATES]

All persons born or naturalized in the United States, and subject to the jurisdiction thereof, are citizens of the United States and of the State wherein they reside. No state shall make or enforce any law which shall abridge the privileges or immunities of citizens of the United States; nor shall any State deprive any person of life, liberty, or property, without due process of law; nor deny to any person within its jurisdiction the equal protection of the laws.

Section 2

[APPORTIONMENT OF REPRESENTATIVES IN CONGRESS]

Representatives shall be apportioned among the several States according to their respective numbers, counting the whole number of persons in each State, excluding Indians not taxed. But when the right to vote at any election for the choice of electors for President and Vice-President of the United States, Representatives in Congress, the Executive and Judicial officers of a State, or the members of the Legislature thereof, is denied to any of the male inhabitants of such State, being twenty-one years of age, and citizens of the United States, or in any way abridged, except for participation in rebellion, or other crime, the basis of representation therein shall be reduced in the proportion which the number of such male citizens shall bear to the whole number of male citizens twenty-one years of age in such State.

Section 3

[PERSONS DISQUALIFIED FROM HOLDING OFFICE]

No person shall be a Senator or Representative in Congress, or elector of President and Vice-President, or hold any office, civil or military, under the United States, or under any State, who, having previously taken an oath, as a member of Congress, or as an officer of the United States, or as a member of any State legislature, or as an executive or judicial officer of any State, to support the Constitution of the United States, shall have engaged in insurrection or rebellion against the same, or given aid or comfort to the enemies thereof. But Congress may by a vote of two-thirds of each House, remove such disability.

Section 4

[WHAT PUBLIC DEBTS ARE VALID]

The validity of the public debt of the United States, authorized by law, including debts incurred for payment of pensions and bounties for services in suppressing insurrection or rebellion, shall not be questioned. But neither the United States nor any State shall assume or pay any debt or obligation incurred in aid of insurrection or rebellion against the United States, or any claim for the loss or emancipation of any slave; but all such debts, obligations and claims shall be held illegal and void.

Section 5

[POWER TO ENFORCE THIS ARTICLE]

The Congress shall have power to enforce, by appropriate legislation, the provisions of this article.

AMENDMENT XV

[Proposed by Congress on February 26, 1869; declared ratified on March 30, 1870.]

Section 1

[BLACK SUFFRAGE]

The right of citizens of the United States to vote shall not be denied or abridged by the United States or by any State on account of race, color, or previous condition of servitude.

Section 2

[POWER TO ENFORCE THIS ARTICLE]

The Congress shall have power to enforce this article by appropriate legislation.

AMENDMENT XVI

[Proposed by Congress on July 12, 1909; declared ratified on February 25, 1913.]

[AUTHORIZING INCOME TAXES]

The Congress shall have power to lay and collect taxes on incomes, from whatever source derived, without apportionment among the several States, and without regard to any census or enumeration.

AMENDMENT XVII

[Proposed by Congress on May 13, 1912; declared ratified on May 31, 1913.]

[POPULAR ELECTION OF SENATORS]

The Senate of the United States shall be composed of two Senators from each State, elected by the people thereof, for six years; and each Senator shall have one vote. The electors in each State shall have the qualifications requisite for electors of the most numerous branch of the State Legislature.

When vacancies happen in the representation of any State in the Senate, the executive authority of such State shall issue writs of election to fill such vacancies: Provided, That the Legislature of any State may empower the executive thereof to make temporary appointments until the people fill the vacancies by election as the Legislature may direct.

This amendment shall not be so construed as to affect the election or term of any Senator chosen before it becomes valid as part of the Constitution.

AMENDMENT XVIII

[Proposed by Congress December 18, 1917; declared ratified on January 29, 1919.]

Section 1

[NATIONAL LIQUOR PROHIBITION]

After one year from the ratification of this article, the manufacture, sale, or transportation of intoxicating liquors within, the importation thereof into, or the exportation thereof from the United States and all territory subject to the jurisdiction thereof for beverage purposes is hereby prohibited.

Section 2

[POWER TO ENFORCE THIS ARTICLE]

Congress and the several states shall have concurrent power to enforce this article by appropriate legislation.

Section 3

[RATIFICATION WITHIN SEVEN YEARS]

This article shall be inoperative unless it shall have been ratified as an amendment to the Constitution by the legislatures of the several states, as provided in the Constitution, within seven years from the date of the submission hereof to the states by Congress.*

* [Repealed by the Twenty-first Amendment.]

AMENDMENT XIX

[Proposed by Congress on June 4, 1919; declared ratified on August 26, 1920.]

[FEMALE SUFFRAGE]

The right of the citizens of the United States to vote shall not be denied or abridged by the United States or by any state on account of sex.

Congress shall have power, by appropriate legislation, to enforce this article by appropriate legislation.

AMENDMENT XX

[Proposed by Congress on March 2, 1932; declared ratified on February 6, 1933.]

Section 1

[TERMS OF OFFICE]

The terms of the President and Vice-President shall end at noon on the 20th day of January, and the terms of Senators and Representatives at noon on the 3rd day of January, of the years in which such terms would have ended if this article had not been ratified; and the terms of their successors shall then begin.

Section 2

[TIME OF CONVENING CONGRESS]

The Congress shall assemble at least once in every year, and such meeting shall begin at noon on the 3rd day of January, unless they shall by law appoint a different day.

Section 3

[DEATH OF PRESIDENT-ELECT]

If, at the time fixed for the beginning of the term of the President, the President-elect shall have died, the Vice-President-elect shall become President. If a President shall not have been chosen before the time fixed for the beginning of his term, or if the President-elect shall have failed to qualify, then the Vice-President-elect shall act as President until a President shall have qualified; and the Congress may by law provide for the case wherein neither a President-elect nor a Vice-President-elect shall have qualified, declaring who shall then act as President, or the manner in which one who is to act shall be selected, and such person shall act accordingly until a President or Vice-President shall have qualified.

Section 4

[ELECTION OF THE PRESIDENT]

The Congress may by law provide for the case of the death of any of the persons from whom the House of Representatives may choose a President whenever the right of choice shall have devolved upon them, and for the case of the death of any of the persons from whom the Senate may choose a Vice-President whenever the right of choice shall have devolved upon them.

Section 5

[AMENDMENT TAKES EFFECT]

Sections 1 and 2 shall take effect on the 15th day of October following ratification of this article.

Section 6

[RATIFICATION WITHIN SEVEN YEARS]

This article shall be inoperative unless it shall have been ratified as an amendment to the Constitution by the legislatures of three-fourths of the several States within seven years from the date of its submission.

AMENDMENT XXI

[Proposed by Congress on February 20, 1933; declared ratified on December 5, 1933.]

Section 1

[NATIONAL LIQUOR PROHIBITION REPEALED]

The eighteenth article of amendment to the Constitution of the United States is hereby repealed.

Section 2

[TRANSPORTATION OF LIQUOR INTO "DRY" STATES]

The transportation or importation into any State, Territory, or Possession of the United States for delivery or use therein of intoxicating liquors, in violation of the laws thereof, is hereby prohibited.

Section 3

[RATIFICATION WITHIN SEVEN YEARS]

The article shall be inoperative unless it shall have been ratified as an amendment to the Constitution by conventions in the several States, as provided in the Constitution, within seven years from the date of the submission hereof to the States by the Congress.

AMENDMENT XXII

[Proposed by Congress on March 21, 1947; declared ratified on February 26, 1951.]

Section 1

[TENURE OF PRESIDENT LIMITED]

No person shall be elected to the office of the President more than twice, and no person who has held the office of President or acted as President for more than two years of a term to which some other person was elected President shall be elected to the Office of the President more than once. But this Article shall not apply to any person holding the office of President when this Article was proposed by the Congress, and shall not prevent any person who may be holding the office of President, or acting as President, during the term within which this Article becomes operative from holding the office of President or acting as President during the remainder of such term.

Section 2

[RATIFICATION WITHIN SEVEN YEARS]

This Article shall be inoperative unless it shall have been ratified as an amendment to the Constitution by the legislatures of three-fourths of the several states within seven years from the date of its submission to the States by the Congress.

AMENDMENT XXIII

[Proposed by Congress on June 21, 1960; declared ratified on March 29, 1961.]

Section 1

[ELECTORAL COLLEGE VOTES FOR THE DISTRICT OF COLUMBIA]

The District constituting the seat of Government of the United States shall appoint in such manner as the Congress may direct:

A number of electors of President and Vice-President equal to the whole number of Senators and Representatives in Congress to which the District would be entitled if it were a State, but in no event more than the least populous State; they shall be in addition to those appointed by the States, but they shall be considered, for the purposes of the election of President and Vice-President, to be electors appointed by a State; and they shall meet in the District and perform such duties as provided by the twelfth article of amendment.

Section 2

[POWER TO ENFORCE THIS ARTICLE]

The Congress shall have power to enforce this article by appropriate legislation.

AMENDMENT XXIV

[Proposed by Congress on August 27, 1963; declared ratified on January 23, 1964.]

Section 1

[ANTI-POLL TAX]

The right of citizens of the United States to vote in any primary or other election for President or Vice-President, for electors for President or Vice-President, or for Senator or Representative in Congress, shall not be denied or abridged by the United States or any State by reason of failure to pay any poll tax or other tax.

Section 2

[POWER TO ENFORCE THIS ARTICLE]

The Congress shall have power to enforce this article by appropriate legislation.

AMENDMENT XXV

[Proposed by Congress on July 7, 1965; declared ratified on February 10, 1967.]

Section 1

[VICE-PRESIDENT TO BECOME PRESIDENT]

In case of the removal of the President from office or his death or resignation, the Vice-President shall become President.

Section 2

[CHOICE OF A NEW VICE-PRESIDENT]

Whenever there is a vacancy in the office of the Vice-President, the President shall nominate a Vice-President who shall take office upon confirmation by a majority vote of both houses of Congress.

Section 3

[PRESIDENT MAY DECLARE OWN DISABILITY]

Whenever the President transmits to the President pro tempore of the Senate and the Speaker of the House of Representatives his written declaration that he is unable to discharge the powers and duties of his office, and until he transmits to them a written declaration to the contrary, such powers and duties shall be discharged by the Vice-President as Acting President.

Section 4

[ALTERNATE PROCEDURES TO DECLARE AND TO END PRESIDENTIAL DISABILITY]

Whenever the Vice-President and a majority of either the principal officers of the executive departments or of such other body as Congress may by law provide, transmit to the President pro tempore of the Senate and the Speaker of the House of Representatives their written declaration that the President is unable to discharge the powers and duties of his office, the Vice-President shall immediately assume the powers and duties of the office as Acting President.

Thereafter, when the President transmits to the President pro tempore of the Senate and the Speaker of the House of Representatives his written declaration that no inability exists, he shall resume the powers and duties of his office unless the Vice-President and a majority of either the principal officers of the executive department or of such other body as Congress may by law provide, transmit within four days to the President pro tempore of the Senate and the Speaker of the House of Representatives their written declaration that the President is unable to discharge the powers and duties of his office. Thereupon Congress shall decide the issue, assembling within 48 hours for that purpose if not in session. If the Congress, within 21 days after receipt of the latter written declaration, or, if Congress is not in session, within 21 days after Congress is required to assemble, determines by two-thirds vote of both houses that the President is unable to discharge the powers and duties of his office, the Vice-President shall continue to discharge the same as Acting President; otherwise, the President shall resume the powers and duties of his office.

AMENDMENT XXVI

[Proposed by Congress on March 23, 1971; declared ratified on June 30, 1971.]

Section 1

[EIGHTEEN-YEAR-OLD SUFFRAGE]

The right of citizens of the United States, who are eighteen years of age or older, to vote shall not be denied or abridged by the United States or by any State on account of age.

Section 2

[POWER TO ENFORCE THIS ARTICLE]

The Congress shall have power to enforce this article by appropriate legislation.

AMENDMENT XXVII

[LIMITING CONGRESSIONAL PAY CHANGES]
[Proposed by Congress on September 25, 1789; ratified on May 7, 1992.]

No law varying the compensation for the services of the Senators and Representatives shall take effect until an election of Representatives shall have intervened.

Acknowledgments

Annas, George J. "Jumping Frogs, Endangered Toads, and California's Medical-Marijuana Law" from *The New England Journal of Medicine*, Vol. 353, Issue 21, Nov. 24, 2005, pp. 2291–2296. Copyright © 2005 Massachusetts Medical Society. All rights reserved. Reprinted with permission.

Bolick, Clint. "The Health Care Freedom Act: Questions and Answers," The Goldwater Institute, Feb. 2, 2010. Reprinted by permission of Clint Bolick, director, Scharf-Norton Center for Constitutional Litigation at the Goldwater Institute, Phoenix, Arizona.

Borosage, Robert and Katrina vanden Heuvel. "Change Won't Come Easy." Reprinted with permission from the February 1, 2010 issue of *The Nation*. For subscription information, call 1-800-333-8536. Portions of each week's magazine can be accessed at http://www.thenation.com.

Burtless, Gary. "Growing American Inequality: Source and Remedies." From *Brookings Review*, (Winter 1999). Reprinted with the permission of The Brookings Institution, Washington, DC.

Davidson, Chandler. "The Historical Context of Voter Photo-ID Laws," *PS: Political Science & Politics* 42(1), Jan. 2009: 93–96. Copyright © 2009 The American Political Science Association. Reprinted with the permission of Cambridge University Press.

Dworkin, Ronald. "The Decision That Threatens Democracy," May 13, 2010. Reprinted with permission from *The New York Review of Books*. Copyright © 2010 NYREV, Inc.

Edwards, Chris and Jeff Patch. "Corporate Welfare and Earmarks," *Cato Handbook for Policymakers, 7th Edition*, pp. 277–279, 283–287. Reproduced with permission of The Cato Institute.

Elazar, Daniel. "The Political Subcultures of the United States" from *American Mosaic: The Impact of Space, Time, and Culture on American Politics*, pp. 229–36, 239–46. Copyright © 1994 by Westview Press. Reprinted by permission of Westview Press, a member of the Perseus Books Group.

Englund, Will, et al. "Czar Wars." Excerpted with permission from *National Journal*, February 14, 2009. Copyright 2010 by National Journal Group, Inc. All rights reserved.

Fallows, James. "How to Save the News," *The Atlantic*, June 2010, pp. 44–56. Copyright 2010, The Atlantic Media Co. as published in *The Atlantic*. Distributed by Tribune Media Services.

Fiorina, Morris P. "Letter to the Editor," in *Commentary* (May 2006). Reprinted by permission of the author. "The Decline of Collective Responsibility in American Politics," *Daedalus* 109:3 (Summer 1980), pp. 25–34, 37–43. © 1980 by the American Academy of Arts and Sciences. Reprinted by permission of MIT Press Journals. "What Culture Wars?" in *The Wall Street Journal* (July 14, 2004). Reprinted by permission of the author.

Foley, Edward B. "Is There a Middle Ground in the Voter ID Debate?," Election Law @ Moritz, Ohio State University, Sept. 6, 2005. Reprinted by permission of the author.

Friedman, Leon. Reprinted with permission from Leon Friedman, "Overruling the Court," *The American Prospect*: August 2011, Volume 12, Number 15. www .prospect.org. *The American Prospect*, 1710 Rhode Island Avenue, NW, 12th Floor, Washington, DC 20036. All rights reserved.

Friel, Brian. "Inhofe: Earmarks Are Good For Us." Reprinted with permission from *National Journal*, March 5, 2010. Copyright 2010 by National Journal Group, Inc. All rights reserved.

Gallup, George H. "Polling the Public" from *A Guide to Public Opinion Polls*. © 1944 Princeton University Press, 1948 revised 2nd Edition, 1975 renewed. Reprinted by permission of Princeton University Press.

Gertner, Jon. "The Rise and Fall of the G.D.P., *New York Times Magazine*, May 16, 2010, pp. 60–68, 70–71. © 2010, *The New York Times*. Reprinted by permission.

Greenberg, David. "The Honeymooners," *The Atlantic*, January/February 2010, pp. 80–83. Copyright 2010, The Atlantic Media Co. as published in *The Atlantic*. Distributed by Tribune Media Services.

Hartz, Louis. Excerpts from "The Concept of a Liberal Society" in *The Liberal Tradition in America: An Interpretation of American Political Thought Since the Revolution*, copyright © 1955 and renewed 1983 by Louis Hartz, reprinted by permission of Harcourt, Inc.

Hibbing, John and Elizabeth Theiss-Morse. "Too Much of a Good Thing: More Representative Is Not Necessarily Better." *Political Science & Politics* (March 1998). Reprinted with the permission of the authors.

John, David C. "Providing Social Security Benefits in the Future." From The Heritage Foundation, March 25, 2004. Reprinted with the permission of the publisher.

Jones, Charles. "Perspectives on the Presidency." From *The Presidency in a Separated System*. Reprinted with the permission of The Brookings Institution, Washington, DC.

Jost, Timothy S. "Can States Nullify Health Care Reform?" from *The New England Journal of Medicine*, Vol. 362, Issue 10, March 11, 2010, pp. 869–871. Copyright © 2010 Massachusetts Medical Society. All rights reserved. Reprinted with permission.

Judis, John B. "Tea Minus Zero," *The New Republic*, May 27, 2010. Reprinted by permission of *The New Republic*, © 2010 TNR II, LLC.

Kammen, Michael. Excerpt from "Introduction" by Michael Kammen, from *The Origins of The American Constitution*, edited by Michael Kammen, copyright © 1986 by Michael Kammen. Used by permission of Viking Penguin, a division of Penguin Group (USA) Inc.

Key, V.O., Jr. Reprinted by permission of the publisher from *The Responsible Electorate: Rationality in Presidential Voting, 1936–1960* by V.O. Key, Jr., with the assistance of Milton C. Cummings, Jr., pp. 1–8, Cambridge, Mass.: The Belknap Press of Harvard University Press, Copyright © 1966 by the President and Fellows of Harvard College.

King, Martin L., Jr. "Letter from a Birmingham Jail." Reprinted by arrangement with the Heirs to the Estate of Martin Luther King, Jr., c/o Writers House as agent for the proprietor, New York, NY. Copyright 1963 Dr. Martin Luther King, Jr., copyright renewed 1991 Coretta Scott King.

Lane, Eric and Michael Oreskes. From *The Genius of America: How the Constitution Saved Our Country and Why It Can Again*. Copyright © 2007 by Eric Lane and Michael Oreskes. Reprinted by permission of Bloomsbury USA.

Levin, Yuval. "Repeal: Why and how Obamacare must be undone." This article is reprinted with permission of *The Weekly Standard*, where it first appeared on 4/5–12/2010. For more information visit www.weeklystandard.com.

Levinson, Sanford. Chapter 1, "The Ratification Referendum," *Our Undemocratic Constitution: Where the Constitution Goes Wrong (And How We the People Can Correct It)* by Sanford Levinson, pp. 11–24. Copyright © 2006 by Oxford University Press, Inc. Reprinted with permission of Oxford University Press.

Lindblom, Charles. "The Science of Muddling Through." *Public Administration Review*, Vol. 19, No. 2: 79–88. Reprinted with permission of publisher, American Society for Public Administration c/o Sun Trust Bank.

Lomborg, Bjørn. "Mr. Gore, Your Solution to Global Warming Is Wrong," *Esquire*, August 2009, Vol. 152, Issue 2, pp. 104–107. Reprinted by permission of the author.

Lowi, Theodore. "American Business, Public Policy, Case Studies & Political Theory." *World Politics* 16(4), 1964: 677–715. Copyright © 1994 Trustees of Princeton University. Reprinted with permission of Cambridge University Press.

Lowry, Rich and Ramesh Ponnuru. "An Exceptional Debate," *National Review*, March 8, 2010, pp. 31–38. © 2010 by National Review, Inc., 215 Lexington Avenue, New York, NY 10016. Reprinted by permission.

Mayhew, David. "Congress: The Electoral Connection," from *Congress: The Electoral Connection* (1974). Copyright © 1974 by Yale University Press. Reprinted with the permission of Yale University Press.

McKibben, Bill. "Climate Change," *Foreign Policy*, January/February 2009, pp. 32–38. © 2009 The Slate Group, LLC. www.foreignpolicy.com. Reprinted by permission via Copyright Clearance Center.

Menand, Louis. "The Unpolitical Animal: How Political Science Understands Voters." Copyright © Louis Menand. Granted with the permission of the author.

Morin, Richard. "Choice of Words: If You Can't Understand Our Poll Questions then How Can We Understand Your Answers." From *The Washington Post*, © 1999 The Washington Post. All rights reserved. Used by permission and protected by the Copyright Laws of the United States. The printing, copying, redistribution, or retransmission of the Material without express written permission is prohibited.

Neustadt, Richard E. "The Power to Persuade" from *Presidential Power* by Richard E. Neustadt. Copyright © 1986 by Macmillan Publishing Company. Reprinted by permission of Pearson Education, Inc.

Song, Sarah. "What does it mean to be an American?," *Daedalus*, 138:2 (Spring, 2009), pp. 31–40. © 2009 by the American Academy of Arts and Sciences. Reprinted by permission of MIT Press Journals.

Soros, George. "The Age of Open Society." From *The New Era*. Reprinted with the permission of the author.

Starr, Paul. "Goodbye to the Age of Newspapers (Hello to a New Era of Corruption)," *The New Republic*, March 4, 2009. Reprinted by permission of *The New Republic*, © 2009 TNR II, LLC.

Sutherland, Peter. "Reality Check." *Harvard International Review* (Winter 2000). Reprinted with permission of the publisher.

Taibbi, Matt. "Wall Street Bailout Hustle." Article by Matt Taibbi. From *Rolling Stone* issue dated, March 4, 2010. © Rolling Stone LLC 2010. All Rights Reserved. Reprinted by Permission.

Tocqueville, Alexis de. "Political Associations in the United States" (pp. 189–195) from *Democracy in America* by Alexis de Tocqueville. Edited by J. P. Mayer and Max Lerner. Translated by George Lawrence. English translation copyright © 1965 by Harper & Row, Publishers, Inc. Reprinted by permission of HarperCollins Publishers.

Truman, David B. "The Alleged Mischiefs of Faction" from *The Governmental Process* (Knopf, 1971). Reprinted with permission of Edwin M. Truman.

von Spakowsky, Hans. "Requiring Identification by Voters," Testimony before the Texas Senate, Delivered March 10, 2009. © 2010, The Heritage Foundation. Reprinted by permission of The Heritage Foundation.

Warshawsky, Steven M. "What Does It Mean To Be An American?," *American Thinker*, July 2, 2007. Reprinted by permission of the author.

Wilentz, Sean. "States of Anarchy," *The New Republic*, April 29, 2010. Reprinted by permission of *The New Republic*, © 2010 TNR II, LLC.

Wilson, James Q. "How Divided Are We?" Reprinted from *Commentary*, February 2006, by permission; copyright © 2006 by Commentary, Inc. "What Government Agencies Do and Why They Do It," from *Bureaucracy: What Government Agencies Do & Why They Do It* by James Q. Wilson. Copyright © 1991 James Wilson. Reprinted by permission of Basic Books, a member of the Perseus Books Group.

Wood, Gordon S. From *The Creation of the American Republic, 1776–1787* by Gordon S. Wood. Published for the Omohundro Institute of Early American History and Culture. Copyright © 1970 by the University of North Carolina Press; new preface copyright © 1998 by the University of North Carolina Press. Used by permission of the publisher.